WINDOWS 2000

DNS Server

WILLIAM **WONG**

D1530286

Osborne/**McGraw-Hill**

Berkeley   New York   St. Louis   San Francisco
Auckland   Bogotá   Hamburg   London   Madrid
Mexico City   Milan   Montreal   New Delhi   Panama City
Paris   São Paulo   Singapore   Sydney
Tokyo   Toronto

For information on translations or book distributors outside the U.S.A., or to arrange bulk purchase discounts for sales promotions, premiums, or fund-raisers, please contact Osborne/**McGraw-Hill** at the above address.

Windows 2000 DNS Server

1234567890 AGM AGM 019876543210

ISBN 0-07-212432-6

Publisher
Brandon A. Nordin
Associate Publisher and
Editor-in-Chief
Scott Rogers
Acquisitions Editor
Jane Brownlow
Project Editor
Jody McKenzie
Acquisitions Coordinator
Tara Davis
Technical Editor
Ron Ellenbecker

Copy Editor
Sally Engelfried
Proofreader
Pat Mannion
Indexer
Karin Arrigoni
Computer Designers
Jani Beckwith
Roberta Steele
E. A. Pauw
Illustrator
Michael T. Mueller
Series Design
Peter F. Hancik

This book was composed with Corel VENTURA™ Publisher.

For my wife, Ann, whose constant support made this book possible.

For Jennifer, Robert, and Laura, who make life interesting.

To Tabatha, our cat, who is no longer with us and
Samantha, who still likes to sleep on my keyboards.

About the Author

William Wong is the Embedded Systems/Software Technology Editor for *Electronic Design* magazine. He has written a number of books on networking, telecommuting, and software development. He was Director of PC Labs for *PC Magazine* and Windows User Labs for *Windows User Magazine*. Bill has installed and managed networks running Windows 2000, Windows NT, Linux, Novell NetWare, and OS/2.

About the Technical Reviewer

Ron Ellenbecker has worked with personal computers for more than 20 years. He earned his MCSE in 1996 and has kept up to date, passing all the Windows 3.11 and 9x tests along with NT 3.51 and NT 4.0 tests. Ron is currently a senior systems engineer with Tushaus Computer Services and assists with designing and implementing networks of all sizes. He also assists with the maintenance and upgrading of Tushaus's internal network, which consists of more than 15 servers and numerous workstations in various locations.

CONTENTS

ACKNOWLEDGMENTS

Writing a book is something I say I will never do again until the next one rolls around. They are always more work that you originally anticipate. Now that this is finally finished, I look forward to seeing my collection of text and drawings turned into a real book.

I want to thank Jane Brownlow, Jody McKenzie, and Tara Davis from Osborne/**McGraw-Hill**, whose support, patience, and determination to keep things moving finally got this book out the door.

A big thanks to Ron Ellenbecker, my tech editor. His close scrutiny kept this book technically on track. He pointed out the obscure and the obvious.

Many thanks to Shaun Hayes of Microsoft. He provided answers to questions that were difficult or impossible to answer with the standard Windows 2000 documentation.

To our children, Jennifer, Robert, and Laura, who have grown up with networks all around the house. They put up with my continual tinkering and reconfiguration and somehow got their homework done.

Finally, to the love of my life and my wife, Ann. It's time for the two of us to take a real vacation.

William Wong

INTRODUCTION

The Domain Name System (DNS) is the unsung hero of the Internet. Without DNS we would be slinging around IP addresses like phone numbers. Most users never know that a DNS server is required to access most of the services on the Internet or an intranet.

Microsoft's decision to build Windows 2000 Active Directory support on top of DNS indicates its dedication to standards, although it has pushed the limits with its implementation. This includes its implementation of secure dynamic DNS updates and the naming convention used for Active Directory services and domain controller addresses.

Microsoft has made major improvements to the Windows 2000 DNS service, compared to its predecessor on Windows NT. In fact, there are so many changes that the Windows NT version cannot hold a candle to its new big brother. Still, third-party DNS servers do not have to be left out of a Windows 2000 network. Newer versions of third-party DNS servers such as BIND can not only interoperate with the Windows 2000 DNS service, but these third-party DNS servers can support Windows 2000 Active Directory without using the Windows 2000 DNS service.

Those new to DNS will find most of the book useful. It covers everything from basic DNS operation through integration with Windows 2000 DHCP and WINS services.

Chapter 1 provides an overview of things to come.

Those new to DNS need to take a close look at Chapter 2. The rest of the book assumes a background at least to the level presented in this chapter.

Chapter 3 introduces Windows 2000 and DNS, including how domain controllers are referenced via DNS SRV resource records. It also explains why Windows 2000 Active Directory domain controllers use dynamic DNS updates.

It is possible to use Windows 2000 DNS without discussing or using Windows 2000 Active Directory, but this situation arises only in small networks or where Windows 2000 DNS is used as a stand-alone DNS server. Windows 2000 networks with even a few servers will utilize Active Directory, which is discussed in Chapter 4.

Chapter 5 takes a look at the initial configuration of Windows 2000 DNS and Active Directory. It addresses migration issues. It also introduces the small, medium, large, and distributed network environments described in later chapters.

These environments represent the typical Windows 2000 networks of ever larger size and graphical disbursement.

Chapters 6, 7, 8, and 9 present the small, medium, large, and distributed network environments introduced in Chapter 5. Active Directory and DNS setup are described and migration issues are addressed.

The Microsoft Management Console (MMC) is integral to managing all Windows 2000 services, not just Windows 2000 DNS. Chapter 10 takes a look at MMC and how it works. It also looks at Active Directory MMC snap-ins that will be used with Windows 2000 DNS configuration.

Chapter 11 concentrates on the Windows 2000 DNS MMC snap-in. This is where most of a DNS administrator's work is done, so everyone should take a close look at this chapter.

DNS Security is addressed in Chapter 12. This includes security related to outside access of DNS information from a standard DNS client as well as Active Directory–related access management. It takes a look at Active Directory–integrated DNS zone security.

The Windows 2000 DNS service supports any standard DNS client. Chapter 13 takes a look at configuration of clients found in a typical Windows 2000 network. These include Windows 2000, Windows NT, and Windows 9x.

Chapter 14 takes a look at Windows 2000 DHCP service. This service is more closely integrated with the Windows 2000 DNS service because of the DHCP service's dynamic DNS update proxy support.

Dynamic DNS update provides an automatic naming mechanism that can greatly simplify maintenance of workstation DNS address resource records. Chapter 15 takes a look at how dynamic DNS works as well as how the Windows 2000 WINS service is used. WINS will be important to DNS administrators who have to deal with Windows 9x and Windows NT clients and NetBIOS-based applications.

Chapter 16 takes a look at DNS replication and indirection. This includes standard primary and secondary DNS zone replication as well as Active Directory–integrated DNS zone replication through the Active Directory domain database. This chapter takes a look at sites and security.

Zone migration is addressed in Chapter 17. Not all migrations will be from a Windows NT to a Windows 2000 environment. This chapter examines the alternatives.

Chapter 18 discusses Windows 2000 DNS and the Internet. This includes placement of DNS servers.

The Windows 2000 MMC provides a graphical management interface, but that is not the only way to manage the Windows 2000 DNS service and other services such as DHCP and WINS. Chapter 19 looks at command line management utilities. Even dyed-in-the-wool DNS administrators should read through this chapter. Batch files can do wonders in solving many otherwise tedious chores.

Chapter 20 presents remote DNS management alternatives as well as some third-party DNS utilities. These are only the tip of the iceberg, but they present features that Windows 2000 utilities lack.

Chapter 21 presents an overview of BIND. BIND is probably the most common DNS implementation around and one that Windows 2000 DNS administrators are most likely to encounter.

Check out the appendixes for the details such as DNS resource record definitions.

CHAPTER 1

Active Directory, DNS, and Windows 2000

Windows 2000 is a major advancement in Microsoft's stable of operating systems. Its ambitious feature set is built around a new, integrated management architecture called Active Directory. One of Active Directory's requirements is a Domain Name System (DNS) environment because of Active Directory's use of IP-based networking. Without DNS servers, a Windows 2000 Active Directory changes from a tightly integrated environment to a collection of isolated servers. For this reason, a robust DNS environment will be needed on any Windows 2000 Active Directory network.

Network administrators charged with installing or upgrading to Windows 2000 must take a close look at Active Directory and the DNS environment. If a DNS environment already exists on the network, consideration must be given to requirements placed on the DNS servers by the Windows 2000 Active Directory support, such as the need to support SRV resource records in DNS zones.

DNS and Active Directory planning are interrelated because of their dependency on each other. Administrators will need to address DNS and Active Directory together or face the consequences of improper design. Incorporating DNS and Active Directory over and existing Windows NT network will often require additional DNS servers, consolidation of domains, and creation of management hierarchies to accommodate a very new environment.

This book presents the basics of Active Directory so that those unfamiliar with this aspect of Windows 2000 will be able to understand its complexities and impact. Those tasked with design and management of Active Directory will definitely want to check out a book dedicated to Active Directory.

The majority of this book addresses the installation and configuration and migration details associated with Active Directory as it relates to Windows 2000 DNS. This includes examination of third-party DNS tools and BIND, a major DNS server implementation. Heterogeneous networks that include UNIX or Linux servers will most likely incorporate BIND in one fashion or another.

DNS and related services run remarkably well with minimal management, but changes are always needed with actions such as the addition of new servers. This book looks at managing Windows 2000

DNS and other services using the Microsoft Management Console (MMC) support as well as command-line management tools and remote management options.

ACTIVE DIRECTORY

The Windows 2000 DNS service can operate on a standalone Windows 2000 server, but this is an unlikely configuration for all but the smallest networks. The typical Windows 2000 network will incorporate Active Directory throughout the network.

Active Directory is a major change from Windows NT. Active Directory supports a hierarchical domain system that mirrors a DNS domain hierarchy. In addition, each domain will normally sport an additional hierarchy that includes all types of network objects that can be grouped in organizational units (OU). Organizational units can contain other organizational units, which leads to this internal hierarchy.

Active Directory is also central to Windows 2000 security. Hierarchical security-related inheritance makes management easier to handle and understand. The security system also incorporates Kerberos, an advanced authentication system that originated at MIT. Kerberos is so important to the inner workings of Windows 2000 that these services are advertised in Windows 2000 DNS zones.

Windows 2000 can operate in native mode that requires a homogeneous collection of Windows 2000 workstations and servers. In this case, IP-based communication is required, as is DNS support.

Many Windows 2000 networks will operate in mixed mode. Windows 2000 workstations and servers can still operate with the latest security support, but non-Windows 2000 computers will use the less secure Windows NT protocols and security.

Active Directory is not just a management hierarchy. It incorporates a multimaster database that spans a domain as well as a global catalog database, which in turn spans an entire network. This scope was not lost on the Windows 2000 designers, and Windows 2000 DNS allows you to take advantage of this database when Active Directory–integrated DNS zones are used.

This book looks at the impact and uses of Active Directory support, including replication aspects found in large or distributed networks, because of the impact Active Directory can have on Windows 2000 DNS.

NEW DNS FEATURES

The Windows 2000 DNS service includes a host of new features compared to the older Windows NT DNS server. Many of the new features were added to support and to take advantage of Active Directory. With minor exceptions, the implementation is completely in line with existing DNS standards. This makes Windows 2000 DNS services suitable for enterprise DNS support in addition to Active Directory support within a Windows 2000 network.

The three major enhancements include:

▼ New DNS resource record support

■ Dynamic DNS update support

▲ Active Directory–integrated DNS zones

One of the new DNS resource records supported is the SRV (service resource record). It advertises the existence of a service such as a Windows 2000 domain controller or a Kerberos server. Any DNS system that will be used with Active Directory will need to support these new, standard DNS enhancements.

Dynamic DNS updates allow clients to automatically change the contents of DNS zones. Prior to dynamic DNS update support, changes to a DNS zone were made manually. Dynamic DNS update support provides a feature similar to that found in Microsoft's Windows Internet Naming Service (WINS). (Windows 2000 supports WINS primarily for mixed-mode Windows 2000 networks.)

Active Directory–integrated DNS zones not only place DNS zone information into the Active Directory domain database, they also makes the zone more robust by providing multimaster primary zone support. A change made through any Windows 2000 DNS server to an Active Directory–integrated DNS zone will automatically show up on other Windows 2000 DNS servers supporting the same zone. This is an Active Directory–specific enhancement that DNS administrators will find very worthwhile.

WINDOWS 2000 DHCP

Other major Windows 2000 DHCP service improvements include support for superscopes and multicast scopes. These features are useful, but it is Windows 2000 DHCP service's dynamic DNS update proxy service that makes DHCP interesting—especially since it can perform secure dynamic DNS updates when used in conjunction with the Windows 2000 DNS service.

The Windows 2000 DHCP service is examined in detail in this book because it complements Windows 2000 DNS so well, and many network administrators will deploy both.

DHCP support will undoubtedly be found in larger networks. If DHCP is not already used in a network, it will probably be added, given Windows 2000's dependence on IP.

Those unfamiliar with DHCP should take a closer look at its operation and management. Those who have implemented individual DHCP servers on a subnet should consider configuration of multiple DHCP servers with DHCP scopes that overlap and provide a more robust dynamic IP address environment.

WINDOWS 2000 WINS

Windows 2000 includes a WINS service. WINS is not required in a native Windows 2000 network, but it can be invaluable in a mixed-mode environment. This is especially true for networks that are running NetBIOS-based network applications.

WINS could effectively replace DNS support under Windows NT but, given the rise of the Internet, WINS and DNS have learned to coexist. WINS can be replaced by a combination of Windows 2000 DNS and DCHP services using the latter's dynamic DNS update proxy support. This book looks at Windows 2000 WINS, including its relationship with Windows 2000 DNS. WINS coverage is not exhaustive, but it should be sufficient for network administrators to manage and configure Windows 2000 WINS.

SUMMARY

Windows 2000 Active Directory does not have to be used with a Windows 2000 network, but only small networks with one or two servers will do without. All others will allow Active Directory to be a central part of the network.

DNS is a major requirement for Active Directory support; hence the importance of this book and its coverage of the Windows 2000 DNS service. Windows 2000 DHCP, WINS, and Active Directory are addressed because they all relate to the Windows 2000 DNS server in one way or another.

This book attempts to address the relevant planning, installation, and management tasks needed to support a homogeneous or heterogeneous Windows 2000 network. The information in this book is based on the initial release of Windows 2000. There may be enhancements in the future, but the Windows 2000 DNS server is not expected to change radically because it is based on existing DNS standards.

CHAPTER 2

How DNS Works

D NS is a necessary component for Windows 2000 Active Directory support, but it is also a significant part of any TCP/IP network, including the Internet. The specifications and operation of DNS are independent of Windows 2000, although Windows 2000 requires specific DNS support. This makes some DNS server implementations inadequate for supporting Window 2000 with Active Directory.

This chapter addresses the DNS specifications in their general form, with minimal references to Windows 2000. It is designed for those who may be unfamiliar with all the features of DNS and the RFC mechanisms used to present the specifications. Those familiar with DNS support, including dynamic DNS updates, can skip to Chapter 3, although even veteran DNS managers may find a useful tidbit of information here. This chapter is not designed to be an exhaustive description of DNS and all its related RFCs. The RFCs do a good job of that. Instead, this chapter provides an overview of how DNS works and references the appropriate RFCs.

The following sections are included in this chapter:

▼ DNS specifications and RFCs

■ DNS 101

■ DNS server operation

■ Dynamic DNS

▲ DNS implementations

DNS specifications are found in Request for Comment (RFC) documents that are maintained at **http://www.rfc-editor.org**. These RFCs are approved by the Internet Engineering Task Force (IETF) working groups. The RFCs that are supported by Windows 2000 DNS are discussed in the section "DNS Specifications and RFCs."

NOTE: This section and most of the book address the IPv4 address implementation that uses four 8-bit numbers to designate a node. IPv6 uses four 16-bit numbers. RFC 1886, DNS Extensions To Support IP Version 6, covers differences between the addressing methods.

DNS-related RFCs provide all the details of how DNS clients and servers operate, but they tend to be rather verbose. The "DNS 101" section presents a simple overview of the various interactions that occur between DNS clients and servers, beginning with an overview of DNS domain names.

DNS client and server interaction is only part of the puzzle. The section "DNS Server Operations" addresses details like forward- and reverse-DNS zone use and delegation and caching. This includes interaction between DNS servers to handle secondary DNS zones.

DNS has been around for many years. Dynamic DNS support is a relatively new but important feature that is used by Windows 2000. The section "Dynamic DNS" addresses the basics, including its relationship to DHCP. Chapter 15 covers Windows 2000 Dynamic DNS in more detail.

Obviously, Windows 2000 DNS is not the only DNS implementation and, as it turns out, Windows 2000 and Active Directory can work with other DNS implementations. The "DNS Implementations" section looks at some of the alternatives commonly found on Windows-based networks. Chapter 21 is more specific and detailed on this topic and addresses using BIND, one of the most popular DNS implementations, to support Windows 2000.

DNS SPECIFICATIONS AND RFCS

Approved RFCs are the result of extended discussion of interested parties. The IETF handles RFCs that address a variety of technologies. RFCs provide a specification that can be superceded or nullified by subsequent RFCs. There are dozens of RFCs that address various aspects of DNS. This book narrows this set to those required and supported by Windows 2000 DNS. As with any software that will be upgraded, this set of RFCs may change as Windows 2000 is improved.

Table 2-1 contains a list of RFCs implemented by Windows 2000. These RFCs address all aspects of the Windows 2000 DNS implementation, including requirements for Active Directory support such as RFC 2052, which defines the use of the DNS SRV (service locator) resource record, and RFC 2136, which defines Dynamic DNS updates.

RFC	Title
1034	Domain Names—Concepts and Facilities
1035	Domain Names—Implementation and Specification
1101	DNS Encoding of Network Names and Other Types
1464	Using the Domain Name System to Store Arbitrary String Attributes
1536	Common DNS Implementation Errors and Suggested Fixes
1591	Domain Name System Structure and Delegation
1629	Guidelines for OSI NSAP Allocation in the Internet
1664	Using the Internet DNS to Distribute Mail Address Mapping Tables
1706	DNS NSAP Resource Records
1712	DNS Encoding of Geographical Location
1713	Tools for DNS Debugging
1794	DNS Support for Load Balancing
1886	DNS Extensions to Support IP Version 6
1912	Common DNS Operational and Configuration Errors
1995	Incremental Zone Transfer in DNS
1996	A Mechanism for Prompt DNS Notification of Zone Changes
2052	A DNS RR for Specifying the Location of Services (DNS SRV)
2136	Dynamic Updates in the Domain Name System (DNS UPDATE)
2181	Clarifications to the DNS Specification
2308	Negative Caching of DNS Queries (DNS NCACHE)

Table 2-1.   RFCs Supported by Windows 2000

Compatibility with RFCs is important for two reasons. First, it allows Windows 2000 DNS to provide DNS services to any DNS client or server, not just Windows 2000 systems. Second, it allows network administrators to identify third-party DNS servers that will work with Windows 2000.

The RFCs listed in Table 2-1 are referenced throughout this book to clarify where standards come into play and to allow you to check out the related standard that often provides more details. The remainder of this section presents a short overview of each of the RFCs listed in Table 2-1.

RFC 1034, Domain Names—Concepts and Facilities, provides an excellent overview to DNS. It, along with RFC 1035, defines the hierarchical name space that is the basis for all current DNS implementations. It does not address all aspects of DNS because DNS, like other RFC-based technologies, is designed to be enhanced—hence the collection of RFCs in Table 2-1.

RFC 1035, Domain Names—Implementation and Specification, addresses the details of how DNS records are laid out. For example, it sets the maximum domain name length at 255 characters and makes domain names case insensitive.

RFC 1101, DNS Encoding of Network Names and Other Types, addresses the encoding scheme for DNS name records as well as other useful DNS records such as name server records.

RFC 1464, Using the Domain Name System to Store Arbitrary String Attributes, shows how DNS can be used to store information that is unrelated to resolving domain names. Although DNS is not a general network name database, it can be used to house information that is related to systems or services.

RFC 1536, Common DNS Implementation Errors and Suggested Fixes, is an informative look at problems that DNS implementers may encounter.

RFC 1591, Domain Name System Structure and Delegation, shows how the hierarchical nature of DNS allows distribution of services and responsibilities. Although it does not define the Start of Authority record, it describes how it impacts delegation of DNS authority.

RFC 1629, Guidelines for OSI NSAP Allocation in the Internet, defines the NSAP formats.

DNS is used to define mail exchanges so that queued mail delivery can proceed even if the primary mail destination is not available. RFC 1664, Using the Internet DNS to Distribute Mail Address Mapping Tables, describes the procedures of this process.

RFC 1706, DNS NSAP Resource Records, defines the DNS lookup procedure for NSAP resource records. These are not used by most DNS clients associated with Windows 2000, but the Windows 20000 DNS server is compliant.

Want to use a global positioning system to determine where a service or PC is located? Well, RFC 1712, DNS Encoding of Geographical Location, does just that. While not required by Windows 2000 clients, RFC 1712 support allows Windows 2000 DNS to store and deliver this information.

RFC 1713, Tools for DNS Debugging, describes available tools for debugging a DNS installation. Not all the tools listed are available under Windows 2000, but they can be used from a PC that is running another operating system such as UNIX to test out a Windows 2000 DNS installation.

RFC 1794, DNS Support for Load Balancing, defines fast zone updates as a way to randomly distribute access to services mapped by a DNS service. Windows 2000 has its own load balancing support that is not discussed in this book, although it is possible to use this DNS support to provide basic load distribution to IP-based services.

IP Version 4 provides the well-known four-byte IP address associated with DNS names. RFC 1886, DNS Extensions to Support IP Version 6, allows DNS and Windows 2000 DNS to support the latest IP implementation that doubles the number of bits used to encode an address.

As mentioned earlier, RFC 1536 addresses implementation problems; RFC 1912, Common DNS Operational and Configuration Errors, on the other hand, addresses problems and procedures that the typical DNS administrator will encounter.

RFC 1995, Incremental Zone Transfer in DNS, defines how incremental changes are propagated to other DNS servers. This is a major DNS enhancement, but it's one that most DNS administrators do not have to worry about, since it is a low-level implementation detail.

RFC 1996, A Mechanism for Prompt DNS Notification of Zone Changes, is a similar feature that defines a way for DNS servers to replicate changes. It is primarily used for interaction between DNS services using this standard interface versus Active Directory–integrated zones that use Active Directory for replication.

RFC 2052, A DNS RR for Specifying the Location of Services (DNS SRV), is one of the RFCs that has a major impact on Windows 2000. The SRV (service resource record) is one that Windows 2000 uses to advertise its systems services such as the domain controllers, Kerberos servers, and LDAP servers.

2136, Dynamic Updates in the Domain Name System (DNS UPDATE), is another RFC that Windows 2000 uses and is one feature that is not supported by the Windows NT DNS service. Dynamic DNS updates allow both clients and servers to register their information with the DNS service. The specification described in this RFC addresses unsecured DNS updates and not the enhanced, secured DNS updates supported by Windows 2000 between Windows 2000 servers and Windows 2000 clients.

RFC 2181, Clarifications to the DNS Specification, allows binary strings for DNS domain names. Windows 2000 DNS provides Unicode transformation format (UTF-8) support using RFC 2181, although UTF-8 is only a subset of the functionality available via RFC 2181. Given Windows 2000's Unicode support, it is not surprising that UTF-8 support is extended to the Windows 2000 DNS support. Unicode supports multiple languages via multibyte encoding, whereas RFC 1035 provided only 8-bit character encoding.

DNS servers, including the Windows 2000 DNS service, employ caching to improve performance when requests for nonlocal information are processed. Prior to RFC 2308, Negative Caching of DNS Queries (DNS NCACHE), positive responses were cached but negative responses were not. Instead, each request was processed even though the negative response was always the same. This RFC allows the DNS server to cache the negative response and return it when the DNS server detects that a new request matches a cached request that received a negative response.

DNS 101

This section takes a look at how DNS operates from a DNS client perspective. First, however, we will take a look at domain names and Internet domain names to see what DNS clients will be asking about or using in a query. Most of this will be familiar to anyone who has used a Web browser, since domain names are an integral part of browsing.

Domain Names

Domain names are at the core of the Domain Name System. They are kept in the DNS database and are used in queries and in responses. They describe *hosts* and *domains*. Hosts and domains are defined later in this section. Without domain names, DNS is not very useful.

Domain names fit a very specific pattern that matches the bottom-up concatenation of node names in an inverted tree structure like the one shown in Figure 2-1. The circled nodes have a node name and the

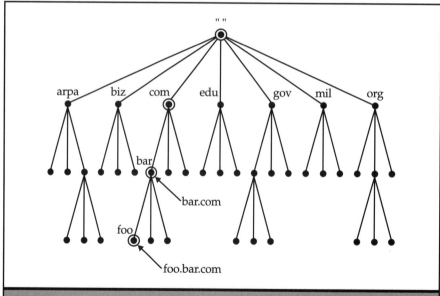

Figure 2-1. Inverted tree structure used for domain names

matching domain name. For example, foo.bar.com defines one of the bottom nodes in the tree. The parent node is bar.com. The domain name is the collection of individual node names separated by periods.

The domain name tree follows a few simple rules that are spelled out in the DNS-related RFCs mentioned in the "DNS Specifications and RFCs" section. These include a maximum of 127 levels, a node name length limit of 63 characters, a domain name length limit of 255 characters, and a valid set of characters. An exception to the latter is spelled out in RFC 2181, which allows arbitrary binary strings to define domain names. For our discussion, we will concentrate on conventional domain names normally used for DNS servers. The node names must also be unique with respect to their parent. This prevents having two foo child nodes for bar.com. The same node name can appear anywhere else in the tree, however, so foo.com and foo.org are both valid domain names.

The root of the tree has no name, although the trailing period is included. Domain names that include the trailing period are referred to as a *fully qualified domain name* (FQDN). Names without the trailing period are referred to as a *relative domain name*. Relative domain names are used with respect to another domain.

A *domain* is a subtree of the domain name space. The domain name for the domain is the same as the domain name of the subtree's root node. Figure 2-2 shows the domain bar.com. This domain also contains the domain foo.bar.com. Both bar.com. and foo.bar.com are domains.

Domains are collections of nodes that refer to other domains and *hosts*. Nodes can also be aliases that refer to other nodes. Hosts are network devices that are addressed by one or more IP addresses. Although the main purpose of DNS is to provide IP address information about hosts, DNS can provide other details about hosts, such as the type of operating system being used or the services provided. Nodes can also provide mail routing information.

Leaf nodes refer to hosts, host information, and aliases, but interior nodes may refer to them as well. For example, the domain foo.com may have leaf nodes like www.foo.com, ftp.foo.com, and server1.foo.com, but it can also refer to a host. In small networks, this is often the case, and some leaf nodes like www.foo.com may refer to foo.com.

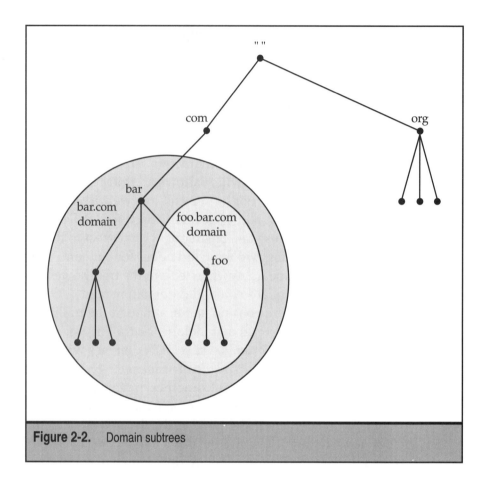

Figure 2-2. Domain subtrees

Domains are a way to logically group related hosts and domains, although nodes within a domain are not required to have any specific relationship to each other. Relationships can be arbitrary or they may be based on some common attribute such as geographical location, device type, or organizational unit. For example, a Taiwanese company might have a domain with a name like sample.com.tw. Organizations in a company with a domain of foo.com might have domain names like software.foo.com and marketing.foo.com, with host names like server1.software.foo.com and www.marketing.foo.com.

Domain names can also be described by their level within the domain tree. A top-level domain (TLD) is a child of the root. In Figure 2-1, the top-level domains include arpa, biz, com, edu, gov, mil, and org. The first-level domains, such as bar.com, are children of top-level domains. A second-level domain, such as foo.bar.com, is a child of a first-level domain. This process can continue to 127 levels—more than anyone would care to use. A summary of this is shown in Table 2-2.

Domain names used on a network without connections to the outside world can utilize any naming convention desired and still make use of standard DNS servers. The rules change when the network is connected to a larger network like the Internet.

Internet domain names are no different than the ones already discussed, with the exception that the top-level domains are fixed and first-level domains must be registered. After that, the node names are up to the DNS managers for the first-level domains. Table 2-3 shows a list of the generic top-level domain (gTLD) names.

The generic top-level domain names were created when ARPAnet, a U.S. Department of Defense (DOD) project, was developed. Another domain name included at that time was *arpa*. This domain was originally all the hosts on the ARPAnet when the network was rather small. Once the ARPAnet grew into the much larger Internet, it was no longer feasible to use this domain name to keep track of all the hosts, although the arpa domain name has survived.

The list in Table 2-3 is not comprehensive because the number of TLDs is being expanded. One reason for the expansion is trademark preference. Many companies would like their company name or a variation of it to be their Internet domain name. Unfortunately, the

Name	Child of	Example
Top-level domain	Root	com
First-level domain	Top-level domain	bar.com
Second-level domain	First-level domain	foo.bar.com
Third-level domain	Second-level domain	server1.foo.bar.com

Table 2-2.   Domain Levels

Top-Level Domain	Description	First-Level Domain Name Examples
com	Commercial organization	foo.com
edu	Educational institutions such as universities and colleges	gatech.edu
gov	Government organizations	nasa.gov
mil	Military organizations	army.mil
net	Networking organizations, also used for businesses	nsf.net
org	Noncommercial organizations	isc.org
int	International organizations	nato.int

Table 2-3.   Generic Top-Level Internet Domain Names

name may already be in use by a third party that may be unable or unwilling to sell the right to use the domain name. Expanding the number of TLDs allows companies to get a first-level domain name that matches their requirements even if the domain name belongs to another organization in a different TLD.

As the Internet grew from a U.S. DOD project to an international network, the top-level domains expanded to accommodate different countries. An international standard, ISO 3166, defined a two-letter abbreviation for every country in the world. This includes the United States (our abbreviation is, of course, us). Many companies, in the U.S. and elsewhere, prefer to use the nongeographical top-level domain names.

NOTE: Great Britain (gb), which includes Northern Ireland, is the only country with a second top-level domain name. The United Kingdom (uk) is commonly used in place of Great Britain in common language and Internet domains.

The convention for first-level domain names in country domains is to follow the gTLDs, which gives us domain names like com.uk for companies in the United Kingdom. The United Kingdom also uses first-level domain names like co.uk for corporations and ac.uk for academic organizations versus com.uk and edu.uk, respectively.

NOTE: The United States (us) top-level domain contains first-level domain names for each of the 50 states plus Washington, D.C., and the United States territories. The two-letter node names for the 50 states match the two-letter abbreviations used by the United States Postal Service. This approach is typically taken one step further with second-level domains for cities within the states or territories.

Many new users of the Internet assume that everything is addressed using second-level names like www.gatech.edu. Of course, anyone who has worked with DNS knows that this is not true, and that it is common to have domain names that hit six levels. While the only level-related restriction is set at 127 levels, six levels tends to be a practical limit. However, given Windows 2000 Active Directory's dependence on DNS, six levels may just be the starting point.

DNS Resource Records

The DNS database consists of resource records (RR). Each resource record is a member of a class. The Internet class is the most popular and is the one addressed in this book. Other classes pertain to different networks or software and tend to remain for historical reasons or for limited use, such as the Hesiod software class still utilized by MIT.

NOTE: Address resource records are the most common DNS database entries, but they are not the only ones. The use of other resource record types is covered throughout this book as appropriate.

Each class is broken down into types. The type corresponds to the type of data stored in the record. Each type has an abbreviation, such as A for address information. A typical text representation of a resource record is:

```
foo.com.    IN A 123.45.67.89
```

The associated key, a domain name, is foo.com in this case. The IN keyword stands for Internet, and the data associated with the record is the IP address, 123.45.67.89. A complete list of resource records and types is included in Appendix A of this book. Resource records are also referred to and described throughout this book as necessary.

NOTE: IP version 4 addresses are four octets, where each octet value is listed with a period separator. Thus, the maximum value is 255.255.255.255. IP version 6 uses four 16-bit words, which raises the values to 65535.

Domains, Zones, Delegation, and Name Servers

Domains cover an entire subtree in the domain name space, but managing an entire subtree for the Internet can be rather cumbersome and is usually impractical for top-level domains and even some first-level domains. The concept of *zones* allows management of the domain name space to be delegated.

A zone is a range of responsibility within the domain name space that spans a subtree or a portion of a subtree, as shown in Figure 2-3. An organization is delegated the task of managing a *zone database* that contains DNS resource records. The zone database is stored in and accessed through a *name server*, also called a DNS server or service.

Zones do not have to encompass a contiguous set of levels and domains. Figure 2-4 shows how the bar.com zone encompasses the bar.com node and the entire soap.bar.com domain. Delegations may not overlap. Delegation allows a DNS administrator to manage the entire domain covered by a zone, including the delegation of domains within the zone.

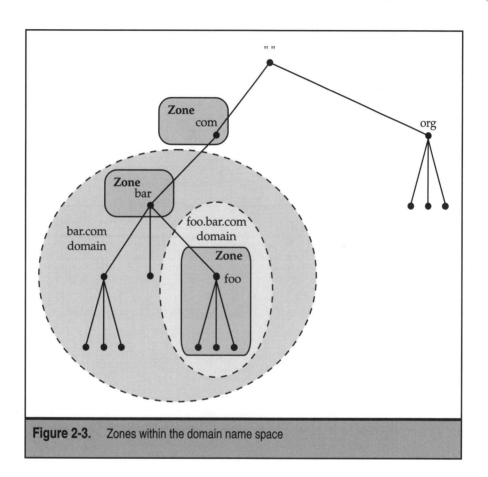

Figure 2-3.   Zones within the domain name space

A more detailed discussion of name servers and zones is covered in the section "DNS Server Operations."

Domain Name Client Operation

DNS uses a client/server architecture. In this section, we take a look at the client side and how it interacts with the server. The "DNS Server Operations" section looks at the inner workings of the server and how it interacts with other DNS servers.

Domain name clients are also called *name resolvers* or simply *resolvers*. They provide applications running on the same system

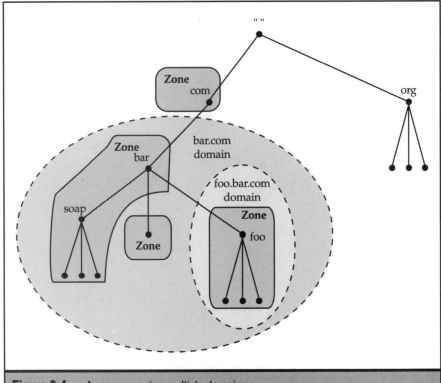

Figure 2-4.   A zone spanning multiple domains

with information obtained from a DNS server. The resolver handles querying the DNS server, interpreting the response, and returning the information to the requesting application. This process is called *name resolution* or simply *resolution*.

The resolver is usually a module or set of routines that can be accessed by an application versus an independent program. Typical applications that use the resolver include Web browsers, ftp clients, and telnet clients.

Resolvers vary in complexity. The simplest version processes a request from an application and returns a response. A more advanced resolver maintains a local cache because repeated accesses to the same host are common since the Universal Resource Locator (URL) incorporated DNS domain names as a primary component, as with Web browsers.

Resolvers can also be found in DNS servers. These are used to contact other DNS servers if the first server does not have the requested information. This transparent forwarding is covered in the next section.

DNS client and server interaction is rather simple. A DNS client requests information from a DNS server's database. The request includes the type of information required and a key. The key is either a domain name or an IP address. The DNS server returns a positive response plus the requested information if it can find the record with the matching key; otherwise, it returns a negative response. One possible negative response is a referral to one or more DNS servers that may provide a positive response. DNS clients capable of using the referral will then contact another DNS server until all options are tried or success is returned. This referral process can also be done by the DNS server.

One of two typical requests made by a DNS client includes a key that is a domain name, with the type of information requested being the IP address associated with the domain name. The DNS server looks for an address resource record with the matching domain name and returns the IP address stored in the resource record. This domain name-to-IP address conversion occurs when an application like a Web browser wants to request information from a Web server. A user typically supplies the URL of the form http://domain-name/ local-path. The domain-name is shipped off to a DNS server that returns the IP address, and the Web browser then sends its request off to that IP address.

The second typical request works in the opposite direction, with a key that is an IP address and the type of information being requested the domain name associated with the IP address. This type of request is often used by a Web server to determine the name of a requester based upon the IP address in the request packet.

There are additional kinds of DNS requests but, for the most part, they are variations on these two requests. These are covered in more detail later in the book.

DNS SERVER OPERATIONS

DNS servers provide database lookup services for name resolvers that include DNS clients and other DNS servers, as described by the resolution process in the previous section. This section examines the following items:

▼ Types of name servers and zones

■ Zone database files

▲ Caching and time to live (TTL)

Name servers support one or more of the following: primary zone, secondary zones, and caching. The section "Types of Name Servers and Zones" addresses what these are and how they operate. The section "Zone Database Files" takes a closer look at the zone files used by most third-party DNS servers as well as the Windows 2000 DNS server when a zone is not an Active Directory–integrated zone. The section "Caching and Time to Live (TTL)" examines how and why servers cache DNS information and how long this cached information is valid.

NOTE: Windows 2000 DNS supports Active Directory–integrated zones if the DNS service is running on a Windows 2000 Active Directory domain controller. Active Directory is covered in Chapter 4. Active Directory–integrated zones are addressed in Chapter 5. Windows 2000 DNS supports conventional primary and secondary zones described in this chapter as well as Active Directory–integrated zones. Secondary zone replication between DNS servers is equally applicable to Windows 2000 DNS, although Windows 2000 Active Directory replication offers nonstandard, multiple master support within an Active Directory domain that is lacking in standard DNS support.

Types of Name Servers and Zones

Most DNS implementations such as Windows 2000 DNS, Window NT DNS, and BIND support a mix of services on one DNS server.

This includes support for primary zones, secondary zones, and caching. In this section, we take a look at how zones work and how DNS servers interact. Caching is covered in the section "Caching and Time to Live (TTL)."

Thus far, we have presented DNS operations that assumed a single DNS server for a domain. A DNS client contacts the DNS server that returns a response, either positive or negative. In practice, a single DNS server for a domain is rare. In a more typical case, a DNS server maintains zone information more than one domain. We use figures and some snippets of DNS zone files to explain concepts in this section. A more concise description of the DNS zone file is contained in the section "Zone Database Files."

Multiple DNS servers can provide information about the same zone. These servers have a master/slave relationship with respect to zones, and there is one master per zone. A zone master has a primary zone database that defines the zone. One or more zone slaves maintain a secondary zone database whose contents are obtained from either the primary zone database or another secondary zone database. In the latter case, the information in the database must eventually come from the primary zone database. Figure 2-5 shows the master/slave relationship between primary and secondary zones managed by different DNS servers.

DNS Server 3, with the two secondary zones, receives its DNS database contents from the other two DNS servers. DNS Server 1 maintains the zone soap.bar.com while DNS Server 2 maintains the foo.bar.com domain. Queries for foo.bar.com can be handled by DNS Server 2 and DNS Server 3 but not DNS Server 1 since it does not know the contents. foo.bar.com is a primary zone database because it does not have a secondary zone. Chapter 16 addresses secondary zone file transfers. DNS Server 1 and 2 are considered master name servers while DNS Server 3 is considered a slave name server.

NOTE: This description of name resolution with primary and secondary zone servers only considers resolution based upon the zone files contained in the server. Caching and forwarding are not addressed.

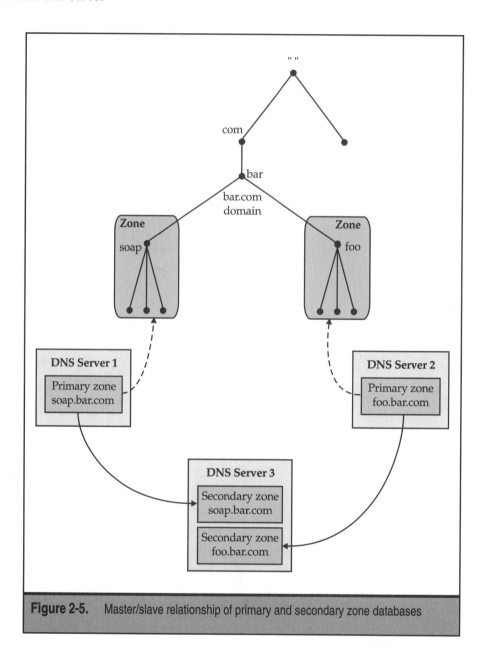

Figure 2-5.   Master/slave relationship of primary and secondary zone databases

     Figure 2-5 shows that a slave name server can obtain the information for different secondary zones from different sources. Figure 2-6 takes this one step further and mixes primary and secondary zones on the same DNS server. It also shows a DNS server with a secondary zone getting its information from another secondary zone.

DNS Server 3 will receive the information for the zone soap.bar.com from DNS Server 2 only after DNS Server 2 receives it from DNS Server 1. DNS Server 3 receives the information for the zone foo.bar.com directly from DNS Server 2.

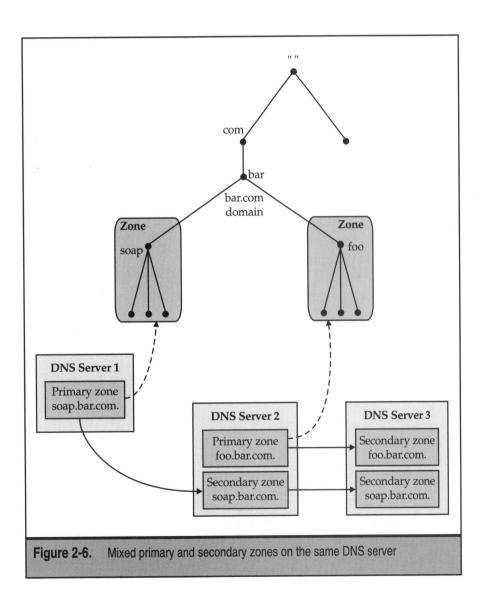

Figure 2-6.   Mixed primary and secondary zones on the same DNS server

Secondary zones do not contain information about the primary zone location. This is kept separate, allowing secondary zones information to be used without change by a slave name server. Most DNS servers support a list of sources to be specified for a secondary zone for redundancy purposes. The entries in the list are used in order, and the first server that can deliver the secondary zone information will be used. The rest will be ignored. This server may change depending upon the availability of the servers when the secondary zone needs to be updated.

Secondary zones can be updated by sending the entire zone file to a slave name server. The slave name server can request an update at any time. Assuming the size of the file is small or the bandwidth available between the name servers is high, the time it takes to update the slave name server will be small. In many cases, however, the size of the zone file may be large or the bandwidth may be limited, making frequent updates impractical. DNS servers that support the RFC 1995 Incremental Zone Transfer specification can reduce the overhead by only transferring changes that are usually much less than the entire zone file. One source for incremental updates is dynamic DNS updates, which are discussed later in the section "Dynamic DNS."

The source for secondary zone updates is different from zone authority definitions. The Start Of Authority (SOA) resource record (there may be only one) that appears in a zone file specifies the primary name server for the zone. The following is a sample SOA definition.

```
@ IN SOA foo.bar.com. dnsmanager.foo.bar.com. (
        1              ; serial number
        3600           ; refresh (1 hour)
        600            ; retry (10 minutes)
        86400          ; expire (1 day)
        3600 )         ; min TTL (1 hour)
```

The @ sign indicates the current domain name. IN indicates an Internet class, while SOA is the resource record type. This is followed by the FQDN for the primary name server for the zone. This is followed by the e-mail address for the person responsible for the zone. The rest of the details of the SOA resource record are covered in the next section.

NOTE: The SOA e-mail address name format is different than that used by most e-mail applications. In this case, the e-mail address would be dnsmanager@foo.bar.com. There is no requirement that the mail address has any relationship to the zone being defined, although any use of the address requires proper name resolution of the e-mail address.

Resolution

A DNS server can actually receive two types of requests: *recursive* and *iterative* (also called *nonrecursive*). DNS clients always make recursive requests. DNS servers use both types of requests. The following is a list of responses.

- ▼ Positive authoritative
- ■ Positive
- ■ Referral
- ▲ Negative

A positive authoritative response indicates that the information returned is from an authoritative source. A positive or positive nonauthoritative response indicates that information returned is valid but was obtained from a nonauthoritative server. A referral is the IP address of another DNS server that is more suitable for handling the request. A negative response indicates that an authoritative source determined that either the domain name in the request does not exist, or the specified node does not exist.

A DNS server first attempts to process resolution requests locally by using the information in its zone files, whether they're primary or secondary, and its cache. If the information is found, the results are successfully returned to the requester.

If the information is not found locally, the next step is based upon whether the name server is forwarding requests and, if it's not, whether the request was recursive or iterative. Forwarding is the easiest method because the DNS server simply hands off the request to another DNS server.

TIP: Forwarding is a handy way to build up a cache, but it is not a good idea to chain forwarders. For example, do not have A forward to B and B forward to C. This leads to potential loops such as C forwarding back to A. It can also make DNS management difficult and DNS debugging a real nightmare.

For a recursive request, the DNS server attempts to process the request via the closest known authoritative name servers and returns one of the positive or the negative results. The closest known name servers are those that match a portion of the domain name being used in the request. For example, if the request is for server1.foo.bar.com, then a local search is made for name servers that handle server1.foo.bar.com, foo.bar.com, bar.com, and com. The name server can then send the request to the closest known name server.

A recursive or iterative request is then sent to the closest known name server. An iterative request is preferable because the requesting name server then handles any referral or negative responses. In addition, name servers can be set up to reject recursive requests.

If a recursive request is sent, the closest known name server is expected to return a positive or negative result. If an iterative request is sent, a referral request can also be returned. The referral will be to a name server that is an authoritative name server for the request or a name server that is logically closer to the authoritative name server. For example, an iterative request for server1.foo.bar.com that is sent to a name server for the bar.com domain could return a referral to the foo.bar.com name server. The name server that issued the iterative request would then send the request to the foo.bar.com name server. The iterative process can start at the root or at any point that is already known to the name server (possibly from prior requests that are cached). Eventually, the name server either locates an authoritative name server for the domain in question and responds based on its local information or returns a negative response because an authoritative name server for the domain could not be located. The latter can occur because the name server is inaccessible or the domain does not exist.

For an iterative request, the name server simply returns the best answer it knows. This can be a positive answer if the name server is authoritative for the domain and the information is found locally or if the information is cached from a prior, recursive request. If neither of these is the case, the answer can be a referral if the name server has a reference to another name server that handles a portion of the requested domain name. In this case, the best match should be returned. For example, if the request is for server1.foo.bar.com and the name server knows about the name servers for the domains foo.bar.com and bar.com, the IP address for foo.bar.com should be returned in the referral response.

In either approach, the root name server may have to be contacted. There are actually 13 root name servers around the world. These hold the Internet's DNS system together, and at least one must be available for the entire system to operate properly. There are multiple servers used to distribute the load and provide redundancy. Because these name servers are heavily used, they return referrals only to top-level name servers.

Figure 2-7 shows the resolution process of a recursive request from a DNS client where the name server uses iterative requests that start from a root name server. Figure 2-8 shows the same process, but the initial name server knows about an authoritative name server that partially matches the DNS client's request.

The following steps occur in Figure 2-7:

1. DNS Client sends recursive request for server1.foo.bar.com. to DNS Server 1.

2. DNS Server 1 checks the local database for server1.foo.bar.com. or any of the domains that it is part of but fails to find anything.

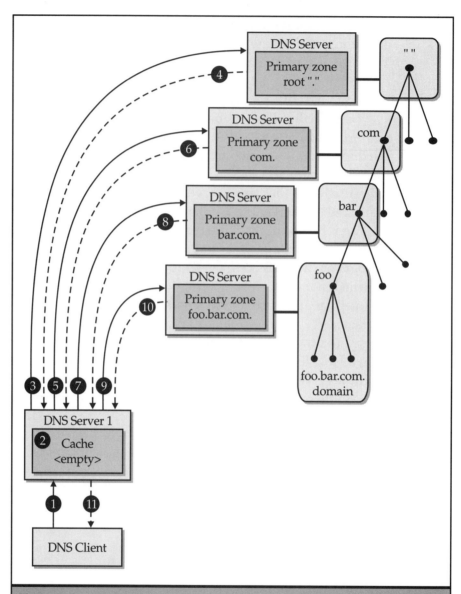

Figure 2-7. Iterative name resolution example starting from a root name server

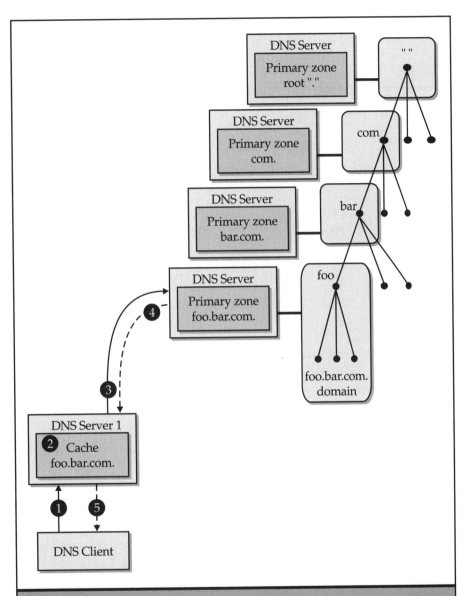

Figure 2-8. Iterative name resolution example starting below the root name server

3. DNS Server 1 sends an iterative request to the root (".") DNS Server.

4. Root DNS Server returns a referral to com DNS Server 1.

5. DNS Server 1 sends an iterative request to com DNS Server.

6. com DNS server returns a referral to bar.com DNS Server 1.

7. DNS Server 1 sends an iterative request to bar.com DNS Server.

8. bar.com DNS server returns a referral to foo.bar.com DNS Server 1.

9. DNS Server 1 sends an iterative request to foo.bar.com DNS Server.

10. Root DNS server returns a positive authoritative response for server1.foo.bar.com to DNS Server 1.

11. DNS Server 1 returns a positive authoritative response for server1.foo.bar.com to DNS Client.

Recursive requests can be sent instead of iterative requests but the process would then stop at step 2 since the root DNS server will not service a recursive request. Figure 2-8 assumes that the request processed in Figure 2-7 saved the address of the foo.bar.com DNS server. This allows a subsequent request for the same domain to be routed directly to an authoritative name server. The following steps occur in Figure 2-8:

1. DNS Client sends a recursive request for server2.foo.bar.com to DNS Server 1.

2. DNS Server 1 checks the local database for server1.foo.bar.com or any of the domains that it is part of and finds foo.bar.com.

3. DNS Server 1 sends an iterative request to foo.bar.com.

4. foo.bar.com DNS server returns positive authoritative response for server2.foo.bar.com to DNS Server 1.

5. DNS Server 1 returns positive authoritative response for server2.foo.bar.com to DNS Client.

NOTE: DNS Server 1 could have additional primary and secondary zone databases, but we assume that they are not related to the requests processed in Figure 2-7 and Figure 2-8. Likewise, a request for the same resource record of server1.foo.bar.com of Figure 2-7 in Figure 2-8 would result in an even shorter process in Figure 2-8 because the cache would also have included the cached server1.foo.bar.com information along with references to each of the name servers used in the process outlined in Figure 2-7.

The resolution process can occur without caching but, as Figure 2-8 shows, the time involved and the number of name servers involved in the resolution of a nonlocal domain can be significantly reduced through caching. Likewise, caching provides a more robust system since name servers lower in the tree can be accessed if their references are cached without the contacting name servers higher up—even if the name servers higher in the domain tree are not accessible. However, DNS caches do not retain information indefinitely, as outlined in the next section, so it is still important that these name servers are available at some point.

Referrals are not restricted to a single name server. In fact, most referrals include a list of name servers that typically includes the primary master name server and one or more secondary slave name servers. This allows the resolution process to proceed even if one of the name servers in the list is not accessible as shown in Figure 2-9.

The procedure followed in Figure 2-9 is the same as for Figure 2-7 except that two secondary slave name servers are available for the domain foo.bar.com. The secondary zone information is obtained from DNS Server A. The abbreviated response for step 8 shows that it will be the last one to be tried by the resolution process. The X on DNS Server C indicates that the server is not responding so the

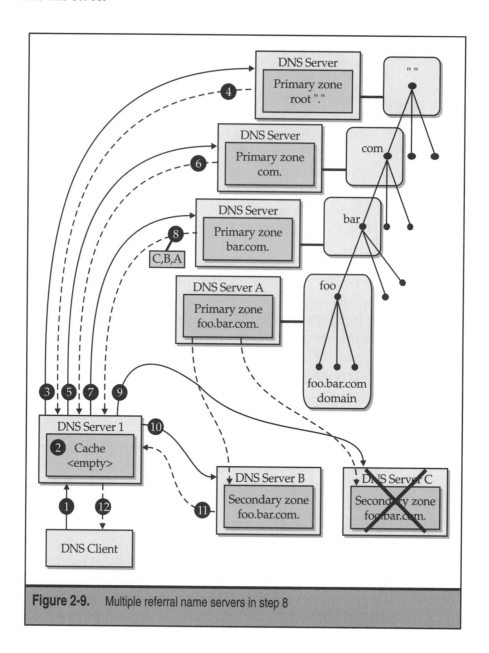

Figure 2-9.   Multiple referral name servers in step 8

request sent in step 9 fails, causing a subsequent request to be sent in step 10. This succeeds, so DNS Server A will not have to be contacted.

Caching and Time to Live (TTL)

Name servers can cache the results of requests that are made to it. This information then augments any primary or secondary zones that it manages. Cache-only name servers or cache-only servers only maintain a cache and do not manage primary or secondary zones.

Cache-only servers are advantageous because they require minimal management. Just set them up and they work. They start with an empty cache and process requests by checking the cache first. If the information is not found in the cache, then the cache only-name server performs the same iterative name resolution outlined in the previous section. Referral information and positive results are saved in the cache. The cache grows as the name server is used increasingly. Initially, the cache-only server winds up contacting other name servers for most requests. If requests continue to access the same domains, however, then the cache-only server handles more of the resolution process via the cache and makes fewer requests of other name servers. This is when a cache-only name server becomes advantageous.

A regular name server is a better choice if most of the requests the name server handles are for information contained in one of the primary or secondary zones that it manages. The name server will be able to respond to these requests immediately, unlike a cache-only server that must first query one or more servers to get the information.

So what are the limitations of a cache-only server and caching in general? There are actually two issues. The first is time to live (TTL). The second is the issue of positive and negative caching.

TTL indicates how long a cached entry can be kept. Each resource record in a zone can have a TTL associated with it. This allows certain records, such as those associated with a server with a fixed IP address, to be retained for a long period of time, while allowing dynamically assigned IP addresses, such as those assigned by a DHCP server and added to the DNS database via dynamic DNS updates, to expire more quickly.

The SOA record in a zone file has a minimum TTL that is used when a resource record specification does not include a TTL value or if a TTL value is less than the TTL specified in the SOA record. This allows an administrator to customize how information will be cached.

Positive caching occurs when positive results are obtained from a name server and these results are saved in the cache. Negative caching occurs when an authoritative name server indicates failure. This can occur if the requested subdomain or node does not exist. Negative caching does not occur if a request cannot be fulfilled, because an authoritative name server cannot be contacted. Negative caching is only available if the DNS server implements RFC 2308.

TIP: Set up at least one slave name server with a secondary zone for each primary zone within a network before adding cache-only name servers. A cache-only name server can obtain local information from either the primary or secondary zone, but it cannot do anything if these servers, or a lone master name server with the primary zone, are inaccessible.

Zone Database Files

Many Windows 2000 DNS administrators will choose to deal with primary and secondary zones using the graphical Windows 2000 Microsoft Management Console (MMC) DNS plug-in. The plug-in is the only way to deal with Active Directory–integrated zones directly, although all zones can be manipulated indirectly using the command line programs presented in Chapter 19. Still, many Windows 2000 DNS administrators will deal with primary and secondary zone files directly. There is a variety of reasons for this preference, including the use of custom or third-party applications that may manipulate or process the zones files.

This section is designed to provide an overview of a zone database file, its use, and the format for commonly used resource records. Appendix B provides a detailed list of the syntax and semantics for resource records. This section does not address configuration files normally used by third-party DNS servers such as BIND.

Forward and Reverse Zones

There are two types of zone files: forward and reverse. Thus far, we have concentrated on resolution requests that start with a domain name and result in an IP address. This type of query uses forward zone. Reverse queries take an IP address and obtain a domain name. This type of query uses a reverse zone. These queries are summarized in Table 2-4. Sample resource records are shown as well.

NOTE: Both forward and reverse zones can be primary and secondary zone files.

In reality, forward and reverse zone files are defined in the same fashion and searched in a similar fashion. The main difference with a reverse zone is that the zone file contains PTR resource records instead of A (address) records. Reverse zones are part of the in-addr.arpa. domain. Figure 2-10 shows how the in-addr.arpa. zones are constructed.

NOTE: Remember that the arpa domain was used for the ARPAnet address lookups. The in-addr domain stands for Internet address.

The same resolution procedure for forward zones can be used with reverse zones. In fact, the only real difference is the type of record requested. For forward queries, data from the A (address) resource record is requested. For reverse queries, data from the PTR resource record is requested.

This approach does lead to a slight reversal. For example, the IP address for server1.foo.bar.com shown in Figure 2-10 is 123.45.67.89.

Type	Key	Positive Result	Sample Resource Record
forward	server1.foo.bar.com.	123.45.67.89	server1.foo.bar.com. IN A 123.45.67.89
reverse	123.45.67.89	server1.foo.bar.com.	123.45.67.89 IN PTR server1.foo.bar.com.

Table 2-4.   Zone Lookup Types

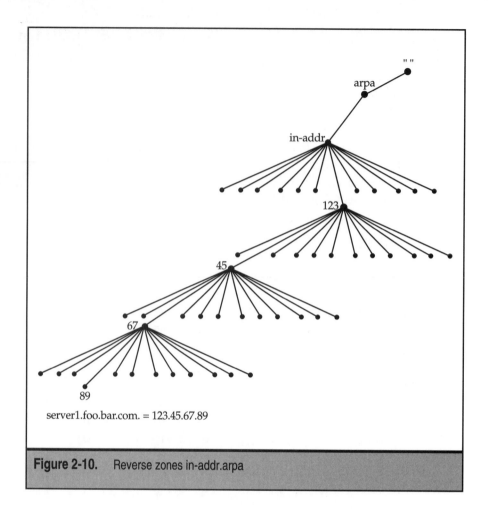

Figure 2-10. Reverse zones in-addr.arpa

This is found in the domain 67.45.123.in-addr.arpa. Notice how the order of the numbers in the domain name is reversed compared to the IP address. This is necessary because the most significant octet in the IP address is the least specific designator in the name, and the domain tree goes from the least specific, the root, to the most specific. This reversal shows up in the query as well. Requesting 123.in-addr.arpa. obviously uses the most significant portion of the IP address.

Zone Files

Zone files are text files with a very simple layout and a very simple syntax. Comments start with a semicolon and blank lines are ignored.

DNS resolution is case insensitive, so the text associated with zone resource records is also case insensitive. Zone files can be set up in a long form or an abbreviated short form. The next section examines the short form, which is more common but is often cryptic to new DNS managers.

The layout of the zone file itself is as follows:

▼   SOA record that indicates the zone's authority

■   NS records that indicate the name servers for this zone

▲   Other records

Each record, including the SOA and NS records, has the following format:

<name> <class> <TTL> <type> <data>

The <name> is the domain name for the resource record. It must start in column one. In the long form, it will be a FQDN. The <class> is optional, but if it exists, it will be IN (IN stands for Internet). There are other classes, but none is commonly used. The <TTL> field is optional and is almost never found in a zone file. It specifies the time to live for the resource record. Usually, the minimum TTL in the SOA record is used for all resource records in a zone file. The <type> is a keyword that indicates the resource record type. Some keywords for common resource records are SOA, NS, A, CNAME, MX, and PTR. The <data> is <type> specific. For example, an address type, A, has an IP address as its <data>.

NOTE: Remember that the name for a resource record must start in column one and a FQDN always ends in a period. One of the most common mistakes in editing a zone file is the omission of trailing periods. Omitting the trailing period changes the name from a FQDN to a relative domain name with respect to the zone defined by the zone file.

The following is a simple zone file.

```
foo.bar.com. IN SOA ns1.foo.bar.com. dnsmanager.foo.bar.com. (
            1               ; serial number
            3600            ; refresh (1 hour)
```

```
          600              ; retry (10 minutes)
          86400            ; expire (1 day)
          3600 )           ; min TTL (1 hour)

; NS Records
foo.bar.com. IN NS ns1.foo.bar.com.
foo.bar.com. IN NS ns2.foo.bar.com.

; Other records
ns1.foo.bar.com.   IN A   123.45.67.12
ns2.foo.bar.com.   IN A   123.45.67.25
server1.foo.bar.com.     IN A    123.45.67.1

; Aliases
www.foo.bar.com.   IN CNAME server1.foo.bar.com.
ftp.foo.bar.com.   IN A      123.45.67.1
```

The name of the SOA record is the domain name. There are a number of items in the data section of the SOA record that actually span six lines in this example. The first name after the SOA keyword is the primary name server for the domain. This is followed by the mail address of the person responsible for the domain. This address does not look like most mail addresses used on the Internet because it lacks the @ separator. In this case, the period that separates the first part of the name replaces the @. In this example, the mail address would be dnsmanager@foo.bar.com. Newer DNS implementations support the RP (responsible person) resource record that performs the same function but is more flexible. Appendix B provides a complete description of resource record types, including RP.

The SOA arguments in parentheses include comments to describe their function and values. These parameters are used by slave name servers when handling a secondary zone. The serial number is an arbitrary integer designed to distinguish different iterations of a zone file. In general, it is incremented each time a change is made. Some DNS managers prefer to encode the date as the serial number specifying the month, day, and year, in addition to a sequence number. The other parameters are discussed in Chapter 16.

This example zone file contains two name server NS records. This indicates that two name servers will have a copy of this zone file. Although these name servers are part of the domain defined by the zone file, there is no requirement that this be the case. If the name servers are outside the domain, then the name field for the NS record must be a FQDN.

There are three address resource records, A, in the next group. The address record data is the IP address associated with the FQDN. The two name servers are listed here. This would be how the domain names for the name servers would be converted to IP addresses.

The next group shows two ways to define aliases. An alias is a domain name that maps to an existing IP address. The CNAME resource record maps via a name. Changing the IP address for server1.foo.bar.com will cause it and the www.foo.bar.com name to map to the new IP address. On the other hand, the second alias, ftp.foo.bar.com, maps to the same IP address as server1.foo.bar.com. Unfortunately, changing the IP address of server1.foo.bar.com will not have the same effect on ftp.foo.bar.com. This may be the desired action, but aliases are typically best when implemented via CNAMEs.

We mentioned PTR records, but none shows up in this sample zone file because it is used for forward queries. We need to turn to a different zone file for reverse queries such as the following zone file.

```
67.45.123.in-addr.arpa. IN SOA ns1.foo.bar.com. dnsmanager.foo.bar.com. (
            1              ; serial number
            3600           ; refresh (1 hour)
            600            ; retry (10 minutes)
            86400          ; expire (1 day)
            3600 )         ; min TTL (1 hour)


; NS Records
67.45.123.in-addr.arpa. IN NS ns1.foo.bar.com.
67.45.123.in-addr.arpa. IN NS ns2.foo.bar.com.


; Other records
123.45.67.12.in-addr.arpa.    IN PTR    ns1.foo.bar.com.
123.45.67.25.in-addr.arpa.    IN PTR    ns2.foo.bar.com.
123.45.67.1.in-addr.arpa.     IN PTR    server1.foo.bar.com.
```

The start of the file is very similar to the forward zone file with the exception of the SOA's name. In this case, it is a familiar subdomain of in-addr.arpa. The name server records are the same, and we assume that both name servers will handle both the forward and reverse zones.

The difference occurs with the other records. In this case, there are just three PTR records, as only three hosts are actually used in the forward zone file. The only item to note is that server1.foo.bar.com. will be the only name associated with the IP address 123.45.67.1. The aliases, www.foo.bar.com and ftp.foo.bar.com, in the first zone file do not have a corresponding entry in this file.

> **NOTE:** Some DNS servers, such as the Windows 2000 DNS service, will automatically update the reverse zone by adding PTR records when address resource records (A) are added to a forward zone; this simplifies some management chores. Unfortunately, the converse is not always true, so be careful when deleting address resource records. A matching PTR record may have to be removed as well.

The sample zone files are short, but actual zone files can be rather large, so minimizing a zone file's contents can help to minimize the work needed to manage it as well as reduce potential problems. The next section looks at how the zone files presented in this section can be minimized.

> **NOTE:** Only a limited number of resource records are presented in this chapter. Other resource records are presented in other chapters and the complete list is found in Appendix B.

Zone Files: Short Form

The use of a number of abbreviations can considerably reduce the size and complexity of a zone file. The rules are simple—they have to be, or simplification would wind up in obfuscation.

The first abbreviation is the @. When used alone in the first column of a resource record, it refers to the current domain name associated with the zone.

The second abbreviation is a resource record without a name. In this case, it is necessary to look at the previous resource record because the one being discussed takes its name from it. This situation may appear to be unique, especially given a long chain of address resource records where the names are all different, but the situation is actually more common than the simple examples indicate. For example, additional resource record types not yet mentioned can apply to a node in addition to an address resource record.

The third abbreviation is the use of relative domain names instead of FQDNs. As mentioned in an earlier section, a relative domain name is converted to a FQDN by concatenating it with the domain name for the zone. The syntactical difference between a relative domain name and an FQDN is simply the trailing period found at the end of a FQDN.

The following is the same forward zone file that was presented earlier but with these three abbreviation methods used.

```
@ IN SOA ns1.foo.bar.com. dnsmanager.foo.bar.com. (
            1              ; serial number
            3600           ; refresh (1 hour)
            600            ; retry (10 minutes)
            86400          ; expire (1 day)
            3600 )         ; min TTL (1 hour)


; NS Records, Note @ is implied
            IN NS ns1.foo.bar.com.
            IN NS ns2.foo.bar.com.


; Other records
ns1         IN A   123.45.67.12
ns2         IN A   123.45.67.25
server1     IN A   123.45.67.1
; Aliases
www         IN CNAME server1
ftp         IN A    123.45.67.1
```

The SOA record utilizes the @ abbreviation, while the two NS records that appear directly after the SOA record need no name because they inherit the @ from the SOA. The address records no longer use FQDN. The same is true for the aliases. Even the CNAME data uses a relative domain name.

It is clear that the short form is more concise and more flexible. Change the domain name and the zone file requires little if any change. Even the reverse zone file can benefit from these abbreviations. In fact, the size reduction is often more significant because of the elimination of the in-addr.arpa. portion of the name.

```
@ IN SOA ns1.foo.bar.com.  dnsmanager.foo.bar.com. (
                1               ; serial number
                3600            ; refresh (1 hour)
                600             ; retry (10 minutes)
                86400           ; expire (1 day)
                3600 )          ; min TTL (1 hour)


; NS Records
                IN NS ns1.foo.bar.com.
                IN NS ns2.foo.bar.com.


; Other records
12              IN PTR          ns1.foo.bar.com.
25              IN PTR          ns2.foo.bar.com.
1               IN PTR          server1.foo.bar.com.
```

NOTE: It is possible to mix abbreviated and nonabbreviated definitions in the same file. In fact, this may be necessary. For example, a CNAME record may refer to a host that is not in the domain even though the name for the CNAME record is. In this case, the CNAME data must be a FQDN.

Two other features worth mentioning are the $ORIGIN and the $INCLUDE statements. These are meta statements, not resource record definitions. They are supported in BIND but not Windows 2000 DNS. They modify how the zone file is processed. The syntax for these two statements is:

$ORIGIN <domain-name>

$INCLUDE <file-name> [<domain-name>]

The $ORIGIN statement is used to change the domain name used with relative domain names. By default, this is initially the domain associated with the zone file, but the $ORIGIN statement allows this setting to be changed. It can be very useful when defining subdomains within a zone file. The following is a sample excerpt from a zone file:

```
; Resource records relative to the default domain foo.bar.com.
ns1        IN A  123.45.67.12
ns2        IN A  123.45.67.25
server1    IN A  123.45.67.1
;
; Resource records relative to subdomain1.foo.bar.com.
$ORIGIN  subdomain1.foo.bar.com.
www        IN A  123.45.68.1
ftp        IN A  123.45.68.2
server1    IN A  123.45.68.3
```

The $INCLUDE statement allows another file to be incorporated into the zone definition. It is a handy way to reduce the overall size of the main zone file. The optional <domain-name> is essentially the same as preceding the $INCLUDE statement with an $ORIGIN statement.

TIP: The $INCLUDE statement is a handy way to partition a zone file that contains subdomains. Each file is laid out just as a zone file except that there is no SOA record. This is because the zone can only have one SOA record in the main zone file.

We wrap this section up by looking at two useful resource record types: MX and SRV. The MX record is a mail exchange record used in conjunction with mail delivery. The SRV (service resource record) specifies the location of resources in the network. The SRV is used by Windows 2000 Active Directory to indicate where Windows 2000 resources are located.

The following is the syntax and an example of an MX record:

```
; Syntax: [<name>] IN [<TTL>] MX <preference> <exchange>
;
foo.bar.com.       IN MX 0     server1
                   IN MX 10    smtp.other.domain.com.
                   IN MX 10    ms1.another.domain.com.
                   IN MX 15    ms2.another.domain.com.
```

NOTE: The mail exchange can be a relative domain name. A mail exchange for the current domain can be specified using an @ as the name.

Specifying more than one mail exchange allows mail to be delivered to an alternate site even if the preferred mail server is unavailable. It is assumed that the alternate sites will attempt to deliver the mail to the primary site or that users will be able to pick up mail from the alternate site. The <preference> field is an arbitrary number indicating a site's relative preference. The lower the number, the higher the preference. The MX record is discussed in more detail in Chapter 18.

The following is the syntax and an example of an SRV:

```
; Syntax: [<name>] IN [<TTL>] SRV <priority> <weight> <port> <target>
;
; Windows 2000 Syntax:
; [<service>.<protocol>.<name>] IN [<TTL>] SRV <priority> <weight> <port> <target>
;
_ldap._tcp.dc._msdcs       IN SRV 0    0    389   server1
                           IN SRV 0    20   389   server2
                           IN SRV 10   0    389   ldap.other.domain.com.
_kerberos._tcp.dc._msdcs   IN SRV 0    0    389   server1
                           IN SRV 0    20   389   server2
```

In general, the name can be any valid node name. Windows 2000 services follow a stricter definition. In particular, the resource record name is divided into subdomains that include the type of Windows 2000 service and protocol. Two of the Windows 2000 services, _ldap and _kerberos, are shown in the example. Two Windows 2000 protocols include _tcp and _udp. Chapter 15 provides more details on the service records used with Windows 2000 Active Directory. These are normally added via dynamic DNS updates, which are discussed next.

DYNAMIC DNS

Dynamic DNS refers to a feature specified by RFC 2136, Dynamic Updates in the Domain Name System (DNS UPDATE), that allows zones to be updated by a third party. Normally a zone can only be modified by a DNS manager who makes changes to the zone file and then restarts or notifies the name server of the change. Windows 2000 DNS and BIND 8 support RFC 2136.

The initial intention of the dynamic DNS update feature was to support DHCP clients that wanted to register their names with the DNS server, thereby allowing others to locate the client. Microsoft also utilizes dynamic DNS updates to store Windows 2000 Active Directory domain information in a zone so Windows 2000 clients can locate Windows 2000 domain services. This is important because the Windows 2000 client logon process starts with a Kerberos password service located through the client's DNS server. Details of the entries added by Windows 2000 Active Directory can be found in Chapter 15.

NOTE: Dynamic DNS update eliminates the need to use Microsoft's WINS (Windows Internet Naming Service) that performs the same function. WINS is only supported with Windows operating systems, including Windows NT and Windows 2000, whereas dynamic DNS updates are supported by most current DNS servers.

This section presents an overview of the dynamic DNS update protocol.

Dynamic DNS is a facility whereby authorized systems can add or delete resource records via a name server that is authoritative for the zone being modified. Unauthorized or secondary servers that support dynamic DNS will forward updates to the authoritative server. A dynamic DNS client can find the authoritative server via the name server records in the zone database nonauthoritative name servers. Figure 2-11 shows how this process operates with a

DNS client that obtains its IP address from the DHCP server. The steps include:

1. The client requests an IP address from the DHCP server.

2. The DHCP server returns an IP address to the client.

3. The client sends a dynamic DNS update with an address resource record that includes the client's domain name and new IP address.

4. DNS Server 1 is not authoritative, so it forwards the dynamic DNS update request to DNS Server 2.

5. DNS Server 2 is authoritative and returns a positive result to DNS Server 1.

6. DNS Server 1 returns the positive result to the client.

Additions and deletions can be performed on individual resource records. It is also possible to delete all records or a set of records associated with a particular domain name. The latter takes into account the class and type of resource records. Additions can be made conditional based upon whether a set of resource records exists

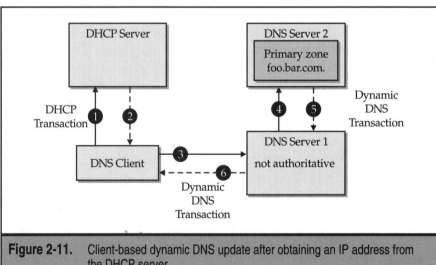

Figure 2-11. Client-based dynamic DNS update after obtaining an IP address from the DHCP server

or does not exist. For example, a mail exchange (MX) resource record could be added only if the mail server resource record was already defined.

Dynamic DNS update messages are effectively hidden with Windows 2000 clients and when Windows 2000 DHCP acts as a proxy, as shown in Figure 2-12. In the latter case, the DHCP service contacts the DNS server after the DHCP service delivers a new IP address to a DHCP client. The client's name, combined with the domain name set by the DHCP administrator, is sent as a dynamic DNS update to the DNS server.

1. The client requests an IP address from the DHCP server.

2. The DHCP server returns an IP address to the client.

3. The DHCP sends a dynamic DNS update with an address resource record that includes the client's domain name and new IP address.

4. DNS Server returns the positive result to the DHCP Server.

UNIX and Linux systems utilize a program called nsupdate to perform their dynamic DNS update chores. This program can also be used as a utility to perform arbitrary updates remotely.

Dynamic DNS updates could wreak havoc if improperly used. Third-party DNS servers like BIND 8 can selectively allow or prevent

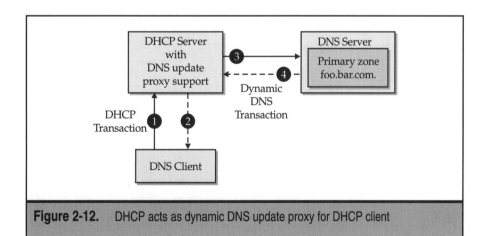

Figure 2-12.   DHCP acts as dynamic DNS update proxy for DHCP client

updates. The restrictions are based upon IP addresses, so even this limitation may not be sufficient in some high security environments.

Windows 2000 DNS service has the ability to implement similar security restrictions, and it adds secure dynamic DNS updates that are linked to Windows 2000 Active Directory–based security. In this case, the client making the dynamic DNS update request must already be recognized by Active Directory through the login process. Windows 2000 Kerberos identification verifies that the request is coming from a valid client, and further checking of access rights allows this form of secure update to allow finer grain security management.

TIP: Windows 2000 clients support dynamic DNS update directly. Windows 2000 DHCP service supports proxy updates for non-Windows 2000 clients such as Windows 95 and Windows 98. Switch from Microsoft WINS to Windows 2000 DHCP support if possible. This will minimize management chores.

DNS IMPLEMENTATIONS

There are a number of DNS service implementations available for both the Windows environment as well as other operating systems typically found in a Windows network. Many of these can support Windows 2000 networks, but others cannot. In the latter case, a DNS server may still be a useful adjunct to the former if the unsupported features are not needed. For example, a caching server that sits between a Windows 2000 network and the Internet does not have to support advanced DNS features like dynamic DNS updates and SRVs.

Two popular DNS services stand out because of their usefulness in Windows NT environments, the precursor to Windows 2000. These services are BIND and Windows NT DNS service. BIND versions 8.1 and later provide support to Windows 2000 and Active Directory by supporting both SRV and dynamic DNS updates. Windows NT's DNS service does not fare as well.

Using BIND with Windows 2000 is covered in more detail in Chapter 21. BIND is often used in larger organizations that utilize

Windows 2000 for application, file, and print services but that use
UNIX and BIND to provide Web and DNS services. Replacing BIND
is often difficult or politically incorrect but, luckily, BIND can handle
even a large Windows 2000 network.

The DNS service that comes with Windows NT is rather basic.
While Windows NT supports TCP/IP, it is not its native protocol,
and the level of DNS implementation reflects this lack of importance.
Windows NT DNS service is capable, but it is on a par with earlier
versions of BIND and is unsuitable as a DNS service for Windows
2000 Active Directory support. In particular, Windows NT DNS
service lacks SRV and dynamic DNS support.

It is possible to keep Windows NT DNS servers around by using
third-party DNS services such as the Windows port of BIND or
commercial products like Checkpoint Software Technologies, Ltd.'s
(**www.metaip.checkpoint.com**) Meta IP Standard. Meta IP Standard
includes Meta DNS, which is a version of BIND 8.1.2. Meta DNS
incorporates a very nice user interface, good reporting, and
management tools and integration with Meta IP Standard's
DHCP support.

DNS CLIENT NAME RESOLUTION PROCESS

We have discussed DNS client operation as though a DNS is always
used for name resolution. Unfortunately, DNS is not always the first
method used by many operating systems when trying to resolve names
to addresses or vice versa. In fact, a client can perform this resolution
process without even contacting a DNS server if two things occur. First,
the client must be set up to use a host cross-reference file. Second, the
name being resolved must be located in the host cross-reference file.

The host cross-reference file is normally a simple list with each
line containing an IP address and a domain name. The name and
location of the file may vary from operating system to operating
system or even from one protocol driver implementation to another.
For example, under Linux and many UNIX implementations, the
file is /etc/hosts. For the Windows 98 TCP/IP support, the file is
LMHOSTS.SAM and is located in the \Windows directory.

The host cross reference is normally used before DNS is used. This can cause a client not to recognize changes in the DNS server since the file is used first.

TIP: Set clients up to always use DNS by deleting the host cross-reference file or making sure the file is empty. It can be very disconcerting debugging a DNS server when a change to the DNS server zone files has no effect on the DNS clients because they are finding what they need in the host cross reference file.

Windows 98 host file format actually extends the comment syntax to include the domain name or workgroup name. The extension is hidden in a comment, so the same file can be used with TCP/IP stacks that do not handle the extension. The pound sign (#) indicates the start of a comment. For example, a line associated with the server Server4 in domain FOO would look like:

```
123.45.67.8  Server4   #dom:FOO
```

With the exception of the Windows extensions, the host file does not provide anything beyond name resolution, not even references to other services like name servers or mail servers. A DNS server can provide these added benefits; these details are addressed later in the book.

SUMMARY

DNS name resolution is a relatively simple process. The RFCs mentioned at the start of the chapter describe the process in more detail. Even so, keeping DNS servers working properly is a complex task, as the rest of this book shows. It is especially important that DNS systems work properly in a Windows 2000 network as Windows 2000 services are often discovered using DNS queries.

CHAPTER 3

DNS and Windows 2000

This chapter presents an overview of Windows 2000 and its relationship to DNS. Each of the topics presented in this chapter are covered in more detail in the rest of the book.

Unlike Windows NT, Windows 2000 and Active Directory are tightly melded to IP and DNS. Without these components, Windows 2000 and Active Directory do not work. Windows 2000 can support non-Windows 2000 clients in a mixed-mode environment using a Windows NT compatibility mode. However, while suitable for migration purposes, the mixed-mode environment only provides features and security on a par with Windows NT and not the feature-rich, high-security mode inherent in a native Windows 2000 environment.

We will first look at what goes on underneath a Windows 2000 Active Directory client logon sequence in the section of that name. Unlike a Windows NT logon, which works just fine without DNS, IP and DNS are required to get things started.

NOTE: Windows 2000 supports a Windows NT compatibility mode. Non-Windows 2000 clients such as Windows NT, Windows 98, and Windows 95 can log on to Windows 2000 using this mode without needing DNS—or IP, for that matter. This type of connection, however, does not use the more secure Windows 2000–based Kerberos authentication.

To get some insight into the depth that IP and DNS are involved with Windows 2000, we'll take a look at the Windows 2000 domain hierarchy. It is closely related to the DNS domain hierarchy, but there are distinct differences, including Windows 2000 Active Directory's use of organizational units (OU) to manage groups of users and resources.

Not surprisingly, Windows 2000's dependence on IP and DNS tends to push the envelope, along with the other features in Windows 2000. In the section "Windows 2000 DNS Requirements," we'll look at what the minimum requirements are for a DNS server that supports Windows 2000. This can be the Windows 2000 DNS service, but many third-party DNS implementations work as well.

Next, we'll delve into the basics in the section "Windows 2000 DNS and Active Directory integration." Windows 2000 DNS adds a bit more spice to DNS with proprietary extensions that are tightly integrated with Windows 2000 Active Directory support.

Most Windows NT network managers will be familiar with Windows NT's Windows Internet Naming Service (WINS). While Windows 2000 still supports WINS, there are reasons its use should be limited or eliminated within a Windows 2000 network. The features that Microsoft incorporated into the proprietary WINS system have been migrated to the standards-based Windows 2000 DNS service.

In the section "What Is Special About Windows DHCP Service?" we'll take a look at the new Windows 2000 DHCP service. It will play an important part in mixed-mode Windows 2000 networks with non-Windows 2000 clients because of its ability to perform dynamic DNS updates supported by the Windows 2000 DNS service. It is one area where WINS was needed in Windows NT, although WINS can be replaced with a combination of the Windows 2000 DNS service and the Windows 2000 DHCP service.

Next, we include a brief discussion about Windows 2000 DNS clients and why they provide an advantage over other Windows clients, including Windows 95, Windows 98, and Windows NT.

Finally, there are the migration issues when moving to a Windows 2000–based network. These issues are presented in this chapter, but the details and answers will be found later in the book.

WINDOWS 2000 ACTIVE DIRECTORY LOGON SEQUENCE

Although users will not see it, the importance of DNS is apparent almost immediately when looking under the hood as a user sits down in front of a Windows 2000 workstation or server to log into an Active Directory domain.

The first thing that a Windows 2000 user sees after pressing CONTROL-ALT-DELETE is the logon screen from the local Winlogon service. It looks very similar to a Windows NT logon screen, but the similarity is only skin deep. What goes on in the background is significantly different, and understanding what happens provides an insight into why Windows 2000 is so different from Windows NT. We will forego the details that occur inside the local workstation for local authentication and concentrate on what happens with respect to a Windows 2000 domain controller. Figure 3-1 shows the interaction between the Windows 2000 client, the domain name server (DNS), and the Windows 2000 domain controller.

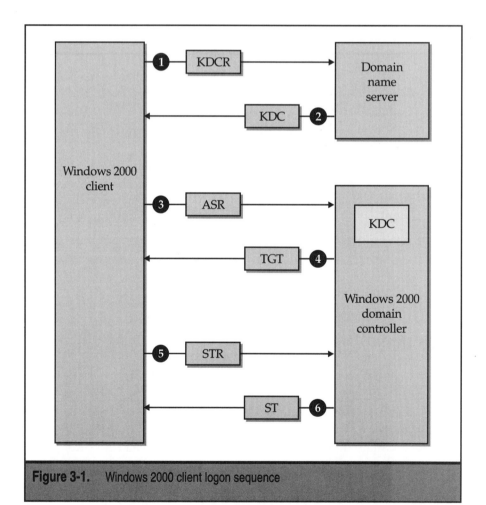

Figure 3-1.   Windows 2000 client logon sequence

Locating a Domain Server

First, an Active Directory domain controller must be located. This is done using a DNS service that the client already knows about. The DNS server's IP address can be set in the Windows 2000 network configuration if either the client has a static IP address, or the DNS Server's IP address can be obtained from the DHCP server that supplies a dynamic IP address. If a DNS server cannot be contacted, the domain log in process cannot proceed. The DNS service is sent a DNS request (KDCR) (step 1 in Figure 3-1) to locate one or more Kerberos key distribution centers (KDCs). The KDC is located on a Windows 2000 domain controller, as shown in Figure 3-1.

The DNS service can return the locations of the KDCs (step 2) if its zone database contains a service resource record (SRV) for the requested domain and service type. More details on SRVs are in the "Windows 2000 DNS Requirements" section. The SRV information is normally supplied to the DNS service using dynamic DNS updates by the Windows 2000 domain controller when the Windows 2000 domain controller starts up. Alternatively, the DNS administrator can add this information to the zone database. In either case, the information is necessary so that the DNS service can return the KDC response with one or more IP addresses.

The use of DNS SRV resource records for the Windows 2000 log in process is just one of the reasons Windows 2000 requires DNS. In addition to the domain controllers, the DNS service will have SRV resource records for other Windows 2000 services such as LDAP. This allows Windows 2000 applications to have a single, standards-based source for service location information.

Getting a Ticket

The user has entered a name, domain name, and a password. This information is collected together in an authentication service request (ASR) that is sent to the KDC (step 3). Part of the ASR is encrypted, and part of it is not. Details of this Kerberos authentication operation are covered in Chapter 4. The encryption key is generated using a one-way hash that includes the user's password. The hash algorithm is known to all clients and servers, but the encryption key can only be generated if the algorithm and the password are known. Of course, the KDC will have access to this information since the user's name and password are stored in the Active Directory database.

The KDC receives the ASR and verifies the request by generating the same encryption key, based on the user name and domain name in the unencrypted portion of the ASR. The key is used to decrypt the message. The request can then be processed. Assuming everything is in order, including validating the user's logon rights in the Active Directory database, the KDC generates a ticket granting ticket (TGT). The TGT can be used by the client to access other services within the domain. The KDC returns the TGT (step 4), which is encrypted, to the client.

The first thing the client does it to turn around and send a session ticket request (STR) to the KDC (step 5) so a session can be opened on the client. The STR is generated using a key that is part of the TGT.

The KDC receives the STR and decrypts the request. It can do this because it generated the original TGT. The request is checked against the rights in the Active Directory database, and a session ticket (ST) is returned to the client (step 6), who can then log on to the workstation, assuming everything went smoothly. Details that are checked include whether the user account is valid, whether the current time is within the allowable logon times, and whether the user is allowed to log on to the client workstation.

The client logon routine uses the ST to open a new session on the client. The TGT is retained so that subsequent communication with the domain server or other servers can be performed. All native Windows 2000 authentication is done using Kerberos and tickets starting with the ASR and TGT. A Windows 2000 client cannot use any Windows 2000 services if a TGT cannot be obtained.

NOTE: The Window NT logon and authentication process is completely different from the Windows 2000 logon process outlined here. Windows NT and other non-Windows 2000 clients can only access a Windows 2000 server if the server is operating in compatibility mode. This supports the less secure Windows NT access protocol.

TIP: Switch to native Windows 2000 as soon as possible if security is a major issue. The Windows 2000 Kerberos-based authentication is significantly more secure than the Windows NT authentication.

The logon process outlined in this section is the only mechanism available if the Windows 2000 Active Directory service is operating in native Windows 2000 mode. If the domain is running in compatibility mode, then Windows NT support is provided and the Windows 2000 server appears to be a Windows NT primary domain controller (PDC), as shown in Figure 3-2.

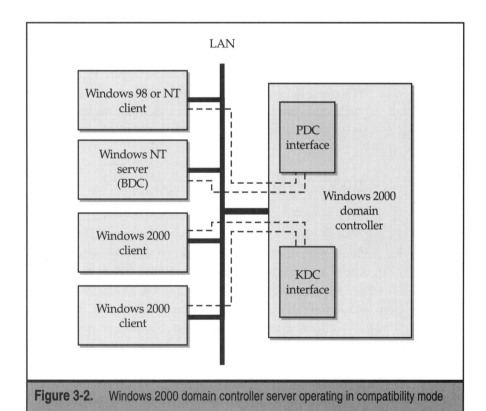

Figure 3-2.   Windows 2000 domain controller server operating in compatibility mode

If Windows 2000 is installed in an existing Windows NT domain, the Windows 2000 domain controller will be set up to replace the Windows NT PDC. The Windows 2000 PDC support allows Windows NT backup domain controllers (BDC) to exist on the network and operate with the Windows 2000 PDC support. The Windows NT BDCs can be upgraded to a Windows 2000 domain controller as necessary. Unlike Windows NT, which allows only a single PDC, Windows 2000 domain controllers operate at the same level.

NOTE: Replacement of a Windows NT PDC is typically done by upgrading a Windows NT PDC to a Windows 2000 domain controller. The Windows 2000 server then services the BDCs until they can be upgraded to Windows 2000 domain controllers. At that point, the distinction between primary and secondary goes away, as Windows 2000 domain controllers operate as peers. The Windows 2000 upgrade process from a PDC or BDC to a Windows 2000 domain controller is not addressed in this book. Windows 2000 Active Directory services are installed after the upgrade takes place. Active Directory installation is covered in Chapter 5.

WINDOWS 2000 DOMAIN HIERARCHY

Like Windows NT, Windows 2000 is domain-based, but whereas Windows NT provided distinct domains, Windows 2000 provides hierarchical domain support when more than one domain is needed. The complete details of the Windows 2000 domain hierarchy and Active Directory support are covered in Chapter 4. The basics are presented here so that the related DNS issues can be discussed in this chapter.

The Windows 2000 domain hierarchy has a matching DNS hierarchy in both form and function although the Windows 2000 domain hierarchy is much more rigid. In fact, once the Windows 2000 domain hierarchy is in place it cannot be changed, only destroyed and rebuilt. The Windows 2000 domain hierarchy must also have a matching DNS hierarchy to match or Active Directory will not operate properly. In general, each Windows 2000 domain has a matching DNS domain with the same name. Defined in the DNS domain will be the published services as mentioned in the previous section.

Windows NT Trusts

Figure 3-3 shows a number of Windows NT domains that contain a collection of PDCs and BDCs along with trust relationships between domains. Notice that the trust relationships are explicit and that there is no implied relationship between Domain B and Domain C even though both trust Domain A. Each domain is dependent upon its

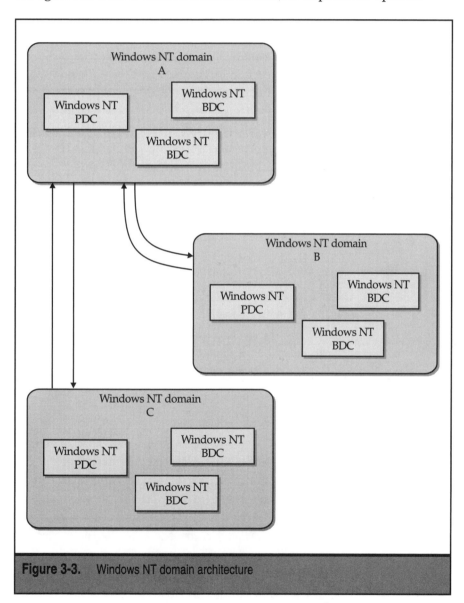

Figure 3-3.   Windows NT domain architecture

PDC. A BDC can be upgraded to a PDC if a PDC fails, but this process must be performed by a network administrator.

Windows 2000's Active Directory domain architecture is modeled after the hierarchical domain architecture used by DNS. In fact, in a hierarchical Windows 2000 domain design, the domain names are managed by a DNS server. Windows 2000 Active Directory supports both domain trees and forests. A domain tree is the same type of hierarchy used with DNS. A typical domain name for the root of a tree is mycompany.com. Domains in the next level down incorporate this name, as in administration.mycompany.com.

Domain forests are used in larger Windows 2000 networks. A forest consists of any number of Windows 2000 domain trees. The only difference between the trees is the domain name of the root. These must be distinct. This situation often arises when two organizations merge. It can also occur when a corporation has a Web site that uses a product name instead of the company name. In this case, the two domains can still be part of a single Windows 2000 network, providing the same level of security throughout the network.

NOTE: Deep or wide domain trees or domain forests should be used frugally. Management becomes a much more complex task as the number of domains increases, and Windows 2000 can handle a larger number of nodes per domain than Windows NT. It is usually preferable to have a single domain with twice as many nodes rather than splitting the nodes into two domains. Also, the use of organizational units can be used to address management-related issues rather than using multiple Windows NT domains.

TIP: Use DNS domains instead of Windows 2000 domains for a multiple domain–architecture if a domain is used to provide access to Web-based services. For example, www.product.com is the name of a Web site that a company provides, but the company domain name is company.com. A single Windows 2000 domain and matching DNS domain can handle company.com. This domain will service all the users. A Web server is associated with www.product.com and a matching product.com DNS domain can be used. In fact, the Web server can still be a part of the company.com domain by supporting two IP addresses.

Transitive Trusts

Windows 2000 Active Directory also changes how trusts are set up and used compared to Windows NT. Transitive trusts are inherent in a Windows 2000 domain tree. The bidirectional trusts match the branches of the tree, and the administrator of the root domain can manage domain controllers in child domains. The transitive nature of the trusts allows implied trusts between domains within the same tree. A transitive trust is also set up between root domains in a domain forest.

Transitive trusts can only be used between Windows 2000 domains. Explicit trusts can still be used between a Windows 2000 and Windows NT system, but two trust relationships, one in each direction, must be set up for bidirectional trusts. These trusts cannot be transitive.

Windows 2000 domain controllers within a domain operate in a multiple master configuration. If one Windows 2000 domain controller fails or is turned off, the others continue to support the domain. No upgrading is necessary as with Windows NT, even if the Windows 2000 domain controller never comes back online. Figure 3-4 shows a simple domain hierarchy including the trust links that also represent the domain child relationships of the domain tree. The bidirectional arrows in the figure indicate a bidirectional trust between domains. The solid lines indicate transitive trusts. The dashed line indicates an implied trust due to the transitive trusts. In particular, both the sales.foo.com and software.foo.com domains trust the foo.com domain. There is an implied trust between the sales.foo.com and software.foo.com domains because they both trust foo.com. There would not be an implied trust if the other trusts were not transitive. Trusts are covered in Chapter 4.

Organizational Units

Windows 2000 continues the hierarchy within a domain allowing resources to be grouped and managed. The grouping is done using Window 2000 organizational units (OU). Organizational units use the same naming convention, so an OU may have a name like sales.software.mycompany.com within a domain mycompany.com.

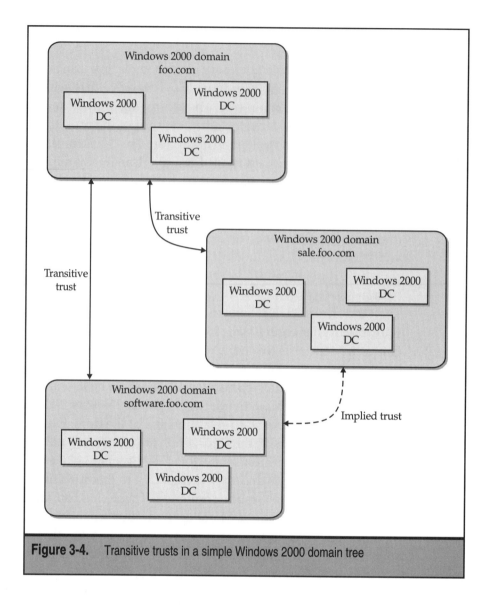

Figure 3-4.   Transitive trusts in a simple Windows 2000 domain tree

The main difference between Windows 2000 domain names and OUs with respect to DNS is that DNS is only used to track domains, not OUs. This is not to say that DNS entries may not follow the OU naming convention within a Windows 2000 domain tree. For example, a Web server might have a name like www.sales.software.mycompany.com. This name would be kept in a DNS database along with the domain mycompany.com, but the intervening OU names would not.

This difference is due to how the Windows 2000 hierarchy is constructed versus the DNS hierarchy. In the case of Windows 2000, the hierarchy is part of the architecture. OUs must be defined under a domain or another OU. The name of an OU is the implicit concatenation of domain and OU names. With the DNS hierarchy, entries within the domain can include any combination of names such as a.very.long.dns.name.in.domain.mycompany.com. This is only possible within the domain. DNS domains with subdomains delegated to other DNS servers must be defined within a strict hierarchy. In this sense, the DNS hierarchy does match the Windows 2000 hierarchy in form and function.

Another difference between the Windows 2000 hierarchy and a DNS hierarchy is DNS's ability to support aliases. For example, under the Windows 2000 hierarchy, a computer has a distinct name. With DNS, an IP address associated with a computer may be used with a number of DNS names. For example, a computer may host a web service and an FTP service so the DNS database would have two entries: www.server1.mycompany.com and ftp.server1.mycompany.com. These would both map to the same IP address. The computer may have other DNS names associated with it as well.

WINDOWS 2000 DNS REQUIREMENTS

While OUs are not tracked via DNS, Windows 2000 does use DNS to track more than just the domain name. You can find a host of services that allow Windows 2000 clients to locate these services under the DNS domain for the matching Windows 2000 domain name. These services are stored in the DNS SRVs mentioned in Chapter 2. This makes SRV-support mandatory for any DNS service used to support Windows 2000's Active Directory services. This includes DNS servers that Windows 2000 clients use to log on to a Windows 2000 domain.

NOTE: A Windows 2000 client can also be a Windows 2000 server. In this case, the Windows 2000 server is accessing another Windows 2000 system. It uses the same access protocols and procedures as a Windows 2000 Professional workstation.

Windows 2000 requires a hierarchy of DNS definitions below the domain name associated with a Windows 2000 domain. While it is useful to know that these definitions and subzones exist, the actual way these definitions are used is well hidden by Active Directory. The use of dynamic DNS updates allows a Windows 2000 Active Directory domain controller to add the information automatically. DNS managers will not usually need to set up or modify this information if the primary DNS zone is managed by a Windows 2000 DNS service or if a third-party service supports dynamic DNS updates.

A naming convention has been adopted by Microsoft that uses underscores as the first character of the domain name, for example, _sites. The rest of the name indicates the function or protocol, as in _tcp. Table 3-1 enumerates the subzones that a Windows 2000 domain controller will need. Be aware that Windows 2000's use of the underscore character can cause problems with third-party DNS servers.

The _udp subdomain contains one or more SRV records named _kpasswd that enumerate the Windows 2000 domain controllers providing Kerberos password support used for log in. The _tcp includes a copy of these as well, along with _ldap and _gc references. The _ldap SRVs indicate servers that provide a LDAP

Subdomain Name	Description
_msdcs	Domain controller services
_sites	Windows 2000 sites
_tcp	TCP-based services
_udp	UDP-based services

Table 3-1.   Windows 2000 Domain Subdomains

support file, and the _gc reference is for the Active Directory global catalog support.

The _sites subdomain contains a subdomain for each site defined under Windows 2000 Active Directory. The Default-First-Site-Name is created when the first Windows 2000 domain controller is installed, but this site can be renamed or eliminated after other sites have been defined. Each individual site subdomain has a _tcp subdomain that includes entries for _ldap, _gc, and _kerberos.

The _msdcs subdomain contains a number of subdomains. These are listed in Table 3-2.

The domain controller subdomain dc contains a list of sites under a _sites subdomain and a list of LDAP and Kerberos servers under the _tcp protocol subdomain. These entries are also found under the _sites and _tcp subdomains listed in Table 3-1. The subdomains under the domains subdomain look a bit cryptic, but the names are actually GUIDs for the domains. The gc subdomain provides a way to locate Active Directory global catalog servers. This is also based on _sites and _tcp protocol subdomains. Finally, there is the pdc subdomain. Although Windows NT–compatible clients do not look at this subdomain to locate a PDC, Windows 2000 can.

The various subdomains listed above include SRVs for each domain controller within a Windows 2000 domain. This allows a Windows 2000 client to locate all Windows 2000 Active Directory domain controllers and contact them as necessary. The SRVs contain information that allow Windows 2000 clients to prioritize the domain

Subdomain Name	Description
dc	Windows 2000 domain controllers
domains	Windows 2000 domains
gc	Windows 2000 global catalog
pdc	Windows 2000 primary domain controllers

Table 3-2.   _msdcs Subdomain Definitions

controllers so that the most desirable domain controller will be contacted first. This prioritization typically leads to access to a local domain controller first.

Windows 2000 domain controllers can set up DNS SRV definitions using dynamic DNS support, which is described in more detail in Chapter 15. Although not required, this method of updating the DNS zone database that contains the Windows 2000 domain definition makes a DNS manager's job easier and forces the DNS server to maintain accurate records with respect to the Windows 2000 domain services.

If dynamic DNS support is not available, a DNS manager must place these records in the DNS zone database. Any changes in the domain controllers must be reflected in the database, which makes more work for the DNS manager. Luckily, Windows 2000 domain controllers normally have a single, fixed IP address, and domain controllers are not added and removed on a regular basis. Although this makes the problem manageable, the job tends to be rather large when a network includes a large number—possibly hundreds—of domain controllers.

Windows 2000 DNS supports both SRV and dynamic DNS updates. Windows 2000 DNS also supports integration with Active Directory.

WINDOWS 2000 DNS AND ACTIVE DIRECTORY INTEGRATION

Windows 2000 DNS supports both SRVs and dynamic DNS updates, but the Windows 2000 implementation does more. The most notable difference from a standards-based DNS implementation is the integration of the Windows 2000 DNS zone storage with Windows 2000 Active Directory database. While the Windows 2000 DNS service still supports the standards-based primary and secondary zone replication support, the new Active Directory integration allows the Windows 2000 DNS service to operate zones in a multimaster mode instead of the master-slave mode associated with a primary-secondary approach. The details of this integra-

tion are presented in Chapter 4 and addressed in other chapters
dealing with the distribution of DNS servers throughout various
size networks.

Figure 3-5 shows how standard DNS servers can operate in a
master-slave relationship. The master copy of a DNS zone database is
maintained by the DNS server with the primary zone. DNS servers
with a secondary zone obtain a copy from either the DNS server with
the primary zone or another DNS server with an updated copy of the
secondary zone.

For static operation, the master-slave relationship works well.
Even if the primary zone is unavailable for some time, the secondary

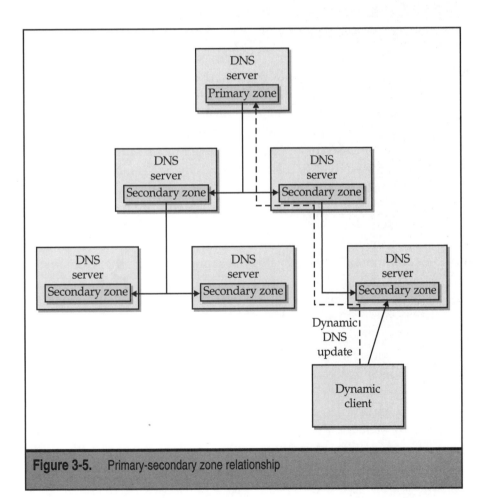

Figure 3-5.   Primary-secondary zone relationship

zones can provide DNS services with exactly the same information. The only service that cannot be performed is updating the zone information because that must be done in the primary zone. The change is then replicated among the secondary zones.

Dynamic DNS updates change the situation substantially. First, the updates must done at the primary zone, so any dynamic DNS client must eventually get its information forwarded to the primary zone. The information is then replicated down through the primary-secondary zone hierarchy. If you make the primary zone inaccessible, dynamic updates cannot occur.

Active Directory-Integrated Zones

Active Directory–integrated zones operate in a different fashion. Figure 3-6 shows how Windows 2000 DNS servers use Active Directory. All Windows 2000 domain controllers within a domain maintain a copy of the same Active Directory database. Changes can be made at any domain controller and are replicated by the Active Directory service at all sites. Windows 2000 DNS servers using an Active Directory–integrated zone must reside on a domain controller so the Active Directory–integrated zone can be stored in the Active Directory database.

Dynamic DNS updates from clients are handled by any of the Windows 2000 DNS servers in Figure 3-6. These changes are added to the Active Directory database, and the Active Directory service automatically replicates the changes to the other domain servers that, in turn, provide the new information to the DNS servers.

Windows 2000 DNS service also allows secure dynamic DNS updates. This secure update only works with an authenticated Windows 2000 client like a Windows 2000 Professional workstation, which uses the Kerberos authentication that is based upon the initial logon procedure for any Windows 2000 client. In addition, the updates are checked against the rights set by the DNS manager for each domain, making it possible to specify which workstations can update the DNS database. Conventional dynamic DNS updates can have IP-based restrictions, but there is no comparable authenticated security. This makes the Windows 2000 approach unique.

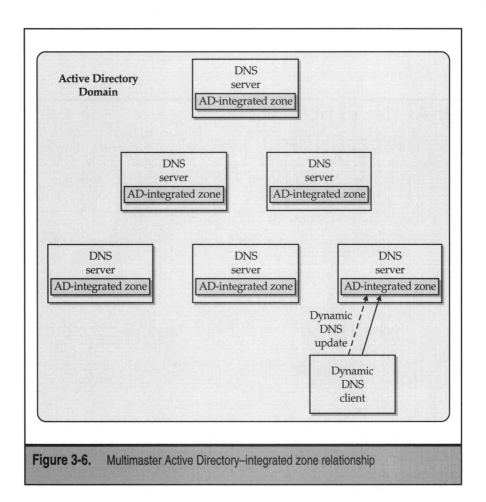

Figure 3-6.   Multimaster Active Directory–integrated zone relationship

Active Directory–integrated zones are required for secure
updates. Active Directory–integrated zones also have the advantage
of Active Directory's access security, so it is possible to permit certain
actions by various people allowing fine control over who can be a
DNS manager and what they can change. For example, they may be
restricted from deleting server records but permitted to change
resource records for local PCs.

The dynamic DNS update support effectively eliminates the need
for the Windows Internet Naming Service (WINS) that was made
available under Windows NT so that IP-based workstations could be
found by name instead of IP address. The next section addresses

WINS, which is retained by Windows 2000. Keep in mind, however, that it is preferable to minimize or eliminate the use of WINS.

WHAT HAPPENED TO WINS?

The Windows Internet Naming Service (WINS) is not gone, but it may soon be forgotten as the migration to Windows 2000 workstations is completed. Details about WINS can be found in Chapter 15. This section presents an overview of how WINS works, why it is effectively replaced by dynamic DNS support, and how it is integrated with Windows 2000 DNS. For those network administrators with a large WINS installation, Windows 2000 WINS support may be around for quite awhile as some applications are dependent on WINS.

Essentially, WINS is a service and protocol that was used with Windows NT to allow workstations to provide their names to a central naming system (WINS) that could be accessed by IP-based clients. WINS is specifically designed for TCP/IP, as the NETBIOS support under Windows NT already has a broadcast-oriented naming facility. Unfortunately, NETBIOS is not a routable protocol while TCP/IP is preferable in larger networks. TCP/IP can also be used to link a network to the Internet via a router or proxy server without the need for special drivers on the client.

NOTE: There exist a number of NETBIOS- and IPX-based products that provide router service to a network without requiring installation of TCP/IP on the workstations. These products are normally designed to work with Windows 3.x, Windows 95, and Windows 98 systems through a custom implementation of WinSock. WinSock is the interface most Web-based applications use on these operating systems, and the products make use of the existing protocols (IPX or NETBIOS) to communicate with the router. The router then communicates with the Internet using TCP/IP. These types of products are primarily used with older, small- to medium-sized networks running IPX or NETBIOS. Most new networks use TCP/IP exclusively.

WINS operates in a fashion very similar to dynamic DNS updates. The client provides the WINS server with its IP address and can then access WINS to determine the IP address of other PCs.

Without WINS, a TCP/IP-based Windows client used to have to depend on the contents of the LMHOSTS file to perform name-to-IP translation. The LMHOSTS file on each workstation had to be updated when changes were made, which made this approach impractical for large networks. WINS effectively provides a dynamic LMHOSTS file. The WINS database is updated when workstations log in to a Windows domain.

Windows 2000 WINS can be integrated with the Windows 2000 DNS service just like the Windows NT WINS and Windows NT DNS services. WINS still maintains its database, but it makes this information available to the Windows DNS service allowing a DNS request to be processed using names and addresses in the WINS database. In this case, a DNS lookup request is first checked against the DNS service database. Failing this check, the DNS service then checks with the WINS service.

Although it's preferable to eliminate WINS, it will likely be around as long as a Windows 2000 network incorporates Windows 95, Windows 98, and Windows NT workstations. It is possible to use Windows 2000's DHCP service with dynamic DNS update proxy service instead of WINS, however. In this case, non-Windows 2000 systems that obtain an IP address from the Windows 2000 DHCP server will have a DNS entry added by the DHCP service using dynamic DNS update support.

Replacing WINS in a small network may be a nonissue, but it can be significant in larger networks. WINS does scale to handle large networks, and migration from WINS to DNS and dynamic DNS updates is not a chore to be taken lightly. Still, managing a large WINS network is often more work than managing a comparable DNS environment, and it is definitely more work if both the WINS and DNS environments must be maintained.

WHAT IS SPECIAL ABOUT WINDOWS 2000 DHCP SERVICE?

The Dynamic Host Control Protocol (DHCP) provides IP clients with an IP address upon demand. It allows workstations to be set up without a fixed IP address. DHCP can also set a number of other parameters from the client's DNS server to the gateway that is to be used for IP addresses outside the current subnet. The Windows 2000 DHCP server provides all these services.

In the last section, we mentioned one of the new major features of the Windows 2000 DHCP service, the dynamic DNS update proxy service. This facility is available to any system that uses the DHCP service that does not have dynamic DNS update support. Chapter 14 contains a more detailed description of the DHCP service.

In its most basic form, the dynamic DNS update proxy service allows non-Windows 2000 workstations to request an IP address and have that IP address and the name of the workstation that is provided by the request to be registered with the nearest DNS server using dynamic DNS updates. The DHCP server handles all the details once the client is sent the IP address, along with the other detailed information it may have requested.

The Windows 2000 DHCP service includes a number of other new features, including additional performance monitoring, multicast scope support, support for BOOTP clients, and automatic detection of unauthorized DHCP servers. The latter requires Active Directory integration and cannot be used if the DHCP server is used in a standalone Windows 2000 system.

WINDOWS 2000 DNS CLIENT CONSIDERATIONS

Windows 2000 Active Directory clients include Windows 2000 DNS client support and dynamic DNS update support. The DNS client is needed to access a DNS server to locate the Active Directory domain controller that the Windows 2000 Active Directory client will log in to.

While many Windows 2000 networks will be a heterogeneous mix of Windows 2000 and non-Windows 2000 systems, consideration should be given to a homogeneous Windows 2000 network. The difference is the ability of Windows 2000 to operate in native mode versus compatibility mode. This issue is covered in more detail in Chapter 13. This is mainly a security issue since a homogenous Windows 2000 network operating in native mode employs strong Kerberos authentication throughout.

NOTE: A homogeneous Windows 2000 network operating in native mode can incorporate non-Windows 2000 systems if those systems do not log in to the Windows 2000 domain. The non-Windows 2000 systems can still access Windows 2000 applications such as the Windows 2000 Internet Information Server (IIS) via direct IP addressing. Likewise, the non-Windows 2000 systems can still make use of Windows 2000 DNS services and Windows 2000 DNS services can interact with non-Windows 2000 DNS servers.

While non-Windows 2000 clients cannot participate in secure dynamic DNS updates, they can perform a standard dynamic DNS update if they have dynamic DNS update support. Non-Windows 2000 clients can use the Windows 2000 DNS server without taking advantage of the Windows 2000-specific features.

The Windows 2000 DNS client support comes with all Windows 2000 implementations from the Professional version on up. The Windows 2000 DNS client supports all standard DNS server implementations plus added features specific to Windows 2000, including the secure Windows 2000 dynamic DNS update support. The client also implements the following features:

▼ Client-based caching

■ RFC 2308–compliant negative caching support

▲ Bypassing of unresponsive DNS servers

DNS servers normally implement positive caching and sometimes negative caching. The Windows 2000 DNS client also implements caching support, including RFC 2308–compliant negative caching. Positive caching occurs when a DNS request returns a valid response that is saved in the cache. Subsequent accesses to the same site use the IP address saved in the cache.

Negative caching operates in a similar fashion except that a negative response is saved in the cache so that subsequent accesses to the same site will also fail. While a user will not typically continue to access an unknown site, it is possible that the site will become available at some later time. For example, if the site is a workstation that supports dynamic DNS updates or uses the Windows 2000 DHCP server, its DNS entry will not be available until after the workstation is turned on. Negative cache entry timeouts are normally much shorter than positive cache entry timeouts. A typical negative cache entry timeout is five minutes.

Most DNS clients have a list of DNS servers. Entries in the list are checked in the order they appear until a DNS server is found. If the DNS server fails, the DNS client is often left without an option. Bypassing unresponsive DNS servers allows the DNS client to continue to operate as long as a DNS server is available. The support also checks how quickly a DNS server responds so that the client can switch to a DNS server that responds more quickly. This can help balance the load on DNS servers.

WINDOWS 2000 DNS MIGRATION ISSUES

DNS is an integral part of Windows 2000 with Active Directory, with or without Windows 2000 DNS servers. As such, DNS installation or migration must be considered when installing or upgrading to Windows 2000. This includes how and when to migrate DNS support and what kind of DNS servers will be used.

NOTE: Windows 2000 can be used without Active Directory. In this case, existing DNS support will often be sufficient, but the use of Windows 2000 without eventual use of Active Directory will be rare except in small networks such as a single server environment. Windows 2000 can also be deployed with Active Directory with the clients using Windows 2000 compatibility mode. In this case, the Active Directory–specific DNS requirements must only be addressed by Windows 2000 domain controllers until workstations begin to employ Active Directory login.

One of the first issues to address is whether Windows 2000 DNS will provide some or all of the DNS services on the network. Windows 2000 DNS has many advantages, especially when Active Directory integration is used, but replacing a large DNS infrastructure with a new, unverified DNS system can be risky. This is especially true when the existing DNS infrastructure is not based on Windows NT DNS.

Organizational direction and politics can also come into play with a heterogeneous DNS environment, especially when the existing structure has been providing reliable performance. It can be even more confusing if some DNS support is already being supplied by Windows NT servers that will be upgraded to Windows 2000. In these cases, long term planning and cooperation within an organization will be invaluable for the ultimate support of Windows 2000 Active Directory.

NOTE: Windows 2000 DNS can be unverified for a particular organization even though it has been well tested by Microsoft and Windows 2000 users. Windows 2000 DNS has many more features than Windows NT DNS, so even experienced Windows NT administrators will want to work with Windows 2000 in a controlled setting before using it in a production environment.

There are three main alternatives when choosing which DNS system to use. The first is to maintain the existing DNS system, assuming it meets the minimum criteria for Active Directory support. The second is to go with Windows 2000 DNS. The third is to have a mix of Windows 2000 DNS and third-party DNS support. The use of third-party DNS servers like BIND is covered in Chapter 21.

The key requirement for Windows 2000 DNS support includes the SRV support outlined in the section "Windows 2000 DNS Requirements." Dynamic DNS update support is extremely desirable, since the Windows 2000 domain controllers can add the necessary SRVs for Active Directory services instead of having them added manually. Third-party DNS support should be well tested with Windows 2000 before mixing the two in a production environment.

Assuming Windows 2000 DNS services will be used in place of existing DNS services, DNS zone information on existing DNS servers will have to be moved to the Windows 2000 DNS service. Chapter 17 addresses this type of zone migration. Essentially, the DNS zones managed by the existing DNS servers must be moved to matching DNS zones handled by the Windows 2000 DNS services. This information may include DNS zones that are not associated with the Active Directory domains. The main difference between migrating these DNS zones and the ones associated with an Active Directory domain is that the latter must include or be updated with the SRVs that the Windows 2000 Active Directory support requires.

Another key issue will be the existing Windows NT domain architecture and the target Windows 2000 domain architecture. A large Windows NT network will often have more domains than a comparable Windows 2000 network. Much of the difference is due to Active Directory. A typical Windows NT upgrade process that is performed before moving to Windows 2000 is to collapse Windows NT domains into a smaller number of domains. Chapter 20 addresses third-party tools that can assist this process. These tools essentially move users, groups, and other domain-related information from one domain to another. This includes changing the security settings for files and directories. There is little or no change for DNS services unless unique DNS domains were set up to match the Windows NT domains. In this case, the DNS domains must be adjusted accordingly.

Collapsing Windows NT domains prior to migration to Windows 2000 should not be taken lightly. It is a major change to the network configuration requiring major resources and time, and instabilities induced by this change must be corrected prior to moving to Windows 2000.

The resulting Windows 2000 domain architecture will impact how Windows 2000 DNS Active Directory integration may be used. Active Directory integration is easiest to use with a small number of domains because an Active Directory–integrated zone can support a large number of systems with minimal management.

Finally, there is the issue of whether Windows 2000 will be operating in native or compatibility mode. Native mode implies a

homogeneous Windows 2000 environment with only Windows 2000
clients. This makes the use of secured dynamic DNS updates possible
across the board. Of course, secured dynamic DNS updates can be
used in a heterogeneous environment, but they must be used only in
selected areas, since secured dynamic DNS updates cannot be mixed
with regular dynamic DNS updates for the same zone.

The bottom line is that planning DNS installation and migration
must be a key aspect of planning a Windows 2000 installation.
Windows 2000 will not operate without DNS support, so it is
important to make it available reliably and continuously. Luckily,
most DNS clients have more than one DNS server, so replacing the
first DNS server will have a minimal impact on the network because
the second or third DNS server can still run while the first DNS
server is taken down for an upgrade. The key is to make sure that the
first DNS server is operating properly before bringing it back online
as part of the network where regular workstations can access it.

SUMMARY

Windows 2000 Active Directory is tightly tied to both IP and
DNS. IP and DNS support can also be used with the Windows 2000
compatibility mode, but it is not a requirement. Still, many
Windows 2000 sites will prefer to migrate towards a full, native
Windows 2000 Active Directory environment because of
considerations such as security and better remote management of
Windows 2000 clients. This book does not address the advantages
of a native Windows 2000 Active Directory environment in detail,
although some of the advantages, such as Kerberos authentication,
are presented in this chapter.

The Windows 2000 Active Directory client logon sequence
presented in this chapter shows the dependency on both IP and DNS.
Although the use of the Active Directory–specific DNS subzones is
not examined in great detail, this information is critical to the
underlying operation of Active Directory. The DNS zone for a
domain provides a way for any Active Directory client or server to
locate a necessary service.

DNS support is a requirement for Windows 2000 Active Directory clients and servers, but the Windows 2000 DNS service also benefits from Active Directory support through the use of Active Directory–integrated domains. Active Directory–integrated domains were introduced in this chapter and detailed in Chapter 4.

The Windows Internet Naming Service (WINS), detailed in Chapter 15, is still a part of Windows 2000. It will remain an important part as long as the Windows 2000 environment is operated in compatibility mode to serve non-Windows 2000 clients such as Windows NT, Windows 98, and Windows 95. Many installations will continue with WINS and compatibility mode well past initial migration to Windows 2000 servers. Other sites may convert completely to Windows 2000 clients and servers so that only native Windows 2000 Active Directory mode will be needed, providing a more secure environment. This type of migration is most likely to occur when all servers and workstations are currently running Windows NT.

The DNS service is not the only service to gain features with Windows 2000. The Windows 2000 DHCP service provides improved security and can also act as a dynamic DNS update proxy service to DHCP clients that do not support dynamic DNS updates. Dynamic DNS update support can eliminate the need for WINS.

It requires more than one chapter to address the details of DNS migration issues. Migration can be complicated by the different types of DNS servers that may already be in use. Windows 2000 operates very well with the Windows 2000 DNS service, but it can work equally well with third-party DNS services as well.

CHAPTER 4

Active Directory

Microsoft Windows 2000 contains a large number of enhancements over Windows NT 4, but one of the most important enhancements is Active Directory. Active Directory is an extensible and scalable directory service that is integrated with Windows 2000 and the major TCP/IP networking components including DNS, DHCP, and WINS. Active Directory does much more than manage information network services. Although this chapter touches on some of these other services, it focuses primarily on the networking aspects, specifically DNS support.

Complete coverage of Active Directory is beyond the scope of this book, but a basic knowledge of Active Directory design, operation, and management is critical to supporting the networking components. This chapter presents a basic overview of Active Directory and how it operates. It addresses the other major uses of Active Directory such as user, group, and machine management and security related issues.

After the basic overview, subsequent sections explore the relationship between Active Directory and DNS, DHCP, and WINS. The last section addresses the impact of Active Directory design and setup on DNS support. This relationship is covered in more detail in the next chapter.

WHAT IS ACTIVE DIRECTORY?

Active Directory is Windows 2000's directory service. It provides an all-encompassing directory service that affects the way users, groups, computers, and resources are managed. Active Directory maintains a database in which an object exists for each entity that is managed by Active Directory, such as a user or a computer. The database is called the global catalog, and it is replicated on each Windows 2000 domain controller server. A Windows 2000 server can also be a member server or stand-alone server. Domain controllers and member servers are part of a domain, which is an Active Directory security concept. Client workstations, including Windows 95, Windows 98, Windows NT, and Windows 2000 clients, can be part of a Windows 2000 domain. Users at these workstations will have matching Active Directory user objects so that the clients can access resources in the domain.

Active Directory objects are defined by the Active Directory schema. The schema describes the fields associated with a class, and each object is a member of a single class. Network administrators can customize a class by adding fields, thereby allowing the Active Directory database to be used for purposes other than just basic Windows 2000 management.

Active Directory is a hierarchical database. Organizational unit (OU) objects contain Active Directory objects that may include additional OUs. The design of the Active Directory hierarchy using OUs is important to a network administrator with respect to DNS because the names used in the hierarchy are reflected in the DNS names. For example, if the base DNS name for the domain is *foo.com* and there is a *server1* in the top level OU *admin*, then the DNS name would be *server1.admin.foo.com*, as shown in Figure 4-1. Note how the two hierarchies of the Windows 2000 Active Directory domain and the DNS domain are identical.

NOTE: Although identical hierarchies are shown in Figure 4-1, it is possible for the DNS domain names to map to any object in an Active Directory domain structure. For example, a DNS domain name of www.foo.com could be associated with the IP address of server1.admin.foo.com.

A domain requires one or more Windows 2000 servers acting as a domain controller and a base DNS name. A network can encompass one or more domains. Multiple domains can be managed in two methods. The first method is to incorporate multiple domains into a *domain tree* if the base DNS names for each domain share a common root name such as *foo.com* with domains *company1.foo.com* and *company2.foo.com*. This method is said to have a contiguous DNS domain name hierarchy.

The second method is to group the domains in a *domain forest*. A domain forest is a collection of domain trees that have different roots. For example, foo.com and bar.net can be in the same domain forest but not the same domain tree. The two methods can be combined, so it is possible to have a domain forest that contains one or more multiple domain trees. This method is said to have a discontiguous DNS domain

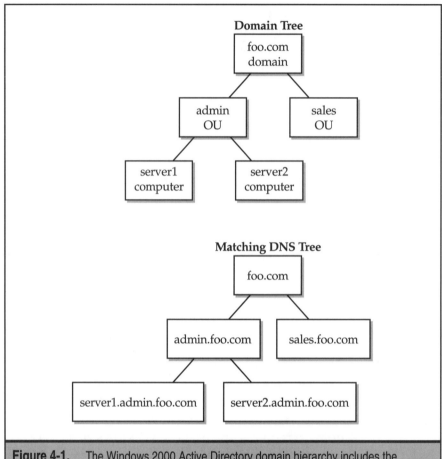

Figure 4-1. The Windows 2000 Active Directory domain hierarchy includes the organizational units (OU), whereas the DNS domain hierarchy incorporates domain names. Note how the two hierarchies are identical

name hierarchy. Figure 4-2 shows an Active Directory using a single domain tree and an Active Directory using a domain forest. A domain forest may have both domains and organizational units (OU), but an OU may only have OUs beneath it. The domain names for domains that are not at the root are based upon their location in the hierarchy. A domain forest consists of multiple domain trees, but each root of each domain tree must have a distinct name.

Each multiple domain method has advantages and disadvantages. Domains within a domain tree have automatic trust relationships

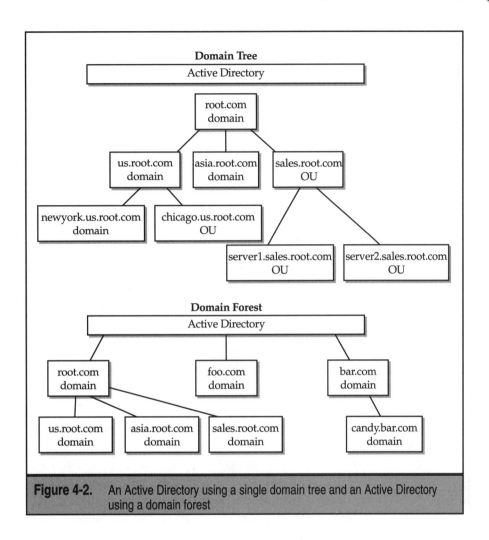

Figure 4-2. An Active Directory using a single domain tree and an Active Directory using a domain forest

between domains in the tree. In addition to distribution of management rights, this allows users and applications associated with one part of the tree to access resources that are in another part of the tree even though the two are in different domains.

In a domain forest, only the root domains initially have a trust relationship. It is possible to create trust relationships between all the trees in the forest, but the relationships must be set up individually by a network manager who has the appropriate rights. The process is not difficult when only a couple of domains are part of the network, but it can be quite cumbersome when there are dozens of domains and trees involved.

Trust relationships can have one or more of the following qualities:

▼ Transitive

■ Intransitive

■ One-way

▲ Two-way

Transitive trusts are two-way trusts that imply a trust relationship between any pair of domains linked by transitive trusts. For example, if there is a transitive trust between domain A and domain B and between domain B and domain C, then domain A will trust domain C. Figure 4-3 shows the relationships between domains and trust links.

Transitive trusts can be explicitly created between any pair of Active Directory domains. Transitive trusts are also set up implicitly, for example, when an Active Directory child domain is created. In that case, there is a transitive trust created between the parent and child domains.

A transitive trust is implicitly set up between domains in a Windows 2000 domain tree or domain forest. You can create a transitive trust when domain trees are created or when domain trees are added to a domain forest. Transitive trust relationships are inherited up a domain tree and can be explicitly created between Windows 2000 domains.

Explicit transitive trusts are often created for more efficient verification when users are accessing resources in other Active Directory domains. Although verification can occur even if the transitive trusts are between domains higher in the respective domain tree hierarchy, this is less efficient, since the verification must be done through additional Active Directory domain controllers in the hierarchy instead of directly between controllers in the respective domains.

Intransitive trusts are one-way and must be created explicitly. They can be created between domains that are not within the same domain tree or domain forest. For example, domains for different companies that have a secure link between networks can set up an intransitive trust to share resources. A pair of intransitive trusts provide two-way trusts between domains. Intransitive trust relationships are not inherited up a domain tree. All trusts between a Windows 2000 domain and a Windows NT domain are intransitive.

One-way trusts are between one domain and another. A one-way trust is always intransitive. For example, domain A can trust domain B but, without a two-way trust, domain B will not trust domain A. If that's the case, domain A can allow access rights to be enabled for users in domain B.

A two-way trust consists of a pair of one-way trusts between two domains; these trusts may be transitive or intransitive. A two-way trust between domain A and domain B consists of a one-way trust between domain A and domain B and a one-way trust between domain B and domain A.

Windows 2000 uses the Kerberos V5 security protocol to implement trust relationships between Windows 2000 servers and clients. A Windows 2000 domain controller acts as a Kerberos server providing *tickets* that identify a client and server pair. Windows 2000 uses Kerberos so that it identifies both the client and server involved

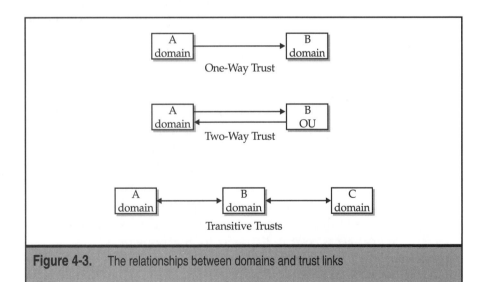

Figure 4-3.   The relationships between domains and trust links

in a transaction. Windows 2000 utilizes the DNS server to identify the default Kerberos server in a domain.

Active Directory domain controllers maintain a directory data store to hold the directory and security data. This collection of information is simply called the *directory*. The directory contains both private and public directory data. The private data is used for the server on which the directory resides and allows enterprise administrators access to the server even though the server may be disconnected from the network.

The public portion of the directory contains objects such as users, groups, computers, organizational units, security information, and domains. Each domain controller has a copy of the directory for its domain. This replicated information also gets distributed to domain controllers that include the domain as part of a domain tree or domain forest.

There are three types of data in the public directory:

▼   Schema data

■   Domain data

▲   Configuration data

Schema data is the formal definition of all objects and attributes contained within the directory. The default schema data, or simply *schema*, describes the minimum class structure required by Windows 2000 for objects such as users, groups, organizational units, and domains. For example, user objects have attributes like user name and password without which Windows 2000 could not operate. Enterprise administrators can extend the schema by adding attributes like project codes and product responsibilities to user objects. These attributes may be useful in an organization, but they are not part of the standard definition. The standard Windows 2000 schema for user objects already includes attributes like title, company name, address information, and phone numbers. Access to schema data, as with other objects in the directory, is protected by Windows 2000's access control list security mechanism.

Domain data makes up the bulk of the directory and includes all objects defined by the schema. The domain data is what most users and many administrators consider to be the Active Directory database because this information is accessible to both users and administrators. For example, Windows 2000 provides access to the domain data using the Lightweight Directory Access Protocol (LDAP) that is used by many e-mail programs. LSAP allows users to obtain the e-mail addresses of others users. E-mail users see, via LDAP, the names and e-mail address information stored in domain data users objects in their e-mail programs that provide the user interface. As with most data in Windows 2000, access to this information is controlled by Windows 2000 access control lists, so unauthorized users will not be able to view object attributes even though the object is stored in the public directory.

Configuration data is of concern only to domain managers. It contains the logical description of the network topology referencing objects in the domain data. The latter include objects such as computers and domains. The configuration data describes the domain trees and domain forests that the domain controller is a part of. It also includes references to the global catalog servers.

The *global catalog* is the collection of information associated with a domain tree or domain forest. It contains a replica of public directory information for those domains. The global catalog contains all the information for the host domain controller but only a partial set of information from other domains. Information reduction is done by replicating only selected attributes. The selection is part of the schema data. Key information in objects like domain groups, users, and organizational units is always replicated so that the global catalog can be used for user logon.

The global catalog is stored on a global catalog server. The server that is set up as the first domain controller in a domain is also set up as the first global catalog server. A server can provide one or both types of services. The global catalog provides a fast way to locate information about objects in related domains without server-to-server traffic.

Windows 2000 supports multimaster updates of Active Directory data between all domain controllers in a domain, with some exceptions. These exceptions are processed by a domain controller designated as the *operations master*. Updates become even more complicated when the update needs of a domain forest must be handled. In this case, there are five operation master roles that can be distributed among domain controllers. These include:

▼ Schema master

■ Domain naming master

■ Relative identifier (RID) master

■ Primary domain controller (PDC) master

▲ Infrastructure master

These roles are sometimes referred to as *flexible single master operations* (FSMO) because they can be moved from one domain controller to another within a domain tree or domain forest. A single domain controller can handle all the roles.

The schema master handles updates to the Active Directory schema data for a domain tree or domain forest. All domains in a domain tree or domain forest must use a single schema, and having a single Schema master prevents inconsistency in domain data. The Schema master notifies all domain controllers of changes so that the objects in the domain data can be updated accordingly.

The domain naming master handles domain additions and deletions. It guarantees consistent and unique DNS names for all domains and computers within these domains. The domain naming master only deals with DNS names at the domain level; this allows domain controllers to adjust DNS names for lower level organization units and computers.

A relative identifier (RID) is combined with a domain controller's domain security identifier to form a unique security identifier (SID). Every Active Directory user, group, or computer object has its own SID. The relative identifier master is responsible for assigning a range of RIDs to a domain controller thereby allowing the domain controller to generate SIDs as needed. The domain controllers need RID ranges very infrequently, but a single master makes sure no two domain controllers generate duplicate SIDs.

The primary domain controller (PDC) master is used when there are non-Windows 2000 clients or servers within the network. This situation will be quite common as Windows 2000 is rolled out to larger organizations since it is rare to replace or upgrade all Windows NT servers at the same time. The PDC master allows a Windows 2000 domain controller to act as a Windows NT–compatible PDC. It can service Windows NT backup domain controllers (BDC), and it provides preferential password updates to occur within Windows NT domains that coexist with Windows 2000 domains.

The infrastructure master handles the addition and deletion of users from groups. This prevents conflicting group changes from occurring in two different domain controllers. Centralizing group updates into a single master does incur a delay in updates, especially with a large network, but it does guarantee that domain controllers have the accurate, although not always up-to-date, data. The infrastructure master distributes updates to all domain controllers, but it performs this synchronization using the multimaster replication so that it occurs at approximately the same time in each domain controller.

Multimaster replication of domain directory information and the global catalog allow Active Directory information to be replicated across the network at domain controllers and global catalog servers. This allows user logon, secure communication, and access to directory information by applications to occur quickly with limited network traffic. Windows 2000 directory replication is a major network configuration issue when the number of domain controllers grows beyond two, especially in large networks with different speed network connections. Replication considerations are addressed in more detail later in this chapter.

Active Directory is designed with an open application programming interface (API) called the Active Directory Service Interface (ADSI). It provides access to all aspects of Active Directory, from DNS support to multimaster replication. Third-party directory services can be integrated into the Windows 2000 directory management tools by providing ADSI support. However, both ADSI and Microsoft's Active Directory ADSI implementation are beyond the scope of this book. They are both aspects of Active Directory that are not necessary to use in order to manage Windows 2000 DNS.

Active Directory Objects

Active Directory objects populate the Active Directory database and the global catalog. Access and modification of the database and catalog are strictly controlled by Windows 2000's security system. Each object is an instance of a class, and the structure of the objects of a class is defined by the Active Directory Schema.

Enterprise administrators can modify the Active Directory Schema to add or delete attributes for an existing class. They can also create new classes and new objects. We will concentrate our examination of Active Directory objects to a small subset of the standard set of Windows 2000 Active Directory objects. These include objects such as users, groups, and DNS-related objects.

The user class defines attributes that cannot be deleted, such as the user name and password. To uphold Windows 2000's security system, each user object requires these attributes. The objects are referred to as security principal objects.

Objects, such as user objects, are described by a structural class. A structural class defines what an object of that class contains. Windows 2000 also has abstract and auxiliary classes. These classes are not used to define objects but other classes. Abstract classes are used to define new structural or new abstract classes. The new classes contain the attributes of the parent Abstract class plus any that are added to the new class definition. Auxiliary classes define a list of attributes. Adding an auxiliary class to another class adds the attributes to that class. Class definitions can be combined to form new class definitions.

Each object class has a unique Object Identifier (OID). The OID is a dotted decimal string, such as 1.2.3.4, that uniquely defines a class. Every attribute type also has a unique OID. New objects are also assigned unique identifiers, and all principal security objects must have a text name. The name can contain up to 20 characters, not including the following: " / \ [ ] : ; | = , + * ? < >. A name cannot consist solely of a period or spaces, although these can be used as part of a name. Security principal objects also have SID, a globally unique ID (GUID), an LDAP distinguished name, and a canonical name.

DNS objects show up in Active Directory in a number of areas. A DNS service has a service object, as do all Windows 2000 services. The security associated with the DNS service object specifies which users can control the service. The DNS service object exists on servers running this service.

What other DNS-related Active Directory objects exist in a domain controller's Active Directory database depends upon how the DNS service is configured. There are two methods to configure the DNS service. The first method uses text-based DNS zone storage files. In this case, Active Directory plays little part in DNS management, and there are no other DNS-specific objects created.

The second method is where the zone storage for the DNS service is maintained in Active Directory. In this case, each zone has a DNS zone container object (dnsZone) created for it by the DNS service. DNS entries are kept in DNS node objects (dnsNode) that are collected together in a dnsZone container object. The dnsZone object's name is stored in the dnsProperty attribute. This attribute corresponds to the DNS zone's domain name.

The dnsNodes map to the various DNS records is normally found in a DNS zone file in the text-based DNS storage method used with standard primary and secondary DNS zones. Each dnsNode has a dnsRecord and dnsProperty attribute, as shown in Figure 4-4. The

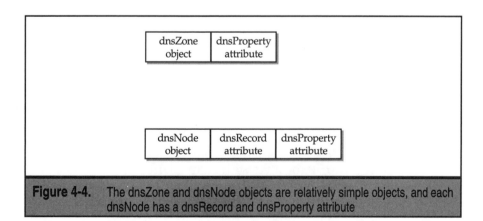

Figure 4-4.   The dnsZone and dnsNode objects are relatively simple objects, and each dnsNode has a dnsRecord and dnsProperty attribute

dnsZone and dnsNode objects are relatively simple objects with text names stored in the dnsProperty attribute. The dnsNode's dnsRecord attribute contains the information associated with a DNS resource record.

The dnsRecord attribute defines the type of dnsNode record, such as an address record, type = A, or a mail exchange record, type = MX, along with binary information associated with the record. For example, the IP address for an address record is contained in the dnsRecord attribute. The dnsProperty attribute is used to store configuration information such as whether dynamic update is enabled or disabled.

NOTE: Active Directory–integrated zones are stored in a special organizational unit called WindowsDNS, which is located just below the Active Directory's root. Because of the default setting of the WindowsDNS access control list, this organizational unit is initially accessible only by administrators. The contents of WindowsDNS are normally accessed only by the DNS MMC snap-in.

NOTE: Non-Active Directory–integrated zones, including standard primary and secondary zones, are stored in text files located in the %System Root%/system32/dns directory.

Data and Management Security

Windows 2000 utilizes Access Control Lists (ACL) and a new security authentication protocol call Kerberos to implement data and management security across a network. The type of security and its implementation are important to DNS administrators when there are multiple DNS servers in the network, when DNS services are managed from Windows 2000 workstations instead of the servers where the DNS services are running, and when DNS administrators must manage DNS services in different domains.

ACLs are associated with Active Directory objects. An ACL limits how users or groups specified in the ACL can query or manage an object. For example, when an ACL is associated with the DNS service, the ACL specifies which users can start and stop a service, thereby preventing unauthorized users from aborting a critical service. The same is true for the DNS Active Directory records when the DNS service utilizes Active Directory to store the DNS database. ACLs are also used to control other Active Directory objects such as shared files and directories.

Kerberos is a protocol used to authenticate one entity to another, such as a user to server during the logon process. The authentication can be performed across an unsecured network, but the user name and password are not sent as cleartext (unencrypted). Authentication information is sent as ciphertext (encrypted).

Although not a definitive description of ACLs and Kerberos, the rest of this section provides a general overview for administrators who may not be familiar with these two important topics.

Access Control Lists, Users, and Groups

Active Directory provides access security to Active Directory objects using access control lists (ACL). An ACL is associated with each Active Directory object that requires security restrictions, such as server objects and even DNS objects. The ACL specifies which actions can be taken, such as deleting an object, and which users can perform these actions. An ACL is a list because different users or groups can have different access rights for the same object. Each entry in the list has a matching set of access rights.

Active Directory utilizes inheritance to minimize the amount of information kept in an ACL and to simplify ACL management. The ACL inheritance hierarchy is based on Active Directory's object hierarchy. Each branch in the hierarchy occurs at an OU. Objects contained in an OU inherit the ACL settings of the OU. Inherited capabilities filter down through the hierarchy until an explicit specification is set for an OU or object. For example, an enterprise administrator manages most objects but, in this example, the users of a specific OU are managed by administrator X. In this case, the OU's ACL would include administrator X.

Active directory supports fine grain control of a variety of attributes and management attributes that are often object-specific.

For example, a shared folder will have some attributes that are different compared to a network printer. Both would have write attributes but only the folder would have a read attribute. ACLs allow an enterprise administrator to set up different DNS service administrators.

ACLs can contain groups and users. Individual users are easy to contend with because there is only one type. Groups, on the other hand, fit into two different group types and three different group scopes. The two types of groups are security groups and distribution groups. Security groups can be used in ACLs; distribution groups cannot.

The group scopes are universal, global, and domain local. Universal groups are the most flexible, and the domain local groups are the most restrictive. How each group operates depends on whether Windows 2000 is in a native mode or mixed mode domain.

A native mode domain is used where only Windows 2000 servers are used. A mixed mode domain is used where Windows NT servers will coexist with Windows 2000. Native mode is the more flexible of the two.

In native mode, universal groups can contain users accounts, computer accounts, universal groups, and global groups from any domain. Global groups can contain users and groups from the same domain. Domain local groups can contain users, universal groups, and global groups from any domain in addition to domain local groups from the same domain.

In a mixed mode domain, the global groups can only contain users. Domain local groups can contain users and global groups. Universal groups are not supported in a mixed mode domain.

It is possible to change the scope of a group as long as its contents match the restrictions associated with a group. This is typically a factor when converting more flexible group types to more restrictive ones.

In addition to these groups, Windows 2000 supports a number of dynamic, built-in groups whose contents change based upon the current state of users on the network. These groups include Everyone, Network, and Interactive. These groups can be used as security groups. The Everyone group contains all current network users, including guests and users in other domains. The Network group contains users currently accessing resources on the network, and the Interactive group contains all users currently logged in who are using resources on the local computer.

Windows 2000 also supports a number of static, built-in groups. These are groups that are necessary for Windows 2000 operation but whose contents can be modified, unlike the dynamic, built-in groups. There are a number of static, built-in groups such as Domain Users and Domain Admins. New users are normally added to the Domain Users group when the user object is created. The initial enterprise administrator user is placed in the Domain Admins group.

Some Windows 2000 groups, as noted above, can contain other groups. For security groups, this creates a group hierarchy that is different than the Active Directory OU hierarchy. Understanding the two hierarchies and their impact on Windows 2000 security can help alleviate enterprise administrator confusion.

Kerberos

Kerberos (the name of the three-headed guard dog of Hades) was developed at the Massachusetts Institute of Technology in the early 1980s as a way to provide reliable and secure authentication across unsecured lines. Windows 2000 follows the current Kerberos specification, IETF RFC 1510. This section addresses the Windows 2000 implementation of Kerberos, unless otherwise specified.

NOTE: Kerberos is primarily used behind the scenes for Active Directory authentication. Most users and even most administrators will not address it directly at any time. The issue usually arises when cross-platform authentication will be used and the Windows 2000 Kerberos system is interfaced with a third-party implementation of Kerberos.

Windows 2000 implements Kerberos as one of a number of Security Service Providers (SSP). Other SSPs supported by Windows 2000 include Secure Socket Layer (SSL) and NT LAN Manager (NTLM) protocol. SSL is used for secure Internet communication. NTLM was the security for Windows NT and can be used with Windows 2000 to provide backwards compatibility. SSPs are accessed by applications using the Security Support Provider Interface (SSPI). Typically, applications utilize SSPI indirectly via Microsoft DCOM when DCOM objects are used within an application.

The Windows 2000 implementation of Kerberos supports both public key and private key encryption. Public key encryption uses two keys, one public and one private. The private key must be kept secret, but the public key can be given to anyone. The public key encryption system allows a user with the public key to send encrypted information to the holder of the private key or to authenticate anything digitally signed using the private key. Private key encryption utilizes a single private key that must be in the possession of both sender and receiver, and the distribution of the private key must be done over a secure communications link or the private key could be compromised.

Private key protocols include the Data Encryption Standard (DES), which uses 56-bits. DES provides interoperability but is susceptible to brute force decryption. Triple DES uses DES three times to provide a more secure encryption scheme. The default key protocol used by Windows 2000 is RC4, which utilizes a 128-bit key.

Authentication using encryption is rather simple, even if you're using private keys. Encrypt a known message and send it. Since the message is encrypted, it can be sent over an unsecured line. The receiver can then decrypt the message and verify that the message is accurate. A message decrypted with an improper key will result in garbage.

Although using keys and encrypted messages is a viable method for authenticating a pair of computers, it becomes impractical when a large number of applications are communicating among a number of computers. Using the simplified authentication example, each pair of computers that needs to securely authenticate each other would need to share a key. It gets worse when different individuals on each computer need to log in or when different applications need to access a database on a database server.

Kerberos gets around the multiple-key problem by using tickets and delegation. Tickets are used to authenticate users and applications. Initially, tickets are issued to an application running on a PC by a Kerberos domain controller (KDC) service that runs on a Windows 2000 domain controller. This ticket can then be used to obtain more tickets for communicating with other applications on other computers. Information from these tickets is then combined to create new tickets that are sent to the other computers to gain access to resources on the other computers. This process is examined in more detail in the remaining portion of this section, but a more comprehensive examination of Kerberos and its implementation is beyond the scope of this book.

Delegation is another important feature of Kerberos. Essentially, tickets can be used so that application A can work with application B, which, in turn, works with application C. Application A must be authenticated with B and C, but through the process of delegation, A does not communicate directly with C. Instead, B is delegated authority by A to work with C on A's behalf. Again, this is done using tickets so that B cannot forge A's tickets to fool C. The tickets used by B to act on A's behalf with C are created from tickets A provides to B that B can decrypt. Portions of the decrypted ticket are actually encrypted by another key that A and C possess. The latter is forwarded to C by B as part of the delegation authentication process.

Tickets, whose general structure is shown in Figure 4-5, are messages that contain encrypted and unencrypted data. The unencrypted data includes the domain name and the principal name. The unencrypted data is replicated in the encrypted data so that decryption of the unencrypted data can be used to verify that the unencrypted data has not been corrupted. The encrypted data also contains a session key, start and end times, host address information, authorization data, various Kerberos flags, and fields not discussed in this overview. The session key is a secret key generated when a session between two applications takes place and is used to encrypt and decrypt tickets used during the session. The session key is different from the one used to encrypt and decrypt the original ticket. The start and end time set the lifetime for the ticket. The start time is set when the ticket is created, and the ticket is considered invalid after the end time. Communication that runs longer than the lifetime of a ticket will require a new ticket, but this renewal process is taken care of automatically by Windows 2000. The host address information is a list of one or more IP addresses associated with the application. The authorization data indicates what services are available and what rights are given to the holder of the ticket.

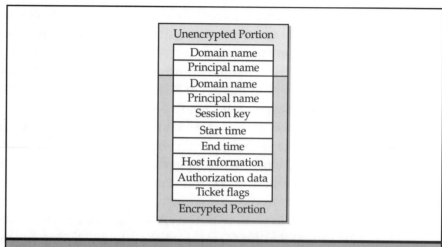

Unencrypted Portion
Domain name
Principal name
Domain name
Principal name
Session key
Start time
End time
Host information
Authorization data
Ticket flags
Encrypted Portion

Figure 4-5.   A Kerberos ticket consists of an unencrypted part and an encrypted part

The whole process starts when a user logs on to a network. In this case, the client PC accepts the domain name, user name, and user password from the login screen and generates a ticket that is sent to the domain controller's Kerberos server. This login ticket, or request of a ticket granting ticket (TGT), actually uses a key that is the hash of the user password. The principal name of the ticket is the user name and the domain name is the same as that provided in the login screen. Preauthentication information is also included in the login ticket. This information tells Windows 2000 about the current login process. This process and the subsequent access of a service on another server is shown in Figure 4-6. The last exchange shown in the figure occurs after the client receives an authorization ticket from the KDC to access the server.

The login ticket is sent to a KDC that uses Active Directory to look up a password for the principal name in the specified domain using the unencrypted information in the login ticket. The same hash algorithm is then used with the password to generate the key to decrypt the rest of the login ticket. Assuming all of this works, the user provides the proper name, password, and domain name so that the KDC can return a TGT.

The TGT has the same structure as any other ticket, including the login ticket. Only the contents of the ticket change. The TGT is returned

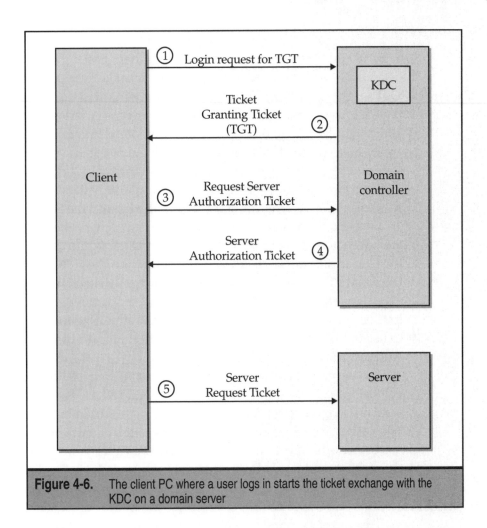

Figure 4-6. The client PC where a user logs in starts the ticket exchange with the KDC on a domain server

to the user's PC using the password hash key. The TGT includes a random session key for subsequent communication between the KDC and the user's PC that is now authenticated with the KDC. The TGT also contains the SIDs for the user and the groups the user is a member of based upon information kept in the Active Directory.

Now that the user's PC has a TGT, it can communicate with KDC to obtain information about other servers that are recognized by Active Directory. For example, an administrator on a client PC wants to work with the DNS service on a Windows 2000 server. To get access to the DNS service, the application on the client PC allows the administrator to enter or select the name of the server with the DNS service, called Server in this example. This information is then placed into a request ticket that is sent to the KDC. The request ticket is encrypted using the TGT session key. The KDC has already authenticated the client PC, so the KDC then looks up the requested Server's information in Active Directory, along with the security information related to the user's ability to access the DNS service. Assuming that the Server and DNS service do exist, the client PC is sent an Authorization ticket that contains authorization information and a randomly generated session key for communication between the PC and the Server.

Portions of this return ticket, including a copy of the session key, are encrypted using the Server's key that is known to the KDC and the Server. The Server's key is not given to the client PC. Instead, the client PC creates a Request ticket for the Server that contains the encrypted information from the KDC and sends the Request ticket to the Server. The Request ticket also contains authorization information to use the DNS service, but this information is encrypted using the Authorization session key.

The Server receives the Request ticket and extracts the session key using the Server key that is known to the KDC. The session key is then used to extract request information provided by the client PC. The Server can then provide its services to the client since the client has been authenticated to the Server by the KDC using the exchange tickets that could only be created using the keys discussed in the example. The advantage to this is that the server does not have to communicate with the KDC to service the authorized client.

This ticket exchange occurs at a very low level in Windows 2000 and is transparent to users and to most programmers. It is reassuring to know how this process takes place and that it is possible to efficiently and reliably authenticate DNS management across a large network. Kerberos essentially provides a means to distribute session keys and to authenticate. Keys can also be used to digitally sign or encrypt data for more secure communication.

Active Directory Database Replication

Windows 2000 performs Active Directory database replication when there are multiple domain controllers in a domain or if a domain is part of a domain forest. Although the replication process proceeds automatically, enterprise administrators can set up different replication strategies. Replication, as it specifically applies to Windows 2000 DNS support, is covered in Chapter 8. This section provides an overview of the Active Directory replication process and issues related to performance.

Active Directory database replication is based around sites. A site is contained within a domain, and a domain may contain more than one site. Each domain controller in a domain is part of a single site. The minimum configuration is a single server that is a domain controller that is part of a single site that is part of a single domain.

NOTE: A default site is created when Active Directory is installed on the first domain controller. New domain controllers are added to this site. The issue of sites does not have to be addressed until multiple sites are needed. This may occur because a remote location is being added to the network or a large network is partitioned for management and performance reasons.

In a multiple site environment, each site has at least one site link to another site, and there must be a route through the site links from every site to every other site. A site may have more than one route to another site, which makes the Active Directory replication network fault-tolerant. Site links and routes are configured by the enterprise administrator.

Windows 2000 makes ongoing replication management relatively easy. It evaluates routes to determine the most efficient distribution of Active Directory changes. Windows 2000 also minimizes replication traffic by sending only change information to other sites.

Site links are created automatically when a domain controller is added to subsequent sites. The domain controller can be either a new domain controller or one moved from another site. In the latter case, the domain controller retains site links that it originally had so that the new site may have more than one site link. Sites and site links are explicitly created and managed using the Microsoft Management Console (MMC) Active Directory Sites and Services snap-in, as shown in Figure 4-7.

Active Directory replication occurs between domain controllers within a site and from site to site. Each domain controller has a complete copy of its domain directory, enterprise configuration, and Active Directory schema. Changes are made through any domain controller; these changes are then sent using multimaster replication to domain controllers within a site and to adjacent sites.

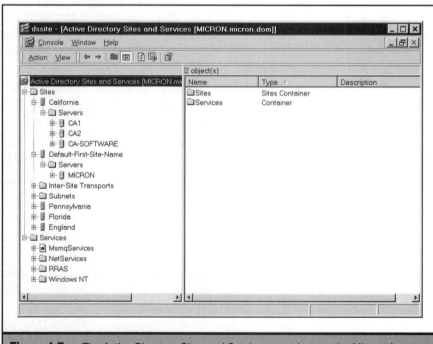

Figure 4-7. The Active Directory Sites and Services snap-in uses the Microsoft Management Console interface

Changes are replicated automatically. They can also be requested by a domain controller. This normally occurs when a domain controller that was offline is brought online.

A Windows 2000 network will also contain one or more global catalogs that contain a copy of the Active Directory information for the domains that are part of the catalog. The Active Directory information contained in the catalog is actually a subset of the properties associated with each object. The network administrator can control which attributes are included in the catalog. The catalog contains enough information so that a domain controller can authenticate a user when a login request is received.

The global catalogs are updated using a different mechanism, although replicated information will eventually make its way into a global catalog after a site is synchronized.

ACTIVE DIRECTORY AND DNS

Active Directory requires a DNS service to operate properly. Active Directory can be tightly or loosely integrated with the Windows 2000 DNS service, or it can operate with a third-party DNS service that's possibly running on a server with a different operating system. Tight integration with the Windows 2000 DNS service provides enterprise administrators with the most power and flexibility. The Windows 2000 DNS service is managed using MMC DNS plug-in, as shown in Figure 4-8.

Since the Windows 2000 Active Directory system is dependent upon DNS, there must be at least one DNS server on the network. If this DNS server is not a Windows 2000 DNS service, the DNS server must be managed using its third-party tools and configured according to Windows 2000 Active Directory conventions that will be discussed in Chapters 5 and 6.

When Windows 2000 DNS service is used, Active Directory encounters the DNS service in a number of places, depending upon the configuration of the DNS service. Minimally, the DNS service shows up an object in Active Directory's list of services. Windows

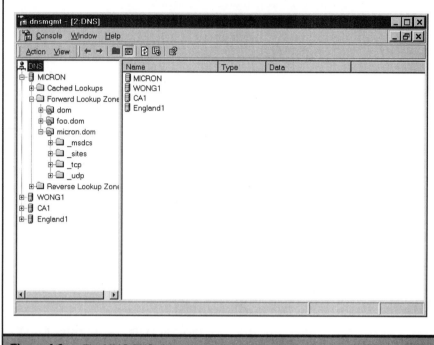

Figure 4-8. The MMC DNS plug-in is used to manage local or remote Windows 2000 DNS services, regardless of whether they use loose or tight Active Directory integration

2000 security allows access to this object to be controlled using a Windows 2000 ACL.

With a loosely integrated Windows 2000 DNS service, the DNS zone information is kept in a file on the file system of the PC running the service. With a tightly integrated Windows 2000 DNS service, the DNS zone information is kept in the Active Directory database. The DNS objects mentioned earlier in this chapter are subject to replication so that additional DNS services can utilize the information.

DNS services provided by third-party DNS applications must meet the minimum standards for Active Directory as outlined in Chapter 3. While Windows 2000 DNS service offers many new features, it often makes sense to retain existing third-party DNS environments because of cross platform, stability, and maintenance issues.

ACTIVE DIRECTORY AND DHCP

The Windows 2000 Dynamic Host Control Protocol (DHCP) service has minimal interaction with Active Directory. It exists as a service object in the Active Directory list of services for a server, but the DHCP service maintains its own database, much like the loosely integrated Windows 2000 DNS service. The Windows 2000 DHCP service is managed using MMC DHCP plug-in, as shown in Figure 4-9.

The DHCP service can operate independently of the DNS service, or it can work with the DNS service if the DHCP service's proxy-based, dynamic DNS update support and the matching DNS service support are enabled. The dynamic update support allows the DHCP service

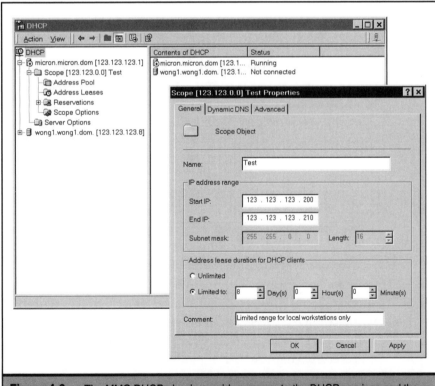

Figure 4-9.   The MMC DHCP plug-in provides access to the DHCP services and the contents of the configuration files

to issue an IP address to a client and then notify the DNS service of both the name associated with the PC and the IP addresses issued by the DHCP service.

The Windows 2000 DHCP service can use secure dynamic DNS updates that utilize Active Directory's authentication service. Secure dynamic DNS updates will prevent unauthorized updates. Active Directory access control lists for the Windows 2000 DNS service are used to control which computers can perform such updates. It is possible to restrict such updates to only Windows 2000 DHCP servers.

NOTE: Third-party DHCP services can also implement proxy-based, dynamic DNS update support that will work with the Windows 2000 DNS service or any DNS service that supports dynamic DNS updates. A third-party DHCP service will not be able to implement secure dynamic DNS updates.

Some clients, such as Windows 2000 workstations, can handle the dynamic update process without the DHCP service's intervention, but many clients, such as Windows 95, cannot handle this without the help of the DHCP service and its proxy-based, dynamic DNS update support.

ACTIVE DIRECTORY AND WINS

Microsoft's Windows Internet Naming Service (WINS) is a holdover from Windows NT, when it was necessary because of the initial lack of DNS dynamic update support in DNS server applications. NetBIOS was literally the name of the game when TCP/IP started gaining network support with Windows operating systems. NetBIOS required each workstation to be assigned a unique name. As TCP/IP support was added, WINS was responsible for matching a workstation's IP address and NetBIOS name and storing these in a WINS database.

NOTE: WINS is a Windows-specific feature. It is not employed by systems other than Windows NT, Windows 2000, or environments that try to be compatible with WINS. Unlike DNS, which spans the Internet, WINS is almost exclusively used within a network.

WINS was usable by itself, but DNS eventually won out; this is evident by Windows 2000's dependence on DNS rather than WINS. In fact, WINS is a service that is better left unused, if possible. However, WINS provides a valuable service in existing networks where migration from Windows NT to Windows 2000 is taking place.

TIP: Windows 2000 WINS support will be very important when migrating Windows NT networks that currently use WINS to Windows 2000. Migration to Windows 2000 DNS and DHCP service from WINS can be beneficial, but in most cases it's better to migrate Windows NT WINS support to its Windows 2000 counterpart since WINS expertise will normally be available. In larger networks, WINS replication may be well tuned, and conversion to DNS and DHCP with proxy-based, dynamic DNS updates will entail new configuration and performance issues. This conversion can be performed after the Windows 2000, Active Directory, and WINS migration has taken place and is stable. In some cases, the clients that depended upon WINS may be converted to Windows 2000 clients that already support dynamic DNS updates and will not require WINS.

Essentially, WINS continues to operate in its normal fashion, tracking NetBIOS names and IP addresses of workstations that log in to the Windows 2000 server. WINS can be integrated with the Windows 2000 DNS service by enabling DNS name resolution using WINS. In this case, the WINS names and addresses are associated with a designated zone handled by the DNS service. When the DNS service needs to resolve a name to an IP address for a name in the zone, the DNS service checks with the WINS service to get the IP address. Reverse lookup, IP-to-name, using WINS is also supported.

WINS employs its own replication system that exists in both the Windows NT and Windows 2000 WINS implementations. This replication process is similar to what occurs with DNS secondary zones. Chapter 15 takes a closer look at WINS under Windows 2000 and the issues faced by migration from Windows NT.

WINS interacts with Active Directory only as a Windows 2000 service. The WINS database is independent of both Active Directory and the Windows 2000 DNS service. WINS also acts indirectly with any DHCP server, Windows 2000, or a third-party DNS server, when workstations are assigned IP addresses via DHCP.

Windows 2000 DNS and DHCP services can essentially replace WINS if NetBIOS support is not required. Even if NetBIOS support must be maintained, the DNS and DHCP dynamic update support is usually sufficient to replace the functionality of WINS. Often the decision of when to eliminate WINS from a site is dependent on the timing of a migration plan.

SUMMARY

Active Directory is one of the major enhancements in Windows 2000. It provides enterprise-wide security and administration services. Its multimaster design provides a more robust environment than the two-level primary/backup domain controller architecture of Windows NT.

Active Directory's hierarchical domain system depends upon DNS support primarily for locating Active Directory services located on Windows 2000 domain controllers. These IP-based services provide the backbone of Windows 2000.

Windows 2000 DNS and DHCP services remain a major component of Windows 2000 Active Directory support. Both take advantage of and provide new services under Windows 2000. The DNS service can utilize the Active Directory database for Active Directory–integrated DNS zones, and DHCP can provide secure, proxy-based, dynamic DNS updates to the DNS service where the security is provided by authentication provided through Active Directory.

CHAPTER 5

Windows 2000 DNS and Active Directory Setup

Windows 2000 DNS and Active Directory are intertwined. While it is possible to utilize a third-party DNS system, most network administrators will use Windows 2000's own DNS server because of its integration with Active Directory. As such, this chapter initially concentrates on setting up Active Directory and DNS servers together. We then examine issues related to using a third party DNS system instead of Windows 2000 DNS. Finally we examine how Windows 2000 DNS and third party DNS systems can coexist.

Complete Active Directory planning considerations are beyond the scope of this book, but we do look at aspects of such planning as they impact planning and configuration of DNS servers. This and other general DNS setup considerations are examined in the first section of this chapter. These include security and management considerations, whether DNS will track only server IP addresses, and how the network is being set up. The latter addresses whether a network administrator is setting up a new network, upgrading an existing network from Windows NT 4.0 to Windows 2000, or migrating from an existing DNS architecture that might be running on Windows NT or UNIX. The section also covers related issues, such as the use of DNS forwarding versus clients that can reference multiple DNS servers.

The subsequent chapters in this book look at DNS deployment based on network size and configuration. Setting up DNS servers in a small network is significantly easier than it is in a medium or large network. We also take a look at issues related to geographically distributed networks where link speeds between portions of the network are typically much slower than local area network speeds. We use the following network model definitions in this chapter:

▼ **Small**   Single domain, single domain controller, single DNS servers

■ **Medium**   Single domain, multiple domain controllers, multiple DNS servers

■ **Large**   Multiple domains, multiple domain controllers, multiple DNS servers

▲ **Distributed**   Large networks that are geographically dispersed

Figure 5-1 shows the layout for a small network. In this case, a single Windows 2000 Server handles everything from Active Directory to file and print services, which is the simplest and the most common case.

The smallest configuration is where one server provides all services, that is, everything from file and print services to Web and DNS services. If possible, it is a good idea to spread these services among multiple servers, especially if you're using an intranet Web server. This improves security, as a Web server tends to be more susceptible to accidental or intentional security breaches than other services with fixed interfaces like Active Directory, DNS, and file and print services.

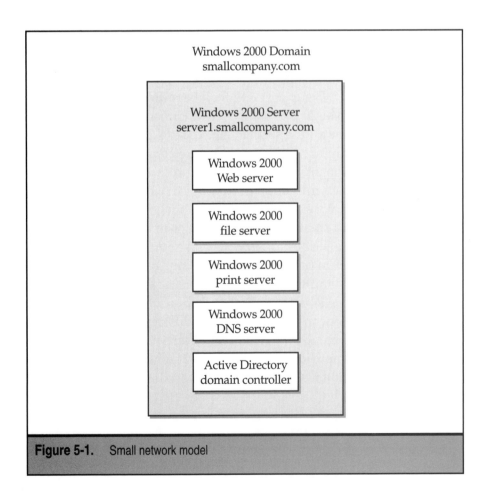

Figure 5-1.   Small network model

A small network typically has fewer than 25 users, although a typical server can often handle hundreds of users. While most small networks use only a single DNS domain, it is very easy for the Windows 2000 DNS server to provide support for more than one domain without increasing the number of Windows 2000 domains.

The small network model, from a domain point of view, is identical to a medium network model. The difference is the number of domain controllers involved. Small Windows 2000 networks will often be implemented *without* Active Directory. This is not to say that DNS services will not be needed for other reasons, but that DNS will not be required for Active Directory since it is not being used.

The advantage of not using Active Directory in a small network model is a simplification of the installation and management process. It is also more likely that the clients used in this type of network will not be Windows 2000 clients. Most likely, a Windows NT server will have been upgraded to Windows 2000. This simplified environment can always be upgraded to Active Directory support at any time although DNS support will then be required.

The advantage of using Active Directory in a small network model is the added security between Windows 2000 clients and the server. Administrators can also take advantage of Active Directory's organization units to manage resources in a hierarchical fashion. It makes future migration to a medium network model very simple.

The primary reason to move to a medium network configuration, even with a small number of users, is to make the network more robust by distributing services and adding redundancy.

A medium network, as shown in Figure 5-2, maintains services and data in multiple locations. It has a single Windows 2000 domain but multiple Windows 2000 domain controllers and DNS servers. The services can be spread across different servers or a collection of services can be replicated on different servers.

The sample shown in Figure 5-2 shows a mix of replicated servers and distributed services. Putting everything in a single Windows 2000

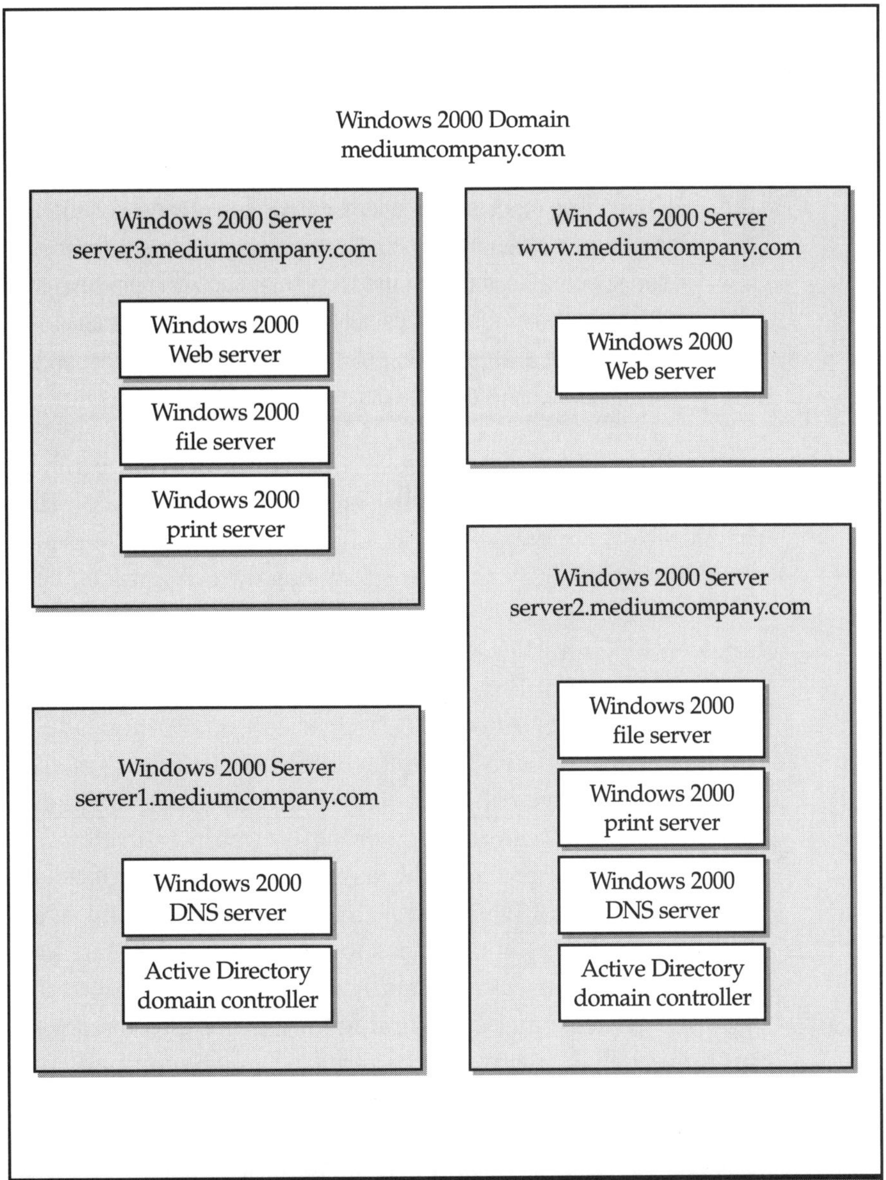

Windows 2000 Domain
mediumcompany.com

Windows 2000 Server
server3.mediumcompany.com

Windows 2000
Web server

Windows 2000
file server

Windows 2000
print server

Windows 2000 Server
www.mediumcompany.com

Windows 2000
Web server

Windows 2000 Server
server2.mediumcompany.com

Windows 2000
file server

Windows 2000
print server

Windows 2000
DNS server

Active Directory
domain controller

Windows 2000 Server
server1.mediumcompany.com

Windows 2000
DNS server

Active Directory
domain controller

Figure 5-2.   Medium network model

domain keeps management simple. A single domain can handle hundreds of users, and multiple servers can provide sufficient performance when properly distributed.

NOTE: The medium network model will be the most common as it provides the easiest management model, comparable to the small network model, and it can support thousands of users given enough domain controllers. Use of the large network model is usually not warranted unless special conditions exist, such as a large number of existing domains or the need to support domain name hierarchies or different root domain names.

Medium model networks are often employed to provide redundancy. A comparable Windows NT network would have one primary domain controller (PDC) and one or more backup domain controllers (BDC). Active Directory has the advantage of providing multiple peer-level domain controllers removing the distinction between PDCs and BDCs.

Normal user and resource management can be partitioned and delegated using Windows 2000 organizational units. DNS names can be partitioned in a hierarchical fashion similar to a large network model without resorting to a large network model. However, Windows 2000 DNS management will remain centralized with a medium network model, whereas a large network model allows decentralization of DNS and Active Directory domain management.

A large network model, as shown in Figure 5-3, can support the same number of users as a medium network model, but the large network model may be preferable for a number of reasons. First, multiple DNS domains may be required due to company organization where pre-existing DNS names are in use. The same may be true of Windows 2000 domain names in an environment that is upgrading from Windows NT. Second, a large network model allows distribution of management that a medium model does not allow. For example, DNS servers in a medium network model would fall under the purview of a single administrator or group. With a large network model, the job could be split along domain lines.

A large network model can handle larger networks than a medium model because of the benefits of service distribution and minimization of replication. With a medium network model, the Windows 2000 Active Directory database is replicated among all domain controllers. With a large network model, there are separate Active Directory databases for each domain making a large network model simply a collection of small and medium networks. A global catalog is shared among all domain controllers within the network, but this information is a collection of subsets of information from each Active Directory domain database. Another way to view the domains in a large network is shown in Figure 5-4, where the Active Directory domain forest is shown more clearly.

NOTE: While a large model network can handle larger networks than a medium network model, this is only a reason to use a large network model in very large networks. Windows 2000 Active Directory single domain support can handle thousands of users in a medium model, single domain configuration. This covers most large networks. The preference for a large model network is due to other considerations such as delegation of management chores, easier security management of resources within domains and a reduction of network traffic due to Active Directory database replication.

While a large network model has advantages over a medium network model, the large network model is more complex and can require significantly more network administrative talent and effort. In many cases, this delegation of network management chores is actually desirable. Domains are often included specifically to allow management by local network administrators more familiar with the domain's requirements as well as providing better turnaround time for network management changes.

The distributed network model is simply a large network model that is geographically distributed. Typically, the speed of connections between domains can vary and will be slower or have a lower bandwidth than the backbone of a larger network that is not geographically dispersed. Figure 5-5 shows a distributed network model. The view is a physical distribution that happens to match the logical distribution of domains. This is typically the case with distributed Windows 2000 networks. Note that the domain structure is the same as for the large network model presented previously.

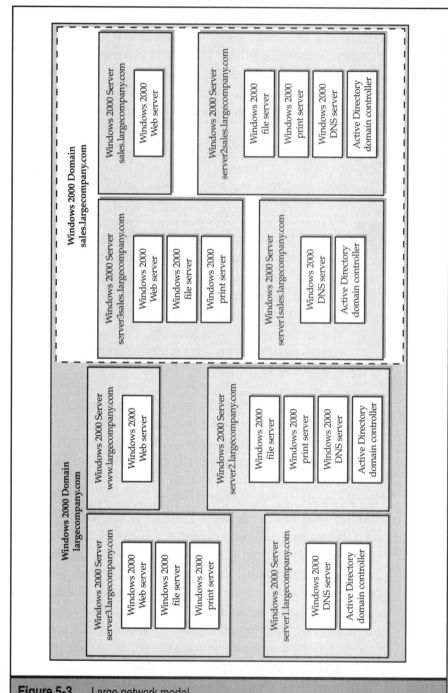

Figure 5-3. Large network model

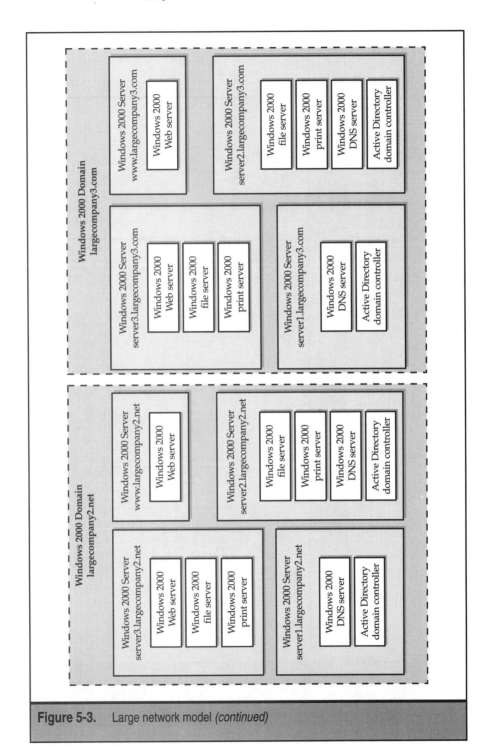

Figure 5-3. Large network model *(continued)*

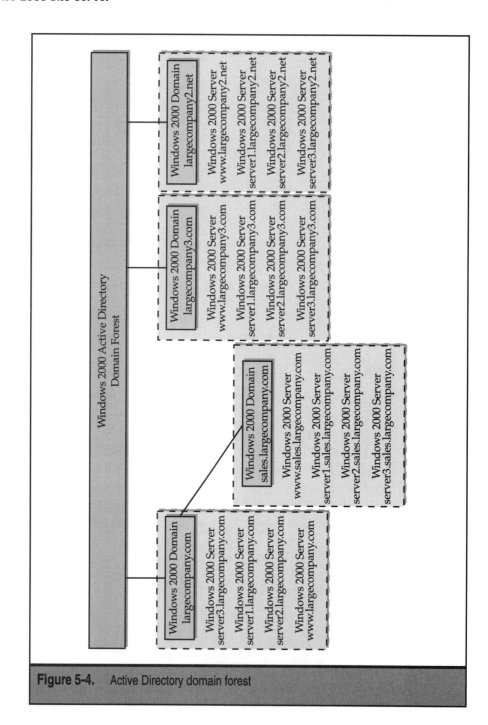

Figure 5-4. Active Directory domain forest

NOTE: Distributed Active Directory networks do not have to follow the distributed network model presented here but a distributed medium model network is not very common. Distributed networks typically support larger organizations that lend themselves to multiple domains. Assigning domains on a per site basis is a logical way to lay out a network and it makes it easier to delegate network management to local administrators.

Setup and management of a distributed network is very similar to that of a large network, but there are more considerations with the distributed network model, especially regarding DNS. For example, in a distributed network model there is typically one or more DNS servers located at each site. The same is true for Active Directory domain controllers.

PLANNING AND SETUP CONSIDERATIONS

Unlike Windows NT, where DNS server support was performed after Windows NT was installed, a Windows 2000 Active Directory installation requires DNS support from the start. Thus, it is important that the planning for both Active Directory and DNS be done before installation actually begins. An Active Directory domain controller and DNS service can be on the same or different servers, and the DNS service can be Windows 2000 DNS service or a comparable DNS service such as BIND. A comparable DNS service can run on any suitable operating system, not just Windows 2000.

The first step is to lay out the basic plan for Active Directory hierarchy based on an organization's personal or network structure. Determining what domains will be required and what resources they will encompass must occur first. Grouping resources within a domain can be done later using Active Directory organizational units. As many Windows 2000 installations will be upgrades from Windows NT, the existing Windows NT domain structure will normally be the basis for the Windows 2000 domain structure. Windows NT domains may be consolidated prior to conversion to Windows 2000 as Active Directory provides a more powerful and flexible environment for managing users

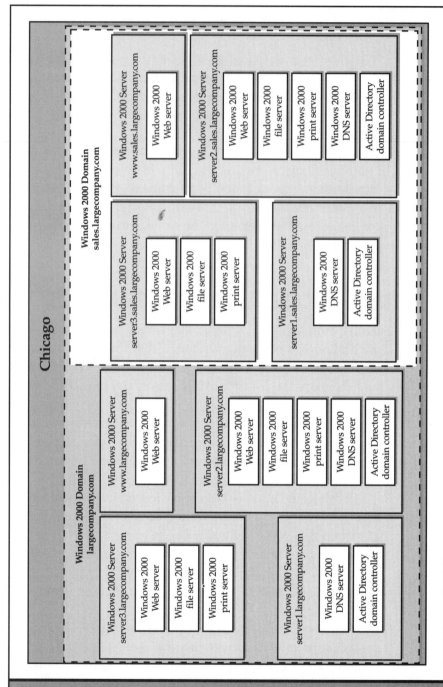

Figure 5-5. Distributed network model

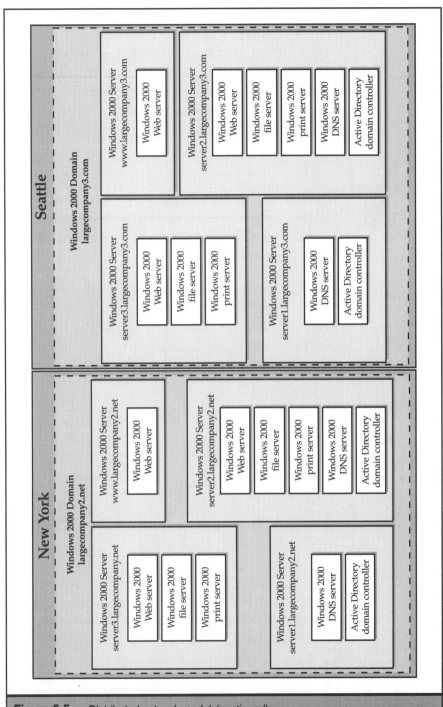

Figure 5-5.   Distributed network model *(continued)*

and resources. Figure 5-6 shows how a group of Windows NT domains might map to a Windows 2000 domain structure.

In this case, one of the Windows NT domains maps to the Windows 2000 root domain, company.com. The sales domain maps to a child domain and the remaining two domains are combined into one Windows 2000 domain. Windows 2000 Active Directory organizational units can provide the same type of separation that the two Windows NT domains did.

TIP: Active Directory domain planning should take into account Active Directory's hierarchical nature as managing a single domain is easier than managing multiple domains and managing a domain tree is easier than managing a domain forest.

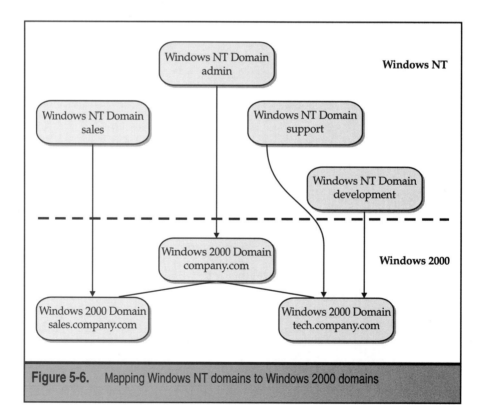

Figure 5-6. Mapping Windows NT domains to Windows 2000 domains

The next step is to plan DNS deployment. This covers issues such as DNS performance with respect to network traffic (an issue in larger networks), security and management considerations, what IP addresses will be tracked by DNS servers, and how and if DHCP servers will be deployed.

Finally, there are the migration issues related to DNS servers. Obviously, network administrators setting up a new network will not need to address migration issues. However, a network administrator will rarely set up a new network—with the exception of small networks being placed into a new site. The typical configuration is a migration from Windows NT 4.0 to Windows 2000. If TCP/IP is already used on this network, the type of DNS server used may impact the setup of the Windows 2000 DNS servers. The DNS servers in use prior to the migration to Windows 2000 may be running on Windows NT or another operating system such as UNIX or Linux. We will examine what issues may arise from migrating from these DNS servers to Windows 2000 as well as the possibility of maintaining the DNS servers in place of or in conjunction with the Windows 2000 DNS servers.

Aspects of migrating Windows NT to Windows 2000 that are not addressed in this book include user, group, and file migration; upgrade procedures; mixed Windows NT and Windows 2000 incremental migration; and mixed Windows NT and Windows 2000 networks. We assume that network administrators performing migrations on large networks will look to this book for guidance in planning the DNS aspect of the migration.

BASIC PLANNING FOR ACTIVE DIRECTORY

Active Directory planning is actually the design of a hierarchical domain structure that will track all objects within a network. Each domain, user, group, organizational unit, computer, server, and service has at least one Active Directory object associated with it. See Chapter 4 for an overview of Active Directory and its relationship to DNS.

Each domain maintains an Active Directory database that is replicated on one or more domain controllers within a domain. The Active Directory objects are organized in a domain tree with the root at the top of the tree. This root must have a DNS name, and that name is used as part of DNS names for objects that are automatically maintained by Windows 2000 Dynamic DNS for items within the tree. For example, the name of a domain tree for the FooBar Corporation might be foobar.com. The DNS name for a Web server within the domain might be www.foobar.com.

Planning a Single Domain Network

A single domain addresses small- and medium-size networks and is the simplest configuration. It supports integration of a single domain name and centralized network management of both Active Directory and DNS support. Replication control and requirements are minimized. A single set of password requirements is used for the entire domain.

In this configuration, Windows 2000 Active Directory requires at least one domain controller and one DNS server. This configuration can support multiple nondomain servers and workstations. We consider a small network to be one with a minimal, single domain configuration capable of supporting under 100 users.

NOTE: A single, or multiple, Windows 2000 server can operate without Active Directory and a DNS server. This network can handle hundreds of users but management tends to be more involved than with Active Directory.

A single domain can support more than one domain controller and DNS server. Multiple domain controllers maintain a replica of the Active Directory database and multiple DNS servers maintain a replica of the DNS database. A medium size network uses this type of implementation to support a larger number of users and to provide a more robust and redundant computing environment.

TIP: It is preferable to use Active Directory when a network has more than one Windows 2000 server. There is no difference in licensing costs between non-Active Directory and Active Directory Windows 2000 servers but there are significant replication, security, and management benefits to using Active Directory.

NOTE: Windows 2000 can upgrade a Windows NT PDC to a Windows 2000 domain controller and the domain controller can emulate a Windows NT PDC so existing Windows NT BDCs are still supported. Windows NT BDCs cannot be upgraded in the same fashion with BDC operation being preserved. Instead, BDCs must be upgraded to Windows 2000 domain controllers so the upgrade path for a Windows NT network to a Windows 2000 Active Directory network will always start with the Windows NT PDC and then all BDCs.

The main issue that must be addressed with respect to DNS support is the domain name. This is the primary DNS zone name, such as foobar.com. The Windows 2000 DNS server can manage additional zones, but it must support at least the zone with the matching domain name.

The planning of organizational units and groups is less of an issue regarding DNS, but Active Directory does affect DNS in two other areas: management and storage.

The Windows 2000 DNS service has a matching Active Directory object that is automatically created when the DNS service is installed. By default, the domain administrators group will have the ability to manage the DNS service.

The Windows 2000 DNS service can store its zone information in one of two places: in the Active Directory database or in a disk file. The former provides backup and replication features, while the latter is compatible with conventional DNS servers. How to determine the storage method is discussed in the section "Planning DNS Deployment."

Planning a Multiple Domain Network

A multiple domain network is applicable to larger networks or those with special needs. A multiple domain architecture should not be chosen lightly, as it greatly increases the level of sophistication of the network and requires a corresponding increase in the level of expertise and network management chores. Most of these issues are unrelated to DNS configuration or management, but DNS configuration and management chores will also have to be more sophisticated.

Typical reasons for choosing a multiple domain network architecture include:

▼ **WAN connections**   WAN connections are normally used to connect geographically dispersed sites. While it is possible to place servers from the same domain at each site, the Active Directory management and replication requirements usually make onsite management preferable. This is a form of decentralized network administration, but it's not the only one.

■ **Decentralized network administration**   Decentralized network administration may also be needed when the entire network is part of a single network if the groups using the network need or prefer to manage their own network resources. For example, colleges within a large university typically have resources that are best managed by the college faculty.

■ **Multiple Internet domain names**   A multiple domain network requires multiple Internet domain names, one for each domain. This situation arises when domains are hierarchically stacked and share a root domain name such as english.mycollege.edu and science.mycollege.edu or when companies or organizations with existing domain names, such as mycompany.com and yourcompany.net, are merged but must retain the domain names.

■ **Very large number of Active Directory objects**   A very large network typically has a very large number of Active Directory objects. Separating the network into domains allows the objects to be distributed among the domains, and only those in the Active Directory catalog are shared among domains. Catalog replication is independent of the Active Directory database replication that occurs within a domain.

■ **Better control over Active Directory replication**   The effort to replicate an Active Directory domain database can be significant so keeping this information within a smaller domain allows better control over where this information is kept. The Active Directory catalog will be replicated throughout a domain forest but this contains a subset of the information contained in a domain.

▲ **Different system policy requirements for each domain, such as different password lengths** There are instances where different domains within a network utilize different system policies such as having different minimum password lengths and password changing schedules. For example, the human resources and accounting groups in a university may have very high standards for security, whereas the security level needed for the students within the college may be lower.

Once the need for multiple domains has been established, the domain names must be determined. Domain names that are distinct, such as mycompany.com and yourcompany.net, must be implemented as a domain forest where each domain has its own tree. Domain names that share a root name, such as sales.mycompany.com and accounting.mycompany.com, must be implemented in a domain tree—in this instance, a common root domain, mycompany.com, must also be defined and managed even if most users and services are maintained in lower level domains. These domains cannot be placed in different domain trees within a domain forest because they share a common root.

NOTE: Multiple Windows 2000 domains are not required to provide hierarchical name support for IP-addressed services. For example, a medium network model with a single domain, mycompany.com, can contain multiple organizational units like sales.mycompany.com and accounting.mycompany.com. DNS can provide support for matching DNS domains with the same names so the organizations could have Web servers with names like www.sales.mycompany.com and www.accounting.mycompany.com. DNS-based naming support should be used for this type of environment instead of multiple Windows 2000 domains.

TIP: Create multiple Windows 2000 domain and DNS domain designs when creating a plan for a large network. The first iteration may not always be the best. Note tradeoffs between different plans especially those aspects that are fixed versus ones that are desirable. For example, if existing Windows NT domains must map to Windows 2000 domains then this fixed requirement may help determine whether Active Directory domain tree or domain forest hierarchy is required.

While multiple domains provide flexibility and tight integration with Windows 2000, network administrators should closely examine the need and implementation details of different domain names. For example, Internet domain names are often used to identify resources that will be made public on the Internet, such as mail, Web, and FTP servers, whereas internal organization resources and users do not have to share these domain names. For example, www.sell.com might be the name of a Web server that will be part of a network whose domain name will be mycompany.com. Windows 2000 DNS can accommodate this by maintaining two DNS zones: sell.com and mycompany.com. The Windows 2000 domain will require that mycompany.com be used, while the Web server's name is maintained in the sell.com DNS zone. The Web server can use IP addresses, so the IP addresses maintained in the two DNS zones are unique. Using DNS to maintain different Internet domain names works best when an organization can utilize one or just a few Active Directory domains. Changing and updating DNS names is significantly easier than changing Active Directory domains.

On the other hand, if a domain name is being used for more than just accessing one or more Internet servers, Windows 2000 domains may provide better management and security.

PLANNING DNS DEPLOYMENT

DNS performance will be determined by the number of clients actively using the DNS server, the distance between the DNS server and the clients in terms of network segments, and whether the DNS server can resolve the requests using local or cached information versus forwarding requests to other DNS servers. The latter may be more of an issue if Dynamic DNS support is used, since one of many DNS databases will be updated when a workstation registers its name and IP address. This information must then be passed to other DNS servers with a forwarded request or through DNS database synchronization.

DNS servers need to be placed where they can provide naming services efficiently while redundant DNS servers need to be placed where they can properly back up the primary DNS server. Security and management should be considered with respect to initial setup and configuration of these servers. DNS servers should be on or near domain controller systems for the domains supported by the DNS server. This allows the DNS servers to be part of the Active Directory domain, which allows local management. Most Windows 2000 DNS servers will be inside a firewall, but some may not. Special security considerations may be necessary to address those servers located outside the firewall because they are more susceptible to attack. In fact, it may be preferable to have these DNS servers act as standalone domain servers rather than have them be part of an internal domain so that internal security will not be compromised should the server outside the firewall be compromised.

The forwarding of DNS requests may also affect placement of DNS servers. Because of caching, forwarding can be more efficient than allowing clients to access multiple DNS servers. DNS servers that will be forwarding requests should be able to efficiently access DNS servers where these requests are sent.

The relationship between DNS servers supporting secondary DNS zones and DNS servers with a matching primary zone is similar to the relationship between forwarding DNS servers and the DNS servers to which requests are forwarded. The major difference is that secondary DNS zone information is downloaded in a block instead of one request at a time. This is usually more efficient than using forwarding DNS servers, but it can have more of an impact on network traffic. The update frequency is set at the DNS server with the primary DNS zone.

Finally, there is the issue of whether the DNS servers will track a small number of servers with static IP addresses or whether a larger number of workstations will be tracked as well. In the latter case, the use of DHCP and Dynamic DNS updates can minimize problems of reconfiguration and maintenance. Placing the DHCP server on the same system as the DNS server also minimizes Dynamic DNS update traffic on the network.

USING WINDOWS 2000 DNS SERVICES TO SUPPORT ACTIVE DIRECTORY

If Windows 2000 DNS support is used, it can be installed at the same time as Windows 2000 and Active Directory. If a different DNS package is used instead, it must be up and running prior to the installation of Windows 2000. As Windows 2000 will be installed on a PC prior to installing Active Directory, it is possible to have the Windows 2000 DNS service installed prior to installing Active Directory.

NOTE: If the Windows 2000 DNS service is installed prior to installing Active Directory then the Windows 2000 DNS service will only support primary and secondary DNS zones. Primary DNS zones can be converted to Active Directory–integrated DNS zones after Active Directory is installed. The Windows 2000 DNS service primary DNS zones will support Active Directory. Windows 2000 DNS primary DNS zones lack secure dynamic DNS update support.

A number of factors must be considered when deploying multiple Windows 2000 DNS servers. This will be true for all but small Windows 2000 networks. In this case, a single server handles most network services including DNS.

Factors to consider include DNS performance, reliability, security, and reconfiguration. These will impact the number of DNS servers, their placement, and the type of management necessary to keep the system in synch.

In general, DNS servers will find a home in one of three places in a homogeneous Windows 2000 DNS network (see Figure 5-7). The first place will be on Windows 2000 domain controllers. This allows the DNS service to support Active Directory–integrated DNS zones.

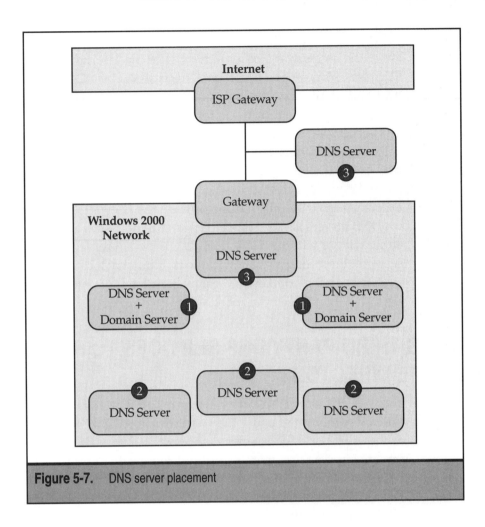

Figure 5-7. DNS server placement

It also provides DNS services to locate domain controllers and at least one will be available with this configuration so network logons will not be a problem.

The second place Windows 2000 DNS servers will be found is within the network. They will normally be placed so they improve DNS lookups in their local area. This type of DNS server will often be forwarding or caching servers or DNS servers with secondary DNS zones. They may also provide primary DNS zone support for local services within the network such as internal web sites.

The third place the Windows 2000 DNS servers will be found are at the gateways to other networks or the Internet. In this case, the DNS servers may provide caching and secondary DNS zone support for name resolution for sites outside the network. These servers may also provide name resolution for clients outside the network. In this case, access is provided through the gateway. If this incoming access is from a less secure environment like the Internet, the DNS server may be on the other side of a firewall. In this case, the server may not be an Active Directory domain controller as keeping a copy of Active Directory security information outside the firewall is rarely desirable.

DNS servers also are often located at remote sites and branch offices either with or without a Windows 2000 domain server. Having a DNS server at these locations allows logons to quickly locate domain servers even though the domain server may be at a remote site.

USING THIRD-PARTY DNS SERVICES TO SUPPORT ACTIVE DIRECTORY

Using third-party DNS services to support Active Directory is not much different than using the Windows 2000 DNS service as long as the third-party DNS services support SRV records. Dynamic DNS update support is preferable but not required although in the latter case, the DNS administrator will have to add the SRV records to the DNS service's database.

Placement of third-party DNS services is the same as for Windows 2000. Many third party DNS servers can run on Windows 2000 systems but Active Directory can be supported just as well using DNS servers that run on operating systems other than Windows 2000. Even Windows NT platforms are suitable although Windows NT's DNS service will not support Windows 2000 Active Directory because the Windows NT's DNS service does not support SRV records or dynamic DNS updates.

Many companies have well-established DNS infrastructures because TCP/IP was the chosen network transport. UNIX and Linux platforms are popular for DNS services. In many instances, the network uses these platforms for other services in addition to DNS services.

Once it is determined that an existing DNS infrastructure will support Windows 2000 Active Directory, additional planning will be needed to determine what DNS servers will be involved in supporting Windows 2000 Active Directory and whether additional DNS servers will be required. For example, because DNS servers are needed by Windows 2000 clients to located Windows 2000 Active Directory domain controllers, additional DNS servers may be needed where there are concentrations of these types of clients and servers. This may be the case when existing DNS servers are primarily providing support for Internet access or for local web services.

In a homogeneous Windows 2000 network, DNS servers are often combined with domain controllers so a Windows 2000 client will have access to a domain controller if they have access to the DNS server. A similar design works well with third-party DNS services if the DNS software runs on Windows 2000. Alternatively, pairing servers often makes sense.

TIP: Keep existing DNS support in perspective when bringing Windows 2000 into a network. Mixing different DNS servers, as discussed in the "Mixing Third-Party DNS and Windows 2000 DNS Services" section, is often the best approach to supporting Active Directory in a mixed environment. If using Windows 2000 DNS services is not desirable due to other organizational pressures then make sure that the existing DNS services will support Windows 2000 and find out how the existing DNS software works. For example, dynamic DNS updates may be supported but disabled for security or management reasons. In this case, determine whether the DNS software can restrict dynamic DNS updates to Windows 2000 domain controllers. BIND is one DNS service that can handle this type of restriction.

While Windows 2000 DNS services with Active Directory support offer many advantages, well-established third-party DNS environments have already addressed the issues associated with these advantages such as DNS zone replication, backup of DNS zone files, DNS security, and support for DHCP.

MIXING THIRD-PARTY DNS AND WINDOWS 2000 DNS SERVICES

A mixed DNS environment will be very common in medium to large size networks where Windows 2000 will have a home. In many cases, Windows NT servers have been a mainstay in the network, and they will be upgraded to Windows 2000. In most cases, this upgrade can be done without changing the existing environment until Active Directory is added. When this occurs, Active Directory's need for DNS support will be a significant issue especially if the existing DNS infrastructure has little or no Windows NT–based DNS services.

There are two approaches to mixing Windows 2000 DNS services with third-party DNS services. The first is to migrate third-party DNS services to Windows 2000 DNS services as part of the migration from Windows NT to Windows 2000 with Active Directory. The second is to restrict Windows 2000 DNS support to where Windows 2000 Active Directory is needed.

Migration from third-party DNS services to Windows 2000 DNS services should be done in a well-planned and well-tested fashion. Users will most likely be very dependent on existing DNS services so replacing them with Windows 2000 DNS services must result in an environment that is just as dependable and robust as its predecessor. Windows 2000 DNS services are up to the chore but DNS administrators must make sure that the existing DNS zone information and configuration get moved to the new Windows 2000 DNS service properly.

Peaceful coexistence is often the preferred method of bringing Windows 2000 DNS services to a network with a well-established DNS environment. In this case, DNS naming conventions will come into play as Windows 2000 Active Directory domain names are chosen so as not to conflict with the existing DNS domain environment. This allows the existing DNS environment to remain intact while being complemented by Windows 2000 DNS services for those new DNS zones added specifically for Windows 2000 Active Directory support.

For example, consider a network with a DNS zone named sample.org. The domain may have any number of subzones, such as admin.sample.org or sales.admin.org. Adding a win2000.sample.org domain for Windows 2000 support allows the Windows 2000 DNS support to be part of the existing domain structure. In this case, the root domain for the Windows 2000 Active Directory domain tree will be win2000.sample.org.

This approach allows a Windows 2000 DNS administrator to handle all the details of the win2000.sample.org domain and any subdomains and related DNS subzones. This information can be replicated among existing, non-Windows 2000 DNS servers using secondary DNS zones. Typically, the Windows 2000 DNS support will be used to support only Windows 2000 servers and clients. This effectively places a homogeneous Windows 2000 environment within a larger heterogeneous network. Information from the existing DNS infrastructure can be brought into the Windows 2000 environment using standard DNS tools like forwarding, caching, and secondary DNS zones.

The use of naming conventions like win2000 in win2000.sample.org makes it easy for network managers but is of little use to most users. One alternative is to use more representative names or to migrate specific domains to Windows 2000.

Although it is possible to mix and match DNS server support for Active Directory, it is best to choose a single approach for an organization and apply it consistently throughout the network. Mass migration of Windows NT servers to Windows 2000 Active Directory domain controllers will be more common in a homogeneous Windows environment. It will be less common for a heterogeneous environment.

MIGRATION ISSUES

Migration normally occurs from a Windows NT server running Microsoft's Windows NT DNS service or a third-party DNS service running on any number of platforms such as Windows NT, UNIX, Linux, and OS/2 to a Windows 2000 DNS service. Migration can also occur from these platforms to newer, third-party DNS services that are capable of supporting Active Directory assuming the existing services do not have the requisite DNS support for Active Directory.

The most common third-party DNS service is BIND, the latest version of which is suitable for use with Active Directory.

Luckily, the DNS database for existing DNS servers can be stored or saved as DNS zone text files. The format of these files is presented in Appendix B. This is the same format used by the Windows 2000 DNS service, so it is possible to easily migrate an existing DNS database to Windows 2000, assuming that the domain names are to remain the same.

The big change occurs with the additional DNS information that Windows 2000 maintains via DNS. Luckily, it is possible to create a new primary DNS zone for a Windows 2000 domain and then edit the domain zone file and add information from the zone file being migrated to Windows 2000. This is a relatively straightforward process that can be done with a text editor. Just copy the zone definitions from one text file to the other when the Windows 2000 DNS server is stopped. The server then starts and loads the updated file.

SUMMARY

While DNS services alone are useful in a network, Active Directory cannot operate alone. It must have DNS support, so planning where DNS servers will be placed is important to Active Directory operation.

DNS planning tends to be broader than just Active Directory support because of the importance of TCP/IP and the Internet. It is unusual that networks are isolated, so connection to the Internet is almost a given. DNS servers in the network will interact with those on the Internet. This allows local DNS servers to provide network workstations with both local DNS information as well as cached DNS information obtained from the Internet.

Adding DNS and Active Directory to a network that has not used TCP/IP tends to be the easiest from a design and political standpoint since DNS services are a new addition and there are no DNS services to update or displace.

Adding Active Directory to a network that has DNS services can be a bit more complicated. Major issues will be how the DNS services will support Active Directory and what DNS services will be used.

CHAPTER 6

Windows 2000 DNS and Active Directory Setup for a Small Network

Setting up a small Windows 2000 network is a relatively easy task. A small network has by definition a single domain, a single domain controller, and a single DNS server. While the domain controller and the DNS server can run on different PCs, in a typical small network configuration a single PC hosts both services. The PC also normally hosts other services such as file and print services. For the purposes of this chapter, we will assume that this is the case.

Windows 2000 handles the basic server setup during installation, but Active Directory and DNS support are set up by the Windows 2000 Configure Your Server Wizard. This wizard can set up a variety of services, as listed on the left side of the window in Figure 6-1. To configure the Active Directory, just select it from the list and the right side of the window will then be updated to display information

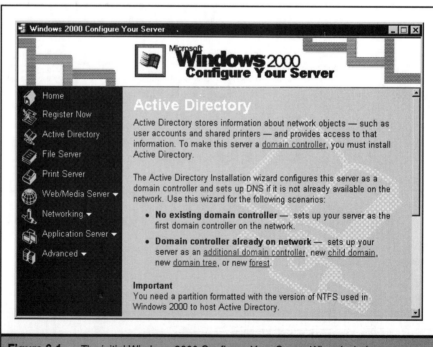

Figure 6-1. The initial Windows 2000 Configure Your Server Wizard window

about Active Directory, as shown in Figure 6-1. The wizard assumes that Active Directory is not yet installed on the domain controller.

The hyperlinks in the right side of the window provide access to online help. To get to the link for installing Active Directory, you must scroll down and reveal the rest of the page, as shown in Figure 6-2.

The Learn More link provides access to Active Directory online help. If you're unfamiliar with Active Directory and the Active Directory Wizard, it's a good idea to explore this link. The Start link runs the Active Directory Wizard. Click on the Start link to bring up the first Active Directory Wizard window.

Throughout the wizard, you can click the Next button to move to the next screen or click the Back button to return to the previous screen. Click the Cancel button to exit the wizard without effecting any change. On the welcome screen, click on the Next button to bring up the Domain Controller Type screen shown in Figure 6-3.

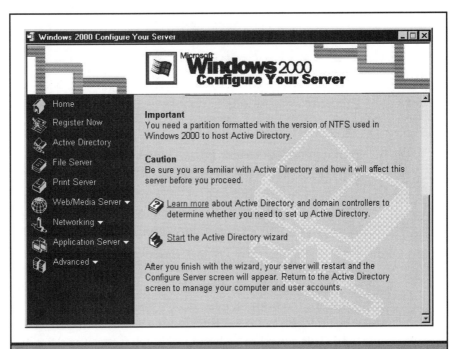

Figure 6-2.   Configure Your Server Wizard with Active Directory Wizard link

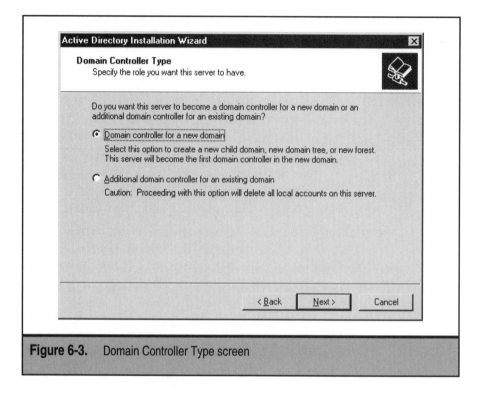

Figure 6-3. Domain Controller Type screen

There are two options to choose from in the Domain Controller Type screen:

▼ Domain Controller For A New Domain

▲ Additional Domain Controller For An Existing Domain

For a small network, choose the Domain Controller For A New Domain option. This creates a new domain and sets up the server as a domain controller. The other option, Additional Domain Controller For An Existing Domain, is used in medium, large, or distributed networks where an additional server is being set up after the initial domain controller for the domain has already been set up. The additional server must be attached to the network where an existing domain controller is attached. This selection is discussed in Chapters 7 and 8, which cover medium and large network installations respectively.

Click on the Next button to bring up the Create Tree or Child Domain screen shown in Figure 6-4.

There are two options to choose from in the Create Tree or Child Domain screen:

▼   Create A New Domain Tree

▲   Create A New Child Domain In An Existing Domain Tree

For a small network, choose the Create A New Domain Tree option. This creates a new domain tree with a domain name that you will enter later in this process. This option is also selected when creating a new top-level domain that has a different domain name than an existing Active Directory domain. Top-level, Windows 2000 domains can be merged into a forest of domain trees for large and distributed networks.

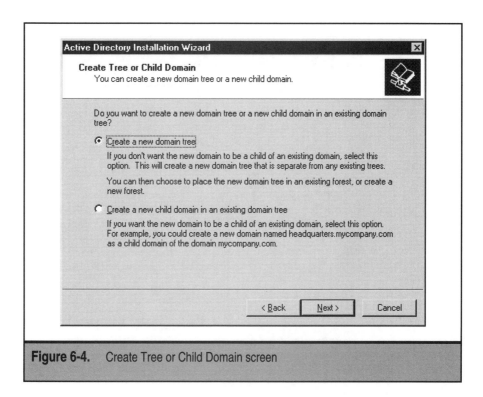

Figure 6-4.   Create Tree or Child Domain screen

The other option, Create A New Child Domain In An Existing Domain Tree, requires an existing and named domain and at least one domain controller. The child domain must have a domain name whose root matches the DNS name for the existing domain tree. For example, a child domain named child.root.com can be part of a root.com domain tree. This approach is taken when working with large and distributed networks with multiple domains.

Click on the Next button to bring up the Create or Join Forest screen shown in Figure 6-5.

The Create or Join Forest screen is only presented when a new domain tree is created. There are two options to choose from in the Create or Join Forest screen:

▼ Create A New Forest Of Domain Trees

▲ Place This New Domain Tree In An Existing Forest

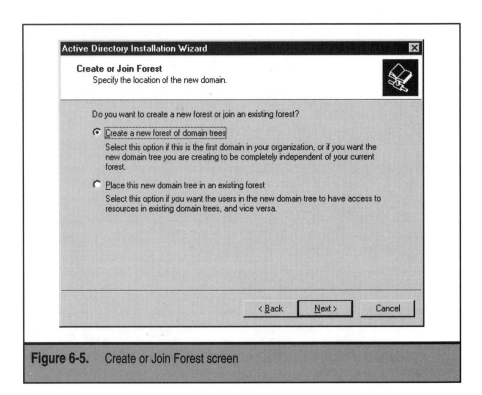

Figure 6-5. Create or Join Forest screen

For a small network, choose Create A New Forest Of Domain Trees. This creates a new domain forest with a single domain tree, the new domain. Subsequent domain trees can be added to this forest in the future if a small network grows into a large one.

The Place This New Domain Tree In An Existing Forest option is used in a large or distributed network where multiple domain trees are maintained in a common domain forest. This allows domains to share resources and users with appropriate rights to administer resources in different domains.

Click on the Next button to bring up the New Domain Name screen shown in Figure 6-6.

This is the easy part: just enter the full domain name for the new domain in the New Domain Name window. A commercially registered domain name will end in a standard extension like .com, .net, or .org. Higher education institutions end in .edu. A domain that will be

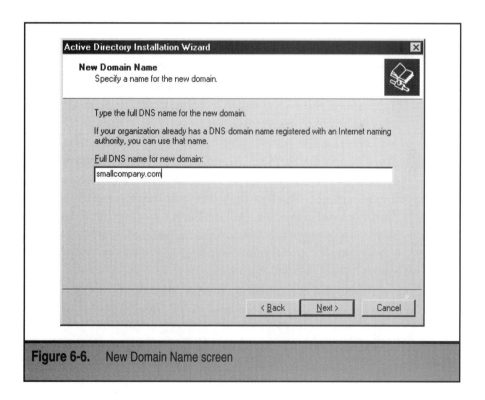

Figure 6-6.   New Domain Name screen

used internally but not on the Internet can have a nonconflicting domain extension such as .dom. Check out www.register.com for a list of other domain extensions that can be used internally. Since these are internal domain names only, there would be no conflict if two companies used company.dom because the domains are on separate networks that are not accessible anywhere else. However, this does not mean that servers on the network cannot be accessible to the outside world such as the Internet. It simply means that any servers that can be accessed from an external source must have an additional domain name and usually an additional IP address. This additional domain name can be stored in both local and external DNS servers.

The example in Figure 6-6 uses smallcompany.com. It is not registered, but the network is in the lab and not connected to the Internet so there are no conflicts. The domain name may have more than two levels such as support.software.smallcompany.com.

It is important that the domain name entered is correct. While it is a simple matter to adjust the zones in the Windows 2000 DNS server, it is a more difficult process to change the Active Directory domain name, especially of a domain tree that is part of a domain forest or in a domain tree hierarchy. Get it right the first time. Cancel the process if there is any question about what domain name should be used.

Click on the Next button to bring up the NetBIOS Domain Name screen shown in Figure 6-7.

The domain name entered in the NetBIOS Domain Name screen must be a valid NetBIOS name. This is a different name from the domain name used by both the Active Directory domain name and the matching DNS domain name, although typically the NetBIOS name is a portion of the Active Directory and DNS domain name, as shown in Figure 6-7. A similar name makes it easier for users to recognize a domain when switching between older clients and newer Windows 2000 clients.

The NetBIOS name is used when the Windows 2000 server is used within a NetBIOS network. This is typically the case when older Windows clients such as Windows 95 and Windows 98 are used versus Windows 2000 clients. The 15-character name may need to be shortened to 8 characters if even older LAN Manager clients are being used.

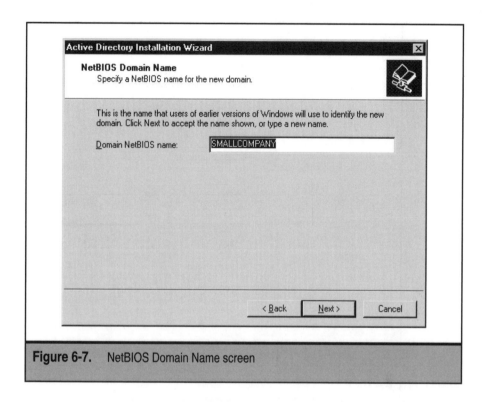

Figure 6-7.   NetBIOS Domain Name screen

Click on the Next button to bring up the Database and Log Locations screen shown in Figure 6-8.

The Database and Log Locations screen allows you to set the location of the Active Directory database and log files. By default, both are set to the same address, the NTDS directory in the Windows 2000 installation directory. However, both the Database and Log Locations screen and the Windows 2000 Best Practices recommendations indicate the two should be different. In particular, the Active Directory database must be on an NTFS partition for security reasons. Keeping the log file on a separate partition also prevents large log files from impacting on the size of the Active Directory database. The Browse buttons make it easy to locate the directories where you want to store each.

Click on the Next button to bring up the Shared System Volume screen shown in Figure 6-9.

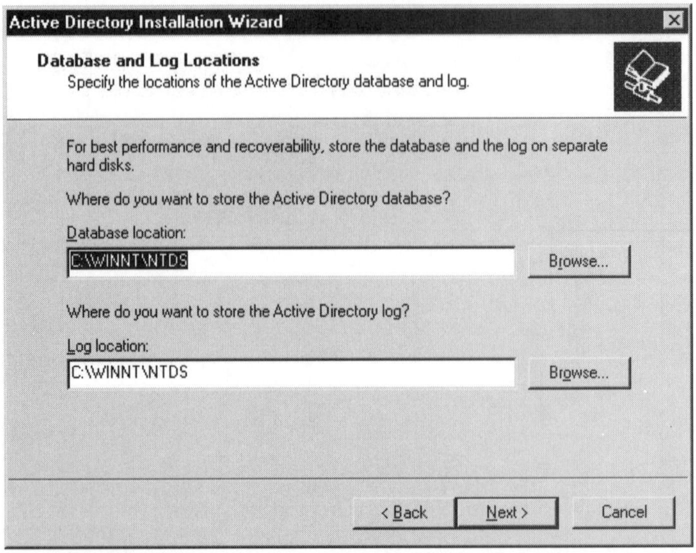

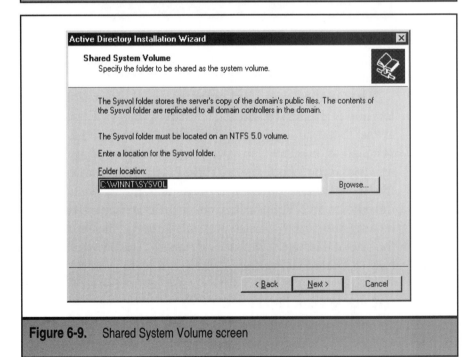

Figure 6-8. Database and Log Locations screen

Figure 6-9. Shared System Volume screen

The Shared System Volume screen allows you to select to which directory the domain's public files will be replicated. These files will be replicated to all domain controllers in an Active Directory domain. The default location is presented and does not typically need to be changed. The directory is a local one and can be different on each domain controller. The replication process is not addressed by this wizard.

Click on the Next button to bring up the Configure DNS screen shown in Figure 6-10.

Setting up the DNS service is a snap at this point; most of the work is already done. The server has its TCP/IP support already configured, and all the information about the base domain has been entered through this wizard. If you select Yes, Install And Configure DNS On This Computer (Recommended), you will add the Windows 2000 DNS service to this domain controller. This is the typical way of setting up the DNS service even if most users will use a different DNS service on another server. Having a DNS service running on

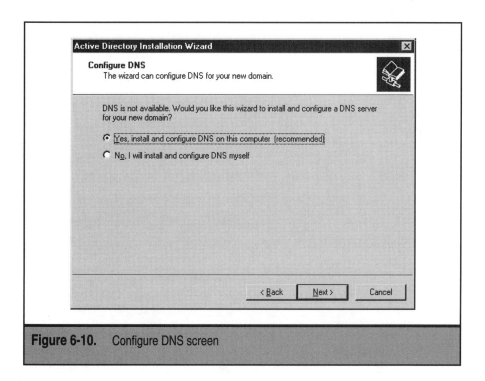

Figure 6-10.   Configure DNS screen

the domain controller means the domain controller has access to a DNS service.

If you choose No, I Will Install And Configure DNS Myself, you will have to manually configure the DNS service. The DNS service can be installed on this PC or another PC. The DNS service can also be a DNS service other than Windows 2000 DNS service. If you wish to choose this option, it is preferable to set up the DNS service before you configure Active Directory. (It is possible to set up the DNS service after Active Directory is installed, but there is a potential for a nonfatal error when the Active Directory service is run without a DNS service.)

Click on the Next button to bring up the Permissions screen shown in Figure 6-11.

The Permissions screen addresses communication security used between servers when it comes to accessing domain information. There are two options to choose from:

▼ Permissions Compatible With Pre-Windows 2000 Servers

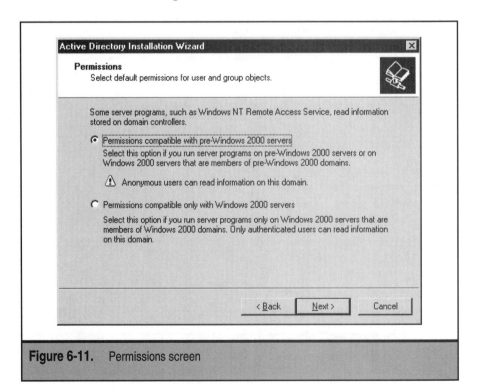

Figure 6-11. Permissions screen

▲ Permissions Compatible Only With Windows 2000 Servers

The Permissions Compatible With Pre-Windows 2000 Servers option should be used if other non-Windows 2000 servers are to be used on the network and if these servers are working with this server. This option allows anonymous users access to information on this domain, which is the way Windows NT Server operates. Choose this option when migrating more than one server and you are completing the process incrementally.

The Permissions Compatible Only With Windows 2000 Servers option forces the servers to use the Windows 2000 implementation of Kerberos. Only servers that have been authenticated can access information from this server. This prevents users from finding information that may be private. This option should be chosen if all Windows NT servers are being upgraded at the same time or if servers without Windows 2000 do not need to access this server. Windows 2000's security implementation is preferable to Windows NT and should be used if at all possible. It is possible to change the permissions setting at another time.

Click on the Next button to bring up the Directory Services Restore Mode Administration Password screen.

As with any service, the Active Directory service restricts access to certain portions of the registry and other key areas of Windows 2000 to those users with administrative rights. To assign a password for the Administrator account, enter it (twice) on this screen. The service will use the Active Directory Services Restore Mode when starting up.

Click on the Next button to bring up the Summary screen shown in Figure 6-12.

The Summary screen provides a list of selections you made while using the Wizard. You may have to scroll down the window to see all the details. To make changes, click on the Back button. This can be tedious if the necessary window is over ten screens back, but, in general it is a simple process to make changes. The Wizard retains all values previously entered except the ones you change. Click on the Next button to bring up the Configuring Active Directory window.

The Configuring Active Directory window provides real time status of the configuration process. Your only option is to cancel the installation; if you choose to do this, the configuration information

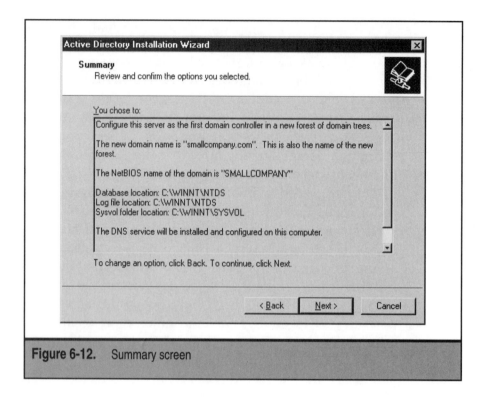

Figure 6-12. Summary screen

will be lost, and the wizard must be run again to properly configure the servers.

Once the Active Directory and DNS service installation process is completed, the Completing Active Directory Installation Wizard screen shown in Figure 6-13 will be displayed.

At this point, everything has been installed, and the only active button is the Finish button. Once you click the button, Windows 2000 prompts the server to reboot. As well as starting up the new services, rebooting allows some final changes to be made to the registry and system files when the system restarts that cannot be done while the system is running.

After the server reboots and the Administrator has logged in, it is possible to view the results of the installation by using the Microsoft Management Console (MMC), which supports a variety of snap-ins. There are a number of Active Directory snap-ins, including one for users and another for machines. Figure 6-14 displays the DNS snap-in.

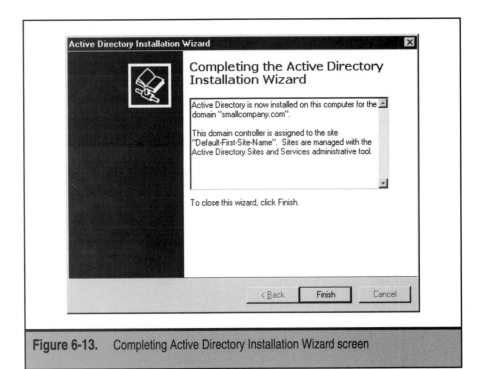

Figure 6-13. Completing Active Directory Installation Wizard screen

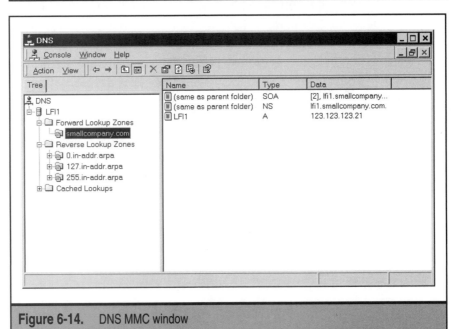

Figure 6-14. DNS MMC window

You can run the DNS MMC snap-in by choosing Start |
Programs | Administrative Tools | DNS. Details of the DNS MMC
support are covered in Chapter 11, but you can see that the Forward
Lookup Zone for the desired domain, smallcompany.com, is already
set up. There is a DNS entry for the server based on its IP address
that was set up when Windows 2000 is installed.

ACTIVE DIRECTORY SETUP FOR SMALL NETWORKS

While most MMC snap-ins deal with Active Directory—at least
with respect to related services like DNS—there are some Active
Directory–specific MMC snap-ins that are in the Start | Programs |
Administrative Tools menu. These include the following:

▼ Active Directory Domains and Trusts

■ Active Directory Sites and Services

▲ Active Directory Users and Computers

These are addressed in more detail in Chapter 10. The Active
Directory Domains and Trusts are of minimal use in a small network
since there is only one domain and no trusts, but they can be used if the
small network is ever incorporated into an existing medium network.

The Active Directory Sites and Services are also of minimal use in
a small network. Sites are a concept reserved for multiple domains,
and the Services noted in the title are really site-related services, not
the application services running on a server such as the DNS service.
There is a Service MMC snap-in that handles application service
control. The Service MMC is started by choosing Start | Programs |
Administrative Tools | Services, as shown in Figure 6-15.

The screen shown in Figure 6-15 lists all the services that are
installed on the local computer including the DNS Client and DNS
Server. The Status column indicates which services are running and
the Startup Type column shows what Windows 2000 will do with the
service when Windows 2000 starts. Automatic startup is normal for
services that are always running in the background, whereas Manual
startup services are normally started by other services or applications

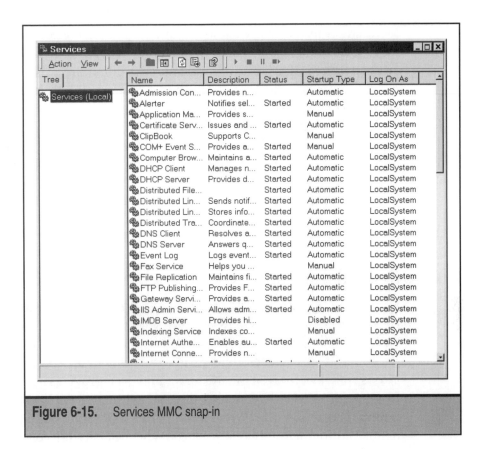

Figure 6-15.   Services MMC snap-in

as needed. A Disabled startup mode prevents a service from running even though it is installed.

When Active Directory is installed, the wizard creates the Default-First-Site-Name in the Sites folder. The Server folder within the Sites folder contains a list of servers associated with the site. You can find the newly installed server in this list. The site name can be renamed at any time, but for most small network installations the name is never changed.

You will probably perform the majority of the configuration work for Active Directory using the Active Directory Users and Computers MMC snap-in. Each domain is listed in this snap-in's window. Each domain contains standard folders such as Users, Computers, and Domain Controllers. This is also where the organizational unit hierarchy is listed. Organizational units can be used effectively even in a small network model to organize users and manage administrative rights. The organizational unit hierarchy is created using the Active Directory Users and Computers MMC snap-in to add new organizational unit folders.

By default, the Administrator user is defined when Windows 2000 is installed. There are a number of predefined users and groups that are also defined, such as Guest and Domain Users. The former is defined but disabled by default.

Users, groups, and organizational units can be defined once the Active Directory Service Wizard has finished its work.

DNS CONFIGURATION FOR SMALL NETWORKS

The Windows 2000 Configure Your Server Wizard sets up only the most basic DNS configuration. This includes setting up the domain name in the Start of Authority record, Name Server record, and host record for the server in the domains zone in the Forward Lookup Zones list. This is sufficient for running the server and even provides access to any intranet services running on the server such as the Internet Information Service (IIS) Web server and the FTP server. Additional definitions for these services, such as www.smallnetwork.com and ftp.smallnetwork.com, can be included at this time by simply adding new DNS host records using the DNS MMC snap-in. You can find more details on how the DNS MMC snap-in works in Chapter 11.

By default, the Windows 2000 Configure Your Server Wizard sets up the domain's zone type as Active Directory–integrated. This allows the zone information to be stored in the Active Directory database. This is helpful for backup purposes on a small network model, but it is less of an issue here than it is with more complex models where replication becomes an issue. The alternative to the Active Directory–integrated zone type is the Standard primary type that stores the DNS database in a text file. In this case, the file must be managed and replicated using file management tools. There is also a Standard secondary zone type but this is used to replicate information from another DNS server. While Standard secondary zones are useful in small network models to replicate DNS information for a different domain maintained on another DNS server, a secondary zone is of little use as the primary zone for the server unless the DNS service is not located on the Windows 2000 server. This type of configuration is possible but rarely used since the purpose of using the small network model is keeping it simple.

MIGRATION TO WINDOWS 2000 DNS FOR SMALL NETWORKS

DNS services may be migrated from a Windows NT DNS service or from a third-party DNS service such as BIND. If the server is the only entry within the DNS system, there really is nothing to migrate. Typically, however, the old DNS service has a number of DNS entries that must be migrated to the Windows 2000 DNS service.

The easiest way to perform the migration is to install the Windows 2000 Active Directory and DNS services as described in this chapter. Next, change the Active Directory–integrated zone type for the default zone to Standard primary type. This saves the current domain database in a text file that can be found in the system32/dns directory in the Windows 2000 directory. The DNS zone text file has an extension of .dns.

This file can be merged with the contents of the old DNS zone text file using a standard text editor like Windows 2000 Notepad. This is a relatively straightforward process. The format of the files is found in Appendix B.

You can create the Standard primary zone file by changing the zone type on the General tab of the Properties page, as shown in Figure 6-16.

To do this, click on the Change button to bring up the Change Zone Type dialog box shown in Figure 6-17.

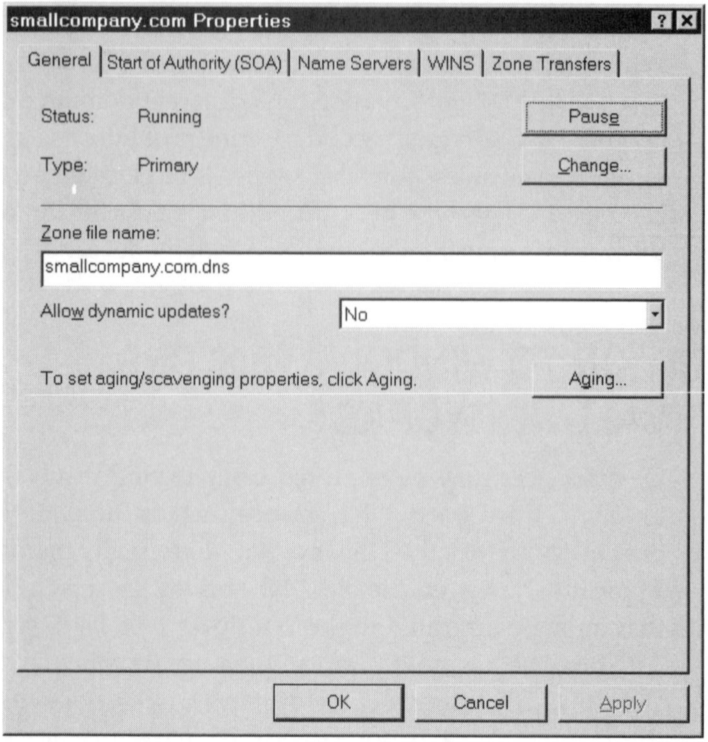

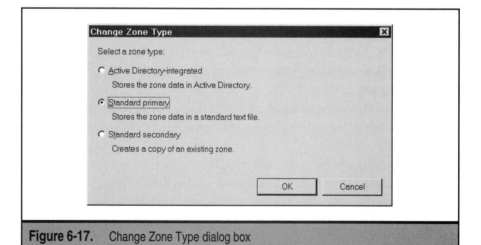

Figure 6-16. Standard Primary Zone Type for smallcompany.com

Figure 6-17. Change Zone Type dialog box

The Active Directory–integrated option is selected by default. Change this to Standard Primary, and then close the dialog box by clicking the OK button. This will return you to the General tab of the Properties page. Click the Apply button. This switches the zone type and saves the current database contents in the text file smallcompany.com.dns, as shown here.

```
;
;  Database file smallcompany.com.dns for smallcompany.com zone.
;      Zone version:  105
;
@                       IN  SOA server1.smallcompany.com.
administrator. (
                              105             ; serial number
                              900             ; refresh
                              600             ; retry
                              86400           ; expire
                              3600        ) ; minimum TTL

;
;  Zone NS records
;
@                       NS      server1.smallcompany.com.

;
;  Zone records
;
@                       600   A    123.123.123.1
9955dad9-50d5-11d3-b049-00c0f0161239._msdcs 600      CNAME
        server1.smallcompany.com.
_kerberos._tcp.default-first-site-name._sites.dc._msdcs 600 SRV      0
100 88
        server1.smallcompany.com.
_ldap._tcp.default-first-site-name._sites.dc._msdcs 600      SRV      0
100 389
        server1.smallcompany.com.
_kerberos._tcp.dc._msdcs 600  SRV    0 100 88
server1.smallcompany.com.
_ldap._tcp.dc._msdcs     600   SRV   0 100 389
server1.smallcompany.com.
_ldap._tcp.9f540ae0-50d5-11d3-b049-00c0f0161239.domains._msdcs 600
SRV  0 100 389    server1.smallcompany.com.
gc._msdcs              600   A    123.123.123.1
_ldap._tcp.default-first-site-name._sites.gc._msdcs 600      SRV      0
```

```
100 3268
        server1.smallcompany.com.
_ldap._tcp.gc._msdcs        600    SRV    0 100 3268
server1.smallcompany.com.
_ldap._tcp.pdc._msdcs       600    SRV    0 100 389
server1.smallcompany.com.
_gc._tcp.default-first-site-name._sites 600    SRV    0 100 3268
        server1.smallcompany.com.
_kerberos._tcp.default-first-site-name._sites 600    SRV    0 100 88
        server1.smallcompany.com.
_ldap._tcp.default-first-site-name._sites 600SRV    0 100 389
        server1.smallcompany.com.
_gc._tcp                    600    SRV    0 100 3268
server1.smallcompany.com.
_kerberos._tcp              600    SRV    0 100 88
server1.smallcompany.com.
_kpasswd._tcp               600    SRV    0 100 464
server1.smallcompany.com.
_ldap._tcp                  600    SRV    0 100 389
server1.smallcompany.com.
_kerberos._udp              600    SRV    0 100 88
server1.smallcompany.com.
_kpasswd._udp               600    SRV    0 100 464
server1.smallcompany.com.
server1                            A      123.123.123.1
```

For this example, we merged the DNS zone file with a simple DNS zone file listed here.

```
;
;  Database file smallcompany.com.dns for smallcompany.com zone.
;
@                       IN   SOA server1.smallcompany.com.
administrator. (
                            105            ; serial number
                            900            ; refresh
                            600            ; retry
                            86400          ; expire
                            3600        )  ; minimum TTL
;
;  Zone NS records
;
@                       NS     server1.smallcompany.com.
```

```
;
;   Zone records
;
@                         A              123.123.123.1
; Add the following to the end of the Windows 2000 zone file
www                       CNAME server1.smallcompany.com.
ftp                       CNAME server1.smallcompany.com.
router1                   A              123.123.123.98
router2                   A              123.123.123.99
printer1                  A              123.123.123.52
```

Note the differences between the two files. The Windows 2000 zone file has a large number of predefined definitions specific to Windows 2000, including mappings for LDAP. These are not found in the old DNS file since they are not needed for UNIX or Windows NT. Still, they need to remain intact so it is easiest to move the necessary lines from the old file to the new one.

First, stop the Windows 2000 DNS service so the DNS zone file will not be in use. We took a short cut and added a line in the old DNS file to make it easy to find the lines to add to the new DNS zone file. Everything after the line `; Add the following to the end of the Windows 2000 zone file` should be copied from the old DNS zone file to the Windows 2000 DNS zone file. Once the edited file is saved, you can start the Windows 2000 DNS service again. It will then read the new zone file, and the new DNS entries such as router1.smallcompany.com and www.smallcompany.com will be available to DNS clients.

The zone type can now be changed back to Active Directory–integrated if you wish. We recommend this, as does Microsoft in its Best Practices section of the Windows 2000 online help. This moves the information in the DNS zone file into the Active Directory database where service can be managed more effectively. This also makes dynamic DNS updates more secure.

Getting Windows 2000 DNS up and running for a small network model is a relatively simple process as outlined in this chapter. Even migrating old DNS zone information can be done in a matter of minutes, although it will take longer if the old DNS zone file contains lots of information. It is possible to debug DNS problems using tools like DNS Expert discussed in Chapter 22, but of course it will be easier if such problems do not arise in the first place.

SUMMARY

The small network model is very limited but it addresses a large number of existing Windows NT installations. Migration to Windows 2000 is often warranted for its many new features including improved DNS and DHCP support but the use of Active Directory is another issue. Active Directory tends to be overkill for a small network. Still, incorporating Active Directory does have some advantages as discussed in this chapter.

Active Directory allows Active Directory–integrated DNS zone support. Granted, replication is not an issue because there is only one server in this model but it does allow DNS information to be backed up in conjunction with the rest of the Active Directory database contents. It also provides finer security control. Of course, if Windows 2000 native mode is used, Active Directory and Windows 2000 DNS server support is required even in a small network.

DNS configuration and migration from Windows NT with a small network are significantly easier than in any other network model. It is simply a matter of using the upgrade support on the Windows 2000 installation CD-ROM. DNS zone information is brought under control of the Windows 2000 DNS service that replaces its Windows NT counterpart.

The small network model has been presented to contrast a simple configuration with the more advanced configurations associated with multiple servers and domains supported by the other network models where Active Directory is more appropriate and DNS support is required.

CHAPTER 7

Windows 2000 DNS and Active Directory Setup for a Medium Network

etting up a medium model Windows 2000 network is more time consuming than setting up a small model network, primarily due to the setup time associated with each server. The increased time needed to configure Active Directory and DNS servers compared to a small model network, however, is minimal.

The medium model network consists of a single domain with one or more domain controllers and one or more DNS servers. While domain controllers and DNS servers can run on different PCs, we assume that a single PC hosts both services when addressing the installation process. The PC normally hosts other services such as file and print services as well, although these are often placed on another server when performance or security is an issue.

NOTE: The medium network model will likely be the most common Active Directory implementation as it provides redundancy as well as being able to support a large number of users without dealing with the complexity of a multiple domain environment like that found in the large network model. The medium network model is also the best for Active Directory–integrated DNS zones since these zones will be available to any DNS service that is installed on an Active Directory domain controller.

The first step to installing a medium model network is to set up the first domain controller. The process is the same as outlined in Chapter 6 for a small model network. Chapter 6 also addresses the setup and configuration of subsequent domain controllers and DNS servers. The same procedure is followed for each additional server within a medium model network. In this section, we assume that the first Windows 2000 domain controller is set up with a Windows 2000 DNS service that uses a primary Active Directory–integrated DNS zone and that each additional server is attached to the same network. Each server also has a fixed IP address, and the DNS server IP address is set to an existing DNS server that names existing domain controllers. The DNS server should have regular dynamic DNS update support enabled so the new domain controller will be able to add its SRV resource records to its DNS zone. This information can be added by hand either before or after Active Directory is set up on the new domain controller, but it must be in place so the domain controller can be found. This is important for both logins as well as Active Directory synchronization.

Although DHCP can be used to obtain an IP address, it is rarely used in a server since the lack of a DHCP server and the lack of dynamic DNS update capability can prevent the server from being accessible to other servers and workstations. In general, it is best to have a range of IP addresses for use with servers and to use DHCP only with workstations. It is possible to keep DNS information updated for a server given an IP address via DHCP using dynamic DNS update support, but this should be avoided because replication of a domain controller's information will only occur immediately at the DNS server where it is registered. Any replication via DNS secondary zones or through Active Directory replication for Active Directory–integrated DNS zones will take some time in a situation where it would be possible to have conflicting information from a prior registration if the IP address is different than a prior address.

NOTE: A Windows NT SAM database for a Windows NT domain will be retained if the first Windows 2000 server is an upgraded Windows NT primary domain controller (PDC). This information will be retained when the Windows 2000 Active Directory service is installed. Windows NT backup domain controllers (BDCs) can continue to work with the first Windows 2000 server if the server is set up in compatibility mode. Windows 2000 can be installed on BDCs as new installation. A BDC can also be upgraded if services on the BDC are to be retained. Installation of Active Directory and DNS support discussed in this chapter will not be affected by the upgrade or installation method used.

The medium model network differs from the small model network in that server-to-server communication is necessary to maintain the integrity of the Active Directory database maintained on each Active Directory domain controller. DNS servers must also synchronize their databases, as shown in Figure 7-1. There are three ways to achieve this synchronization: Active Directory–integrated synchronization, secondary zone synchronization, and manual

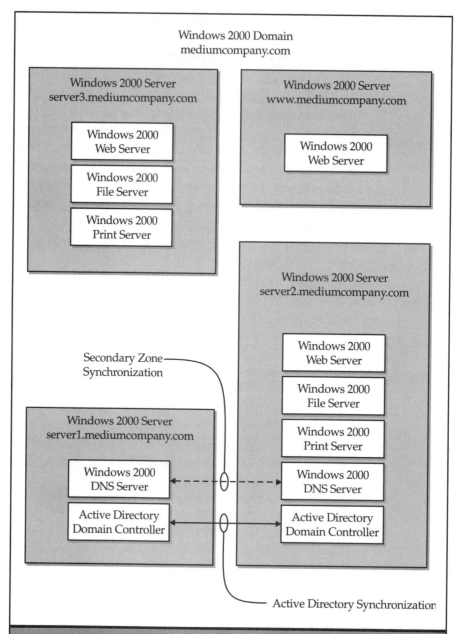

Figure 7-1. Medium model showing DNS and Active Directory server communications

synchronization. Active Directory–integrated DNS zone implementation allows DNS synchronization to be completed with Active Directory. Secondary zone configuration allows DNS servers to synchronize themselves with the added advantage of working with non-Windows 2000 DNS servers. Manual synchronization requires administrative action that can lead to lack of synchronization if DNS administrative duties are ignored or delayed. While Active Directory–integrated synchronization is preferred over secondary zone synchronization and manual synchronization, the other two approaches have merits as well.

As with the small network model covered in Chapter 6, installation of the Windows 2000 Active Directory and DNS services is initiated from the Windows 2000 Configure Your Server Wizard, which you can bring up by choosing Start | Programs | Administrative Tools | Configure Your Server. The Windows 2000 Configure Your Server Wizard can be run any time after Windows 2000 is installed, but the computer name should be set before installing Active Directory. This is because the computer name cannot be changed once Active Directory is installed unless the domain controller is demoted to a regular server. The same is true for the choice of domain name that will be entered later in this sequence. Once set, the Active Directory domain name remains fixed until the domain is destroyed. It is relatively easy, however, to change the DNS domain name.

TIP: As with any major network configuration, make sure that backups have been made prior to starting the Active Directory Installation Wizard. This includes backing up at least one of the domain controllers in the Active Directory domain that the computer will be added to as well as the computer. The backup for the existing domain controller should include a backup of the Active Directory database, not just a file backup.

On the welcome screen of the Active Directory Installation Wizard, click on the Next button to bring up the Domain Controller Type screen, shown in Figure 7-2.

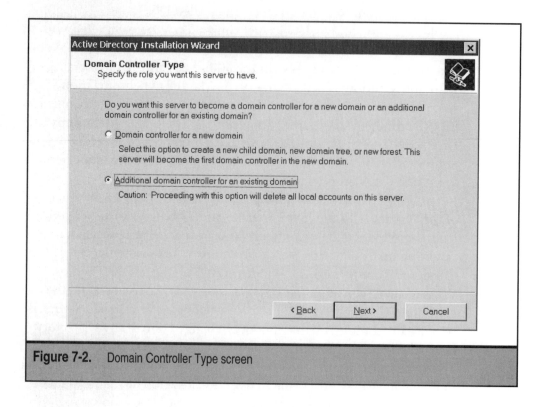

Figure 7-2.   Domain Controller Type screen

Just as in the small network model, you would select the Domain controller for a new domain button for the first domain controller in a medium model network. For subsequent domain controllers, however, select the Additional domain controller for an existing domain button. This changes several of the subsequent dialog boxes from what they would be if you were setting up a new domain controller. In particular, a new domain controller allows any domain name to be used, but an additional domain controller must use an existing domain name assigned to the initial domain controller.

NOTE: A second Active Directory domain name can be used when creating a new domain controller but the domain controller will now be part of a child domain or a root domain in an Active Directory domain forest. This is what a large network model uses. Check out Chapter 8 for details on a large network model.

After selecting the Additional domain controller for an existing domain button, click on the Next button to bring up the Network Credentials screen shown in Figure 7-3.

Filling in the user name, password, and domain logs you in to the domain so that subsequent synchronization can be performed. The user must have administrative privileges for the domain. The information you enter here is the same information that an administrator would use to log into the domain from another workstation. Note that the domain name is the simple domain name that is also used for the NetBIOS domain name; it is not the same domain name used in the next dialog box or the one supported by the Windows 2000 DNS primary domain. The wizard will not proceed to the next dialog box if the information entered is incorrect.

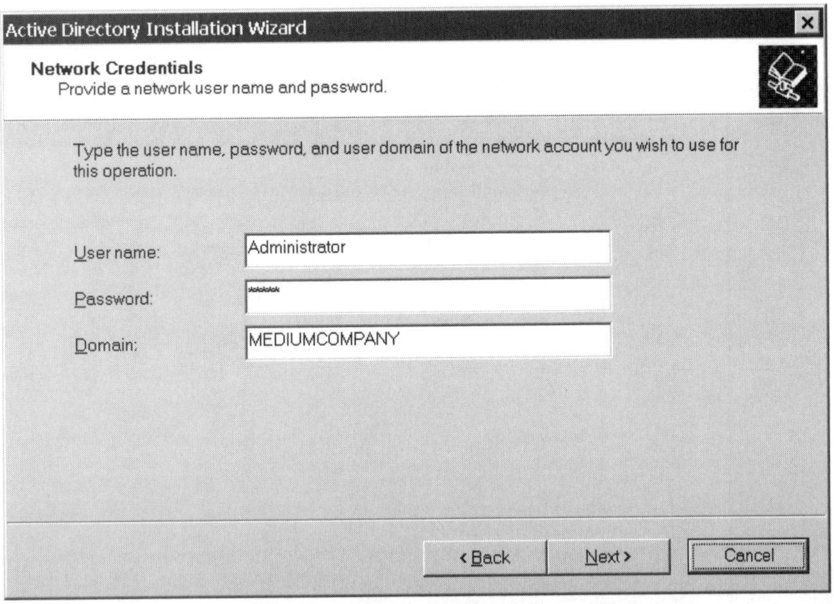

Figure 7-3.   Network Credentials screen

NOTE: Another domain controller must be accessible by the Windows 2000 computer being turned into an Active Directory domain controller. This is usually the case because the network can be checked out by logging into the domain from the computer. A problem will normally arise because the network connection was lost after the user logged in. A similar problem can occur if the DNS server fails. The DNS server will be needed to locate another Active Directory domain controller when the user initially logs in.

Click on the Next button to bring up the Additional Domain Controller screen shown in Figure 7-4.

This screen is where you enter the DNS name for the domain. You can either type in the name or use the Browse button to locate the desired domain. For our purposes, only one domain exists, mediumcompany.com, so it is not necessary to browse in this situation.

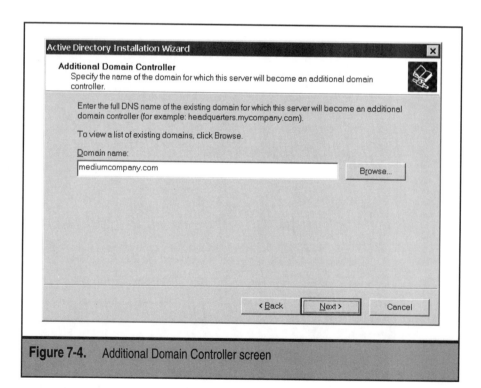

Figure 7-4. Additional Domain Controller screen

However, if you do choose to click on the Browse button and the domain name does not show up in the list, it means the network connection between this server and the existing domain controller for the selected Active Directory domain has a problem. It is also possible that the domain controller is offline for some reason. Subsequent wizard operations will only be possible if at least one of the domain's domain controllers is online and available to this server. Browsing is a simple way to check the availability of the domain with respect to the computer.

CAUTION: It is best to add new domain controllers to a domain only if they can communicate with the existing domain controllers. It is much easier to isolate network problems prior to installing Active Directory.

From the Additional Domain Controller screen, click on the Next button to bring up the Database and Log Locations screen shown in Figure 7-5.

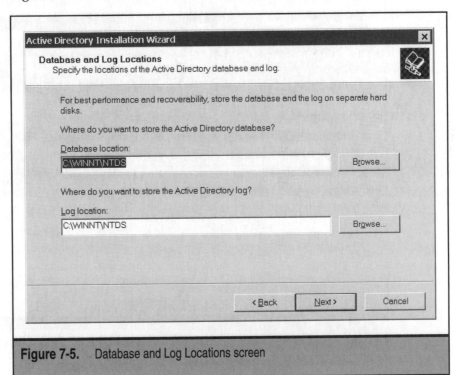

Figure 7-5. Database and Log Locations screen

The Database and Log Locations screen is identical to the one shown in Chapter 6. The locations of the database and log are on the local server that is being configured, so the directory names can be the same as on an existing domain controller. As mentioned in Chapter 6, it is a good idea to put the database and log files on different disk drives to prevent large log files from impinging on the small database files. As with the Shared System Volume in the next screen, the database and log file locations must be on an NTFS volume. This also guarantees that security can be set for individual files and directories.

Clicking on the Next button brings up the Shared System Volume screen shown in Figure 7-6.

The location of the Shared System Volume is another local directory used by the Windows 2000 Active Directory service to replicate directory information among domain controllers within the domain. As noted in the window, the volume must be in an

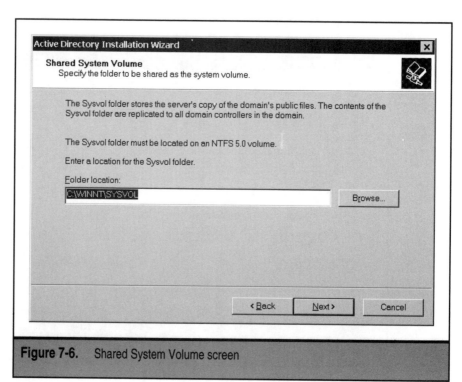

Figure 7-6.   Shared System Volume screen

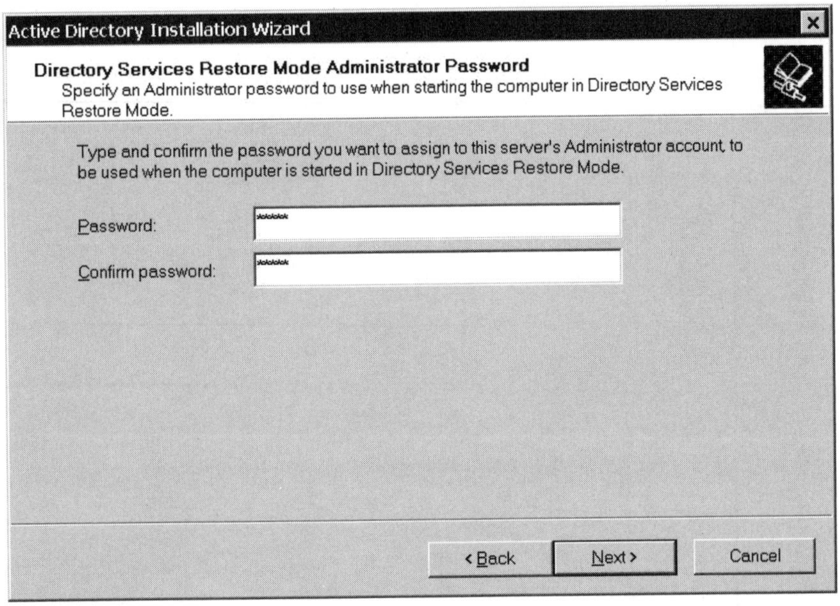

Active Directory Installation Wizard

Directory Services Restore Mode Administrator Password
Specify an Administrator password to use when starting the computer in Directory Services Restore Mode.

Type and confirm the password you want to assign to this server's Administrator account, to be used when the computer is started in Directory Services Restore Mode.

Password:

Confirm password:

< Back   Next >   Cancel

Figure 7-7.   Directory Services Restore Mode Administrator Password Screen

NTFS partition. The location can be the same as that of other domain controllers because the directory is on the local hard disk.

Click on the Next button to bring up the Directory Services Restore Mode Administrator Password screen shown in Figure 7-7.

The password to be entered in the Directory Services Restore Mode Administrator Password window is for the Administrator account in the existing domain. If the account name is Administrator, you can enter the same account you entered in the Network Credentials screen.

Click on the Next button to bring up the Summary screen shown in Figure 7-8.

The Summary screen lists the actions to be performed by the wizard. Note that the DNS service is not part of this list. At this point, it is not necessary to have a DNS service on the server since it is making use of the DNS server associated with a domain controller

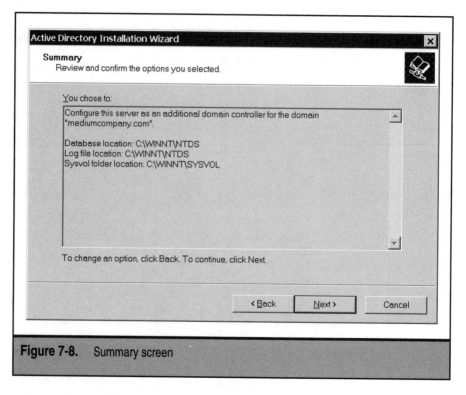

Figure 7-8. Summary screen

set up prior to this server. It is recommended that you set up the DNS
service on this server after the Active Directory Wizard is finished
because it allows the server to operate even if other domain
controllers or DNS services fail. Click on the Next button to bring
up the Configuring Active Directory screen.

The Configuring Active Directory screen displays status
information about the steps that the Active Directory Wizard
is performing to install Active Directory on the server and to
synchronize the Active Directory database with the domain by
accessing one of the domain controller servers for the domain. The
amount of time needed to complete this process can range from ten
minutes in small networks to an hour or more in large networks that
have thousands or millions of objects. Some of the status indicators
indicate how much information must be copied.

> **NOTE:** This portion of the installation should never be interrupted. A partial installation can be difficult to fix. It is often easiest to reinstall Windows 2000, give the computer a new name, and then install Active Directory.

Eventually, the process completes and the Active Directory Wizard presents the Completing the Active Directory Installation Wizard screen.

The Active Directory database and the various communication options have been set up to link the domain controller to other controllers in the domain, and the user database on the server has been replaced by the one associated with the Active Directory domain. However, although the Active Directory service is now installed, it is not yet running. To make the domain controller active, click on the Finish button to bring up the Active Directory Installation restart screen shown here:

Click on the Restart Now button to reboot the PC. You can choose to reboot at a later time if you prefer, but the Active Directory service will not be available until the system reboots.

After the new domain controller reboots, it begins communication with the other domain controllers in the network. It will automatically resynchronize with the domain if any changes have occurred between the time the installation downloaded the Active Directory database and when the domain controller came online. This is part of Active Directory's automatic synchronization support.

There are now two domain controllers and one DNS server installed on the network: the initial Windows 2000 domain controller named SERVER1 with a DNS service running and SERVER2, the second domain controller you just installed. Note that the names of the servers are set up when Windows 2000 is first installed on the server and are not specified during the Active Directory installation. Figure 7-9 shows the status of the DNS server on SERVER1.

At this point, the DNS database is a bit sparse. There are only two host records, one each for SERVER1 and SERVER2. The additional domains that begin with an underscore under mediumcompany.com are defined by Active Directory when it is installed on the first domain controller, SERVER1. The DNS database will have many more entries if additional workstations have been working with the DNS server. Entries would have to be added manually or via dynamic DNS update requests. Windows 2000 clients support

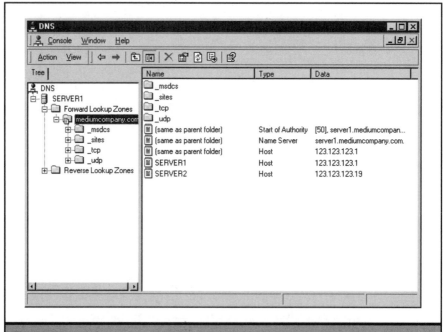

Figure 7-9. The status of the DNS server on SERVER1

dynamic DNS update. Windows 2000 DHCP server can perform the same operation for its non-Windows 2000 clients including Windows 95 and Windows 98 workstations.

SERVER1 provides DNS services for both servers and the rest of the network. This is sufficient to run the network, but it provides no backup should SERVER1 fail. SERVER2 provides Active Directory services and replicates the Active Directory database but doesn't provide another DNS server. A second DNS server could be installed on another PC, but it is easiest to have SERVER2 provide this service and, if necessary, additional DNS servers can be included in the network.

NOTE: The Windows 2000 DNS service can run on a Windows 2000 server without an Active Directory service or it can run on a Windows 2000 domain controller with the required Active Directory service. The Windows 2000 DNS service only supports Active Directory–integrated zones on a Windows 2000 domain controller. A typical Windows 2000 network configuration has a Windows 2000 DNS service running on each Windows 2000 domain controller. For security reasons, it is a good idea to keep other services on non-domain controller servers.

ADDING THE WINDOWS 2000 DNS SERVICE

The Windows 2000 DNS Service can be added when Windows 2000 is installed as part of the networking services. It can also be added after Windows 2000 is installed or after Active Directory is installed. There are two other ways to add the DNS Service: you can use the Configure Your Server Wizard or the Control Panel Add/Remove Programs applet. If the DNS Service is already installed, skip to the section "DNS Configuration for Medium Networks."

Adding DNS Service with the Configure Your Server Wizard

The Configure Your Server Wizard automatically starts when Windows 2000 first starts up. It can also be run by choosing Start | Programs | Administrative Tools | Configure Your Server.

This brings up the Windows 2000 Configure Your Server window shown in Figure 7-10.

Click on the Networking item on the left side of the window to see the list of Networking options, including DNS. Clicking on the DNS item updates the right side of the window to display the DNS page shown in Figure 7-10, which features a Manage DNS link. If the DNS service is already installed, click on this link to start up the DNS MMC snap-in to manage the DNS service. If the DNS service is not installed, you can install it by clicking on this link to bring up the Windows Server Setup window.

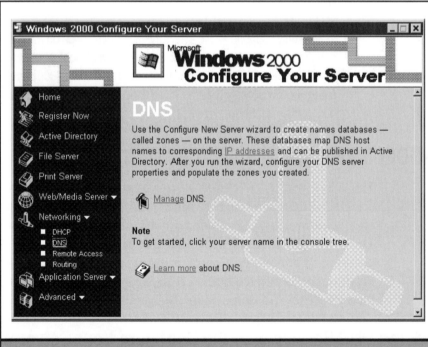

Figure 7-10. Windows 2000 Configure Your Server window

NOTE: The Windows 2000 DNS service can be added before Active Directory is installed but it cannot support Active Directory–integrated zones until after the Active Directory service is installed, making the server a domain controller. The domain controller uses dynamic DNS updates to place its service information into its DNS server's zone database. Although a conventional primary domain zone on a Windows 2000 DNS service can handle dynamic DNS updates, any changes made will be lost if the zone is converted to an Active Directory–integrated zone. The domain controller will update the zone once the server is rebooted. It is better to use the Active Directory–integrated zone of a DNS service on an existing domain controller and have the newly installed local DNS service access the same Active Directory–integrated zone. The domain controller's DNS server reference in its network configuration can be changed to reference its own domain name.

Status information will be displayed in the Windows Server Setup window as the DNS service is installed and initialized. Once the installation process has finished, you can configure the DNS service; see the section "DNS Configuration for Medium Networks" for details on how to do this.

Adding DNS Service with the Control Panel

The other way to install the DNS service is through the Add/Remove Programs control panel applet. To do this, open the Windows 2000 Control Panel, and double-click on the Add/Remove Programs icon.

This brings up the Add/Remove Programs window shown in Figure 7-11.

Installed applications are listed on the right side of the window and the Change Or Rename Programs option is selected by default. To access DNS Service support, click on the Add/Remove Windows Components button. This starts up the Windows Components Wizard shown in Figure 7-12.

The Windows Component Wizard is the same one that is presented during the Windows 2000 installation process. Scroll through the Components list until the Networking Services selection is visible, as shown in Figure 7-12. Note that even if the check box to the left is checked, the DNS service may still have to be installed.

Figure 7-11. Add/Remove Programs window

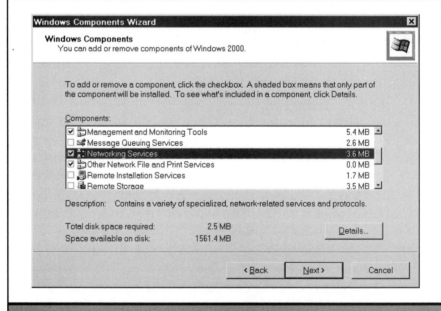

Figure 7-12. Windows Component Wizard window

Click on the Details button to see the Networking Services windows shown in Figure 7-13.

Although you have installed several networking services, you can see if the DNS service is one of them if the Domain Name System (DNS) entry is checked as shown in Figure 7-13. If not, click on the Domain Name System check box so the checkmark appears in the box and then click on the OK button. This will take you back to the Windows Component Wizard. Click on the Next button to initiate the installation of the DNS service. Once the DNS service is installed, you can configure it.

Installation of the DNS service only takes a few minutes. It will require the Windows 2000 installation CD-ROM. The installation process may take longer if you select additional services such as the DHCP server service.

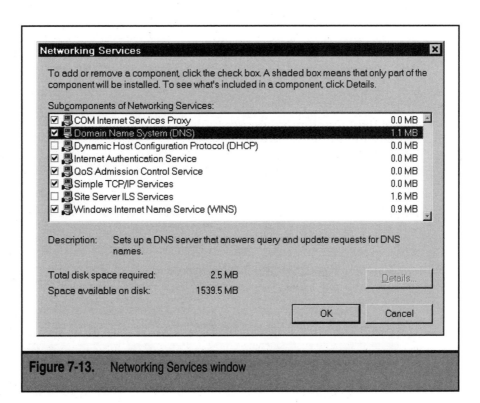

Figure 7-13.   Networking Services window

DNS CONFIGURATION FOR MEDIUM NETWORKS

After you install the DNS service on SERVER2, you can configure it using the DNS MMC snap-in that is accessible by choosing Start | Programs | Administrative Tools | DNS. This gives you the window shown in Figure 7-14. The DNS MMC snap-in is covered in more detail in Chapter 11. Chapter 10 details the Microsoft Management Console operation. The DNS MMC snap-in can be used to manage the local DNS service as well as any Windows 2000 DNS service on the network if the user has the appropriate access rights.

Note that mediumcompany.com, the primary zone for the Windows 2000 domain, has already been set up. You can also see that the Start of Authority is set to SERVER2, and that both SERVER1 and SERVER2 have Name Server entries since they both run the Windows 2000 DNS service. There are also a number of predefined domains, including _msdcs, _sites, _tcp, and _udp, that are identical to the configuration of SERVER1. These DNS settings are almost

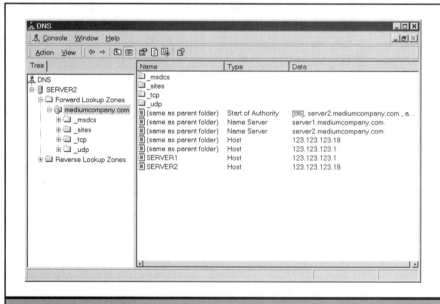

Figure 7-14. The status of the DNS server on SERVER2 DNS

identical because DNS service with Active Directory installed has a default configuration of the primary zone being an Active Directory–integrated DNS zone. Since both SERVER1 and SERVER2 are using this integration, they both wind up using the same DNS database that is stored in the Active Directory database.

NOTE: It is possible that the primary DNS zone for mediumcompany.com has not been set up on SERVER2 at this point, but it is easy to add. Select the Forward Lookup Zones entry under SERVER2. Make sure this entry is expanded so you can see the zones that are handled by this DNS server. This is where the mediumcompany.com zone will be found. If it is not there, create it by selecting Action | New Zone. This starts the New Zone Wizard. The details of this Wizard are outlined in Chapter 11. Create an Active Directory–integrated DNS zone with the name mediumcompany.com. The zone will be created and will be populated automatically since the information will already be in there from SERVER1 and its matching, Active Directory–integrated DNS zone.

Changes such as adding a new host to one server are soon reflected in the other server when the Active Directory services synchronize with each other. However, there are some caveats, such as the Start of Authority entry. If you view the DNS service on SERVER1 now, it will still show its Start of Authority to be SERVER1. The Start of Authority entry indicates what DNS servers provide authoritative responses for the zone. A domain controller is authoritative for its Active Directory–integrated zones, which is why each domain controller is shown as its own Start of Authority.

The type of integration can be viewed and changed using the DNS server properties, which are accessed by selecting the server, in this case SERVER2, and right-clicking to display the pop-up menu shown here:

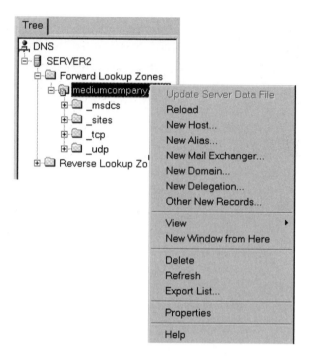

Selecting the Properties menu entry brings up the DNS Server Properties window shown in Figure 7-15.

You can access various settings, such as the Start of Authority and Security attributes, by clicking on the tabs of the DNS Server Properties window. Click the General tab to specify the type of the DNS zone database. In this case, Active Directory–integrated is selected indicating the zone is an Active Directory–integrated zone that is functionally identical to a primary zone except for Active Directory replication and security support. If this installation wasn't on an Active Directory server, the default is a Standard primary indicating a primary zone, where the primary zone database is maintained as a text file in the DNS system directory. The other alternative is a Standard secondary. The Standard secondary, indicating a secondary zone, stores the DNS zone database in the same fashion as the Standard primary except that its contents are

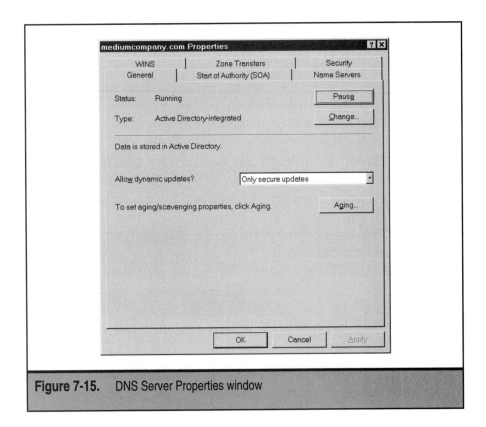

Figure 7-15.   DNS Server Properties window

obtained from another DNS server and cannot be edited on the server. Secondary zones are used when the primary zone is maintained by another DNS server.

Changing to a Standard Secondary Zone Database

The source of the information for a Standard secondary zone database is actually maintained by another DNS server and the contents of the zone database are periodically downloaded to the DNS server that is maintaining a secondary zone. In this case, you can set up SERVER2's DNS service to use a Standard secondary zone that is copied from SERVER1's DNS service. SERVER1 maintains an Active Directory–integrated zone database so both DNS servers gain the benefits of Active Directory integration. You would typically take this approach if the server with the secondary zone database were not a Windows 2000 domain controller. It can also be used with Windows 2000 DNS services that do not use Active Directory–integrated zones.

The disadvantage of using a secondary zone instead of an Active Directory–integrated zone is that the server with the secondary zone only provides DNS services if the primary zone server fails. No changes can be made to the secondary zone because a secondary zone cannot be edited and the server does not provide redundancy for Active Directory.

Secondary zones do have advantages, though. They maintain themselves automatically and, while they do not provide redundancy for Active Directory, they do provide redundancy for DNS services. Overall management is minimized since any changes made via the Active Directory integration, including any Windows 2000–specific DNS records, are eventually replicated on the secondary zone DNS server.

Another advantage of the secondary zone approach is that it works with third-party DNS servers, including Windows NT DNS service. This is handy in environments where there is a heterogeneous mix of DNS servers or where migration to Windows 2000 is proceeding systematically instead of occurring all at once.

TIP: Stick with primary and secondary zones when initially installing Windows 2000 Active Directory if you are more familiar with this approach. It is also a good idea if an existing DNS structure is in place. The primary zone can be set up as an Active Directory–integrated zone using this approach, and secondary zones can be converted to Active Directory–integrated zones at a later date.

To convert an Active Directory–integrated or Standard primary zone type to a Standard secondary zone type is relatively simple. First, click on the Change button in the DNS Zone Properties window shown previously in Figure 7-15. This brings up the Change Zone Type window shown in Figure 7-16.

Select the Standard Secondary entry and click on the OK button. The verification window appears:

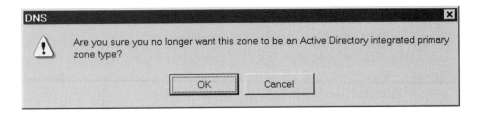

Click on the OK button to begin the conversion. The domain name of the zone remains the same, although you can change it from the General Properties page. The next step is to add the IP address of one or more DNS servers that maintain a copy of the zone. These

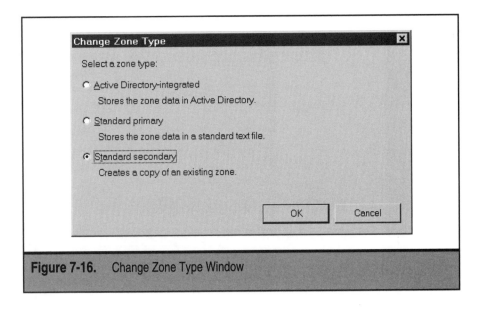

Figure 7-16.   Change Zone Type Window

DNS servers can maintain Active Directory–integrated, Standard primary, or Standard secondary zones.

The IP address of a DNS server is added from the General Properties page shown in Figure 7-17. Fill in the IP address field to enable the Add button, which adds the address to the IP address list. The list is order-dependent, meaning that the DNS service attempts to contact the DNS servers in the order they are listed when the information in the secondary zone becomes stale. The Browse button lets you select a server from a list, and that server's IP address will then be added to the IP address list. The Up and Down buttons move the selected entry in the corresponding direction when there is more than one entry is in the list.

SERVER2 will periodically download the contents of the zone file from the first source it finds available. How often it does this is

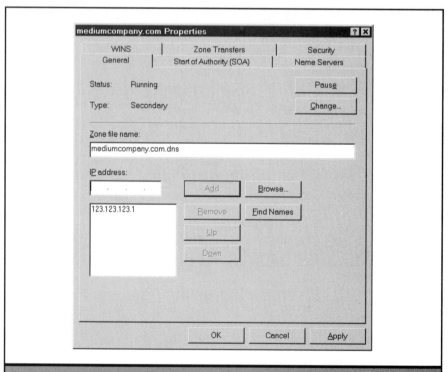

Figure 7-17. The General Properties page for secondary zone

determined by the expiration date listed in the Start of Authority page of the zone's Properties window. The expiration date is set at the source, in this case SERVER2, not at the secondary zone DNS server.

An update can be forced by selecting the secondary zone and right-clicking. The pop-up menu has a new menu item, Transfer from Master, which allows you to update before the expiration date; this is typically done to force synchronization when a server is brought up or when changes are known to be available from the source.

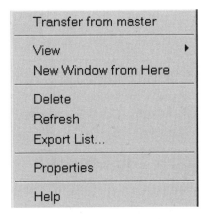

Secondary zones can also be created from scratch, but a domain name is required when the zone is created. The source DNS server IP addresses are also needed before the zone can be active.

Multiple secondary zones can be hosted by a DNS server, and the Windows 2000 DNS server can host any mix of zone types. More details on secondary zones can be found in Chapter 16.

Converting to Standard Primary Zone Database

Converting an existing Active Directory–integrated or secondary zone database to a Standard primary zone is as simple as changing the type associated with the zone. This is done from the General page of the

Properties for the zone. The conversion moves the zone information into a text file on the server that can then be maintained using a text editor.

The advantage of using a Standard primary zone is that management of the DNS database is on a par with other third-party, text-based DNS services. The disadvantage is the loss of integration with Active Directory that provides automatic updates when Windows 2000 services are added or deleted and when Windows 2000–specific DNS data is updated. In general, Standard primary zones are only used on Windows 2000 servers that are not domain controllers.

NOTE: Standard primary zones support dynamic DNS updates but not secure dynamic DNS updates. Secure dynamic DNS updates are only supported by Active Directory–integrated zones.

Setting up Additional DNS Servers in a Medium Network

Once a domain controller is set up and has the Windows 2000 DNS server installed, the domain controller's DNS client should be set up to use its own DNS service as its primary DNS server. This allows the domain controller to operate by itself even if separated from the other domain controllers in the domain because of network communication failure or failure of the other domain controllers. The domain controller's DNS server will also be able to provide DNS services to local clients on the network, allowing the clients to log into the Active Directory domain.

Additional DNS servers are often utilized in a medium network to increase performance and reliability. The installation procedure outlined in the "DNS Configuration for Medium Networks" section of this chapter can be used to add more DNS servers that reside on Windows 2000 domain controllers.

TIP: If additional DNS servers are being set up on Windows 2000 computers and Active Directory is installed, and the DNS services are provided only for computers on the network, then set up these computers as domain controllers and utilize Active Directory–integrated DNS zones for managing zone information. This is more secure and more efficient than using standalone Windows 2000 computers with DNS services using secondary DNS zones. If outside access to the computer will be possible, then placing security-related information like the Active Directory database on the computer may not be a good idea.

There are a variety of other ways DNS servers can be utilized in a medium network especially since a single Windows 2000 domain can encompass dozens of servers and hundreds of users. Caching DNS servers is one way to provide improved performance to clients accessing the Internet, while DNS servers with secondary zones can provide better performance for intranets. Chapter 16 addresses caching DNS servers and secondary zones in more detail.

Placement of additional DNS servers in a network is more an issue of efficiency and security. Additional DNS servers come into play in two areas: the first is located between the Internet and the network; the second is within the network.

DNS servers that sit between the Internet and the network are typically implemented as caching DNS server. Under Windows 2000, this type of Windows 2000 DNS server does not support any zones directly, even secondary zones. As such, making the server act as an Active Directory domain controller is overkill. While Active Directory and Windows 2000 provide enhanced security, these DNS servers are occasionally placed outside a firewall, which is not a great place to keep the Active Directory database. One approach is to keep the domain controller and DNS servers inside the firewall and only provide access to the DNS server through the firewall. Another alternative is to place a second DNS server outside the firewall and provide its secondary DNS zone with information from the DNS server inside the firewall.

DNS servers that sit between the Internet and the network can use secondary zones to provide improved Internet performance if the Internet Service Provider (ISP) allows zone transfers. This must be enabled at the ISP's DNS server. Also, zones with a .com or .org suffix are very large and take a while to download.

DNS servers that replicate local zones do not have such problems since the source of information is under the control of the network administrator and the amount of information in the zone file is comparatively small. Also, local network backbone is typically much faster than are links to an ISP and the Internet.

The DNS services discussed in this section are not dependent on Active Directory. As such, it is possible to incorporate non-Windows 2000 DNS servers for these tasks. A homogeneous Windows 2000 network has management advantages, but utilizing other operating systems like Linux may provide cost advantages.

ACTIVE DIRECTORY SETUP FOR MEDIUM NETWORKS

Since a medium network simply adds domain controllers to the mix and Active Directory handles replication, the Active Directory setup for medium networks is the same as the setup for small networks, which was covered in Chapter 6. There is really no additional configuration, and other issues, such as replication schedules, routing, and site management, usually come up only with large network planning and management. Still, for medium model networks with a very large number of users, it may be desirable to split the network into sites so Active Directory replication can be managed. Chapter 16 addresses replication in more detail. This includes both DNS zone replication as well as Active Directory database and catalog replication.

The lack of configuration issues related to Active Directory does not imply that Active Directory will not require configuration for other aspects of the network. Obviously, user and group management is still required. Partitioning will still be possible using organizational units. These will all have to be planned and implemented for general network operation.

Additional configuration will not be required to support Active Directory–integrated DNS zones. Replication of this information is part of the standard Active Directory database replication that is handled transparently although site-to-site communication can be controlled and scheduled. The only requirement for automatic replication is that the Windows 2000 DNS services be running on a domain controller and that the Active Directory–integrated DNS zones have the same name on each DNS server.

MIGRATION TO WINDOWS 2000 DNS FOR MEDIUM NETWORKS

Migration of existing DNS server zones to a medium Windows 2000 network is identical to the migration of a small network that was discussed in Chapter 6, since both address a single domain. In fact, a medium network often requires fewer adjustments than a small network, since a network with multiple DNS servers may already be set up to use caching servers and secondary zones. The only place information must be migrated from would be primary zones, and this is normally a single server in a medium network.

It is worth closely examining existing DNS server function and placement to determine how and in what order DNS servers need to be migrated or if migration to Windows 2000 is even necessary. If the servers provide services other than DNS, migration to Windows 2000 may be useful for other reasons.

There is also the issue of easier management of a homogeneous Windows 2000 environment with Active Directory. Typically, the DNS server with the primary zone will be migrated first, but it does not have to be the first Windows 2000 domain controller. Remember, Windows 2000 needs a DNS server to run Active Directory, but it does not need an Active Directory–integrated zone. The Active Directory–integrated zone simply provides long term advantages.

A possible scenario is to bring up a Windows 2000 domain controller that is named in the primary zone of an existing DNS controller. This domain controller may or may not have the DNS service installed. In either case, if the server with the primary zone is a Windows NT server then it can be migrated to Windows 2000 and be made a domain controller. The DNS service can be installed and the primary zone database can be merged with the DNS service's zone database.

If possible, it is a good idea to keep both the old DNS server and the new Windows 2000 DNS server running while the new DNS server is tested. Use of third-party utilities like DNS Expert, discussed in Chapter 20, can make the migration less error prone. An easy way to do this is to run the servers side-by-side. When the network administrator is confident that the new server is ready, the old DNS server can be temporarily removed from the network, and the new server can be given the old server's IP address. In fact, a Windows 2000 system can support multiple IP addresses so it is simply a matter of adding a new IP address. The old server can then quickly be returned to service should the new server fail to meet expectations.

SUMMARY

The medium network model will be the most common Windows 2000 network configuration. It provides the simplicity of a single domain with support for multiple domain controllers for improved performance and reliability, in addition to supporting multiple Windows 2000 servers that provide other services, such as file and print services. DNS services tie all of these servers together by providing references to these services.

Active Directory–integrated zones provide significant advantages compared to primary/secondary zone configurations with multiple DNS servers, including better replication, multiple master update support, and Active Directory security. These advantages provide a compelling reason to use this approach.

Primary/secondary zone configurations support multiple DNS servers in networks with lots of workstations and servers. It is a technology that is very familiar to network administrators. Existing TCP/IP-based networks will typically use this approach so the configuration will be reliable and well understood. As long as the DNS servers support the needs of Active Directory domain controllers, the existing DNS configuration can remain in place. A typical exception is a network using Windows NT DNS services because the Windows NT service does not support SRV records or dynamic DNS updates. Upgrading to Windows 2000 solves this problem.

Operating a mixed environment is possible with a primary zone being handled by a Windows 2000 DNS service on a Windows 2000 domain controller. The primary zone could then be an Active Directory–integrated zone. This approach allows subsequent upgrades so secondary zones could be converted to Active Directory–integrated zones. The key is that the Windows 2000 DNS service must run on a Windows 2000 domain controller.

The medium network model with a single Windows 2000 domain is significantly easier to maintain than the large network model covered in the next chapter because Active Directory–integrated zones are restricted to the domain in which they occur. Cross domain replication must use the primary/secondary zone approach.

CHAPTER 8

Windows 2000 DNS and Active Directory Setup for a Large Network

etting up a large model Windows 2000 network requires more planning than a medium model Windows 2000 network because multiple domains are involved. This guarantees that multiple domain controllers are involved. More likely, there are multiple domain controllers for each domain. In theory, a single DNS server can service the entire network, but in practice, DNS servers will be as prevalent or more prevalent than domain controllers.

Multiple domains in one large network can be combined in one of two ways. The first collects domains in a common domain tree with the root domain at the top of the tree. The second is multiple domain trees within a domain forest. This chapter addresses the setup procedures for both configurations. The simplest configuration is a single domain tree containing multiple domains starting with a common root. This is addressed in the sections "DNS Configuration in a Domain Tree for Large Networks" and "Active Directory Setup in a Domain Tree for Large Networks." Multiple domains are addressed in the sections "Active Directory Setup in a Domain Forest for Large Networks" and "DNS Configuration in a Domain Forest for Large Networks." Migration issues are common to both approaches and will be addressed in the section "Migration to Windows 2000 DNS for Large Networks."

Large networks tend to have a large number of DNS servers for a variety of purposes including support for Active Directory. The bulk of this chapter addresses DNS support with respect to Active Directory. The "Placement and Other Uses for DNS Servers in a Large Network" section takes a look at some of the other uses for DNS servers in a large network.

DNS setup is complicated by the fact that multiple domain names are involved and that these are usually made available to users throughout the network. This means that DNS servers must obtain the appropriate DNS information to provide to users accessing the DNS server. This can be done using Active Directory or DNS protocols. Both approaches will be examined in this chapter, including tradeoffs for each approach.

The basic Active Directory and DNS setup procedures outlined in Chapters 6 and 7 are referenced here because building a large network of domain controllers is done in an incremental fashion using the same steps. The additional details of linking various domains together will be covered in more detail in this chapter.

One aspect of large networks not addressed in this chapter is Active Directory sites. Sites are a collection of domain controllers that participate in Active Directory replication. Site configuration and intersite communication are topics beyond the scope of this book. While site configuration affects the efficiency and performance of Active Directory replication, it does not affect the initial configuration of Active Directory or DNS services.

Active Directory–integrated DNS zones are the preferred mode of operation, especially with large networks, because they provide a robust naming system compared to most third-party DNS servers. Active Directory–integrated DNS zones also support secured DNS updates, a feature not found in most third-party DNS servers. Still, most third-party DNS servers can support Active Directory even in a large network, and future enhancements to third-party DNS servers may elevate them to the same level of security and support as a Windows 2000 DNS server.

CAUTION: The use of a third-party DNS server may introduce a single point of failure for dynamic updates necessary for Active Directory support compared to Active Directory–integrated zones supported by Windows 2000 DNS. Typical third-party DNS servers support a single primary server for a zone that can then receive dynamic update requests, whereas a Windows 2000 Active Directory–integrated zone can be updated by Windows 2000 DNS server in the domain when any one of the servers receives a dynamic update request. A third-party DNS server must also support SRV records.

The assumption at this point is that one or more root domain controllers and one or more DNS servers are up and running to handle the root domain. The process of setting up one or more root domain controllers is addressed in Chapters 6 and 7.

The next step is to create a child domain or another root domain within the same domain tree. These processes are outlined in the subsequent sections. These same processes are used when setting up a child domain to another child domain or when adding yet another domain tree to a domain forest. Child domains can be repeated to any level, although it is rare to have a depth of more than four.

DNS CONFIGURATION IN A DOMAIN TREE FOR LARGE NETWORKS

Setting up a single domain tree as part of a large network is the easiest way to incorporate multiple domain names that have the same root. The root domain name must be part of each child domain's domain name. For example, if the root domain name is largecompany.com then child1.largecompany.com and child2.largecompany.com would be child domain names. Of course, when possible, child domain names should provide a more useful designation that may be related to location or use such as sales.largecompany.com, chicago.largecompany.com, or switzerland.largecompany.com.

TIP: Use Active Directory–integrated zones in root domain controllers if the Windows 2000 DNS chores will be centrally managed. A root domain controller with the Windows 2000 DNS service will be required to handle dynamic updates for child domains at each site.

TIP: Use Active Directory–integrated zones in child domain controllers if the Windows 2000 DNS management chores will be distributed. Child and root DNS zone interaction can be accomplished using secondary zones.

DNS configuration is normally done before the Active Directory configuration of a child domain because Active Directory requires a DNS server to locate a domain controller of the parent domain and to store the information for the child domain. This information can be spread across different DNS servers or placed in a single domain server. Your options are as follows.

▼   Create a new subzone within the root zone on the root domain controller DNS server.

- ■ Create a primary zone on the child domain controller DNS server.

- ▲ Create a zone on a DNS server that is on neither the root domain controller nor the child domain controller.

Creating a new subzone within the root zone on the root domain controller DNS server allows DNS services to be centrally managed. It is especially effective when the root zone is an Active Directory–integrated zone. The root zone is replicated at every root domain controller, so including a DNS service on each domain controller provides one level of redundancy. Secondary zones on other DNS servers can maintain copies as well.

Figure 8-1 shows the DNS MMC snap-in window for the DNS server running on a root domain controller named server1. Typically a domain controller will have a domain name directly underneath the domain name. In this case, the fully qualified domain name would be server1.largecompany.com. A new zone, chicago.largecompany.com, has been created as a sample child

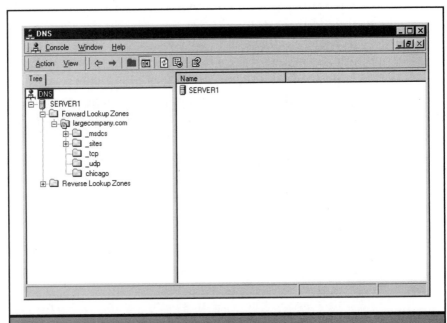

Figure 8-1. DNS MMC snap-in window on root DNS server

domain in the largecompany.com domain. It is possible to add a host resource record for the server, in this case server4, since the IP address is known. The fully qualified domain name for the server would be server4.chicago.largecompany.com. The details for adding the resource record is covered in Chapter 11. In general, it is good practice to use fixed IP address for all domain controllers and DNS servers.

Creating a new primary zone on a child domain controller's DNS service also allows Active Directory to be used, but if the information is to be provided through the root domain and other DNS servers, secondary zones must be used.

Placing the primary zone support on the DNS server on the child domain controller works for distributed domains that will be managed locally instead of globally. Other DNS servers, such as the ones for the root domain, can keep a copy of this zone using a secondary zone, but only subsequently installed domain controllers in the same child domain will have access to the Active Directory–integrated zone. Initially, only a primary zone can be created (as shown in Figure 8-2), as an Active Directory has not been installed. A secondary zone would be chosen if this DNS server were not the one used to manage the child zone.

With this configuration, we recommend that a secondary zone of this newly created zone be created on the root domain's DNS server or the one servicing the root domain. This way, root domain administrators will be able to remotely manage the child zone. (The root domain administrators have this right initially but it can be revoked.)

The primary zone for the child domain can be converted to an Active Directory–integrated zone after Active Directory has been installed. Note that the primary zone must have the dynamic updates option set to Yes.

Finally, the root and child zones can be on a DNS server that is running on neither the root domain controller nor the child domain controller. As in the two previous cases, it is still possible to split the root and child zones, but using a separate DNS server usually means that DNS server management is being centralized. Thus, making the child a subzone of the root or parent zone makes the most sense.

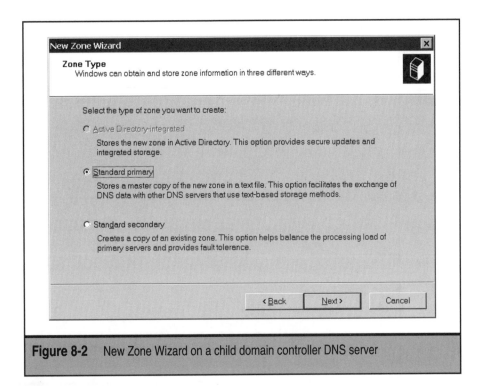

Figure 8-2 New Zone Wizard on a child domain controller DNS server

REMEMBER: Remember to have the child domain's designated DNS server IP address set to the appropriate DNS server, be it the server itself or another server. Make sure the zone allows normal dynamic updates.

For Windows 2000 DNS servers, check out the Properties window for the new child zone, as shown in Figure 8-3.

The Active Directory setup process can now proceed since the server will have access to a DNS server that can handle both the references to the parent domain controller and subsequent updates to the child domain's zone when the domain controller registers its services.

ACTIVE DIRECTORY SETUP IN A DOMAIN TREE FOR LARGE NETWORKS

Now that the DNS support is ready, setting up Active Directory support for a child domain controller is a relatively straightforward process. Start by running the Windows 2000 Configure Your Server Wizard by

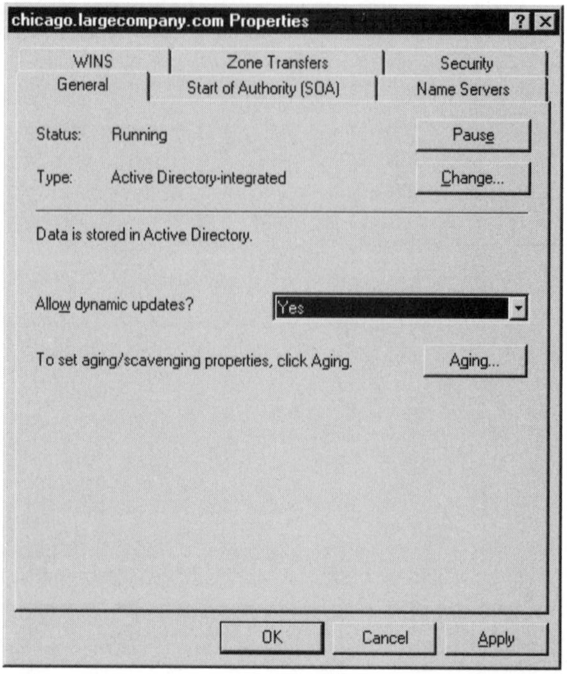

Figure 8-3. Child Zone Properties window

choosing Start | Programs | Administrative Tools | Configure
Your Server. This presents the Windows 2000 Configure Your Server
window. Select the Active Directory option on the left to see Windows
2000 Configure Your Server window.

Scroll down the right part of the window and click on Start the
Active Directory Wizard. Click the Next button to get past the first
information screen to view the Domain Controller Type screen shown
in Figure 8-4.

There are two options in the Domain Controller Type screen.
Choose Domain controller for a new domain, since this is for a
child domain. (The other option, Additional domain controller for
an existing domain, was used in Chapter 7 to increase the number of
domain controllers in an existing domain for added redundancy and
improved performance.) Click the Next button to bring up the Create
Tree or Child Domain screen shown in Figure 8-5.

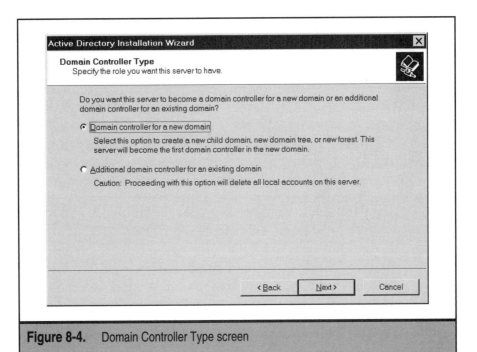

Figure 8-4.   Domain Controller Type screen

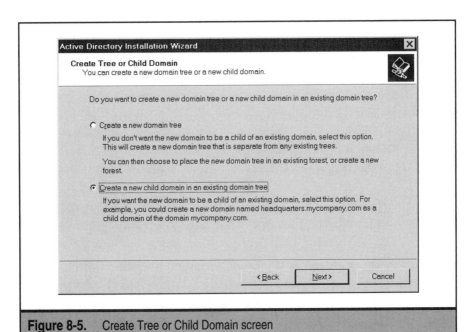

Figure 8-5.   Create Tree or Child Domain screen

Unfortunately, the wizard asks lots of compound questions, so this window is needed to determine whether the new type of domain you want to create is a new domain tree or a new child domain. The Create a new domain tree option will be used later in this chapter to set up a new domain tree in a domain forest, but here you want to select Create a new child domain in an existing domain tree. The domain name will be supplied later. For now, just click on the Next button to bring up the Network Credentials screen.

In the Network Credentials screen, enter the user name and password for an administrator already defined in the parent domain. The parent domain name must also be supplied. The administrator's account must be capable of adding the new domain to the parent's Active Directory. Click the Next button to start the logon process. An error dialog box will be presented if the parent domain cannot be contacted to authenticate the user. A valid user may not be authenticated if an incorrect DNS setup has been performed on the child domain server.

Assuming all the information is correct, the Child Domain Installation screen shown in Figure 8-6 will be presented.

The wizard makes you fill in the blanks for this screen since the administrator's domain does not have to be the immediate parent for this installation procedure. For example, the administrator's account could be in the root domain, whereas the parent domain is a child domain of the root domain. Active Directory utilizes inherited rights, which means that a root administrator will be able to configure all lower-level child domains, so the administrator's domain may be different than the child domain's parent domain. In this example, the parent domain is the root domain.

For this window, enter a fully qualified parent domain name in the Parent Domain field. Then enter the child domain name in the Child Domain field, but don't enter the fully qualified child domain name. The fully qualified child domain name is the combination of these two fields and is presented in the view-only field at the bottom of the window as the fields are filled in. Note that if you use periods to separate names and then click on the Next button, you get an error window. This is because it is not possible to create child domains like sales.chicago.largecompany.com or techsupport.software.

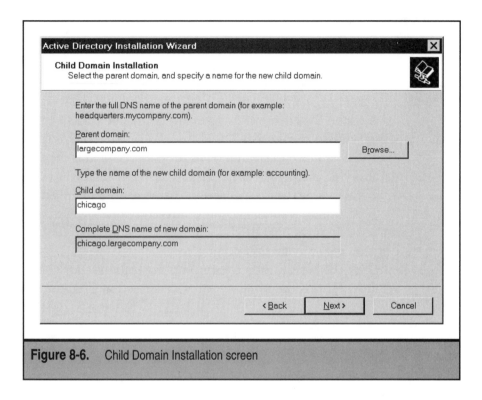

Figure 8-6.   Child Domain Installation screen

largecompany.com under a parent domain of largecompany.com without creating the intervening child domains of chicago .largecompany.com or software.largecompany.com respectively. This restriction is with respect to Windows 2000 and not the Windows 2000 DNS server and its zones that can be disjointed.

TIP: If longer descriptive names are desirable, use different separation characters or juxtapose words instead of using a period that imposes the use of another domain. For example, techsupport-software.largecompany.com or saleschicago.largecompany.com can be used instead of techsupport. software.largecompany.com or sales.chicago.largecompany.com. The latter two names would require intervening child domain definitions. Unnecessary child domains complicate setup and regular management chores.

CAUTION: Make sure the child domain name is correct because, as with any new domain installation, it is not possible to rename a domain. Delete and re-create a domain immediately if a misspelling is discovered. Moving resources from one domain to another is tedious at best.

Click on the Next button to bring up the NetBIOS Domain Name screen shown in Figure 8-7.

The default for the Domain NetBIOS Name field is the child domain name and is usually left as is. A more descriptive name can be used or another name may be needed if a name conflicts with an existing NetBIOS domain name. The latter situation can arise because a similarly named Windows 2000 child domain can exist in a different part of the domain tree or in another domain tree.

Click the Next button to bring up the Database and Log Locations window. This is the same window discussed in Chapter 6 and

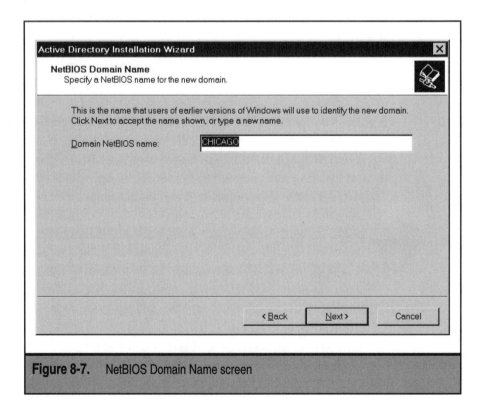

Figure 8-7.   NetBIOS Domain Name screen

Chapter 7 that displays when installing a domain controller. The default directories are usually sufficient. Change these if needed and then click the Next button to bring up the Shared System Volume window. This window, along with the Permissions window and the Directory Service Restore Mode Administration Password window, are also addressed in the previous chapters, and the defaults are usually sufficient.

> **REMEMBER:**   Database, log, and shared system volumes must be NTFS partitions. These partitions must be formatted or converted accordingly prior to installation of the Active Directory service.

Click the Next button to eventually bring up the Summary screen shown in Figure 8-8. Note the references to both the child and parent domain names. Double-check to make sure all the spellings are

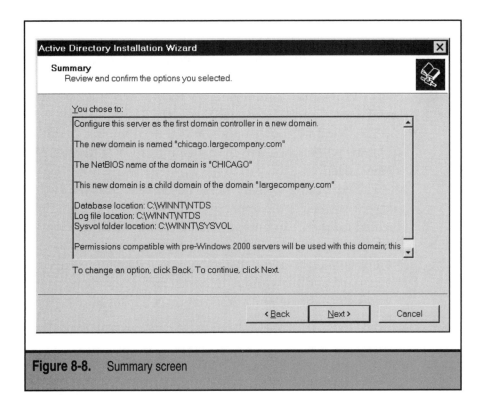

Figure 8-8.   Summary screen

correct. Click the Next button when satisfied. This presents the Configuring Active Directory window.

The configuration process takes a while and the window is updated as various actions are begun and completed. This process sets up the Active Directory database on the child domain controller and updates the Active Directory database on the parent domain. The Completing the Active Directory Installation Wizard window is presented once the installation process is complete.

CAUTION: Do not interrupt the configuration process once it is started. Remove and reinstall the Active Directory support if the process does not present the Completing the Active Directory Installation Wizard window.

Click on the Finish button. You will receive a prompt for a reboot that is necessary to get things started. The DNS server will also be updated with the domain DNS zone information when the reboot occurs.

It is now time to check out whether the child domain has been properly configured. This is done by starting the Active Directory Domains and Trusts MMC snap-in shown in Figure 8-9 by choosing Start | Programs | Administrative Tools | Active Directory Domains and Trusts.

This window shows parent and child domains. Additional domains will be included in the list if this is not the first child domain being added.

The next thing to check is the DNS zone. Start up the DNS MMC snap-in and select the appropriate DNS server. If a new zone was created for the child domain then the DNS MMC snap-in display will look like Figure 8-10. If the new zone was created as a subzone of the parent domain then the display will look like Figure 8-11. You will have to expand the various folders to achieve the layout in the figures since the default presentation collapses all information.

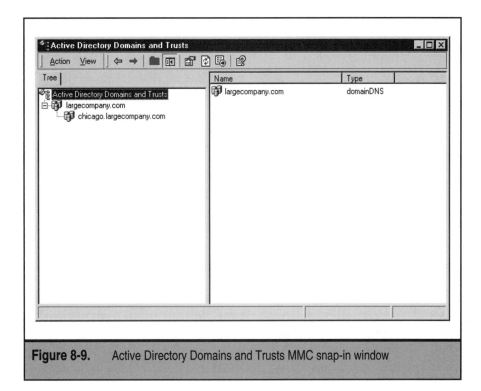

Figure 8-9.   Active Directory Domains and Trusts MMC snap-in window

The subzone approach shown in Figure 8-10 shows a single zone, largecompany.com. The parent domain matches the zone name. The child domain is a subzone, in this case, chicago. Note the set of underscored subzones under both the parent domain and the child domain. This is where the various domain services are advertised. These entries are added by the servers when they first communicate with the DNS server.

This figure also shows how a single zone can encompass many Windows 2000 domains, making centralized management and replication easier. A single zone, largecompany.com, can be replicated to a secondary zone on any number of DNS servers that then provide DNS information about root domain as well as all of its children.

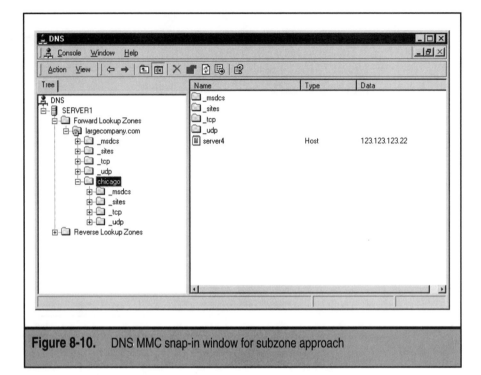

Figure 8-10. DNS MMC snap-in window for subzone approach

Separating the zones, as shown in Figure 8-11, makes setup and replication more difficult, but it has the advantage of distributing both the management and the support. In this case, the root domain controller, server1, handles the largecompany.com zone as an Active Directory–integrated zone and the chicago.largecompany.com zone is a secondary zone. The secondary zone obtains its zone information from the primary zone on server4 that is also the domain controller of the child domain, chicago.largecompany.com.

Note that the view from server1 and server4 will be identical because the Windows 2000 DNS MMC snap-in does not differentiate primary or secondary zones via icons. The primary zone, chicago.largecompany.com, on server4 can now be converted to an

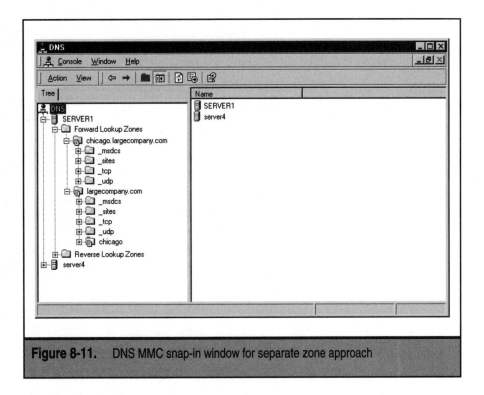

Figure 8-11.   DNS MMC snap-in window for separate zone approach

Active Directory–integrated zone. Any new domain controller added
to chicago.largecompany.com will be able to have its DNS server use
the Active Directory–integrated zone instead of having to resort to a
secondary domain.

ACTIVE DIRECTORY SETUP IN A DOMAIN FOREST FOR LARGE NETWORKS

Domain trees of any depth can be constructed by adding child
domains, but in many cases it is not possible or desirable to create
child domains. For example, an organization consists of two groups

that already have different domain names such as foobar.com and swiftcomp.com. These two domain trees can be combined into one domain forest at one of two points in time. The first is when one or both of the organizations have yet to install Windows 2000 Active Directory support. The second is when Active Directory is being initially employed by organizations. This distinction is necessary because the original release of Windows 2000 does not have tools for migrating a domain tree from one domain forest to another.

CAUTION: Only create a domain forest when necessary. Management of multiple domains within a domain forest is much more difficult than managing a domain tree. Domain forests require multiple primary DNS zones, and distributing DNS information across domain trees can lead to a veritable rat's nest of secondary zone links. Keeping the number of domain trees in the forest to a minimum will make DNS management significantly easier.

The section "Creating a New Domain Tree" addresses the first situation, when Active Directory has not been installed on servers that are part of a new domain tree. The section "Merging Existing Domain Trees" addresses the second situation, when Active Directory is already in use on all servers involved and a migration of a domain tree from one domain forest to another is required.

In either case, the DNS support for the domain tree being added to the domain forest should be handled within the domain tree, not by a DNS server that is already part of the domain forest. Keeping the DNS support within the forest makes DNS server configuration and management easier. In fact, the Active Directory Wizard can install the Windows 2000 DNS service when the new domain tree is set up.

Creating a New Domain Tree

Adding a new domain tree to an existing domain forest is the easiest method of mixing two domain names. The process is started by building a single domain tree in the domain forest as described in the previous chapters. Domain trees with a common root can then be added if necessary, as described previously in the sections "DNS Configuration in a Domain Tree for Large Networks" and "Active Directory Setup in a Domain Tree for Large Networks." Finally, additional domain trees can be added to the domain forest using the process outlined in this section.

REMEMBER: Only create additional domain trees in an existing domain forest as necessary. Domains within an existing tree are easier to manage and support via DNS than domains in separate domain trees.

Start by running the Windows 2000 Configure Your Server Wizard to start the Active Directory Wizard. Click the Next button to get past the first information screen to view the Domain Controller Type screen.

Select Domain controller for a new domain and click the Next button to bring up the Create Tree or Child Domain screen.

In this case, choose the Create a new domain tree. (The Create a new child domain in an existing domain tree was used at the start of the chapter for adding domains within an existing domain tree.) Click the Next button to bring up the Create or Join Forest screen shown in Figure 8-12.

Finally, something new. The Create a new forest of domain trees option was selected when the very first domain controller was set up. All subsequent domain tree root domains will be added in this fashion by selecting Place This New Domain Tree In An Existing Forest. Click the Next button to bring up the Network Credentials screen.

This user name, password, and domain name must be associated with a user in the current Enterprise Admins group of a root domain that is part of the domain forest where the new domain tree will be added. It is not associated with a user in the current server that Active Directory is being added to. We used the original Administrator account, but it is a good idea to have an additional enterprise administration account as a backup.

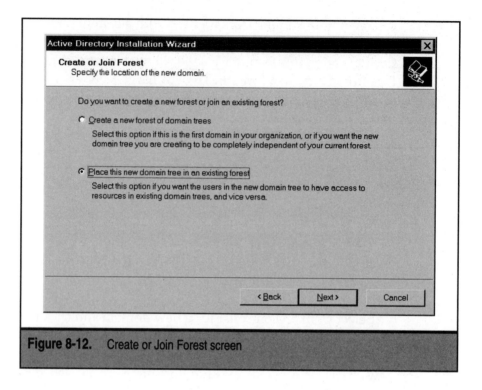

Figure 8-12. Create or Join Forest screen

Click the Next button so that the Wizard will check the credentials. This also verifies that the server can communicate with a domain controller within the domain forest. If everything works correctly, the Wizard presents the New Domain Tree screen shown in Figure 8-13.

In the New Domain Tree screen, enter the DNS name for the new domain. This name cannot incorporate part of a domain name that already exists in the domain forest. Note that the example used here, anotherlargecompany.com, is distinct from the domain name, largecompany.com, in the sample domain forest. There would be a conflict if the new domain name was another.largecompany.com. Click the Next button to bring up the NetBIOS Domain Name screen.

The Domain NetBIOS name field default is the child domain name and is usually left as is. A more descriptive name can be used

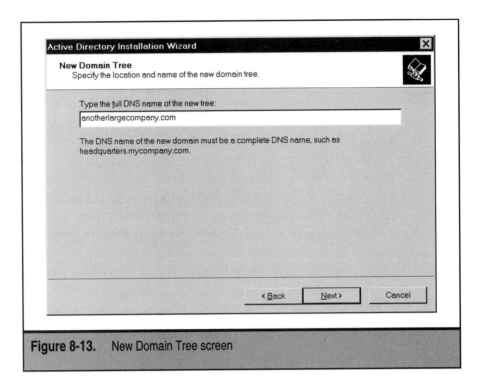

Figure 8-13.   New Domain Tree screen

or another name may be needed if the name conflicts with an existing NetBIOS domain name. The latter situation can arise because a similarly named Windows 2000 child domain can exist in a different part of the domain tree or in another domain tree.

Click the Next button to bring up the Database and Log Locations screen. This is the same screen that is discussed in Chapters 6 and 7 when installing a domain controller. As before, the default directories are usually sufficient. Change these if needed and then click the Next button to bring up the Shared System Volume window. Click the Next button again to see Configure DNS window.

REMEMBER: Database, log, and shared system volumes must be NTFS partitions. These partitions must be formatted or converted accordingly prior to installation of the Active Directory service.

As this is the first server in the new domain tree, the Active Directory Wizard can install the Windows 2000 DNS server. It is best to let the wizard do so, as the DNS server will be set up for the current domain zone using Active Directory integration. It is possible to use another DNS server if the zone has been set up already or if the zone is set up before Active Directory is started, but the DNS server must support dynamic update, as previously described.

Click the Next button three times to get through this window, the Permissions window, and the Directory Service Restore Mode Administration Password window (the defaults are usually sufficient). The Summary screen in Figure 8-14 will then be displayed.

The Summary screen shows both the new domain name, anotherlargecompany.com, and the trust link to a domain, largecompany.com, in the domain tree to which the new domain tree will be added. Note that the DNS service will also be installed. Click on the Next button to begin configuring the server.

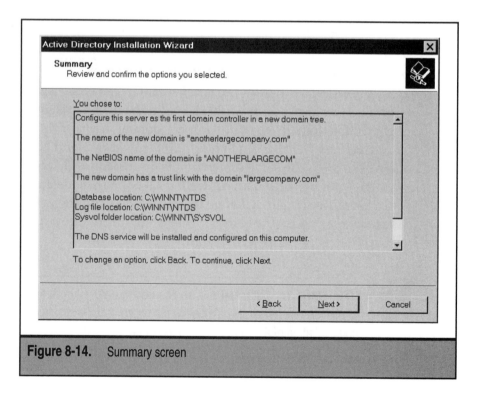

Figure 8-14. Summary screen

CAUTION: Make sure the contents of the Summary window are correct. It is easy to back up or cancel at this point, but it is very difficult or impossible to change things once the Next button is clicked. For example, changing the domain name after Active Directory is set up requires removing the domain and reinstalling Active Directory on the domain controllers. The process is even more complex as the number of domain controllers for the domain increases.

The Server Setup window displays the changes being made to the server to set up Active Directory services; it also displays changes made to the Active Directory support in the existing Active Directory support in the domain controllers of the domain forest. The setup of the DNS service is also noted. The Completing the Active Directory Wizard screen in Figure 8-15 is presented when all the setup chores are done. Note that the default site name is Default-First-Site-Name. This will match the site name of the site containing the other domain

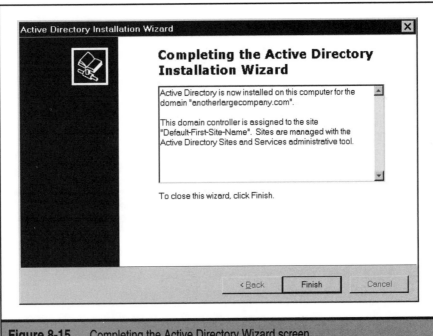

Figure 8-15.   Completing the Active Directory Wizard screen

controllers if the site name was never changed. The implication of sites and DNS support is addressed in Chapter 9.

After the server reboots, the results of this process can be checked by starting up the Active Directory Domains and Trusts MMC snap-in by choosing Start | Programs | Administrative Tools | Active Directory Domains and Trusts. In this case, the Active Directory Domains and Trusts window is presented (Figure 8-16).

The window shows the first domain we created, largecompany.com. It also shows the first child domain we added at the start of this chapter,

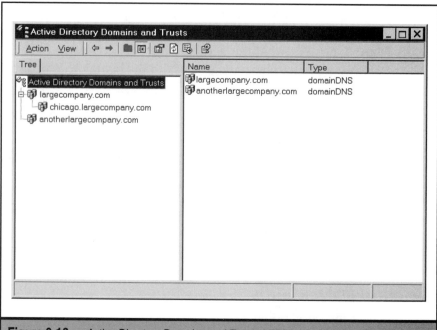

Figure 8-16.   Active Directory Domains and Trusts MMC snap-in

chicago.largecompany.com. Finally, there is the new domain tree whose root domain name is anotherlargecompany.com. Repeat the steps in this section to add any number of new domain trees to the forest.

NOTE: The DNS services were set up for both root domains, largecompany.com and anotherlargecompany.com. The section "DNS Configuration in a Domain Forest for Large Networks" addresses DNS service configuration so that the domains can access servers within the domain forest.

Merging Existing Domain Trees

Unfortunately, the release of Windows 2000 that was used with this book does not have the ability to combine domain trees in different domain forests. This type of feature is promised in future versions of Windows 2000. In the meantime, it is possible using tools like FastLane's DM/Manager (**www.fastlane.com**) and Mission Critical's OnePoint Enterprise Administrator (**www.missioncritical.com**). These tools are addressed in more detail in Chapter 22, which covers third-party utilities.

Essentially, these tools can migrate a domain from one domain forest to another. The process retains the Active Directory objects and their logical access control lists.

The other approach is to perform the migration without the help of these tools. This requires building up a new, empty domain tree as described in the section "Creating a New Domain Tree" and then populating it with information from the old domain tree. The repopulation may be done manually or by using batch files, custom applications, or tools similar to FastLane's and Mission Critical's.

Microsoft may also be providing more advanced tools for performing this type of reconfiguration.

In any case, migration of DNS information will be one of the first things to occur. This migration will be similar to migrating from another operating system and will typically be done by editing the text file associated with a primary domain.

DNS CONFIGURATION IN A DOMAIN FOREST FOR LARGE NETWORKS

Assuming that Windows 2000 DNS servers are used with root domain controllers in the domain forest, the Enterprise Admin group will be of great importance to DNS administrators. This group is automatically created in the first domain of the domain forest. Its members initially include the Administrator account for the first domain. This is the one account that spans domain forests, because the Enterprise Admin group is also a member of each of the Administrator groups in each of the newly created root domains.

So what does Enterprise Admin have to do with DNS servers? Assuming that the DNS servers will be managed locally, it has little to do with them. On the other hand, if centralized management is desired, some changes will need to be made. It is possible to use the Enterprise Admin group to manage DNS services, but it is a better idea to create an Enterprise DNS group, as shown in Figure 8-17.

Users that can manage DNS servers across the enterprise can be made members of this group. This group must also be added to the DnsAdmins group that is created by default when the DNS service is created.

By default, the Active Directory Wizard DNS server setup will create an Active Directory–integrated zone for the domain being set up. To use DNS names across domain forests, it is necessary to bring the DNS zones to DNS servers within each domain tree. The amount of work that needs to be done will depend upon how the zone information is distributed.

One way to handle distribution of zone information is at the client end. Some clients can reference more than one DNS server, although

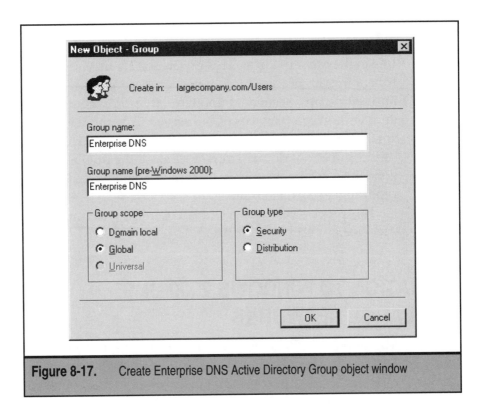

Figure 8-17.   Create Enterprise DNS Active Directory Group object window

some additional DNS servers are used only if the primary DNS server cannot be contacted. Managing clients with this type of DNS access is an administrative nightmare that gets worse because only IP addresses are used to specify the DNS server. Using DHCP helps, but moving the chore to the DNS server is a better idea, especially in large networks. This is why forwarding and secondary zones are a much better alternative.

NOTE: Windows 95, Windows 98, and Windows NT can reference multiple DNS servers, but the additional servers will only be contacted to service DNS requests if a prior DNS server fails to respond.

Forwarding and secondary zones can be used on the DNS server to get DNS information from another DNS server; the details on this are covered in Chapter 16. In this case, it is a matter of adding secondary zones to a DNS server in the root domain of each domain tree in the domain forest. This means setting up a secondary zone for anotherlargecompany.com in a largecompany.com DNS server and setting up a secondary zone for largecompany.com in the anotherlargecompany.com DNS server. This chore is simple for a small number of domain trees, but it can get to be quite cumbersome as the number of domain trees rises since the number of secondary zone links grows exponentially if each domain tree DNS zone is replicated at each DNS site.

This process can be even more complex when migration is included as part of the equation.

MIGRATION TO WINDOWS 2000 DNS FOR LARGE NETWORKS

Migration from Windows NT or other DNS servers to Windows 2000 DNS servers on a large network will be time consuming because the existing DNS support system must remain in place while the new system is being installed. Typically, the migration and elimination of older DNS servers is done in an incremental fashion since it is rare to have two complete sets of servers for a network migration.

The first decision to make is what, if any, DNS servers will be retained and which ones will be replaced. It is possible to use existing, non-Windows 2000 DNS servers for Windows 2000 Active Directory support as long as the DNS servers support dynamic updates and the range of DNS record types used by Windows 2000. This may mean upgrading the existing DNS server software, but this is often less of a problem than replacing the servers with Windows 2000 DNS servers. For example, the latest version of BIND does support dynamic DNS updates.

The next step is to determine in what order DNS servers are to be upgraded or replaced and whether this process can be done prior to conversion to Windows 2000 Active Directory. Remember, Windows 2000 servers can run without Active Directory, but Active Directory cannot run without DNS support. DNS zone migration issues and procedures are covered in Chapter 17.

It is possible to completely replace an old DNS server with a Windows 2000 server running a DNS server and simply copy the zone files and use them for the Windows 2000 DNS server's primary zone files. Make sure that the dynamic update support is enabled.

If incremental updates will occur, it may be necessary to carefully schedule the DNS server update or replacement so that it will occur in a particular network segment prior to installing the Active Directory domain controllers. The exception to this is if the domain controller will also be running the Windows 2000 DNS service. In that case, Active Directory and the DNS service can be installed at the same time.

If the existing DNS server is handling a number of different zones, it may have to remain in place even if the Windows 2000 DNS server will eventually replace it. This is because the initial installation of the Windows 2000 DNS service will only address the Active Directory domain for the domain controller. Once the Windows 2000 DNS and Active Directory services are installed, the zones from the existing DNS server can be moved to the Windows 2000 DNS service, as discussed in Chapter 17.

If existing DNS services are to be retained, it is now possible to install Active Directory on the Windows 2000 domain controller. The installation of Active Directory proceeds as outlined in the beginning of this chapter starting with the root domain and proceeding to child domains and adding domain trees to the domain forest.

PLACEMENT AND OTHER USES FOR DNS SERVERS IN A LARGE NETWORK

DNS servers need to be placed throughout a large Active Directory network to provide the location of domain controllers so computers can log into the network. Windows 2000 DNS services are often located on the same computer as a domain controller for two reasons. The first reason is to provide a reliable source of DNS service when the domain controller is available so computers can locate the domain controller and other domain controllers in the network. The second reason is to provide DNS information for other computers in the network or computers outside the network. One advantage of putting Windows

2000 DNS services on the same computer as the domain controller is that Active Directory–integrated DNS zone support can be utilized.

DNS services are often located on servers other than Windows 2000 domain controllers when the DNS infrastructure already exists. For example, in many large organizations, UNIX servers provide a well-established DNS environment. Windows 2000 Active Directory will work with the latest version of most third-party DNS services so Windows 2000 can be added to a network without changing the DNS infrastructure.

DNS support for computers other than Windows 2000 domain controllers will be important when these computers are providing IP-based services such as local web or FTP servers. In large networks, local network administrators will handle management of the DNS servers with primary DNS zones that contain information for these computers. This information is typically replicated throughout the network although the DNS server is often located on the subnet where the computers are located. Chapter 16 addresses details of replication and redirected DNS queries.

Distribution of local DNS information is just one reason that additional DNS servers will be required. DNS servers may also be placed at gateways to other networks such as the Internet. Chapter 18 takes a closer look at DNS and the Internet. In this case, the DNS servers are normally located on the same subnet as the gateways. The DNS servers can be on either side of the gateway, and its placement will depend upon the kind of service being provided. For example, a DNS service outside the network may provide DNS information about computers inside the network for computers outside the network. Likewise, a DNS service inside the network may provide DNS information about computers outside the network for computers inside the network.

DNS servers set up to work through gateways often cache information obtained from DNS servers on the other side of the gateway. DNS can be set up to act exclusively as a caching DNS server or it can provide a combination of DNS services. Large networks with an existing IP infrastructure typically have many of these DNS servers already in place. Large networks without an IP infrastructure will need to consider these additional DNS servers when building an IP infrastructure to support Windows 2000 Active Directory.

One other consideration for DNS server placement and use is the Windows Internet Naming Service (WINS). WINS will normally be found in a large network where IP is being used with Windows NT. WINS provides NetBIOS-based name resolution in an IP environment. WINS will typically remain if all servers and workstations are not migrated to Windows 2000. WINS will be required for DOS, Windows for Workgroups, Windows 95, Windows 98, and Windows NT computers that utilize IP. WINS is covered in more detail in Chapter 15. Windows 2000– and Windows NT–based WINS can be integrated with Windows 2000 DNS so placement of DNS servers involved with WINS can be critical.

SUMMARY

Large networks are built incrementally over time and will be in place when Windows 2000 is installed, so a migration strategy must be used. Since Windows 2000 depends upon TCP/IP, it is best to have TCP/IP in place prior to Windows 2000 installation. This means that you need to have DNS services in place before Windows 2000 is installed.

Constructing a large Windows 2000 network without Active Directory is unthinkable, and setting up Active Directory on a large network without DNS support is impossible. DNS support can be provided by the Windows 2000 DNS server or by most third-party DNS products such as BIND. The key is to make sure that dynamic DNS updates are supported and that either the DNS service is set up prior to setting up Windows 2000 Active Directory support or the Windows 2000 DNS service is installed at the same time as the Windows 2000 Active Directory support. In either case, the installation or upgrade of Windows 2000 servers will normally be done in an incremental fashion versus a complete, system-wide update. This means that planning is of paramount importance, and tracking changes will be key to fixing any Active Directory or DNS problems that arise after Windows 2000 server installation or update.

CHAPTER 9

Windows 2000 DNS and Active Directory Setup for a Distributed Network

Chapters 6, 7, and 8 address the mechanics of setting up Windows 2000 DNS and Active Directory on small, medium, and large networks. The primary concern when setting up these networks was getting everything to work together. Placement and the number of DNS servers become even more important when dealing with a distributed network because improper design can impact the overall performance of a network. In general, it is a good idea to provide sufficient local Active Directory domain controllers and DNS servers so that clients can minimize communication over slower-speed network links.

This chapter addresses Active Directory and DNS service planning and implementation issues. It deals with aspects of Windows 2000 that the prior chapters ignored, such as Windows 2000 sites, replication, and delegation of authority.

Our definition of a distributed network is one with local networks of PCs connected by high-speed network connections such as Ethernet or Fast Ethernet. This also includes local networks that may be connected by high-speed backbones using technologies such as Gigabit Ethernet or Asynchronous Transfer Mode (ATM). These local networks are then connected by links with less bandwidth. These links impact any communication between local networks in two ways: increased latency and possible congestion.

While complete elimination of network-to-network communication is not possible (why have the connections otherwise?) it is possible to minimize traffic with respect to DNS servers. In general, this is done by having DNS servers provide information to local clients about the entire network, or at least portions that are important to the clients within a network group. Windows 2000 uses the network-to-network communication links to exchange this information.

Normally, each local network is defined as a Windows 2000 site. A single site was sufficient for the other network models presented earlier. For the distributed network model, there are at least two sites.

In this chapter, the section "Active Directory Planning for Distributed Networks" addresses Active Directory and site layout considerations, including Active Directory–integrated DNS zones. Windows 2000 DNS servers will be the norm here.

The section "DNS Configuration for Distributed Networks" examines DNS services in the context of site design. In particular, it examines the use of non-Active Directory–integrated zones and third-party DNS servers.

ACTIVE DIRECTORY PLANNING FOR DISTRIBUTED NETWORKS

Windows 2000 introduces the concept of sites to Windows network design. A site is a collection of computers that are typically connected on a local network in the same geographical area. Sites were designed to facilitate scheduled interchange of information such as Active Directory databases including Active Directory–integrated DNS zones.

Sites are organized around IP subnets. A site consists of one or more IP subnets. While it is possible for subnets to span sites, it is preferable that they do not. It is common for a domain to span a site, but it is not a requirement; for large networks it is quite common for a single domain to span multiple sites. Likewise, it is possible for a site to contain more than one domain. This is quite common in large organizations that require a domain forest with users from different domains who are located at the same site.

For example, a sales site, as shown in Figure 9-1, might contain two domains such as sales.foo.com and sales.bar.com because the employees of a merged foo.com and bar.com were moved to the same building. The root domain names are foo.com and bar.com, so the sales.foo.com and sales.bar.com are part of those domain trees respectively, and the two domain trees are part of a common domain forest. Having the two domains at the same site allows Active Directory replication between this site and other sites to occur on a scheduled basis with respect to the site rather than to a particular domain. This is more efficient because there can be more domains than sites. Similarly, allowing Active Directory replication in an ad hoc rather than a scheduled fashion could lead to excessive communication overhead.

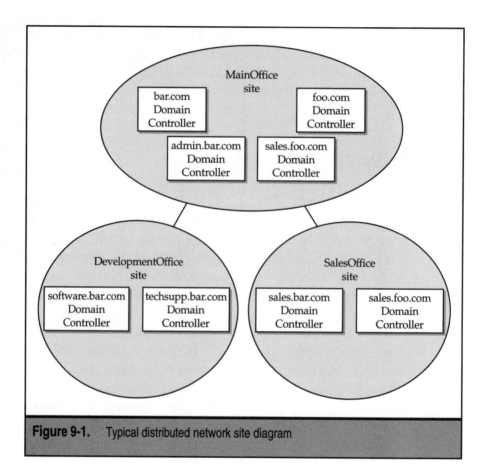

Figure 9-1. Typical distributed network site diagram

Note how the Active Directory domain tree diagram shown in Figure 9-2 differs from the site diagram in Figure 9-1. Obviously, it would be more difficult to manage site-to-site communication using this hierarchy, especially given the fact that the sales.foo.com domain actually spans two sites as shown in Figure 9-1.

NOTE: It is very useful to use multiple diagrams when planning Active Directory domains and placing Active Directory domain controllers and DNS servers. It's easy to see if you have a lack of DNS servers with a site diagram, but a domain tree diagram provides no such insight. More detailed site diagrams are useful if a DNS server will be handling more than one primary domain.

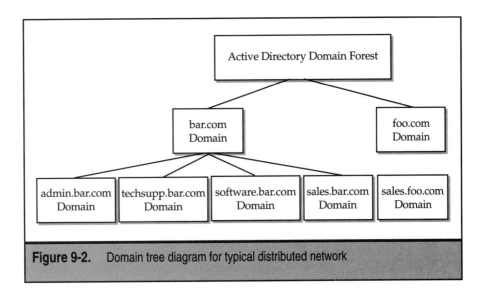

Figure 9-2. Domain tree diagram for typical distributed network

Typically, a site contains at least one domain controller. It is possible for a site to contain no domain controllers, but then any client PCs must log on using a domain controller in another site. This may be acceptable for a small workgroup of less than six PCs with a solid connection to another site where logon times are not critical. The lack of a domain controller in a site is not acceptable when there are more PCs at the site or where the connection to another site is transient.

Likewise, a site typically contains at least one DNS server since Active Directory clients locate a domain controller using the DNS server. It is possible to have the domain controller and DNS server on the same PC, but they often exist on different PCs. In the previous example, it would be possible to have a single DNS server for the SalesOffice site with the DNS server providing information about both the sales.bar.com domain and the sales.foo.com domain. Unfortunately, while it is possible for one DNS server to handle multiple zones, Windows 2000 is not set up to allow a domain controller to service more than one domain. However, there is no requirement that a DNS server only handle zones that are not part of its domain. Minimally, the SalesOffice site will have two servers, one for each domain controller. One or both of the servers could have a DNS service installed.

Looking at the bigger picture of our example, the MainOffice site requires at least four domain controllers and one DNS server. The DevelopmentOffice is similar to the SalesOffice site with at least two domain controllers and one DNS service.

Replication between sites will be primarily for the Active Directory catalog for the domain forest and synchronization between the sales.foo.com domain controllers in the SalesOffice and MainOffice sites. Active Directory–integrated DNS information for the sales.foo.com domain is exchanged in this fashion, which makes these two PCs ideal spots for a DNS service. All other DNS information must be synchronized using secondary zones. This will be addressed in the section "DNS Configuration for Distributed Networks."

TIP: One possible solution to DNS replication via Active Directory–integrated zones without the use of secondary zones is to assign DNS chores to one domain. This will require an Active Directory–integrated zone for each domain being supported and a domain controller with a DNS service at each site, but it can simplify overall management and replication chores. Configuration is significantly more complex if secured DNS updates are used because security and trust relationships for these updates for the respective zones must be enabled.

Before addressing the complexities of multiple domain trees spread across multiple sites, we will look at the simpler cases such as the one in the next section that addresses a single domain spread across multiple sites.

The assumption made for these next few sections is that Active Directory–integrated zones are the primary method of DNS synchronization. We will examine how this integration meshes well with the general site and domain planning that must naturally occur for Windows 2000 networks to address Active Directory in general. We will not address the needs of a site designer beyond the need for general replication in areas such as bandwidth allocation, replication scheduling, and other aspects important in a distributed network design, as these are beyond the scope of this book.

Single Domain over Multiple Sites

Figure 9-3 shows the site diagram for a sample distributed network with a single domain. A domain tree diagram is unnecessary since it is the single domain foo.com.

A single domain is the easiest to manage. It makes centralized management easy, but delegating network management chores to people at different sites can be more difficult. In particular, a single Active Directory–integrated DNS zone is all that is necessary to handle the entire network. This is possible since the DNS service is not concerned with the actual IP addresses associated with the names in the DNS zone database. Sites can still utilize their own subnets, as shown in the example.

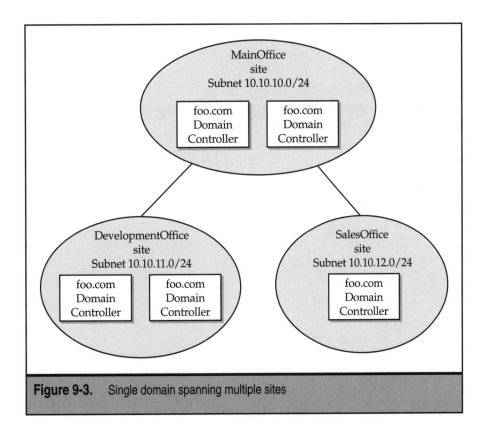

Figure 9-3.   Single domain spanning multiple sites

The subnets in the example include 10.10.10.0/24 for the MainOffice site, 10.10.11.0/24 for the DevelopmentOffice site and 10.10.10.12/24 for the SalesOffice site. The number of mask bits in all cases is 24. Figure 9-4 shows the Sites and Services MMC plug-in with this same setup.

At least one DNS service on a domain controller per site would be required to handle the DNS requirements of the network. The existence of multiple domain controllers for the same domain could be due to redundancy concerns, in which case redundant DNS services may be appropriate. Alternatively, multiple DNS services may be needed to provide support for a large number of clients within a site. In either case, the DNS services within the site would be updated quickly when changes occurred through dynamic DNS updates when a Windows 2000 client logged into the domain.

Movement of Active Directory data between sites occurs at scheduled intervals. This means that updates that occur at one site

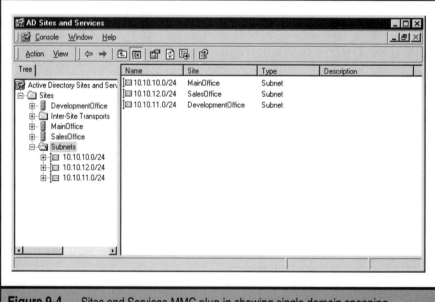

Figure 9-4. Sites and Services MMC plug-in showing single domain spanning multiple sites

may not be reflected at another site until well after they occur. This delay typically has more impact on security due to addition, deletion, or changes to users and groups. The delay will also impact DNS users by potentially delaying access to a resource named in the DNS database or by providing an incorrect IP address if a DNS database entry is not updated in time. Little can be done to eliminate this problem other than to provide a high-speed link between sites.

Replication intervals are set by the enterprise administrator, and the replication takes into account the transport mechanism used for replication. The default transport replication mechanisms are IP and SMTP (i.e., e-mail). IP transport is comparable to secondary zone updates in terms of speed, since both use the network directly. SMTP imposes a delay, but it is often sufficient in distributed networks where information does not change regularly. It can also be used where the links between sites may use a third-party network such as the Internet. In this case, important DNS information normally changes very little since clients will typically be accessing servers across the link and the server's IP addresses will be fixed. Access to clients that have IP addresses assigned by DHCP are less likely targets for site-to-site communication. In any case, the overall system works given the delay necessary to make updates.

Conflicts, with respect to Active Directory–integrated zone information, tend to be minimized with a properly designed distributed Windows 2000 network because subnets should be nonoverlapping and server IP addresses are typically fixed. This means that only dynamic client IP addresses will be part of Active Directory updates.

A single distributed domain is preferable from a DNS service standpoint since a single Active Directory–integrated zone is all that is needed to provide the entire enterprise with DNS information for all sites. While distributed management of the DNS zone is possible, it is recommended that a single manager handle updates to minimize confusion. This is typically not a problem since addition or removal of servers from a network is a rare occurrence. These updates require infrequent and minimal changes, especially compared to dynamic DNS updates associated with clients, which can occur every minute.

NOTE: Although a single distributed domain is preferable from a DNS management standpoint, it may not be suitable for political or management reasons. A single domain may also be impractical due to communication bandwidth or security between sites. Multiple domains may require more work to manage in a single site, but they may involve less work when the domains are found in individual sites.

Configuration of Windows 2000 sites and DNS servers in this environment is extremely simple. The first domain controller can be used to define the various sites, and each additional domain controller can be added to the appropriate site. The DNS service should be installed when Active Directory is installed; this will allow the installation wizard, started via Start | Programs | Administrative Tools | Configure Your Server, to include the single root domain as the initial Active Directory–integrated zone.

As each new domain controller is added, the Active Directory database will be updated, as will the Active Directory–integrated DNS zone. Secure dynamic DNS updates are allowed by default, so Windows 2000 clients will be able to update the zone automatically.

Single Domain Tree over Multiple Sites

Adding additional domains within a single domain tree complicates matters a bit when it comes to site design and management. It also adds benefits by allowing distributed management of domains and DNS zones. Multiple domains within a single domain tree may also be desirable from a performance standpoint if the network and Active Directory database is very large. In this case, splitting up the network into multiple domains can also make sense.

Network administrators should examine what type of distributed management is needed before deciding upon the use of multiple domains. In many cases, distributed management and logical distribution of resources with respect to DNS names can be accomplished through the use of organizational units and DNS domains, not to be confused with Active Directory domains.

Organizational units provide multilevel names within an Active Directory domain and administrative security is assigned with respect to organizational units. In other words, an enterprise administrator can set up organizational units so that each can be managed by a network administrator, thereby distributing the management workload.

In a similar fashion, additional DNS domains can be defined within a DNS zone or another DNS domain. Although these domains present a hierarchical naming system, they are stored within a single DNS zone database. Windows 2000 DNS management granularity is limited to a DNS zone, not a DNS domain. It is possible to use Windows 2000 DNS delegation with multiple DNS zones to accomplish the desired goal of distributed zone management. For example, a foo.com zone would include a delegation record of sales.foo.com that refers to another DNS zone, sales.foo.com. The sales.foo.com DNS zone could be maintained on the same DNS server as the foo.com zone, and both could be Active Directory–integrated zones. The advantage is that the sales.foo.com DNS zone security is independent of the foo.com DNS zone security, so an enterprise administrator could have another network administrator manage only the sales.foo.com zone and not the foo.com zone. The same configuration holds true for any number of DNS zones and domains. The DNS zones can be distributed among different DNS servers if necessary.

A comparative example using multiple domains in a single tree is shown first in the site diagram in Figure 9-5 and then in the corresponding domain tree diagram in Figure 9-6. In these cases, there are five Active Directory domains including the root, foo.com. Both the sales.foo.com and the foo.com domains span more than one site. Each Active Directory domain has its own group of management users with overall enterprise management being available to the initial enterprise administrators. In these cases, distributed management is essentially mandated unless centralized management by enterprise administrators is performed or domain administrators are given enterprise privileges. Neither is preferable.

Active Directory–integrated DNS domains can be set up and managed at the root domain level with DNS domains to match the Active Directory child domains. Alternatively, Active Directory–integrated DNS domains can be set up to match all the Active Directory domains. The former is preferable for centralized

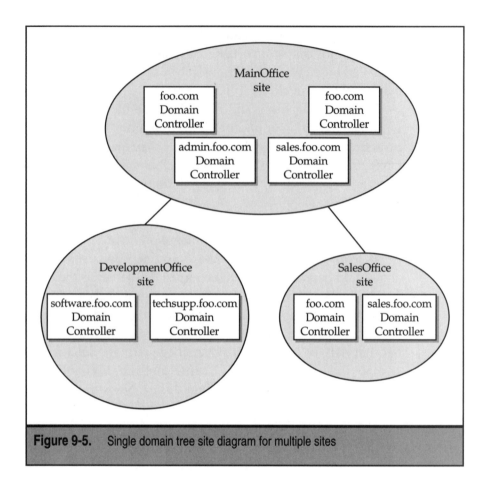

Figure 9-5.   Single domain tree site diagram for multiple sites

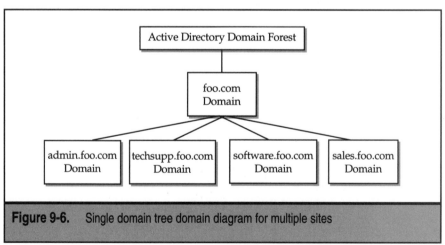

Figure 9-6.   Single domain tree domain diagram for multiple sites

DNS management, while the latter is preferable for distributed DNS management.

A comparable configuration using the organizational unit approach presented at the beginning of this section would result in a single domain, foo.com, as shown in Figure 9-7. It would incorporate organizational units named admin.foo.com, sales.foo.com, software.foo.com, and techsupp.foo.com. This diagram differs from Figure 9-6 in that the Active Directory child domains are organizational units.

Of course, organizational unit administrators of these organizational units can define additional organizational units under these, just as domain administrators can define organizational units within their respective Active Directory domain.

In this example, the default Active Directory–integrated DNS zone for the foo.com domain will not include any of the organizational units since the Active Directory Installation wizard only deals with domains. Instead, these DNS domain records must be created manually. Resources that need DNS names that are within these domains can then be configured, including dynamic DNS updates. In particular, if DHCP is used for IP address assignments, the domain name for these clients should match the desired DNS domain name, such as sales.foo.com. Likewise, alias DNS entries can be included for servers so that a server could have a DNS name like server6.sales.foo.com.

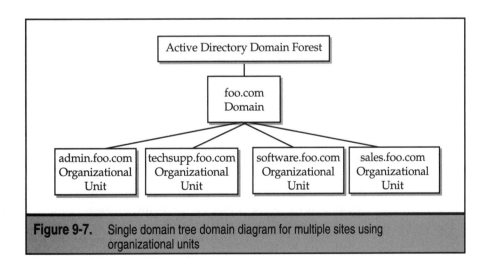

Figure 9-7. Single domain tree domain diagram for multiple sites using organizational units

NOTE: The Active Directory–integrated DNS zone for foo.com
is only accessible to DNS servers in the domain foo.com as an Active
Directory–integrated zone. The zone will not be accessible as an
Active Directory–integrated DNS zone to any DNS servers in child
domains of foo.com, although this information can be shared via
secondary zones. From a user's point of view, there is no difference.
A server or workstation can still have a logical hierarchical name, and
a local administrator can be responsible for making local changes.

Multiple Domain Trees over Multiple Sites

Let's get back to the Active Directory domain forest with multiple
Active Directory domain trees spanning multiple sites, as shown
previously in Figures 9-1 and 9-2. As mentioned in the sections "Single
Domain over Multiple Sites" and "Single Domain Tree over Multiple
Sites," the single domain tree can span a rather large distributed
network and provide quite a bit of flexibility when it comes to
management and distribution of administrative chores. Still, there
are times when this level of complexity is insufficient and the
multiple domain tree approach is necessary.

An Active Directory domain forest has the advantage of forcing
the distribution of Active Directory resources and management
requirements. An enterprise administrator who attempts to manage
even a small Active Directory domain forest by themself is either
very foolish or has figured out how to work with one hour of sleep
per week. Windows 2000 does a good job of making network
administration easier, but it does not eliminate the need for it.

An Active Directory domain forest spanning multiple sites
actually differs little in terms of complexity from the single domain
tree spanning multiple sites presented in the section "Single Domain
Tree over Multiple Sites." In fact, the major change is with respect to
DNS support.

First the simple part: Active Directory administration. The main
difference between the single domain tree and the domain forest is
the existence of multiple enterprise administration groups. There is
one for each root domain. A true enterprise administrator will be
made part of each group or will have accounts in each root domain.

Transitive trusts exist between all domains within the forest, so it is simply a matter of having the appropriate rights for enterprise management.

Administrators of individual domains will have control over a small portion of the network and the domain may span more than one site.

Now for the complex part: DNS configuration. Even the use of Active Directory–integrated zones does not help simplify the job because Active Directory–integrated zones cannot be shared via Active Directory across the domain forest. Instead, providing cross-domain DNS information must be accomplished using the techniques outlined in the section "DNS Configuration for Distributed Networks," typically using secondary DNS zones and DNS caching.

One approach to simplifying DNS configuration in a domain forest is to minimize interdependency between DNS servers that are being updated using secondary DNS zones. For example, the network shown in Figure 9-1 has no site-to-site connections between the DevelopmentOffice site and the SalesOffice site. This means that any communication between these two sites moves through the MainOffice site. For IP traffic, this is easily accomplished via routers, although obviously there is inherent latency due to forwarding. Still, adding a link between the DevelopmentOffice site and the SalesOffice site should not imply that DNS information should be transferred using this link. In particular, it may be easier to manage if the primary DNS zone for software.bar.com in the DevelopmentOffice site is sent to a DNS server in the MainOffice site, where it is then forwarded to a DNS server in the SalesOffice site as a secondary DNS zone. Either approach provides a secondary DNS zone copy of the software.bar.com to the SalesOffice site.

One of the main issues of DNS updates versus Active Directory updates between sites is the measure of control available to administrators. While secondary DNS zone updates can be scheduled for specific intervals, each secondary DNS zone has its own interval. Toss in a dozen secondary DNS zone linkages, and any coordinated communication is lost, especially compared to Active Directory.

On the other hand, Active Directory synchronization and replication are scheduled on a per-site-link basis regardless of the number of domains or Active Directory–integrated DNS zones involved. For the most part, the use of Active Directory for DNS support is preferable, and it would be even better if it had a replication procedure of non-Active Directory–integrated zones.

The next section takes a look at how DNS configuration can be set up without Active Directory integration, as well as how it can augment Active Directory–integrated zones.

DNS CONFIGURATION FOR DISTRIBUTED NETWORKS

The previous section examined how Active Directory replication can be used to distribute DNS information across a large distributed network. This approach works well with single domain networks, although distributed Windows 2000 networks tend to have multiple domains to help distribute management chores.

Unfortunately, Active Directory replication of Active Directory–integrated DNS information within a multiple domain network does not address the issue of providing DNS information across domains. This job must be performed using other techniques such as using secondary DNS zones or DNS request forwarding with DNS caching.

A reminder: Windows 2000 DNS services provide all the necessary support to handle a large distributed network that utilizes Active Directory with or without Active Directory–integrated DNS zones. Also, the latest versions of third-party DNS services like BIND can provide the same level of service if they support dynamic DNS update. This support is required by domain controllers so they can register their IP information and so that Windows 2000 clients can access the information that is necessary in the Windows 2000 login process.

Both third-party and Windows 2000 DNS services can be mixed in a large distributed network. The main difference between using Windows 2000 DNS services and third-party is Windows 2000's Secured DNS update support and Windows 2000 security for the DNS service and any Active Directory–integrated DNS zones.

The first step for DNS configuration in a distributed network is to support domain controllers. This can be accomplished using

Windows 2000 DNS services and Active Directory–integrated DNS zones, as described in the previous section. It can also be done using third-party DNS servers like BIND. BIND is discussed in more detail in Chapter 21.

The second step for DNS configuration in a distributed network is to provide DNS information about the rest of the network to each site. This task can be accomplished using secondary DNS zones and DNS request forwarding plus DNS caching. The procedures for implementing these are covered in Chapter 16. In the next chapter, we look at the architectural issues.

The advantage of secondary DNS zones is that they obtain distributed DNS information as a block. The disadvantage is the complexity of setting up secondary DNS zones with more than half a dozen zones or more than two or three sites.

The advantage of using DNS forwarding and caching is the simplicity of configuration and the lack of any management requirements. The disadvantage is that caching DNS servers obtain DNS information on an incremental basis, that is, one request at a time.

Figure 9-8 shows how secondary DNS zone links can be used on a fully connected, multiple-site network. The dashed links represent bidirectional paths for secondary DNS zone updates. Note that the DNS zone name associated with the DNS controllers are not necessarily the DNS name of the DNS server but rather the primary DNS zone managed by the server. This designation is only for illustrative purposes within this chapter.

With this architecture, each DNS server obtains its secondary DNS zone copy of another DNS server's primary DNS zone directly. The advantage is quick updates. The disadvantage is an exploding number of links as the number of DNS zones increases. Note that additional DNS servers supporting the same site provide redundancy and possibly better performance within the site. They will also require the same setup as the first DNS server at the site.

Figure 9-9 shows an alternative way to link secondary DNS zones. In this case, the bar.com DNS server provides the bar.com primary DNS zone and secondary zones for all the other DNS zones. These

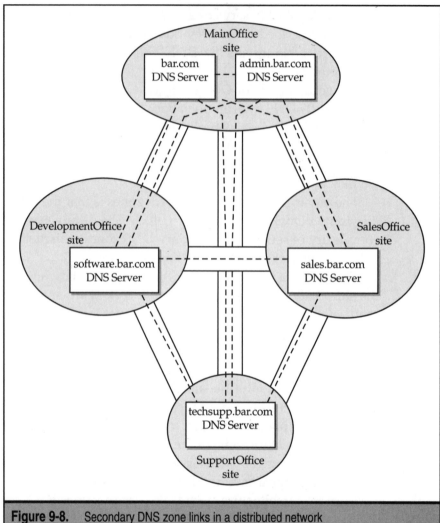

Figure 9-8.   Secondary DNS zone links in a distributed network

secondary DNS zones in the bar.com DNS server are updated
from their respective primary DNS servers respectively. These other
servers also obtain the information for their secondary DNS zones
from the bar.com DNS server.

This approach depends upon a reliable bar.com DNS server. It is
possible to have multiple DNS servers at the MainOffice site that

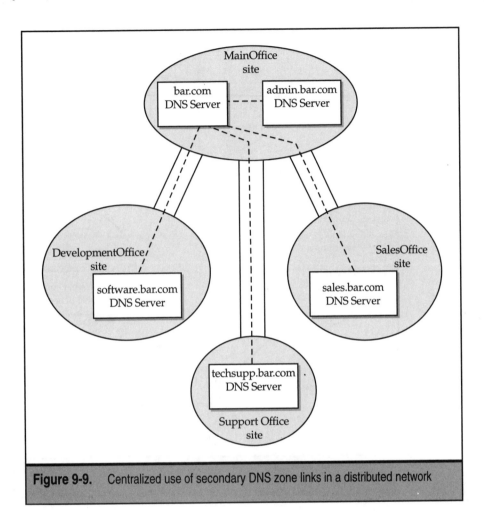

Figure 9-9. Centralized use of secondary DNS zone links in a distributed network

provide the same services as most DNS servers, including Windows 2000 DNS service, implement secondary DNS zone support with the option for multiple sources. To provide a more robust environment, the DNS servers would reference both the primary bar.com DNS server as well as any alternate bar.com DNS servers.

Secondary DNS zone links to a primary DNS zone can be indirect, as shown in Figure 9-10. In this case, the primary DNS zone in techsupp.bar.com is provided to the secondary DNS zone in the bar.com DNS server through the secondary DNS zone in software.bar.com.

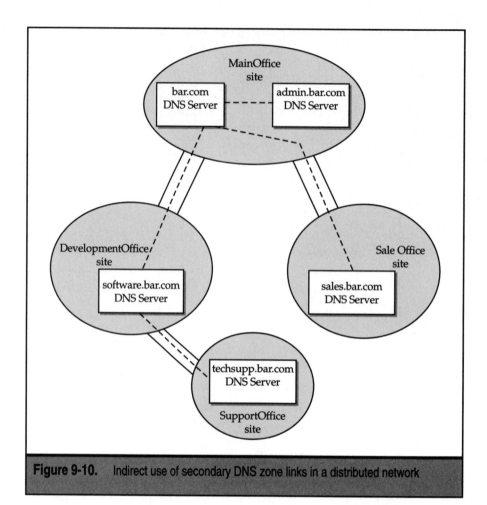

Figure 9-10. Indirect use of secondary DNS zone links in a distributed network

Updates from techsupp.bar.com are first delivered to software.bar.com DNS server. This same information is, in turn, provided to the bar.com DNS server. Of course, with appropriate router configuration between sites, it is possible for the bar.com DNS server to communicate directly with the techsupp.bar.com DNS server. Still, there may be a number of reasons why this is not possible or desired. In particular, most DNS servers, including Windows 2000 DNS service, can restrict secondary DNS updates to a specific set of DNS servers via a list of IP addresses. If the techsupp.bar.com DNS server is set up to allow secondary DNS zone updates only with the software.bar.com

DNS server, the bar.com DNS server will be denied access. This is of little consequence on a network where an administrator has authority over all the DNS servers, but it can be an issue where control is distributed. Connections such as these must be discussed and possibly negotiated.

The approach presented thus far depends upon secondary DNS zone updates between DNS servers. The alternative method of servicing DNS requests transparently is to use DNS forwarding and DNS caching. Figure 9-11 shows an example with a DNS client in the MainOffice site.

For this example, the client requests the IP address of www.techsupp.bar.com from the local bar.com DNS server. The DNS server fails to find this information in its primary DNS zone database and, for this example, lacking the secondary DNS zones of the prior examples, must forward the DNS request to adjacent DNS servers. Both admin.bar.com and sales.bar.com will indicate that they do not have this information. However, the software.bar.com DNS server has a link with the techsupp.bar.com DNS server, so the request is forwarded from two DNS servers to get to the server with the matching primary DNS zone. The www record is found (we assume that it exists), and the techsupp.bar.com DNS server returns the information to the software.bar.com DNS server where it is added to the cache and also returned to the bar.com DNS server where it is again added to the bar.com DNS server's cache. The bar.com DNS server returns the information to the DNS client and all is well.

Subsequent requests for the same www.techsupp.bar.com IP address will now be found in the cache for both the bar.com and software.bar.com DNS servers. DNS clients that request this information will now be serviced more quickly via information in cache. Of course, access to the www.techsupp.bar.com Web server at the support office site from the MainOffice site will still have to flow through two sites for each Web page being viewed unless a caching Web proxy server is used. DNS caching will still reduce the overall latency for the Web page access as well as reduce the overall intrasite traffic.

As mentioned earlier, the forwarding and caching approach only updates the cache based upon a request, and the first request will

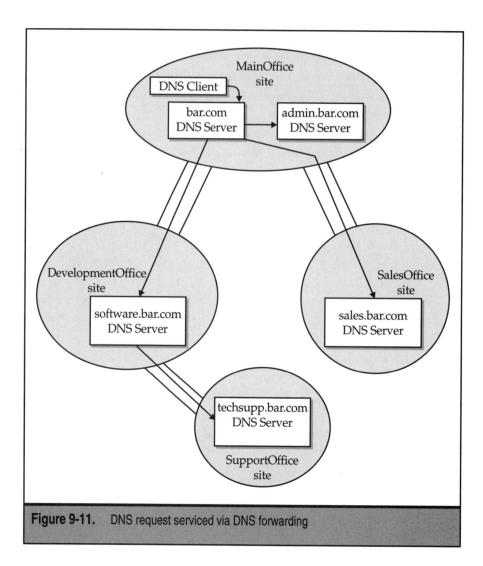

Figure 9-11. DNS request serviced via DNS forwarding

have additional delay as the DNS servers communicate among themselves. Also, each subsequent request for a different name within the DNS zone will result in this same delay as the process is only done on a per name basis. This is of little consequence if the number of different requests per site is small. For example, if the techsupp.bar.com zone has only DNS records, the Windows 2000 domain controllers and the Web server then forwarding and caching work very well. On the other hand, if individual workstations are enumerated at the techsupp.bar.com DNS server via dynamic DNS updates and clients at other sites need to access these workstations directly, as when using teleconferencing software, then the use of secondary DNS zones becomes more advantageous.

NOTE: Replication of dynamic DNS updates is not immediate, so the amount of time between a workstation registering its IP address and name with the primary DNS server for the domain and its replication to other secondary zones will vary. Some DNS servers implement notification of changes that will reduce the delay between updates, but there will always be some amount of time when a secondary server is out of synch with the primary server.

In large distributed networks, a combination of forwarding and caching and secondary DNS zones will be used. Typically, network administrators can estimate where secondary DNS zones will be most advantageous. Luckily, both approaches require no maintenance, but occasional performance monitoring is useful to determine whether the right approach has been used.

SUMMARY

Planning, configuring, and maintaining a distributed network is one of the hardest jobs around. This is especially true for Windows 2000 with Active Directory. While Active Directory can greatly improve configuration and management chores, its initial planning and configuration must be done carefully as it will impact how the system operates in the long run.

As noted, using a single domain across multiple sites is the easiest to design and implement, but a single domain can be a drawback when distributed management is needed. It also makes automatic distribution of the Active Directory database an issue especially if the database is large and the intranetwork connections are slow.

A domain tree is the preferred configuration for a distributed network. A single domain tree addresses many of the replication and management distribution issues while not increasing complexity to the level of a domain forest.

A domain forest with multiple domain trees is often a requirement in larger organizations especially those that have merged with other organizations. Active Directory planning is critical in this environment and just keeping track of who manages what can be a major chore.

DNS configuration for distributed Windows 2000 Active Directory networks is complicated by the fact that domain controllers must have access to a DNS server that provides information about other domain controllers including those within a domain tree. Placing a Windows 2000 DNS server on each domain controller is a good idea even if the DNS server will only provide services to domain controllers. An additional DNS server can provide DNS services to workstations but the DNS servers must be configured to exchange information, usually using secondary DNS zones, so that workstations can access Windows 2000 servers.

Using non–Windows 2000 DNS servers in a distributed environment will be a given for most organizations. Maintaining DNS support for a large organization was never easy with Windows NT, and other operating systems such as UNIX were often called to task.

Unfortunately, tools for planning DNS installation in a distributed network are not very good. It takes a good understanding of Active Directory and DNS to make sure that domain controllers and Windows 2000 workstations have enough information to log in and use the resources provided by Windows 2000 servers.

CHAPTER 10

Configuring Active Directory Using Microsoft Management Console

lthough this is a book about Microsoft Windows 2000 DNS, DNS's tight relationship with Active Directory makes it imperative that a DNS administrator understand the operation of Active Directory and how to manage it using the Microsoft Management Console (MMC).

The MMC is a framework application that does little by itself. It gains its power from a long list of MMC snap-ins that provide management and monitoring services to everything from Windows 2000 Sites and Services to Windows 2000 DNS service. The architecture and application programming interface (API) for MMC snap-ins called the Windows Management Infrastructure (WMI) is readily available from Microsoft so that third-party MMC snap-ins can be created. In fact, most third-party Windows 2000 server-based applications come with an MMC snap-in.

This chapter takes a look at the MMC and three Windows 2000–specific MMC snap-ins including the MMC snap-in for Domains and Trusts, the MMC snap-in for Sites and Services, and the MMC snap-in for Users and Computers. These snap-ins will be examined with respect to their relationship to Windows DNS, although their general functionality is not explored in depth, as general Windows 2000 management is beyond the scope of this book.

The first section on the Microsoft Management Console examines how MMC looks and works. It addresses how MMC snap-ins can be mixed to provide an integrated management environment. This approach is more complex than the standard, single MMC snap-in approach that's used by the default management configuration setup when Windows 2000 is installed. For example, the Administration Tools menu contains shortcuts for MMC snap-ins for each major Windows 2000 component including installed services like DNS, DHCP, and WINS.

MICROSOFT MANAGEMENT CONSOLE (MMC)

The Microsoft Management Console (MMC) was created to provide a consistent interface to administration tools. It was originally developed for later versions of Windows NT 4.0 as part of the Windows NT 4.0 Option Pack, but it was not until Windows 2000 that the majority of operating system services were supported by MMC snap-ins.

MMC uses a multidocument interface similar to that found in applications such as Microsoft Word. The main difference between MMC and Microsoft Word is that a document window in MMC is typically driven by an MMC snap-in with a two-pane interface that's similar to Windows Explorer, whereas a Microsoft Word document window contains only one document. With Microsoft Word, a new window is displayed when a new document is created or an existing document is opened. With MMC, a new entry is added when a new MMC snap-in is opened. The entry is added to the existing window that contains other MMC snap-in entries. It is possible to clone windows in the MMC, but we'll discuss that later in this chapter.

Unlike Microsoft Word, where documents are opened and closed individually, MMC allows the configuration of all MMC snap-in windows to be saved in an .msc file. Start MMC with the .msc file, and the management environment will be re-created. MMC is associated with the .msc extension, so double-clicking on an .msc file from an application like Windows Explorer will start MMC using the matching file.

TIP: To provide quick access to management tools, set up desktop shortcuts to .msc files for common management configurations that are useful to specific users, such as an MMC configuration that includes both a DNS and DHCP snap-in.

To start MMC without any snap-ins, click on Start | Run, enter **MMC** in the Program field, and click on the OK button. The resulting window looks like the one shown in Figure 10-1.

The MMC window contains a basic Console Root window and a minimal toolbar for both the main window and child Console Root window. The Console Root window shows a typical snap-in window configuration with a navigation pane on the left and a content pane on the right. This configuration is not a requirement, and third-party snap-ins may have different configurations that are more appropriate for the snap-in. For example, the content pane may have a graph on top and a data table on the bottom.

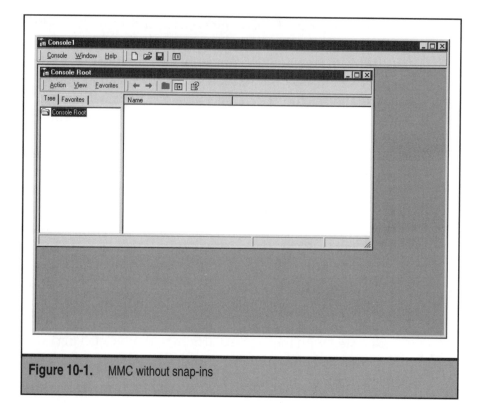

Figure 10-1. MMC without snap-ins

NOTE: Right-clicking on an entry in a snap-in window will typically bring up a pop-up menu of related actions. This normally includes access to a Properties page dialog box.

The MMC can support one or more MMC snap-ins. The next section shows how to add MMC snap-ins.

Adding MMC Snap-ins

To add an MMC snap-in, click on the Console menu in the main MMC window. This brings up the Add/Remove Snap-in window shown in Figure 10-2.

The MMC Add/Remove Snap-in window shows a list of currently selected snap-ins for the specified console window. A console window can support more than one snap-in, and a snap-in can appear more than once in the list. In the latter case, duplicate

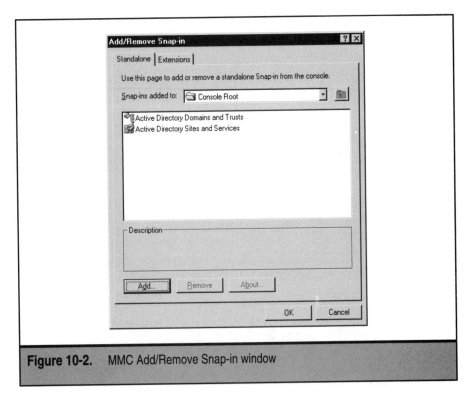

Figure 10-2. MMC Add/Remove Snap-in window

snap-ins can be used to examine different aspects of the items managed by the snap-in. For example, two DNS snap-ins can be used so that one snap-in instance is presenting information for a local Windows 2000 DNS service while the other presents information for a remote DNS service.

The console window is named in the Snap-ins Added To field. The list associated with this field will include entries for each open console window. Changing the selected entry will change the list of snap-ins accordingly.

To add a snap-in, click on the Add button. This brings up the Add Standalone Snap-in window, which displays a list of available snap-ins, as shown in Figure 10-3.

A snap-in entry includes the name of the snap-in and the name of the company that created the snap-in. Selecting an entry and clicking on the Add button adds the snap-in to the Console window snap-in list. Add as many snap-ins as necessary and then click on the Close button.

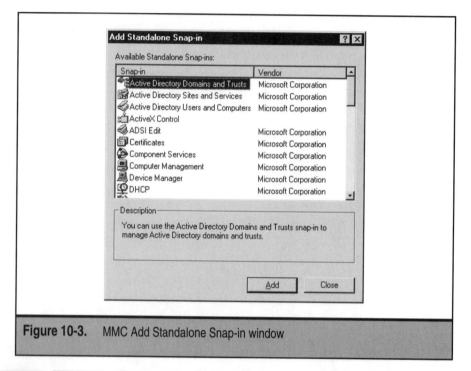

Figure 10-3. MMC Add Standalone Snap-in window

NOTE: It is possible to add the same snap-in more than once. This allows the same snap-in to be used to manage or monitor different parts of the network. For example, adding two DNS snap-ins would allow viewing of both a local DNS service and a Windows 2000 DNS service in a different domain (assuming the user has sufficient access rights for the latter). This environment is useful when dealing with two services that interact with each other, such as a primary DNS zone handled by the local DNS service and a secondary DNS zone that is handled by the other DNS service.

The services of the snap-in can be used once the snap-in window is closed. By default, the snap-ins are listed at the highest level of the navigation window just below the Console Root. The snap-in information can be viewed by clicking on the plus sign in front of the entry to expand the list of snap-in items.

Active Directory snap-ins, like the Domain and Trust snap-in or the Site and Services snap-in, are initially linked to the server's domain controller. To change the domain controller for an Active Directory domain controller, right-click on the snap-in entry. This will reveal a number of options, including the one that changes the domain controller, Connect To Domain Controller. Other snap-ins may have similar attributes or links between different servers or domains. In general, these features are snap-in–specific.

Saving MMC .msc Files

An MMC environment that's built up by adding snap-ins can be a useful management environment. Unfortunately, unless the configuration is saved, the environment will have to be reconstructed from scratch each session.

Saving the current configuration of .msc files is as simple as selecting Save or Save As from the Console menu in the main MMC window. Saved .msc files can be opened from the Console menu, or they can be used to start up the MMC with the .msc file configuration via file associations using applications like Windows Explorer. They can also be opened by adding a shortcut to the file on the desktop or in a system menu. The default save location is Start | Programs | Administrative Tools.

NOTE: The saved configuration includes the selected snap-ins as well as the child window layout. Multiple configurations can be handy for dealing with subnetwork management or quickly viewing administrative details related to debugging a network management problem. Remember, snap-ins are not restricted to Active Directory tools.

MMC will check to see if the current snap-in configuration has been changed before it exits. If a change has occurred, MMC will prompt to save the configuration as an .msc file.

Dealing with Multiple MMC Child Windows

Being able to deal with many snap-ins at once is useful, but it can also complicate navigation to specific items managed by different snap-ins because of the hierarchical structure of the navigation window. MMC supports multiple child windows to make such navigation simpler.

There are two ways to create a new child window. The first is to select New Window in the Window menu. This opens a new window with the same set of snap-ins as the current window. The snap-ins in this child window display the same information as the other windows. The difference between them is what details are displayed in the child window. For example, expanding the Active Directory Domain and Trusts snap-in can fill up the child window with details that cause the other snap-ins to be hidden. Of course, scrolling up the contents of the window will reveal these hidden details and hide the Active Directory Domain and Trusts snap-in details. By using two child windows, each window can display the details the user is interested in viewing. Switching between windows is just a mouse click away.

NOTE: The effect of viewing different parts of the environment becomes more important as the number of details increases. Keep in mind that all the child windows display the same information with a different view. Changing an attribute in one child window may change the information that's displayed in another window.

The second way to create a new child window is to use the right mouse button menu for snap-ins and most snap-in items. Check for the New Window From Here menu item. This will create a new child window, but it will be from the point of the selected snap-in or snap-in item instead of the Console Root of the first child window.

NOTE: Selecting New Window From Here from the right mouse button menu for the Console Root is the same as selecting Window | New Window.

The main difference between the first approach and the second is that the root for the new window of the second approach is not the Console Root. In this case, it is not possible to navigate higher in the hierarchy shown in the initial child window. Restricted navigation can still be handy. For example, the DNS snap-in can display all the DNS servers within a domain. Using New Window From Here, each server can now be displayed in its own child window.

The typical window organization actions are available. For example, selecting Windows | Cascade organizes the child windows as shown in Figure 10-4.

Restricting MMC Access and Operation

The MMC operation mode presented thus far is called *author mode*. It is possible to restrict author mode to a select number of individuals using Windows 2000's normal security support. It is also possible to restrict access to specific snap-ins. This can be useful to DNS network administrators who want to restrict access to the DNS snap-in or possibly specific DNS servers.

To control MMC access, perform the following steps:

1. Start up MMC in author mode.

2. Select Console | Add/Remove Snap-in.

3. Click on the Add button in the Add/Remove Snap-in window.

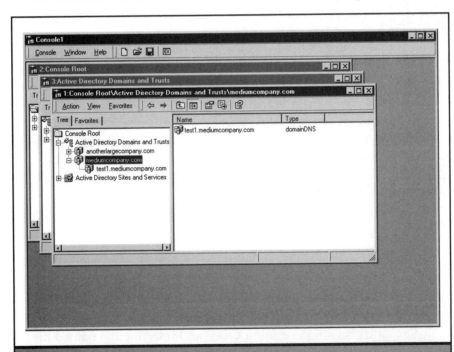

Figure 10-4.   Cascaded child MMC windows

4. Locate the Group Policy snap-in in the Add Standalone Snap-in window.

5. Click on the Add button in the Add Standalone Snap-in window.

6. Select the object to manage in the Select Group Policy Object window. This will usually be the Local Computer.

7. Click the Close button in the Add Standalone Snap-in window.

8. Click on the OK button in the Add/Remove Snap-in window.

9. Select the Local Computer Policy item in the navigation window to display the MMC entry found under Local Computer Policy | User Configuration | Administrative Templates | Windows Components | Microsoft Management Console.

10. Select Restrict The User From Entering Author Mode in the right window pane and, using the right mouse menu, select the Properties menu item. The options are Not Configured, Enabled, or Disabled. Enabled prevents users from using author mode.

Figure 10-5 shows the expanded Local Computer Policy items with author mode restrictions enabled. More selective restrictions can be managed using the Restricted/Permitted snap-in entry in the right window pane. We will not go into all the details of MMC management, but the ones presented thus far should be sufficient to see how the control can be exercised and where these settings can be found.

Command Line Arguments

MMC can be started with a limited number of command line options. The general syntax is

mmc path\filename.msc [/a][/s]

This opens a new console window using the specified .msc configuration file. This is the same as starting MMC with no arguments and choosing Console | Open and selecting the named file.

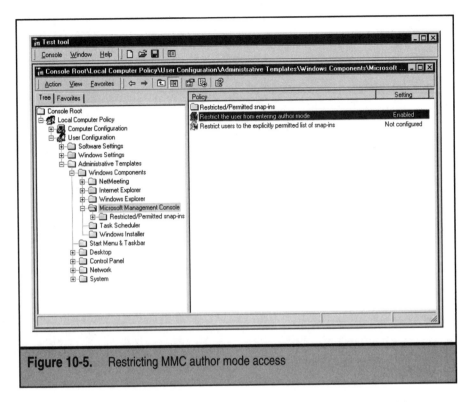

Figure 10-5.   Restricting MMC author mode access

The /a option indicates that the configuration file should be opened in author mode. The standard .msc configuration files for tools such as DNS and DHCP are set up so that they do not start in author mode by default. Using the /a option allows these configurations to be modified through the addition of snap-ins.

The /s option simply eliminates the standard MMC splash screen.

Console Mode

Author mode is the only console mode that has been discussed thus far. While in author mode, it is possible to change the mode associated with an MMC configuration for the next file for which the configuration file is used. This mode is accessed by choosing Console | Options. This brings up the Options window, as shown in Figure 10-6.

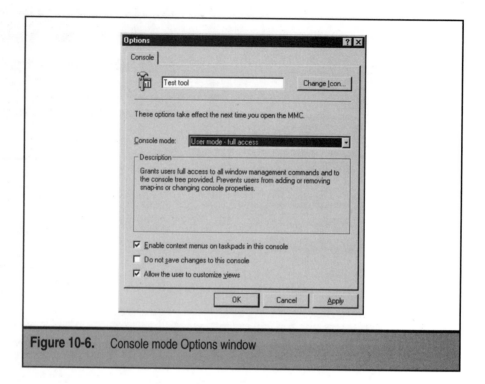

Figure 10-6. Console mode Options window

The four console modes include:

▼ Author mode

■ User mode – full access

■ User mode – limited access, multiple window

▲ User mode – limited access, single window

We have already discussed author mode. User mode allows various degrees of access to the various snap-ins that have already been added to a configuration file in author mode. User mode – full access allows all options to be used, but snap-ins cannot be added or removed. User mode – limited access, multiple window restricts users from using some of the features we have not discussed, including use of tasks and the task pad. User mode – limited access, single window prevents the creation of additional child windows.

This mode is often used to present administrators who have selective responsibilities with only one snap-in.

The MMC is covered throughout the rest of this book since most Windows 2000 management, including Active Directory, DNS, DHCP, and WINS management, is done using MMC snap-ins. The remainder of this chapter addresses the most commonly used Active Directory snap-ins and their relationship to DNS services. The snap-ins presented typically have more features and address more aspects of Windows 2000 than what we present here since our presentation is primarily targeted at the snap-ins' relationship to DNS services.

NOTE: Other MMC aspects not discussed in this book include formatting of information presented by snap-ins, such as what columns are displayed. This type of customization is described in the online help for MMC and associated MMC snap-ins.

MMC SNAP-IN FOR DOMAINS AND TRUSTS

The MMC snap-in for Domains and Trusts handles Active Directory domains and trusts between Active Directory and non-Active Directory domains. The configuration of the trusts between Active Directory domains is set up automatically when Active Directory is installed and domains are created. These trusts are transitive, as discussed in Chapter 4.

The default Domains and Trusts snap-in MMC console window can be accessed using Start | Programs | Administrative Tools | Active Directory Domains and Trusts. This brings up the MMC console shown in Figure 10-7. The snap-in can also be added to an existing console configuration running in author mode, as discussed in the previous section.

NOTE: The MMC window shown in Figure 10-7 is operating in User mode – limited access, single window. Additional windows cannot be opened, nor can additional snap-ins be added.

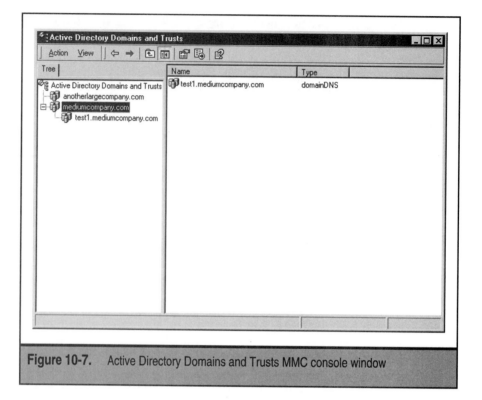

Figure 10-7. Active Directory Domains and Trusts MMC console window

The domains listed in the navigation pane of the child window are Active Directory domains for the currently selected Active Directory domain forest. Two domain trees are shown in Figure 10-7, including mediumcompany.com and anotherlargecompany.com. Expanding a top level domain reveals child domains such as test1.mediumcompany.com.

Active Directory domains cannot be created or deleted from this snap-in. This can only be done using the Windows 2000 Configure Your Server Wizard, as covered in a number of earlier chapters. Instead, the snap-in is used to manage domains and to create and manage additional trust relationships. Both of these are accessed by selecting a domain and then selecting an item from the right mouse button menu.

Selecting the Manage item from the menu provides access to the User and Computers MMC snap-in for the respective domain. The Properties item provides access to a domain's trust and management information. The initial page of the tabbed dialog box presented with this selection is shown in Figure 10-8. The General page is presented first.

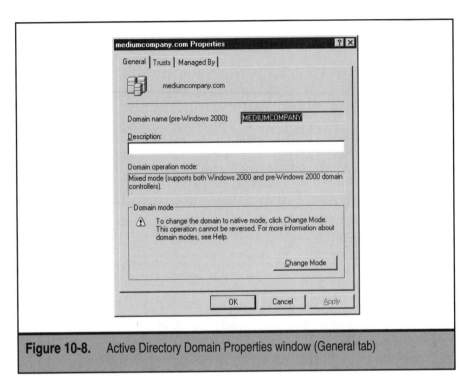

Figure 10-8.   Active Directory Domain Properties window (General tab)

The only major item of interest is the Change Mode button. This allows the domain to be changed from mixed mode to native mode. This is not a change that should be made casually, as it is not reversible. Mixed mode is the default when the domain is created. This mode allows inclusion of non-Windows 2000 systems such as Windows NT workstations and servers. Determining when to convert to native mode is a discussion that is beyond the scope of this book but, in general, it is a shift that occurs only after a major portion or the entire network has been migrated to Windows 2000 and Active Directory. Once converted to native mode, the Windows 2000 clients and servers will be inaccessible to non-Windows 2000 computers such as Windows 9x and Windows NT clients.

Selecting the Trusts tab presents Figure 10-9. The trusts shown in the example include transitive trusts created by the Windows 2000 Configure Your Server Wizard when the domains, domain tree, and domain forest were created, as well as a nontransitive trust example for a non-Windows 2000 domain (ntdomain1, in this example). The latter is used with Windows NT servers that do not support the Windows 2000 Kerberos authentication system.

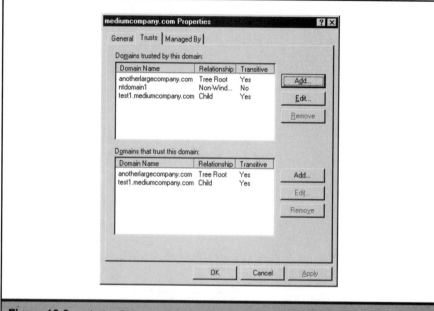

Figure 10-9. Active Directory Domain Properties window (Trusts tab)

Default transitive trusts will appear between root domains and child domains. Additional transitive trusts can be created by clicking on the Add button. To do this, the name of the domain and the domain management password are required. Typically, transitive trusts between different domains in a tree and forest are created when communication between the domains is frequent and authentication through the domain tree structure is inefficient.

Nontransitive trusts with domains outside the Active Directory domain forest allow access to other domains, but a trust between the respective domain and the local domain must also be created for bidirectional authentication.

NOTE: Trusts are needed for management communication between domains. Trusts are not required for nonmanagement related communication between domains. For example, a trust is not required between domain A and domain B if a workstation in domain A is accessing a Web server in domain B, assuming that domain-level authentication is not in use. This would be the case for non-Windows NT or non-Windows 2000 Web servers or if this type of Web server was either allowing Anonymous access or using the Challenge Handshake Access Protocol (CHAP).

In general, trust relationships affect only management of remote DNS services or other administration interaction outside of the domain forest. Transitive trust relationships allow administration in the domain forest within the limits provided by the current security settings for the user performing the administrative chores.

Finally, we look at the Managed By tab shown in Figure 10-10. A single user is designated as the manager for a domain. The information presented is the same information associated with a user record and can be modified by the Users and Computers MMC snap-in discussed in the "MMC Snap-in for Users and Computers" section. This tab provides informational details only and does not change the security controls associated with domain and trust management. The user is usually an administrator.

MMC SNAP-IN FOR SITES AND SERVICES

The MMC snap-in for Sites and Services handles Active Directory sites, well connected subnets, and site-related Active Directory services—not to be confused with server-based services such as the Windows 2000 DNS service or the Windows 2000 file and print

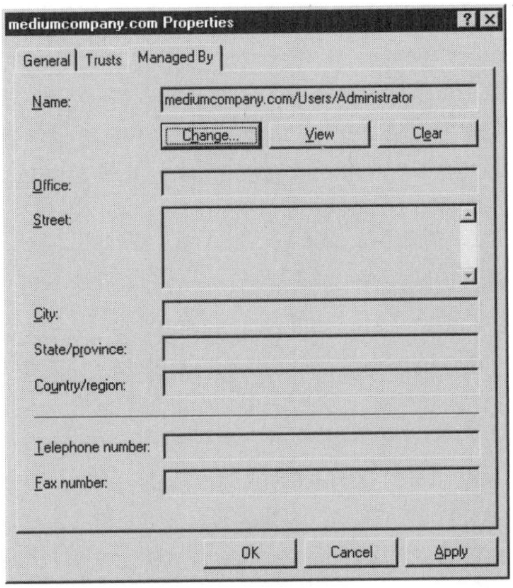

Figure 10-10.   Active Directory Domain Properties window (Managed By tab)

services. The primary purpose of the Sites and Services snap-in is to manage the Active Directory database and Active Directory global catalog replication. The effect of this replication is directly related to DNS Active Directory–integrated zones. This is of particular interest when domains span sites.

Site and replication schedule design allow physical network and WAN topology to impact the operation of a logical Active Directory domain forest design. For example, network bandwidth on a WAN is typically limited compared to a local network. Replication of information over a WAN should occur less often than on the local network if the amount of Active Directory information being replicated will have a significant impact on the amount bandwidth used for replication.

How replication occurs is a detail that the network administrators can control. For example, in a well connected WAN, alternate connections are available between different sites. In this case, one connection may be preferred over another because of bandwidth considerations. Alternate connections can be used if a preferred connection fails or is not responsive.

This section addresses the general operation of the Sites and Services snap-in and considerations regarding Windows 2000 DNS service support for Active Directory–integrated zones.

NOTE: Windows 2000 Active Directory site replication has no effect on the operation or performance of non-Active Directory–integrated zones. This includes primary and secondary DNS zones.

REMEMBER: Replication of Active Directory information occurs throughout a domain forest, but Active Directory–integrated zones may only be used within a domain, not across domains or up or down domain trees.

TIP: Site considerations regarding replication will be of little concern for a small network model with a single site, but replication schedules should be examined for multiple sites of medium or large models.

Network Circuit Maps

Network circuit maps come into play when a WAN is part of a network. Very large international companies can have large, complex network circuit maps, while a small, distributed organization may have one or two circuits between a pair of sites.

Circuits can be switched, nonswitched, or shared. ISDN dial-up connections are an example of switched circuits; these connections are often transient. They are used as necessary, such as when Active Directory replication occurs, and are often used as backup to nonswitched circuits.

Nonswitched circuits are dedicated connections from one site to another. T1 lines (1536Kbps) are an example of nonswitched circuits. Nonswitched circuits are used by most large WANs because of speed and reliability concerns. Multiple nonswitched circuits between the same sites are often grouped together to increase total bandwidth between the sites. Nonswitched circuits are generally used when organizations want control over the connection as well as the bandwidth that will be dedicated to the connection, as opposed to switched circuits, where connection is not guaranteed, or shared circuits, where bandwidth is often not guaranteed.

NOTE: Nonswitched circuits are often used for information other than network communication. For example, a T1 line could be used for voice and network communication.

Shared circuits are connections to a shared network like the Internet or a frame relay network. Logical, usually dedicated, connections are made through the shared network between two local networks. In many cases, the shared network connection is made using virtual private network (VPN) software that uses strong authentication methods and data encryption to ensure secure communication.

NOTE: WAN engineers and administrators often handle site-to-site communication. DNS managers and network administrators should work with WAN engineers when designing and managing a Windows 2000 network so that site-to-site communication can be done effectively.

WAN connections will handle routed IP traffic. Knowing the bandwidth of connections, as well as where they are located, is important to both Active Directory operation and DNS service operation when information must pass from one site to another.

For logical Active Directory connections, bridge server placement will be important. A bridge server is a domain controller that acts as a server for outgoing or incoming Active Directory information. This information is then passed on to other servers within the site. A comparable configuration for DNS secondary zone replication occurs between DNS servers, although the replicated information is specific to the DNS servers, whereas Active Directory information supports a wide variety of Active Directory services.

NOTE: Placement of bridge servers or DNS servers with respect to WAN circuits should take into consideration the logical connection speed of the LAN versus the physical location of a site connection. For example, a circuit that is terminated at a router that is attached to a network will allow a bridge server to be located anywhere on the network, as most networks operate at the same speed regardless of the placement of individual nodes. LANs often have various bandwidth connections such as high-speed backbones and slower speed connections to workstations. In this case, the location of the router and the bridge server can be critical, but placement is still logical with respect to the connections available in the network.

Site-to-Site Transport Links

Windows 2000 Active Directory can use SMTP (e-mail) and IP connections for replication purposes. Windows 2000 DNS service and most other DNS services support IP connections for replication of secondary DNS zones. Secondary DNS zone replication uses standard protocols. Active Directory replication is specific to Windows 2000 systems.

The Sites and Services MMC snap-in is used to specify how Active Directory can use site-to-site links. Multiple links between two sites provide redundancy and improved aggregate throughput for Active Directory replication.

NOTE: Active Directory site-to-site replication information is compressed prior to transmission. Compression ratios of 10–15 percent are typical. Active Directory also minimizes replication time by exchanging only changes. Active Directory's ability to use multiple site-to-site links can also improve the speed at which information flows between sites.

Active Directory allows costs to be assigned to site links. A slow link is normally given a higher cost than a high-speed link. Preferences are given to low-cost routes, thereby allowing a mist of high- and low-speed links, with the latter being used as backups.

A typical configuration with a site-to-site link is where multiple domain controllers reside at both sites. In this case, bridgehead servers are normally specified at each site. A bridgehead server is an Active Directory domain controller. Replication information flows between these bridgehead servers and is then distributed to other servers within the site. This approach makes it so that replication information passes from one site to another only once.

Multiple bridgehead servers can be designated, but only one is the preferred point of contact; the others are used as backups. If no bridgehead servers are specified, Active Directory chooses an Active Directory domain controller.

NOTE: The choice of bridgehead servers for IP links is usually done with respect to the speed of site-to-site links. The choice of bridgehead servers for SMTP links is often done with respect to the ability to support an SMTP link since SMTP links are often used through firewalls.

Making Changes to Sites and Services

Sites and replication services are managed from the Sites and Services MMC snap-in. Choose Start I Programs I Administrative Tools I Active Directory Sites and Services to display the window shown in Figure 10-11.

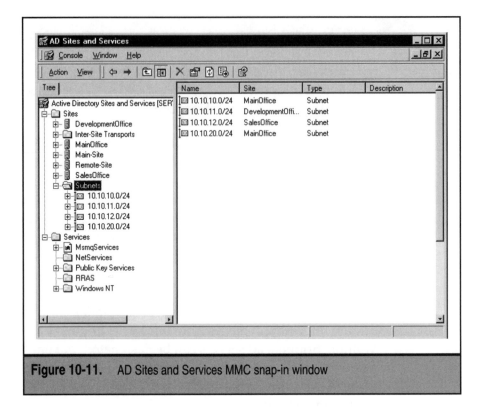

Figure 10-11. AD Sites and Services MMC snap-in window

Not surprisingly, there are two containers in the Sites and Services MMC snap-in window, a Sites container and a Services container. The Sites container addresses site details such as site-to-site links and Active Directory domain controller servers within a site. The Services container is used to manage Active Directory services.

There are three main items handled by the Site container: InterSite Transports, the Subnets for the site, and a list of sites.

Under the InterSite Transports are the IP and SMTP connection methods. Under each connection method is a list of named links. The connection methods are not shown in Figure 10-11, although expanding a site like Main Site will reveal these details. A site link can link more than one site, but a site link must contain at least two sites. Site links must be set up after sites have been defined.

The Subnets section is a list of IP subnets found in the network. These subnets do not control DNS, DHCP, or fixed IP addressing for a site but rather indicate to Active Directory where IP addresses are expected to be found. A subnet is specified in terms of a net mask and an IP address that specifies the fixed portion of the net mask. For example, 10.10.11.0/24 specifies a range of IP addresses from 10.10.11.0 to 10.10.11.255 with a 24-bit net mask. This is the typical syntax used with IP addressing. A particular subnet must be associated with a single site. Subnets cannot span multiple sites. A site may contain multiple subnets, and a site may be defined without defining a subnet.

NOTE: The subnet restrictions are similar to those imposed by most routers or switches used to implement sites and site links. In theory, it is possible to set up workstations or servers with arbitrary IP addresses, but in practice the problems this causes makes doing so impractical.

At least one site always exists. A default site is created when the first Active Directory domain is created. All domain controller servers are placed into the default site as they are set up. Servers can be moved from one site to another using the Sites and Service MMC snap-in. A server can only be found in one site, although, as mentioned earlier, servers from a specific domain may be spread across multiple sites.

NOTE: All references in the Sites and Service MMC snap-in to servers in a site refer to Active Directory domain controllers, as these are the only Windows 2000 servers of concern to us with respect to sites and Active Directory replication.

Sites can be renamed after they are created, unlike Active Directory domains, which can only be deleted and added. A Servers container appears under each site entry. The Servers container contains a list of Active Directory domain controller servers that reside at the site.

To display the Properties window for a server as in Figure 10-12, select the desired server entry and use the right mouse button menu to select the Properties item. This window displays a server that is set up as a bridgehead server. The designation is protocol-specific, and a bridgehead server can be set up to use both protocols.

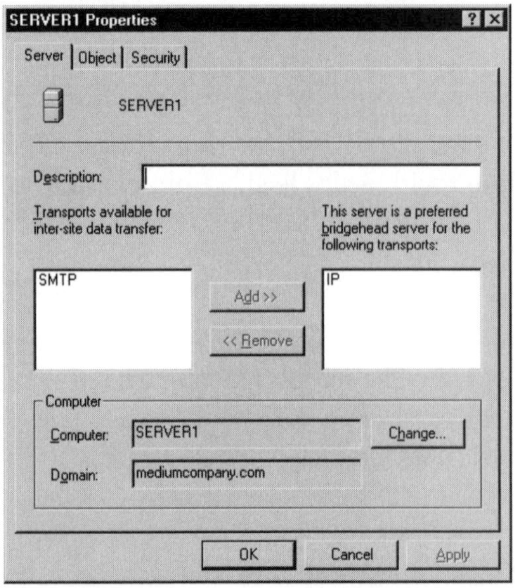

Figure 10-12.   Sites and Services MMC snap-in Server Properties window

Once the sites and servers are in place, it is possible to set up links between sites. These are found under the respective InterSite Transports protocol, such as IP. Each site link has a name. The Properties window for the site link, as shown in Figure 10-13, is accessed with the right mouse button menu and the Properties entry for the site link.

The replication schedule is associated with the site-to-site link. Replication is set up based on a schedule, which is accessible by the Change Schedule button, and by filling in the number of minutes in the Replicate Every field. The sites involved in the replication using the link are shown in the right list box under Sites In This Site Link. The Cost field provides a relative ranking for the use of the link. Another link can be defined with the same set of sites and even the same cost and schedule. Often the cost or schedule is different, which allows Active Directory to choose between links.

Once the sites and servers are set up, Active Directory handles replication automatically. As for DNS Active Directory–integrated zone replication, it is just part of the package. Nothing special has to

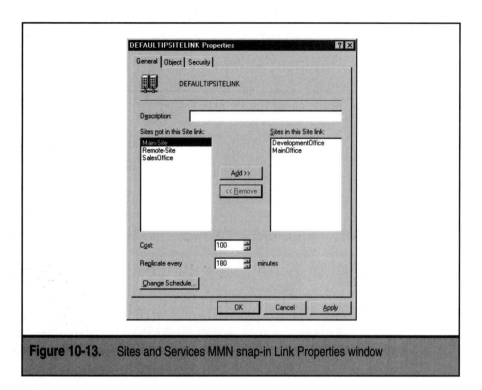

Figure 10-13. Sites and Services MMN snap-in Link Properties window

be done to make it happen. On the other hand, DNS managers need to know how often replication occurs because this will affect how often DNS servers will receive updated information regarding these integrated zones. In some cases, DNS managers will not have control over the Active Directory replication details discussed here. This may have an impact on whether Active Directory–integrated zone replication is chosen over secondary zone replication. DNS managers always have control over the latter.

We will not delve into the Services aspect of the Sites and Services MMC snap-in because they have no impact on DNS services. The types of services managed by this snap-in include services like Net Services and the Public Key Services.

MMC SNAP-IN FOR USERS AND COMPUTERS

The MMC snap-in for Users and Computers handles Active Directory objects such as users, groups, and computers. It also handles resource objects such as shares, printers, and the all-important

Active Directory organizational units (OU), which may contain any of the aforementioned items. OUs are indispensable in larger Windows 2000 networks as they partition objects into logical groupings.

The Windows Explorer is used to locate objects. The Windows Explorer can send e-mail to users, locate a user's home page, browse a shared folder, or use a shared printer.

Active Directory groups are also used for security purposes. The Domain Admins group contains a list of users with administrative rights. Groups are also where DNS, DHCP, and WINS comes into play. For example, by default, DNS administration is restricted to members of the DNSAdmins group. DHCP is handled by members of the DHCP Administrators group.

Actually, Active Directory–based security for Windows 2000 is a bit more complicated, as each Active Directory object can have multiple groups or users associated with it, including inherited associations, and each user or group can have individualized permissions. For example, the default Windows 2000 DNS service setup is associated with a number of security groups including DNSAdmins, Domain Admins, and Enterprise Admins. It is even possible to restrict dynamic DHCP updates by computer if desired.

Given the importance of security and its link to DNS, DHCP, and WINS, DNS administrators should be knowledgeable about users, groups, OUs, and Active Directory–based security and how it is managed with the Users and Computers MMC snap-in. This section provides a brief overview that provides sufficient details for a DNS administrator to determine which users have access to DNS-related (DNS, DHCP, WINS, etc.) resources and how to adjust the settings, assuming they have sufficient access rights to perform these operations. More detailed coverage of Active Directory security and the use of the Users and Computers MMC snap-in is beyond the scope of this book.

Start the Users and Computers MMC snap-in by choosing Start | Programs | Administrative Tools | Active Directory Users and Computers. This presents a window like the one shown in Figure 10-14. Under an Active Directory domain (mediumcompany.com in the example), the Users folder shows a large list of security groups. These

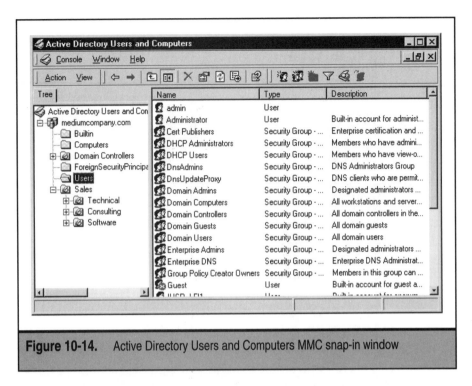

Figure 10-14.   Active Directory Users and Computers MMC snap-in window

are created by default when Active Directory is installed and the initial administrative user is created. Additional users and groups can be added to this folder, but typically an organization will have a number of top-level OUs defined within the Active Directory domain, and these OUs can contain groups, users, and other objects.

The Windows Explorer provides a similar presentation of the Active Directory hierarchy, although its operations are more limited in some ways and more extensive in others compared to the Users and Computers MMC snap-in. Figure 10-15 shows what the Windows Explorer presents on the same domain shown in Figure 10-14. E-mail can be sent to a user by selecting the matching icon and selecting Send Mail from the right mouse button menu. A printer can be used in a similar fashion: just select Connect from the right mouse button menu.

The Windows Explorer is limited because it cannot create new users or groups. It can just browse them. On the other hand, the Windows Explorer can open shared folders and then create new

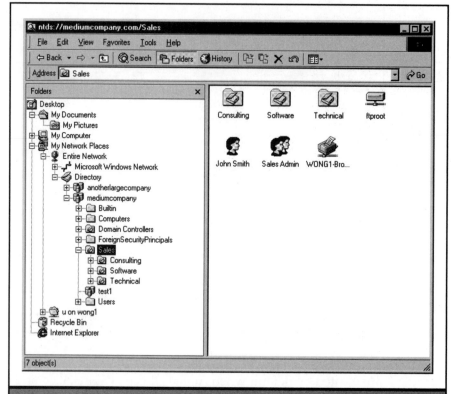

Figure 10-15.   Windows Explorer viewing an Active Directory hierarchy

subfolders, copy files, etc.—all jobs that the Users and Computers MMC snap-in will not do. Luckily, the Users and Computers MMC snap-in can start up the Windows Explorer using the right mouse button or Action menus when an OU or shared folder is selected.

NOTE: Active Directory shared folders can be placed anywhere in the Active Directory domain hierarchy regardless of where the shared folder actually resides. This provides Active Directory users with location transparency since an administrator can move a shared folder from one server to another simply by changing the shared folder object so its reference is to the new server. This is done by adjusting the Properties for a shared folder object.

OUs are created like any other Active Directory object found in the Users and Computers MMC snap-in. First, the container object is selected. This can be the domain, a folder like the Users folder, or an OU. Selecting Action | New presents a submenu of object types that can be created including Users, Groups, and OUs. The same options are available via the right mouse button menu under the New menu item.

Users can be added to groups from the user Properties window that has a Member Of tab. The Member Of Properties page shows a list of groups that the user is a member of; the Add and Remove buttons are used to change group membership. Conversely, a group object's Property page contains a Members tab. The Members Property page contains a list of members that can include users and groups. The Add and Remove buttons on this page are used to change group membership, too.

NOTE: A group's scope can be domain local, global, or universal. A group's use can be for security or for distribution. The groups discussed here are global security groups.

For DNS administrators, the users and groups that can use and manage the DNS services start here in the Active Directory Users and Computers MMC snap-in, but we need to look at the DNS MMC snap-in to see where the actual security list resides. Chapter 11 has more details on this snap-in, but for now take a look at Figure 10-16. This is an example of the Properties page for a zone managed by the Windows 2000 DNS server. It was accessed from the DNS snap-in. The zone was selected and then the Properties option was selected from the right mouse button menu. The Properties option is also found on the Action menu when the zone is selected. We then selected the Security tab on the Properties window.

The area to note is the list of names in the security page. These names should look familiar, with groups like DNSAdmins and Domain Admins. The Permissions list in the bottom half of the window shows the properties for the selected name. Each name has its own properties associated with it.

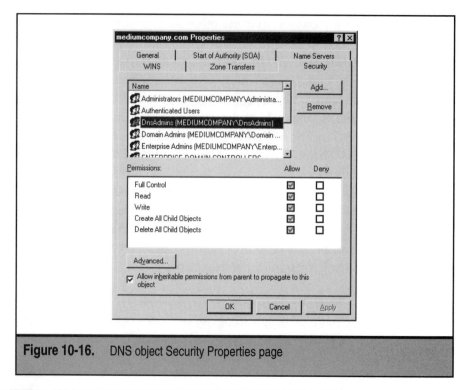

Figure 10-16. DNS object Security Properties page

NOTE: As with all of the Active Directory security, inheritance plays a major part. This allows the global DNSAdmins group to manage DNS services that are found lower in an Active Directory domain tree.

Changing the members in a group associated with a DNS service or zone using the Users and Computers MMC snap-in affects who can access and manage the respective DNS resource. DNS administrators typically have access to the Users and Computer MMC snap-in, but they may be restricted to viewing. If this is the case, then user and group management is delegated to another person or group and a DNS administrator will have to work with them if security changes are needed.

Cross-domain DNS management is possible if transitive trusts link the domain of the user and the DNS service, as with two domains in an Active Directory tree or forest. In addition, the user or a group that the user is a part of must be found in the DNS service's security list. A user that will be regularly managing a DNS service across a tree may prefer to have a trust established directly between the domains using the Domain and Trust MMC snap-in. This will allow faster authentication when the service needs to be managed by the user.

It is also possible to manage Windows 2000 DNS services outside the Active Directory forest if explicit trusts are configured. This will typically be a rare occurrence, as most DNS management will be within the local Active Directory forest.

SUMMARY

The Microsoft Management Console (MMC) is a ubiquitous part of Windows 2000, and understanding its features and operation will be important to any DNS or Active Directory administrator.

The Active Directory MMC snap-ins discussed in this chapter will be of limited use to DNS administrators, but they are very important within these limits. The Domains and Trusts MMC snap-in provides a way to improve authentication performance between domains within an Active Directory forest; this is handy for DNS administrators that handle cross-domain DNS management.

The Sites and Services MMC plug-in provides DNS administrators with an overview of sites and links between sites. While a DNS administrator may not implement or manage this structure in a multiple site network, they must be aware of the structure, especially when domains span sites and Active Directory–integrated zones are used. Understanding the type, bandwidth, and location of links between sites can also be useful when setting up secondary DNS zone replication.

The Users and Computers MMC plug-in provides control over users and groups. This is important because it is this set of users and groups that are used to specify the security settings for DNS-related services including DNS, DHCP, and WINS. Improper security configuration can be too restrictive, thereby preventing proper operation, or too loose, allowing irresponsible access to DNS-related services. While default settings are usually sufficient for small networks with a single domain on only a few DNS servers, a large network will often have various DNS security requirements with a number of different DNS administrators sharing the DNS management chores.

CHAPTER 11

Configuring Windows 2000 DNS Using Microsoft Management Console

This chapter takes a look at the DNS snap-in for the Microsoft Management Console (MMC). It addresses how to find the various features supported by the snap-in. Check out Chapter 10 for general MMC operation. The DNS snap-in is just one of many.

The DNS snap-in appears in many of the chapters in this book. For example, Chapter 12 addresses DNS security. This chapter covers where these features are found; the other chapters address how to use them. Some of the details addressed in this chapter are how to set up an Active Directory–integrated zone and how to manage Windows 2000 DNS services remotely.

The default method to start up the MMC DNS snap-in is via Start | Programs | Administration Tools | DNS. Figure 11-1 shows a typical startup window. All the interesting items are found under the Forward Lookup Zones and Reverse Lookup Zones. There is also a third item, Cached Lookups, that will appear if the Advanced menu item is selected in the View menu.

The window shown in Figure 11-1 shows a single child window and a single DNS service. The tree has been expanded under the DNS server to show the Forward and Reverse Lookup Zones. This is a typical setup for a small network or the first time the DNS snap-in is used in a larger network with multiple DNS servers. Additional DNS servers can be added to the first, which allows quick access to multiple servers.

In addition to viewing multiple servers, the DNS MMC snap-in can display information in multiple child windows, and other snap-ins can be mixed with the DNS MMC snap-in to provide quick access to related services. The section "Multiple MMC Child Windows and Snap-ins" shows how this is done.

WHERE IS EVERYTHING?

The DNS snap-in's child window Action menu is selection-dependent. The Action menu is the same as the one you get by pressing the right mouse button. This section takes a look at each of the menu selections

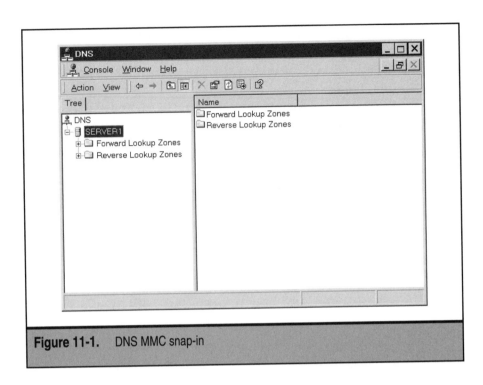

Figure 11-1.   DNS MMC snap-in

and their actions in general. Many of these actions are covered in more detail in other parts of the book, including this chapter.

The Action menu changes depending upon what item is selected in the child window. For example, the following illustration shows the menu that is displayed when the DNS root is selected (again, you can view the Action menu by either clicking on the menu itself or pressing the right mouse button).

The menu has a number of common items. The first is Connect To Computer, which is used to manage another DNS server. This is covered in the section "Accessing Another DNS Server" later in this chapter.

The View submenu displays the same View menu that you get if you select View from the toolbar, shown next. The New Window From Here item is discussed in Chapter 10.

The Refresh menu item causes the snap-in to refresh its data. Changes can occur for a variety of reasons such as a dynamic DNS update or another user managing an Active Directory–integrated DNS zone from another workstation. Export List provides a way of saving the contents of the list pane on the right side of the window opposite the navigation pane. Finally, there is context-sensitive, online Help.

The DNS snap-in has the potential for displaying an enormous amount of information. The hierarchical structure of the navigation pane helps to manage the number of entries. The View menu shown in Figure 11-3 provides additional control over presentation.

Most of the options found in the View menu are common to other MMC snap-ins. The Choose Columns menu item is sensitive to the item selected and displays the Choose Column dialog box. For example, the Name column is the only column available when the DNS root or a DNS server is selected. The columns for the Forward Lookup Zones include Name, Type, and Status. The columns for a zone are Name, Type, and Data. The Choose Column dialog box lets you select which columns will be displayed and in what order. This feature is more useful in snap-ins with many columns, but it can be handy with the DNS snap-in when multiple child windows are being displayed in a tiled layout.

The layout options are identical to those found in standard Windows 2000 applications such as Windows Explorer. These include Large Icons, Small Icons, List, and Detail.

The Advanced menu item has a check mark in front of it when enabled. Selecting Advanced toggles the setting. When checked, the Cached Lookups item is listed below each server entry.

The Filter menu item presents a dialog box that lets you select the maximum number of items to display. Items past the maximum are ignored. You also get the option of filtering by the name column.

The Customize menu item displays the DNS Customize window, shown next. The Customize window is not too interesting; it controls whether or not you can view items like the Standard toolbar and the Status bar. The options in the dialog box are self-explanatory.

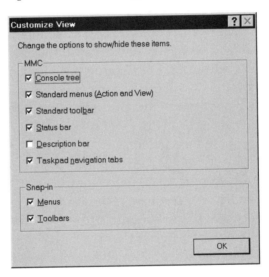

DNS Server Action Menu

The DNS server Action menu is available when a DNS server is selected in the navigation pane. The DNS server Action menu provides access to DNS server-wide features such as the DNS cache, aging and scavenging for dynamic DNS support, and the server's Property page dialog box.

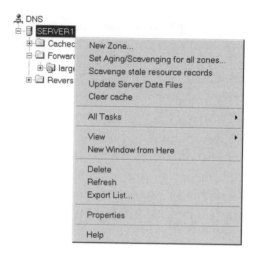

The New Zone menu item is used to create a new DNS zone in the DNS Forward Zone Lookup. Selecting this menu item starts up the New Zone Wizard; you can also start up this wizard by selecting New Zone from the DNS Forward Zone Lookup Action menu. The details of the New Zone Wizard's operation are covered in the sections "Working with an Active Directory–Integrated DNS Zone," "Working with a Primary DNS Zone," and "Working with a Secondary DNS Zone" later in this chapter.

The Set Aging/Scavenging For All Zones and Scavenging State Resource Records menu items control aging and scavenging settings that handle DNS resource records added via dynamic DNS updates. The details of these items are addressed in the section "Aging and Scavenging" later in this chapter.

The Update Server Data Files menu item forces any changes made via the DNS snap-in out to the files that were used to initialize the DNS server. This primarily affects any primary DNS zones where the information is maintained in a file on disk versus the Active Directory–integrated zones. Secondary DNS zone files are unaffected as they are updated automatically—although it is possible to refresh the secondary DNS zone files from the Action menu when a secondary DNS zone is selected.

The Clear Cache menu item clears the Cached Lookups of all items. This is handy for debugging purposes to see what happens when an item is not in the cache. It can also free up disk space used by the cache, which can grow rather large.

NOTE: Clearing the cache can affect performance and network traffic when the DNS server is connected to other DNS servers or the Internet by a low-speed WAN connection such as a branch office that's connected to a main office by a 56Kbps modem or frame relay link or a 128Kbps ISDN link. This occurs because the cache builds up incrementally as requests are made by local clients over a period of time. This process must then repeat itself to refill the cache. Clearing the cache when high-speed connections are used tends to have minimal effect on network performance and a limited effect on DNS resolution response time.

The All Tasks submenu is used to control the DNS service. The submenu includes the following items: Start, Stop, Pause, Resume, and Restart. Only the appropriate items will be available. For example, if the DNS service is not running, the Start menu item will be the only one available. Selecting Restart or Stop and Start for a DNS service is one way to force it to use updates that were performed on its primary DNS zone files when these changes were not made using the DNS snap-in.

The All Tasks submenu has no provision for controlling the system startup options for the DNS service. This must be done using the Windows 2000 Services application by choosing Start | Programs | Administrative Tools | Services. The Services application can also start and stop the DNS service, but it is the Services' General page of the Properties window that controls the startup type. The startup type is normally Automatic. The other options are Manual and Disable. The All Tasks submenu tends to be common to all service-based MMC snap-ins.

NOTE: Task-related actions are restricted by the Domain Security Policy and the Local Security Policy applications found in the Start | Programs | Administrative Tools menu. This can be used to prevent unauthorized users from starting and stopping the DNS service.

The New Window From Here menu item is discussed in Chapter 10. It starts up a new child window that is a copy of the state of the current child window. This is handy when you're drilling down in a zone that contains a large number of records or a deep hierarchy when you want to be able to back up quickly so you can look at values at the top of the hierarchy.

The Delete menu item deletes the DNS service. This is a major step, as much of the configuration information can be lost. In general, it is a better idea to stop the DNS service and then change its startup option to Disable, as discussed earlier.

The Refresh menu item refreshes information related to the selected DNS service. This option is often used instead of the DNS root Action | Refresh menu item when multiple DNS services are being monitored. Refreshing a local service is very quick, and it is handy because it lets you see changes made via other source such as dynamic DNS updates or scavenging. However, the process can be very time consuming if a remote DNS service is connected to the local server via a slow speed WAN link.

NOTE: There are also zone and subzone level Action | Refresh menu items. This finer granularity is useful for debugging purposes or when very large zones are being managed.

The Export List and Help menu items provide the standard context level services. This leaves the ever-present Properties menu item. Selecting this, of course, brings up the Properties window for the DNS server. The DNS server Properties window has a number of pages that we will examine individually. Most of the details and the use of the respective page settings are covered in other chapters in the book.

We will start with the Interfaces page shown in Figure 11-2. This controls which IP addresses the DNS server watches for DNS requests. The default is to check all IP addresses, and the typical Windows 2000 server has only one IP address. Multiple IP addresses may be used for a variety of reasons such as when the Windows 2000 server is acting as a proxy server or a firewall and the two network adapters are used, each with its own IP address. Multiple IP addresses can also be used with a single adapter when the server is accessible from different subnets. In this case, the Windows 2000 server may also be acting as a router.

NOTE: The All IP Addresses selection must be used if the DNS server is to handle any dynamically assigned IP addresses. This case is extremely rare for a server, although it can occur when the server has two network connections: one fixed IP address for the local network and a dynamic IP address obtained from an Internet Service Provider. In this case, the typical configuration has the DNS server supporting just its fixed IP address so it will be accessible only from the local network. This does not restrict the DNS server from using the dynamic IP address link to resolve or forward DNS requests. It is also a good practice since exposing the DNS service to the dynamic IP link would allow a system connected by the WAN to query the DNS service and determine which domain names and IP addresses were being used on the other side of the firewall or proxy server.

The Forwarders page shown in Figure 11-3 is used to manage a list of DNS servers that this server will forward requests to. This service is

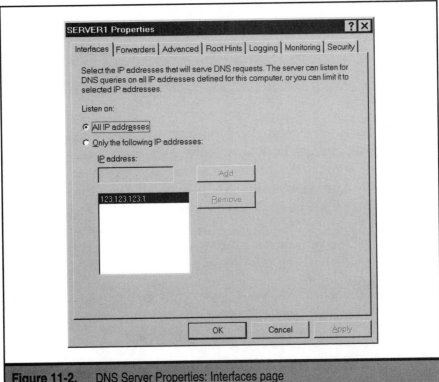

Figure 11-2.   DNS Server Properties: Interfaces page

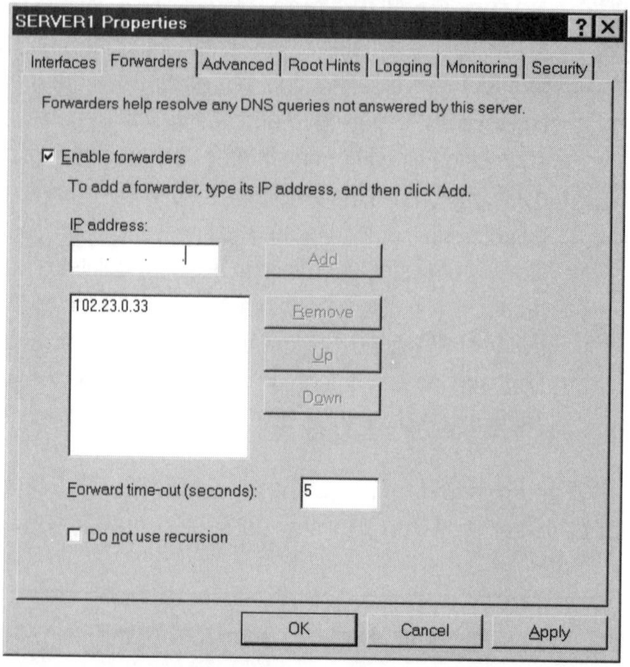

SERVER1 Properties

Interfaces | Forwarders | Advanced | Root Hints | Logging | Monitoring | Security

Forwarders help resolve any DNS queries not answered by this server.

☑ Enable forwarders

To add a forwarder, type its IP address, and then click Add.

IP address:

| · · | Add

102.23.0.33   Remove

Up

Down

Forward time-out (seconds): 5

☐ Do not use recursion

OK   Cancel   Apply

Figure 11-3.   DNS Server Properties: Forwarders page

discussed in more detail in Chapter 16. Forwarding is normally used with multiple DNS servers on a high-speed local network that has a slow link to the Internet or a company intranet at the main office. In this case, a forwarding DNS server will aggregate all requests over the slow link. The other servers forward nonlocal recursive requests to the forwarding DNS server. This approach also utilizes the forwarding DNS server's cache to service all the outgoing requests.

NOTE: The term forwarding DNS server is used to differentiate the servers involved in the scenario describing the forwarding operation. It is not a term normally associated with a DNS server.

The Advanced Properties page shown in Figure 11-4 provides a catch-all list of options that do not fit under the other Properties pages. The default settings for most of the options are sufficient for

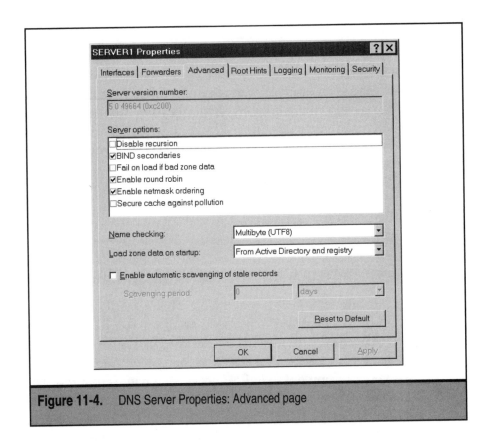

Figure 11-4.   DNS Server Properties: Advanced page

general DNS service operation, and the Reset To Default button is a handy way of restoring the settings to a known configuration. In general, changing the settings should only be done if you understand the implications that such a change will cause.

We will start looking at the rest of the items on the Advanced page from the bottom up. The Enable Automatic Scavenging Of Stale Records is normally reset. When the option is checked, the scavenging period can be set in terms of hours or days. Scavenging is done to remove DNS resource records added by dynamic DNS updates.

Load Zone Data On Startup allows the zone configuration information to be loaded from the Windows 2000 Registry, from a file, or from Active Directory and the registry. The latter is the default choice. It rarely needs to be changed, although loading from a file allows the configuration to be managed through file editing and distribution. This is the way that other DNS servers operate, and it may be suitable in environments where the configuration options are more readily exchanged through files that are distributed by methods such as e-mail or in order to remain compatible with other third-party DNS servers in the network. Loading from the registry only allows configurations to be adjusted by remote registry management.

Name Checking list box determines how domain names will be verified for correctness. The options include:

▼ Strict RFC (ANSI)

■ NonRFC (ANSI)

■ Multibyte (UTF8)

▲ All Names

Multibyte (UTF8) is the default. This provides Unicode support used by Windows 2000. It also handles the standard ASCII character set. Strict RFC provides name checking that is compliant with RFC 1123 and is the best selection for a mixed-mode DNS client and server environment. NonRFC accepts all names that the Strict RFC handles as well as those that it does not, but it will not handle the Unicode names that Multibyte (UTF8) will. Of course with All Names, anything goes. Details on checking name and zone data are covered in Chapter 17.

Finally, there is the list of Server options. These include:

▼ Disable Recursion (default: unchecked)

■ BIND Secondaries (default: checked)

■ Fail On Load If Bad Zone Data (default: unchecked)

■ Enable Round Robin (default: checked)

■ Enable Netmask Ordering (default: checked)

▲ Secure Cache Against Pollution (default: unchecked)

Recursion is enabled by default (i.e., Disable Recursion is unchecked) so that the DNS service will query other DNS servers in response to a client request; otherwise, the DNS service will return a referral that is its closest guess to what the request is. For example, if the client wants to know the IP address for www.mediumcompany.com, and the DNS service knows a DNS server that handles mediumcompany.com zone, then the DNS server address is returned as a referral because recursion is disabled. With recursion enabled, the DNS server is queried for the www.mediumcompany.com IP address and the result is returned to the client.

NOTE: Recursion or referrals are not used if the DNS server can resolve a client's request using local information.

Fast zone transfers for sending secondary zone information to secondary DNS servers is enabled using the BIND Secondaries entry. When checked, a DNS server distributing zone information will put multiple resource records in each TCP record sent to the secondary DNS server. This is efficient because it reduces the number of transfers and the amount of overhead associated with each transfer. The BIND reference in the entry name refers to the Berkeley Internet Name Domain (BIND), a standardized, third-party DNS server that can be found on a variety of platforms. BIND and its operation with Windows 2000 DNS are covered in Chapter 21. BIND 4.9.4 or later supports fast secondary zone transfers.

The Fail On Load If Bad Zone Data option is normally unchecked to allow the DNS server to start up even if one or more pieces of data in one or more zone files are invalid. This will not occur if the contents of the zone files are managed through the DNS snap-in, but it is relatively easy to corrupt a zone file if it is edited using a text editor. It is also possible that the zone file is delivered from another source that generated an incompatible file from the perspective of the Windows 2000 DNS service. This might be the case if a primary zone file was used by both a UNIX-based BIND DNS server and a Windows 2000 DNS service.

One reason to check Fail On Load If Bad Zone Data is to check the validity of an existing set of zone files since the service will not start if a problem is detected. However, it is not a good idea to leave the option checked if the DNS service will not be monitored on a regular basis, especially if any problems are assumed to be minor, as the DNS service simply ignores invalid records.

Multiple resource records can have the same name. For example, www.mediumcompany.com may have multiple resource records with different IP addresses. This is a typical configuration for a server configuration where each Web server contains the same information and round-robin load distribution is done through the DNS server—assuming the Enable Round Robin entry is checked.

If Enable Round Robin is not checked, the list of IP addresses that is returned for a multiple resource record name will be the same each time. If the entry is checked, the list of IP addresses will be rotated by one entry each time. This means that each IP address will eventually be the one at the beginning of the list. The client normally scans the list from the start to the end trying each address until a server responds. In general, clients will be sequentially assigned to each server, thereby distributing the load. It is not sophisticated, but it works. Of course, the multiple resource record entries must be entered into the DNS zone database for this to work.

Enable Netmask Ordering is similar to Enable Round Robin except that rather than a simple rotation of the IP list, the priority scheme for reordering the list is a matching that is based on the IP address and netmask associated with the client. The client's IP address is part of the client's request. Given the following resource records

```
server1    IN    A    10.0.1.13
server1    IN    A    171.121.33.68
server1    IN    A    192.168.0.1
server1    IN    A    171.121.44.68
```

the resulting list of resource records for a client with the address of 171.121.33.1 would be

```
server1    IN    A    171.121.33.68
server1    IN    A    171.121.44.68
server1    IN    A    10.0.1.13
server1    IN    A    192.168.0.1
```

NOTE: Subnet mask reordering takes priority over round robin reordering, although both may be used at the same time. If both are selected, the round robin reordering occurs with respect to the local subnet.

Finally, there is the Secure Cache Against Pollution option. This is unchecked by default and is used to minimize the contents of the cache based on information returned by a referral request when performing a recursive resolution. In particular, a referral that does not exactly match the original request may be used but not cached. For example, a request for the IP address of www.mediumcompany.com might return a referral to a DNS server handling .com or another server that might be handling largecompany.com. In the former case, the match is exact since .com matches a parent domain of www.mediumcompany.com. The DNS server for mediumcompany.com would work as well but the latter does not match because mediumcompany.com and largecompany.com are different domains. Still, because the DNS server handling largecompany.com matches for the root domain, .com, the server may still be able to resolve the client request.

The Root Hints page shown in Figure 11-5 shows a list of the standard root DNS servers on the Internet. The use of the root DNS

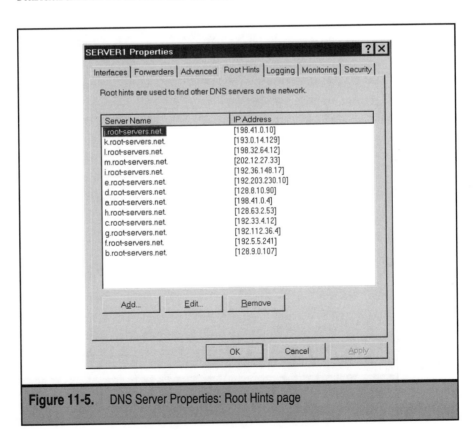

Figure 11-5. DNS Server Properties: Root Hints page

servers is discussed in Chapter 2. In general, these entries do not have to be modified in any fashion unless changes are made to the list of root DNS servers. In that case, new servers can be added.

The Logging page shown in Figure 11-6 is used to enable logging of DNS activity, including client requests. The "DNS Logging" section in this chapter discusses logging in more detail. In general, all entries should be unchecked to disable logging because logging slows down the operation of the DNS service and the server itself. This is one reason for the Reset To Default button, which clears all the check boxes as shown in the figure. There are no additional controls available for logging such as limiting the size of the log file (as there are with other services such as Windows 2000's Web server, the Internet Information Service [IIS]).

The Monitoring page shown in Figure 11-7 is actually misnamed; it should be the Testing page. The operation of this page is covered in

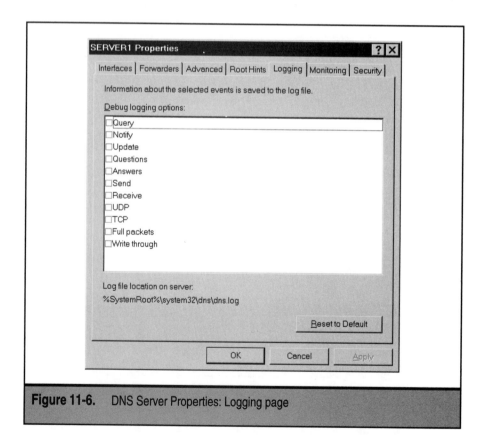

Figure 11-6.   DNS Server Properties: Logging page

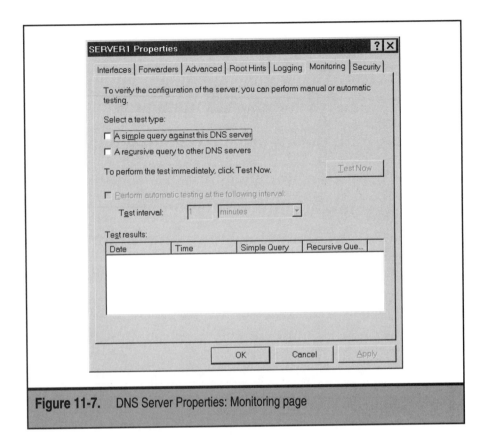

Figure 11-7.   DNS Server Properties: Monitoring page

more detail in the "DNS Monitoring" section later in this chapter. In general, this page is used to test the operation of the DNS server without resorting to external test applications such as NSLOOKUP, which is described in Chapter 19, or third-party tools such as those described in Chapter 20. This page is most often used to immediately test the effects of changes made elsewhere in the DNS snap-in.

Finally, there is the Security page shown in Figure 11-8. The operation of this page is covered in Chapter 12. Through this page, you can control who can access the DNS server and who can make changes to the zones managed by the server.

NOTE: The DNS Server Properties Security page shows both specific and inherited attributes. Most management-related attributes are inherited from Active Directory security groups like Administrators and DnsAdmins.

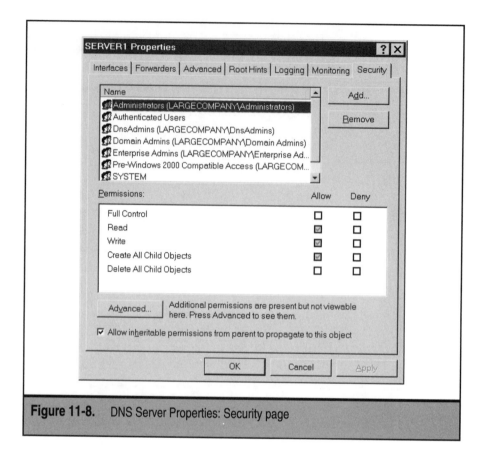

Figure 11-8. DNS Server Properties: Security page

Forward and Reverse Zone Action Menu

The Forward and Reverse Zones have the same Action menu, and the Cached Lookup entries has a similar Action menu. The Action menu for the former follows.

The New Zone menu item starts up the DNS Zone Wizard, but its operation is specific to which entry, Forward Lookup Zones or Reverse Lookup Zones, was selected. One of the differences is that the wizard requires a domain name to create a Forward Lookup Zone, whereas only a partial IP address is needed for a Reverse Lookup Zone. The latter is covered in more detail in the section "Working with a Reverse DNS Zone" in this chapter. The former is addressed in the sections "Working with an Active Directory–integrated DNS Zone," "Working with a Primary DNS Zone," and "Working with a Secondary DNS Zone" later in this chapter.

All the other menu items have been described in the prior sections. The Refresh menu action is specific to the selected entry and its contents.

DNS Zone Action Menu

The DNS Zone Action menu shown next includes a number of sections. It is available when an existing zone is selected. The items in the list in the middle were either addressed in previous sections or perform a straightforward function like Delete, which removes a zone and all its contents. In this section, we will take a look at the first group of menu items and the Properties menu item.

NOTE: The DNS zone menu shown in Figure 11-14 is the same for zones in the Reverse Lookup Zones with the exception of automatically created reverse zones. These include 0.in-addr.arpa, 127.in-addr.arpa, and 255.in-addr.arpa. The Action menu for these zones only includes the New Window From Here, Refresh, and Help menu items.

The Update Server Data File menu item will only be enabled for a primary DNS zone. The action is to write out the current settings for the DNS zone to the primary DNS zone file in the DNS directory. Secondary DNS zones have this menu item disabled because all updates are based on information obtained from another DNS server. Active Directory–integrated DNS zones have all changes saved to the Active Directory database as they are made.

The Reload menu item is used to force an update from the zone's source. This is a primary DNS zone file for a primary DNS zone. It is a download from the source DNS server for a secondary DNS zone file. It is a refresh operation if the zone is an Active Directory–integrated zone. In general, the Reload action is only used when making changes to a zone through means other than the DNS snap-in or if the DNS snap-in is being used to manage a remote Windows 2000 DNS service, and a secondary DNS zone is located on a DNS service also being viewed by the DNS snap-in.

The following entries are used to add new resource records to a primary or Active Directory–integrated zone. Entries cannot be added to a secondary DNS zone, and these menu items will be disabled.

▼ New Host

■ New Alias

■ New Mail Exchange

■ New Domain

■ New Delegation

▲ Other New Records

The types of records and their use are discussed in a number of areas within this book including Chapters 2, 3, and 17, and Appendices A and B.

Finally, there is the Properties menu. This brings up a zone's Properties page window. The DNS Zone Properties window has a number of pages starting with the General page shown in Figure 11-9.

The Windows 2000 DNS service provides individual controls for each zone. The Pause button on the General page allows changes to be made without having the zone available for lookup operations. This is handy when changing a number of related records.

The type of zone can be changed using the Change button. In general, conversion between a primary DNS zone and an Active Directory–integrated zone in a single DNS server environment is simply a matter of having the DNS service move information from one location to another. The movement can be in either direction. Making changes in a more common, multiple DNS server environment is more critical since the change affects other servers. In particular, changing from an Active Directory–integrated DNS zone to a

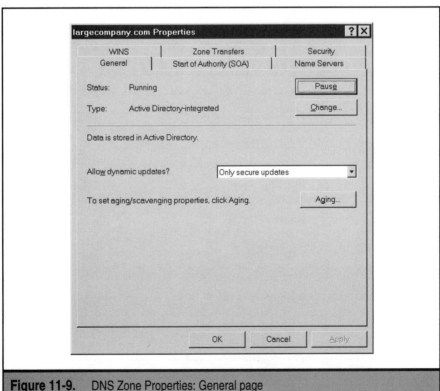

Figure 11-9. DNS Zone Properties: General page

file-based primary DNS zone can be difficult. In general, it is best to make changes when a single DNS server is handling a particular zone.

The Allow Dynamic Updates? field has three possible selections for an Active Directory–integrated DNS zone and two of the three for a primary DNS zone. The selections possibilities are Only Secure Updates, Yes, and No. Only Secure Updates is not an option for the primary DNS zone. Dynamic DNS updates are discussed in more detail in Chapter 15.

The Aging button brings up the Aging and Scavenging dialog box that controls the settings for the selected zone. The section "Aging and Scavenging" in this chapter covers this in more detail.

Switching to the Start of Authority (SOA) page presents the window in Figure 11-10. This is the same window presented if the Properties Action menu item is used when the SOA resource record in a zone is

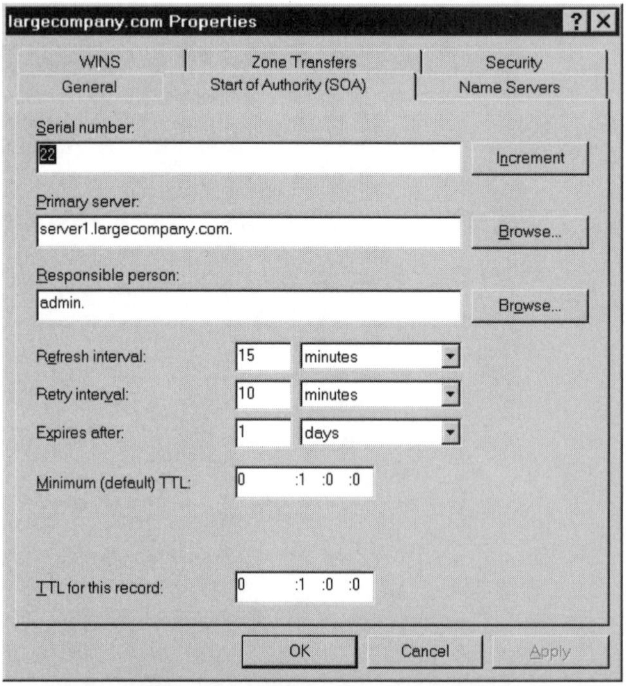

Figure 11-10. DNS Zone Properties: Start of Authority (SOA) page

selected. The SOA resource record is presented in Chapter 2 and Appendixes A and B. All of the attributes associated with the SOA resource record are accessible from this page.

The Name Servers page shown in Figure 11-11 contains a list of authoritative servers for the selected zone. For a primary or Active Directory–integrated DNS zone, the list will start with the DNS server's own IP address. The list will also contain the name and IP address of any secondary DNS zone servers that are also considered to be authoritative. These are set up using the NS resource record discussed in Appendix A.

The WINS page shown in Figure 11-12 is used if the Windows 2000 WINS service is installed and if WINS name resolution is to be used in conjunction with the DNS name resolution. This is typically used in an environment where mixed DNS clients exist and WINS is required to

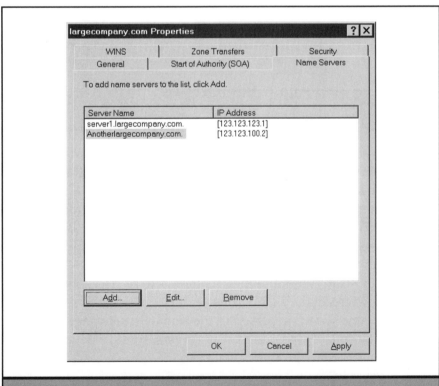

Figure 11-11.   DNS Zone Properties: Name Servers page

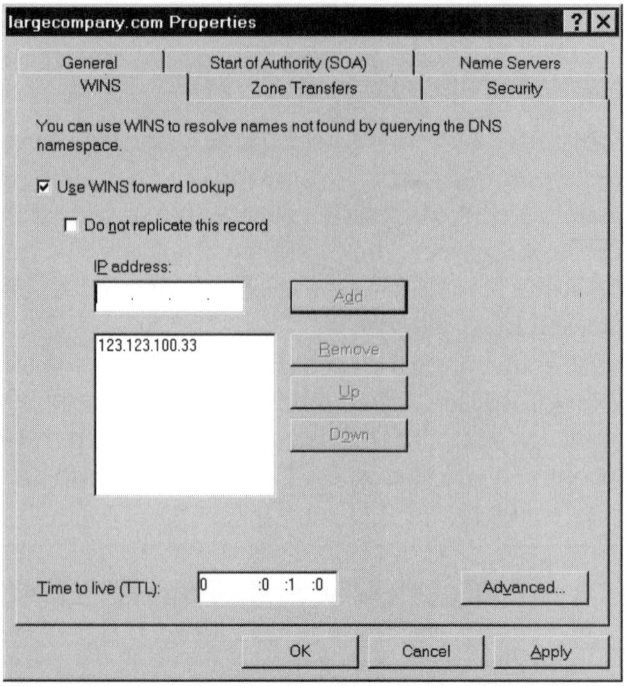

Figure 11-12. DNS Zone Properties: WINS page

handle the Windows clients other than Windows 2000–based clients. The latter normally utilize dynamic DNS support. A more detailed discussion of WINS and this property page is covered in Chapter 15.

The Zone Transfers page show in Figure 11-13 is used to control access from secondary DNS zone servers. The default configuration allows transfers of a copy of a DNS zone to any DNS server that requests it. A more refined method is to restrict zone transfers to known secondary DNS zone servers. One option is to use the list of name servers specified in the Name Servers page. The alternative is to explicitly include a list of servers, some of which may not be authoritative.

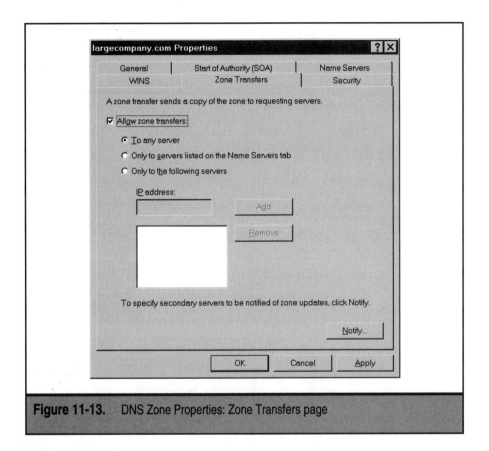

Figure 11-13.   DNS Zone Properties: Zone Transfers page

NOTE: DNS server identification in the Zone Transfer page is to explicit IP addresses. The Windows 2000 DNS service does not allow restriction by subnet.

Updates are usually requested on a scheduled basis. It is also possible for the DNS server to notify secondary DNS zone servers when changes have been made. The Notify button brings up a window that allows the selection of the servers that will receive the notification. Not all servers need be sent the notification, although they will not be updated until a normal update occurs.

Finally, there is the ever-popular Security page shown in
Figure 11-14. Security issues are covered in Chapter 12. The page
and tab will only be available for Active Directory–integrated DNS
zones. Likewise, the Security page will not be available for subzones
within the zone as the finest security granularity is a zone.

Accessing Another DNS Server

The default configuration for the DNS snap-in is managing a single
DNS service on the local server. It is not the only way to manage a
Windows 2000 DNS service. In fact, as long as an administrator has
the proper access rights and a connection to a server, remote DNS

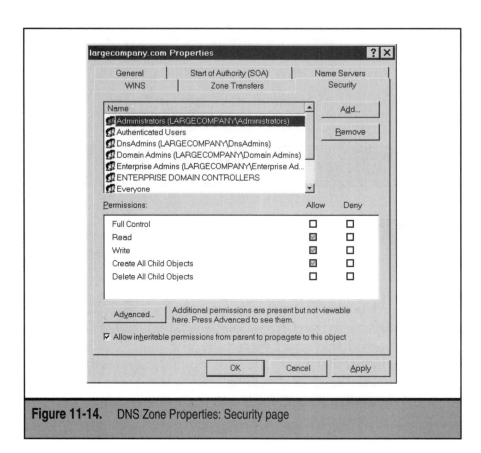

Figure 11-14.   DNS Zone Properties: Security page

management is possible. Typically, remote management occurs within a domain. In general, an enterprise administrator has access to all servers within an Active Directory domain forest.

NOTE: It is possible to manage a Windows 2000 DNS service across domain forests if explicit trusts are set up between domains. However, this would be a very unusual situation.

Any number of DNS servers can be added to the MMC snap-in. First, select the DNS root. Next, using Action | Connect to New Computer, open the Select Target Computer window, shown next.

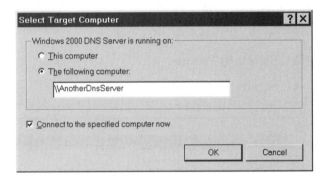

You must select The Following Computer radio button, and the server name must be entered in the field below. There is no Browse button, but it is possible to use the Active Directory Sites and Services, accessible via Start | Programs | Administrative Tools | Active Directory Sites and Services, to locate all the servers within an Active Directory domain forest.

Mixing a number of DNS servers in the same MMC DNS snap-in instance is possible, and performance will be good if all servers are connected to the management PC by a high-speed connection.

TIP: Open multiple MMC DNS snap-in windows in author mode to access different DNS servers. Save the configurations in individual .msc files. This will allow you quick access to any DNS server or set of servers in the network.

Working with an Active Directory–Integrated DNS Zone

Creating an Active Directory–integrated DNS zone is simple with the New Zone Wizard. Active Directory–integrated DNS zones can be created under both Forward Lookup Zones and Reverse Lookup Zones. The same is true for the primary and secondary DNS zones covered in the next two sections.

To start up the New Zone Wizard, select a server, either Forward Lookup Zones or Reverse Lookup Zones, and Action | New Zone. This brings up the Welcome to the New Zone Wizard.

Click on the Next button to step through the rest of the New Zone Wizard windows. The next screen of the wizard, Zone Type, has the following selections, as shown in Figure 11-15:

▼ Active Directory–Integrated

■ Standard Primary

▲ Standard Secondary

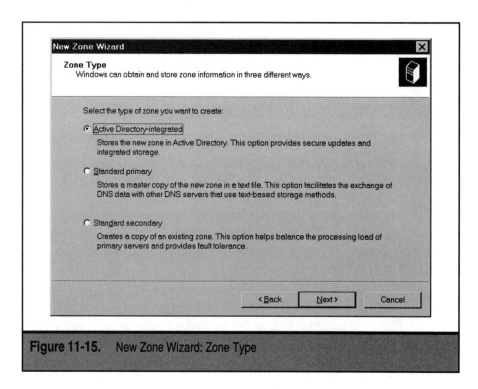

Figure 11-15. New Zone Wizard: Zone Type

Active Directory–Integrated is selected for this scenario. The primary and secondary options are examined in the next two sections. You should select Active Directory–Integrated even if the Active Directory–integrated DNS zone you want has already been created on another DNS server within the same Active Directory domain. It just means that the contents of the zone will already be filled in instead of being empty.

The next step is entering the zone name, as shown in Figure 11-16. The name must be a fully qualified domain name. It can be any valid name, and it is not restricted to the domain associated with the DNS server, although this is usually the first zone created. In fact, when Active Directory is first installed and a DNS server must be installed, the Active Directory Installation Wizard will create the zone when the DNS service is set up.

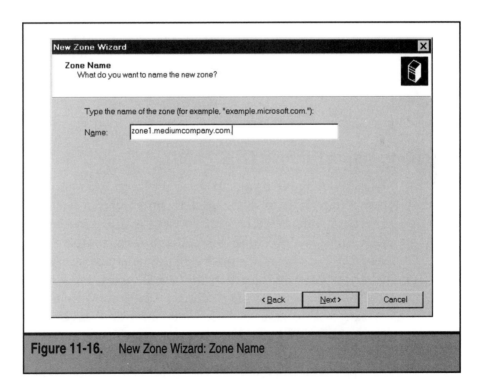

Figure 11-16.   New Zone Wizard: Zone Name

> **WARNING:** Be careful when entering the domain name. A domain cannot be renamed. There are alternatives, however, assuming resource records have been added to a domain. For example, an Active Directory–integrated zone can be converted to a primary zone so that the information is saved in a file. The zone file can then be used when the properly named primary zone is created. The primary zone is then converted to an Active Directory–integrated zone.

The Completing the New Zone Wizard screen simply summarizes the choices already made. Make sure the details are correct because, although changes are not too difficult to make, they are tedious to make. Click the Finish button to create the new zone.

The Active Directory–integrated DNS zone is now available for modification. It can also be added as an Active Directory–integrated DNS zone to any other Windows 2000 DNS server within the same domain. It will not be accessible to Windows 2000 DNS servers within different domains. These must use secondary DNS zones to obtain a copy of the Active Directory–integrated DNS zone.

Assuming the other Windows 2000 DNS servers within the same domain are already running, it is possible to immediately add a DNS server to the DNS root and add the Active Directory–integrated DNS zone to the server.

Working with a Primary DNS Zone

One advantage of using a primary DNS zone is that the zone file is compatible with zone files used by other DNS servers. While Active Directory–integrated DSN zones have many advantages, primary DNS zones may wind up being the preferred implementation method. Primary DNS zones can be created even if Active Directory is not installed on the server that the DNS service is running on.

The steps for creating a primary DNS zone with the New Zone Wizard are the same as those for creating an Active Directory–integrated DNS zone. After you enter the Zone Name, as shown in Figure 11-17, click the Next button to bring up the Zone File screen.

The Create A New File With This File Name option allows a brand new, empty zone file to be created. The other option, Use This

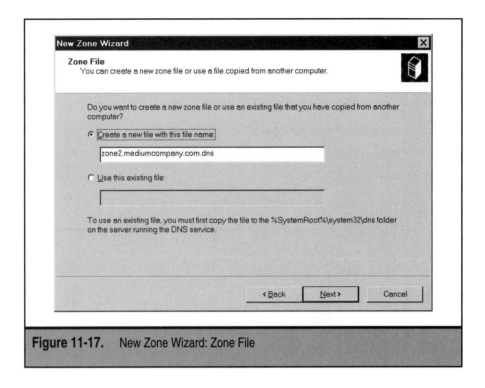

Figure 11-17.   New Zone Wizard: Zone File

Existing File, allows information from an existing primary zone file
to be used instead. The zone file name can be changed in the zone's
Properties General page. The contents of the file must parse properly
for an existing file to be used.

New resource records can be added immediately after the primary
DNS zone is created. By default, the zone is available for replication to
a secondary DNS zone on another DNS server.

Working with a Secondary DNS Zone

Creating a secondary DNS zone is as simple as creating a primary
DNS zone. Follow the same steps as those outlined in the "Working
with an Active Directory–Integrated DNS Zone" section. Then select
Standard Secondary in the Zone Type screen shown in Figure 11-15.
After the Zone Name screen shown in Figure 11-16, the Master DNS
Servers screen shown in Figure 11-18 will appear.

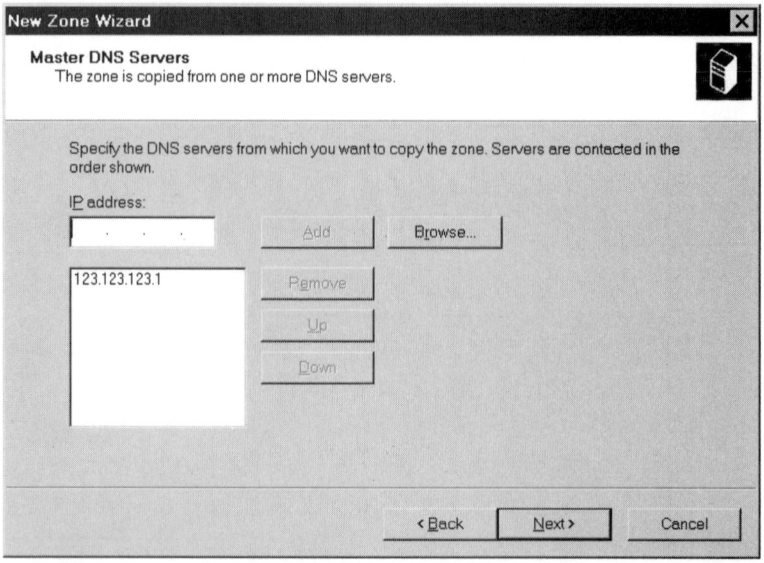

Figure 11-18.   New Zone Wizard: Master DNS Servers

The DNS servers that will be added to the list in this window are servers that have or will have a matching zone. The DNS server tries to obtain a copy of the zone file from each server in the list until one server delivers the information. Multiple DNS servers provide a basic level of redundancy.

You can either enter the IP address or use the Browse button to locate a Windows 2000 server within the network. The IP address approach must be used to identify all other types of DNS servers.

The contents of the secondary DNS zone will be updated after the Finish button is clicked on the last step of the New Zone Wizard. The zone will still be created even if the source DNS servers are unavailable, but the zone will not contain any information until a valid update occurs. An update can be forced by selecting the secondary DNS zone and using Action | Transfer from master.

Working with a Reverse DNS Zone

Reverse DNS zones must be created if IP addresses are to be resolved to domain names. Reverse DNS zone operation is described in Chapter 2. The naming convention has a base zone name of in-addr.arpa. Three reverse DNS zones are set up by default when the DNS server is set up; these zones are named 0.in-addr.arpa, 127.in-addr.arpa, and 255.in-addr.arpa.

Creating a zone for an existing subnet is done using the same procedure outlined for Active Directory–integrated DNS, primary, and secondary zones. In fact, all three can exist under the Reverse Lookup Zones entry. The tradeoffs for each choice are the same as for forward zones.

You can create a reverse zone by choosing Action | New Zone and using the New Zone Wizard. With a reverse DNS zone, after the Zone Type screen (Figure 11-15), the Reverse Lookup Zone screen shown in Figure 11-19 will appear.

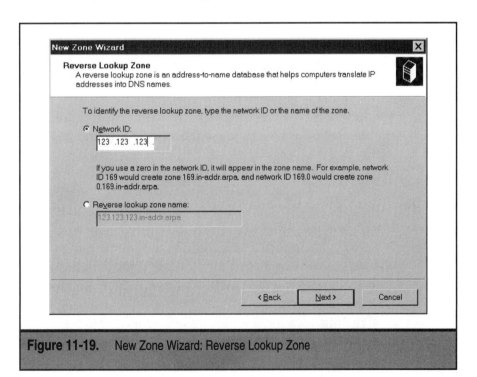

Figure 11-19.   New Zone Wizard: Reverse Lookup Zone

One, two, or three numbers must be entered if the Network ID choice is used. It is also possible to explicitly give the reverse lookup zone name in the Reverse Lookup Zone Name field. In either case, the New Zone Wizard proceeds through the remaining steps based upon the type of zone chosen in the first step. For example, a primary DNS zone file name will be requested, or a list of secondary DNS zone masters must be filled in.

Reverse lookup zones with three numbers can have PTR resource records added immediately. For example, a reverse lookup zone with a name of 10.11.12.in-addr.arpa. with a PTR resource record named 5 would define the name for IP address 12.11.10.5.

Reverse lookup zones with one or two numbers specified will require the definition of one or more subdomains. For example, 11.12.in-addr.arpa. would require that a subdomain of 10 be created to match the previous example.

MULTIPLE MMC CHILD WINDOWS AND SNAP-INS

In this section, we will look at some concrete MMC DNS snap-in examples that use multiple child windows and multiple snap-ins. In the last chapter, we looked at how this is done. In particular, Action | New Windows From Here provides a way of creating multiple windows with different views of the same information. In this chapter, MMC author mode will be used to combine DNS, DHCP, and WINS snap-ins.

Navigating a Large DNS System

MMC provides a number of methods to navigate large DNS systems. The first method is to create multiple windows using the Action | New Windows From Here menu item. This action is available from most DNS snap-in entries with the exception of leaf nodes such as host resource records.

Creating additional windows has a number of advantages. First, it eliminates the clutter associated with DNS snap-in hierarchy, especially when multiple snap-ins are used. Second, it allows an administrator to hone in on a particular area of the DNS database.

Third, it provides a quick way to change views on the same details. For example, entries can be sorted by ascending or descending order based on any column. You can get a sorted list of host resource records by clicking on the Name column to sort by name and then clicking on the Type column to sort and group by type. Just check for the A type to see the host resource records.

Figure 11-20 shows a simple example of multiple child windows. To view this, locate the zone largecompany.com and select Action | New Windows From Here. Then select Windows | Tile Horizontally.

One serious drawback of the MMC is that there is no Find function. A limited one-character search is available, however. Just press any key, and the cursor will position itself on the next item that starts with the matching character. The cursor does not move if no entry starts with that character.

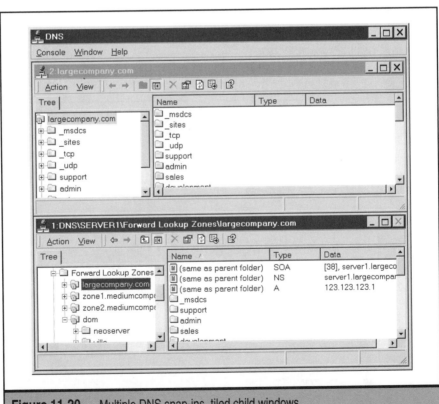

Figure 11-20.   Multiple DNS snap-ins, tiled child windows

Closing the MMC program will save the current configuration including child window position. This lets a manager navigate to desired locations in different windows and exit the program so that the same information can be quickly presented when the DNS MMC snap-in is started up again.

Configuring MMC with DNS, DHCP, and WINS Snap-ins

The standard method of using MMC with the DNS-related snap-ins is to start up individual copies using the respective configuration files referenced in the Start | Programs | Administrative Tools menu. Using MMC author mode, it is possible to bring all these snap-ins into a single MMC console window to provide an environment that looks like Figure 11-21.

The advantage to this is the ability to start up one instance of MMC and have access to all the relevant management tools. Multiple child windows can be used to display individual snap-ins, as described in the previous section.

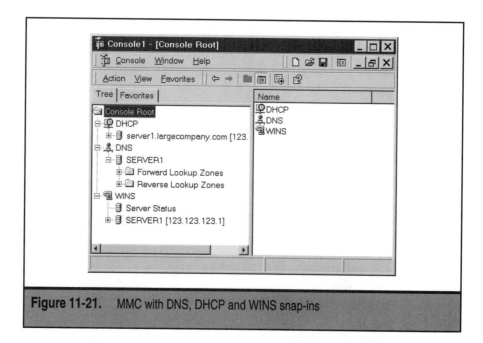

Figure 11-21. MMC with DNS, DHCP and WINS snap-ins

NOTE: Mixing snap-ins is not limited to related MMC snap-ins as shown in this example. Security and performance snap-ins are only a couple useful tools that can be combined with DNS-related snap-ins.

To set up an MMC window with multiple snap-ins, start MMC by choosing Start | Run | Select Console | Add/Remove Snap-in. Next, click on the Add button in the Add/Remove Snap-in window. Select a snap-in to add, and click on the Add button. Repeat the last step until all the desired snap-ins have been added. Close the windows and take a look at the list of snap-ins under the Console Root entry.

Make sure to save the configuration file when all the snap-ins have been added and the desired window layout has been completed. Now all the details and actions DNS management will be available simply by starting up MMC using this configuration file.

REGULAR DNS MAINTENANCE

DNS effectively operates without any regular maintenance. Static IP references can be added and deleted when necessary, but for the most part DNS works like any good service and does everything in the background.

Two areas where regular maintenance may be necessary are debugging and scavenging. The Windows 2000 DNS service has two built-in debugging tools. The first is the DNS logging support, and the second is the DNS monitoring support. Aging and scavenging are related to dynamic DNS updates and how long resource records added in this fashion are valid.

The next sections take a look at these DNS snap-in features. If the DNS service is operating as expected, the debugging features will not be needed. Likewise, if dynamic DNS is working well with the defaults, it is possible to overlook aging and scavenging.

DNS Logging

Unlike other Windows 2000 services with low overhead logging features that can track usage or performance, the DNS logging feature is strictly for debugging purposes. As such, it has a limited number of configuration options. Because of its overhead and lack of log file controls, it should be used only as necessary and only under the strict control and monitoring of the DNS administrator. Still, the logging feature can be invaluable in tracking down operational problems or unwanted interactions with other DNS servers or clients.

To access the DNS logging facility, select the desired server, choose Action | Properties, and click on the Logging tab. The DNS Server Properties Logging page shown earlier in Figure 11-10 will be displayed. Logging is enabled if any of the items in the list on the Logging page are checked.

NOTE: The Reset To Default button on the Logging page clears all entries. Remember to hit the Apply or OK button to save the settings, or logging will continue.

The log file name is %ServerRoot%\SYSTEM32\dns\dns.log. The dns.log file is a text file that can be viewed using any text editor, such as Notepad or Wordpad. Figure 11-22 shows a sample excerpt from a dns.log file.

Entries in the log file are verbose. This is handy for debugging purposes, but it makes the log file size increase quickly. Entries are appended to the end of the log file, so it continues to grow until it is deleted by the user. Turning off logging and turning it back on does not delete the log file. The only filtering available is the selection of which items are logged.

TIP: Rename or delete the dns.log file as soon as you are finished using it. Disable all logging as soon as possible.

Log file entries include all relevant details, such as the IP address of a DNS request, the request type and data, and the returned information. A text editor's search tool can come in handy to locate potential problems.

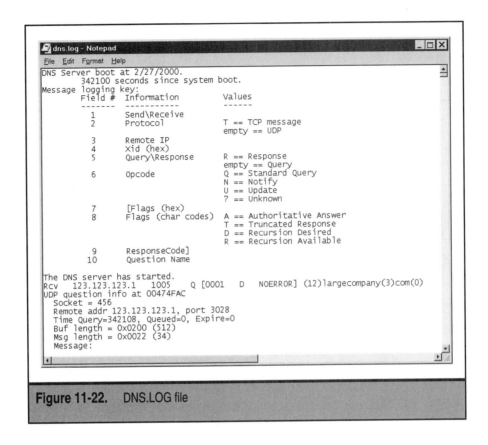

Figure 11-22. DNS.LOG file

DNS Monitoring

As mentioned earlier, the DNS monitoring feature should be named DNS diagnostic tool because it is really a probe that generates queries and displays responses. It is primarily used to test out changes made using the DNS snap-in without having to resort to another application.

Access the DNS Server Properties: Monitoring page by choosing the desired server to test and selecting Action | Properties and then the Monitoring tab. This will display the DNS Monitoring window, as shown in Figure 11-7. This debugging tool is often used in conjunction with the logging support described in the previous section.

Simple or recursive queries can be tested, but there is no control over what zone will be tested. Clicking the Test Now button starts a test that will occur once unless you check Perform Automatic Testing At The Following Interval. In the latter case, the test will be repeated at the rate specified. You can also start automatic testing by checking this item and clicking on the Apply button.

The results for each test, whether single or automatically recurring, are listed in the Test Results list box. Automatic testing will continue even when the dialog box is closed. You must uncheck Perform Automatic Testing At The Following Interval and click the Apply button to stop testing.

In general, the external tools such as those discussed in Chapters 19 and 20 provide better testing features.

Aging and Scavenging

Dynamic DNS updates have the potential of creating resource records that just do not go away. In general, this is not much of a problem, as a workstation will try to renew their DHCP-obtained IP address. Excess resource records can exist because a workstation has had a name change or the workstation is replaced with a new workstation. In other cases, a workstation that adds a resource record via a dynamic DNS update does not remove it when shutting down.

In general, the performance and space issues only come into play in large networks. Extra resource records can lead to the following problems:

▼ A large number of useless or inaccurate resource records degrade performance.

■ A large number of useless or inaccurate resource records can use up server disk space.

■ Queries made about expired records result in invalid results.

▲ A resource record can cause another dynamic DNS update to fail if it uses the same name.

Windows 2000 DNS server time stamps all dynamic DNS updates. This allows the age of a resource record to be calculated and scavenged.

NOTE: Dynamic DNS updates can only be used with Active Directory–integrated zones or primary DNS zones.

By default, aging and scavenging are disabled. To make it operate, the feature must be enabled in two places, the server and the zone. More than one zone can be scavenged at a time. It is also possible to initiate scavenging manually.

To enable scavenging on a server, either select the desired DNS server and then choose Action | Set Aging/Scavenging for all zones, or click the Aging button on the General property page for the zone. This presents the Zone Aging/Scavenging Properties window shown in Figure 11-23.

The settings for each zone must be changed after the server's Aging and Scavenging settings have changed. At this point,

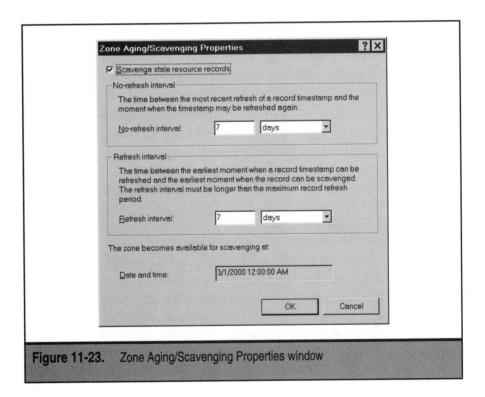

Figure 11-23.   Zone Aging/Scavenging Properties window

with both server and zone settings enabled, the DNS service will periodically scavenge expired resource records.

Scavenging can also be initiated manually from the server's Action menu. Select Scavenge Stale Resource Records, and the window shown here will appear. Click on the OK button, and the scavenging process will run once for all scavengable zones.

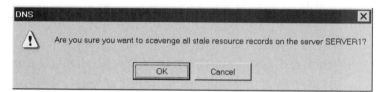

SUMMARY

The DNS MMC snap-in provides a powerful interface to the Windows 2000 DNS service. Chapter 19 addresses the other alternative to managing the service, command line applications.

The MMC interface has the advantage of being easy to use as well as providing the ability to view more than one part of the DNS domain tree. MMC also has the ability to include other snap-ins to provide integrated access to other Windows 2000 resources such as the DHCP and WINS services.

Most of the DNS support is up front when a zone is created. Additional management chores include adding and deleting static IP resource records. However, other than debugging chores and an occasional scavenge for unused resource records, the DNS service requires almost no routine maintenance.

While the Window 2000 DNS service has a logging facility, it is useful only as a debugging tool as there is no log file management and it imposes too much overhead for general use. For example the DNS snap-in does not even provide a way of viewing the text log file; it must be done using a text editor such as Wordpad.

Aging and scavenging of dynamic DNS updated information is automatic, and most DNS administrators will let Windows 2000 handle this chore without even knowing that it is being done. Still, it is worthwhile to know about it, especially when dealing with a large DNS server.

CHAPTER 12

Windows 2000 DNS Security

W indows 2000 DNS security addresses a number of different areas:

▼ Who can manage the DNS service and zones

■ Limits to what users can examine

▲ Controls that can be set on dynamic DNS updates, including settings that address how secondary zones operate.

This chapter addresses all these security-related concerns. The section "DNS Service Access Control" looks at how the rights of DNS managers and users are controlled and what rights they provide. In general, users need to be able to access the DNS service, and managers need to be able to make changes to the DNS service settings. In larger networks, the rights of DNS managers may differ from network or enterprise administrators. The implications and details of the Active Directory security for DNS services in small to large networks are also examined in this section, including the default security configuration.

The section "DNS Zone Access Control" examines limits that can be placed on a DNS zone. The Active Directory–integrated zones have the most sophisticated access security, as the zone information is maintained within the Active Directory database. File security is addressed as well, as primary zone files are stored in a Windows 2000 directory. Finally, we'll discuss issues associated with secondary zone security.

Some other DNS services such as BIND, covered in Chapter 21, allow client restrictions by subnet. Windows 2000's ability to limit client access is less restrictive. The section "DNS Client Access Security" addresses Windows 2000's limited control over client access.

The section "Dynamic DNS Security" looks at the dynamic DNS update feature and how it can be controlled. In particular, it examines the ability of Windows 2000 with Active Directory to provide updates from only authorized clients.

DNS services are designed to be used by the largest possible number of clients, and a well managed system will allow such access. On the other hand, a securely managed system will allow only authorized users to make or manage changes. In this way, the information distributed by the DNS services will be accurate. Remember, bad information is usually worse than no information.

DNS SERVICE ACCESS CONTROL

Access to the DNS service resources and control of the DNS service are based upon Windows 2000's security mechanism. Each object has a list of users and groups that have specific access rights. In addition, rights can be inherited. The inheritance hierarchy is based on the Windows 2000 domain and organizational unit hierarchy.

In this section, "Windows 2000 Security and Inheritance" addresses the basics of Windows 2000's security system, security groups, and how to deal with user groups and security. The security management interface is the Microsoft Management Console (MMC), which is covered in Chapter 10. This chapter deals with the mechanics of the interface, while the section in this chapter deals with the theory of operation.

"Group Policy" addresses another aspect of security. Because it deals with server-based services such as the DNS service, it is an important part of security administration.

The ability to control who can start and stop a service such as the DNS or DHCP service is covered in "DNS Service Control."

"DNS Service Access" shows how the Windows 2000 security system is implemented with respect to the DNS service. This section addresses how domain administrators can delegate authority to DNS administrators.

In many cases, especially with smaller networks, the default security settings are sufficient. Adding users to the various security-related management groups for services like DNS is often all that will be done by domain administrators because this is the easiest way to provide permission to get a job done.

Windows 2000 Security and Inheritance

Windows 2000 security is implemented using access control lists (ACL). An ACL is associated with Windows 2000 Active Directory objects. Each entry in the list has a set of attributes associated with a particular type of object, such as the ability to read or control an object.

Entries in the ACL specify explicit access rights. Windows 2000 Active Directory also supports inherited access rights. The inheritance is based on the Windows 2000 object hierarchy, which starts with domains and progresses down through organizational units and objects.

The combination of explicit and inherited access rights makes up an object's effective access rights. A user can manipulate an object based on their effective access rights to that object. A user with no effective access rights to an object cannot do anything with the object. A user with full access rights to an object can do just about anything with the object, including deleting it. Users in the Enterprise Admins group typically have full access rights to all objects, while the average user has limited access to most objects.

In addition to access rights, an object can have group policy rights associated with them. For example, Windows 2000 services such as the DNS service are found in the Windows 2000 Group Policy's list of services. The next section, "Group Policy," examines these rights in more detail. The key point here is that rights associated with an object may be found in more than one place under Windows 2000.

Group policies are domain-specific and are not inherited across domains. Figure 12-1 shows how inheritance spans Windows 2000 Active Directory domains within a domain tree. In particular, it shows some of the standard security groups defined when a domain is created. The Enterprise Admins group is set up within the root domain, and Domain Admins is set up within each domain. In addition to being used within their respective domains, the Domain Admins group's access rights are inherited by child domains. In this case, a typical object that is managed by a local Domain Admins group can also be managed by the root's Domain Admins group if the default settings are used.

For example, the object in the sales.largecompany.com domain has explicit rights associated with the local Domain Admins group. It also has inherited access rights associated with the largecompany.com Domain Admins group. This inheritance is

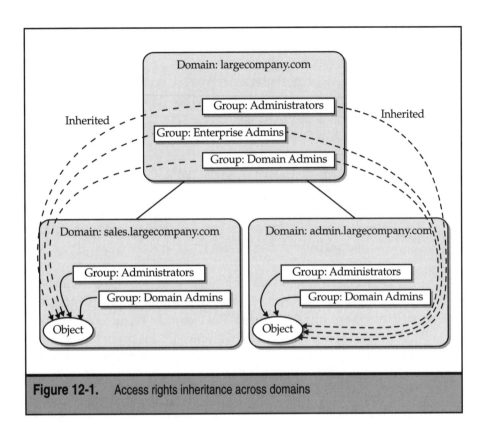

Figure 12-1.   Access rights inheritance across domains

due to the link between the root domain, largecompany.com, and the child domain, sales.largecompany.com.

The access rights of the Enterprise Admins group also span the root domains of an Active Directory domain forest. This allows management across domains in the forest as well as all the child domains in the forest through inheritance. Of course, this provides those in the Enterprise Admins group with considerable power. In most large organizations, the breadth of control is often limited, with delegation of authority replacing complete centralized management. You can assign this type of restriction by setting explicit access rights and owners in addition to restricting inheritance. Owners have special access rights because they can change the access rights of an object.

NOTE: Improper security setups can occur when an owner is given restricted access rights to the object they own. This is a problem because the owner can change the access rights and restore their access rights to the object. In general, if access rights are to be limited to an object, then inheritance, access rights, and the owner should be set accordingly.

TIP: Limit the number of objects that have a limited number of groups or users with full access rights. If you don't, it can lead to inaccessible objects. For example, if an administrator is the only one who can access an object, and the administrator's account is eliminated or made inaccessible, the object will become inaccessible.

Domains tend to be rather large entities. Within domains are two major items: servers and organizational units. Security tends to be organized around these items. For example, services are specific to a particular server. Organizational units, on the other hand, are designed to group objects such as users and computers. Objects can be moved from one organizational unit to another, whereas services must stay on the server where they reside.

Figure 12-2 shows how inheritance plays a role in organizational units and the objects contained therein. Users and groups can be explicitly linked to an object just as the Sample Group is to the organization unit admin.largecompany.com in the example. Objects contained within this organizational unit inherit this link in addition to any links that are inherited by the organizational unit itself, such as the Domain Admins group that is defined as part of the domain.

The Active Directory User and Computers MMC snap-in covered in Chapter 10 is used to manage the organizational unit hierarchy. It can be modified as necessary versus the domain hierarchy that is fixed once it is created. Domains can be added and deleted using the Active Directory tools, but domains cannot be moved around as organizational units can.

It is possible to control the effects of inheritance explicitly through two methods. The first is to change the setting of the Allow Inheritable Permissions From Parent To Propagate To This Object check box found

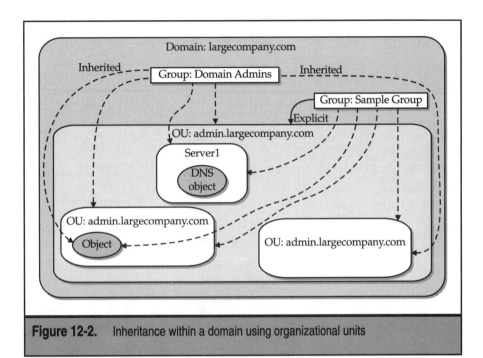

Figure 12-2. Inheritance within a domain using organizational units

in most object's Properties on the Security page. The other method is to include explicit entries in an object's ACL that disable the desired access.

Figure 12-3 shows a sample of the Security page in the Properties window of a domain controller computer object. By default, the Allow Inheritable Permissions From Parent To Propagate To This Object check box is checked. Unchecking the box prevents inherited access rights from applying to this object. If the object is an organizational unit, the inheritance is prevented from the organizational unit and any objects that it contains.

The Enterprise Admins group selected in Figure 12-3 is an example of an inherited access right. Enterprise Admins is selected in the Name list on the top part of the window, and the Permissions box shows the access rights of the selected item. The dimmed check boxes indicate that the permissions are inherited. Individual access rights can be set by checking Deny check boxes to specify rights that should be inaccessible. The only difference between this approach and using the Allow Inheritable Permissions From Parent To Propagate check

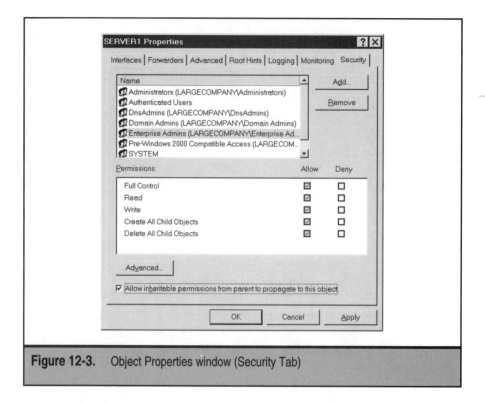

Figure 12-3. Object Properties window (Security Tab)

box is that the latter applies to all inherited rights including those that may be added in the future. The Allow Inheritable Permissions From Parent To Propagate check box does not affect the subsequent inheritance of users or groups added explicitly to the Name list.

NOTE: Unchecking the Allow Inheritable Permissions From Parent To Propagate check box will cause Windows 2000 to present a dialog box allowing one of three options. One option is to turn all inherited references into explicit references. Another option is to remove all inherited references. The last option is to cancel the operation.

Only users, computers, and organizational units are presented by the Active Directory Users and Computers MMC snap-in. Services, such as DNS, are not part of this hierarchy. Instead, they are part of the server on which they reside. The DNS MMC snap-in, which is accessible via

Windows 2000 DNS and Active Directory are tightly linked. Although third-party DNS servers can support Active Directory, Windows 2000 DNS Active Directory–integrated DNS zones can make management of Windows 2000 networks easier. Large model networks are the most common. The Large Model figure shows how automatic replication of Active Directory–integrated DNS zones can be used in place of secondary DNS zone replication.

DNS administrators of distributed networks will need to deal with Windows 2000 sites. Active Directory domains will often span sites, as shown in the Distributed Network figure, making DNS server placement critical.

DNS administrators should be aware of the storage and replication mechanisms used by primary, secondary, and Active Directory–integrated zones. This can affect placement and use of different zone types. The replication mechanisms are highlighted in the DNS Database Replication figure. Windows 2000 Active Directory domain controllers make use of dynamic DNS updates. Windows 2000 clients support this feature, but most other clients do not. DNS administrators can make use of the Windows 2000 DHCP dynamic DNS update proxy support to gain the benefits of dynamic updates. This feature is highlighted in the Dynamic DNS Update Protocol figure.

Table of Contents

Large Network

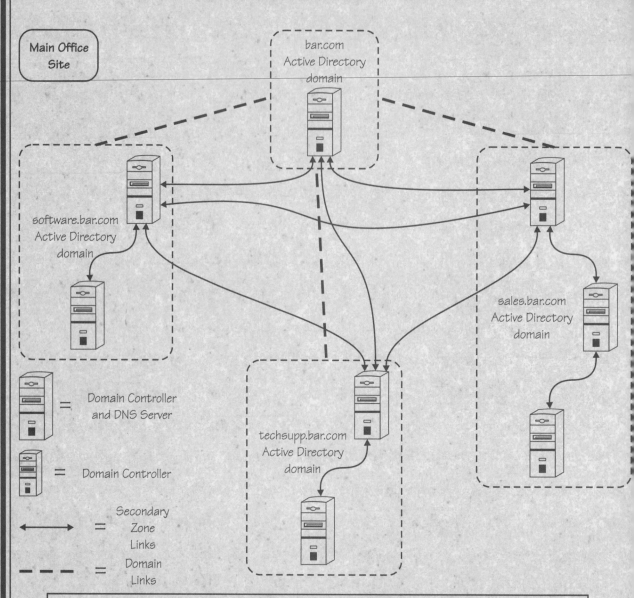

Main Office Site

bar.com
Active Directory
domain

software.bar.com
Active Directory
domain

sales.bar.com
Active Directory
domain

techsupp.bar.com
Active Directory
domain

= Domain Controller
and DNS Server

= Domain Controller

= Secondary
Zone
Links

= Domain
Links

This large-size network encompasses a single Active Directory domain tree with multiple Active Directory domains. Each Windows 2000 domain controller has its own Windows 2000 DNS service, but replication of information across domains is performed using secondary zones. The approach allows domain-level management of Active Directory–integrated zones, but secondary zone linkages can be numerous if there is a large number of Active Directory domains. In many instances, it is not necessary to publish DNS information beyond the Active Directory domain that the DNS domain covers. In other instances with minimal cross-domain requests, forwarding of DNS requests is sufficient.

2

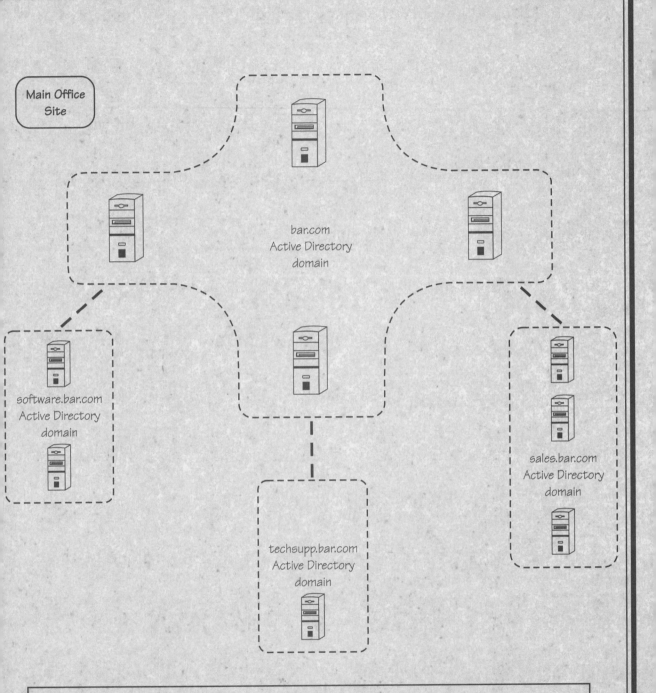

Main Office
Site

bar.com
Active Directory
domain

software.bar.com
Active Directory
domain

techsupp.bar.com
Active Directory
domain

sales.bar.com
Active Directory
domain

Using a single Active Directory–integrated DNS zone bar.com for the root domain of a large-size network allows centralized DNS support plus redundant operation. In this case, servers and workstations in a child domain like sales.bar.com send dynamic updates to a root domain DNS server, and Active Directory replication handles distribution of these updates to other DNS servers. This eliminates the need to set up secondary zones to distribute child domain DNS information to the root and siblings.

Distributed Network

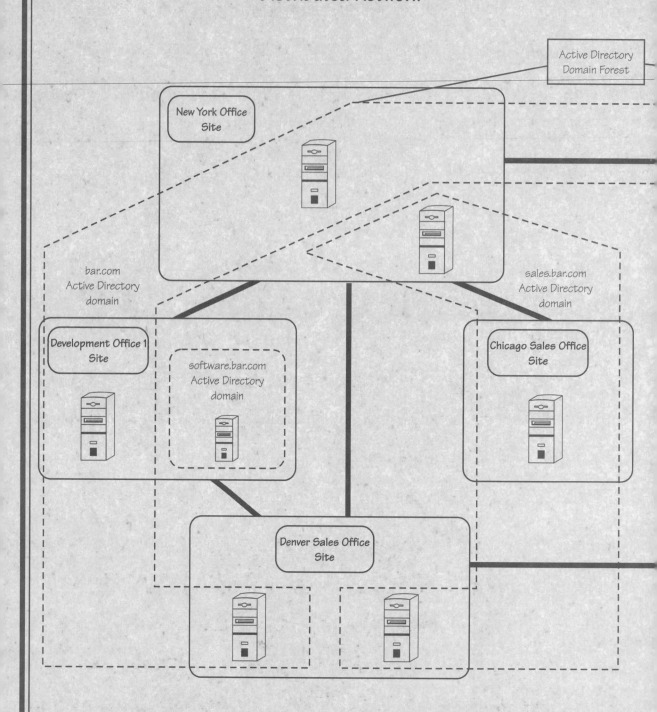

Active Directory
Domain Forest

New York Office
Site

bar.com
Active Directory
domain

sales.bar.com
Active Directory
domain

Development Office 1
Site

software.bar.com
Active Directory
domain

Chicago Sales Office
Site

Denver Sales Office
Site

4

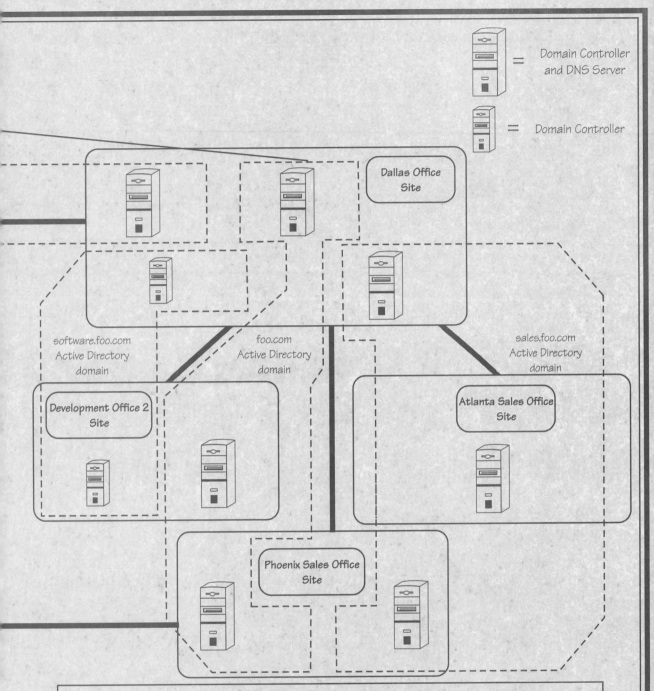

Domain Controller
and DNS Server

= Domain Controller

Dallas Office
Site

software.foo.com
Active Directory
domain

foo.com
Active Directory
domain

sales.foo.com
Active Directory
domain

Development Office 2
Site

Atlanta Sales Office
Site

Phoenix Sales Office
Site

Distributed networks that encompass an Active Directory domain forest must distribute DNS servers throughout the network so workstations and servers have access to at least one DNS server. The Development Office 1 site's bar.com DNS server can support both bar.com and the software.bar.com domains. All domain servers within the forest have direct or transitive trusts with each other, so it is possible to use secured dynamic DNS updates. Secondary DNS zone links (not shown) provide a mechanism whereby domains in different domain trees can resolve names in different domains.

DNS Database Replication

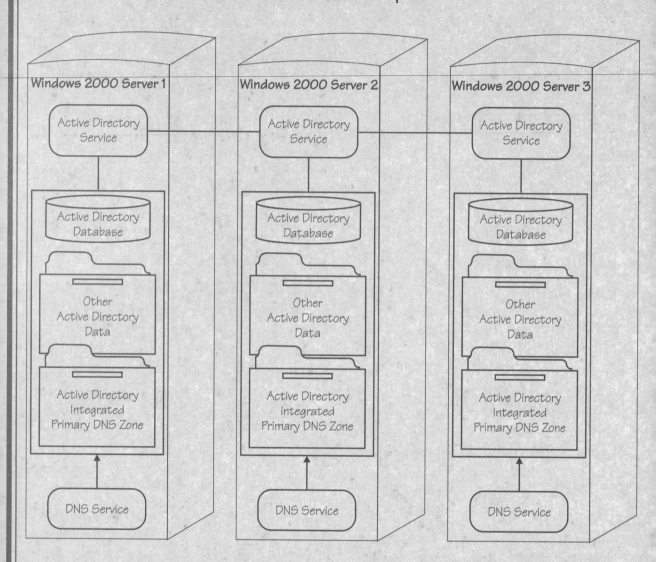

Active Directory—integrated zones are stored in a domain's Active Directory database. This information is replicated in each domain controller's database where the local Windows 2000 DNS service can access it. Dynamic DNS updates sent to any of these DNS services will be automatically distributed to all other locations in an incremental and secure fashion. Active Directory—integrated zones are also easier to manage because the services are already authenticated and managed using Active Directory. Note that Active Directory replication occurs only within a domain.

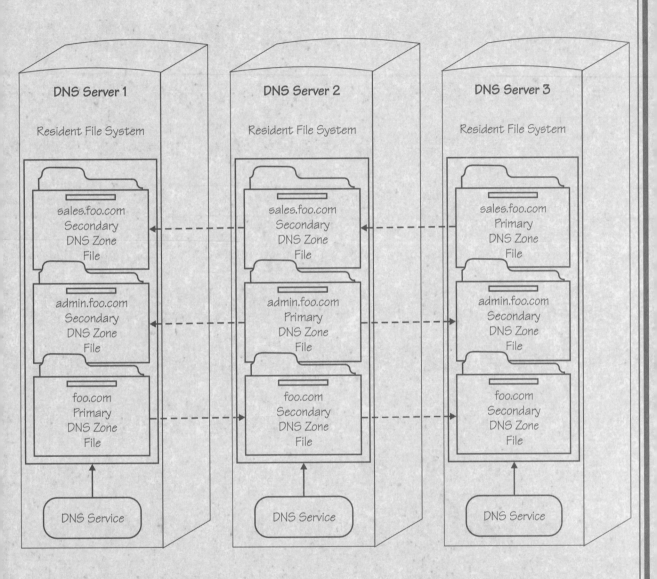

DNS Server 1

Resident File System

sales.foo.com
Secondary
DNS Zone
File

admin.foo.com
Secondary
DNS Zone
File

foo.com
Primary
DNS Zone
File

DNS Service

DNS Server 2

Resident File System

sales.foo.com
Secondary
DNS Zone
File

admin.foo.com
Primary
DNS Zone
File

foo.com
Secondary
DNS Zone
File

DNS Service

DNS Server 3

Resident File System

sales.foo.com
Primary
DNS Zone
File

admin.foo.com
Secondary
DNS Zone
File

foo.com
Secondary
DNS Zone
File

DNS Service

Primary and secondary DNS zones are stored as text files. Security and backup arrangements are independent of the DNS server, whether it's a Windows 2000 DNS server or third-party DNS server. The advantages of using primary and secondary DNS zones is that the DNS information can be exchanged with any DNS server, not just Windows 2000 DNS servers. Although secondary DNS zones provide redundant access to a zone, the holder of the primary zone such as foo.com on DNS server 1 is the only one that can receive dynamic DNS updates for the zone. DNS server 1 is also a potential point of failure for the primary DNS zone it handles. Note that secondary zones can be copied from the primary zone or another secondary zone.

Dynamic DNS Update Protocol

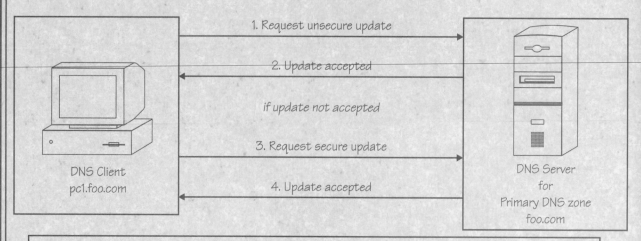

1. Request unsecure update

2. Update accepted

if update not accepted

3. Request secure update

4. Update accepted

DNS Client
pc1.foo.com

DNS Server
for
Primary DNS zone
foo.com

Dynamic DNS update protocol—The DNS client pc1.foo.com sends an update request to a DNS server for foo.com when the client's name changes, the workstation starts, or the user initiates an update. A Windows 2000 DNS server can be set up for unsecured or secured updates. In this case, the Windows 2000 DNS server will reject an unsecured update, and the client must submit a secured update request. This request is then verified using Windows 2000's security system before a change is made to the primary zone.

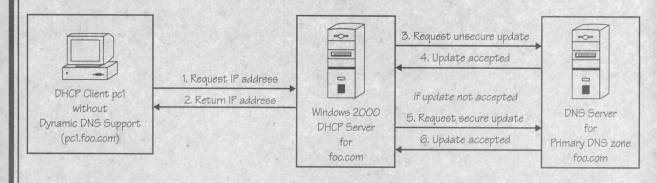

DHCP Client pc1
without
Dynamic DNS Support
(pc1.foo.com)

1. Request IP address
2. Return IP address

Windows 2000
DHCP Server
for
foo.com

3. Request unsecure update
4. Update accepted

if update not accepted

5. Request secure update

6. Update accepted

DNS Server
for
Primary DNS zone
foo.com

DHCP-provided dynamic DNS update—Windows 2000's DHCP service can provide dynamic DNS update support for clients that do not support this facility. The DHCP server contacts the DNS server on behalf of the DHCP client pc1.foo.com after the IP address is sent to the client. The Windows 2000 DHCP server can operate using an unsecured request with any dynamic DNS update—capable DNS server. It can operate using a secured request when operating with a Windows 2000 DNS server. The Windows 2000 DHCP server and DNS server do not have to be on the same Windows 2000 server. Note that the DHCP server maintains the domain name used for all requests and this, combined with the name of the DHCP client, generates the name in the dynamic DNS update request sent to the DNS server.

Start | Programs | Administrative Tools | DNS, provides access to all
DNS services; the Computer Management MMC snap-in, which is
accessible via Start | Programs | Administrative Tools | Computer
Management, provides access to services specifically on the local
computer. This same snap-in can be accessed using the Action |
Manage menu option in the Users and Computers MMC snap-in
when a server is selected.

The Properties page for a DNS service can be accessed from the
DNS MMC snap-in. If you check this out, you will notice that the
DNS root has no Properties page, but each DNS service running on a
particular server does. Some of the objects under the DNS service in
the hierarchy will also have a Security tab in their Properties window
but others will not. In the latter case, the security is inherited based
upon the first object farther up in the tree that does have a Security
tab in its Properties window.

Objects that have security properties under a DNS service are
limited to Active Directory–integrated DNS zones. Primary and
secondary DNS zones use other mechanisms for security. Each of
these zones is discussed in the "DNS Zone Access Control" section.

Group Policy

Group policies are used within a domain or on a computer
to implement security policies. These effectively are access
control restrictions similar to the ones discussed in the previous
section, except that the group policies tend to be a bit broader in
functionality. For example, instead of basic check boxes to enable or
disable a right, group policy entries can have values that are used by
Windows 2000 to implement the desired policy such as the amount
of idle time required before disconnecting a session. (The default is
15 minutes.)

Group policies are managed using two MMC snap-ins: the
Domain Security Policy MMC snap-in and the Local Security Policy
MMC snap-in. Both are found in the administrative tools menu
accessible via Start | Program Files | Administrative Tools. Domain
group policies are not inherited by child domains in a domain tree

and are not shared with peers in a domain forest. Local group policies are specific to a computer.

TIP: Don't muck around with group policies if you don't know what you are doing. It is possible to make changes so that no one can log into the server. While it is possible to cause a similar problem by making changes to the security settings accessible within the Active Directory Users and Computers MMC snap-in, the process is much more involved.

To access the Group Policy MMC, first start up the Active Directory User and Computer MMC snap-in shown in Figure 12-4. The domain largecompany.com is selected in the example. The Group Policy you are pursuing with this process is actually a superset of the details presented by the Domain Security Policy MMC snap-in and the Local Security Policy MMC snap-in mentioned earlier.

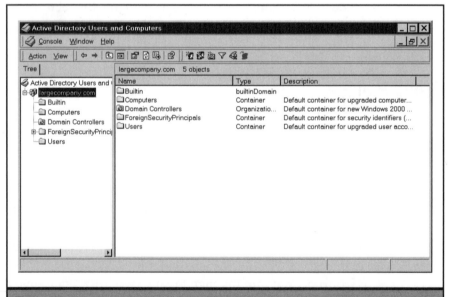

Figure 12-4. User and Computer MMC snap-in window

Select Action | Properties to view the largecompany.com's
Properties page. Select the Group Policy tab to show the window in
Figure 12-5. The Default Domain Policy is set up when the domain is
created, but it is possible to add policies to the list using the buttons
below the Group Policy Object Links list. Multiple policies allow
specific attributes to be set in a policy and enabled or disabled based
on the policy, instead of having just one policy and having to locate
and set the individual attributes. For example, a highly secure server
may be set up with a policy that prevents unnecessary services from
being started maliciously or by accident. Configuring a new policy
with the New button allows the settings to be placed into the new
policy and implemented only when the policy is in effect. If the
configuration is incorrect, it is a simple matter to disable it and return
to the original policies so that subsequent changes can be made while
the server or domain continues to operate. The Add button is used to
include a policy that has already been created. The Delete button can
both delete the entry from this list and delete it from the list of
available policies.

NOTE: It is possible to disable a policy by selecting the policy and clicking on
the Options button. Another option is to prevent other policies from overriding
settings in the selected policy.

The Block Policy Inheritance check box operates in a similar fashion
to the Allow Inheritable Permissions From Parent To Propagate To
This Object check box mentioned in the previous section. Of course,
the semantics are reversed, but the Block Policy Inheritance check box is
usually empty by default. Domain level policies are typically inherited
by a computer within the domain.

REMEMBER: Policies are not inherited across domain boundaries.

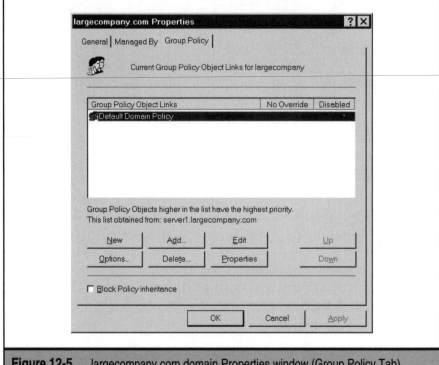

Figure 12-5. largecompany.com domain Properties window (Group Policy Tab)

NOTE: A policy is an Active Directory object that has an ACL associated with it. As with other Active Directory objects, there is a Security tab on the policy's Properties page (which you can access by clicking the Properties button shown in Figure 12-5). This controls who can change the policy; it does not affect what is implemented by the policy.

Policies are applied in a top-down fashion. The Up and Down buttons in Figure 12-5 would be enabled if more than one policy was in the list. The selected policy can be moved in the corresponding direction using these buttons.

Clicking on the Edit button after selecting a policy brings up the Group Policy MMC snap-in window shown in Figure 12-6. Only the first level of the hierarchical contents is shown in the window when it

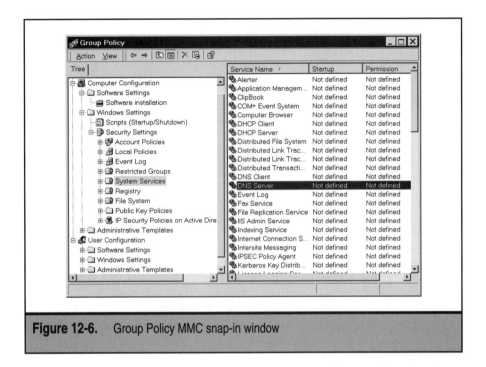

Figure 12-6.   Group Policy MMC snap-in window

first comes up. The window in Figure 12-6 is obtained by expanding Windows Settings | Security Settings and selecting System Services.

The system services are those that can run within a domain versus services that are actually running. Remember, this particular presentation of the Group Policy is for the entire domain. Any changes applied here filter down to the Windows 2000 computers running in the domain unless policies specific to the computer override the domain specified policy.

In particular, the DNS service is selected in Figure 12-6. The current startup setting and permission column entries indicate undefined. Select Action | Security to bring up the Security Policy Setting window shown in Figure 12-7.

By default, the check box for Define This Policy Setting is unchecked. This disables the Automatic, Manual, and Disabled radio buttons and the Edit Security button. The Edit Security button is used in the next section. To enable it, check the Define This Policy Setting check box.

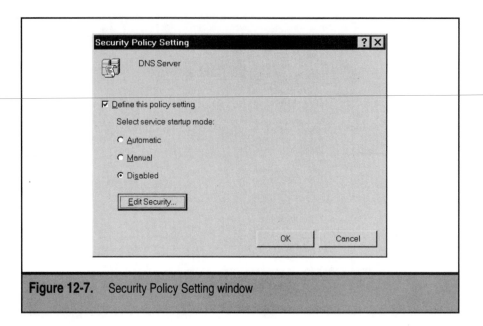

Figure 12-7.   Security Policy Setting window

DNS Service Control

Click on the Edit Security button to bring up the Security for DNS
Server window shown in Figure 12-8. The default setting allows the
Everyone group to control the service. This is generally changed to a
group such as DNS Admins. The ability to start, stop, and pause the
service should always be enabled for at least administrators.

Selecting one of the entries in the Permissions box and
clicking the Advanced button presents the Access Control Settings
for MicrosoftDNS window shown in Figure 12-9. Adding or
removing entries from the Permission Entries list will have the same
effect as adding or removing the same entry in the window shown
in Figure 12-8. The added features for this window include the
Auditing tab, which can fine-tune auditing for this service, and
the View/Edit button.

Click on the View/Edit button to display the more detailed list
of permissions shown in Figure 12-10. This allows a more detailed
selection of rights than those available in the Security for DNS Server
window shown in Figure 12-8.

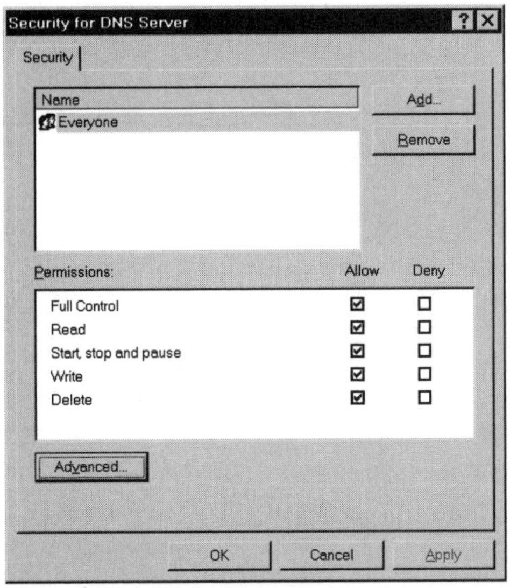

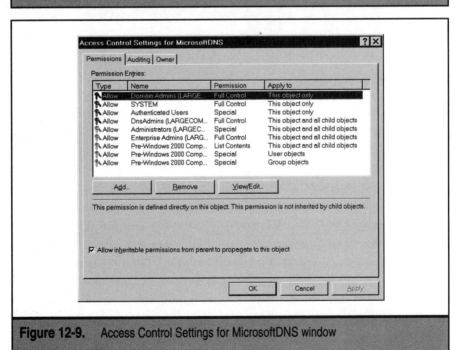

Figure 12-8. Security for DNS Server window

Figure 12-9. Access Control Settings for MicrosoftDNS window

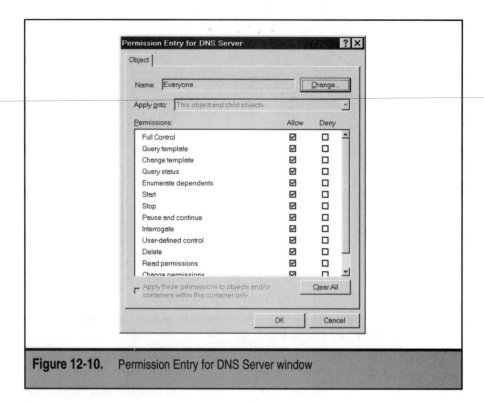

Figure 12-10.   Permission Entry for DNS Server window

DNS Service Access

The quest to limit DNS service access starts with the DNS MMC snap-in. Start by selecting the desired DNS server. Select Action | Properties to display the Properties window and then select the Security tab. This brings up the window in Figure 12-11.

Note that the Permissions list looks similar to the list in the prior section except that this list does not include service control rights such as the ability to start or stop the service. This list is specifically for access control such as the ability to read information from the DNS server. In general, Authenticated Users will only have Read rights.

Clicking on the Advanced button brings up a window similar to the one shown in Figure 12-9. Again, the main difference will be that this path addresses more detailed rights.

The windows presented in this section are used to limit who can manage the information distributed by the DNS server. Users or

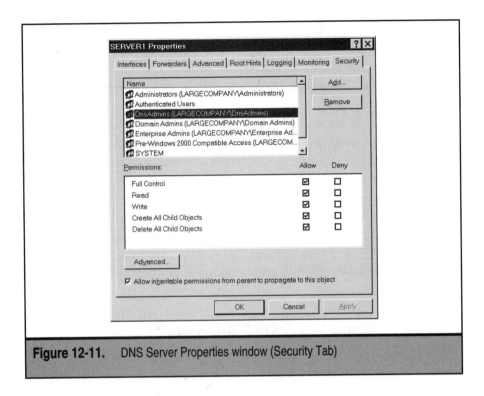

Figure 12-11. DNS Server Properties window (Security Tab)

groups given permission to Create and Delete All Child Objects can create and delete DNS zones covered in the next section.

DNS ZONE ACCESS CONTROL

DNS administrators can create and delete DNS zones if they have Create and Delete All Child Objects permissions, as described in the previous section. This includes Active Directory–integrated DNS zones, primary DNS zones, and secondary DNS zones.

This section takes a closer look at the access controls that can be applied to these types of zones. Each has different attributes; for example, Active Directory–integrated DNS zone permissions are managed via Active Directory. Permissions are associated only with the zone entry, not with individual resource records. In this sense, the control a DNS manager has over a zone is not different from the restrictions that can be placed on file-based primary or secondary DNS zones. The main difference is that the data in an Active Directory–integrated DNS zone can be managed from any point in the network that provides access to Active Directory, whereas file-based management requires access to the server on which the DNS server resides.

Primary and secondary DNS zones, on the other hand, are controlled by file permissions. File permissions can be set using Windows Explorer. Of course, the primary and secondary zones files must be placed in the %SystemRoot%\system32\dns directory, so managers must have access to that directory to make changes. Restrictions can be placed on individual files. Luckily, DNS administration is rarely along zone boundaries.

"Zone Transfer Control" shows how to restrict access to a zone hosted by the DNS server by another DNS server for a secondary DNS zone.

Securely Delegating Zone Management

Windows 2000 DNS service does not allow delegation of subzones or control over individual resource records, but it does provide zone-level security for Active Directory–integrated DNS zones. DNS administrators can be given control over specific zones while being prevented from changing other zones. The person doing the delegation must have control over the DNS service.

Each Active Directory–integrated DNS zone has a Security tab in its Properties window. Users or groups who have authority to manage a zone must be listed on this page and have permission to Read, Write, and Create and Delete All Child Objects. The DNS administrator for this zone does not need control over the DNS service, as changes to the DNS zone are immediately available to the DNS service.

Zone Transfer Control

All DNS zones can act as the source for a secondary DNS zone on another DNS server. Each zone transfer can be controlled on a per-zone basis. The Zone Transfers tab of a zone's Properties window is shown in Figure 12-12.

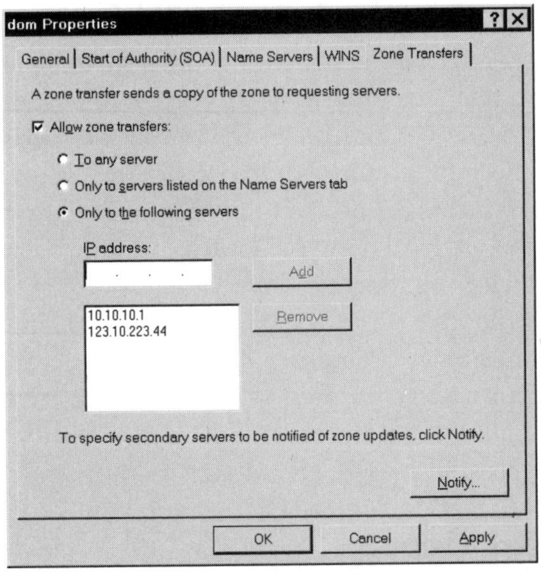

Figure 12-12. DNS zone Properties window (Zone Transfer Tab)

Restricting zone transfers can prevent unwanted replication. There are four selections that are possible. The first is to leave the Allow Zone Transfers check box unchecked, which prevents all replication. The second possibility is to check the box and allow any server to access the zone. The other two possibilities restrict access to computers that are identified by their IP address. Selecting the Only To The Following Servers radio button causes a list such as the one shown in Figure 12-12 to be displayed. Selecting Only To Servers Listed On The Name Servers Tab causes the list to be displayed on the Name Servers page.

In addition to restricting zone access to specific servers, the Zone Transfers tab can configure notification messages when changes are made to the local copy of the zone information. Clicking the Notify button accesses the list of servers to notify. The Notify window offers the same kinds of options as the Zone Transfers tab. The notification list can be a subset of the computers in the allowable zone transfer list.

DNS CLIENT ACCESS SECURITY

In general, DNS client access is unrestricted, but there are some cases where it is preferable to restrict access to DNS information. For example, the DNS server may be storing resource records for the local network, and this information should not be accessible outside the network. If the DNS server is connected to the Internet to provide name resolution beyond the local network, local information can be accessible outside itself. Firewalls are one way to limit incoming DNS access.

Some DNS servers, such as BIND, can restrict access based upon a list of subnets. Windows 2000's restrictions are more basic. In particular, the Windows 2000 DNS service can restrict access by the interface it monitors. This works well when the server has two network interfaces, such as where the server is acting as a proxy server or firewall. In this case, the DNS server would only monitor the local network interface.

The interface settings are found in the DNS server's Properties page that is accessed from the DNS MMC plug-in. Select the server and then select Action | Properties. The Interfaces tab allows a list of IP addresses to be included, as shown in Figure 12-13.

Clients will be able to access the DNS server only if they can access the server through one of the IP addresses specified in the Interfaces tab screen when the DNS server is set up to use the list of IP addresses. Typically a client will be able to access a DNS server through only one of the IP addresses that the DNS server supports. If that IP address is not in the list then the clients will not be able to access the DNS service.

NOTE: A DNS client may access a DNS server through a router. In this case, the IP address in the interface list may be one that the router can access, in which case the DNS client can access the DNS server through the routed connection.

DYNAMIC DNS SECURITY

Dynamic DNS updates are possible for Active Directory–integrated and primary DNS zones. Dynamic DNS updates are very useful, but

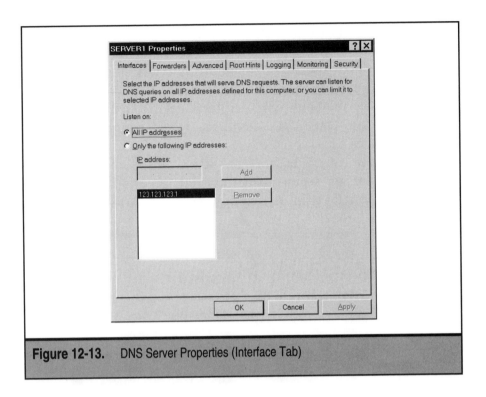

Figure 12-13.   DNS Server Properties (Interface Tab)

unintended and unrestricted updates can lead to large zone files and long resolution times.

Some third-party DNS servers such as BIND can restrict dynamic DNS updates by IP addresses, but the Windows 2000 DNS service does not have a comparable feature. On the other hand, the Windows 2000 DNS service has a more advanced feature available with Active Directory–integrated DNS zones. In this case, updates can be restricted to computers that have been authorized by the Windows 2000 Active Directory service. These *secure updates* require prior Kerberos authentication of the computers requesting the updates. Primary DNS zones on a Windows 2000 DNS server cannot use this feature, although there seems to be no reason why this feature could not be made available since dynamic DNS update control occurs at the zone level.

Dynamic DNS updates are controlled from the Properties window for a zone. This is most easily accessible from the DNS MMC snap-in. Select an Active Directory–integrated or primary DNS zone and select

Action | Properties. The General tab, shown in Figure 12-14, has an Allow Dynamic Updates? combo box field. For primary DNS zones, you can choose Yes or No; Active Directory–integrated DNS zones add the Only Secure Updates option.

One additional way to restrict dynamic DNS updates is to use the Windows 2000 DHCP service and have it perform proxy dynamic DNS updates. This is primarily used for non-Windows 2000 clients that are not authenticated. The DHCP server runs on an authenticated computer so it can request an update. Nonauthenticated DHCP servers can still perform this type of proxy service if the zone allows updates from any source.

RESTRICTING CLIENTS

Restricting access to the DNS server is difficult since IP access to the DNS server is unrestricted. However, it is possible to set some limits

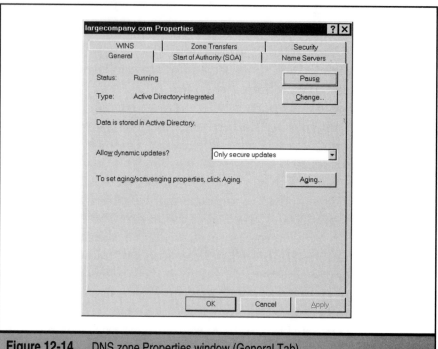

Figure 12-14. DNS zone Properties window (General Tab)

depending on how the IP support is configured on the computer. The Interfaces Tab on the DNS service's Properties page specifies which IP addresses the DNS service will listen to. By default, All IP Addresses will be selected.

If the DNS computer has a single IP address, the only restriction is the associated subnet based upon the IP address of the computer and its subnet mask. It is possible to have more than one subnet on the same network segment. In this case, the subnets will be independent of each other unless a router is used to link one subnet to the other.

If the DNS computer has multiple IP addresses, the restrictions can be more selective but only based on the subnets that are supported by the computer's IP configuration. For example, by selecting Only The Following IP Addresses in the Interface Tab on the Properties page, a list of IP addresses can be specified. In this case, the DNS service will only listen for DNS requests on IP addresses in the list. In general, this feature is used to restrict access to a particular network adapter in a computer with multiple network adapters. In fact, the usual configuration is a computer with a pair of network adapters where the computer is acting as a firewall or proxy server. In this case, the DNS service may be provided on just one of the two network adapters. The selection is based upon the IP address assigned to one of the network adapters.

Restricting access based on a network adapter is relatively secure since access to the server can only be gained if a computer is on the same subnet as the network adapter or if a router connects a computer to the DNS server's subnet network segment.

Some third-party DNS servers can restrict access to specific IP ranges, but this feature is of limited use given the ease of setting a computer's IP address.

SUMMARY

Windows 2000 DNS service security is somewhat limited compared to some third-party DNS servers, such as BIND, when it comes to restricting access by IP address. On the other hand, Windows 2000 DNS does have an edge when it comes to dynamic DNS updates when Active Directory–integrated zones are used.

Although most of this chapter discusses Active Directory security, the Windows 2000 DNS service will even run on a standalone Windows 2000 server that does not have Active Directory installed. The only limitations in that case will be the lack of support for Active Directory–integrated DNS zones and the elimination of dynamic DNS updates from authenticated computers; all other features are available.

This chapter also examines how restrictions can be placed on DNS service management and service control. These restrictions are typically put in place when DNS management is delegated to different users.

CHAPTER 13

Windows 2000
DNS Clients

T he Windows 2000 DNS service will work with any standard
DNS client, although some features, such as dynamic DNS
updates, may not be available with the client or interoperable
with the Windows 2000 DNS server. This depends on the client and
the configuration of the Windows 2000 DNS service.

This chapter takes a look at the DNS clients that will most often
be used with Windows 2000 DNS services. It examines how they
are configured and how they work. We will also address the client
interaction with the Windows 2000 DHCP service. The DHCP service
is discussed in more detail in Chapter 14.

Understanding how DNS clients work is important because
improper configuration can prevent them from properly resolving a
domain name, even if the DNS server can perform the job. It is the
DNS client that must submit the request to the DNS server. Most DNS
clients support local name lookup support in addition to access to a
DNS server. This support can be useful when configured properly,
but it can also be a source of problems.

Luckily, most sites will have DNS clients configured properly.
Added Windows 2000 DNS and DHCP services should work just fine
with the existing client base. Workstations that run Windows 2000
Professional will be new, however, so initial configuration will
be important.

In general, DNS client configuration will be divided into two
camps: workstations and servers. Workstations typically obtain IP
addresses from DHCP servers that can also set up other information
in the client, including which DNS servers are to be used. Servers
typically have fixed IP addresses, and you must configure your DNS
server and set the IP address. Workstations may also be configured
with fixed IP addresses; in this case, their DNS configuration
procedure is usually identical to that of a server.

TIP: Use DHCP services whenever possible. It makes adding or removing
DNS servers much easier, since DHCP-serviced workstations can have their
DNS references changed at the DHCP server instead of having to make
changes at each workstation.

The DNS clients discussed in this chapter are divided into four sections: Windows 2000 clients; Windows 95 and Windows 98 clients; Windows NT clients; and other potential DNS clients. Windows 2000 clients are designed to work with the Windows 2000 DNS service and support dynamic DNS updates. They are also compatible with the Windows 2000 DNS service's secure dynamic DNS updates.

Windows 95 and Windows 98, and Windows NT clients can use the Windows 2000 DNS service, but they do not support dynamic DNS updates. The Windows 2000 DHCP service will often be used with these clients so that the Windows 2000 DHCP service's dynamic DNS update proxy can be used. We will also take a look at WINS operation and configuration with these clients. WINS server configuration is covered in Chapter 15.

Finally, we will take a general look at other potential DNS clients, including their support for dynamic DNS updates. Most will need to use the Windows 2000 DHCP service's dynamic DNS update proxy if the DNS updates are required. WINS support is usually not an issue. Other potential DNS clients include Apple's MacOS, Linux, and UNIX. This discussion is general, and testing of each of these platforms was not done because of the many versions and flavors of each of these platforms. Most network administrators will have a small subset of these platforms if they exist in the network, so testing the clients should not be a major job.

NOTE: A number of other platforms that are not mentioned can also make use of the Windows 2000 DNS and DHCP services. Most of the issues discussed in the "Other DNS Clients" section will pertain to these as well. Some platforms not specifically addressed are PC-DOS, MS-DOS, Caldera DOS, Windows 3.x, FreeBSD, and BSDI.

In general, a client interacts with the DNS and DHCP server in the following fashion. The client determines whether it has a fixed IP address or whether it must obtain one from a DHCP server. In the latter case, a packet is broadcast to request a response from a DHCP server that in turn sends a packet to the client with its IP information. This information includes at least the IP address and net mask needed to use TCP/IP. Additional information can include details like the IP addresses for name servers and gateways. Access to IP-based services can now begin.

At this point, dynamic DNS support can come into play. Either the client or a DHCP server with dynamic DNS update proxy support can register the IP address with the DNS server. Which approach is used or if it is done at all will be dependent upon the client and, potentially, on the DHCP server. The Windows 2000 DHCP server provides dynamic DNS update proxy support. In any case, proxy support is provided transparently for a client if this route is taken.

IP addresses are needed to access IP-based services like Web servers and FTP servers. The client follows a name resolution procedure to convert domain names to IP addresses. This procedure generally includes accessing DNS servers but there are usually other sources of domain name-to-IP resolution used by the client. Each client has its own set of procedures, and the specific clients presented in this chapter are covered in the appropriate section. In some cases, the DNS server will resolve the domain name to an IP address. In other cases, the information may be found locally on the client, and in still other cases, another service such as WINS (on Windows clients) may be used to perform the resolution.

WINDOWS 2000 CLIENTS

Windows 2000 clients are the most robust of the Windows DNS clients when it comes to using Windows 2000 DNS services. This is especially true when Active Directory is used and the Windows 2000 DNS service can service secure dynamic DNS updates. This feature requires authentication provided by the Windows 2000 Active Directory support of the client.

As with most DNS clients, the Windows 2000 DNS client supports its own name resolution sequence that includes the use of local as well as remote name resolution services such as DNS. The first part of this section addresses the name resolution services that are automatically used when a domain name must be resolved to an IP address. The "Windows 2000 DNS Client Configuration" section examines how these services are configured.

Windows 2000 Client Name Resolution Services

The following sequence is used for IP name resolution depending upon what protocols are installed on the workstation. This sequence applies to Windows 2000 and the default configuration for most Windows implementations. Check out tech note Q139270, "How to Change Name Resolution Order on Windows 95 and Windows NT," to see how this sequence can be rearranged.

1. Local machine name
2. HOSTS file
3. Local DNS cache
4. DNS server
5. NetBIOS name cache
6. WINS server
7. B-node broadcast
8. LMHOSTS file

The following sequence is used for NetBIOS name resolution depending upon which protocols are installed on the workstation. This sequence is used by most Windows-based operating systems, not just Windows 2000. It is similar to the process used on other operating systems such as UNIX or Linux, although these platforms tend to skip the NetBIOS and WINS related resolution support.

1. Local machine name
2. NetBIOS name cache
3. WINS server
4. B-node broadcast
5. LMHOSTS file
6. HOSTS file
7. Local DNS cache
8. DNS server

The first three are NetBIOS related services and are used if the NetBIEU protocol is installed on the client. NetBIOS over TCP/IP (NetBT) makes the first three steps possible. NetBT is the session-layer network service. These services can be disabled. NetBIOS uses a broadcast mechanism for NetBIOS names. The NetBIOS names used by the local PC are stored in the NetBIOS name cache. When NetBIOS is used with the TCP/IP protocol, the cache contains name-to-IP mappings that can be used to resolve domain names. NetBIOS names are simple names, not the fully qualified domain names used with DNS. The domain associated with local NetBIOS-based names is the same as the domain set for the client. Hence, this mechanism is only useful for resolving names associated with the local domain.

WINS is the next step up and involves a WINS server. A WINS server operates much like a DNS server with dynamic DNS update support. The main difference is the protocol which is WINS-specific. Clients that have access to a WINS server will register their IP address and name with the WINS server. Clients can then query the WINS server for name resolution, and the WINS server will handle the resolution request using the registered names. As with DNS servers, WINS servers are identified by fixed IP addresses. Windows 2000 supports multiple WINS servers and accesses them in order until an active WINS server is found. WINS is not used if a WINS server IP address is not supplied. WINS does not support reverse name resolution, although the Windows 2000 WINS service can work with the Windows 2000 DNS service so the Windows 2000 DNS service can provide reverse name resolution for names in the WINS database.

B-node broadcasts are actually part of a process of name resolution implemented for NetBT by Microsoft. B-node refers to the type of NetBT client. The client can actually have one of the following designations:

▼ B-node: uses broadcast messages to resolve names

■ P-node: uses point-to-point communications with a name server to resolve names

■ M-node: uses b-node broadcast messages first and then p-node if needed

▲ H-node: uses p-node first and then b-node if needed

P-node operation works with a WINS server. B-node works without a WINS server. B-node operation is primarily used for small networks where broadcast traffic would not overwhelm the network. A large network will normally have clients configured as p-nodes. In general, WINS servers should be used if NetBT is used. If TCP/IP is used without NetBT, these issues can be ignored. Since Windows 2000 clients can operate strictly with TCP/IP and Active Directory, WINS should be avoided if possible. If it's not possible, the Windows 2000 clients can still deal with Windows 2000 DNS if Windows 2000 WINS and Windows 2000 DNS services are linked together. Chapter 15 discusses WINS and this issue in more detail.

Originally, the LMHOSTS and HOSTS configuration files were set up to provide name resolution without the need for name resolution services like WINS or DNS. They are often used for providing name resolution for local workstations and servers in a small network where management and distribution of a text file are simpler than setting up and configuring a service as in a peer-to-peer environment. Clients can still use DNS services, but in this type of environment the DNS server is often located on another network such as the Internet and provides name resolution for nodes on that network, not the local network. Therefore, the configuration files are used to support name resolution of local nodes.

NOTE: Local maintenance of LMHOSTS and HOSTS files can be centralized if the logon script for the workstations copies these files from a file on a network server.

TIP: Avoid using LMHOSTS and HOSTS files, if possible. As they are processed before sending a name resolution request to a DNS server, they can make it appear to a user that the DNS service is not working for a particular domain name when in actuality the resolution is being performed on the client without the help of the DNS server.

The LMHOSTS and HOSTS files provide a similar service to DNS. Both are supported by a Windows 2000 client. In general, these files are used to provide a static list of name and IP address pairs that can be used for name resolution. They are handy if DNS is not used, but with Windows 2000 Active Directory this is not an option. The use of these files is typically reserved for environments that have previously used them, such as older Windows or UNIX clients and the information contained within the files used under Windows 2000. Placing this information in a DNS server makes much more sense from a management standpoint.

TIP: When debugging DNS-related problems, check the LMHOSTS and HOSTS files on the client. They may be the cause of the problem, since they can mask changes made on a DNS server.

Using these files occasionally makes sense for client/server applications that use a fixed name to access a service and need an alias because the DNS server has a different name or does not contain a name for the server being referenced. In this case, the workstation with the application can have the server's name and IP address listed in one of the two files, and the application will be able to reference the server using this name. These configurations are very rare, but they do occur. For example, a client application C needs to access a service S using the name SERVICE1. The server with the service S has a different domain name from SERVICE1, and the DNS server does not include the name SERVICE1. In this case, if the name SERVICE1 and the IP address are included in the LMHOSTS or HOSTS file, the client application will work properly.

The situation becomes more complex if there are multiple services and multiple clients. For example, some clients might be set up to access SERVICE1 on server A, while other clients access SERVICE1 on server B. In this case, the first set of clients have server A's IP address and the SERVICE1 name in their local LMHOSTS or HOSTS configuration file, while the other set of clients have server B's IP address in their configuration file. This situation can become confusing to users if they attempt to ping SERVICE1 from different machines, but the approach works for applications that are not configurable.

The LMHOSTS and HOSTS file have a common format, although the LMHOSTS file can support a number of additional configuration options. The other difference is that the HOSTS file can contain a fully qualified domain name such as foo.bar.dom, whereas the names in the LMHOSTS file are individual names such as foo or bar. The HOSTS file is the same format as the 4.3 Berkeley Software Distribution (BSD) UNIX /etc/hosts file. It usually contains a single entry for localhost: 127.0.0.1.

Let's take a look at the basics first. Essentially, these are text files. Comments are noted using a leading pound sign (#). Blank lines are ignored. The rest of the lines contain an IP address and matching name. Sample files, LMHOSTS.SAM and HOSTS.SAM, are often available. Our sample is the following:

```
# This is a sample HOSTS file
123.45.67.8        server1
123.45.67.1        router1    # Ethernet router
123.45.67.44       workstationA
```

The LMHOSTS file adds its extra features by hiding them inside comments. For example, #INCLUDE MOREHOSTS will add the contents of the MOREHOSTS file to the contents of the configuration file. A common procedure is to include an LMHOSTS file located on a file server. In this case, the file name is usually a complete UNC file name that includes the file server's name, as in \\SERVER1\ SHARE1\DIR-X\PUBLIC-LMHOSTS.

The types of comment-based configuration lines in an LMHOST file include the following:

▼ #PRE

■ #DOM:<domain>

■ #INCLUDE <file name>

■ #BEGIN_ALTERNATE

▲ #END_ALTERNATE

The #PRE command is used on the same line as an entry. It indicates that the entry should be preloaded into the name resolution cache. Normally the cache is empty and is filled as names are resolved, including those resolved through the LMHOSTS file. The command is usually used in conjunction with the #DOM command.

The #DOM command is used to indicate that the entry is for a domain controller needed for logon support. A typical entry would look like this:

```
123.45.67.11    server1    #DOM:mycompany
```

When combined with the #PRE command, the #DOM command allows an entry to become available for subsequent #INCLUDE commands. If this feature was not available, the #INCLUDE commands could not refer to a server named in the file.

The #BEGIN_ALTERNATE and #END_ALTERNATE commands are used to bracket a block of lines with #INCLUDE lines. The first #INCLUDE that references a file that can be opened will terminate the processing of the block. This effectively provides a service similar to the secondary DNS zones on a DNS server where the name resolution information in the zone is downloaded from a host. With the DNS server, the list of DNS hosts is scanned until one is found that can provide the secondary DNS zone information. The block of #INCLUDEs provides a limited form of redundancy.

Windows 2000 looks for the LMHOSTS and HOSTS files in the %System Root%\System32\Drivers\Etc directory. This is also where the sample files are installed. If no files are found, this feature is not used. These files are scanned each time they are used to resolve a name. This can be a long process if the files are large, or, in the case of the LMHOSTS file, if there are a large number of #INCLUDEs. In general, the files should be kept as small as possible with minimal comments.

NOTE: A large HOSTS or LMHOSTS file is of little consequence if most of the name resolution traffic is local, if it's for the same name as the resolved name, and if the IP addresses are stored in a cache that is used before the files are scanned. On the other hand, large files can have a major impact when browsing the Internet where most of the names will be found on a remote DNS server. Each name resolution process will first have to go through these configuration files before sending a noncached request to the remote DNS server.

The final steps in the name resolution process are the local DNS cache and a DNS server. The cache will contain resolved names and IP addresses obtained from previous requests serviced by the DNS server.

The Windows 2000 DNS client supports multiple DNS servers and will dynamically adjust the DNS server used based on the response time of the current server. Most Windows-based DNS clients support multiple DNS servers but only the first accessible one is used. This DNS server is selected once and does not change.

The local DNS cache and remote DNS server support is very important to Windows 2000 clients in an Active Directory network because of the support and requirements of the SRV resource records. These records cannot be found by any of the other name resolution services listed in this section. In fact, access by the Active Directory support on a Windows 2000 client will deal only with the DNS cache and DNS server support.

Windows 2000 DNS Client Features

The Windows 2000 DNS client has some new features compared to the Windows NT DNS client. These include the following:

▼ Dynamic DNS update support

■ System-wide cache support

■ RFC 2308–compliant negative cache support

▲ Avoidance of unresponsive DNS servers

The dynamic DNS update support is the most interesting new feature. It is designed to work with the dynamic DNS update support in the Windows 2000 DNS server as well as any RFC-compliant DNS server. The Windows 2000 DNS client and the Windows 2000 DNS server also support authenticated dynamic DNS updates when both the client and server are using Active Directory support. Authenticated dynamic DNS update support requires authentication of the client by the server using Kerberos. This and the dynamic DNS updates are performed in the background, so most users are unaware of this feature. The result is the ability to locate workstations via DNS without the need to employ WINS or LMHOSTS or HOSTS files.

The system-wide cache support allows the Windows 2000 DNS client to maintain its own DNS cache based upon the time-to-live information associated with resource records. Usually, a DNS cache will be cleared each time the system is started. This support provides a more accurate picture of the network, especially for servers or workstations that are not turned off since the cache information will be aged and eliminated properly.

The Windows 2000 DNS client's DNS cache supports negative caching as specified by RFC 2308. A negative cache entry is added if an authoritative source indicates that a name under its control does not exist. For example, if a DNS server is authoritative for the foo.com domain and it receives a request to resolve the name something.foo.com, it can return an authoritative negative response if something.foo.com is not in its database. Likewise, an authoritative source may indicate that foo.com does not exist, which also eliminates something.foo.com as a defined name. Any subsequent requests such as other.foo.com would be immediately rejected based upon the information in the local cache.

The Windows 2000 DNS client keeps track of the performance of DNS servers with respect to the client and avoids those that are unresponsive. The list of servers is part of the client configuration or the configuration downloaded by a DHCP server when an IP address is initially obtained. The basic Windows 2000 DNS client configuration has a preferred and alternate server. These are actually the first two entries in the DNS server list. An Advanced button leads to the complete server list.

The DNS server list is first used to locate a DNS server. This DNS server is used until it no longer responds, at which point the DNS server is temporarily removed from the list, and the DNS client tries to locate another active DNS server. Most other DNS clients find the first responsive server and stick with it indefinitely.

Windows 2000 comes with a number of command line utilities like IPCONFIG that can be used to manage and query the DNS client and other aspects of the TCP/IP support. The program is more extensive than the Windows 95 and Windows 98 versions. The

Windows 2000 version is covered in more detail in Chapter 19, along with other command line utilities.

Windows 2000 DNS Client Configuration

The first step to configuring the Windows 2000 DNS client is to set up the computer's name and domain suffix. Typically, this is done when Windows 2000 is installed, but we will do a quick run-through to see where to make changes if necessary. One reason for doing this on a server is to make sure that the computer name is the desired name prior to installing Active Directory and turning the computer into a Windows 2000 Active Directory domain controller. Once this is done, the computer name and its domain are cast in concrete. It can only be changed if you remove the Active Directory support first.

NOTE: If an Active Directory domain controller's computer name must be changed and the domain information is to be retained, make sure there is at least one more domain controller set up for the domain. The domain controller can then be converted to a regular computer, at which time its computer name can be changed. Active Directory can then be reinstalled, and the computer will be added to the existing domain. Its local Active Directory database will then be replicated from the domain via another domain controller in the domain.

The following steps can be used to change the computer name and its associated domain suffix. The fully qualified domain name for the computer is the concatenation of these two items. Computers can be managed using Active Directory with limits placed on what resources the computer can access as well as which users can use the computer.

1. Chose Start | Settings | Control Panel.
2. Run the System applet.
3. Click on the Network Identification tab.
4. Click the Properties button.

5. Set the computer name in the Properties window.

6. Click the More button to show the DNS Suffix and NetBIOS Computer Name window.

7. Set the Primary DNS suffix for this computer.

8. Close down the various windows.

TCP/IP settings, including DNS settings, are handled through the Network and Dial-Up Connections applet. This can be started using Start | Settings | Control Panel and running the Network and Dial-Up Connections applet or by using Start | Settings | Network and Dial-Up Connections.

The Network and Dial-Up connections applet lets you create new network connections. If a network adapter is installed, at least one icon will be displayed by the applet in addition to the Add Connection icon. The default icon is named Local Area Connection. Double-clicking on this icon or selecting File | Properties brings up the Local Area Connection window. Next, click on the Properties button to display the Local Area Connection Properties window shown in Figure 13-1.

The Local Area Connection Properties window is used to configure the matching network adapter and to install, uninstall, and configure network components used with the network adapter. Separate network connection objects like this are set up for each network connection, such as a modem link to the Internet, a second network adapter, or even a virtual private network (VPN) connection over an existing network connection.

This chapter specifically addresses the TCP/IP support, which is one of the components that can be installed with a network connection like an Ethernet adapter. TCP/IP support must be installed to support Active Directory. If TCP/IP support is not installed, click on the Install button, select Protocol in the Select Network Component Type, and select TCP/IP protocol.

The TCP/IP protocol configuration is where DNS and WINS settings are found. The settings are specific to the current Network Connection, so it is possible—and usually desirable—to have different settings for each connection. To get to the details, select the Internet

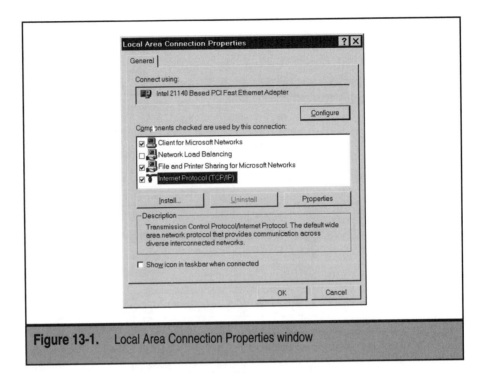

Figure 13-1.   Local Area Connection Properties window

Protocol (TCP/IP) entry in the Components Checked Are Used By
This Connection list box in the window shown in Figure 13-1. Then
click on the Properties button. This presents the Internet Protocol
(TCP/IP) Properties window shown in Figure 13-2.

The Internet Protocol (TCP/IP) Properties window allows the
computer to use a fixed IP address with the matching network
adapter when the Use The Following IP Address radio button is
selected, as shown in Figure 13-2. The IP address and the subnet
mask must be entered. The IP address of the local gateway can be
entered here as well. If the Obtain An IP Address Automatically
option is selected, Windows 2000 tries to obtain an IP address from
a DHCP server. Normally, only one DHCP server will service a
network segment in small networks. In larger networks, two or
more DHCP servers will service a network segment. Chapter 14
covers DHCP configuration, including multiple DHCP servers. In
this case, the DHCP servers will distribute from nonoverlapping
lists of IP addresses.

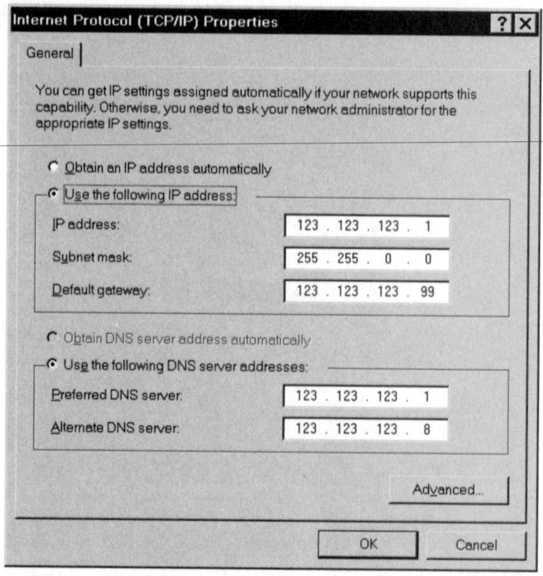

Figure 13-2. Internet Protocol (TCP/IP) Properties window

The DHCP server can provide a number of pieces of useful information in addition to the IP address and subnet mask. Which DNS servers to use is one of these pieces; however, it will be used only if the Obtain DNS Server Address Automatically option is selected. The Use The Following DNS Server Addresses can be selected whether the computer's IP address is fixed or obtained from a DHCP server. This allows a user to override the DNS settings from a DHCP server when necessary.

NOTE: In general, Use The Following DNS Server Addresses should not be selected if DHCP support is used (and Obtain DNS Server Address Automatically is selected). This can add to user confusion when trying to fix DNS related problems, as any changes made by a DHCP administrator will not be reflected on the local computer, and there is no way to determine this except by looking at this screen.

This main screen is all that needs to be examined, assuming WINS is not used and a single IP address is used. Still, it is a good idea to click the Advanced button and check out the Advanced window to make sure that additional customization has not been performed. Advanced settings can cause confusion when debugging DNS problems. The Advanced TCP/IP Settings (IP Settings tab) screen shown in Figure 13-3 is presented when you click the Advanced button.

The Advanced TCP/IP Settings (IP Settings tab) screen shows two major items: the computer's IP addresses and the gateways used to contact computers outside of the subnets accessible from the ones listed in the top list.

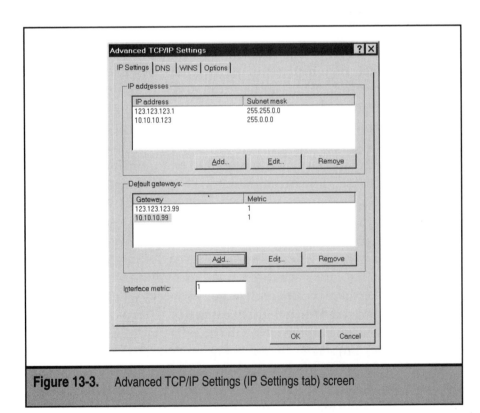

Figure 13-3.   Advanced TCP/IP Settings (IP Settings tab) screen

NOTE: In general, a computer will have a single IP address for a single subnet that will have zero or one gateways. The lists will be empty if IP addresses are obtained automatically. Multiple IP addresses are typically used if the server is acting as a router between subnets using a single network adapter or when the server is providing multiple IP-based services where each service has a unique IP address. For example, the server can present two distinct Web servers when two IP addresses are assigned to the server using the Advanced TCP/IP Settings (IP Settings tab) screen. In this case, the IP addresses are normally on the same subnet that is specified by the subnet mask.

Multiple IP addresses and multiple gateways can cause confusion when debugging DNS problems. This is due to the multiplicity of subnets on which DNS servers can be located. The DNS servers are actually configured on the DNS tab screen, but these addresses are routed based upon the subnets and gateways listed. For example, if a DNS server is on a subnet not directly accessible from the computer's subnets on which it has an IP address, any DNS requests must be routed to the DNS server through one of the gateways. This situation typically occurs when a gateway is providing access to the Internet and one of the DNS servers is the Internet service provider's DNS servers.

The Interface metric is used to determine what gateways are to be used first. This determination will need to be done when accessing a DNS server through a gateway. The gateway with the lowest metric value can provide access to the DNS server's subnet and will be used first, assuming the gateway is accessible. This assumes that multiple gateways provide access to the same DNS server's subnet. This situation rarely occurs on small to medium size networks but it can be quite common on larger networks where multiple routes are provided for reliability purposes.

Clicking on the DNS tab presents the Advanced TCP/IP Settings (DNS tab) screen shown in Figure 13-4. The DNS Server Addresses In Order of Use list at the top contains the IP addresses for DNS servers that will be used in name resolution. For Windows 2000, this list is used dynamically based upon the responsiveness of the DNS servers. In general, one DNS server will be used until it fails to respond to repeated DNS requests. The DNS servers are tested starting with the first one in the list. DNS server IP addresses entered in the main screen shown in Figure 13-2 will be listed here as the first two entries. Additional entries can be added, but this is rarely done unless the DNS servers are often unavailable or multiple networks are being accessed through gateways.

The second half of the screen controls how domain suffixes are used with any unqualified domain names such as workstation1. In the case shown in Figure 13-4, the domain suffix used will be the domain associated with the computer name, as discussed earlier. For example, if the computer's name is workstation1 and the computer's domain is mycompany.com, then a DNS request of workstation2 would be converted to a fully qualified domain name of workstation.mycompany.com.

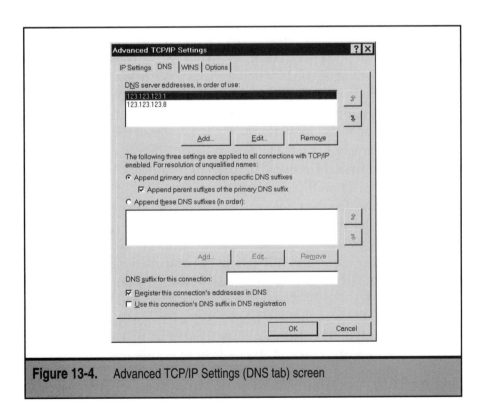

Figure 13-4.   Advanced TCP/IP Settings (DNS tab) screen

If the Append Parent Suffixes Of The Primary DNS Suffix box is checked, a failure of the initial DNS request would be followed by one or more requests using the parent domain names. For example, a domain suffix of a.b.c.com would generate the following fully qualified domain names with workstation2:

▼ workstation2.a.b.c.com

■ workstation2.b.c.com

■ workstation2.c.com

▲ workstation2.com

The second list may contain domain suffixes that are used when the Append These DNS Suffixes (In Order) option is selected. If parent domain suffixes are to be used, they must be listed explicitly.

The WINS settings shown in Figure 13-5 are accessed via the WINS tab. These settings are needed if WINS is used. This tab also controls the use of the LMHOSTS file and whether NetBIOS over TCP/IP will be used at all. In general, a WINS server IP address should be included if the computer needs to be registered with a WINS server or if a WINS server will be used for name resolution. This is most likely to occur on a network where WINS is currently in use and other non-Windows 2000 workstations are being used with WINS.

For WINS to work, the list at the top of the screen under WINS Addresses In Order Of Use in Figure 13-5 must have at least one IP address. Multiple IP addresses provide redundancy in a fashion similar to multiple DNS servers. The order of the servers in the list is critical, just as it is with multiple DNS servers. Windows 2000 handles routing of the WINS requests to the appropriate subnet and gateway if necessary.

The use of LMHOSTS can be controlled from this screen as well. The LMHOSTS will not be used even they are if enabled from this screen if the file does not exist. The Import LMHOSTS button brings up a directory browser from which a file can be chosen. This is typically an LMHOSTS configured file located on a network server or possibly one supplied on diskette and simply saves copying the file to the %System Root%\System32\Drivers\Etc directory.

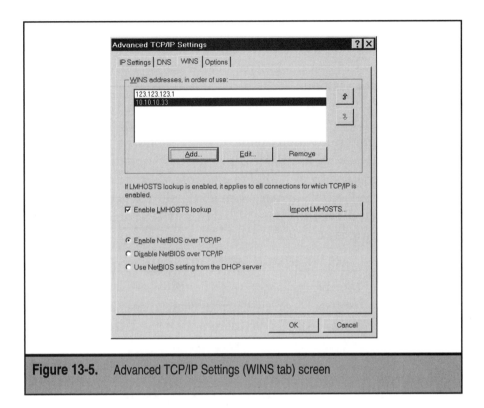

Figure 13-5.   Advanced TCP/IP Settings (WINS tab) screen

The three selections on the bottom of the screen can enable or disable NetBIOS over TCP/IP support or allow the status to be determined by information received by a DHCP server. The latter assumes that DHCP is used to obtain an IP address.

TIP: Disable NetBIOS over TCP/IP whenever possible. It eliminates one possible point of confusion and problems if name resolution is limited to the HOSTS file and DNS support.

The Options tab screen includes arcane details like IP security and whether IPsec is enabled or disabled. The one potential item related to DNS found on this screen is TCP/IP Filtering, which allows individual TCP, UDP, and IP protocols to be enabled. This feature is normally used on computers that act as gateways to limit the type of traffic that can be routed, including DNS requests. In general, a workstation will not filter any ports or protocols. Additional items may wind up on this screen in the future, but at this time there are no other settings.

While the Windows 2000 TCP/IP support and the DNS client have a large number of options, their configuration is not really that different from DNS clients on other platforms. Windows 2000 DNS client features like secure dynamic DNS updates and negative caching are enabled by default. For example, a secure dynamic DNS update is sent to the DNS server when an IP address is received from a DHCP server. If this fails, a regular dynamic DNS update is performed. Nothing is done if this fails.

TIP: When debugging difficult DNS problems on a Windows 2000 computer, record the current settings on paper; change the settings to the minimal configuration such as a single IP address, gateway, and DNS server; and see whether this works properly.

WINDOWS 95 AND WINDOWS 98 CLIENTS

TCP/IP configuration of Windows 95 and Windows 98 is essentially the same and is covered in this section as one. The screens in the "Windows 95 and Windows 98 DNS Client Configuration" section were obtained using Windows 98.

The name resolution services provided by Windows 95 and Windows 98 DNS clients are the same as those presented in the "Windows 2000 Client Name Resolution Services" section. This includes support for NetBIOS, NetBT, WINS, HOSTS, and LMHOSTS. The HOSTS and LMHOSTS files are stored in the main Windows directory, typically C:\WINDOWS. HOSTS.SAM, and LMHOSTS.SAM files are installed when TCP/IP support is installed.

In general, Windows 95 and Windows 98 DNS clients and TCP/IP support differs only in depth of configurability and certain features that are only found in Windows 2000 clients. For example, Windows 2000 can be easily configured for multiple IP addresses, whereas

Windows 95 and Windows 98 are most readily configured with a single IP address.

Windows 95 and Windows 98 DNS clients do not support advanced features such as dynamic DNS updates or negative caching. They do support DHCP, and they will work with the Windows 2000 DHCP service's dynamic DNS update proxy support that is actually transparent to DNS clients. This configuration is preferable to using WINS, although switching from WINS to Windows 2000 DHCP service's dynamic DNS update proxy is a process that should be tested and done in stages. Both can be used at the same time.

TIP: When switching from WINS to Windows 2000 DHCP service's dynamic DNS update proxy, leave the WINS servers running and turn off the WINS support in the clients. This can be easily done if Windows NT or Windows 2000 DHCP is used, as WINS services can be configured via DHCP. It is then a matter of disabling WINS from the DHCP server—but remember that DHCP settings are not activated immediately. They only take effect when a computer renews or initially obtains an IP address from the DHCP server. Renewals can be forced by running the WINIPCFG program and clicking on the Renew or Renew All button.

The "Windows 95 and Windows 98 DNS and TCP/IP Utilities" section covers useful applications for these platforms.

Windows 95 and Windows 98 DNS Client Configuration

Windows 95 and Windows 98 are easier to configure than Windows 2000; this is primarily due to the more limited configuration available under these operating systems. For example, all the settings for these operating systems are found in one place, whereas in Windows 2000 they're split.

Everything starts at the Control Panel Network applet shown in Figure 13-6. This is obtained by choosing Start | Settings | Control Panel and double-clicking on the Network applet. TCP/IP support must be listed in the components list, or it can be added using the Add button, selecting the Protocol items, and then selecting

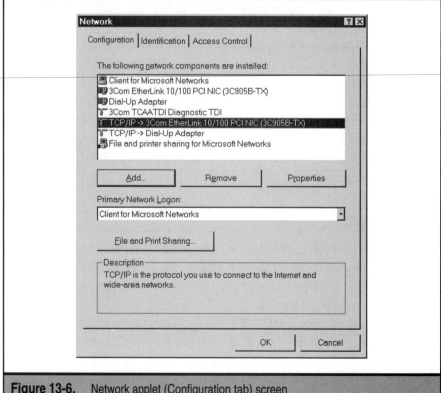

Figure 13-6.   Network applet (Configuration tab) screen

Microsoft TCP/IP support. TCP/IP protocol options are automatically added for every network adapter. They can be selectively deleted as can any other network protocol such as IPX.

NOTE: If the TCP/IP settings for a particular adapter are accidentally deleted, the TCP/IP support can be added again. If the settings have not been saved, clicking the Cancel button will close the configuration window and discard any changes, including the deletion.

TCP/IP and DNS settings for a specific network adapter are configured by selecting the TCP/IP option with the matching network adapter and clicking on the Properties button. This brings up the TCP/IP Properties (IP Address tab) screen shown in Figure 13-7.

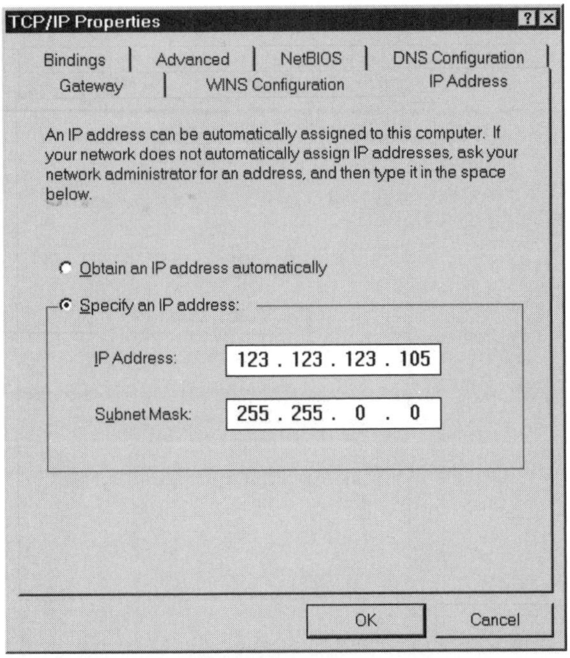

```
┌─────────────────────────────────────────────────────────────┐
│  TCP/IP Properties                                    [?][X]  │
│ ┌───────────────────────────────────────────────────────────┐│
│ │ Bindings │ Advanced │ NetBIOS │  DNS Configuration │      ││
│ │ Gateway      │   WINS Configuration        IP Address      ││
│ │                                                            ││
│ │  An IP address can be automatically assigned to this       ││
│ │  computer. If your network does not automatically assign   ││
│ │  IP addresses, ask your network administrator for an       ││
│ │  address, and then type it in the space below.             ││
│ │                                                            ││
│ │     ○ Obtain an IP address automatically                   ││
│ │   ┌─○ Specify an IP address: ──────────────────────────┐  ││
│ │   │                                                     │  ││
│ │   │  IP Address:      [ 123 . 123 . 123 . 105 ]         │  ││
│ │   │                                                     │  ││
│ │   │  Subnet Mask:     [ 255 . 255 .  0  .  0  ]         │  ││
│ │   └─────────────────────────────────────────────────────┘  ││
│ │                                                            ││
│ │                              [   OK   ]   [  Cancel  ]     ││
│ └───────────────────────────────────────────────────────────┘│
└─────────────────────────────────────────────────────────────┘
```

Figure 13-7.   TCP/IP Properties (IP Address tab) screen

The TCP/IP Properties (IP Address tab) screen is used to set the IP address and subnet mask. DHCP support is used if the Obtain An IP Address Automatically option is selected. Gateways, NetBIOS, DNS servers, and WINS servers are selected by clicking the appropriate tab and filling in the fields on the screen. The NetBIOS screen has a single check box to enable NetBIOS over TCP/IP. The Gateway screen has a list of gateway IP addresses. Clicking on the DNS Configuration tab brings up Figure 13-8, the TCP/IP Properties (DNS Configuration tab) screen.

Disabling DNS does not actually disable DNS support; rather, it allows DHCP configuration of DNS support. Enabling DNS allows fixed DNS settings specified in the rest of the screen. The Host and Domain name can be set independently of the computer name that is set from the main Network applet screen Identification tab. The latter

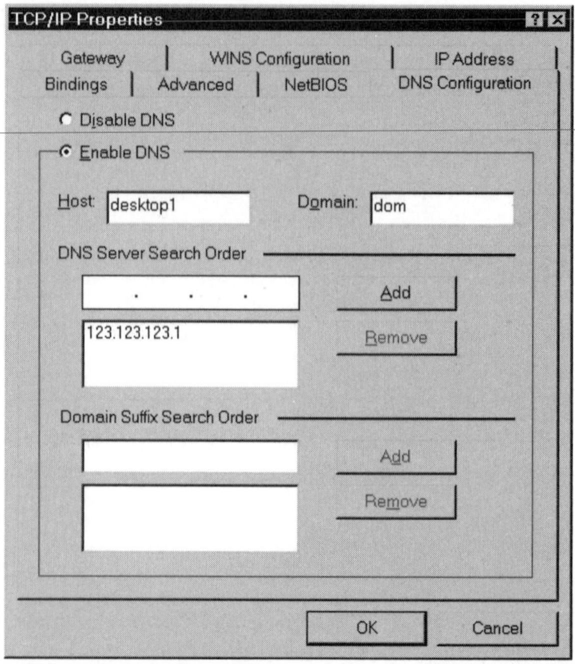

Figure 13-8. TCP/IP Properties (DNS Configuration tab) screen

is used for the NetBIOS name, while the Domain name is used as a suffix for unqualified names. The Domain Suffix Search Order list at the bottom of the screen can expand the list of suffixes that will be tried if the first try is unsuccessful. The DNS Server Search Order list contains the IP addresses for the DNS servers that Windows will initially try. It stops at the first one it finds and uses that for the duration.

WINS can be disabled from the TCP/IP Properties (WINS Configuration tab) screen shown in Figure 13-9. When enabled, the list of WINS servers is searched in order, in the same fashion as the DNS server list. WINS information can be delivered via DHCP as well.

HOSTS and LMHOSTS use cannot be disabled from these screens, so it is important that the HOSTS and LMHOSTS files do not exist if these services are not used.

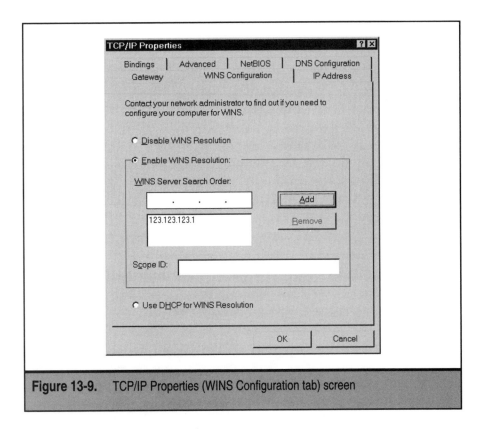

Figure 13-9. TCP/IP Properties (WINS Configuration tab) screen

Windows 95 and Windows 98 DNS and TCP/IP Utilities

There are a number of command-line TCP/IP utilities that are installed with the Microsoft TCP/IP service. These include standard TCP/IP utilities like ARP, PING, and ROUTE. As we are specifically concerned with DNS, however, let's bypass these and concentrate on two applications that can help with DNS operation. The first is a command line utility, IPCONFIG. The second is a graphical application, WINIPCFG. IPCONFIG has limited functionality compared to its Windows 2000 cousin. Specifically, the Windows 95 and Windows 98 version is limited to displaying the current TCP/IP network configuration, including DNS servers, as well as releasing and renewing IP addresses obtained from DHCP servers. The latter is important because this is one way to test DHCP operation and its DNS configuration.

WINIPCFG is essentially a graphical version of IPCONFIG. Figure 13-10 shows the advanced WINIPCFG screen. The top part of the screen is normally presented when the application is started. The More Info button shows the advanced screen as shown in Figure 13-10. The More Info button is then hidden. The information includes the IP address, the DHCP server from which it was obtained if a fixed IP address was not used as well as DNS servers.

The WINIPCFG program shows the details for one network adapter at a time. This includes modem-based connections. The combo box in the middle of the screen is used to select the network adapter.

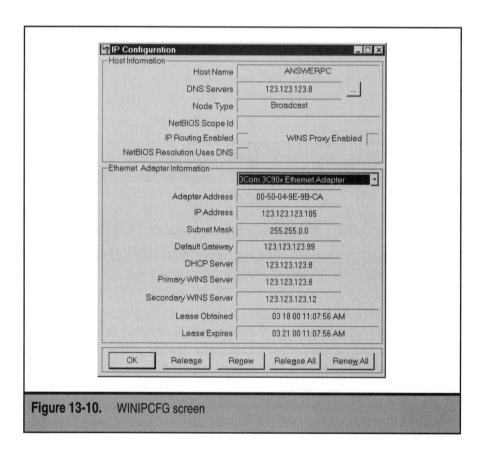

Figure 13-10. WINIPCFG screen

WINDOWS NT CLIENTS

Windows NT TCP/IP clients fall somewhere between Windows 95 and Windows 98 TCP/IP clients and Windows 2000 TCP/IP clients. Users have more control over Windows NT configuration than do Windows 95 and Windows 98 users, but Windows NT still lacks the advanced features of Windows 2000 such as dynamic DNS updates. As such, Windows NT workstations will still require Windows 2000 DHCP server's dynamic DNS update proxy support if WINS is to be eliminated by DNS updates.

Other than the specific details given in the "Windows NT DNS Client Configuration" section, the support for Windows NT DNS clients is the same as that outlined in the "Windows 95 and Windows 98 Clients" section. The "Windows 2000 Client Name Resolution Services" section details the operation of the same name resolution used with Windows NT. Windows NT utilities are comparable to command line utilities outlined in the "Windows 95 and Windows 98 DNS and TCP/IP Utilities" section. IPCONFIG is there but not WINIPCFG.

Windows NT DNS Client Configuration

Windows NT's configuration is similar to Windows 95 and Windows 98. Start the Network applet by using Start | Settings | Control Panel and running the Network applet. The computer's NetBIOS name is found on the Identification tab page, while network services are found on the Services tab page. Windows NT supports multiple network adapters and the Adapters tab page lists those. The Bindings tab page shows the linkage between network adapters, services, and protocols.

Figure 13-11 shows the Network applet (Protocols tab) screen, which lists some protocols. DNS support, as well as other TCP/IP settings, is configured from the TCP/IP Protocol Properties page. The Add button can be used to add TCP/IP support if it is not already in the list of active protocols as shown in the figure. Windows NT can operate very well with protocols other than

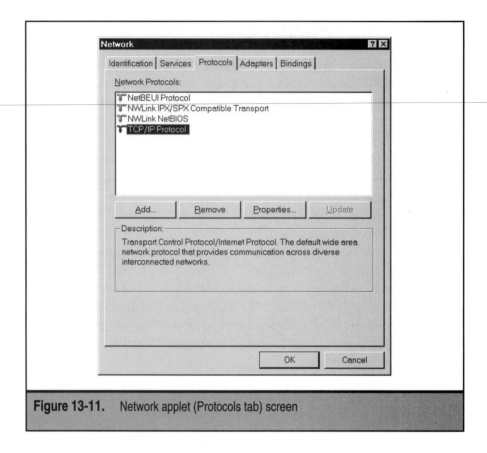

Figure 13-11. Network applet (Protocols tab) screen

TCP/IP; there is no requirement for TCP/IP as there is with Windows 2000 with Active Directory support.

To display the Microsoft TCP/IP Properties screen, select TCP/IP Protocol and click the Properties button. This brings up the Microsoft TCP/IP Properties (IP Address tab) screen shown in Figure 13-12. From this screen, you can set the IP address and subnet mask for the computer. A single gateway address can be set from this point but the configuration options are more like those in Windows 2000 rather than those in Windows 95 and Windows 98.

Clicking on the Advanced button brings up another screen that allows multiple IP addresses to be assigned for each network adapter. This is especially handy for servers that need to provide multiple services using different IP addresses such as independent Web servers. The screen also allows multiple gateway addresses to

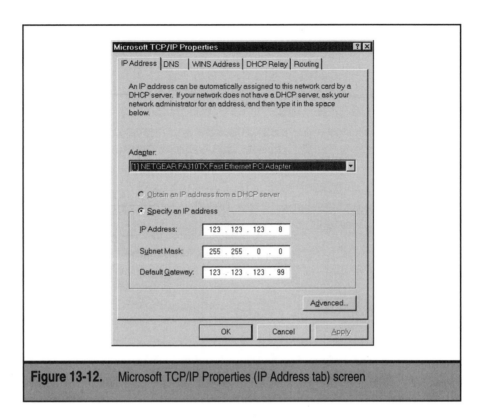

Figure 13-12.   Microsoft TCP/IP Properties (IP Address tab) screen

be set. Filtering can also be controlled from this page, although the Filtering button must be clicked to gain access to the Windows 2000–style TCP and UDP port and IP protocol filtering. Windows NT also supports PPTP filtering.

We skip the DHCP relay support and the routing support. DNS requests can run through the router when Windows NT routes traffic from one network subnet to another, but this is for other DNS clients. The DHCP relay and router support is very useful, but it is not directly related to the task at hand of DNS client configuration. Clicking on the DNS tab shows the Microsoft TCP/IP Properties (DNS tab) screen of Figure 13-13.

There are no surprises on the DNS configuration screen. Multiple DNS servers can be specified but, as with Windows 95 and Windows 98, Windows NT locates the first available DNS server and uses it until the computer is restarted. The Domain Suffix Search Order list

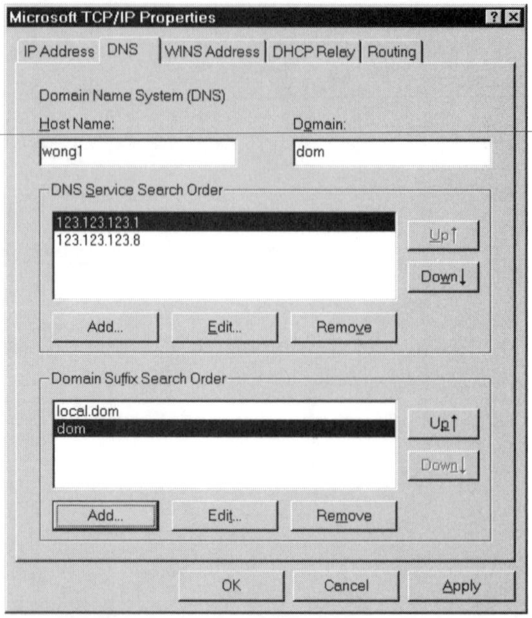

Figure 13-13. Microsoft TCP/IP Properties (DNS tab) screen

allows multiple suffixes to be tested with unqualified domain names.
The Windows NT configuration screen does include Up and Down
buttons to reorder the lists, which makes the job easier than it is on
Windows 95 and Windows 98.

Clicking on the WINS tab brings up the Microsoft TCP/IP
Properties (WINS Tab) screen shown in Figure 13-14. The WINS
configuration is network adapter–specific as selected in the top combo
box. Only two WINS servers can be specified, and Windows NT uses
the first one it finds available. WINS resolution and LMHOSTS
support are controlled from this screen. Windows NT has the Import
LMHOSTS button to import the LMHOSTS file. Like Windows 2000,
the LMHOSTS and HOSTS files are stored in %System Root%\
System32\Drivers\Etc.

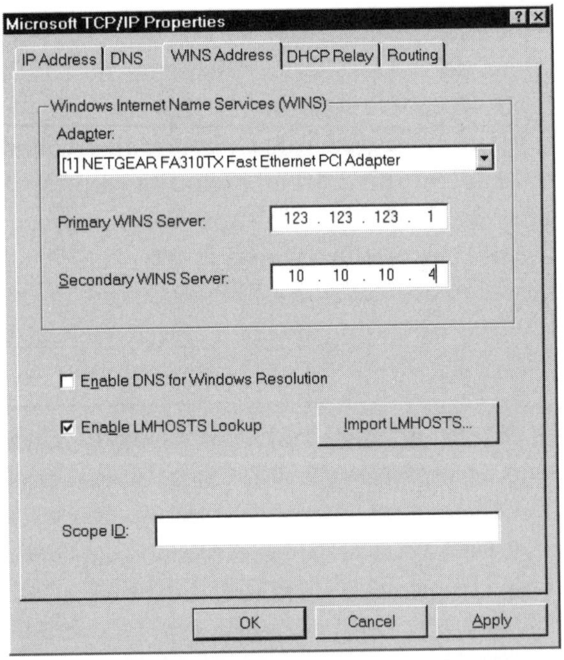

Figure 13-14.   Microsoft TCP/IP Properties (WINS Tab) screen

OTHER DNS CLIENTS

Windows 2000 DNS supports other DNS clients, too. Configuration of clients such as the Macintosh DNS client is similar to Windows configuration, where a graphical user interface makes entry of IP addresses a snap. In this section, we'll take a brief look at UNIX-style DNS clients, including those found on Linux distributions. Some environments provide text-based or graphical network configuration programs that can set up some or all of the DNS support. We do not address these programs, as most of them are specific to a vendor or distribution; the configuration files tend to be more common.

DNS client support is version-specific but the newer versions provide similar features to Windows 2000. For example, BIND 8.2.2 is a third-party DNS service that runs on UNIX and Linux and will support Windows 2000 Active Directory. In particular, it supports SRV records and dynamic DNS updates. Client support has comparable sophistication, including support for dynamic DNS update via a command line application named nsupdate. The nsupdate program is covered in the "Nsupdate" section. For purposes of the following discussion, we group UNIX and UNIX-style operating systems under the heading of UNIX.

NOTE: At the time this chapter was written, Windows 2000's implementation of Kerberos and some UNIX-based Kerberos implementations were compatible with each other. Likewise, the latest version of nsupdate supported secure updates, but there was no general configuration setup for getting this support to work with the Windows 2000 DNS service's secure update support. Showing how to set up such a configuration from source code available from various sources such as MIT is beyond the scope of this book. Sites that need to mix UNIX and Windows 2000–secure dynamic DNS update support should check the Internet for the availability of a more complete solution.

UNIX uses a name resolution that is similar to the Windows name resolution sequence outlined in the "Windows 2000 Client Name Resolution Services" section, although the UNIX process is much more abbreviated, as shown here:

1. HOSTS file
2. Local DNS cache
3. DNS server

The HOSTS file is names /etc/hosts and has the same format as Windows (this format was actually set with UNIX and adopted for Windows). There are a number of other important configuration files. The first is /etc/hosts.conf. This file specifies the order of name resolution, so the sequence just presented is not fixed. The typical content of this file is as follows:

```
order hosts, bind
multi on
```

The first line specifies that the /etc/hosts file is checked first, followed by the DNS servers. The keyword *bind* specifies the BIND DNS server. The order can be reversed, or a single method can be listed. The second line indicates that the /etc/hosts file can contain multiple IP addresses for a particular domain name. This feature is found on most DNS servers and provides a way for the DNS server to indicate that multiple nodes will provide the same service associated with the domain name. A client normally accesses the first address that matches predefined requirements such as being on the same subnet.

The /etc/resolv.conf file is used to specify the domain for the computer as well as the name servers that will be used for name resolution. The following is a sample of this file:

```
domain largecompany.com
nameserver 123.123.123.1
nameserver 10.10.10.21
```

The first line specifies the computer's domain name. The computer's host name is set using the hostname application that is normally run as part of the startup script. Multiple nameserver lines are used to create a list of DNS servers that will be searched to locate the first available DNS server.

The name resolution support is actually found in the resolve library that is linked with applications. The library makes use of the files already presented when resolving a domain name. The nslookup program is one such application. It can be found in other environments, including Windows NT and Windows 2000. Nslookup is used to query a DNS server, and the command line argument is a domain name or an IP address. Nslookup supports various options and can work with a specified DNS server, which makes it a very handy debugging tool. This aspect of nslookup is covered in Chapter 19.

Nsupdate

Nsupdate provides dynamic DNS update client support. The latest version works with the regular Windows 2000 DNS service dynamic DNS update. Support for the secure dynamic DNS update is possible as the latest version of nsupdate, but getting the appropriate Kerberos authenticated ticket is not a straightforward task. It requires configuration of Kerberos on the UNIX system, setting up software to link the local Kerberos realm to a Windows 2000 Active Directory domain, obtaining the appropriate ticket, and formatting it for use with the nsupdate secure dynamic DNS update request. This process is beyond the scope of this book. We do look at the options for performing secure updates with nsupdate, but keep in mind that it is not a simple matter of providing a user name and password to get nsupdate to work securely with Windows 2000 DNS.

Windows 2000 supports the following IETF drafts. These references are provided for those wishing to learn more about the secure dynamic DNS updates. These are also supported by the latest version of nsupdate.

▼ Secret Key Transaction Signatures for DNS (TSIG)

■ Secret Key Establishment for DNS (TKEY RR)

▲ GSS Algorithm for TSIG (GSS-TSIG)

For more details on nsupdate and secure updates, check out the online help for nsupdate and the –k command line option. This aspect of nsupdate will not be addressed in more detail in this book, as the state-of-the-art use of nsupdate at the time this chapter was written required significant UNIX configuration and development skills to integrate Windows 2000's Kerberos-based authentication with its UNIX counterpart. This situation is likely to improve and to provide UNIX users with easier access to UNIX, but the direction and details are not clear at this time.

Nsupdate Operation

For nsupdate to work with the Windows 2000 DNS service's regular dynamic DNS update service, the Windows 2000 DNS service's DNS domain that will support updates must be configured as an Active Directory–integrated or primary DNS domain. The DNS domain must have the dynamic DNS updates option set to yes.

On the UNIX side, the Windows 2000 DNS server must be set up as a name server. This means the Windows 2000 DNS server's IP address will appear in the /etc/resolv.conf file mentioned earlier. At this point, it is simply a matter of running the nsupdate program.

NOTE: The nsupdate program is normally added to the startup script if nsupdate will add the computer's name and IP address to the DNS server. This process should occur after a DHCP server delivers an IP address if the computer is using a dynamic IP address.

The nsupdate program accepts command line options. It can be used interactively or driven by a configuration file. It supports a debug mode that is very handy and that Windows 2000 lacks.

The command line options for nsupdate include the following:

–k keydir:keyname	sign updates using TSIG
–d	use debug mode
–v	use TCP instead of UDP
filename	name of configuration file

Any or all of the command line options can be included. If no filename is provided, nsupdate operates in interactive mode and accepts any one of a number of commands. The syntax and ordering of commands are the same as they are for the configuration file or interactive mode. For example, the following interactive session shows both the interactive mode and the use of the configuration file. Here is the configuration file.

```
prereq nxdomain mycomputer.mycompany.com
update add mycomputer.mycompany.com 300 in a 123.45.67.89
```

Assuming the file was named test.update, the following command would send the request to the DNS server using debug mode:

```
nsupdate -d test.update
```

Here is the interactive session:

```
# nsupdate -d
> prereq nxdomain mycomputer.mycompany.com
> update add mycomputer.mycompany.com 300 in a 123.45.67.89
```

The last blank line is key because each dynamic DNS update request consists of one or more commands. The blank line indicates the end of a request. This allows both the interactive and the configuration file to handle multiple updates. A single update is usually sufficient for a client workstation, but a server will often require multiple updates as the dynamic DNS update can add any resource record.

The following commands are supported by the latest version of nsupdate. These commands can be used in any combination. The first set is prerequisites. The second set is updates that cause changes to occur on the DNS server. The updates are applied if the prerequisites are met. Prerequisites are not required but they can be useful.

prereq yxrrset *name* [*class*] *type*

prereq nxrrset *name* [*class*] *type* [*data*]

prereq yxdomain *name*

prereq nxdomain *name*

update delete *name* [*class*] [*type* [*rdata*]]

update add *name ttl* [*class*] *type rdata*

The command arguments should be familiar to anyone who knows what a DNS resource record looks like. For example, the *name* field is a domain name.

Generally, a prerequisite tests for a domain name used in subsequent update commands. The prereq yxdomain command indicates that at least one resource record must exist for the specified domain. The prereq nxdoman command is just the opposite. No resource records with the matching domain should exist. The prereq yxrrset and prereq nxrrset commands provide the same support but with more specific comparison requirements.

Multiple updates are handy when advertising multiple services. For example, the following configuration file would add Web and ftp address resource records for the same computer:

```
update add mycomputer.mycompany.com 300 in a 123.45.67.89
update add www.mycomputer.mycompany.com 300 in a 123.45.67.89
update add ftp.mycomputer.mycompany.com 300 in a 123.45.67.89
```

One advantage of having a separate application such as nsupdate is that it can be used for a number of purposes and applied selectively. For example, adding the ftp entry can be done only when the ftp daemon is started. The entry can be removed by the script used to shut down the ftp server.

This approach can also be helpful for user applications such as chat or other conferencing applications in which a user will bring up an application and wait for someone to contact them. In this case, the domain name may be based on the user's name or some user ID combined with a domain name suffix resulting in a fully qualified domain name like billwong.largecompany.com. A script will normally be used to start up the application, and the user name or user ID may be obtained from current login information maintained on the computer. Initial configuration requires knowledge of nsupdate and script creation, but it requires no subsequent user interaction. Overall, it's a rather elegant solution.

Nsupdate can also be used in conjunction with a Web-based interface. For example, a Web-based form can be used to enter a domain name and IP address. A script can then update the DNS server using this information. Another alternative is to enter only the desired name; the script would obtain the IP address based on the user's Web browser. The script might even tack on a specific domain name suffix so that the user needs to know only what name to use. This approach is useful when trying to identify a user by name for subsequent communication via IP address.

Using nsupdate is a bit more complicated than using dynamic DNS update support with a Windows 2000 DNS client, but both work equally well once configured. Nsupdate has the edge when it comes to customization, but the Windows 2000 DNS client has the advantage when secure dynamic DNS updates are used with the Windows 2000 DNS service and an Active Directory–integrated DNS zone.

SUMMARY

Configuring DNS clients is not a difficult chore, especially if DHCP is used. By limiting alternatives such as not having LMHOSTS and HOSTS files and using DHCP, DNS administrators can provide configuration flexibly from a centralized point. Chapter 14 provides more on DHCP configuration.

Windows 2000 DNS will support all the Windows DNS clients listed in this chapter, as well as DNS clients on platforms not addressed such as Apple's Macintosh. By staying mostly with the standards, Windows 2000 DNS clients will work equally well with any third-party DNS server as well.

The Windows 2000 DNS client is one of the most robust around and supports advanced features like dynamic DNS updates. While secure dynamic DNS updates are not easily set up except with Windows 2000 DNS clients, it may be the one reason that DNS administrators worried about security will open up the DNS server for dynamic DNS updates.

NOTE: The latest UNIX-based nsupdate application supports the same standards-based, secure dynamic DNS update protocol as the Windows 2000 DNS service, and the UNIX-based Kerberos implementation is compatible with Active Directory's Kerberos implementation. Getting everything to work is still a major task, but it's one that may become significantly easier in the future.

Support for other DNS clients is a bit different than the process outlined for the Windows-based DNS clients, but the results are the same. UNIX- and Linux-based solutions work well with Windows 2000 DNS even to the point of supporting dynamic DNS updates, although configuration tends to be a bit more involved than it is with Windows. This puts them functionally above Windows 95, Windows 98, and Windows NT and almost on par with Windows 2000 clients.

Properly configuring clients is important because improper configuration can cause name resolution to fail or work improperly. The biggest problem that most administrators will face is the lack of monitoring and debugging support on the clients. While tools like nslookup can be used, they are not part of the support regularly used by users.

CHAPTER 14

Windows 2000 DHCP Configuration

Windows 2000 Dynamic Host Control Protocol (DHCP) service provides network administrators with a way to automatically assign workstations with an IP address and to set IP-related information. A DHCP server accepts requests from workstations without a fixed IP address and provides the workstation with a unique IP address based on a collection of IP addresses managed by the DHCP server. This collection is called a *scope*.

A Windows 2000 DHCP server manages one or more scopes that may span one or more subnets. Multiple DHCP servers can be configured to provide redundancy and improve overall DHCP performance.

The Windows 2000 DHCP service is disk intensive. In large networks with hundreds or thousands of IP addresses, the DHCP server may be on a dedicated PC with a substantial hard disk subsystem, possibly a RAID system. Smaller networks often place the DHCP server on the same system as the DNS server, but there is no requirement to do so even when a Windows 2000 DHCP server provides dynamic DNS update proxy services.

The Windows 2000 DHCP dynamic DNS update proxy service is matched with the Windows 2000 DNS dynamic DNS update proxy support. It allows a DHCP server to perform this action for a DHCP client, for example, for a computer running Windows 98 that does not have this ability.

This chapter provides both an overview of the DHCP service in the "DHCP Theory of Operation" section as well as the specifics for the Windows 2000 DHCP server in the "Windows 2000 DHCP Server Configuration" section. Check out the "Creating Scopes and Superscopes" subsection if getting the DHCP service up and running quickly is important.

The "Third-Party DHCP Server Issues" section addresses issues related to using DHCP servers other than the Windows 2000 DHCP server. The "DHCP Client Configuration" section briefly covers DHCP client configuration and references the DNS client configuration presented in the previous chapter since the settings are in the same area.

The Windows 2000 DHCP service has a number of improvements over the Windows NT DHCP service, such as the dynamic DNS update proxy support, but the Windows 2000 DHCP service does not have the same level of integration with Active Directory as the

Windows 2000 DNS service. The Microsoft Management Console (MMC) snap-in for the DHCP service can manage remote services, but each is independent with no sharing of information between one service and another.

NOTE: Microsoft recommends that Windows NT domain controllers be updated to Windows 2000 and Active Directory prior to installing DHCP if an existing DHCP infrastructure is not in place.

As with DNS, the DHCP server implements numerous RFCs. The basic RFCs include RFC 2131, Dynamic Host Configuration Protocol, which obsoletes RFC 1541, DHCP Options, and RFC 2132, BOOTP Vendor Extensions. The latter describes how Microsoft can provide Windows DHCP clients with information about Microsoft Windows–specific services. The DHCP's dynamic DNS update proxy service follows RFC 2136, Dynamic Updates in the Domain Name System.

DHCP TERMINOLOGY

If you are new to DHCP, learning the following terms will help:

▼ Address pool
■ Exclusion range
■ Lease
■ Option type
■ Option class
■ Multicast Address Dynamic Allocation Client Protocol (MADCAP)
■ Reservation
■ Scope
▲ Superscopes

An *address pool* is a set of IP addresses that a DHCP server can provide to DHCP clients. If the pool has 20 IP addresses, the server can provide up to 20 clients with addresses at the same time. The addresses in the pool must be within a scope but not include any exclusion ranges.

An *exclusion range* is a sequential set of IP addresses within a scope that a DHCP server will not use. An exclusion range can define a list of IP addresses used with fixed IP address computers. The range can also specify a list of IP addresses that another DHCP server will be providing to DHCP clients.

A DHCP server *leases* an IP address to a DHCP client for a limited amount of time. When a lease expires, the IP address can be given to another DHCP client. The DHCP client is given the terms of the lease when it receives the IP address, and it can renew the lease any time before it expires. Renewals normally occur about the halfway point on the lease.

An *option type* describes individual pieces of information provided by the DHCP server to a DHCP client in addition to the IP address. The option types are covered in more detail in the "DHCP Options" section.

Option class is a method of grouping option type information by the DHCP server. Windows 2000 DHCP clients can provide Windows 2000 DHCP servers with a class ID so that the client can receive the appropriate class information. A client that cannot specify a class ID will receive the default class options.

Multicast Address Dynamic Allocation Client Protocol (MADCAP) is a new, developing standard for multicast IP support. It is independent of the standard DHCP protocol, although they're very similar. The purpose of the protocol and its support by the Windows 2000 DHCP server is to support dynamic multicast IP address assignment.

A DHCP client normally *reserves* an IP address by taking out an indefinite term lease from the DHCP server. Reservations are usually made for DHCP clients that received the IP address through a means other than by requesting the typical DHCP lease.

A *scope* defines a range of IP addresses that a DHCP server uses to disperse to clients. The address pool for the scope will not include addresses that are excluded by one or more exclusion ranges. A scope can have a set of options defined for it, and clients given leases using the scope will receive the related information.

Windows 2000 DHCP server also supports *superscopes*. Superscopes are a management feature that groups scopes together on a DHCP server. Scopes within a superscope can be enabled or disabled as a group. Options are assigned on a scope basis, not by superscope.

DHCP THEORY OF OPERATION

DHCP operation is relatively simple, as shown in Figure 14-1. A DHCP server maintains a database that includes scope information and lease information. A DHCP client without an IP address broadcasts a request to DHCP servers and waits for a response. A DHCP server responds, and the client receives an acknowledgement called a DHCPOFFER that includes an IP address and any option information that the server has been configured to deliver. The client responds with a message that is designated DHCPREQUEST. The server responds with an acknowledgement, DHCPACK. The DHCP server then logs the lease, including the name of the DHCP client in its database on the DNS server.

NOTE: A DHCP client can receive more than one DHCPOFFER if multiple DHCP servers respond to the client's initial DHCPREQUEST. The client will ignore additional DHCPOFFERs once it has selected one to respond to.

If the client does not receive any DHCPOFFERs, the TCP/IP support may simply fail. Most DHCP clients will continue to retry. Windows 2000 DHCP clients can be configured to use auto-configuration so that the last IP address a client obtained will be used. Although this can be disabled, it is handy in an environment where the DHCP server may not be available on a regular basis, such as when a DHCP relay is providing a subnet with DHCP services via a DHCP server located elsewhere.

If the DHCP server is running the dynamic DNS update proxy, and the DHCP client does not indicate that it can use dynamic DNS update support, the DHCP server will contact its DNS server and perform the update with the client's new IP address. The client's

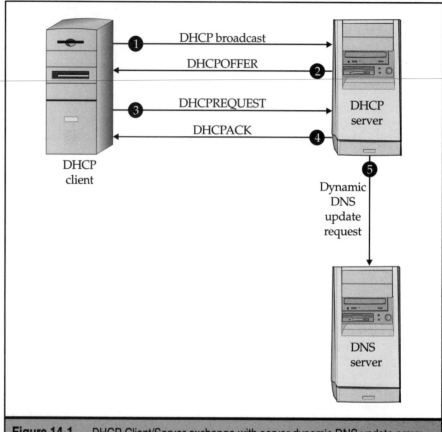

Figure 14-1.   DHCP Client/Server exchange with server dynamic DNS update proxy support

computer name will be sent in the initial request; that name will be used along with a domain name suffix configured at the DNS server. If the DHCP client has dynamic DNS update support, the handshaking looks like Figure 14-2.

One of the items the DHCP client receives when it obtains a lease is the IP address of the DHCP server. The client must contact this DHCP server prior to the expiration date of the lease to renew the lease if the DHCP client wishes to maintain the IP address. A DHCPREQUEST is sent by the DHCP client for a renewal. It will receive back either a positive DHCPACK message from the server indicating that the lease has been extended or a negative acknowledgment (called a DHCPNACK) indicating the lease has expired and will not be renewed.

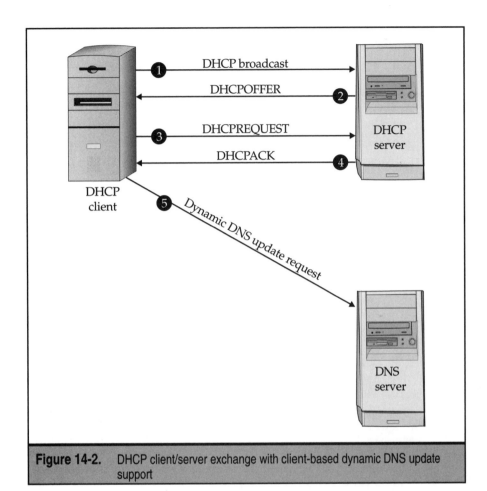

Figure 14-2.   DHCP client/server exchange with client-based dynamic DNS update support

NOTE: DHCP servers do not contact DHCP clients to see if they want to renew a lease that is about to expire. It is up to the DHCP client to perform this task before the expiration date; otherwise, the IP address will be put back into the address pool and given out when needed.

Dynamic DNS update proxy support is a feature of the Windows 2000 DCHP server. It is not a unique feature, although few third-party DHCP servers provide similar support. One aspect that does make the Windows 2000 DCHP server's implementation unique is its support for secure dynamic DNS updates discussed in Chapter 13.

DHCP Options

A DHCP option is information delivered to a DHCP client when a lease is given to the client. Almost every DHCP server supports DHCP options. A DHCP server that supports options will have at least one list of options that will be given to the client. The Windows 2000 DHCP server is configured with multiple option assignment levels, including:

▼ Server options

■ Scope options

■ Class options

▲ Client options

The *server* option level is applied to all scopes handled by the DHCP server. It is handy for network-wide settings.

The *scope* option level is specific to a scope. It is useful for defining details related to a subnet since the scope manages an address pool for a particular subnet. Typical options would be DNS servers that handle the subnet.

Class level options are used for clients that specify what option class they are in. This feature is handy in heterogeneous environments such as those migrating from Windows 9x or Windows NT to Windows 2000. It allows different options to be given to clients based on the operating system they are running.

Finally, there are the *client* level options. These are specific to a particular IP address and are often used for servers that are given addresses via DHCP. They can also be used for clients that do not specify what class they are in or if a particular computer must be distinguished from its peers.

The options that can be specified are described in detail in Appendix C. Table 14-1 is an abbreviated list that provides enough information so that options can be selected and configured using the Windows 2000 DHCP MMC snap-in. The snap-in provides dialog boxes for entering the appropriate data once an option is selected.

Code	Name	Description
0	Pad	Filler to word-align other options.
255	End	Indicates the end of a list of options or a list of suboptions when a vendor-specific option list is included (see option Code 43 for more details).
1	Subnet Mask	Subnet mask for client's IP address.
2	Time Offset	Time offset from Universal Coordinated Time (UCT) for the subnet from the zero meridian (Greenwich mean time).
3	Router	List of IP addresses of routers that a client can use.
4	Time Server	List of IP addresses of RFC 868–compliant timer servers.
5	IEN Name Server	List of IP addresses for Internet Engineering Note–compatible name servers. See code 6 for DNS name server list.
6	DNS Server	List of IP addresses for DNS servers.
7	Log Server	List of IP addresses for MIT-LCS UDP–compatible log servers.

Table 14-1.   RFC 1497 DHCP Options

Code	Name	Description
8	Cookie Server	List of IP addresses for RFC 865–compliant cookie servers.
9	LPR Server	List of IP addresses for RFC 1179–compliant line printer (LPR) servers.
10	Impress Server	List of IP addresses for Imagen Impress servers.
11	Resource Location Server	List of IP addresses for RFC 887–compliant Resource Location servers.
12	Host Name	Fully qualified domain name (FQDN) normally constructed from the computer name provided in the DHCPREQUEST and a domain suffix set at the DHCP server.
13	Boot File Size	Unsigned 16-bit integer value that specifies the number of 512-byte blocks that make up the boot record for the client.
14	Merit Dump File	Specifies the name of a file on the client that is to be dumped in the event of a client failure.
15	DNS Domain Name	Domain name suffix that the client should use for resolving simple domain names.

Table 14-1. RFC 1497 DHCP Options *(continued)*

Code	Name	Description
16	Swap Server	IP address of the swap server for the client.
17	Root Path	Root path for client.
18	Extension Path	Specifies the file name of a boot file that can be downloaded using the Trivial File Transfer Protocol (TFTP). Similar to the BOOTP response from a BOOTP server.

Table 14-1. RFC 1497 DHCP Options *(continued)*

Options used on a Windows 2000 network can be divided into three major groups: standard options, extended options, and Microsoft-specific options. The standard options are those described in RFC 1497, which outlines the basic set of options for DHCP and BOOTP. In the latter case, the options are called vendor extensions. The extended options are specified by the RFCs after 1497. The Microsoft-specific options are those used only with Microsoft DHCP clients and address features such as WINS that have no counterpart in a general DHCP environment. Vendor-specific options are part of the overall DHCP definitions. Like other DHCP options, the client can ignore any option it does not understand, or does not wish to use.

Of the options in Table 14-1, the most important is code 1, Subnet Mask. It specifies the subnet that the client's IP address is associated with. All other options are optional. Code 3, Router, and code 6, DNS Server, are typically used with most networks. For those options with a list of server IP addresses, the client will scan the list and try to contact the first available server.

A number of options are used only by some UNIX-based clients, such as code 17, Root Path, and code 16, Swap Server.

NOTE: Windows clients normally use code 1, 3, 6, and 15. Windows clients do not use the code 12, Host Name, option because a client's name is constructed from the client's computer name. Other options used by Windows clients, which are described later, include WINS client and server specifications.

Other standard DHCP options include the following groups. Options for each group are defined in more detail in Appendix C. While some of these options, such as NetBIOS over TCP/IP, are used by Windows DHCP clients, these options are used less frequently than the RFC 1497 options just covered.

▼ IP host options

■ IP interface options

■ Link layer options

■ TCP options

■ Application layer options

▲ NetBIOS over TCP/IP options

The Microsoft-specific options are delivered as part of a vendor-specific information option, code 43. This option is designed so that clients can ignore the options that they are not using or that they do not support. The vendor-specific information is organized like the vendor independent information in that a code starts each record and the code 255, End, option indicates the end of the vendor-specific information option. The codes listed in Table 14-2 are assumed to encompass a vendor-specific information option record.

Code 1, Disable NetBT, disables NetBIOS support for Windows 2000 clients that do not really need to use it. This option is typically used in a homogeneous environment with Windows 2000 clients and servers or where the Windows 2000 clients will only be using Windows 2000 servers.

Code	Name	Description
1	Disable NetBT	Disable NetBIOS over TCP/IP. Used with Windows 2000 DCHP clients.
2	Release DHCP Lease on Shutdown	Windows 2000 DHCP clients will release its leased IP address before completing a regular shutdown.
3	Default Router Metric Base	Router metric base used by Windows 2000 DHCP clients that receive a router IP address using a code 3 Router option.

Table 14-2. Microsoft Vendor-Specific DHCP Options

Code 2, Release DHCP Lease on Shutdown, is useful where IP addresses may be at a premium and transient laptop users plug into the network on a semiregular basis. Without this Windows 2000 DHCP feature, a laptop user's PC may obtain an IP address and only use it during that session. Subsequent connections may be weeks or months later, but the DHCP server would be forced to maintain the lease until it expired. This option is of little consequence to users on a network with reliable DHCP services since a new IP address can be obtained whenever it is needed.

Code 3, Default Router Metric Base, is used by Windows 2000 DHCP clients to determine the most efficient method of routing nonlocal messages. Generally, the most efficient router will be used, but if it is not accessible then a less efficient router will be selected based upon this metric. This creates a more robust environment when multiple routes are available to a client.

DHCP Class IDs

Microsoft Windows 2000 and Windows 98 support vendor-specific DHCP class IDs. These include:

- ▼ MSFT 5.0
- ■ MSFT 98
- ▲ MSFT

MSFT 5.0 indicates a Windows 2000 DHCP client. MSFT 98 indicates a Windows 98 client (not a Windows 95 client). The MSFT class is handled by the Windows 2000 DHCP server and is associated with both of the other class IDs.

NOTE: A Windows 2000 DHCP client can set its class ID, but it must be done using a command line interface. It uses the ipconfig program with a /setclassid option followed by class name in quotes and the class ID name, for example, >ipconfig /setclassid "New Class" MyClassID.

Class IDs can be defined by DHCP administrators. This may be in response to new DHCP clients, or it may be to provide access to specific features supported by the clients. Microsoft has a few predefined user classes. These include:

- ▼ RRAS.Microsoft
- ▲ BOOTP.Microsoft

RRAS.Microsoft is for dial-in support through a Windows 2000 Routing and Remote Access Server (RRAS). It allows the DHCP server to identify DHCP clients that are using PPP-type connections. Windows 2000 RRAS clients know they are a member of this class, whereas other RRAS clients do not. In the latter case, the RRAS server lets the DHCP server know of the class because it is acting as a DHCP relay to the remote clients.

The BOOTP.Microsoft class is only used by BOOTP clients, not DHCP clients.

Multiple DHCP Servers for One Subnet

A single DHCP server can support an entire network and often does in the case of small networks. A DHCP server is typically assigned to a subnet, and at least one DHCP server will support a subnet in a larger network with multiple subnets, although it is possible for a DHCP server to support multiple subnets. A more robust environment can be created using two or more DHCP servers on the same subnet, just as multiple DNS servers provide a more robust environment.

Most DHCP servers and clients support multiple DHCP servers on a single subnet. This is accomplished by partitioning the IP address space used for address pools among DHCP servers on the same subnet. If the number of addresses is limited, it might be more difficult to split up the addresses among a number of DHCP servers. In general, there are enough IP addresses that they can be split among the DHCP servers.

In general, each DHCP server in the same subnet is set up with the same scope and options. Each DHCP server has its own range of addresses in the scope. Other addresses are ignored using one or two exclusion ranges. Normally these specify the addresses before and after the DHCP server's available address range, as shown in Figure 14-3, which shows three DHCP servers and a single scope.

The exclusion ranges do not have to be split evenly, as shown in the figure. They can be adjusted based upon the availability of more IP addresses than clients, the responsiveness of the DHCP servers, and the planned availability. For example, in a two–DHCP server environment, the primary DHCP server might be given 80 percent of the IP addresses with the other 20 percent going to the other DHCP server.

When a client requests a DHCP address, each DHCP server will see the broadcast and respond in kind. The DHCP client then determines which DHCP server will be used. This is usually the first one that responds.

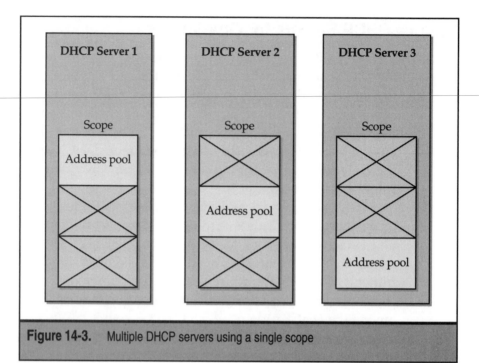

Figure 14-3. Multiple DHCP servers using a single scope

NOTE: The first DHCP server to respond will be responding to the initial request for a new IP address, not renewing a lease. Leases are renewed by communicating directly with the DHCP server from which it obtained the lease.

WARNING: Do not overlap address pools on different DHCP servers or within scopes on the same DHCP server. This will result in major problems when two DHCP servers try to lease the same IP address. If that happens, two different clients will wind up with the same IP address, which is a problem because all IP addresses are supposed to be unique at any point in time.

An alternative to using overlapping scopes for multiple DHCP servers is to use hot standby, or hot spare, DHCP servers. In this case, the hot standby is identically configured with its mate. The hot standby is manually activated when its mate goes down. The hot standby should be shut down if the mate is brought up again, or the mate should be turned into the hot standby.

There's a problem with changing DHCP servers in midstream. While the scopes, address pools, and option information can be replicated, the lease information will not be replicated. In this case, the new hot standby will be starting fresh and will lease IP addresses in the order that they are requested. The clients must release their IP addresses and get a new one from the new server. Unfortunately, this process is manual.

> **NOTE:**   A DHCP service does not have to be started to make a hot spare provide IP addresses if the service can enable scopes on-the-fly. Windows 2000 DHCP server supports control of individual scopes.

A similar process must occur when migrating DHCP services from one computer to another, but the problems can be less severe, especially if the DHCP service is moving from one Windows 2000 computer to another. In this case, the database file used by the Windows 2000 DHCP service is normally copied from one server to another instead of replicating the option and lease information. This approach cannot be taken by hot spare DHCP servers because the DHCP data base is updated continuously. In theory, a clustered pair of servers with a shared, external hard disk subsystem would provide the hot spare with the latest database, but it should be used only if it can be determined that the database has not been corrupted.

The Windows 2000 DHCP service supports superscopes. A superscope contains one or more scopes. A superscope can be enabled and disabled, which enables or disables all the scopes within a superscope.

DHCP on Routed Networks

Routers are normally used to partition a network or to link one part of a network with another part, usually through a lower speed link such as a T1 line or an ISDN line. TCP/IP is a routable protocol, so it makes sense to have computers with IP addresses on both sides of a routed connection.

The issue is how IP addresses are assigned at either end of a routed connection. There are three main possibilities. The first is to use fixed IP addresses. This is practical if the number of computers is small, say, less than a dozen. It is a good approach for a branch office that is connected to the main office by a router.

NOTE: Keep in mind that fixed IP addressing implies more than just setting up a computer with an IP address. Net masks must match so that all the computers are on the same subnet. IP addresses for servers such as routers and DNS servers must be set so the computer can access other services. All must be properly configured and maintained for everything to work properly.

The second option is to place the DHCP server at both ends of the connection. This is the easiest approach and is very advantageous for low-speed connections because computers do not have to obtain an IP address by going through the router and its connection. The possible disadvantage of this option is the need to have a computer to host the DHCP service because this service must be managed, possibly through the routed connection.

The third option is to have a DHCP server at one end and have DHCP client requests from the other end of the connection relayed to the DHCP server. Unfortunately, DHCP requests are broadcasts, and most routers are not set up to relay broadcasts across the connection. This is to prevent overloading the connection. DHCP broadcasts tend to be the exception and many routers can be set up to act as DHCP relays, including Windows 2000 .

This approach has the advantage of minimizing management chores, but it runs the risk of leaving the remote site in the lurch if the router connection is down. While access to computers on the other side is obviously lost when the connection is down, the computers at the remote site can still work with each other if they have IP addresses. Windows 2000 DHCP clients' auto-configuration support, mentioned in the "DHCP Theory of Operation" section, handles this situation gracefully, but other DHCP clients may not. If this is an issue, consider using one of the other two approaches instead.

Another issue with this option is the speed of the routed connection. A low speed increases the delay associated with obtaining an IP address; the computer will not be able to access network services until the IP address is obtained. A low-speed connection will also limit the number of DHCP clients that can be supported.

Whatever approach is taken, DHCP administrators need to be aware of the tradeoffs and their effects on users. If TCP/IP is the only protocol utilized at a remote site, and continuous network operation is a requirement, Windows 2000 clients should be a consideration unless a DHCP server is located at the remote site.

Multicast IP Addresses and MADCAP

MADCAP (Multicast Address Dynamic Allocation Client Protocol) provides multicast IP addresses that are employed by multicast transmissions. It allows a multicast server to broadcast information once and have this information delivered to multicast clients simultaneously. The alternative is to use conventional unicast IP connections. In this case, the server must know the IP address of each client, and information is sent individually to each client. If there are 20 clients, multicast sends information once while unicast sends information 20 times. Multicast is a relatively new technology that has found favor with streaming media applications.

Windows 2000 provides MADCAP client and server support. The MADCAP server is independent of the DHCP server, although both can be installed on the same server.

Multicast clients obtain multicast IP addresses in a fashion similar to the way that conventional IP addresses are obtained from the DHCP service. The main difference is how the IP addresses are used. For example, a multicast client, X, obtains a multicast IP address via MADCAP. This client is also a server that will broadcast information to its clients. These clients contact computer X to register with the server X, and they receive the multicast IP address in return. The clients can then receive information broadcast from X. The clients are part of a *multicast group*.

Multicast information does not get sent to all parts of a network. Multicast-capable routers forward information only as necessary. This information will be sent to a subnet only once, regardless of the number of clients on the subnet that are registered to receive the information.

Multicast IP addresses are part of the IP address space, but they are not part of the address space that a DHCP service can use. In particular, valid multicast IP addresses range from 224.0.0.0 to 239.255.255.255. These are referred to as Class D IP addresses.

A typical private network IP address range is 10.0.0.0 with a subnet mask of 255.0.0.0. A private network multicast IP address range is 239.192.0.0 with a subnet mask of 255.252.0.0. This provides a considerable number of multicast IP addresses. There is no limit to the number of computers that can receive information on a single multicast IP address.

Multicast operation and details are beyond the scope of this book, so the above explanation is all that will be presented here with respect to its functionality. The rest of this section addresses the functional details of the Windows 2000 MADCAP implementation, which complements the regular Windows 2000 DHCP service. MADCAP can be very useful in a network that is using streaming media or other broadcast information, but it is not necessary for the proper operation of Windows 2000 DHCP and DNS clients. It is also not necessary for proper operation of Windows 2000 Active Directory.

The Windows 2000 DHCP service has the MADCAP support built-in, so it is simply a matter of creating a multicast scope. This is done by selecting the DHCP server where the multicast scope is to be defined and then selecting Action | New Multicast Scope. This starts up the New Multicast Scope Wizard.

NOTE: Setting up a Windows 2000 DHCP service to support just MADCAP is simply a matter of creating one or more multicast scopes, not conventional scopes or superscopes. The DHCP service can support MADCAP and not respond to conventional DHCP client requests if there are no conventional scopes or superscopes defined.

The New Multicast Scope Wizard steps through a number of screens including the one shown in Figure 14-4, IP Address Range. This screen sets the starting and ending IP addresses. These must be valid multicast IP addresses, as mentioned above. Subsequent screens check for details such as exclusion ranges, just like the exclusion ranges used with conventional IP scopes. This allows multiple MADCAP servers to

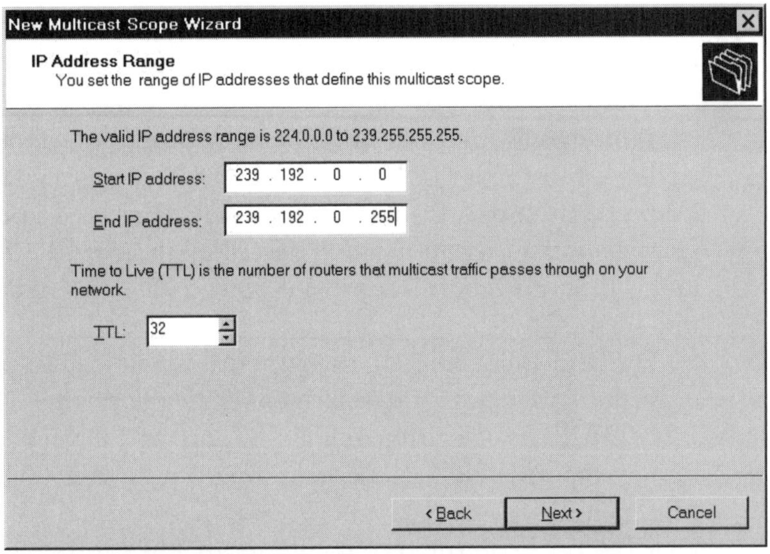

Figure 14-4.   The IP Address Range screen in the New Multicast Scope Wizard

operate on the same subnet in the same fashion that conventional DHCP services can operate on the same subnet, as described in the "Multiple DHCP Servers for One Subnet" section.

Multicast IP scopes cannot be part of superscopes. Multiple multicast scopes can be defined and managed independently. Multicast scopes do not have the options or option classes that conventional IP scopes do, as this kind of information is not delivered to a multicast IP client.

Testing multicast IPs requires MADCAP clients in addition to the multicast clients that would obtain the multicast IP address from the MADCAP client.

Dynamic DNS Update Proxy

Windows 2000 DNS clients support dynamic DNS updates with any DNS server that provides the matching server support. This includes the Windows 2000 DNS server. The Windows 2000 DNS clients also support the secure dynamic DNS update that is implemented by the

Windows 2000 DNS server. Dynamic DNS updates provide an excellent alternative to WINS and to using static IP addresses and DNS entries.

Unfortunately, most of the other DNS clients including Windows 95, Windows 98, and Windows NT do not support dynamic DNS updates. Most older UNIX and Linux DNS clients also lack dynamic DNS update support, although the latest versions do provide support using nsupdate, an application described in Chapter 13. Nsupdate, at this time, does not support Windows 2000's secure dynamic DNS update method.

For DNS clients that do not support dynamic DNS updates, there is an alternative: proxy-based dynamic DNS updates. The Windows 2000 DHCP service provides this support, and it can be implemented for any type of DHCP client, including Windows 2000 DHCP clients. This includes secure dynamic DNS updates since the Windows 2000 DHCP service can run on a computer that has authorized access to an Active Directory domain where the corresponding Windows 2000 DNS service is running.

NOTE: The Windows 2000 DHCP service's dynamic DNS update support will work with other DNS servers such as BIND that support dynamic DNS updates, although the secure version will not, as this feature is exclusive to Windows 2000 at this time. Other DNS servers that support dynamic DNS updates typically provide security for dynamic DNS updates by limiting the IP addresses of computers that can perform such updates.

The dynamic DNS update support is used after a DHCP server acknowledges a lease to a computer. The IP address given to the client and the computer's name are used in the update message to the DNS server to update the A (address) and PTR records. Since all updates will be coming from the DHCP server, the DNS server can be configured to allow only the DHCP servers access to this service. The Windows 2000 DHCP server can be configured to automatically remove the added records when the lease is not renewed in time and the lease expires.

WINDOWS 2000 DHCP SERVER CONFIGURATION

Now that we have gone over the theory, it is time to cover the management details. This section looks at the creation of scopes and superscopes and the management of leases. It does not address MADCAP support. MADCAP is covered briefly in the "Multicast IP Addresses and MADCAP" section.

The "Windows 2000 DHCP Service Enhancements" section presents new features of the Windows 2000 DHCP service as compared to the Windows NT DHCP service. The "Creating Scopes and Superscopes" section covers most of the management work, except for the "DHCP Server Properties and Dynamic DNS Update Proxy" section, which covers this new feature.

Windows 2000 DHCP Service Enhancements

The Windows 2000 DHCP service has a number of enhancements over the Windows NT DHCP service. Unlike the Windows NT DNS server, the Windows NT DHCP supports Windows 2000 . However, given the following list of features, it would be surprising if DNS administrators do not quickly change over to Windows 2000 DHCP service from their current DHCP service.

▼ Automatic client assignment of IP addresses

■ Superscopes

■ Multicast scopes (MADCAP)

■ Active Directory security for DHCP service

■ Support for user- and vendor-specified option classes

■ Dynamic DNS update proxy

■ DHCP service authorization

▲ Enhanced BOOTP support

While the Windows 2000 DHCP service is protected by Windows 2000 Active Directory security, the DHCP service does not take advantage of the Active Directory database for storage as the

Windows 2000 DNS service does. The Windows 2000 DHCP service uses a database file instead.

Some of the new features have already been described, including automatic client assignment of IP addresses, superscopes, multicast scopes (MADCAP), support for user- and vendor-specified option classes, and dynamic DNS update proxy.

The Active Directory security for DHCP service consists initially of two security groups that are created when Active Directory is set up. One provides full access to the DHCP service while the other provides read-only access to the DHCP service. This allows a DHCP administrator to open up the DHCP service for review but prevents inadvertent access to the DHCP service's configuration.

The DHCP service authorization addresses a major security problem that could arise on a Windows 2000 network: the delivery of invalid IP addresses. The Windows 2000 DHCP service does two things to prevent this problem. The first is authorization of the Windows 2000 DHCP service. Authorization is done prior to the DHCP service delivering these leases. Active Directory is used for the authorization process.

The second thing it does is detect unauthorized Windows 2000 DHCP servers. This is done by authorized Windows 2000 DHCP servers that check a new Windows 2000 DHCP server and compare its IP address with the list of IP addresses of authorized DHCP servers. Authorized servers will be shut down. This feature is automatic and does not affect the operation of non-Windows 2000 DHCP servers.

Enhanced BOOTP support improves on the basic, static IP BOOTP protocol by adding dynamic BOOTP support. This allows the Windows 2000 DHCP server to configure BOOTP clients in a fashion similar to DHCP client support using DHCP options.

Installing the Windows 2000 DHCP Service

The Windows 2000 DHCP service is installed using the Windows Component Wizard. It can be installed when Windows 2000 is installed or when the Windows 2000 DNS service is installed.

To install the Windows 2000 DHCP service, start up the Configure Your Server Wizard using Start | Programs | Administrative Tools | Configure Your Server. Under the Networking topic is a list of components, including DHCP and DNS. Select DHCP. If the DHCP service is not running, there will be an option on the topic page to the right to start the Windows Component Wizard; otherwise, there are options to perform management tasks such as configuring scopes.

NOTE: The Configure Your Server Wizard recommends that a new DHCP service not be started if one already exists on another server on the network. While this recommendation is good for network administrators new to DHCP, those trying to build up a more robust system with redundant DHCP servers should check out the "Multiple DHCP Servers for One Subnet" section for details on using multiple DHCP servers on the same subnet. The "DHCP on Routed Networks" section discusses multiple DHCP servers that are separated by a router.

The Windows Component Wizard will display a list of components. You can find the DNS and DHCP services in the Network Services component. Select this component and click on the Details button to see a list of networking components, including DHCP. If there is a check box next to the DHCP entry, the DHCP server is already installed. If not, check the box and click on the OK buttons until the installation process begins.

The DHCP service will be installed and started. It will be set up to automatically start when the server is rebooted. The DHCP service will not respond to any DHCP client requests until at least one DHCP scope is defined and activated.

If MADCAP is to be used then there is nothing else to do except define a multicast scope. The MADCAP support is part of the DHCP server and it remains idle until needed.

Creating Scopes and Superscopes

Scopes, superscopes, and MADCAP scopes are created and managed using the DHCP MMC snap-in. The snap-in is usually started using

Start | Programs | Administrative Tools | DHCP. This brings up a screen that looks like the one shown in Figure 14-5.

Below the DHCP root is a list of DHCP servers. The default configuration shows a single DHCP server that will be the DHCP service running on the local computer. Any Windows 2000 DHCP server in the same network can be managed using the snap-in. Additional servers can be added to this list by selecting the DHCP root and selecting Action | Add Server.

Another action that can be performed from the root is to authorize or unauthorize servers. Select Action | Manage Authorized Servers to see the screen shown in Figure 14-6. The list of authorized Windows 2000 DHCP servers and their IP addresses is presented. Additional DHCP servers can be authorized, or servers in the list can be unauthorized using the buttons to the right. Unauthorized Windows 2000 DHCP servers will be shut down, as described in the "Windows 2000 DHCP Service Enhancements" section. Active Directory must be installed for this to work or the DHCP servers will be acting as standalone entities.

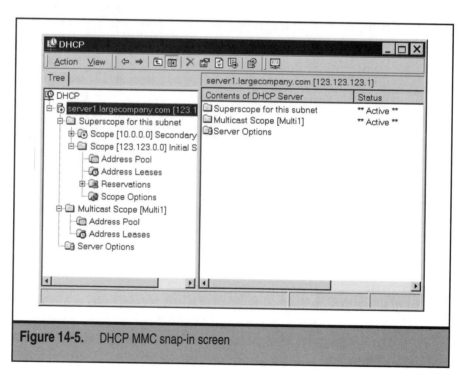

Figure 14-5.   DHCP MMC snap-in screen

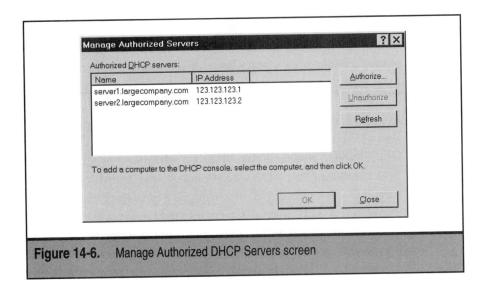

Figure 14-6.   Manage Authorized DHCP Servers screen

In the main MMC window below each server is a list of scopes, superscopes, and MADCAP scopes associated with each server. Initially this list will be empty. The Action menu includes a number of items that are commonly used to create and manage scopes. The menu list includes:

▼ Display Statistics

■ New Scope

■ New Superscope

■ New Multicast Scope

■ Reconcile Scopes

■ Unauthorize/Authorize

■ Define User Classes

■ Define Vendor Classes

■ Set Predefined Options

■ All Tasks

■ Delete

■ Refresh

■ Export List

■ Properties

▲ Help

The last five items, from Delete to the end of the list, provide the usual MMC object services. We will take a closer look at the DHCP server's Properties screen later. All Tasks is a submenu where the DHCP server can be started, stopped, paused, and restarted.

Select Display Statistics to view the Server Statistics screen shown in Figure 14-7. This screen is handy for debugging because it shows the number of requests and the number of DHCPACKs and DHCPNACKs sent. It also shows a summary of the leases. A detailed list of leases is available under each scope definition. This Statistics screen is very similar to other Display Statistics screens when scopes are selected. The main difference is that this main screen provides an overview of the entire server. All of the statistics screens are nonmodal, so they can remain open while accessing the main MMC screen. The Refresh button forces an update of information on any of the screens.

Now we're finally at the meat of this chapter. The New Scope menu selection is used to create a scope that allows the DHCP server to distribute leases. The scope defines the IP address range, subnet

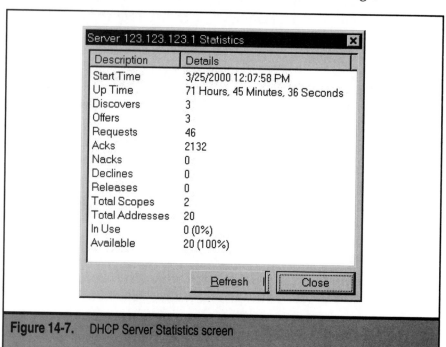

Server 123.123.123.1 Statistics	
Description	**Details**
Start Time	3/25/2000 12:07:58 PM
Up Time	71 Hours, 45 Minutes, 36 Seconds
Discovers	3
Offers	3
Requests	46
Acks	2132
Nacks	0
Declines	0
Releases	0
Total Scopes	2
Total Addresses	20
In Use	0 (0%)
Available	20 (100%)

Refresh   Close

Figure 14-7.   DHCP Server Statistics screen

mask, and other option attributes. Each scope has a description, but this is only for purposes of management. This information is not distributed when a lease is requested.

Choosing the New Scope menu selection starts the New Scope Wizard. It steps through a number of screens, starting with a screen where you enter the name of the scope and its description. This is followed up by the IP Address Range screen shown in Figure 14-8. On this screen, you enter the range of IP addresses, along with the subnet mask. The latter can be specified in bits or using the subnet mask field. Changing either field adjusts its counterpart.

Clicking on the Next button brings up the Add Exclusions screen shown in Figure 14-9. Zero or more exclusion ranges can be added to the scope definition from this screen. Changes can be made after the scope is created. Since there is only one range of IP addresses for each scope, the exclusion ranges are used to map out groups of IP addresses that are off limits, either because they are statically defined or because they may be leased by other DHCP servers. Check out the "Multiple DHCP Servers for One Subnet" section for more details.

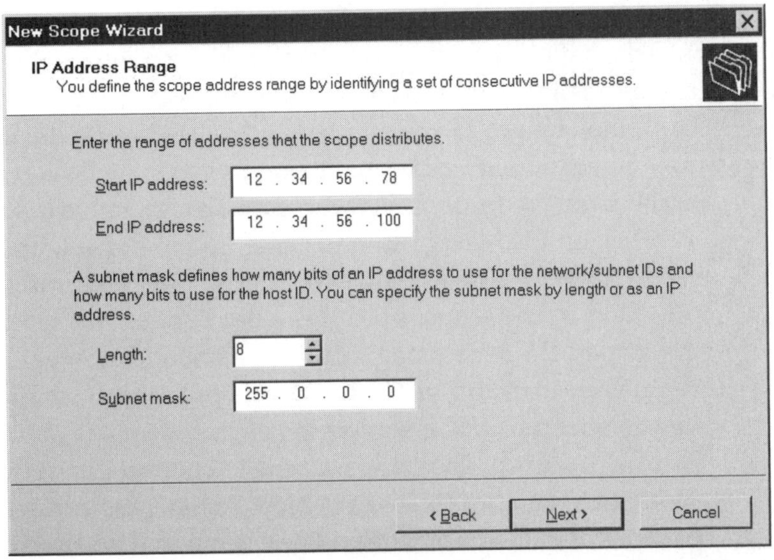

Figure 14-8. New Scope Wizard IP Address Range screen

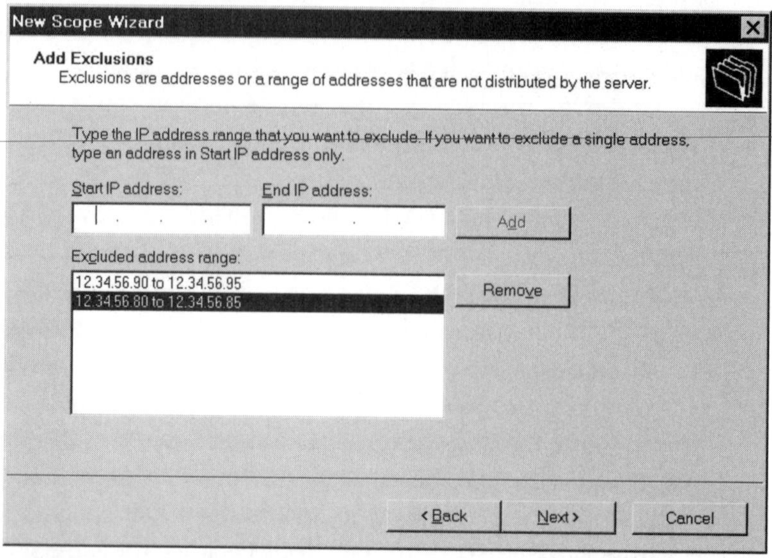

Figure 14-9.   New Scope Wizard Add Exclusions screen

Exclusion ranges are checked for validity when the Add button
is clicked after each range is entered in the top part of the screen.
Exclusion ranges must be within the range specified for the scope.
Unwanted ranges can be selected and deleted using the Remove button.
Any ranges added will be maintained, even if the Back button is used
to check out the prior screen where the scope's range is specified.

Click on the Next button to bring up the Lease Duration screen
shown in Figure 14-10. This screen is where the duration for all leases
provided by the scope is set. It can be changed at a later date using
the scope's Properties page, but it is a good idea to get it correct to
begin with so clients will be given the proper information when they
first contact the DHCP server. In general, choose a shorter lease time
if you are unsure of what lease time to choose. Changing the time at
a later date will not cause a problem as the lease expiration date is
stored in the database when a lease is made. The lease duration is
applied to new leases, and a client with an existing IP lease will use
this new time when a renewal is requested.

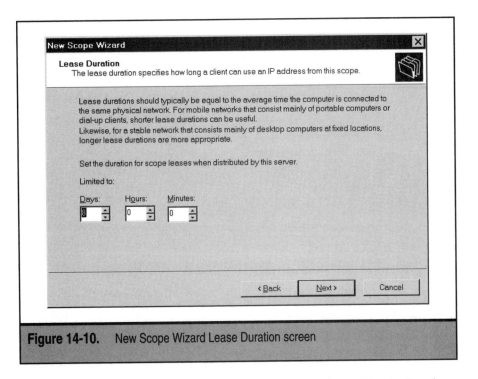

Figure 14-10.   New Scope Wizard Lease Duration screen

The default presented by the wizard is eight days. This is fine for fixed computers, but mobile computers or remote access computers will typically be given a duration of a day or possibly a few hours, depending upon the environment. Decreasing the duration increases the network traffic for renewals.

Clicking on the Next button brings up the Configure DHCP Options screen. There are two options: Yes and No. If you choose Yes, you can select values for the standard options such as code 3, Router, presented in the "DHCP Options" section. These options typically include a list of server IP addresses. These settings can be changed after the scope is created.

One of the more interesting screens in this sequence is shown in Figure 14-11. The Domain Name and DNS Servers screen specifies the parent domain name that the computer should use and the list of DNS servers to select from when resolving domain names. The fully qualified domain name for the computer should be the concatenation of the computer's name and the parent domain name. DNS servers

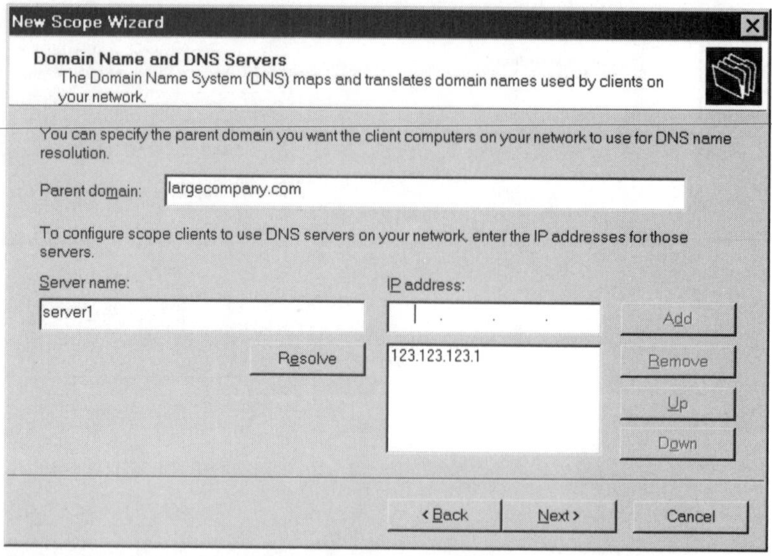

Figure 14-11. New Scope Wizard Domain Name and DNS Servers screen

must be added by IP address, but the Server Name field and the Resolve button can be used to resolve a domain name to an IP address. In this case, a partial domain name is included, and the resolution process adds the domain name suffix set for the computer running the MMC snap-in.

The last wizard screen allows the scope to be created and activated. At this point, the scope properties can be edited and some of the more advanced options can be added to the standard list of options defined through the wizard. We'll talk more about this later.

New superscopes are created using the New Superscope menu item. A superscope has a name and description but no attributes other than the scopes it contains. A superscope is a management tool for grouping scopes. All scopes in a superscope are activated when the superscope is activated. The same is true for deactivation. In addition, the state of an individual scope can be changed independently of the superscope.

A superscope can only be created after a scope exists. The scope cannot already be part of another superscope. Superscopes are deleted automatically when all the scopes defined within a superscope are deleted. Deleting a superscope does not delete the scopes it contains but rather these scopes are moved up a level just below the DHCP server. They can then be added to existing superscopes, added to a new superscope, or they can operate without being part of a superscope.

New scopes can be created within a superscope. To do this, select the superscope and then select Action | Scope. To move a scope that is outside a superscope to a superscope, select the scope and then select Action | Add to Superscope. Multicast scopes cannot be added to superscopes.

The New Multicast Scope menu item is used to create a MADCAP scope. This menu item starts up the Create Multicast Scope Wizard, which is outlined in the "Multicast IP Addresses and MADCAP" section. The steps for creating a multicast scope are similar to creating a normal scope except that the IP range is different and options are not part of the multicast scope definition so the wizard does not prompt for such details.

The Reconcile Scopes item and its related menu items for other DHCP objects are used to determine what conflicts exist between scopes and servers. In general, the DHCP MMC snap-in prevents conflicts from occurring within the server since it has all the details available. You may have to reduce the address range of one scope before increasing the range of another scope if the two scopes are adjacent numerically.

The Unauthorize/Authorize menu item will show up depending upon whether the selected DHCP server is authorized. DHCP servers should be authorized before scopes are enabled.

The Define User Classes and Define Vendor Classes menu items let you add class-specific data. Each requires a display name and an optional description. Information can be entered in text or hexidecimal formats. The screens presented by these menu items include a list of class definitions that already exist. Existing class data can be edited and new classes can be added. A number of predefined Microsoft Windows classes are defined by default. These cannot be edited or deleted.

The Set Predefined Options menu item brings up the Predefined Options and Values screen shown in Figure 14-12. The top combo box lets you select the group of option classes such as the DHCP Standard Options. Options within the class are selected using the second combo box. New options can be added by using the Add button. Options can be edited by using the Edit button or removed by using the Delete button. Predefined options can only have their name or descriptions changed, and they cannot be deleted. Options should be added carefully and only if the DHCP clients can utilize the information. Simply adding information causes it to be delivered to clients, but it does not force them to use it.

The values listed in the bottom part of the screen are dependent upon the option selected. Some options have a single value or text string while others have a list of IP addresses. New options can have single or multiple values of the same type from bytes to IP addresses. Codes for new options should be chosen so they do not conflict with existing definitions. In general, the ability to add options should be used to add new standards-based options that were not defined when the software was released.

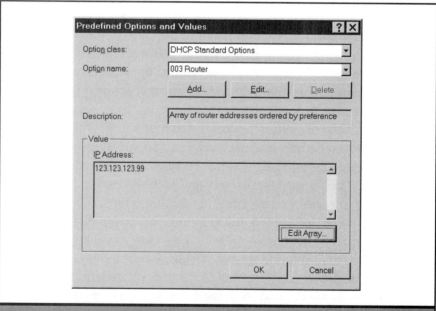

Figure 14-12.   Predefined Options and Values screen

DHCP Server Properties and Dynamic DNS Update Proxy

Selecting a DHCP server in the DHCP MMC snap-in and selecting Action | Properties brings up the DHCP Server Properties screen shown in Figure 14-13. It is used to enable three properties: statistic updates, logging, and BOOTP information support. The statistics update frequency is used with the Display Statistics screens mentioned in the previous section. These are available at the server and scope level.

The logging support allows DHCP transactions to be recorded so that activity can be monitored. It is useful for debugging purposes and provides more details than just the information that is in the lease tables. This option can be disabled if DHCP is running without problems.

The BOOTP information support determines whether the BOOTP table will be listed below the DHCP server along with scopes and superscopes. This information will not be needed if BOOTP is not used on the network. There is only one BOOTP table, and the BOOTP support will not be used if the table is empty.

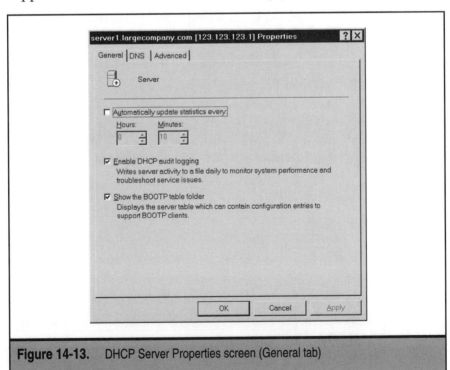

Figure 14-13. DHCP Server Properties screen (General tab)

Clicking on the DNS tab brings up the dynamic DNS update screen shown in Figure 14-14. If all check boxes are empty, the dynamic DNS update support is disabled. If one or more check boxes are checked, some or all the dynamic DNS update support is enabled. This feature normally affects DHCP clients that do not have dynamic DNS update support such as the Windows 2000 DHCP client, although it is possible to use both the dynamic DNS update support of the DHCP server and the DHCP client.

The Automatically Update DHCP Client Information In DNS option allows the DHCP dynamic DNS update proxy to issue an update request either when the client requests one or always. The former case requires a client that can communicate this information to the DHCP server. The latter should be used with clients like Windows 95 or Windows 98 that cannot perform the update themselves and will not indicate whether the DHCP server should perform this function for them.

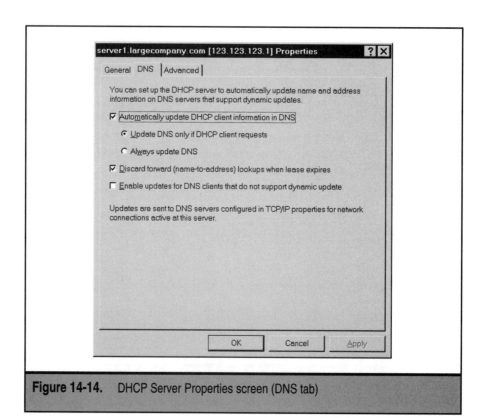

Figure 14-14. DHCP Server Properties screen (DNS tab)

The Discard Forward (Name-To-Address) Lookups When Lease Expires check box is normally checked. If it is, a dynamic DNS update remove message is sent to the DNS server when a lease expires. Only the leased computer's name and IP address will be removed. Any updates that were done using other means will remain. For example, if the DHCP server added workstation1.largecompany.com and later a www.workstation1.largecompany.com DNS entry was added manually, the latter would not be removed by the DHCP server when the lease expired for workstation1.

Enable Updates For DNS Clients That Do Not Support Dynamic Update should be checked if clients that do not support dynamic DNS updates are being serviced by the DHCP server and the names are to be added to the DNS server's database. DOS, Windows 3.x, Windows 95, and Windows 98 do not support dynamic DNS updates.

Clicking on the Advanced tab brings up the screen shown in Figure 14-15. This screen addresses logging and binding details.

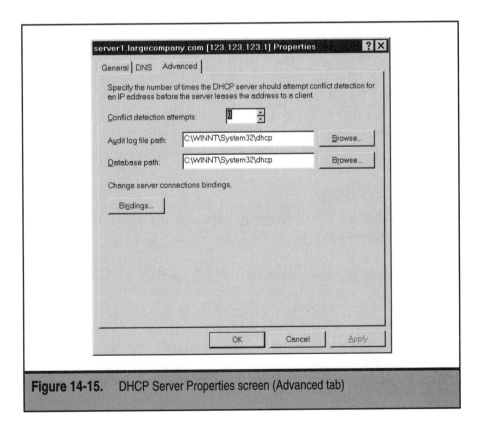

Figure 14-15.   DHCP Server Properties screen (Advanced tab)

The first item is Conflict Detection Attempts. If this value is zero, detection is not attempted. If it is a nonzero value, the DHCP server attempts to contact a computer using an IP address before it gives a lease to a requesting DHCP client. This allows the DHCP server to detect an IP address that has been given to another client accidentally by another DHCP server, or the client may be set up with a fixed IP address that is within the address space of the DHCP server's address pool. The DHCP server tries to ping the IP address and waits for a timeout or a response. A value of 1 or 2 is recommended if this feature is used, as each try takes about a second to time out and the DHCP client will experience the delay and may time out itself. By default, this feature is disabled and the value in the field is 0.

The audit file and database paths are specified on this screen. The respective Browse buttons make searching for the new directories easier. In general, the default settings are sufficient. A change may be required when switching from one set of files to another, such as turning a hot spare into an active DHCP server by using a copy of the primary DHCP server's database.

Finally, there is the Bindings button. This controls which subnets the DHCP server will accept requests on. The subnets match the IP address of the Windows 2000 computer that the DHCP service is running on. There will be multiple entries in the bindings list if the computer has multiple network adapters or multiple IP addresses per adapter. A check box associated with each entry allows the DHCP server to ignore a subnet by simply unchecking the box.

Scope Properties

A scope's Properties page provides access to settings that are initially configured by the New Scope Wizard as well as values not even presented by the wizard. To display the Properties page, select a scope and then select Action | Properties. This presents a screen like the one shown in Figure 14-16.

The General tab screen includes the details entered using the wizard, including the scope name, IP range, and lease duration. Under Lease Duration, the Unlimited option is not available in the wizard. In general, it is better to specify a long lease time rather than to make it unlimited.

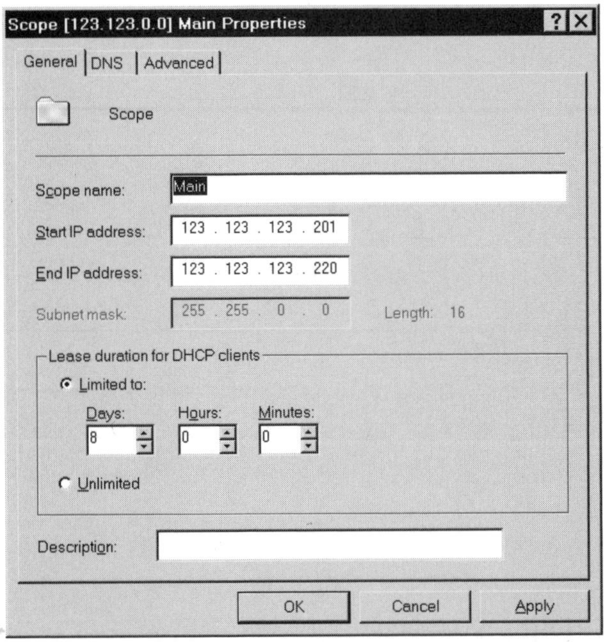

Figure 14-16.   Scope Properties screen (General tab)

Selecting the DNS tab presents a screen that looks just like the one in Figure 14-14, DHCP Server Properties screen (DNS tab). Operationally, it is the same. Functionally, it differs only in scope. In particular, this screen addresses the current scope versus the entire server.

Selecting the Advanced tab presents the screen in Figure 14-17. This screen lets you choose what a scope will be used with: DHCP clients only, BOOTP clients only, or both types. The default configuration is DHCP clients only. If BOOTP clients or both types are selected, the Lease Duration For BOOTP Clients box will be enabled. As with the DHCP settings on the General tab screen, the Unlimited lease duration should be used only when absolutely necessary. The default BOOTP lease duration is longer than the default for a DHCP client but the actual value will be determined by the kinds of BOOTP clients that are on the network.

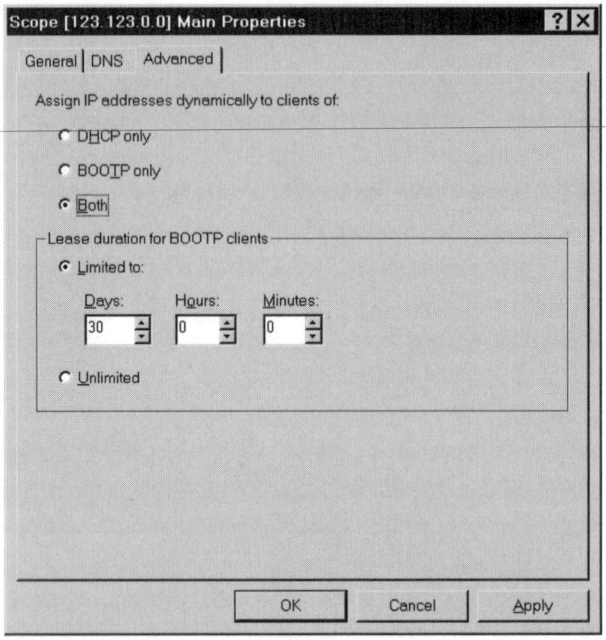

Figure 14-17. Scope Properties screen (Advanced tab)

In addition to the Properties screen, a scope has a number of entries listed beneath it, including:

▼ Address Pool

■ Address Leases

■ Reservations

▲ Scope Options

The Address Pool contains at least one entry, the IP range for the scope. This can only be changed from the scope's Properties screen, and it cannot be deleted. The Address Pool also contains the list of any exclusion ranges. These can be listed when the scope is created or added by selecting the address pool and then selecting Action | New Exclusion Range. New exclusion ranges are checked for validity prior to adding them to this list. Once added they cannot be changed, only deleted. This is done by selecting the entry and then selecting Action | Delete.

The Address Lease contains a list of active leases including the IP addresses and details about the lease including the expiration date and time. The Address Lease list can be refreshed by selecting the entry and selecting Action | Refresh. The refresh time associated with the DHCP server will also cause the list to be updated based upon the refresh setting.

The Reservations entry contains a list of reservation entries that are added explicitly. They make sure a specific network adapter will be given a specific IP address. This can be handy by providing a fixed IP address to a client device while retaining the advantage of DHCP configuration. No special changes must be made to the client other than setting it up to use DHCP. A reservation is added by selecting the Reservations entry and selecting Action | New Reservation. This presents the New Reservation screen shown in Figure 14-18.

The New Reservation screen includes a name to distinguish it from other reservations as well as the IP address to lease. The MAC address allows the DHCP server to determine when the client is requesting a lease. The MAC address is obtained in a variety of fashions depending upon the client. For example, the Windows 95 and Windows 98 WINIPCFG.EXE program will display the MAC address for this type of client. The client type of device will normally be known and is typically

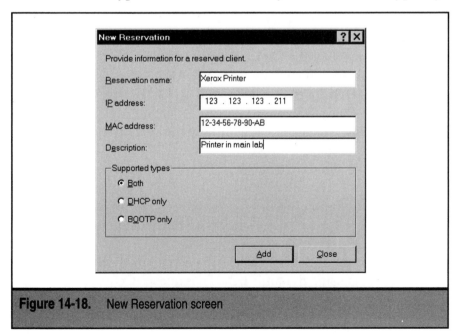

Figure 14-18.   New Reservation screen

a DHCP client. There is no harm in selecting both, as this allows the DHCP server to determine the type when the lease is requested, and a device can normally be set up for one mode or the other. Workstations are almost always DHCP clients.

Once a reservation is added to the Reservations list, the default set of options is copied into the reservation. These can then be adjusted for this specific device by selecting the reservation and selecting Action | Configure Options. Options can be added, deleted, or edited. The Properties screen for the reservation, which you open by selecting the reservation and selecting Action | Properties, provides access to the parameters initially entered when the reservation was created. In addition, there is a DNS tab. The DNS tab screen matches the one in a scope's Property page that allows dynamic DNS updates to be adjusted specifically for this client. This includes disabling or enabling dynamic DNS update proxy support.

The Scope Options entry contains a list of options used for regular leases for the scope. The options can be added, deleted, or edited.

BOOTP Support

BOOTP is defined by RFC 951 and RFC 1542. It is primarily used for diskless workstations and IP devices such as routers that can accept boot programs via the network. The boot program is downloaded using TFTP (Trivial File Transfer Protocol) from a TFTP server. This is done after the device's initial local configuration or it can be obtained dynamically from a BOOTP server such as the Windows 2000 DHCP service that includes BOOTP support. BOOTP and DHCP use different IP ports.

BOOTP clients were initially designed for local configuration including the setting of the device's IP address. Newer BOOTP clients allow dynamic BOOTP configuration that allows a BOOTP server such as the Windows 2000 DHCP server to deliver the BOOTP configuration. The boot program is still downloaded using TFTP, and the boot program does not have to reside on the same server as the DHCP server.

The Windows 2000 DHCP server can allocate IP addresses to clients using dynamic BOOTP requests. Generally, reservations are set up for BOOTP clients using their MAC addresses. Reservations were covered in the previous section covering DHCP scopes.

Scopes can be set up to handle DHCP clients, BOOTP clients, or both types of clients using the same scope. The options sent to the clients will be the same in either case, so if DHCP clients and BOOTP clients need different option information you need to set up separate scopes explicitly for each type of client.

In addition to having IP lease support or an IP reservation, the BOOTP table must be configured. The BOOTP table is initially hidden. The table is displayed in the list that contains a DHCP server's list of scopes by selecting the DHCP server entry and displaying the General tab page of the Properties screen. Make sure that the Show The BOOTP Table Folder check box is checked.

Once the BOOTP table is displayed, entries can be added. Select BOOTP Table and select Action | New Boot Image. This brings up the screen shown in Figure 14-19.

The Boot Image File Name will be the one used by the device to request a boot file. The Full Server Path To Boot Image field is a UNIX-style path name (it uses forward slashes instead of a Windows backslash to separate directory names) that is used to locate a file on the TFTP server that is listed in the third field. The TFTP Server Name is a fully qualified domain name.

The TFTP Server Name and Full Server Path To Boot Image fields are used to fill in the blanks for the respective options: code 66, TFTP Server Name, and code 67, Boot File Name. The BOOTP client identifies the entry by the Boot Image File Name.

NOTE: The DHCP options are called *vendor extensions* in BOOTP terminology.

BOOTP is usually used out of necessity. DHCP support is preferable, but in most cases, BOOTP clients can only be configured to use BOOTP. Network administrators that have networks without BOOTP clients should not enable the BOOTP support, as it simply makes DCHP service management unnecessarily complex.

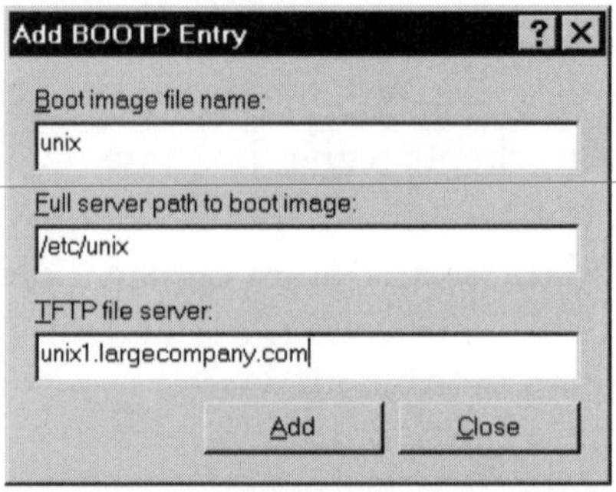

Figure 14-19. Add BOOTP Entry screen

WINDOWS 2000 DHCP SECURITY

The Windows 2000 DHCP service has minimal security associated with it and no security settings within the DHCP MMC snap-in. Security is restricted to read-only access to the MMC snap-in and full access. The former is given to any user in the security group DHCP Users, while the latter is controlled by the DHCP Administrators group.

The security groups are managed from the Active Directory Users and Computer MMC snap-in discussed in Chapter 10. The two security groups are automatically added when the DHCP service is installed. If Active Directory is installed, then the users added to the group can be from different Active Directory domains.

In general, it is a good idea to limit the number of users in the DHCP Users group. Most users do not need to know about the DHCP service. Access is typically given to users who manage devices that are DHCP clients, such as network printers or network attached storage (NAS) devices.

THIRD-PARTY DHCP SERVER ISSUES

DHCP servers are as prevalent as DNS servers are. Windows NT comes with a DHCP server, as do UNIX and Linux. BOOTP servers are normally separate applications. In general, these servers provide most of the services that the Windows 2000 DHCP server does. Unlike the DNS service, the DHCP service has no minimum requirements with respect to Windows 2000 and Active Directory other than meeting the DHCP-related RFC specifications.

Features not usually found in third-party DHCP servers include MADCAP scopes, superscopes, and dynamic DNS update proxy support. MADCAP support is relatively new and will not be used in a large number of sites. Superscopes are a management tool and have no effect on the operation of the DHCP server in terms of providing IP leases. Dynamic DNS update proxy support can be an issue especially when migrating away from WINS to a pure TCP/IP environment. Those DHCP servers that do provide dynamic DNS update proxy support will probably not be able to perform secure dynamic DNS updates to a Windows 2000 DNS server using Active Directory–integrated DNS zones. Still, providing conventional dynamic DNS updates can effectively eliminate the need for WINS in most environments in the same fashion that the Windows 2000 DHCP server can.

Another item that will not be found in most third-party DHCP server implementations are class options specific to Microsoft's DHCP clients. The lack of the default settings tends to be of little consequence, and they can normally be added if necessary.

Some third-party DHCP servers utilize text configuration files and lack a text-based or graphical user interface. While DHCP services rarely require management after they are configured, the user interface will determine the expertise needed by a network administrator to manage the DHCP service.

In general, existing DHCP infrastructures do not have to be replaced by a Windows 2000 DHCP service unless a specific feature is required, such as secure dynamic DNS update support. Windows 2000 DHCP support can be merged into an existing DHCP environment using overlapping scopes and exclusion ranges. Migration of scope information will have to be done manually because the Windows 2000 DHCP service does not have any type of import facility.

DHCP CLIENT CONFIGURATION

DHCP client configuration is specific to the type of client. Settings for the DHCP client are often in the same area as the DNS settings. This is true for Windows 95, Windows 98, Windows NT, and Windows 2000. The DNS configurations are addressed in Chapter 13. The description of these configurations addresses DHCP client configuration as well.

UNIX and Linux DHCP clients are normally separate applications from the DNS clients. Configuration tends to be similar as well, and it often involves editing text configuration files. Graphical front ends are becoming the norm and, as with Windows DHCP configuration, the DHCP client configuration for these clients is typically merged with the DNS configuration, especially since using DHCP support often eliminates the need to configure details like the router and DNS IP addresses used by the client.

TROUBLESHOOTING

Troubleshooting a DHCP server or client can be a tedious task. There are so many combinations that can cause problems that pinpointing a problem is more of an art than a science. Still, there are a number of common problems that have relatively simple solutions. The online help for the Windows 2000 DHCP service is rather good in this respect, so we will not delve very deeply into all the problems and solutions.

Troubleshooting a DHCP Client

The problems presented in this section are fairly generic and apply to most DHCP clients, including the Windows 2000 DHCP client. The common DHCP client problems include:

▼ A client cannot obtain an IP address from the DHCP server.

■ A client is using an incorrect IP address.

▲ DHCP options do not seem to be set properly when a client receives a lease.

A client that cannot obtain an IP address from the DHCP server can have software-or hardware-related problems. Check first for software configuration problems. For example, with Windows 95 and Windows 98, the System Control Panel applet Device Management screen will indicate whether there is a problem with the network adapter configuration. The next item to check is the protocol configuration to make sure that DHCP support is configured.

The possible hardware-related problems include a bad connection to the network or a bad network adapter. The first step to check the former is to set up the client to use a fixed IP address instead of DHCP. The IP address and subnet mask should match the subnet used by the DHCP server. A ping program is then used to see if the DHCP server can be accessed by the workstation. If not, the hardware configuration or connection may be bad. If the ping program succeeds, there may be a configuration problem on the DHCP server including improper scope configuration or a lack of available IP addresses to lease.

The former can be checked by plugging in another computer that works with DHCP into the problem computer's network connection to see if the good computer will work. In some cases, the network connection to the DHCP server may be transient, such as an on-demand ISDN link from a branch office, where the DHCP client is located, to the main office, where the DHCP server is located. Also check DHCP relay configurations on the routers for this type of configuration.

Checking for a bad network adapter is a last resort if none of the other solutions fixes the problem. You can check the adapter by replacing it with a new one or by installing the suspect adapter into a computer that is known to be working properly.

Problems with a client using an incorrect IP address often arise with DHCP clients that support auto-configuration, such as a Windows 2000 DHCP client. In this case, the inability to contact the DHCP server causes the client to revert to its last used IP address or a default address specified within the DHCP client software. The solution is actually the same as the prior problem because the real problem is the inability of the DHCP client to contact the DHCP server.

DHCP options not seeming to be set properly when a client receives a lease is a problem that can be due to configuration of the client, configuration of the server, or implementation limitations of the DHCP client. For example, a list of IP addresses DNS servers is often a DHCP option sent to a workstation. Some DHCP clients, such as the Windows 2000 DHCP client, can specify whether the DNS servers are obtained from the DHCP option information or from the computer's DNS server settings. In this case, the software is working properly, but the desired effect is not achieved because the client settings are incorrect.

In some instances, the DHCP option may not be handled by the DHCP client. This will require a more detailed examination of the option support of the DHCP client. In general, a client will ignore options it does not understand, but the default operation without these settings may be counter to the desired operation.

Finally, the DHCP options may be incorrectly set at the DHCP server. This can be checked on a Windows 2000 DHCP server using the DHCP MMC snap-in. Three things should be checked. The first is whether the client actually has a valid lease. Second, it should be determined whether the IP address is assigned dynamically or if a reservation has been made for the computer. Finally, the options for the scope or the reservation must be checked to determine whether the proper information has been entered.

There are many other problems that can arise with a DHCP client and the Windows 2000 DHCP client specifically, but these problems tend to be less common.

Troubleshooting a DHCP Server

As with the clients, the problems presented in this section are fairly generic and apply to most DHCP servers including the Windows 2000 DHCP server. The common DHCP server problems include:

- ▼ The DHCP server is not running.
- ■ The DHCP server is not responding to DHCP client requests.
- ▲ The DHCP server is not providing proper IP addresses or option information.

If the DHCP server is not running, it may have been stopped or disabled on purpose. Check the service status using the DHCP MMC snap-in. Also check the DHCP service startup settings using the Services application started by choosing Start | Programs | Administrative Tools | Services. Finally, check the DHCP log files and the Windows 2000 Event logs. These should indicate why the service stopped or failed to initialize. This is often due to a corrupted database.

A DHCP server will not respond to DHCP client requests if it is not running. The next step is to check whether the service is configured to respond to the DHCP clients that cannot communicate with the DHCP server. In particular, the DHCP server must have a scope defined, and it must be activated. If a scope is part of a superscope, then the superscope should be checked as well. The next item to check would be the DHCP server's IP address bindings in the DHCP server's Properties screen. A scope cannot be used to provide IP address leases to a subnet that does not match the scope definition. A scope may also have all its IP addresses leased. In this case, new DHCP client requests cannot be filled. A Windows 2000 DHCP server provides this information using the Display Statistics option in the DHCP MMC snap-in. Finally, the DHCP server's scope configuration may conflict with another DHCP server. Check the other DHCP server configurations and temporarily disable them if possible while checking the server in question using a DHCP client.

A DHCP server that is not providing proper IP addresses or option information is usually configured improperly, or else the client is configured improperly. First, check other DHCP clients to see if there are consistent problems. Next, check the server settings to make sure the leases and option information is set as expected. Finally, check the DHCP server's database to verify its integrity.

DHCP server configuration problems are easier to debug if a second computer that is a DHCP client is located near a console that can manager the DCHP server. This allows the client to renew leases and see what kind of information is obtained from the server. Likewise, the IP and MAC address of the DHCP client can be found and compared to the contents of the DHCP server's database. The Windows 2000 DHCP MMC snap-in interface makes this chore easy.

WINDOWS 2000 DHCP DATABASE

The Windows 2000 DHCP server uses a standard Microsoft database; it should be used only by the DHCP service. When the DHPS service is running, it opens the database for exclusive use. The online help for the Windows 2000 DHCP service database is very good and should be used if problems arise related to the database.

In general, the JETPACK.EXE application included with Windows 2000 provides a way to check the database when the DHCP service is offline. It can also repair some problems.

The DHCP database should be backed up as part of the regular server backup if possible. Minimally, a copy of the DHCP database should be saved after any major reconfiguration of scopes or options. This is done by stopping the DHCP service and copying the dhcp.mdb file to a new location.

SUMMARY

DHCP services can be as invaluable as DNS services for both users and administrators. While DHCP services are not required for Active Directory support, it is rare that a Windows 2000 network larger than a dozen machines will not be using a DHCP server.

The length of this chapter indicates the extensive nature of the DHCP server and the variety of options and settings available from the Windows 2000 DHCP server. This includes BOOTP and MADCAP IP support, in addition to conventional DHCP support.

While replacing an existing DHCP infrastructure with a Windows 2000–based DHCP infrastructure has advantages, it is not imperative to migration. The main reason to move to a Windows 2000–based DHCP environment is the secure dynamic DNS update proxy service discussed in this chapter. This is especially true for environments that need to migrate from WINS to a pure TCP/IP environment. In any case, DHCP service management normally falls under the control of the DNS administrator because of the tight relationship between the two services. For example, changes to the DNS environment often result in changes to the DHCP option settings.

CHAPTER 15

Windows 2000 Dynamic DNS and Automatic Naming

Windows 2000 Active Directory's dependence on IP addresses and DNS name resolution support is clear. Without the proper names and addresses, a Windows 2000 network is dead in the water. While Windows 2000 can support IPX and NetBIOS protocols, these are used only for backward compatibility, not forward-looking enhancements.

Most network administrators know that configuring lots of information on a client is bad news when inevitable changes must be made, even in a small network. Centralizing the management and dispersion of this information makes a network administrator's job easier. With Windows 2000, this means dynamic DNS updates and a flexible DHCP server. With the Windows 2000 DHCP server, management via DHCP can include dynamic DNS update support.

But providing IP addresses and configuration information is only half the job. Letting users know where services reside is the other half, and that is the job of the DNS server. In Windows-land, it is also the job of the WINS server. This chapter takes a look at both of these name services and how they relate to each other in a Windows 2000 environment. Typically, Windows 2000 clients will strictly utilize DNS, but in a mixed client environment with Windows 3.x, Windows 9x, and Windows NT clients, WINS will play an important part.

This chapter also addresses WINS configuration. The "Windows 2000 WINS" section takes a look at how WINS works, how it is configured, and issues related to migration from WINS to DNS. As with the migration to Windows 2000, there are many issues related to migration that are not technical, such as training, licensing costs, and support infrastructure. These issues will not be addressed, although they often take priority over technical issues such as converting existing WINS-based applications to use DNS.

WHAT'S IN A NAME?

With TCP/IP, computers are identified by one or more IP addresses. Most workstations have a single IP address, while servers often have more than one depending upon the environment. IP addresses are like phone numbers; they are practical. Remembering a couple of IP addresses is easy, but keeping track of dozens on a network is impossible. Keeping a list of only IP addresses or phone numbers is of little use since one looks like another. This is why most telephone books contain paired entries: a telephone number and a name. DNS and WINS are the telephone books of a Windows 2000 network.

One of the main differences between these digital phone books and a conventional phone book is naming conventions. Telephone books have flat names or arbitrary complexity and, often, characters. WINS and DNS tend to be more restrictive for consistency and function. For example, DNS domain names are defined as part of a hierarchy. A fully qualified domain name (FQDN) includes all of the names and the branches that are part of the domain tree that reach a particular node within the tree. Fully qualified domain names must be unique, but names within the hierarchy can be the same as long as they are not children of the same branch point. Depending upon the standard being followed, a DNS domain name will consist of a restricted set of characters or be an arbitrary binary string.

WINS does not use a hierarchy. Its flat structure mimics the Windows NT domain structure, although a WINS server is oriented towards subnets. This allows a WINS server to support more than one Windows NT domain. WINS uses NetBIOS names that are stored in 16-byte blocks. The last character is a space, so names must be 15 characters or less.

The difference between DNS and NetBIOS in character sets for names and name sizes is one reason Windows clients have two names. The names can be the same since NetBIOS naming restrictions are a subset of the DNS name restrictions.

Having different names for the same computer can be both a blessing and a curse. The advantage is the ability to create a NetBIOS name that does not conflict with other computers. The disadvantage is that both names may show up in a DNS domain if the WINS server is linked to the DNS server.

The ability to have the same name associated with an IP address is very handy. It allows services to be named logically instead of associating resources with a particular computer. This is not possible with standard NetBIOS broadcasts, but it is possible with WINS and DNS. It is also possible using LMHOSTS and HOSTS files.

Multiplicity can work in the other direction as well. Multiple servers can provide the same service. For example, a Windows 2000 domain can have more than one domain controller. The service is known by one name, but each domain controller will have its own IP address. In this case, the naming system needs to provide clients with these addresses.

Keeping track of computer names can be tedious, or you can do it automatically. It is tedious if the information must be manually placed into some known location such as an LMHOSTS file that must then be replicated across the network. That's definitely not a lot of fun and not recommended.

The alternative is to use a system such as WINS or DNS. Using these systems addresses the last half of the problem, distributing information across the network, because they service name resolution requests from clients. The other half of the problem is addressed by dynamic updates coming from clients or client proxies. Although using dynamic updates does not completely solve the problem, it typically addresses the workstation names dilemma. Servers tend to have fixed IP addresses, and, compared to workstations, the number of servers tends to be small.

So much for a name. Unfortunately, on the Internet, a rose is not always a rose.

WINDOWS 2000 DNS

When it comes to names on-the-fly, Windows 2000 DNS provides dynamic DNS update support. Windows 2000 DNS provides the same support as WINS, but DNS is much more sophisticated. It is also based on a public standard that's supported by a wide variety of sources.

This section takes a look at the dynamic update operation of Windows 2000 DNS. This is done primarily because of the dynamic nature of WINS versus DNS, which started out as a static design (dynamic DNS update support was added later). The "Windows 2000 DNS and WINS" section examines the integration of Windows 2000 DNS with Windows 2000 WINS. This integration allows name resolution across DNS and WINS name spaces regardless of what service clients register with.

Windows 2000 Dynamic DNS

Dynamic DNS support has been addressed in previous chapters, including configuration in Chapter 11, client support in Chapter 13, and integration with DHCP and Windows 2000 DHCP server's dynamic DNS update proxy support in Chapter 14. This section examines Windows 2000 DNS server's dynamic DNS update support as well as its relationship to DHCP and DNS clients; we will also contrast it with the operation of WINS.

Windows 2000 DNS dynamic DNS update support works with primary DNS zones and Active Directory–integrated DNS zones. Dynamic DNS update can be enabled or disabled on a per zone basis using the MMC DNS snap-in.

DNS information added via dynamic DNS updates can be replicated on other DNS servers using standard zone replication features. For primary DNS zones, caching and secondary DNS zones provide replication of this information. Both replication methods are part of standard DNS support. Active Directory–integrated DNS zones can be replicated in the same fashion. They can also be replicated throughout the Active Directory domain where the Active Directory–integrated DNS zone is defined.

NOTE: Active Directory–integrated DNS zones are automatically replicated among Active Directory domain controller Active Directory databases within the domain where the zones are defined. The zones are not required to have any relationship to the Active Directory domain in which they are defined, although they are typically associated with the domain or its child domains.

Client support for dynamic DNS updates is a bit sparse at this point. Windows 2000 DNS clients have this support built-in, which makes a homogeneous Windows 2000 network the ideal showcase for dynamic DNS operation. Windows 2000 Active Directory–integrated DNS zones also support secure dynamic DNS updates. Only Windows 2000 DNS clients currently support this feature.

Unfortunately, Windows 9x and Windows NT DNS clients support neither dynamic DNS updates nor secure dynamic DNS updates. Since dynamic DNS updates are used by workstations and these operating systems will be quite common in many Windows 2000 networks, supporting these clients will be very important. This is where WINS and its alternative come into play because WINS does work with TCP/IP support for Windows 9x and Windows NT. The alternative is the Windows 2000 DHCP server's dynamic DNS update proxy support.

With WINS, the Windows 9x and Windows NT clients register with WINS. This, in turn, provides the DNS service with the name resolution information. The clients will still obtain their IP addresses using DHCP. When not using WINS, the Windows 2000 DHCP service will provide the clients with their IP information and register this information with the DNS server. The clients need only be configured to use DHCP; WINS can be disabled. Windows 2000 DHCP configuration for this feature is simple to set up and is covered in Chapter 13. The Windows 2000 DHCP service supports secure dynamic DNS updates.

While WINS support is available for some operating systems, dynamic DNS support is more common. Operating systems such as UNIX and Linux that support BIND also have access to nsupdate. Nsupdate provides dynamic DNS update support. Its operation is covered in Chapter 13. The current version of nsupdate does not support Windows 2000 secure dynamic DNS updates.

The combination of dynamic DNS updates and DHCP makes network-wide changes significantly easier. Subnets and server IP addresses can be changed. It is even possible to migrate from WINS—but more on that later.

Windows 2000 DNS and WINS

As mentioned earlier, Windows 2000 DNS and Windows 2000 WINS will often coexist in a Windows 2000 network. In fact, this type of coexistence is common with Windows NT DNS and Windows NT WINS. The main difference between the Windows NT and Windows 2000 environments is that DNS becomes the primary player where WINS was more important with Windows NT.

Windows 2000 DNS is tied together with WINS through primary DNS zones or Active Directory–integrated DNS zones. This allows the Windows 2000 DNS server to query WINS servers if the DNS server cannot resolve a name. The reverse is not true, so the WINS server can only provide information about WINS clients. Luckily, most WINS clients, such as Windows 9x WINS clients, can be configured to use DNS resolution instead of WINS. In this case, the client normally registers with a WINS server and adds the client's IP address and name to the WINS database. A primary DNS zone in the Windows DNS 2000 is set up to access this WINS server so it can see the client's IP address and name information. The client is set up to use DNS resolution so it will see its WINS registered information when using the DNS server. Of course, the client must be set up with the appropriate IP addresses for the WINS server and the DNS server. Windows client configuration is covered in Chapter 13.

The primary or Active Directory–integrated DNS zones can be set up exclusively for WINS use, or they may contain static and dynamically updated entries. The first step is to set up a DNS zone as outlined in Chapter 11. The next step is to display the zone's Properties page that is accessible from the DNS MMC snap-in and then click on the WINS tab to display the screen in Figure 15-1.

The WINS configuration is disabled by default, so the first thing to do on this screen is to check the Use WINS Forward Lookup check box. This enables the rest of the controls shown in the screen. DNS names that cannot be resolved using information in the standard DNS zone definition will now be checked against the information stored by WINS servers. The IP address of one or more WINS servers must be added to the list of WINS server.

WINS servers are often configured in pairs in larger networks for redundancy. A WINS server can reside on the same computer as the DNS server, but in larger networks the two are often found on separate computers. The WINS servers are accessed in priority order until one is contacted. The DNS server assumes that all WINS servers will provide the same information, so the DNS server will not continue checking the WINS servers if a name cannot be resolved by the first WINS server that responds.

The WINS name resolution support is implemented by adding a WINS resource record to the DNS zone database. One WINS resource record is added per WINS server IP address.

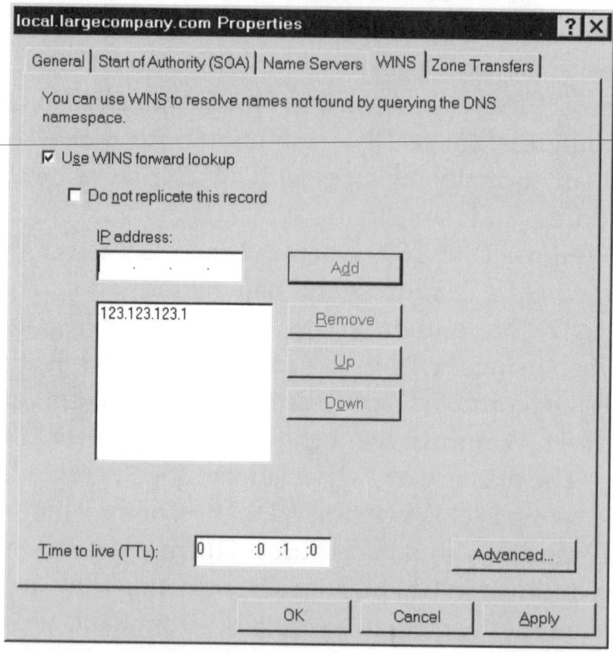

Figure 15-1. Zone Properties screen (WINS tab)

The Do Not Replicate This Record check box controls how WINS resource records are handled if the DNS zone is replicated using standard DNS replication. Usually, the box is unchecked so the WINS information is merged with the DNS information when replication occurs. If the check box is checked, the WINS information is not replicated. This can be useful if the DNS replication is done across an organization and the WINS information is for a local workgroup or if the DNS servers that will receive the replicated information cannot handle the WINS resource record.

Clicking on the Advanced button brings up the screen in Figure 15-2. This screen controls how quickly information is handled. The Time-To-Live (TTL) setting on the WINS tab of the Zone Properties screen is for DNS resource records that are created by this link. The settings in the Advanced screen control how long information is kept by the DNS server in its cache and how long it will wait on the WINS

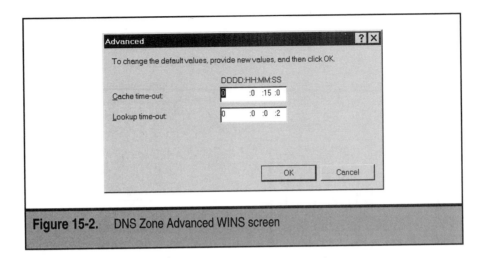

Figure 15-2.   DNS Zone Advanced WINS screen

server when a name resolution request is sent from the DNS server to the WINS server.

The domain name that the WINS names are associated with is dependent upon the zone definition because the WINS naming system is flat. There is no restriction on the number of DNS zones that can refer to a WINS server, but there is little reason to have such a configuration. The latter would also be rather confusing to most users. Figure 15-3 shows a more common configuration. In this case, multiple WINS servers are associated with their own DNS zone. This figure shows the zones residing on the same DNS server, but the DNS zones can be located on different DNS servers.

The WINS coverage in Figure 15-3 is one approach to handling WINS support in a larger organization. From the DNS perspective, it has the advantage of being able to separate the WINS areas into distinct DNS zones. This can be useful if this kind of organizational structure is needed. It is normally done if the WINS servers will be on different subnets.

The WINS/DNS support discussed thus far addresses forward lookups or conversion of domain names into IP addresses. WINS support can also be used for reverse lookups. In this case, a WINS-R resource record is added to a reverse lookup zone's database. As with the WINS resource record, the WINS-R resource record can only be added to primary DNS zones or Active Directory–integrated DNS

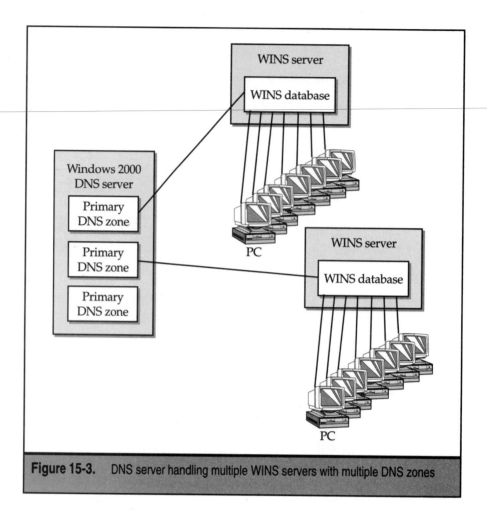

Figure 15-3. DNS server handling multiple WINS servers with multiple DNS zones

zones. The WINS-R resource record is added from the DNS MMC snap-in by selecting the reverse lookup zone entry's Properties page and then selecting the WINS-R tab to present the screen shown in Figure 15-4.

The screen in Figure 15-4 is similar to the one in Figure 15-1 for the forward lookup DNS zone WINS support except that the IP Addresses of the WINS servers field is replaced by the Domain To Append To Returned Name field. When the DNS server receives an IP address to be resolved, it will be partially qualified by the reverse lookup zone's domain name. The WINS server is then queried to find

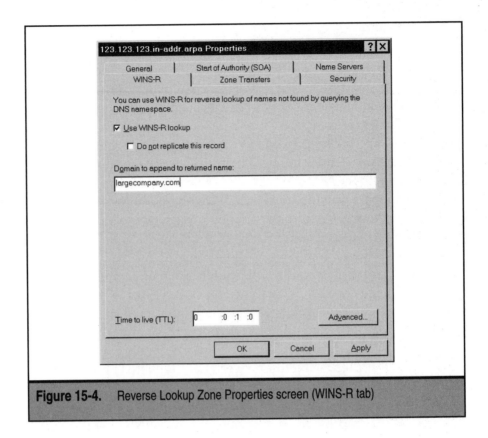

Figure 15-4.   Reverse Lookup Zone Properties screen (WINS-R tab)

the NetBIOS name of the computer in question. This is a single name, and it must be combined with the name in the field to create a fully qualified domain name (FQDN) that is returned as the result of the query.

DNS/WINS configuration occurs on the DNS side, making it more manageable since a single MMC snap-in must be used. The Windows 2000 DNS server can operate with either a Windows 2000 WINS service or a Windows NT WINS service.

WINDOWS 2000 WINS

Another alternative to handling names on-the-fly is Windows 2000 WINS. It is a system that was created before dynamic DNS support was well established and when Windows networks were primarily

NetBIOS-based. TCP/IP was an extra protocol supported by Windows 9x and Windows NT; WINS was set up to address limitations of NetBIOS. In particular, NetBIOS was designed as a broadcast protocol suitable for small workgroups. It provided a dynamic naming environment so computers could automatically recognize computers that had resources available for sharing.

The main purpose of WINS is to provide dynamic naming support similar to the dynamic DNS update support found in the Windows 2000 DNS server. It also provides the name resolution support provided by DNS. WINS-based networks can operate without DNS support, although this tends to be uncommon. One of the advantages of using TCP/IP, however, is TCP/IP's ability to be routed. NetBIOS cannot be routed. This made WINS desirable in larger networks where routers are more common. The rise of the Internet and its dependence on TCP/IP increased the importance of WINS, although DNS became a requirement because WINS is only applicable within a network, not across networks.

WINS does not eliminate NetBIOS, it only encapsulates it. Actually WINS uses the NetBIOS over TCP/IP (NetBT) protocol that puts NetBIOS information inside TCP/IP packets.

This section presents NetBIOS, WINS, and the use of DHCP with WINS to provide an overview of how WINS operates and how it is managed. Network administrators who have an installed base of WINS servers and clients will already be familiar with this and may wish to skip to the next section on "Migrating from WINS to Dynamic DNS." Network administrators unfamiliar with WINS but tasked with migrating a WINS environment to DNS will want to check out the rest of this section. Network design is also presented in this section.

How NetBIOS Works

NetBIOS is a network protocol that was developed when PC networks were first beginning to emerge in the 1980s. It was designed as a simple alternative to IPX and TCP/IP and had many of the qualities found in these protocols. NetBIOS also lacked a number of features found in these protocols, such as the ability to be routed from one network to another.

NetBIOS was initially a broadcast-oriented protocol. Computers are configured with a name up to 15 characters long. NetBIOS names are actually stored in 16-byte blocks, but a NetBIOS name must be stored in the block with a trailing space (20 hex).

The computer responds if a broadcast with this name was received. NetBIOS names can be unique or group names. A unique name is associated with a single computer while a group name is associated with one or more computers. Names are registered dynamically when a computer starts up. A computer can have more than one unique name or group name associated with it. Each name will be associated with a specific application running on the computer. In practice, a workstation normally has a single unique NetBIOS name.

NetBIOS was required for use with MS-DOS and all versions of Windows prior to Windows 2000. Windows 2000 can operate without NetBIOS but only with Windows 2000 clients. Windows 2000 supports NetBIOS for network communication with non-Windows 2000 clients.

NetBIOS actually defines two components: a session level interface and a session management and data transport protocol. The session level interface is an application interface for communications between NetBIOS computers. The session management and data transport protocol works with networking protocols, including NetBEUI and TCP/IP. NetBIOS on TCP/IP is called NetBT. NetBIOS is also sometimes used to refer to the combination of NetBIOS using NetBEUI.

NetBIOS also allows you to specify workgroups or domains. This is simply a way to provide a two-level grouping when browsing. In this case, computers or services can be listed by the workgroup or domain that they belong to.

NetBIOS Name Resolution

NetBIOS name resolution can occur on a network with or without name servers. Broadcasts are used on smaller networks where the broadcast traffic will not overload the network or the workstations. NetBIOS name servers (NBNS) include WINS.

Windows-based NetBIOS name resolution starts with a local file called LMHOSTS, which is described in Chapter 13. If the name cannot be resolved using this file, or if the file does not exist, name resolution continues based on how the computer is configured.

To keep everything straight, RFC 1001 defines NetBIOS specifies four node types. A computer will be one of the following node types:

▼ B-node: broadcast node

■ P-node: peer-to-peer node

■ M-node: mixed node

▲ H-node: hybrid node

The b-node (broadcast node) computers will broadcast any name resolution requests to all computers on the network. The matching computer must then respond. This will be a single computer if the NetBIOS name is unique, or a number of computers can respond if they share a NetBIOS group name. The advantage is simplicity and a response that indicates availability of the queried computer or application. The disadvantage is that each computer on the network must at least check the broadcast. Also, most routers will not route broadcast messages, which is why NetBIOS is normally considered not to be routable.

The p-node (peer-to-peer node) computers contact an NBNS in the same way that a DNS client works with a DNS server. The NBNS maintains a database of network addresses and NetBIOS names in the same fashion as a DNS server maintains a database of IP addresses and domain names. The advantage of a p-node is more limited traffic compared to a b-node. The disadvantages include a higher level of complexity and the lack of routing support. The former was an issue when memory was limited and processor speed was slow. This level of complexity is no longer an issue.

The m-node (mixed node) computer acts first as a b-node and then as a p-node, assuming the broadcast name resolution fails. This can occur if the named computer is busy, down, or configured to not respond to broadcast messages. The advantage of this mode is the ability to work with b-node and p-node computers. The disadvantage is the b-node, with its additional overhead, is used first.

The h-node (hybrid node) computer acts first as a p-node and then a b-node, assuming the former fails. This is possible where a b-node computer does not register with a p-node NBNS but will respond to broadcasts. An h-node is usually preferable to an m-node.

Windows computers, including Windows 2000, are b-nodes when they are not configured to use WINS. They are h-nodes when configured to use WINS.

NOTE: Windows 2000 computers can operate strictly with NetBIOS, but Active Directory domain controllers can only work with non-Windows 2000 computers using NetBIOS when the domain controller is operating in compatibility mode. When a Windows 2000 computer operates in native mode with Active Directory then communication uses native TCP/IP and DNS.

NetBIOS can be disabled for the TCP/IP protocol under Windows 2000 from the TCP/IP protocol's Properties screen. This prevents the Windows 2000 computer from participating in any NetBIOS operations using this protocol, including acting as a WINS server. This feature is enabled or disabled on a network adapter basis. This is handy for Windows 2000 computers that are acting as a proxy server, gateway, or firewall.

Browsing

NetBIOS communication is handy for contacting computers when names are known. The browsing service is used to see what computers and services are available. A computer browsing a server or browser keeps a list of computers so that a browser client can simply poll the browser to see which computers are on the network. Computers that provide services on a network broadcast this information when they start up. A browser simply keeps track of this information in its browse list.

A browser is typically an NBNS but it does not have to be, as is the case on small, peer-to-peer networks. WINS can act as a browser. Applications that use the browser support include the DOS NET VIEW command and the Windows Network Neighborhood. Browsers periodically exchange browse lists.

Browsers can be configured for one of a number of roles. These include:

▼ Domain master browser

■ Master browser

■ Backup browser

■ Potential browser

▲ Nonbrowser

Master browsers are selected by elections that are based on how the browser computer is configured. This dynamic selection means the master browser can change from time to time. This normally occurs in a peer-to-peer network. A server-based network typically has a server as a master browser that is always available. This is why servers and domain controllers are given priority when selecting a master browser.

A domain master browser is normally a primary domain controller (PDC) in a Windows NT domain environment. It maintains the master browser list for the domain as well as names used for other workgroups and domains in the network. As with a master browser, the domain master browser synchronizes browse lists with other master browsers. A domain master browser's list can span subnets.

A master browser operates in the same fashion as a domain master browser except that they can only track computers within a subnet.

Browsers that are not selected to be a master browser wind up as a backup browser. A backup can be converted to a master browser if the master fails to respond.

Potential browsers are similar to backup browsers in that they can be promoted to a master browser. Otherwise, potential browsers act as nonbrowsers.

Nonbrowsers will not convert to a master browser even if no master browser is found on the network. Nonbrowsers can be browser clients.

Windows 2000 computers can fulfill any browser role, although domain controllers are computers that can be domain master browsers. A domain controller can also be set up to emulate a PDC.

WINS can be used to tie together workgroups on a TCP/IP network even when routers are involved. Generally, NetBT will not be able to broadcast browser information through a router so a local master browser is chosen on each subnet. These master browsers must support WINS and be linked to a WINS server by the WINS server's IP address as shown in Figure 15-5.

Browser clients with services within each of three subnets shown in Figure 15-5 broadcast this information to their respective subnets. The master browsers are WINS-enabled and share their browse list with the WINS master browser. This information is then merged so each master browser has the same list. Clients on any subnet can then see any service regardless of what subnet it is located on. It can contact a service across the network because TCP/IP can be routed. This allows NetBIOS to span routed networks.

The browsers on the subnets in Figure 15-5 can be part of a single domain or their own domains. The computers within the subnet must belong to a domain or workgroup for the subnet. The WINS architecture allows more complex connections, but most network administrators will try to simplify WINS site-to-site connections as much as possible.

Browse lists are used when workstations need to log onto a domain. The domain information in a browse list can include the IP address of one PDC and up to 24 backup domain controllers (BDC). Any of these can be used to log in to a domain.

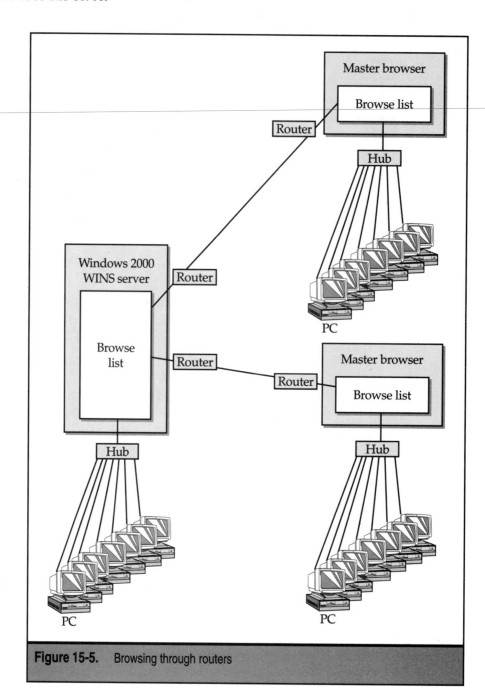

Figure 15-5.   Browsing through routers

New Features in Windows 2000 WINS

The Windows 2000 WINS service includes the following new features compared to the Windows NT WINS service.

▼ **Persistent connections**   WINS can replicate WINS information with other WINS servers. This is usually done using connections that are set up when replication occurs. Persistent connections are maintained continuously, which can improve replication performance.

■ **Improved database engine**   WINS uses the same improved database engine as DNS.

■ **Dynamic record deletion**   The WINS MMC snap-in provides an improved point and click interface. Multiple records can be selected and deleted in one step.

■ **Record and version number validation**   This feature is used for consistency checks for replicated information among WINS servers. It allows the most recent information to be identified.

■ **Multiple WINS server client support**   Windows 98 and Windows 2000 WINS clients can now specify more than two WINS servers for increased reliability especially in larger networks.

■ **Forced updates**   The NBSTAT command line utility can be used from a WINS client to update the client's entry at a WINS server. This is now possible from a Windows NT 4.0 server with Service Pack 4 or later or a Windows 2000 client.

■ **Manual tombstoning**   WINS database records can be tombstoned, marked for deletion, from the WINS MMC snap-in. Records marked for deletion will not be updated. This is useful in multiple WINS server environments to prevent updates of records that are to be deleted.

■ **Command-line administration tool**   WINS servers can be managed using the Netshell command in addition to the graphical WINS MMC snap-in. Most WINS management features can be configured without resorting to editing the registry.

■ **Read-only WINS MMC snap-in access**   The WINS Users group allows members to view WINS configuration.

■ **WINS MMC snap-in filtering and searching**   This feature allows administrators to locate information using advanced criteria. It is essential when managing large WINS databases.

▲ **Export function**   This is a standard MMC snap-in feature that generates comma-delimited text files for processing using other applications.

How WINS Works

WINS uses a client/server architecture similar to DNS. As noted in the previous section, WINS operates in a NetBIOS environment as a NBNS but WINS really shines when used with WINS clients and servers.

WINS servers maintain a WINS database that is similar to a DNS primary zone but, unlike DNS, WINS maintains a flat naming environment like NetBIOS. It uses NetBT for communication between clients and servers. WINS clients register with a WINS server in a fashion similar to dynamic DNS update clients that update a Windows 2000 DNS zone. The main difference between WINS and DNS is the hierarchical nature of DNS and the control over replication.

WINS clients currently include the following platforms:

▼ MS-DOS

■ OS/2

■ Microsoft LAN Manager

■ Windows for Workgroups

■ Windows 95

■ Windows 98

■ Windows NT

- Windows 2000

▲ Linux and UNIX using Samba

NetBIOS clients that do not also have WINS support can use WINS through a WINS proxy server. In this case, the WINS proxy server listens for b-node broadcasts. The proxy server registers a b-node's name with the WINS server when the b-node computer registers its name using NetBIOS. The WINS proxy server will send back a negative response if the name is already registered in the WINS server's database. The WINS proxy server also handles release name requests and name resolution requests. The proxy server normally maintains a cache of previously queried names to speed up the name resolution process in a fashion similar to a DNS server's cache. Windows 2000 WINS servers cannot act as WINS proxy servers, although Windows 2000 WINS servers do support p-node, h-node, and m-node directed requests for name resolution.

As with dynamic DNS updates, WINS clients can register different kinds of information with a WINS server in addition to the client's name and IP network address. As with DNS resource records, multiple WINS records can have the same name as long as the format type is different. Records are registered based on the types of services running on a particular computer. The formats are shown in Tables 15-1 and 15-2. The Name field indicates what the 15-character NetBIOS name specifies.

Name	Format	Description
computer_name	00h	Workstation service.
computer_name	03h	Messenger service—allows sending and receiving messages.
computer_name	06h	Remote access service.

Table 15-1. NetBIOS Unique Names

Name	Format	Description
domain_name	1Bh	Windows NT 4.0 domain controller running as a domain master browser. Used to locate service that handles remote browsing of domains.
computer_name	1Fh	Network Dynamic Data Exchange (NetDDE) service.
computer_name	20h	File server—provides file services.
computer_name	21h	RAS client service.
computer_name	BEh	Network monitoring agent service.
computer_name	BFh	Network monitoring utility—included with Microsoft Systems Management Server.
user_name	03h	User name—allows messages to be sent to user.

Table 15-1. NetBIOS Unique Names *(continued)*

Name	Format	Description
domain_name	00h	Workstation service
domain_name	1Ch	Domain controllers
domain_name	1Dh	Master browsers
domain_name	1Eh	Normal group
domain_name	20h	Internet group
__MSBROWSE__	01h	Master browser for subnet

Table 15-2. NetBIOS Group Names

The combination of records for a particular address indicates what services are supported by a computer. For example, a Workstation Service (00h) will typically have normal group name (1Eh), messenger service (03h), user name (03h), and file server (20h) records defined for the same address. This indicates that the workstation is part of a particular workgroup or domain and that it can send and receive messages and share files. It will also accept messages for the logged on user.

WINS information is usually entered automatically by the computers involved. This information can also be added using the WINS MMC snap-in as static records. In this case, the entries are specified using types shown in Table 15-3. A type may generate more than one WINS record. For example, the Unique type generates three WINS records.

Type	Description
Unique	Specifies a computer name. When added from the WINS MMC snap-in, workstation [00h], messenger [03h], and file server [20h] records are added to the WINS database.
Group	Specifies a normal group. Name resolution for this group is resolved through local subnet broadcasts.
Domain name	Specifies Windows NT domain controllers or Windows 2000 domain controllers emulating a Windows NT domain controller.
Internet Group	Specifies a user defined administrative group. Used to organize resources such as print servers. Generates group [20h] record.
Multihomed	Specifies a computer with multiple IP addresses.

Table 15-3. WINS MMC Snap-In Static Types

When a WINS client starts up, it registers one or more records with the WINS servers. These typically include the services that the client is running. The group that the client is part of is also registered. A user name is registered when a user logs onto the workstation.

A single WINS server is often used on small networks. While a single server does not provide a robust environment, it does make management easier since WINS database replication is not required. On larger networks, it is imperative to have more than one WINS server. Multiple WINS servers can also be used to spread the load when servicing a large number of WINS clients. In general, a single WINS server can handle up to 10,000 WINS clients. Server replication and multiple server placement are discussed in the "Windows 2000 WINS Replication" section.

Windows 2000 WINS Configuration

If the Windows 2000 WINS service is not installed, start up the Configure Your Server Wizard using Start | Programs | Administrative Tools | Configure Your Server. Under the Networking topic is a list of components including WINS, DHCP, and DNS. Select WINS. If the WINS service is not running, there is an option on the topic page to the right to start the Windows Component Wizard; otherwise, there are options to perform management tasks such as configuring scopes.

The Windows Component Wizard displays a list of components. The Network Services component is where the WINS, DNS, and DHCP services will be found. Select this component and click on the Details button to see a list of Networking components, including WINS. If there is a check box next to the WINS entry it means the WINS server is already installed. If not, check the box and click on the OK buttons until the installation process begins.

Windows 2000 WINS is configured using the WINS MMC snap-in that is started using Start | Program Files | Administrative Tools | WINS. This brings up a screen similar to the one shown in Figure 15-6. General MMC operation is discussed in Chapter 10.

The WINS MMC snap-in can manage one or more WINS servers. Selecting the WINS root and then selecting Action | Add Server allows you to select an additional server to manage. Under the WINS

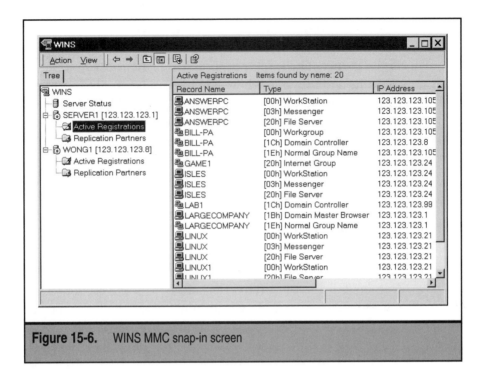

Record Name	Type	IP Address
ANSWERPC	[00h] WorkStation	123.123.123.105
ANSWERPC	[03h] Messenger	123.123.123.105
ANSWERPC	[20h] File Server	123.123.123.105
BILL-PA	[00h] Workgroup	123.123.123.105
BILL-PA	[1Ch] Domain Controller	123.123.123.8
BILL-PA	[1Eh] Normal Group Name	123.123.123.105
GAME1	[20h] Internet Group	123.123.123.24
ISLES	[00h] WorkStation	123.123.123.24
ISLES	[03h] Messenger	123.123.123.24
ISLES	[20h] File Server	123.123.123.24
LAB1	[1Ch] Domain Controller	123.123.123.99
LARGECOMPANY	[1Bh] Domain Master Browser	123.123.123.1
LARGECOMPANY	[1Eh] Normal Group Name	123.123.123.1
LINUX	[00h] WorkStation	123.123.123.21
LINUX	[03h] Messenger	123.123.123.21
LINUX	[20h] File Server	123.123.123.21
LINUX1	[00h] WorkStation	123.123.123.21
LINUX1	[20h] File Server	123.123.123.21

Figure 15-6.   WINS MMC snap-in screen

root is a Server Status entry, along with the servers that have been
added. When the Server Status entry is selected, the list of WINS
servers appears in the right pane and the Status column indicates
whether a server is responding to the WINS MMC snap-in queries.

NOTE: Unlike the Windows 2000 DNS and DHCP MMC snap-ins, the
Windows 2000 WINS MMC snap-in *can* manage Windows NT WINS servers.

Below each WINS server are two entries. The first is the Active
Registrations. This is the WINS database. The second is the Replication
Partners. This will be discussed in more detail in the "Windows 2000
WINS Replication" section.

Selecting an Active Registrations entry lists the contents of the
WINS database because the WINS naming system is flat, unlike the
DNS service system. Displaying the contents of the database for a
10,000-node network could result in tens of thousands of entries since

a node may have more than one entry associated with it. Instead, the program allows entries to be displayed based upon the record name or the owner. The former is accessed by Action | Find By Name and presents a dialog box where a name can be entered. A partial name can be entered, and the program will match the text entered with the leading characters of the names in the database.

Finding by owner is useful for two reasons. First, it can be used to find entries based on a record's owner. The owner is the WINS server that manages the record versus replicated records from other WINS serves. Second, this mechanism can also filter entries based upon their type. Select the Active Registrations entry for a WINS server, then select Action | Find By Owner, and then select the Record Types tab to see the screen in Figure 15-7.

In this example, only the File Servers record type is selected. The Owners tab allows you to select either a single owner or all owners. Clicking on the Find Now button will display all the registered file servers. This is a handy way to find subsets of WINS entries. The two

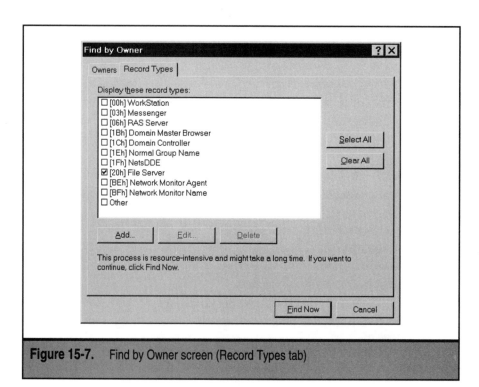

Figure 15-7.   Find by Owner screen (Record Types tab)

Find mechanisms cannot be combined, and it is not possible to refine the search using an existing subset.

Records are usually added automatically, but it is possible to add static definitions using two methods. The first method is to import records from an LMHOSTS file. This is useful when converting a small workgroup that uses LMHOSTS files to WINS. To start the import process, select the Active Registrations entry, then select Action | Import LMHOSTS File and either enter the file's location or browse for it.

The second method to add static definitions is to select the Active Registrations entry and then select Action | New Static Mapping. This presents the screen in Figure 15-8. The Computer Name must be a valid NetBIOS name. The NetBIOS scope is an optional field that is usually left blank. The Type field corresponds to Table 15-3. Changing the type adjusts the parameters of the last field. In this case, the

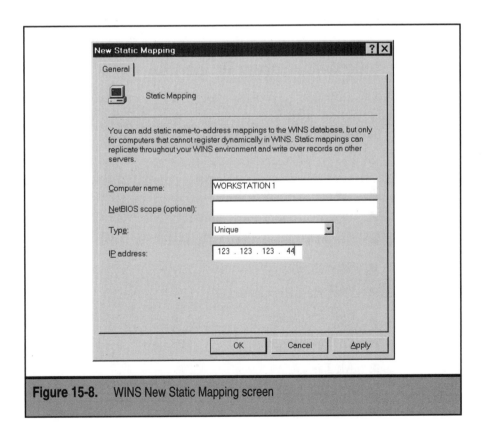

Figure 15-8.   WINS New Static Mapping screen

Unique type has a single IP address. As mentioned earlier, adding a static entry may add more than one WINS record to the database.

Deleting records is a more interesting chore with WINS. It is easiest to do with a single WINS server since deleting a record is the end of the task. When multiple WINS servers are involved, a record must be deleted from all the WINS servers. WINS introduces a process called tombstoning to handle this job.

With tombstoning, a record is marked as extinct or tombstoned. The record will be replicated as a tombstoned record. Tombstoned records will be deleted after the verification interval (you set this in the WINS server Properties screen). This allows replication to occur and all copies of the tombstoned records to be deleted.

Deletions and tombstoning can be applied to a single record, a selected set of records, or all records of a specific owner. The latter is handled by Action | Delete Owner. The dialog box allows you to select the owner and determine whether the records should be deleted or tombstoned.

Windows 2000 WINS Server Properties

This section takes a look at properties and menu actions related to a WINS server. The Action menu when a WINS server is selected includes the following:

▼ Display Server Statistics

■ Scavenge Database

■ Verify Database Consistency

■ Verify Version ID Consistency

■ Start Push Replication

■ Start Pull Replication

■ Backup Database

■ Restore Database

■ All Tasks

- Delete

- Refresh

- Export List

- Properties

▲ Help

The standard set of menu options includes All Tasks, Delete, Refresh, Export List, Properties, and Help. Properties will be discussed at the end of this section.

Display Server Statistics presents a screen that shows various details about the database and operation of the server. It is updated periodically, or you can force a refresh.

Scavenge Database forces a scan of the database to get rid of expired data. This generally happens on a scheduled basis.

Verify Database Consistency and Verify Version ID Consistency are used to scan the database entries to verify the accuracy of the information. This is done by checking with the servers listed in the database. A report is generated based on the response of the servers. A lack of response does not necessarily indicate useless or invalid information but rather that the server could not be contacted.

Replication is addressed in the next section, "Windows 200 WINS Replication." The Start Push Replication and Start Pull Replication menu items are used in this context.

The WINS database can be saved and restored using Backup Database and Restore Database. This process can occur while the service is running.

The WINS server Properties are shown in Figure 15-9. The General tab screen controls statistics update and backup. You can set the server to refresh automatically at a specified interval by checking the Automatically Update Statistics Every box; otherwise, the Refresh button must be clicked on the statistics window to update its contents. One of the server statistics screens can be viewed by selecting a WINS server and then Action | Display Server Statistics. It is unusual for a WINS server to be taken down, but in the event that it is, the Back Up Database During Server Shutdown allows the

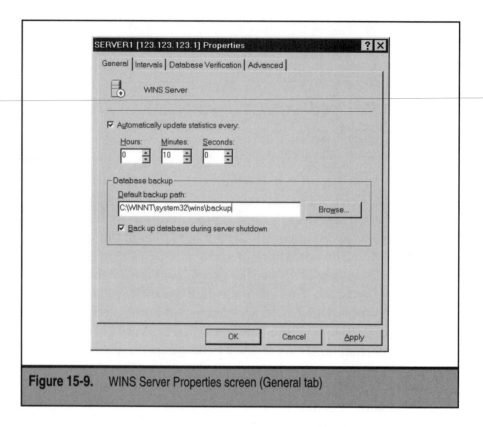

Figure 15-9. WINS Server Properties screen (General tab)

WINS database file to be saved in the specified directory. A handy way to make a backup is to have this check box checked and then stop and start the service.

Select the Intervals tab to display the screen in Figure 15-10. Renewal Interval specifies how often a WINS client should update its information in the WINS database by contacting the WINS server. A long interval is suitable if workstation configuration remains fixed. Extinction Interval is the amount of time that occurs from when a record is released to when it is marked extinct. It should be less than Renew Interval. Extinction Timeout is when extinct records are removed from the database. This is also used for deletion of tombstoned records. Verification Interval is the time a WINS server has to verify names in the database. The minimum value is 24 days.

Selecting the Database Verification tab displays the screen in Figure 15-11. The settings on this screen determine how and when

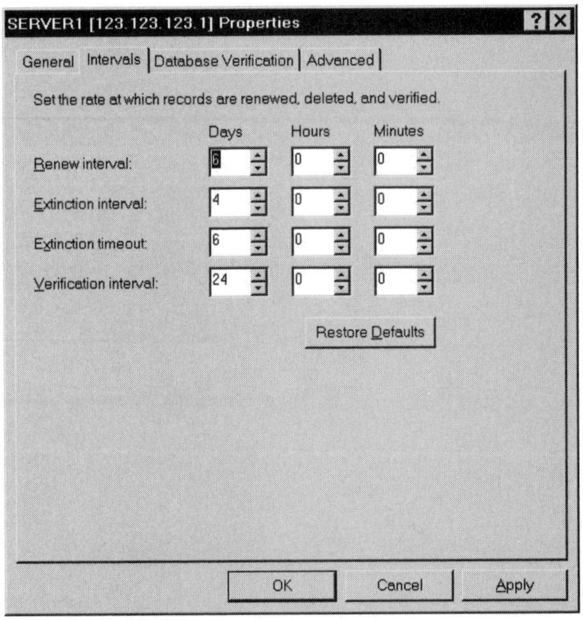

Figure 15-10.   WINS Server Properties screen (Intervals tab)

verification will occur. The verification interval should not be too low, or the WINS server could spend too much time simply doing verification. Verification of replicated data can be done with respect to owners of the data or with randomly selected replication partners. The latter can be useful depending upon how the WINS replication connections are made. The Maximum Number Of Records Verified Each Period field is one way to limit the amount of work done during verification. A value of 30,000 will handle most WINS databases, but this value may be lowered if the overhead is too high or the load on the WINS server is high. Entries not verified in one period will be verified in the next period.

Selecting the Advanced tab presents the screen shown in Figure 15-12. Log Detailed Events To Windows Event Log controls general events associated with the WINS server, such as verification or backup. The WINS service will still report all errors to the Windows 2000 event log, even if this check box is not checked. Enable Burst

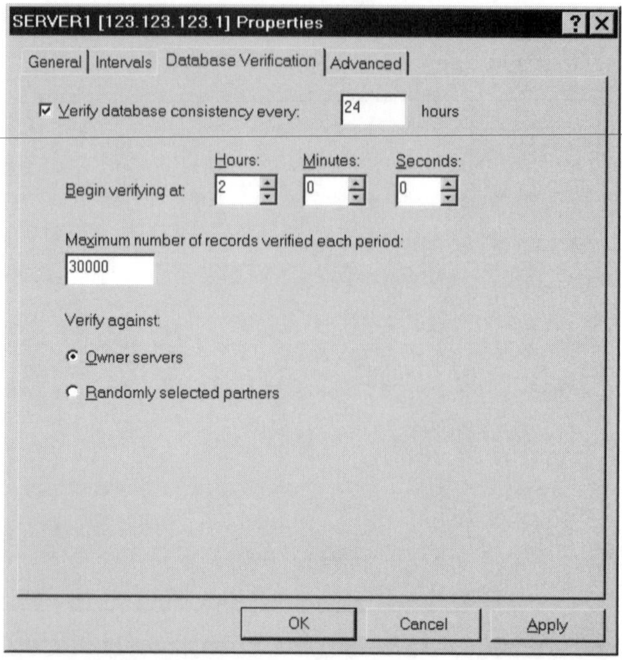

Figure 15-11. WINS Server Properties screen (Database Verification tab)

Handling allows the WINS administrator to limit the number of client requests handled at one time. The Low setting is 300 requests, the Medium setting is 500 requests, and the High setting is 1000 requests. The Custom setting can be used for any amount, but it is usually used for very low or high settings. If the Enable Burst Handling check box is not checked, the WINS server will attempt to service all comers, regardless of load.

The Database Path field allows you to place the WINS database in an arbitrary directory; the default location is %windir%\system32\ wins. The Starting Version ID is associated with records added to the database. The Owners tab in View Records shows the current version ID for the WINS server in the Highest ID column.

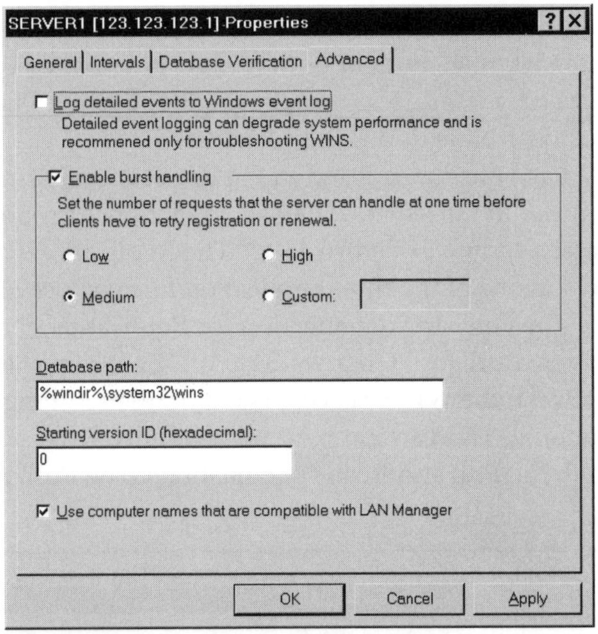

Figure 15-12. WINS Server Properties screen (Advanced tab)

The Use Computer Names That Are Compatible With LAN Manager setting indicates that the 15-character NetBIOS names are used. Some NetBIOS implementations use all 16 bytes for the name.

Windows 2000 WINS Replication

WINS replication can be scheduled or initiated using the WINS MMC snap-in. Replication operates in a push or pull fashion. A push replication is where a WINS server sends its WINS database to its replication partners. A pull replication is where a WINS server requests information from another WINS server.

While it is possible to put together an arbitrary linkage between WINS servers for replication purposes, it is best to use a basic tree structure with a minimum number of levels. WINS partners are WINS servers that are immediately adjacent in the tree. Partners may support push, pull, or both forms of replication. WINS servers are added by IP address by selecting Replication Partners and then Action | New Replication Partner.

Each partner is listed in the Replication Partners list. Select a partner in the list and then select Action | Properties to view the screen shown in Figure 15-13. The Replication Partner Type field selects one of the three replication forms: Push/Pull, Push, or Pull.

The Persistent Connection for Replication check boxes enable a new feature for Windows 2000 WINS. When checked, the connection between the WINS servers is maintained as long as the servers are running. This can improve performance. There is one check box in both the Pull and Push specifications. The Pull option operates on a

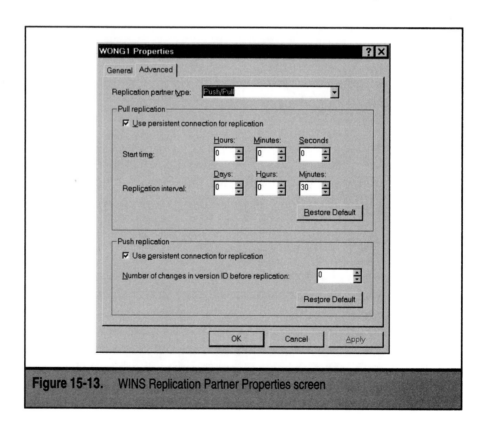

Figure 15-13. WINS Replication Partner Properties screen

scheduled basis. The schedule is based on daily operation, but it can be started at any particular time and repeat for a specified interval. For a Push replication, there is the option to limit replication until a specified number of changes occur. This allows a block of changes to be sent at one time, but it also delays the updates if the threshold is not reached.

Regardless of how replication is set up between servers, the replication settings must be done at both ends before replication can occur. This means that the source and destination WINS servers must have each other in their Replication Partners list with the appropriate replication type enabled.

To view the Properties screen for the Replication Partners entry shown in Figure 15-14, select the entry and then Action | Properties. The General tab screen is used to restrict replication with known

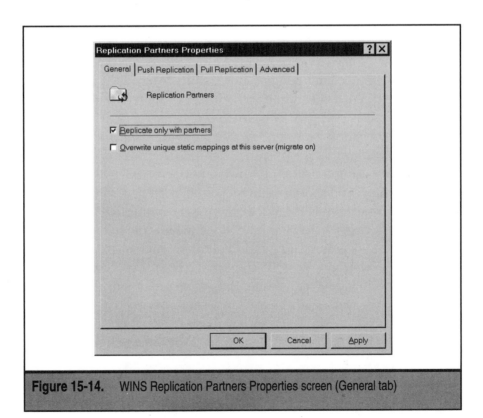

Figure 15-14.   WINS Replication Partners Properties screen (General tab)

partners. If Replicate Only With Partners is unchecked, replication will occur even if the WINS server is not in the Replication Partners list. This normally controls Pull replications with unregistered WINS servers.

The Overwrite Unique Static Mappings At This Server (Migrate On) check box allows information from other WINS servers to overwrite static entries entered on this WINS server. This is normally unchecked so that the WINS server maintains static entries that it was configured with. Such changes can occur if a workstation is moved from one WINS environment to another or if two workstations are configured using the same names.

Select the Push Replication tab to view the screen shown in Figure 15-15. This tab is used to specify when push operations are to begin. The settings are for the entire server, although some settings can be changed for individual replication partners. The At Service Startup check box indicates whether push operation should begin when the WINS service starts up. This is normally when the server is started if the WINS service is set on Automatic. When Address Changes indicates that push updates should occur when a new WINS client registers a new name and address or when the address for an existing name is changed. The Number Of Changes In Version ID Before Replication list box allows changes to be set as a batch. This setting is the threshold for pushing changes. The Use Persistent Connections To Push Replication Partners check box indicates whether a network connection should be made and maintained with push replication partners while the WINS service is running.

Select the Pull Replication tab to view the screen shown in Figure 15-16. The Start Time and Replication Interval are the same as those for the replication partner Properties screen. The Number Of Retries list box specifies how many times this WINS server will attempt replication before waiting for the next replication period. The Start Pull Replication At Service Startup check box is self-explanatory, as is the Use Persistent Connections For Pull Replication Partners check box.

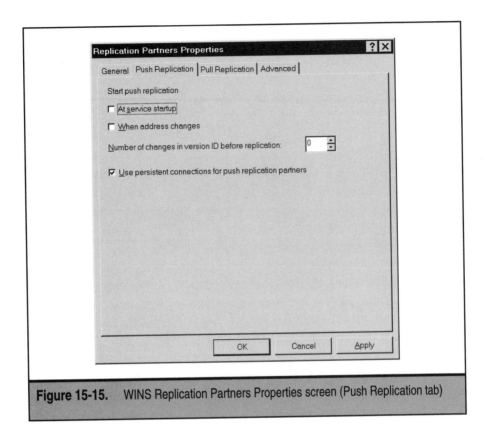

Figure 15-15.   WINS Replication Partners Properties screen (Push Replication tab)

Selecting the Advanced tab presents the screen in Figure 15-17. The Block Records For These Owners list box allows a WINS server to limit the number of entries in its database due to replication. It is primarily used for keeping out entries that should not be available to local WINS clients or that are not needed by local WINS clients. The IP addresses will be for WINS servers, although they do not have to be replication partners. They can be for WINS servers that are linked to the WINS server through replication links with other WINS servers. Ignoring information can be useful for a variety of reasons, especially for a geographically dispersed company. For example,

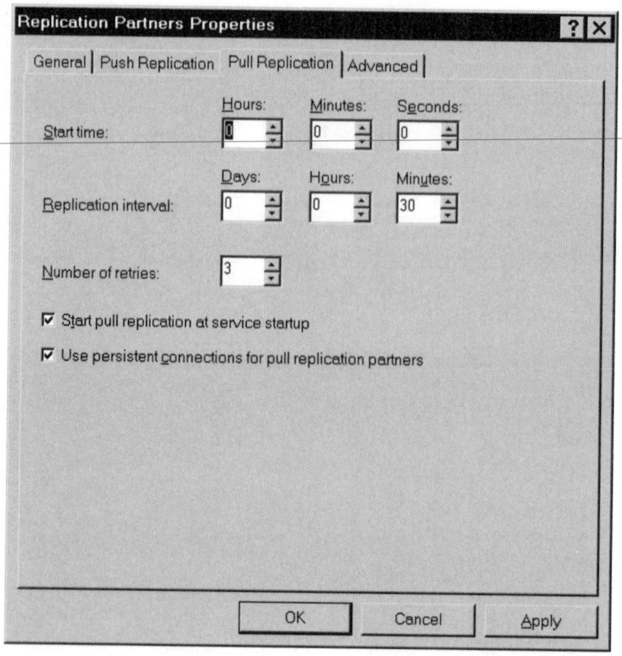

Figure 15-16.   WINS Replication Partners Properties screen (Pull Replication tab)

branch offices may use WINS and the information may be needed by nearby offices but not by offices across the country. Blocking can be used by a WINS server to prevent the movement of WINS information to replication partners.

WINS replication has the advantage of bidirectional updates, but this can lead to confusion when problems occur because blocking is the only control mechanism available to WINS administrators.

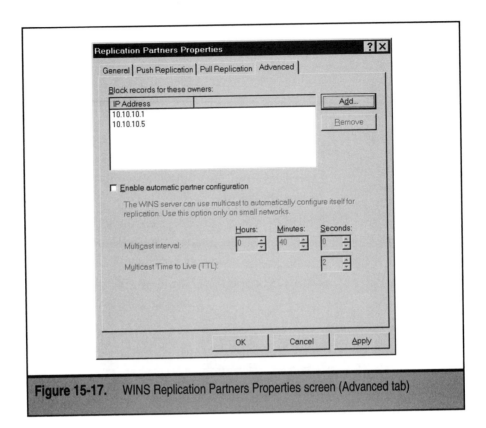

Figure 15-17.   WINS Replication Partners Properties screen (Advanced tab)

Using DHCP with WINS

No special server settings are required for a WINS client to use DHCP to obtain an IP address, but it is possible to configure the DHCP server to deliver additional information to a WINS client. WINS-specific options are listed in Table 15-4.

The settings are made to the DHCP options as outlined in Chapter 14. The WINS clients should be set up to receive their

Code	Option	Description
44	WINS Servers	List of IP addresses of WINS servers to be used by the WINS client
45	NetBIOS Datagram Distribution Server (NBDD)	List of IP addresses for NDBB servers to be used by the WINS client
46	NetBIOS Node Type	Specifies the kind of NetBIOS node the WINS client should operate as
47	NetBIOS Scope ID	Name of the NetBIOS scope associated with the WINS client

Table 15-4. WINS-Specific DHCP Option Codes

settings from the DHCP server. Usually, the WINS client can be set to override the DHCP settings, but this means changes require adjustment of these workstations. Using option codes 44 and 46 is recommended.

MIGRATING FROM WINS TO DYNAMIC DNS

The process of migrating from WINS to DNS is called *decommissioning* by Microsoft. It entails the reconfiguration of WINS clients to use DNS and the elimination of the WINS servers. It is not an easy process, especially in large WINS installations, and it is one that should be carefully planned, as it can affect the operation of network applications.

Decommissioning cannot occur if Windows-based computers on the network are running MS-DOS or earlier versions of Windows or Windows NT or if NetBIOS name services are still used. The NET command line utilities fall into this category, as well as some BackOffice applications. Many third-party mail systems use NetBIOS.

In general, the WINS infrastructure should remain in place until all clients have been moved to DNS. After the release and extinction timeouts have elapsed, the WINS database should be rather sparse. The only entries that should remain are static entries. Any entries left in the database should be checked to verify that the matching computers have been converted to DNS operation. The exception would be WINS servers or WINS proxy servers. The WINS services can then be stopped. The WINS infrastructure should not be removed until it is verified that the DNS infrastructure is handling the reconfigured clients and servers.

NOTE: When removing WINS servers, any records associated with the WINS server can be removed from replication partners by using Delete Owner.

If DHCP is used to configure WINS clients, any WINS- or NetBIOS-related options should be removed from the options list. This will highlight problems associated with dynamic configuration.

Remember, most WINS clients that are not running Windows 2000 will still require NetBIOS or WINS to locate domain servers for logon purposes. If WINS is removed and Windows 2000 is running in compatibility mode, there may still be problems that are not immediately apparent. For example, local NetBIOS clients will still be able to access the local server but not remote servers because local servers can be discovered by NetBIOS broadcasts, whereas locating remote servers requires WINS. DNS does not provide information about NetBIOS-based domain servers to DNS clients.

SUMMARY

Finding the name of a computer and its IP address is clearly defined using DNS or WINS. With Windows 2000, it is clear that the future direction is with DNS. If WINS is not a major issue or it's not used in the existing network, it should be avoided because managing two services is always more difficult than managing one.

For those network administrators with a well-established WINS infrastructure, migration to Windows 2000 WINS is the clear path. Migration to Windows 2000 DNS is a more difficult choice and will be based upon a variety of factors that are outlined in this chapter, including the dependency of clients and client applications on WINS. Networks that must support MS-DOS, Windows, Windows 95, Windows 98, and Windows NT will most likely require WINS as long as these clients exist on the network.

CHAPTER 16

DNS Replication and Indirection

D NS servers rarely operate in isolation, although it is possible to have an intranet with a lone DNS server. In this case, replication of DNS information or forwarding DNS requests is unnecessary, but for the rest of the world, replication and indirection are imperative.

Replication of DNS information is important because most DNS clients deal directly with only a single DNS server. It is up to the DNS server to deal with the rest of the world of DNS servers. Chapter 2 covers DNS client operation.

While replication and forwarding requests may seem like a simple process, improper configuration can result in old or inaccurate name resolution results. Likewise, improper configuration can generate too much network traffic due to replication and name resolution. Finally, Windows 2000 Active Directory's dependence on DNS means that proper DNS operation is imperative for proper Windows 2000 network operation.

The "Active Directory Replication and Active Directory–integrated Zones" section in this chapter examines DNS replication using a feature unique to Windows 2000 DNS, Active Directory–integrated zones and their replication via Active Directory.

The "Secondary DNS Zone Replication" section takes a look at the standard DNS mechanism for replication. Windows 2000 DNS supports the latest DNS specifications for replication. Windows 2000 DNS supports replication with any standards-based DNS service, although limitations may occur due to the implementation of non-Windows 2000 DNS servers. For example, the Windows NT DNS service can send DNS information to a Windows 2000 DNS service secondary DNS zone. Unfortunately, there are problems when the direction is reversed because Windows NT DNS service does not support SRV resource records that can be found in a Windows 2000 DNS server's DNS zone information. This section examines these problems and solutions.

The "Dynamic DNS and Replication" section examines the impact of a new DNS feature in Windows 2000 DNS support, dynamic DNS updates; this feature was introduced in Chapter 2. Dynamic DNS updates impact replication because this information must be replicated in a timely fashion. It is a tough issue when transient, DHCP-based clients are utilized because it is possible for a client's IP address to change. This section examines the proper way to configure DNS and DHCP services to prevent potential confusion.

The "DNS Forwarding" and "DNS Caching" sections take a look at alternate configurations for DNS servers. While these techniques can be combined with regular primary and secondary DNS zone support, it is possible to have DNS servers that use these techniques exclusively. These sections take a look at when and why these techniques should be used.

Windows 2000 DNS can be integrated with Windows 2000 WINS support. WINS supports its own replication procedures that are independent of Windows 2000 DNS replication. WINS replication and WINS operation is covered in Chapter 15. If WINS and DNS operate on the same Windows 2000 network, a good understanding of both services is needed. Planning for the two can be relatively independent, however. The main points of commonality occur when router links are employed and DNS and WINS share these links along with normal network traffic.

ACTIVE DIRECTORY REPLICATION AND ACTIVE DIRECTORY–INTEGRATED ZONES

Active Directory–integrated DNS zones are an important part of Windows 2000 DNS replication in a Windows 2000 Active Directory network. They cannot be used if Active Directory is not used because Active Directory–integrated DNS zones require Active Directory to store zone information and to provide zone replication as part of the Active Directory database replication.

Use of the Active Directory database for storing DNS zone information has several advantages. The first, discussed in this chapter, is Active Directory's replication feature. The second is the elimination of a DNS server as a single point of failure compared to primary/secondary zone replication. Third, backup of DNS information is handled through the backup of the Active Directory database. Finally, Active Directory provides improved security compared to primary or secondary DNS zones.

This section shows how to tune Active Directory replication. "How Active Directory Replication Works" takes a closer look at how Active Directory's replication affects Active Directory–integrated DNS zone replication.

The fact that using Active Directory database replication prevents a Windows 2000 DNS server from being a single point of failure is a major advantage. This is one of the major reasons for considering the use of Windows 2000 DNS over third-party DNS servers. Active Directory prevents DNS servers from being a single point of failure because Active Directory is a multimaster database. Each Active Directory domain controller maintains a complete copy of the domain's database.

NOTE: The Active Directory domain database, or simply Active Directory database, should not be confused with the Active Directory global catalog. The Active Directory database spans a domain and contains all the information associated with objects contained within the domain. The Active Directory global catalog is a subset of the Active Directory databases for all the domains within an Active Directory forest. An Active Directory domain controller contains the domain's Active Directory database and the global catalog. The Active Directory global catalog is used when a client logs onto the network, whereas the Active Directory database handles Active Directory–integrated DNS zone replication.

The other aspect of Active Directory–integrated DNS zone replication is its limitation due to the Active Directory database distribution. Since an Active Directory database remains within an Active Directory domain, so must an Active Directory–integrated DNS zone be limited to an Active Directory domain.

NOTE: Although an Active Directory–integrated DNS zone is limited by replication to an Active Directory domain, the Windows 2000 DNS server that uses an Active Directory–integrated DNS zone is not limited by what clients can access the DNS server and the zone. One approach for cross-domain DNS support using Active Directory–integrated DNS zones is to have a single Active Directory domain provide DNS services for the entire network with individual Active Directory–integrated DNS zones or subzones for each Active Directory domain.

Backup of DNS service information is handled differently for Active Directory–integrated DNS zones and non-Active Directory–integrated DNS. DNS service information is backed up when the Active Directory database is backed up. This can be done through any Active Directory domain controller in the domain. Non-Active Directory–integrated DNS backup is done by saving the DNS zone files located in the DNS system directory. This must be done through the respective server and is independent of the Active Directory database backup.

Active Directory security allows restrictions to be placed on the Active Directory–integrated DNS zones from an access as well as modification point of view (described in detail in Chapter 12). Security is maintained across the domain for the Active Directory–integrated DNS zones, and Kerberos authentication can be used to verify dynamic DNS updates. Primary or secondary DNS zones have limited security controls and do not support secured dynamic DNS updates.

How Active Directory Replication Works

The Active Directory database contains a variety of items including Active Directory–integrated DNS zone information and DNS service and security information. All this information is replicated along with the rest of the Active Directory database contents between domain controllers in the same domain.

The other part of the puzzle is replication of the Active Directory global catalog. This is replicated among all domain controllers within a domain forest versus the Active Directory database that is replicated within a domain.

Most replication configuration issues arise in large or distributed networks where Active Directory information, both database and catalog, may be moved between Active Directory sites. If domains do not span sites, only the Active Directory catalog will be replicated between sites. Database replication occurs between sites when domain controllers from the same domain are located in both sites, as shown in Figure 16-1.

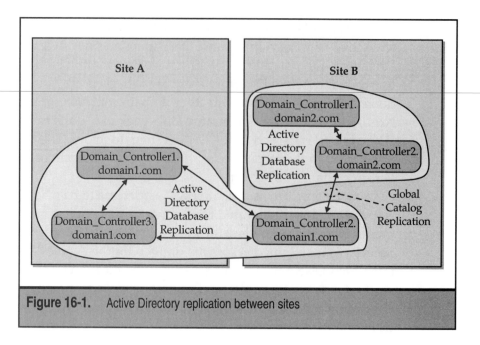

Figure 16-1. Active Directory replication between sites

Figure 16-1 also assumes that Domain_Controller2.domain1.com and Domain_Controller3.domain1.com are set up as bridgehead servers. This allows global catalog information to be exchanged between these servers and distributed to other computers at the respective site.

Intrasite replication uses an uncompressed format, whereas intersite replication uses compressed information. Intersite replication is performed directly between servers. Intersite replication will occur at least through a pair of routers or switches, or the information can be exchanged via e-mail. Intrasite links, communication methods, and scheduling details are configured using the Active Directory Sites and Services MMC snap-in discussed in Chapter 10. Active Directory–integrated DNS zones are configured using the DNS MMC snap-in management, which is covered in Chapter 11.

Updates are done incrementally when possible. Active Directory handles all the details including resolution of differences that can occur due to communication latency or the unavailability of a domain controller. Differences are handled using timestamps with the latest information taking priority. This includes changes made to Active Directory–integrated DNS zones.

Performance and Security Issues

The use of Active Directory–integrated DNS zones has little impact on replication times when all domain controllers are located at the same site. This is because a site is normally connected using high-speed network connections, and the amount of incremental information that must be exchanged is comparatively small. Active Directory–integrated DNS zones may impact the network if the zones receive a significant number of dynamic DNS updates. This can occur if an entire site starts up after a power failure, but Active Directory replication will simply proceed as the network connections will allow.

The main issue with respect to Active Directory–integrated DNS zones for a domain within a single site is that replication is completely transparent. This is good for redundancy purposes, but there is a lack of replication control if a number of Active Directory–integrated DNS zones are used. Finer control of zone replication can be accomplished using secondary DNS zones.

Control of replication is the major issue for domains that span sites and utilize Active Directory–integrated DNS zones. If Active Directory–integrated DNS zones are employed, Active Directory replication has control of the DNS information. If secondary DNS zones are used instead for remote sites, the zone replication is controlled on a per zone basis. Likewise, replication to other sites is controlled on a per zone basis, meaning that all zones do not have to be replicated at all sites. The Active Directory database is replicated at all sites that have domain controllers for the Active Directory domain.

NOTE: The impact of Active Directory–integrated DNS zone replication between sites is only of importance to performance if Windows 2000 DNS servers are used at multiple sites for the domain. This is not a requirement. A domain controller is usually a DNS server, but a domain controller can also use a DNS server on another computer. In fact, it is possible for Active Directory–integrated DNS zones to be used within a site and replicated for support of offsite domain controllers of the same Active Directory domain using secondary DNS zone replication or caching.

There are a number of reasons why it is not desirable to have Active Directory information replicated between sites. For example, a site may not be physically secure, so keeping security information like the Active Directory database away from this site is in the best interest of network security. This actually impacts the placement of domain controllers more than the Windows 2000 DNS server does because the domain controller is the driving factor. If there is no domain controller on a computer, there is no Active Directory–integrated DNS zone support on the computer. In this instance, secondary DNS zone replication is preferable if DNS information can be replicated at the unsecured site.

SECONDARY DNS ZONE REPLICATION

Replication using secondary zones is often preferable because it works equally well with third-party DNS servers like BIND. Configuration of BIND is covered in Chapter 21. This chapter concentrates on the Windows 2000 aspect of secondary DNS zone configuration.

Windows NT DNS administrators will be very familiar with secondary DNS zone configuration under Windows 2000 DNS because all settings are handled through a graphical interface. In the case of Windows 2000, this is the DNS MMC snap-in covered in Chapter 11. Refer to Chapter 11 for the mechanics of setting up secondary DNS zones. This chapter deals with planning and architecture issues.

Secondary DNS Zone Planning

Unlike Active Directory–integrated DNS zones, secondary DNS zone use requires planning and specific configuration of all DNS servers involved. Secondary zone replication can occur from any zone on any DNS server. There may be security requirements that must be met for replication to occur, but this will be discussed later in this section. If security is an issue and secondary zone replication cannot be done, caching or forwarding should be considered.

Secondary DNS zone replication is a top-down process starting with a single primary DNS zone. In the case of a Windows 2000 DNS server, the primary DNS zone can also be an Active Directory–integrated DNS zone. There's a distinction between a top-down process and a hierarchical tree because the source of secondary DNS zone information can come from more than one source, as shown in Figure 16-2.

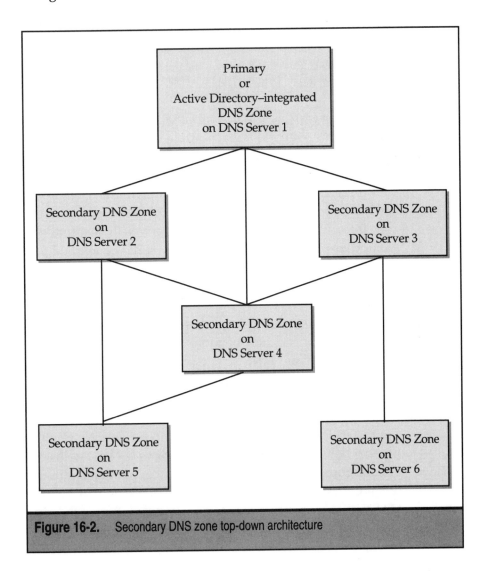

Figure 16-2. Secondary DNS zone top-down architecture

The root of the tree is a primary or Active Directory–integrated DNS zone. Three secondary DNS zones obtain their information from this source. DNS server 4 is set up to receive its information from three sources. This redundancy allows DNS server 4 to obtain information even if one of the links cannot be used. DNS server 5 has a similar configuration to DNS server 4.

NOTE: The network topology and Windows 2000 site architecture is not shown in Figure 16-2. The network topology may limit how DNS servers can communicate with each other, but the Windows 2000 site architecture will have no effect on how secondary DNS zones are configured or managed.

DNS servers 2, 3, and 6 obtain their information from a single source. If this source is not accessible when the secondary DNS zone timeout expires, the updated information will not be available until the source becomes available. The old information will be retained, but it may not be accurate, especially if dynamic DNS updates are used with the root zone. Of course, if DNS server 1 fails, then the zone information in all other DNS servers will eventually expire. No updates can occur because they can only be applied to the zone at DNS server 1.

It is possible to set up multiple DNS servers for the same primary DNS zone, but this will not normally work if dynamic DNS updates are used because only a single primary DNS zone will be updated. The situation can actually be more confusing if dynamic DNS updates are sent to different DNS servers. However, if dynamic DNS update support is not used and the primary DNS zone is relatively static, it is relatively easy to manage multiple DNS servers in this fashion.

Keeping track of multiple secondary DNS zones on a single server can make DNS zone management more complex, especially as the number of DNS servers involved increases because each server must be configured individually. The references to other DNS servers that are sources to the secondary DNS zones are with respect to the DNS server host, which is the specific incarnation of the secondary DNS zone. Unfortunately, while most DNS implementations support multiple sources for the secondary DNS zone information, the implementations do not check to see if the DNS server itself is on the list. If they did, the DNS server would be able to ignore itself as the source and DNS servers for this secondary DNS zone could be set up in an identical fashion.

Luckily, most secondary DNS zone configurations are static. Once configured, a secondary DNS zone definition will normally be changed only when an additional source is added to the list. A change should also be made if a source is removed from the network or if the source no longer manages the matching DNS zone. This has less of an impact because the DNS server will simply move onto the next DNS server in the secondary DNS zone's list of sources when the missing DNS server cannot be contacted. This creates some delay in determining the source for a secondary DNS zone when the zone information must be updated, but the amount of time is minor compared to the time needed to perform the update.

In general, it is advantageous to minimize the number of different secondary DNS zones in a network. It is also a good idea to limit replication where necessary. For example, if a subnet needs to use dynamic DNS updates for workstations and this information is generally used only within the subnet, it makes no sense to replicate this zone outside of the subnet. Secondary DNS zones are still useful in this situation if more than one DNS serves the subnet.

Secondary DNS Zone Replication over WAN Connections

A common DNS configuration in a distributed network has the source and a secondary DNS zone on different ends of a WAN connection. A number of issues may arise because of the type of connection, such as the speed of the WAN connection, its availability, and its reliability.

WAN connections are typically slower than LAN connections. Some large networks have backbone WAN connections that are very fast, but these can be viewed as LAN connections with intervening routers. Slower links, such as 128kbps ISDN or 56kbps frame relay links, will have more of an impact on secondary DNS zone replication planning.

WAN connections can be continuous or transient. The latter is typically on demand, for example, ISDN connections between a branch office and the main office. The WAN connection will normally be available after a short delay, but there is often no guarantee that a connection can be made each time. The inability to make a connection can vary depending upon the technology, but this could be due to a limited number of simultaneous connections supported at the main office. The infrastructure used to make the connection may be shared, as with a modem or dial-up ISDN connection, and overall system load can limit the ability to make a WAN connection.

WAN connections tend to be relatively reliable but this can also vary depending upon the type of connection and the type of service purchased. A discussion of WAN reliability is beyond the scope of this book, but a WAN connection of limited reliability can be compared to a transient connection in a busy system.

The bottom line is that these issues must be considered when setting up one or more secondary DNS zone transfers across a WAN connection. The two controlling values are the refresh interval and the expiration interval that are found in the primary DNS zone's Start Of Authority (SOA) resource record. For LAN connections, a refresh interval of 15 minutes may be acceptable, but this can cause a heavy load on a WAN connection if the zone transfer is large.

The expiration interval is usually significantly longer than the refresh interval and determines when zone information becomes invalid. A DNS server will attempt to update a secondary DNS zone many times before the zone information expires, but with a WAN connection is it possible for an expiration to occur.

In general, the refresh interval should be set as long as possible when using a WAN connection. The duration will depend upon the kind of changes that may occur in the zone. For example, on a relatively static zone, a very long refresh interval of a few hours will have little or no impact on the accuracy of the data. For transient WAN links, it will limit the need for making a connection simply for updating a secondary DNS zone.

TIP: Check out the SOA resource record of any secondary DNS zones if a transient WAN connection is being made on a regular basis. This type of regular connection can significantly increase WAN costs that are based on connection time and the number of connections, such as a dial-up ISDN line.

A shorter refresh interval may be necessary if dynamic DNS updates are used on the primary DNS zone that is the source of a secondary DNS zone. DNS managers may wish to consider splitting a zone if the secondary DNS zone is being used for more static entries. One way to do this is to create a subdomain for dynamic DNS updates and make this subdomain its own primary DNS zone. This will allow independent control and replication of the two primary DNS zones.

Splitting DNS zones can also be used if different WAN and LAN connections are used to replicate information via secondary DNS zones. The split allows SOA intervals for each primary DNS zone to be set independent of the other DNS zones. Unfortunately, this will not work if the same zone must be replicated using different WAN connections. In this case, the SOA settings should be tuned for the most restrictive WAN connection.

Incremental secondary DNS zone updates can significantly reduce WAN traffic, but this approach works best if the WAN connection is reliable, so incremental updates can occur regularly. If incremental secondary DNS zone updates do not occur on a regular basis, the zone replication must be done in total. This tends to show up quickly with a slow WAN connection and a large DNS zone.

Notification should be used if the WAN connection is reliable. Notification combined with incremental secondary DNS zone updates provides the most efficient and timely updates for the secondary DNS zone. However, notification may not be the best choice for transient WAN links if notifications will be occurring often as with a primary DNS zone that is supporting dynamic DNS updates. On the other hand, notification can be useful even on transient WAN links if changes to the primary DNS zone occur rarely.

Secondary DNS Zone Replication with Windows NT

Secondary DNS zone replication between Windows NT and Windows 2000 will depend on the direction of replication and the connection type between the servers and security. The direction of replication is an issue because the capabilities of the Windows NT DNS server are not the same as a Windows 2000 DNS server. The type of connection will be an issue for a low-speed WAN connection. This issue is covered in the "Secondary DNS Zone Replication over WAN Connections" section. Security may be an issue because Windows NT cannot participate in an Active Directory–integrated DNS zone so a secondary DNS zone security approach is the only type of security that can be applied there. Chapter 12 takes a look at security issues.

In this section, we take a look at the direction of replication issue between a Windows NT and Windows 2000 DNS server. Since the feature set for the Windows 2000 DNS server is a superset of the Windows NT DNS server, placing the secondary DNS zone on the Windows 2000 DNS server will result in no restrictions. Any configuration considerations will be associated with issues already discussed.

Going from a Windows 2000 DNS server to a secondary DNS zone on a Windows NT DNS server is another story. First and foremost are SRV resource records that Windows 2000 supports but Windows NT does not. The interesting aspect of this is that, although Windows NT will not support these records, the information is intact in the secondary DNS zone file. If this information is in turn replicated to another secondary DNS zone on a Windows 2000 DNS server or one that supports SRV records, then this information will be usable.

Secondary DNS Zone Replication Issues

The use of secondary DNS zone replication brings up two major topics: security and replication methods. Windows 2000 DNS provides minimal security for replication of secondary DNS zones, but it is comparable to third-party solutions like BIND. Replication methods can be full or incremental, and they can be initiated by the master (secondary DNS zone source) or by the slave (secondary DNS zone).

Windows 2000 DNS secondary DNS zone security is implemented at the source. The Zone Transfers tab of the Properties screen for a secondary DNS zone (discussed in Chapter 11) allows DNS administrators to allow replication from any DNS server or to specific DNS servers. The latter can be listed explicitly by IP addresses, or can be the list of authoritative name servers. They are listed as NS (name server) resource records in the DNS zone. Third-party DNS servers such as BIND allow limitations based upon subnets instead of just individual IP addresses.

Replicated information is sent without using encryption or digital signatures. The lack of encryption is of little consequence because the information is publicly available through the DNS server. Unfortunately, there is no way to determine whether the information received from the source has been tampered with during transit, although keeping replication transmissions within a network is often sufficient from a security standpoint. Still, for replication across the Internet, it may prove to be worth the effort to set up a virtual private network link for this and other traffic between sites in a distributed network. One alternative is to send the zone information in encrypted form using e-mail or some other secure transmission and to have a primary DNS zone at the remote site where the information will be installed.

Another security related issue is authentication of the source. This is not difficult with internal DNS zones since the DNS administrator has control over or can verify the source. The same may not be true for information obtained through a public network like the Internet. This issue arises more often with caching, which is discussed later in this chapter. If the DNS information obtained from a DNS server on the Internet is not accurate, it will cause inaccurate information to be distributed locally. This can have a major impact when users try to access a particular service by domain name because inaccurate information can cause the access to fail or be redirected to another site. Redirecting the access to another site is often worse because such redirection is sometimes done intentionally. This Internet Trojan Horse can have grave security consequences so replication of information from such a source should be considered carefully.

Full zone transfer replication (AXFR) is the basic secondary DNS zone replication method. A more advanced and efficient version is the incremental zone transfer replication (IXFR) specified in RFC 1995. With this method, DNS servers use zone serial numbers to determine what changes are to be sent. A zone's serial number is found in the zone's SOA (Start Of Authority) resource record. A full transfer is used if a destination does not have a valid serial number, such as when a secondary DNS zone is first initialized, or if the source does not have a matching serial number in its database of changes.

Secondary DNS zone transfers can be initiated when the destination determines the information in the zone has expired. The Windows 2000 DNS MMC snap-in also allows the DNS administrator to force an update. Alternatively, the source can be set up to notify destination DNS servers using the NOTIFY packet. Windows 2000 DNS supports this feature, but the only controls are the list of IP addresses a NOTIFY packet will be sent to. There are no controls that dictate when the packet will be sent as there are with WINS. In the latter case, update notification can be held until a specific number of updates has occurred. This limitation is of little consequence for a relatively static DNS zone, but if dynamic DNS updates are used, notification packets can be sent quite often. Incremental updates can minimize zone update related traffic, but it is often a good idea to limit notification when dynamic DNS updates are employed.

DYNAMIC DNS AND REPLICATION

The impact of dynamic DNS updates can be significant for Active Directory–integrated DNS zone replication as well as secondary DNS zone replication. In both cases, dynamic DNS updates cause an Active Directory–integrated DNS zone or primary DNS zone to be out of synch with the rest of the related zones. In the case of an Active Directory–integrated DNS zone, the updates to other Active Directory databases on other domain controllers within the domain occur automatically and usually within a very short time from when the change is made. Domains that span sites will not be updated as quickly as local domain controllers will be, but intersite updates can be controlled, as discussed earlier in this chapter.

Secondary DNS zones obtain their information from a primary DNS zone or another secondary DNS zone. This update process can be initiated by timeouts or by NOTIFY packets. The latter will be generated when a dynamic DNS update occurs on a primary DNS zone if the primary DNS zone is so configured. As notification controls occur on a per zone basis, it may be prudent to split zones based upon whether dynamic DNS updates will occur, so the type of update initiation can be applied selectively. For example, the zone workgroup1.company.com could be used to handle computers within a workgroup that will use dynamic DNS updates, while the company.com zone will not use dynamic DNS updates. This could be because the company.com zone has server definitions that tend to be static, making frequent replication unnecessary.

Configuring DNS and DHCP for DNS Zone Replication

Dynamic DNS updates can be used by servers to register information with a DNS server. A Windows 2000 domain controller can do this. In this case, the information will not change very often, if at all. On the other hand, workstations that obtain their IP address via DHCP may change their IP address on a regular basis, especially if the DHCP lease timeouts are rather short. This is often the case where the number of IP addresses is limited and the number of workstations that will attach to the network is larger than the network or if it's larger than this block of addresses. While it is not possible to have more workstations attached to the network using DHCP than the number of IP addresses the DHCP server can distribute, the situation may be suitable if the turnover rate is high. For example, workstations may be laptop computers and connections may be made and terminated on a regular basis such as when a class starts and ends. In this case, the students come to class, plug their laptops in to the network (or they have a wireless connection), and disconnect when the class is over. A suitably short DHCP lease time will allow the IP addresses to be recovered and reused, but it also results in significant DNS zone changes if dynamic DNS is used.

NOTE: In general, a network with non-Internet–based IP addresses will have more than a sufficient number of IP addresses available so that each computer can have its own unique IP address.

The key to DHCP and dynamic DNS update support is to make sure that the related timeouts are set properly or that secondary DNS zone server notification is used. For the timeout approach, the DHCP lease time must be longer than the secondary DNS zone update time. This means a secondary DNS zone that gets its information from the primary DNS zone will be out of synch for at most one update cycle. Multiple levels of secondary DNS zone linkages complicate matters. In this case, the update cycle needs to be even shorter.

While dynamic DNS update is useful in tracking computers when they are turned off or detached from the network, it may be prudent to limit its use. Dynamic DNS updates are needed only when another computer needs to access resources on the computer by using the computer's domain name.

Controlling how and when a computer will use dynamic DNS updates to register its domain name is another way to address the problem. Unfortunately, a Windows 2000 DNS client with dynamic DNS update support and the Windows 2000 DHCP dynamic DNS update proxy have only two modes of operation: on or off. This simplifies configuration and is usually suitable in most environments. UNIX and Linux implementations of dynamic DNS update support can be applied more selectively and can often be configured based upon the operation of a particular service such as a Web server. Nsupdate (covered in Chapter 13) provides dynamic DNS update support for these operating systems.

DNS FORWARDING

DNS forwarding lets a DNS server forward all requests it receives and cache the results. The idea is that the cache will eventually be filled with the most commonly referenced information so that subsequent forwarded requests will be minimal. A typical use for a forwarding DNS server is on the near side of a slow WAN link such as a local DNS server that forwards requests to an ISP's DNS server to handle Internet name resolution.

DNS forwarding specifies how name resolution query will occur when resolution cannot occur locally. A forwarding-only DNS server will try using only cached information. A forwarding-only DNS can also have primary and secondary zones and, in the case of Windows 2000 DNS Active Directory–integrated zones, still use forwarding. Forwarding is only used if the zone information does not provide an answer to a query. Normally, a DNS server will try recursive resolution using other DNS servers. A DNS server that uses forwarding can also do this but normally only does so after trying all forwarders. A DNS server can normally be set up not to perform a recursive query if the forwarders all fail.

When and Why to Forward

A forwarding DNS server is normally used to provide a subnet with DNS services for queries that are directed to the Internet, as shown in Figure 16-3. In this case, the local DNS servers forward any unresolved requests to the forwarding server that in turn forwards the requests to the two ISP DNS servers.

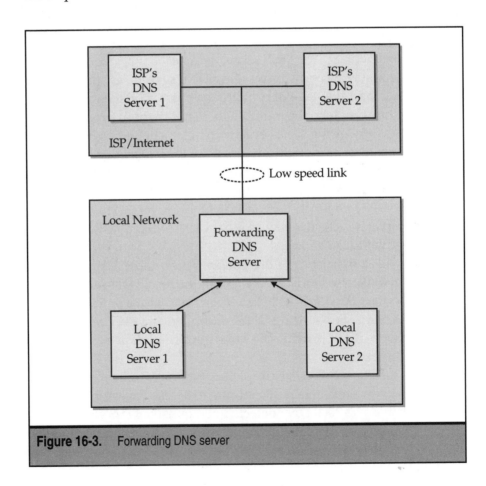

Figure 16-3.   Forwarding DNS server

The effect of the delay due to the low-speed link between the forwarding server and the ISP is minimized by the forwarding server's cache. The two local DNS servers are set up to forward any unresolved requests to the forwarding DNS server. In this instance, the forwarding DNS server is normally set up as a caching-only server.

NOTE: The forwarding server in Figure 16-3 is not set up to forward requests but to recursively resolve requests using the ISP's DNS servers as starting points. The two local DNS servers must be set up to forward to the forwarding server.

For a small network, the forwarding DNS server may be the lone DNS server. In this case, DNS forwarding is not actually used. The DNS server still performs a valuable service as all the local DNS clients utilize the DNS server's cache.

Using multiple forwarding DNS servers, as shown in Figure 16-4, has the advantage of providing a more robust environment. Unfortunately, the multiplicity is not without problems. For example, the forwarding DNS servers do not exchange cache information. To maximize cache utilization, all the local DNS servers need to have their forwarding DNS server IP lists set to the same values in the same order. In this case, the lists should start with Forwarding DNS Server 1 and then Forwarding DNS Server 2. This will cause the first server's cache to grow as it handles DNS requests while the second server idles.

The deficiency of this configuration shows up when Forwarding DNS Server 1 fails. At this point, the local DNS servers will fail to contact Forwarding DNS Server 1 and move onto Forwarding DNS Server 2. Forwarding DNS Server 2 must now build up its cache before it can provide the same performance as Forwarding DNS Server 1.

Many DNS server implementations running on the local DNS server computers will continue to access Forwarding DNS Server 1. Windows 2000 DNS detects unresponsive DNS servers and will quickly determine that Forwarding DNS Server 1 is unresponsive and move Forwarding DNS Server 2 to the top of the priority list.

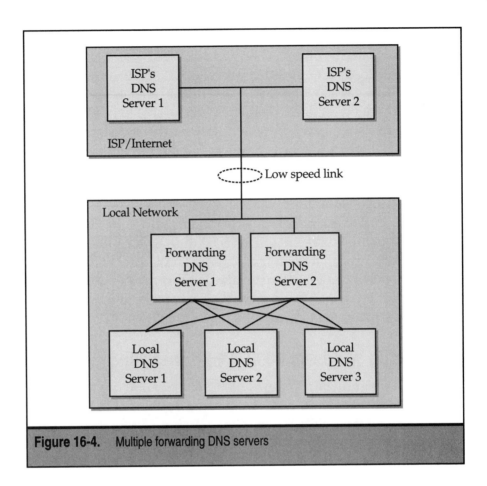

Figure 16-4. Multiple forwarding DNS servers

When Not to Forward

A forwarding DNS server makes little sense if network traffic is not
an issue. For example, if the DNS servers that the DNS server will
access are on the local network, a caching-only DNS server may
be more appropriate. The "DNS Caching" section covers this type
of server.

NOTE: Forwarding links should not be configured into a loop. For example,
DNS Server A forwards to DNS Server B, which forwards back to DNS
Server A. Requests will eventually timeout, but the process will generate
unnecessary network traffic and DNS load.

While a forwarding DNS server does use caching, it also offloads the name resolution chores to other DNS servers. This can cause overloading of these DNS servers if the forwarding DNS server's cache has a low hit rate. If the forwarding DNS server is changed to a caching-only DNS server, it may be able to resolve name requests by contacting different DNS servers, thereby distributing the load.

If the local zone is being accessed on a regular basis, it may prove to be useful for the forwarding DNS server to be changed to a conventional DNS server with a secondary DNS zone for the local zone.

Daisy chaining forwarders is not a good idea if the forwarders only provide caching. This is because passing the query from one forwarding DNS server to another until the resolution request is finally handled will delay the answering of a query. The same is not true if the intermediate DNS servers manage zones that may provide the requested information.

Configuring Windows 2000 DNS Forwarding

Configuring a Windows 2000 DNS server to use forwarding is a relatively simple task. It is done using the DNS MMC snap-in. Select the DNS server and then Action | Properties. Then select the Forwarders tab. This displays the screen shown in Figure 16-5.

Figure 16-5 shows forwarding enabled. The Enable Forwarders check box is checked. This enables IP Address List Of DNS Servers To Forward Requests To. When a request is sent to this DNS server, the server will check any zones it handles and its cache. If the request still has not been satisfied, the first DNS server in the IP Address list will be sent the request. The process is repeated for each DNS server in the list. Finally, if the request was still unsatisfied, the Do Not Use Recursion check box will determine whether the request will fail or further work will be done.

If the Do Not Use Recursion check box is checked, the DNS server will use the computer's DNS client's list of DNS servers to recursively resolve the request. If this fails then there is no recourse.

The main difference between the conventional DNS server name resolution and the forwarding DNS name resolution is the additional forwarding step between the local resolution and the recursive resolution. There is also a Disable Recursion setting in a Windows

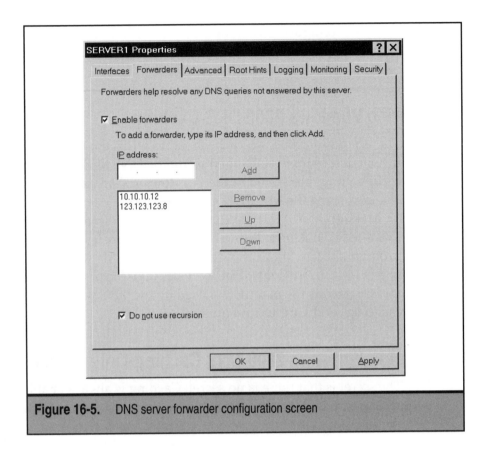

Figure 16-5.   DNS server forwarder configuration screen

2000 DNS server's Property screen. To get to it, click the Advanced tab and go to the Server Options list.

DNS CACHING

Caching is useful in minimizing name resolution traffic by remembering what was done in the past. Almost all DNS servers provide caching support. Windows 2000 DNS servers support caching. Caching is used only for information obtained from other DNS servers. The DNS server will first check any zones that it handles before checking the cache.

The DNS cache cannot be disabled, although if DNS forwarding and recursion is disabled, the cache will not be used. In that case, name resolution requests will be checked against the DNS server's own zones.

The "Configuring Windows 2000 DNS Caching-Only Server" section describes how to set up a DNS server to operate without any local zones.

Configuring Windows 2000 DNS Caching

The Windows 2000 DNS cache is set up when the DNS service is installed. It cannot be changed using the DNS MMC snap-in. The cache settings are stored in the Windows 2000 registry and can be changed using the REGEDIT program.

Making changes is not recommended by Microsoft, but if you are interested in looking at the default settings, crank up the REDEDIT program. Locate My Computer\HKEY_LOCAL_MACHINE\ SYSTEM\CurrentControlSet\Services\Dnscache. The Parameters folder contains the parameters used by the DNS service to control cache size and various timeouts.

Configuring Windows 2000 DNS Caching-Only Server

The secret is that there is no secret. Caching is always enabled, so setting up a caching-only DNS server is simply a matter of installing the DNS service. There are three caveats, however.

First, do not check the Disable Recursion check box in the DNS server's Advanced tab Property screen.

Second, make sure the DNS server root hints are accurate. The defaults will be sufficient if the DNS server will be used in conjunction with the Internet.

Finally, make sure that the computer's DNS client has the IP address of at least one DNS server. As with any DNS server, a caching-only DNS server should have a fixed IP address.

The advantage of a caching-only server is no maintenance. There are no zone transfers to configure. There are no zones to manage.

GENERAL DNS REPLICATION ISSUES

The discussion of DNS replication thus far assumes that the source and destination DNS servers support the same zone information. While this is true for a homogeneous DNS environment, it may not be the case with a heterogeneous DNS environment. In particular, Windows 2000 Active Directory requires SRV resource record support, so at least some of the DNS servers in the network must support this feature.

Differences in resource record support will impact how replication should be configured. For example, Windows NT DNS service does not support SRV resource records. It should not be configured with a secondary DNS zone that will obtain its information from a Windows 2000 zone that will include SRV resource records. A Windows NT DNS service can have a secondary DNS zone that will get its information from a Windows 2000 zone if that zone only contains records that the Windows NT DNS service can handle. The same will be true for other DNS servers such as older versions of BIND. The converse will not be a problem, so a Windows 2000–based secondary DNS zone can accept information from any Windows NT DNS hosted zone.

Another source of incompatibility is domain name encoding. Windows 2000 is very robust when it comes to this support, but other DNS servers can be a bit more fickle. Windows 2000 DNS service's name checking is server-specific. The setting is found in the DNS server's Properties screen. Click on the Advanced tab and check out the Name Checking field.

Another compatibility issue addressed from the DNS server's Properties screen is the fast transfer support for secondary zone transfers. Versions of BIND prior to version 4.9.4 do not support fast transfers. If the Windows 2000 DNS server is used to supply secondary DNS zone information to DNS servers with this restriction, make sure that the Bind Secondaries check box is checked.

SUMMARY

Replication is an aspect of DNS that most DNS administrators learn very quickly because of its importance to proper Windows 2000 Active Directory operation. The first part of this chapter presented new information for DNS administrators already familiar with conventional DNS replication features. While experienced DNS administrators may prefer to utilize the standards-based approach, new DNS administrators may prefer to utilize Active Directory support. This approach is especially effective in reducing replication management and configuration for internal DNS support in small and medium size network models.

Secondary DNS zone replication is necessary if Windows 2000 DNS is part of a heterogeneous DNS environment. While secondary DNS zone replication is possible from an ISP's DNS server, caching will normally be used to replicate information from outside the network. Secondary DNS zone replication offers a good way to distribute information across WANs, and it is imperative in a large and distributed network model where Active Directory replication does not provide network-wide coverage.

Dynamic DNS update support was covered in Chapter 2. It makes a DNS administrator's life easier when it comes to managing computer names, but it makes life more difficult when it comes to replication. Luckily, proper configuration of DHCP, dynamic DNS updates, and DNS replication allows these features to coexist.

DNS forwarding does not really replicate information unless it is combined with DNS caching but, from a client's perspective, the DNS server appears to know all about the DNS environment.

DNS replication has been addressed with respect to Windows 2000. Read Chapter 21 if BIND is used in a Windows 2000 network. Windows 2000 DNS will work with DNS servers other than BIND, but these are not addressed in this book.

DNS replication is one aspect of DNS support that cannot be overlooked by DNS administrators. If a DNS client cannot obtain DNS information then the problem just might be due to replication configuration.

CHAPTER 17

Zone Migration for Windows 2000 DNS

While some sites will continue to use their existing DNS infrastructure, many will migrate their existing DNS infrastructure to Windows 2000 DNS services. This chapter takes a look at the issues involved and how this migration can be accomplished.

The two main DNS migration sources that will be considered in this chapter are Windows NT and BIND. Migration from Windows NT DNS will be of primary concern to DNS administrators because Windows NT DNS does not have sufficient features to support Windows 2000 Active Directory—although Windows NT DNS servers can still act as caching DNS servers or as DNS servers for non–Windows 2000 Active Directory domains. Early versions of BIND will also not support Windows 2000 Active Directory, so the choice is whether to upgrade BIND or migrate to Windows 2000 DNS.

Migration from one DNS platform to another is not always an all or nothing deal, however, unless there are only one or two DNS servers in a network. Windows 2000's dependence on DNS when Active Directory is employed may mean increasing the number of DNS servers to support the additional load imposed by workstations trying to locate and log onto Active Directory domains.

Microsoft would love it if everyone performed a full migration right up front because that means more Windows 2000 installations. It also makes life easier for the network administrator since Active Directory can be pervasive and there is then only one place to look if things appear not to be working. Full migration is easiest to perform when the number of DNS servers is less than a dozen. On the other hand, full migration on a medium to large network can involve dozens or hundreds of servers, which makes full migration a major effort.

Partial migration will typically be the choice for most medium- to large-sized networks. In this case, Windows 2000 DNS deployment will normally lead or occur in step with Windows 2000 Active Directory deployment. From a transparency standpoint, partial migration of Windows 2000 DNS servers prior to Active Directory deployment has the advantage of allowing the DNS migration to be tested before Active Directory is brought into play with its own migration and installation issues.

Partial migration may also be the best choice for heterogeneous environments where DNS is already in place and Windows 2000 will not be the dominant server within the organization. In this case, partial migration will typically occur on or near Windows 2000 domain controller servers.

Finally, there is the possibility of late migration that occurs after Windows 2000 and Active Directory are deployed. This approach normally occurs where an existing DNS environment can handle Active Directory, such as with the latest version of BIND. In this case, Windows 2000 domains can be created, and the domain controllers can work with the existing DNS servers using dynamic DNS update support. At a later time, Windows 2000 DNS can be included to augment or replace existing DNS support.

Most of the migration issues are the same regardless of the migration approach. The main issues of choosing what approach to take will be the size of the migration job, the amount of time the migration will take, and the amount of testing that can be done before turning the new DNS support into a production environment.

This chapter takes a look at some of the migration issues just introduced and examines the impact of the various alternatives, including what happens if migration proves to be a more difficult task than initially envisioned. We'll also examine the mechanics of migration and the issues that will arise before, during, and after migration.

MIGRATION ISSUES AND ALTERNATIVES

Migrating from one DNS configuration to another should not be taken lightly, especially in larger networks. While most non–Windows 2000 Active Directory networks will use IP, they will not be as dependent on DNS as Windows 2000 will be for login purposes. Still, if DNS is being used in the network, it is probably indispensable for other reasons. This makes it imperative to maintain service and reliability during migration to Windows 2000 Active Directory.

In this section, we'll examine whether DNS migration should actually be considered and, if so, to what extent. In some cases, Windows 2000 will be added to an existing network, so additional DNS servers may be warranted. Migrating DNS information from existing DNS servers to the new DNS servers will normally be part of this new configuration. Determining whether to migrate to Windows 2000 DNS is often not a technical issue but a political one. Here you'll examine technical reasons to migrate that may be useful in discussions about whether migration is possible or desirable.

This chapter also covers issues associated with the deployment schedule for Windows 2000 DNS services and migration issues associated with any change to a Windows 2000 DNS platform. It also discusses the impact of changing DNS servers on DNS clients and DHCP servers and looks at how to minimize changes to these clients and servers and the impact that may have on how DNS services are set up and how migration might occur.

Determining Whether to Migrate

Windows 2000 alone does not require DNS support if one of the compatibility modes, such as NetBIOS over TCP (NetBT), NetBIOS, or Novell Netware, is used to allow legacy clients like Windows 95 and Windows 98 access to Windows 2000. DNS support will normally be needed even in this environment to provide name resolution for TCP/IP- and Internet-based resources. If existing DNS infrastructure currently provides this support, the addition of a Windows 2000 server or clients may not require changes to the infrastructure. However, migration to Windows 2000 DNS may be a consideration because of its enhancements or future migration to Active Directory.

DNS support is required for the more secure, native mode operation available only between Windows 2000 clients and servers when Active Directory is installed. Some existing DNS infrastructures will support Windows 2000 Active Directory, including the latest version of BIND. If the current infrastructure will not support Active Directory, there are three alternatives:

1. Upgrade the existing DNS infrastructure to support Active Directory.

2. Migrate all or parts of the existing DNS infrastructure to Windows 2000 DNS.

3. Add Windows 2000 DNS to the existing DNS infrastructure to handle Windows 2000 clients and servers.

Upgrading an existing DNS infrastructure makes sense in a large, heterogeneous environment where DNS is well established and supported. Replacing the existing DNS infrastructure with Windows 2000 DNS typically requires a significant investment in training, software, and time. There are two main reasons for migrating to Windows 2000 DNS in this instance, both related to Active Directory and Active Directory–integrated DNS zones. The first is multimaster support for Active Directory–integrated DNS zones. The second is enhanced security for access, management, and replication.

The dynamic DNS update proxy support of the Windows 2000 DHCP server is another advantage, especially considering that it can use the secure dynamic DNS update support of Windows 2000 DNS. However, this assumes that DHCP migration is also a consideration. In a large network, DHCP deployment is typically intertwined with DNS deployment, so migration considerations for DNS will include DHCP.

NOTE: The decision to retain an existing DNS infrastructure, replace it with Windows 2000 DNS, or support a mix of DNS services will often be based upon human resources and preferences. If most network administrators in the organization are trained in DNS systems and platforms other than Windows NT or Windows 2000, Windows 2000 DNS may not be worth considering, at least in the short term. DNS is not difficult to contend with in a small network, but the administration details can be significant in a large network. Using Windows 2000 DNS can simplify Windows 2000 installation and management. Windows 2000 support is probably the best reason to justify Windows 2000 DNS on Windows 2000 DNS servers, leaving the existing infrastructure for access to other TCP/IP-based services.

Migrating all or part of an existing DNS infrastructure to Windows 2000 DNS makes a lot of sense in many environments.

One instance is where Windows NT currently provides DNS services. Another is where there is an organizational movement from another platform, such as Novell NetWare, to Windows 2000.

In the case of Windows NT providing DNS services, migration will be mandated by limitations of the existing DNS infrastructure. Windows NT cannot handle all the DNS chores needed by Windows 2000 and Active Directory, so at least a part of the network must be modified to support Windows 2000.

In the case of moving from another platform, Windows 2000 will eventually be the server platform of preference within the network, so using Windows 2000 DNS and Windows 2000 DHCP is definitely desirable from a management and support standpoint.

The decision as to whether a partial or full migration takes place will depend upon the extent to which Windows 2000 will be deployed and how DNS is used within the existing infrastructure. Figure 17-1 shows one possible scenario. In this case, Windows 2000 DNS servers replace existing DNS servers where Windows 2000 clients will be deployed. Windows 2000 clients require DNS support, so they are both Windows 2000 clients as well as DNS clients. The existing DNS infrastructure is maintained to tie DNS servers together. A more elaborate reconfiguration may be required as zone replication may leave clusters of Windows 2000 systems in isolation from other Windows 2000 systems. Chapter 16 discusses a variety of ways to replicate information among DNS servers. If Windows 2000 clients are to be able to access all Windows 2000 servers within the network, Windows 2000–specific information, such as SRV resource records used to identify Windows 2000 domain controllers, must be replicated among DNS servers supporting Windows 2000 clients.

Full migration to Windows 2000 and Windows 2000 DNS is a long-term goal for many organizations. This simplifies management and makes the most of Windows 2000 and Windows 2000 DNS services. It is also a good target for smaller networks with a few Windows NT servers since upgrades can be done in a day or two, although such a short time period is impractical at a larger site. Larger sites will typically migrate in steps, and Windows 2000 DNS services will often be deployed in advance or in synch with Windows 2000 Active Directory.

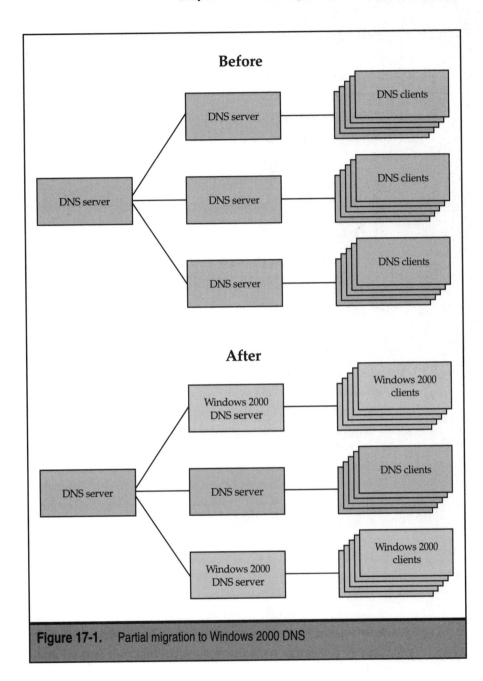

Figure 17-1.   Partial migration to Windows 2000 DNS

One option for incremental migration or partial migration is late migration or migration to Windows 2000 DNS after Windows 2000 Active Directory is installed. This approach may be preferable in environments in which reliability and availability of the existing DNS infrastructure are paramount. The following are the typical steps for migrating to Windows 2000 DNS after Windows 2000 is installed:

1. Verify or upgrade current DNS services to support Windows 2000 Active Directory.

2. Install Windows 2000 servers.

3. Install Active Directory on Windows 2000 servers.

4. Add or replace DNS servers with Windows 2000 DNS.

5. Convert to Active Directory–integrated DNS zones.

This same process is also applicable for DHCP support. Typically, DHCP server migration is less of an issue since most DHCP servers provide basic configuration information. However, this does not include an IP such as the DNS and gateway server addresses. Windows 2000 DHCP can deliver additional information and act as a dynamic DNS update proxy, as discussed in Chapter 14. This support can be useful, but is not as imperative for Windows 2000 support as the advanced features in Windows 2000 DNS are.

Adding new DNS servers is often preferable to partial migration. In this case, the number of DNS servers increases. The number of clients often stays the same, although Windows clients may be upgraded to Windows 2000 Professional.

In a mixed environment, adding Windows 2000 DNS servers to the DNS infrastructure is often the best approach. This may also be a prelude to full migration to Windows 2000 DNS and possibly Windows 2000 Active Directory.

Typically, Windows 2000 DNS servers will be installed in tandem with Windows 2000 domain controllers. These servers will at least manage the zone for the Windows 2000 Active Directory domain. The advantage of this approach is that administrators familiar with Windows 2000 will have control over Windows 2000 DNS, and there is a guaranteed infrastructure for Windows 2000 support. Unfortunately, the Windows 2000 DNS servers will normally require interaction with the other DNS servers on the network. This will require coordination with the DNS administrators for these servers if security controls, such as which DNS servers can access DNS information for secondary DNS zones, are in place.

The "General DNS Migration Issues" section addresses many of the DNS-related concerns that will be encountered even if Windows 2000 DNS servers are added to a network rather than replacing existing servers. For example, workstations that migrate to Windows 2000 will need to access a Windows 2000–compatible DNS server that will have information about Windows 2000 domain controllers. This can often be accomplished with modifications to the subnet's DHCP server, or changes can be made when the workstation is upgraded to Windows 2000.

In general, migration to Windows 2000 DNS is not imperative, but it is advantageous. Most third-party DNS servers can support Windows 2000 Active Directory with sufficient support for good operation. Advantages show up as more DNS servers are replaced by Windows 2000 DNS and as Windows 2000 Active Directory becomes more pervasive.

If you do decide to migrate, the scheduling will be an important part of your installation.

Migration Scheduling Issues

Scheduling DNS migration is on the critical path for Windows 2000 Active Directory installation, assuming the existing DNS infrastructure, if it exists, cannot support Active Directory's requirements. The same is true if Windows 2000 DNS will be added to an existing DNS infrastructure. If the existing DNS infrastructure supports or will be upgraded to support Active Directory, it is also possible to perform a late migration to Windows 2000 DNS.

This section takes a look at the steps involved in migrating, along with technical issues that may arise during that process. The three methods examined include:

▼ Full or partial migration to Windows 2000 DNS

- ■ Adding Windows 2000 DNS to an existing DNS infrastructure
- ▲ Late full or partial migration to Windows 2000 DNS

Full or partial migration to Windows 2000 DNS means replacing an existing DNS server with a Windows 2000 DNS server. This may be on the same machine, although this approach works best when upgrading from Windows NT to Windows 2000. If you're replacing a non-Windows NT DNS server, a better approach is to place the new Windows 2000 DNS server on a new computer, since placing the Windows 2000 DNS server on the old computer often means you'll have the time consuming task of removing the old operating system and installing Windows 2000 on the existing hardware.

If you are upgrading from Windows NT to Windows 2000 DNS, see the section "Windows NT Migration Issues." The main scheduling issue of this approach is the availability of the server and alternative DNS support should an upgrade fail or encounter problems. While uncommon, such upgrade problems can happen. Upgrades are typically scheduled during regularly scheduled downtime or minimal system use, such as the late evening or on the weekends. The server should be backed up prior to performing the upgrade. If this is strictly a DNS server, the zone files need to be saved. Windows 2000 DNS services can be included when a Windows NT server is upgraded or when Windows 2000 DNS is installed over another operating system.

If you are migrating a server from BIND to Windows 2000 DNS, see the section "BIND Migration Issues." Scheduling issues are the same as they are when upgrading from Windows NT to Windows 2000, but more time should be included in the schedule. This is because conversion from BIND zone files to Windows 2000 DNS support is more apt to run into problems due to BIND's larger feature set and support for DNS compared to Windows NT.

In-place migration, that is, adding Windows 2000 DNS to an existing DNS infrastructure, has some advantages. First, the IP address of the server can remain the same. Second, additional servers are not needed and swapping servers does not have to occur. The alternative is to follow these steps:

1. Install Windows 2000 and Windows 2000 DNS on a new computer with a new IP address.

   or

   Install Windows 2000 Active Directory.

2. Migrate the data from the other DNS service to the new Windows 2000 DNS service.

3. Configure a DNS client to use the new Windows 2000 DNS service.

4. Test the Windows 2000 DNS service using the DNS client.

5. Shut down the old service and put the new one in its place by changing IP addresses.

6. Test the Windows 2000 DNS service using an existing DNS client.

NOTE: Installation of Windows 2000 Active Directory may involve the addition of a new zone for the Active Directory domain. This can be done prior to installing Active Directory, or it can be done as part of the Active Directory installation if a new Active Directory domain is being created.

The shutdown in step 5 may not be necessary if IP addresses can be changed on-the-fly. This would allow the new computer to have the IP address of the old computer so DNS clients would not have to be reconfigured. Changing the IP address of a computer while it is running is usually not difficult, but it should be tried prior to performing the migration.

Swapping in the new DNS service can also be done by simply unplugging the old DNS server from the network. You then connect the new DNS server to the network and set it up to use the new IP address.

Assuming the IP address can be changed on both the old computer and Windows 2000, it is simply a matter of changing the old computer's IP address to an unused IP address on the subnet and then changing the Windows 2000 computer's IP address to the new

IP address. A DNS client can then be used to check out the new DNS server.

Adding Windows 2000 DNS to an existing DNS infrastructure still involves modifications to zone information in existing DNS servers. It may also involve changing DNS configuration information in existing DNS clients if they will be using a new Windows 2000 DNS server as either a primary or backup DNS service. To perform this type of migration, follow these steps:

1. Install Windows 2000 and Windows 2000 DNS on a new computer with a new IP address.

   or

   Install Windows 2000 Active Directory.

2. Reconfigure any secondary DNS zone sources for zones that will be set up as secondary DNS zones on the new server so that proper security, replication, and management are possible. This should take into account any network related issues such as low-speed WAN links.

3. Set up any necessary secondary DNS zones on the new Windows 2000 DNS service.

4. Configure a DNS client to use the new Windows 2000 DNS service.

5. Test the Windows 2000 DNS service using the DNS client.

6. Reconfigure any DNS clients that need to use the new Windows 2000 DNS service.

The scheduling issues for a late full or partial migration to Windows 2000 DNS are the same as scheduling prior to Windows 2000 Active Directory installation, although incremental migration in a large network is typically less time-critical. DNS migration from Windows NT will not be an issue for zones supporting Windows 2000 domain controllers because Windows NT cannot support Active Directory. Windows NT may still be in place for handling zones that do not deal with DNS features such as SRV resource records. In this case, in-place upgrading to Windows 2000 is still possible.

The source DNS service may have cached information related to the dynamic DNS updates. Although this is relatively uncommon, it is a scheduling issue that should be considered. The cached information will not move to the Windows 2000 DNS service even though the Windows 2000 DNS can support dynamic DNS updates for primary and Active Directory–integrated DNS zones. To move the information, you must first migrate to the Windows 2000 DNS service, and all the DNS clients that use dynamic DNS updates must perform the update using the new DNS service. In most instances, this can be done by restarting the DNS client. It may also be possible to adjust some settings using the DHCP service if the client computers are obtaining dynamic IP addresses, which is the typical reason for using dynamic DNS update support.

NOTE: Dynamic DNS update support can be used with fixed IP computers, especially servers that may dynamically start and stop IP-based services and advertise these services using dynamic DNS updates only when the service is running. These computers may have to be adjusted individually, as most servers run continuously, and the dynamic DNS update may only occur when the server or service is started.

General DNS Migration Issues

This section takes a look at four general issues of migrating DNS. The sections "Windows NT Migration Issues" and "BIND Migration Issues" look at migration issues of two specific DNS implementations.

The first issue is support for DNS features such as dynamic DNS updates, DNS naming conventions, and SRV resource records. In general, Windows 2000 provides comparable features to other DNS server features. Moving DNS information to the Windows 2000 DNS service should not be a problem, but this is not the end of the issue. A DNS zone on a server being replaced by a Windows 2000 DNS service may be replicated as a secondary DNS zone on another DNS server. This other DNS server may not have the same functionality as the Windows 2000 DNS server. For example, if it is a Windows NT DNS server, features like the SRV resource record will not be handled properly. Such configurations need to be identified, and appropriate action must be taken. For example, if the Windows NT server is to be upgraded, this process should be scheduled at the same time or very soon after the original Windows 2000 DNS service is set up.

The second issue deals with importing DNS information from other DNS servers. Any importation problems can be found and resolved during a trial import process. In general, importing DNS information from another DNS server will be done in a manner that does not disrupt the source of the information.

The third issue is security. The first aspect of this is security related to replication of information from an existing DNS server to a new Windows 2000 DNS server. For non-Windows 2000 DNS servers, this typically involves adjustment of IP addresses for secondary zone access and name servers noted in the zone information. These changes are normally made either just before or just after the Windows 2000 DNS service is set up. If they are made after the Windows 2000 DNS service is set up, the Windows 2000 DNS service may not notice that a secondary DNS zone is not up to date. However, this will change after the security settings are changed and an update has occurred.

The last issue is DNS client configuration. In general, DNS clients that are set up using DHCP will be the easiest to change if the Windows 2000 DNS service is not set up to use the same IP address as the DNS service it is replacing or if the DNS client must also reference the new Windows 2000 DNS service.

Windows NT Migration Issues

There are very few issues regarding migration from Windows NT DNS to Windows 2000 DNS since Windows 2000 DNS support is a superset of the Windows NT DNS support. The main issue will be the type of migration procedure that will be used. These include an in-place upgrade of Windows NT to Windows 2000, copying zone files from a Windows NT DNS server to a Windows 2000 DNS server, or using secondary DNS zone replication from a Windows NT DNS server to a Windows 2000 DNS server.

All three methods are covered in the section on "DNS Migration Methods." The big advantage of in-place upgrades is that the upgrade process handles most of the job. Existing primary DNS zones will be retained. Existing secondary DNS zones will be serviced from the appropriate DNS servers. The main changes will be determining whether additional DNS zones must be created for Active Directory domain support and whether any primary DNS zones need to be converted to Active Directory–integrated DNS zones. The latter may be needed for security reasons.

A few settings must be considered if in-place upgrades are not used. For example, Windows NT and Windows 2000 DNS services both support forwarding. This information is not covered in zone files on Windows NT, so it must be examined and configured on the Windows 2000 DNS service. The same is true for secondary DNS zone notification.

NOTE: If an in-place upgrade from Windows NT to Windows 2000 is not used, make sure that any interactions with DHCP and WINS are taken into account when configuring the Windows 2000 DNS server. One item often overlooked is DNS and WINS integration especially when clients are being incrementally migrated to Windows 2000 and non-migrated clients still use WINS.

One other item to consider is dynamic DNS update support. This is one feature that Windows 2000 has that Windows NT does not have. The DNS administrator will need to determine whether this feature should be enabled or not.

Also consider DHCP and WINS migration. These services upgrade in a similar way to the DNS service in terms of retaining existing configuration information.

BIND Migration Issues

Migrating from BIND to Windows 2000 DNS is a straightforward process, but it could also involve a number of changes. This depends on the security support used and whether it must be maintained, how BIND is configured, and any DNS relationships between the BIND DNS server and other DNS servers. If you are unfamiliar with BIND and need to migrate from a BIND server, see Chapter 21.

The latest version of BIND can limit access to its resolution services by IP address range. Windows 2000 cannot. The same is true for dynamic DNS update support. Other than these, Windows 2000 can handle most other security-related issues.

BIND's configuration details are contained in a number of files. While Windows 2000 can use these files most of the time, there are some instances where Windows 2000 will not. For example, the $ORIGIN and $INCLUDE commands can be used in BIND zone files but not in Windows 2000 DNS. If these commands are in a file, Windows 2000 stops processing the file at the line with the first command that Windows 2000 DNS does not understand.

BIND can have a number of relationships with other DNS servers, such as forwarding references, secondary DNS zone sources, and primary DNS zone notification lists. This information will need to be moved to the Windows 2000 DNS server.

BIND comes in a number of versions. The two primary versions are BIND 4 and BIND 8. Unfortunately, the information in a BIND 4 root file cannot be used by Windows 2000 DNS because the configuration files are different. However, the Windows 2000 DNS server can use a great deal of information from a BIND 8 server. The default name for the BIND 8 root file is named.boot. It needs to be renamed to Boot and placed in the Windows 2000 DNS directory along with the zone files. The zone files must also be renamed. Table 17-1 summarizes the necessary changes.

Description	UNIX/Linux File Name	Windows 2000 File Name
Boot file	named.boot	Boot
Forward lookup zone file	db.*domain_name*	*domain_name*.dns
Reverse lookup zone file	db.*x.y.z*	*z.y.x.in-addr.arpa*.dns

Table 17-1.   BIND to Windows 2000 DNS Migration File Renaming

NOTE: The Reverse lookup zone file name convention for UNIX/Linux is reversed from the Windows 2000 approach. In addition, the Windows 2000 approach includes the in-addr.arpa suffix that is part of the fully qualified domain name (FQDN) used by Windows 2000 for naming all of its domain files.

These changes assume that both the UNIX/Linux files and the Windows 2000 files will be following the normal naming conventions. Both actually allow arbitrary names to be used for zone files, but diverging from the standard naming conventions can cause confusion in the future if another DNS administrator must support the network.

This approach to using the BIND root file can be used only if there are no Active Directory-DNS zones supported by the Windows 2000 DNS server. What is normally done if the latter must occur is to set up the Windows 2000 DNS using the BIND files and then changing the boot method from File to Registry or Active Directory and Registry. This change is made from the Advanced tab of a Windows 2000 DNS server Properties screen in the Windows 2000 DNS MMC snap-in. A change causes the Windows 2000 DNS server to automatically copy the configuration information from the Boot file. The process cannot be reversed after an Active Directory–integrated DNS zone is added. This is of little consequence as most migrations are one way—that is, to the Windows 2000 DNS service rather than from it.

In general, it is a good idea to have the Windows 2000 DNS server running on the same subnet as the BIND server, so that the two can be tested at the same time. Some tools, such as nslookup, can check both servers from a single client. See Chapter 19 for more details on nslookup.

Setting up two DNS servers may require additional configuration on other DNS servers. For example, if secondary DNS zone replication is used and the source is set up to limit DNS servers that may access the zone, this list must be changed to accommodate the Windows 2000 DNS server. The same is true for notification support.

If a Windows 2000 DNS server will replace another DNS server and both servers are kept online until the Windows 2000 DNS server is checked out, IP addresses may become an issue. For example, a typical way to minimize DNS client reconfiguration is to change the Windows 2000 DNS server's IP address to the address of the DNS server it is replacing. As mentioned in the "Windows NT Migration Issues" section, IP addresses can be changed while the DNS servers remain online.

The "DNS Migration Methods" section describes three methods for migrating to a Windows 2000 DNS server. Only two of these methods can be used when migrating from a BIND. These include copying DNS zone files and going through secondary DNS zones.

Copying zone files is the more difficult of the two methods if any of the aforementioned commands such as $ORIGIN and $INCLUDE are used in the BIND primary DNS zone files. Going through a secondary DNS zone eliminates these problems because these commands are processed by the DNS server before sending information off to the secondary DNS zone.

Active Directory Migration Issues

Regardless of the original DNS server being migrated, Active Directory does not directly affect the migration process. However, assuming Windows 2000 DNS is being added to support Active Directory, migration can affect Active Directory deployment. For example, the Windows NT DNS service will not support the SRV resource record needed by Active Directory.

Active Directory domain controllers can optionally use dynamic DNS support, but SRV resource record support is required. If dynamic DNS support is not provided and migration will not occur until after Active Directory is installed, DNS administrators will have to manually enter all the subzones and resource records needed for Active Directory support. These are covered in Chapters 3 and 4.

Active Directory usually comes into play after the migration process is complete. At this point, Windows 2000 DNS is up and running. If the Windows 2000 DNS server is using Active Directory, primary DNS zones can be converted to Active Directory–integrated DNS zones.

Migration Issues Affecting DNS Clients

If a Windows 2000 DNS server is given the same IP address as the DNS server that it is replacing due to migration, DNS clients will typically require no configuration for continued operation. This is the best approach from a DNS client's point of view, especially since it is possible to quickly replace the original DNS server if it is not used for other purposes after the Windows 2000 DNS server is in place.

NOTE: The one exception will be for DNS clients that are using dynamic DNS updates. With the release of Windows 2000, this is currently rare, but dynamic DNS updates are becoming more common for non-Windows 2000 clients. If clients are to be allowed to continue using dynamic DNS updates, Active Directory–integrated DNS zones should be set up to enable dynamic DNS updates but not Windows 2000–secure dynamic DNS updates.

Most DNS clients are typically configured using a DHCP server for all but small networks. If the Windows 2000 DNS server is being added to the network or it is not given the same IP address as the DNS server it is replacing, the DNS clients can be reconfigured by changing the DHCP server settings.

Fixed IP DNS clients, typically servers, will also need to be reconfigured to access a new DNS server. In many instances, the new DNS server will be used only as a backup, so adding the DNS server's IP address to the list of DNS servers that the DNS client is using can occur at a later date.

DNS MIGRATION METHODS

This section looks at the mechanics of migration. It examines the three methods to move DNS information from one DNS server to another:

▼ In-place upgrade of Windows NT DNS

■ Copying zone files

▲ Converting secondary zones to primary zZones

The following sections discuss converting a Windows NT server to a Windows 2000 server along with the upgrade of the Windows

NT DNS service to the Windows 2000 DNS service. This is the easiest migration method, but it is only possible as part of the Windows NT to Windows 2000 upgrade. We'll also look at text-based DNS zone files and what kinds of problems may arise with this approach, such as dealing with special BIND features.

The section "Migration by Converting Secondary Zones to Primary Zones" explores migrating DNS information by creating a secondary DNS zone to move information from one DNS service to the Windows 2000 DNS service. The secondary DNS zone is then converted to a primary DNS zone, and the original primary DNS zone can then be taken down. It is a simple process but, like the other migration methods, must be done correctly for proper DNS operation.

Copying zone files and converting a secondary zone to a primary zone are used to move a primary DNS zone to another DNS server. Migrating other DNS server configuration options such as secondary DNS zones, forwarding server configuration, and security configuration must be done in a more manual fashion. For example, with Windows NT, this information is obtained using the Windows NT DNS Manager that is started via Start | Program Files | Administrative Tools | DNS Manager. Some details, like the forwarding server configuration, are located in the Properties screen for a Windows NT DNS server.

For BIND, this information is contained in the BIND configuration files. It is discussed in more detail in Chapter 21. As with the Windows NT DNS server, this information must be transcribed to the Windows 2000 DNS server.

The Windows 2000 DNS MMC snap-in, discussed in Chapter 11, is where these settings are found. A summary is shown in Table 17-2.

NOTE: The BIND 8 configuration file is normally called named.boot.

BIND has a number of items in the *options* statement that have no direct counterpart under Windows 2000 DNS, such as the restricted query support shown in Table 17-2.

Description	Windows 2000 Location	Windows NT Location	BIND 8 Location
Secondary zones	Under DNS server in DNS MMC snap-in	Under DNS server in DNS Manager	Listed in configuration file
Forwarding DNS servers	Under DNS server Properties screen, Forwarding tab, in DNS MMC snap-in	Under DNS server Properties screen, Forwarders tab, in DNS Manager	Listed in configuration file
Interface support	Under DNS server Properties screen, Interfaces tab, in DNS MMC snap-in	Under DNS server Properties screen, Interfaces tab, in DNS Manager	Listed in configuration file
Restricted queries	Not supported	Not supported	*allow-query* statement in configuration file
Root hints	Under DNS server Properties screen, Root Hints tab, in DNS MMC snap-in	cache.dns file	db.cache file
Logging	Under DNS server Properties screen, Logging tab, in DNS MMC snap-in	Not supported	*logging* statement in configuration file
Dynamic DNS updates	Under DNS primary or Active Directory–integrated DNS zone Properties screen, General tab, in DNS MMC snap-in	Not supported	Primary zone database file

Table 17-2.   DNS Configuration Options Other Than Primary DNS Zone Files

Description	Windows 2000 Location	Windows NT Location	BIND 8 Location
Disabling recursion	Under DNS server Properties screen, Advanced tab, in DNS MMC snap-in	Not supported	*recursion* statement in configuration file

Table 17-2. DNS Configuration Options Other Than Primary DNS Zone Files *(continued)*

In-Place Upgrade of Windows NT DNS

Upgrading a Windows NT server to Windows 2000 is the preferred method of upgrading Windows NT DNS service to the Windows 2000 DNS service. The main advantage of doing this is the ability to retain all the Windows NT DNS service settings. This includes all the zone files used by Windows NT. The other migration methods must be applied a zone at a time. The main disadvantage of this approach is the difficulty of reverting to Windows NT.

TIP: Saving the Windows NT disk image using Symantec Ghost or PowerQuest Drive Image Pro is one way of allowing a quick restoration to Windows NT should upgrading to Windows 2000 prove to be ineffective. A backup image can often be saved on a hard disk, possibly an external SCSI hard disk for SCSI-based servers.

The upgrade process is very easy to initiate. Simply pop the Windows 2000 installation CD-ROM into the CD-ROM or DVD drive. The Windows NT autorun support should start up the installation program. Follow the steps presented by the installation program. If the Windows NT DNS service is installed, the Windows 2000 DNS service will be installed. The DNS zone files and configuration will be used by the Windows 2000 DNS service.

The Windows 2000 DNS MMC snap-in will also be installed as part of the installation process. This snap-in is discussed in Chapter 11;

it can be used to examine the status of the DNS service, its settings, and the DNS zones that it manages.

If the service is not running, check the DNS event logs using the standard Windows 2000 Event Viewer. The Windows 2000 DNS service can be set up so it will not start if the zone files have errors.

Migration by Copying Zone Files

Chapter 2 provided an introduction to text-based DNS zone files. Appendix B contains a more complete list of the resource records that a DNS zone file can contain. In this section, we examine how these and possibly other configuration text files can be moved from one DNS server to the Windows 2000 DNS server for the purposes of migrating primary domains.

NOTE: Only primary DNS zones need to be migrated. Secondary DNS zones need to be set up on a new Windows 2000 DNS server, but this is simply a matter of entering the fully qualified domain name for the zone and one or more IP addresses of source DNS servers. Secondary DNS zone replication does the rest.

There are three ways to migrate zone information when dealing directly with the zone files. The first is to keep the zone file intact. The second method is to edit the file and remove or change entries that are not needed or are incompatible with Windows 2000 DNS. The third is to create a new zone file and copy and paste the appropriate information into the new zone file.

The first approach is the fastest, but it does not work if the original primary DNS zone file was used with BIND and the file contains commands that Windows 2000 DNS does not support, as noted in the section "BIND Migration Issues." In this case, the last approach must be used and only the relevant information is copied.

If zone files are being copied intact to the Windows 2000 DNS directory from a BIND 8 DNS server, there is one more thing to consider. A Windows 2000 DNS server can use both BIND 8 configuration and zone files. Table 17-1 outlined the file name changes that must occur for this to happen. The named.boot file from the BIND server must also be examined to see whether it includes any configuration options that Windows 2000 DNS will not support, such as *xfernet* statements.

In general, it is easiest to try using the BIND files and then check to see whether all the information in the files was translated and loaded by Windows 2000 DNS. To see if all the information from a configuration or zone file has been loaded, use the DNS MMC snap-in to check the last entry in the file and see if it is shown under the DNS server. Windows 2000 translates the files from start to finish and will quit if it encounters an unknown statement. To find the statement that causes the error, locate the last entry that is displayed in the DNS MMC snap-in. The unknown statement should be the next line or close to it.

If the BIND configuration file is not used, individual primary DNS zone files must be copied to the Windows 2000 DNS directory. The primary DNS zone must be created using the DNS MMC snap-in. This is done by selecting the Forward or Reverse Lookup Zones entry depending upon the type of primary DNS zone being added. Next, start the New Zone Wizard using Action | New Zone. Select Standard Primary in the Zone Type screen that appears right after the introduction screen. Click on the Next button to bring up the Zone Name screen shown in Figure 17-2.

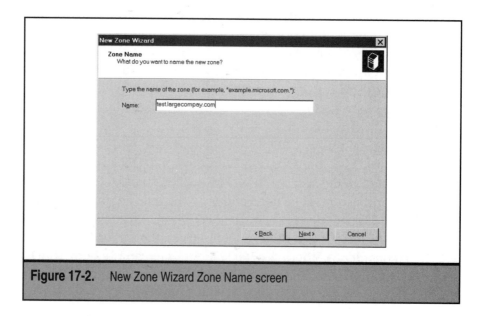

Figure 17-2. New Zone Wizard Zone Name screen

Enter the fully qualified domain name (FQDN) for the zone in the Name field. This should be the same FQDN that is used with the zone file on the original DNS server. Changing the domain name is possible, but it may not have the desired effect on the zone information depending upon how the zone file is configured. For example, if the zone file contains FQDNs for some or all of the entries, changing the domain name will not affect these entries. This is by design, but DNS administrators should examine the zone file prior to using it even if no changes need to be made to the file. Most zone files are set up using relative domain names that are dependent upon the domain name of the zone.

Clicking on the Next button brings up the Zone File screen shown in Figure 17-3. The Create A New File With This File Name radio button is normally selected; this will create an empty zone file. However, you want to use the existing zone file that has been copied into the Windows 2000 DNS directory, so the Use This Existing File radio button must be selected instead, and the file name must be entered as shown in Figure 17-3. By default, the New Zone Wizard creates a file name using the FQDN and appends the .dns file type to it. This is by convention, so any file name can be entered at this point.

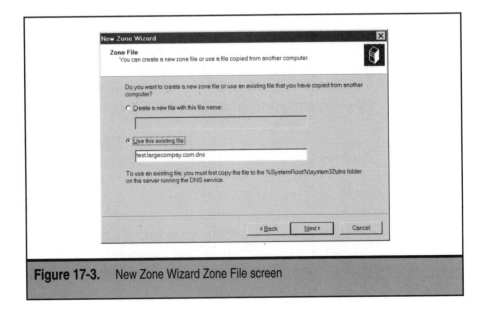

Figure 17-3.   New Zone Wizard Zone File screen

In general, it is a good idea to rename the zone file if necessary prior to completing this screen. The file name will normally be the same if the zone file came from a Windows NT DNS server. The file name will follow the conventions laid out Table 17-1 if the zone file came from a BIND DNS server.

Completing the New Zone Wizard by clicking on the Next button will add the new zone to the list of zones that the Windows 2000 DNS server supports. The contents under the zone should match those specified by the zone file. The contents of the file should be checked more closely for incompatibility errors if all the information is not made available in the DNS MMC snap-in.

Changes can be made to the primary DNS zone file while the Windows 2000 DNS server is running. To have these changes loaded, select the zone in the DNS MMC snap-in and select Action | Reload. Check the zone's contents as displayed in the DNS MMC snap-in to make sure that any changes have been incorporated and that the other information has not been compromised.

NOTE: If a primary DNS zone is to be implemented as a Windows 2000 Active Directory–integrated DNS zone, make sure that the zone migration is complete before converting the primary DNS zone to an Active Directory–integrated DNS zone. Additional zone entries can be added individually using the DNS MMC snap-in via dynamic DNS updates and command line programs (see Chapter 19), but they cannot be added in bulk by editing a zone file because it is not used by the Active Directory–integrated DNS zone. It is possible to convert back to a primary DNS zone to make such changes, but any security or dynamic DNS update settings will be lost.

Converting a zone file by copying is one of the most difficult tasks a DNS administrator will undertake. A good understanding of zone files and the source DNS server is a definite advantage. For example, understanding how the $ORIGIN and $INCLUDE statements are used in BIND files can make migration much easier. Application tools like *awk* and *grep* can be very helpful, especially if a zone file with FQDNs must be converted to relative domain names or if $INCLUDE files need to have their relative domain names converted to FQDNs.

As with any migration operation, a readily available copy of the original files should be maintained until the migration is complete and tested.

Migration by Converting Secondary Zones to Primary Zones

Migrating a primary DNS zone using secondary DNS zone replication requires two DNS servers. The first is usually the DNS server that is being eliminated, and the second is the DNS server that is replacing it. A less common scenario has the second computer being a DNS server that will be used to create the new primary zone that will then be copied to its final destination on another DNS server.

There are two reasons for using secondary DNS zone replication to create a primary DNS zone. First, it is very easy. Second, it eliminates DNS server features such as the $INCLUDE statement that can be used with BIND zone files from the secondary DNS zone file replication information.

The following steps outline the replication process:

1. Set up the new DNS server.

2. Configure the source DNS server's zone to be copied so it can be accessed by the new DNS server.

3. Set up a secondary DNS zone on the new DNS server so that it uses the primary DNS zone or a secondary DNS zone for the desired domain.

4. Convert the secondary DNS zone to a primary DNS zone.

5. Change the SOA resource record.

6. Change Name Server settings.

7. Change Zone Transfers settings.

8. Swap the old DNS server with the new DNS server when all zones are properly configured.

This process can be done with any kind of DNS server being the destination, including a Windows 2000 DNS server or a Windows NT

DNS server. The latter has the usual limitations such as the inability to use SRV resource records.

Steps 5, 6, and 7 are particularly important. The settings for the new zone will be the same as the source zone. In general, the primary server name must be changed in the SOA record, the new DNS server's IP address will have to be added to the Name Server list, and zone transfers will have to be enabled, possibly selectively. Other changes may be made as well, such as enabling dynamic DNS updates. If the zone information is to be moved to a third DNS server, then only some of these settings adjust the zone file. These include the SOA record settings and the Name Servers list. These changes can be made using the Windows 2000 DNS MMC snap-in.

Primary DNS zones can be converted to Active Directory–integrated DNS zones without loss of configuration information. An Active Directory–integrated DNS zone can be changed back to a primary DNS zone, but some configuration and security information will be lost. For example, a primary DNS zone does not support Windows 2000–secured dynamic DNS updates.

One interesting approach using this secondary DNS zone migration method in a large network is to set up a single Windows 2000 DNS server that then imports all the primary DNS zones in the network prior to migration of the DNS servers. This allows the primary DNS zone files to be moved, checked, and configured prior to migration. Configuration details that will not move with the zone files should be recorded so these can be changed on the DNS server where they will be installed.

SUMMARY

Migrating to Windows 2000 DNS will be a major consideration for any network administrator deploying Windows 2000 and Active Directory. While other DNS servers will support Windows 2000 Active Directory, the Windows 2000 DNS service has a number of advantages, such as Active Directory–integrated DNS zones and support for dynamic DNS updates. These features may be sufficient to migrate to Windows 2000 DNS.

This chapter examined issues related to migration including the tradeoffs of migrating to Windows 2000 DNS versus staying with an existing DNS infrastructure. Migration is not always the answer, and even partial migration is often preferable especially in a heterogeneous network.

Migration from another DNS server to a Windows 2000 DNS server is not always a straightforward process. Fortunately, it tends to be easier than dealing with other migration issues such as moving from Novell Netware or Windows NT to Windows 2000.

CHAPTER 18

Windows 2000 DNS and the Internet

Windows 2000 DNS is indispensable for a Windows 2000 network that is connected to the Internet—and these days it is rare for a network of any size not to be connected to the Internet. DNS servers are sprinkled throughout the Internet, starting with the local Internet Service Provider (ISP). An ISP is normally the gateway for DNS services and e-mail. This chapter looks at how local DNS servers will interact with Internet servers as well as how local DNS servers will be used to support Internet-related services such as e-mail.

"DNS Servers on the Internet" takes a look at various interactions between DNS servers, domain names, and Internet subnets. "Things to Avoid with Internet Connections" delves into problems that can arise when first making a connection with the Internet and how preplanning can eliminate these possibilities.

"Local DNS Server Placement" examines more specialized DNS interaction than that presented in prior chapters. For example, DNS services can be impacted by network address translation (NAT). NAT is often used on small networks that use a single IP address to connect an entire network to the Internet. We take a look at DNS proxy servers and how they related to conventional DNS servers examined in this book. This section also takes a look at the use of caching and forwarding servers especially in the context of connecting a network to the Internet.

"DNS and E-mail" examines how Simple Mail Transfer Protocol (SMTP) works and how it uses DNS. This includes the use of DNS MX resource records. DNS is important for Web browsing, but it is also important for e-mail clients and servers. This section looks at how the e-mail clients and servers take advantage of DNS.

DNS SERVERS ON THE INTERNET

DNS servers tie together the Internet name space. It starts with the root servers, also known as root hints, and works its way down from there.

The reason the magical hierarchy of DNS works on the Internet is because domain names are registered—otherwise, duplicate fully qualified domain names (FQDNs) would cause name resolution conflicts that would bring the Internet to a standstill. This section looks at how this process works with respect to a local network connected to the Internet.

One of the big differences between working with the Internet and local network IP subnets is that local subnets are normally set up using DHCP, whereas subnets that are accessible from the Internet are normally assigned fixed IP addresses. DHCP can still be used, but this is typically done for computers that will access the Internet but not necessarily be accessed from the Internet.

Root Hints

The Internet domain naming system is based on 13 root DNS servers that essentially contain the same primary domain ".". The name resolution procedure outlined in Chapter 2 explains how these root domain name servers are used when a DNS server cannot resolve a name locally. Usually, the root domain name servers will not be contacted directly on a regular basis because once a top-level domain (TLD) reference is cached it will be used again and again by the DNS server. TLD names include names such as com, net, edu, gov, and org.

Keep in mind that the root DNS servers do not handle a large number of domains but do handle a large number of DNS clients. The large TLDs such as com, net, edu, gov, and org are handled by multiple DNS servers.

Multiple root servers are used for performance and redundancy reasons. Each root server is authoritative for the root domain. This means that any changes—for instance, adding a new TLD—will mean changing each root server. This requirement, along with the desire to keep the Internet manageable, is why TLDs are not proliferating with wild abandon. New TLDs are being used, but most of the growth is of subdomains of existing TLDs.

A large local network can use the same multiple authoritative DNS server approach for local domains. The same kinds of restrictions apply, including keeping the servers' DNS database in synch and minimizing changes to the root servers.

In general, Windows 2000 DNS servers are configured with the standard set of root DNS servers when DNS support is installed. This rarely needs to be changed. If it does need to be changed, it should be done on each DNS server that will be connected directly or indirectly to the Internet. The root hints are displayed using the DNS MMC snap-in discussed in Chapter 11. Select the DNS server and then select Action | Properties. Then select the Root Hints tab on the DNS server Properties screen. The Add, Edit, and Remove buttons can be used to change the root hints as necessary.

Registering Domain Names

Domain Name Supporting Organization of ICANN (**www.dnso.org**) handles generic Top Level Domains (gTLD) such as com, net, edu, gov, and org. There are also country code TLDs (ccTLDs) for each country, such as jp for Japan. Registration information about domain names under a ccTLD can be found at **http://www.iana.org/ctld/cctld.htm**.

From a DNS administrator's view, TLDs are static. First-level domains (FLD) are what most organizations register. This includes names such as cnn.com or microsoft.com. The organization then defines its own set of subdomains to almost any level. This means that www.microsoft.com is not registered, but its FLD, microsoft.com, is.

InterNIC (**www.internic.net**) was the organization with which FLD names were registered. Today, dozens of registrars handle FLDs, and InterNIC coordinates these registrars. The list of registrars can be found at **www.icann.org/registrars/accredited-list.html** as well as at the IANA (Internet Assigned Numbers Authority) site (**www.iana.org**). Registration forms can be obtained over the Internet but most often this process starts with an ISP.

ISPs will normally provide all the information necessary to set up a domain name, although an organization representative must sign off on the InterNIC form requesting a domain name. An ISP will then, usually for a fee, host the domain. This means that the ISP's name server will be the authoritative name server for the domain.

NOTE: Registering a domain name does not associate the domain name with an IP address. In fact, a domain name like foo.com may not be associated with any IP address. IP addresses may simply be associated with hosts within the domain such as www.foo.com and ftp.foo.com.

A local network for an organization can use a registered domain name as the basis for locally named workstations and servers. Larger networks may be set up to provide name services for the domain directly. In this case, the organization normally has a DNS server outside the local network that's accessible to the Internet. This is discussed in the section "Local DNS Server Placement." Alternatively, a local network can be serviced by a subdomain of a registered domain.

In some cases, an organization will not have a registered domain, or it may not use it or a subdomain for workstations and servers within the local network. In this case, a dummy TLD can be used. A TLD can be chosen arbitrarily, such as .localnet, but the name may conflict with an Internet-based TLD. If this should happen, the Internet-based domain would be inaccessible from the local network because the local DNS servers would resolve domain names to the local network. For example, say net were chosen as a TLD for a local network that was also connected to the Internet. Obviously, this will conflict with the Internet since .net is already a gTLD. It could still be used on a local DNS server, but if the network were connected to the Internet, the local computers accessing the local DNS server would reference the local network and not the Internet. Confusion would reign if the local DNS server were using the ISP's DNS server for subsequent name resolution because domain names that included TLDs like com and gov would resolve to Internet-based addresses, while net-based domain names such as foo.net would not. Figure 18-1 shows how this works. A DNS client on the Internet will find the zone definitions for the Internet-based net and com zones. The local network DNS client will see the local net zone definitions and the Internet com zone definitions.

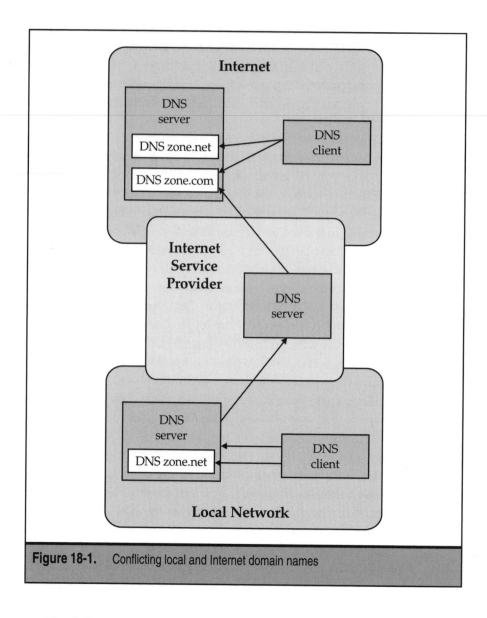

Figure 18-1. Conflicting local and Internet domain names

The following domain names have been reserved for internal use by RFC 2606, Reserved Top Level DNS Names:

▼ test

■ example

- invalid
- localhost

These TLDs cannot be registered by any organization. However, it is possible to use other, nonreserved names such as dom.

DNS servers may map fully qualified domain names to IP addresses. As mentioned earlier, a domain does not have to map to an IP address, but, typically, one or more resource records within a domain do map to IP addresses. For example, foo.com is a domain with host (A) resource records www.foo.com and ftp.foo.com.

As with domain names, IP subnets can be registered, although specific addresses are not requested. Instead, a range of addresses is requested. Most ISPs have been allocated a block of addresses and lease small blocks of these addresses to their customers. ISP's DHCP servers distribute addresses on a per-connection basis for modems and PPPOE (point-to-point protocol over Ethernet).

Internet Subnets

The Internet Assigned Numbers Authority (IANA) and the Internet Corporation for Assigned Names and Numbers (ICANN) track IP addresses for the Internet. Networks that are not connected to the Internet can use any IP address. Networks attached to the Internet can use any IP addresses within their own network, but if they use an IP address that has already been taken on the Internet, the resource on the Internet will be inaccessible from the network because the local IP address takes precedence.

NOTE: Conflicts between an IP address used both in a network and on the Internet are actually complicated by routing issues not discussed in this book. In general, it is a bad idea to arbitrarily select IP addresses on a local network that is or will be connected to the Internet. Instead, a local network should use IP addresses defined by RFC 1918, Address Allocation for Private Internets, or the network should use IP addresses allocated by the ISP that is providing access to the Internet.

IP addresses have been partitioned into classes depending upon the number of bits available for distinct IP addresses within the class. Table 18-1 outlines the three classes.

NOTE: The usable number of IP addresses shown in Table 18-1 is actually slightly lower because of predefined IP addresses such as broadcast IP addresses.

Class A address blocks were originally allocated to large organizations, including major educational institutions. There are few class A blocks and all are currently in use, although all the IP addresses within the block are not in use. Class B address blocks are often owned by ISPs or educational organizations. Class C address blocks are more common.

In general, blocks of IP addresses are not obtained directly except for very large organizations or ISPs. Instead, most organizations lease blocks of IP addresses from an ISP. Class C blocks are sometimes available, but smaller organizations can get fewer IP addresses. These addresses do not have to fit into any of the class definitions presented in Table 18-1, although an ISP will be allocating the leased block from a block of IP addresses that the ISP has registered. The main impact of this ISP connection is that changing ISPs will require changes to the IP addresses used by an organization. The impact of such a change is discussed in the section "Things to Avoid with Internet Connections."

Class	Bits	Example	NetMask	Mask Bits	IP Addresses
A	24	10.x.x.x	255.0.0.0	8	16M
B	16	10.10.x.x	255.255.0.0	16	64K
C	8	10.10.10.x	255.255.255.0	24	256

Table 18-1.   IP Address Class Definitions

Network Address Translation

One approach that is often used to limit the impact of obtaining and managing Internet IP addresses is network address translation (NAT). In this case, the local network uses a private set of IP addresses that will never be used on the Internet. These blocks of IP addresses are defined in RFC 1918, Address Allocation for Private Internets, and are listed in Table 18-2.

NAT can operate in two ways. The first is to map a local IP address to an Internet IP address based on a block of addresses obtained from an ISP. The second uses port mapping. Ports are not discussed in this book, and a description of their operation will be restricted to this chapter. Essentially, each packet sent over the network contains a source and destination IP address. There is also a port address for both the source and destination. There are a number of predefined port addresses associated with well known services such as DNS, Web, FTP, and TELNET services. The source port is not usually fixed. Assuming a single Internet IP address is assigned to the NAT gateway, this allows NAT to change the source IP address to the gateway's IP address for an outgoing message. It changes the source port to an unused port. The gateway sends the packet onto the Internet.

The gateway keeps track of this translation as well as unused ports. Incoming packets from the Internet in response to outgoing packets will be directed to the gateway because of the translation that occurred. The gateway then compares the destination port with its

Class	Bits	Base	NetMask	Mask Bits	IP Addresses
A	24	10.0.0.0	255.0.0.0	8	16M
B+	20	172.16.0.0	255.240.0.0	12	1M
B	16	192.168.0.0	255.255.0.0	16	64K

Table 18-2.   IP Addresses for Private Networks

set of translation ports and finds the matching port and IP address. It then changes the destination port and IP address and sends the packet onto the local network. The process is transparent to the local computer and the Internet computer. The port-based NAT translation process is shown in Figure 18-2.

The port-based NAT works most of the time; we will not go into details associated with limitations of NAT.

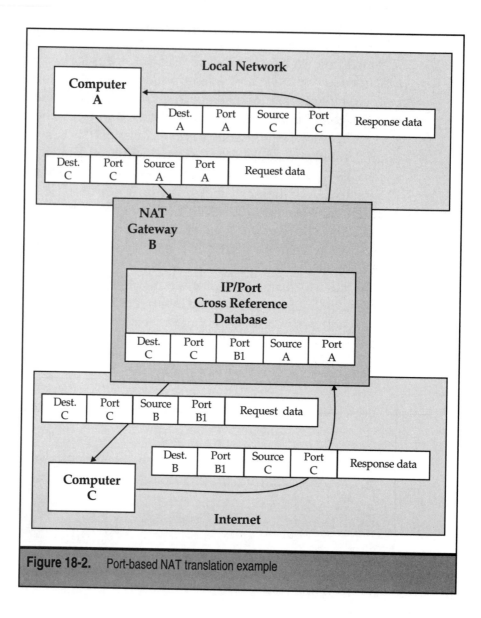

Figure 18-2.   Port-based NAT translation example

In general, NAT allows the local network to use private addresses listed in Table 18-2. A local DNS server can provide name resolution services for local computers and can also be set up to provide name resolution of Internet names for local computers only. Computers on the Internet will not be able to access computers on the local network, including the local DNS server, because the only IP address the computers on the Internet can access will be the gateway's.

There is one exception, which is provided by a fixed mapping feature found on many NAT gateways. This allows a fixed port on the gateway to be mapped to a fixed port on a local computer such as a Web server. Computers on the Internet accessing the gateway port will be translated and forwarded to the local computer. As with conventional NAT support, responses are translated in the same fashion. Often this fixed mapping feature is combined with a secured connection such as a virtual private network (VPN) support. This is typically done when the local computer is a server with important information or one that could provide access to the local network. Figure 18-3 shows how Gateway B maps between two ports: B1 and B2. B1 is visible from the Internet, while B2 is used on the local network. An entry is still necessary in the IP/Port cross-reference database for each computer on the Internet using port B1.

NOTE: The Fixed IP/Port Cross-Reference Database entries in Figure 18-3 are added by the gateway administrator when the gateway is configured. The IP/Port Cross-Reference Database entries are automatically added as needed as packets are sent back and forth through the gateway.

More advanced NAT gateways support a mix of IP address and port mappings. In this case, the NAT gateway is multihomed on the Internet side so it appears to have more than one IP address. One IP address is used for the conventional IP/port-to-IP/port mapping system, while the others are used for IP-to-IP address mappings. In the latter case, ports in the packet address are not remapped.

In the previous examples, ISP was not shown. An ISP router is normally found at the boundary between the NAT gateway and the Internet. The computer on the Internet is normally on the other side of an ISP as well. It can also be on the other side of its own NAT gateway. In this case, the only way this computer can access a computer on the local network shown in the example is if the configuration is the one shown in Figure 18-3.

IPv6 is the next generation of IP addressing. For the most part, a DNS manager's job will remain the same with IPv6. IPv6 increases the number of bits used for an address to 128, but it changes the numbering convention from four 8-bit numbers to eight 16-bit numbers. IPv6 numbering using colons to separate numbers instead

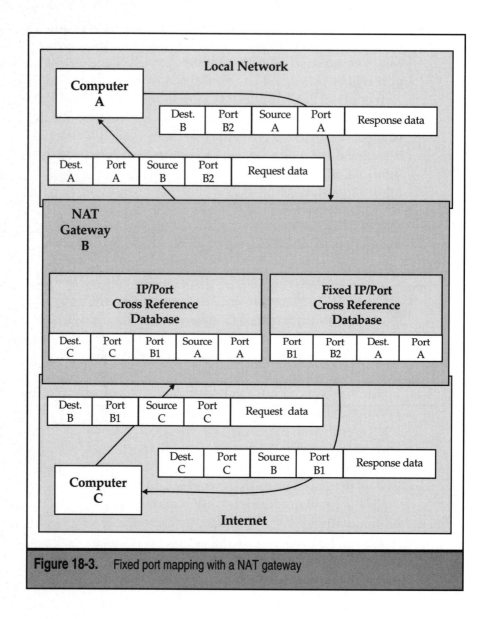

Figure 18-3.   Fixed port mapping with a NAT gateway

of periods. IPv6 host record type designation is AAAA versus the IP host designation of A.

IPv6 incorporates quite a bit more, especially when it comes to routing, but a detailed discussion of IPv6 is beyond the scope of this book. At this point, Windows 2000 DNS supports IPv6 with the AAAA host resource records.

Things to Avoid with Internet Connections

Methods for connecting a local network to the Internet can be divided into two types: those that use NAT gateways and those that use conventional gateways. The latter provides no mapping support so the IP addresses used by local computers must be registered IP addresses and not those for private use such as 192.168.x.x. We will look at the two methods individually.

Proxy servers that provide NAT support can be considered NAT-based gateways. NAT-based gateways provide an isolation mechanism to keep Internet users out of the local network. This allows any IP addressing scheme and any domain naming scheme to be used internally. Avoid being arbitrary at all costs. IP addresses should only be assigned from those listed in Table 18-2. As with any IP address system, use DHCP wherever possible. This simplifies merging two networks, as when two companies or two branch offices merge, since only fixed IP computers will have to be changed. If possible, use DHCP with fixed leases to distribute information such as DNS server addresses.

Conventional gateways can also limit access to certain computers, but this type of restriction is more of an issue for a gateway manager. The use of DHCP to distribute Internet-based IP addresses is a good idea, especially if there are a large number of IP addresses such as when a Class C block is used. Remember that these IP addresses are normally leased from an ISP as part of an Internet access package.

Do not use IP addresses outside the range of those provided by the ISP. Allowing Internet access from local computers using private network IP addresses may not work at all, or it may cause communication or routing problems. If private network IP addresses do end up being mixed with Internet IP addresses, make sure that the private network IP address-based computers on the local network go through a NAT-based gateway to access the Internet.

For both types of gateways, it is a good idea to use at least one caching DNS server inside the local network. This DNS server should be linked to the ISP's DNS servers so the local server can handle name resolution requests for Internet-based domain names through the ISP DNS servers. This configuration also allows the local DNS server to handle name resolution for the local network resources as well. The section "Local DNS Server Placement" addresses this in more detail.

Avoid using domain names with arbitrary TLDs or existing TLDs, such as com or net, on the local DNS server. Using Internet-based TLDs can mask their existence on the Internet from local computers.

To avoid domain name conflicts, register a new domain name even if the name will not be used immediately. This will allow you to configure your local network using this domain name so that conflicts will not arise when the local network is connected to the Internet. Even if a NAT-based gateway is used, the local network's DNS server can use the domain name for naming internal computers. The section "Shadow or Split DNS Servers" shows one way that a domain can be used on both a local network and the Internet.

NOTE: A typical configuration for a NAT-based gateway configuration is an ISP-host Web server and a DNS server on the local network. The ISP's DNS server will contain a zone definition for the domain that includes the Web server's host resource record. The local DNS server also includes a zone definition for the same domain, but it includes host resource records for local computers. If the local DNS server has a zone for the domain, it should include a host record for the Internet-based Web server and any other ISP-hosted services such as an FTP server. This will not be necessary if the local computers are part of a subdomain that has its own zone file. For example, the ISP zone file could handle foo.com while the local DNS zone file could be local.foo.com. The ISP-based Web server name would be www.foo.com, and a local computer would have a name like computer1.local.foo.com. Delegation of the local.foo.com subdomain by the ISP's DNS server is not needed because the local computers cannot be accessed from the Internet.

LOCAL DNS SERVER PLACEMENT

This section looks at how DNS servers can be placed with respect to the Internet and a local network specifically for handling traffic and security issues related to an Internet connection. It also examines dial-up connections to the Internet and their impact on DNS server configuration. Some of the topics in this section are covered in other parts of the book, but this chapter is slanted towards Internet connections of DNS servers.

"Shadow or Split DNS Servers" looks at how the same DNS information may be split between two servers on different sides of a gateway or firewall. It also examines why this approach is useful for many networks.

"Dial-up Connections and DNS Servers" takes a closer look at transient connections and their impact on DNS servers. Proper configuration is important because most dial-up connections are transient and unnecessary calls should be avoided if possible.

"Caching and Forwarding" reexamines these DNS features with respect to the Internet. It takes a look at configurations where a branch office may have Internet access through a central office connection. It also looks at linking DNS servers in different offices that are connected via the Internet.

"DNS Proxy Servers" takes a brief look at DNS proxy servers that are typically found in NAT-based gateways, firewalls, and proxy servers.

Shadow or Split DNS Servers

A *shadow* DNS server, also called a *split* DNS server, is actually one of a pair of DNS servers. One DNS server provides name resolution services for computers on the Internet. The other provides name resolution services for computers on the local network. The DNS server on the Internet side provides a subset of the same domain information as the DNS server on the local network. Figure 18-4 shows how these DNS servers are set up.

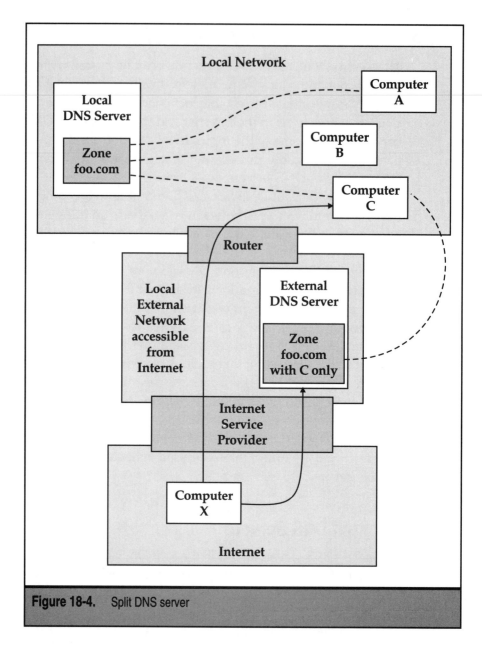

Figure 18-4.   Split DNS server

The local DNS server contains a zone file for the sample domain foo.com. For the sake of simplicity, the zone contains three entries: a.foo.com, b.foo.com, and c.foo.com. The external DNS server contains the same zone for the domain foo.com, but it contains only one entry, c.foo.com. It is assumed that the router allows Internet access to Computer C, also known as c.foo.com. This allows a computer on the Internet, Computer X in Figure 18-4, to access the external DNS server to find the IP address of c.foo.com. Computer X can then access Computer C.

In this scenario, c.foo.com is often a locally maintained Web server that might have a name or alias of www.foo.com. In fact, split DNS server zones often have different domain names associated with the same IP addresses.

Another common configuration is similar to that shown in Figure 18-4. The difference is that Computer C is moved to the local external network along with the external DNS server. The configuration of the split DNS servers is really no different, although the IP address for Computer C may be different because it is now on the other side of the router.

The alias and subset differences between the DNS zone contents is one reason that secondary DNS zones or Active Directory–integrated DNS zones cannot be used to implement split DNS servers. Luckily, the contents of the DNS zone on the external DNS server rarely change, and it is often limited to a small number of entries compared to the DNS zone on the local DNS server.

Split DNS servers are normally implemented by manually configuring DNS zones on both DNS servers. Any changes must be reflected in both DNS servers. BIND actually has an edge because common primary DNS zone entries can be added from a separate file using $INCLUDE. Check out Chapter 21 for details on using $INCLUDE.

If $INCLUDE is not used, BIND and Windows 2000 DNS are in the same boat. Both provide conventional secondary DNS zone replication but no filtering. The only way to configure split DNS servers is to have primary DNS zones for the same domain on both servers.

BIND 9, which was in beta when this book was written, promises to make split DNS server support automatic. It introduces filtering into secondary DNS zone-style replication. This is a significant improvement over manual configuration because the real information is maintained in one location.

One DNS feature that makes split DNS servers more difficult to maintain is dynamic DNS updates. The big question is which DNS server an update should be applied to. Linux or UNIX servers can be configured to update one or both servers, but Windows 2000 clients will normally be configured to update the local DNS server. The same will be true when using the Windows 2000 DHCP server's dynamic DNS update proxy support.

One approach to supporting dynamic DNS updates is to set up a zone specifically for dynamic DNS updates. This does not address the problem of advertising a subset of this zone by the external DNS server, but it does allow easy replication via secondary DNS zones.

Bastion hosts are another item that must to be considered with split DNS servers. A bastion host is one with two or more network adapters that provide it access to the local network and the Internet. In some cases, often on small networks, the bastion host can act as the router.

The configuration issue with bastion hosts is which DNS server a bastion host's DNS client should use. It will typically be the internal DNS server, assuming that the internal DNS server will also resolve domain names on the Internet. The bastion server may resolve a domain name to an IP address on the Internet and then use its Internet connection to access the computer on the Internet. If the bastion host's DNS client is configured to use the external DNS server, then it will only be able to access services for zones managed by the external DNS server.

Dial-up Connections and DNS Servers

Dial-up transient connections are quite common in smaller networks. These are often modem or ISDN connections to the Internet or from a branch office to the main office. Modem and ISDN connections are not the only kinds of transient connections these days. Point-to-point protocol over Ethernet (PPPOE) is common with single IP address DSL and cable modem services. All require special considerations when it comes to DNS support for a small to medium size network.

Transient connections can be set up manually, using a schedule, or on-demand. Manually initiated connections are typically ones that stay up for a long period of time. They are also used when individuals use a transient connection to connect to the Internet. For purposes of this discussion, the manually initiated connection can be viewed as a constant connection, albeit a slow one compared to local network speeds.

Scheduled connections are made based on a schedule stored on a router. A network administrator sets the schedule. A typical schedule would be to make one connection from 8 A.M. to 5 P.M. for regular office use and another from 1 A.M. to 2 A.M. for late-night backups.

On-demand connections are initiated when any computer on the network needs to connect to a computer that is not on the network. A router can be configured to limit the computers that may use a connection, but usually all computers are enabled. The connection is usually terminated after a fixed time limit or after a fixed amount of connection idle time is detected. Be cautious about setting an idle timeout value too short; it can cause a router to repeatedly dial out to restore a connection that a computer needs to complete a set of transactions that take slightly more time than the timeout value. This can be a problem where each call and each connection time costs money, such as with an ISDN line.

Scheduled and on-demand connections are similar in the sense that they are connected for some period of time and disconnected the rest of the time. However, on-demand connections are simply not predictable. Both scheduled and on-demand connections tend to be used for small to medium size networks that often have a DNS server. Networks that do not have a DNS server will use one on the other end of the connection, and only DNS clients will be found on the network. We do not consider this configuration, as there are really no adjustments that can be made to the DNS server that will make the connections more efficient.

On the other hand, having a DNS server on the local network allows the DNS server to provide name resolution services for resources located on the local network. The connection to the outside world need only be used when resources outside the network are needed. A DNS server can reduce the need to set up a connection or use part of its bandwidth if the DNS server's cache and zone information can be used to resolve local requests without using the connection.

There are two configurations to consider with a transient connection and a local DNS server. The first is where the DNS administrator has some control over the DNS server at the other end of the connection. The second is where there is little or no control. The former case shows up in distributed organizations with connections between branch offices. The latter occurs with connections to the Internet through an ISP.

When a DNS administrator does have control over DNS servers at both ends of a connection, secondary DNS zone transfers may be useful, especially if local computers need to access resources defined in the secondary DNS zone. For example, the main office mail server would be defined in a primary DNS zone maintained on the main office DNS server. The local office DNS server could replicate the zone so that local computers could determine a remote computer's IP address through the local DNS server. This approach improves on-demand connection performance in two ways. First, if a connection is not active, it will not be brought up until a computer actually needs to connect with a remote computer. The connection would need to be started sooner if a DNS request had to be processed first to determine the IP address of the remote computer. Second, the connection does not have to be used to service DNS requests since the local DNS server can handle the DNS requests.

The alternative is caching or forwarding. Forwarding does not provide any advantage since the DNS server simply forwards a request over the connection. Caching does help, and often a local DNS server is set up as a caching-only DNS server if local name resolution is not needed. Caching has the advantage over secondary DNS zone replication if items are kept in the cache long enough and requests are made to the same domains on a regular basis. This is often true for Internet connections. Secondary DNS zones tend to work best between a branch office and a main office where traffic is between the two offices. Secondary DNS zone replication can be set up for very long refresh intervals, as primary DNS zones in this type of environment tend to change very little. Secondary DNS zone replication can also be set up to occur in the late evening or on weekends when a remote connection may not be in use.

A special case occurs for small distributed networks that use only secondary DNS zones for replicating DNS information. In this case, a local DNS server can provide all the name resolution services without recursion. If the request cannot be handled by looking in a locally maintained zone, the request fails. For a Windows 2000 DNS server, recursion can be disabled, which prevents a DNS server from contacting a remote DNS server if the local DNS server cannot handle a resolution request. Recursion is disabled from the DNS MMC snap-in discussed in Chapter 11. To do this, select the DNS server and then select Action | Properties. Select the Advanced tab and make sure there is a check mark in the check box for Disable Recursion in the Server Options list. This is normally unchecked. This will not prevent updates for secondary DNS zones.

Caching and Forwarding

The previous section examined caching and forwarding with respect to a small network with transient connections. This section takes a look at larger networks that use transient or fixed connections. In some cases, this configuration will match that of the main office in a branch/main office scenario where the branch office configuration is similar to that described in the previous section.

Figure 18-5 shows a typical configuration for a medium size network connected to the Internet through a single connection. A forwarding DNS server services a group of clients. Often the clients will use another forwarding DNS server as an alternate DNS server.

This configuration allows the caching DNS server to maintain a system-wide DNS cache. The forwarding DNS servers can also maintain a cache. The caching DNS server can also maintain local DNS zones and provide a single point for local DNS zone management. The alternative to using this configuration for local DNS zones is to use secondary DNS zones on the forwarding DNS servers, which complicates the management of these servers. The alternative to forwarding requests to the caching server is for the forwarding servers to resolve nonlocal domain names using recursion so that they would be going to the ISP instead of using the caching server. The end result of this scenario is that the centralized cache will not be maintained because information will only be cached at the forwarding DNS server.

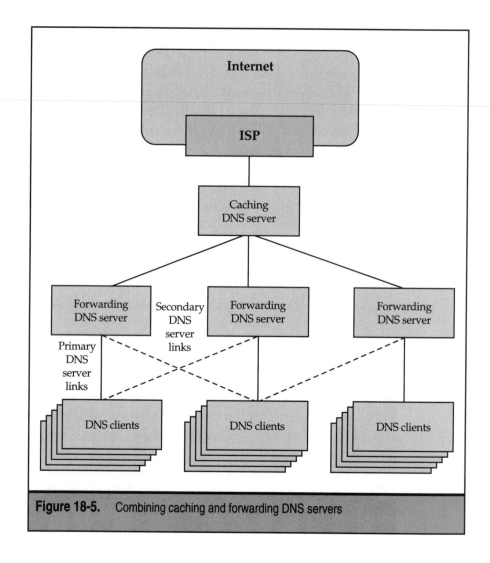

Figure 18-5. Combining caching and forwarding DNS servers

The drawback to the forwarding/caching hierarchy is that it takes time to build up a cache. Once this is done, DNS traffic is minimized.

DNS Proxy Servers

DNS proxy servers are actually a special case of a caching or forwarding DNS server. DNS proxy servers are normally part of a router or proxy server that provides a local network with access to the Internet.

To a DNS client, the DNS proxy server appears to be a DNS server, and it is. The DNS proxy server is configured as a DNS client to use an ISP's DNS server or servers. If the DNS proxy server has limited memory, it is typically set up as a forwarding DNS server. If there is enough available memory for a cache, the proxy server is typically set up as a caching DNS server.

DNS proxy servers often have limited resources and features compared to a full function DNS server such as a Windows 2000 DNS server. Local DNS zones and dynamic DNS updates are rarely supported. These are just a few reasons why a local DNS server may also be employed when a DNS proxy server is available. In this case, it is often more efficient to disable the DNS proxy server, if possible, and have the local DNS server be set up to use the ISP DNS servers instead of the DNS proxy server.

DNS AND E-MAIL

DNS and e-mail go together like bread and butter. In a nutshell, a DNS server stores mail exchange (MX) resource records used by mail clients and servers to deliver mail.

Most users do not even know that DNS servers may be involved in mail delivery. They simply set up the name for an SMTP server to handle outgoing mail and a POP3 server to obtain incoming mail and, as far as they are concerned, what happens in-between is magic.

This section takes a look at how DNS servers are involved in mail delivery. "MX Resource Records" looks at MX resource records and other mail-related resource records that can be found in a DNS zone. As with any DNS resource record, these mail-related resource records will be replicated in secondary DNS zones and can be cached in a DNS server's cache.

"Mail Delivery Using MX Records" takes a look at how MX records are used to actually deliver the mail.

DNS server configuration for mail delivery is an important feature that many DNS managers may not be aware of, especially if e-mail has always been handled by a third party or a single e-mail server has been providing local e-mail services. Configuration for mail services typically pops up in ISPs and in larger organizations with networks that have more than one mail server. Proper configuration can provide redundant mail routing that can be especially useful for networks with multiple routes to different sites and to the Internet.

MX Resource Records

The MX resource record is the most important mail-related DNS resource record. Before delving into it, we'll look at some of the other mail-related DNS resource records. Many of these resource records are obsolete, but they are mentioned here so DNS administrators will not be distracted by wondering what they are.

The MX resource record functionality was originally split between the MD (mail destination) and MF (mail forwarding) resource records. The MD resource record indicated a mail destination for a domain. If the mail destination could not be reached by a mail delivery service, the service would query the DNS server for a MF resource record for a domain. Splitting the job into two parts made the delivery procedure more complicated and resulted in the maintenance of two different types of resource records. In addition, the mail delivery agent needed to contact the DNS twice if a mail destination could not be reached.

The MX record replaces both the MD and MF records by providing a single kind of mail destination. The mail destination may be the delivery point or it may forward the mail.

The mail box (MB) resource records and the mail group (MG) resource records have also fallen from favor and are no longer used. Initially presented in RFC 1035 along with the MX record definition, MB and MG resource records provided a mechanism to implement mail box names and groups using DNS. The task proved unworkable as this type of information had to be updated more often and by more users than a DNS administrator preferred. Mail clients and mail servers now provide similar features. The MX record has remained an important DNS feature because MX records rarely change once configured and because they provide the valuable service of identifying mail servers.

The following syntax is used with an MX resource record:

```
owner class ttl MX preference mail-exchange-name
```

The *owner* specifies the domain that the MX record is associated with. The *class* is normally IN as with other DNS resource records. The *ttl* (time-to-live) number is usually left blank and the default ttl value found in a zone's SOA resource record is used instead. Finally, there is a numeric *preference* and the *mail-exchange-name.*

> **NOTE:**   The mail-exchange-name must have a host (A) resource record definition so that the IP address of the mail server can be obtained. If it doesn't, the mail server cannot be located.

The preference is used if multiple MX resource records for the same owner are included in a zone. Lower values have a higher preference, i.e., zero has the highest preference. Multiple MX resource records for the same owner can have the same preference value, in which case they are used either in random order or in the order they appear in the zone file, depending upon the DNS server being used. Preference values are relative and do not have to be sequential within a zone.

The following is a typical set of MX records:

```
foo.com IN MX  0 mail1.foo.com
        IN MX 40 sales.foo.com
        IN MX 20 admin.foo.com
        IN MX 20 software.local.foo.com
```

In this case, there are four mail servers that can be used to deliver mail for the domain foo.com. None may be the actual destination, but each will attempt to deliver any mail they receive for foo.com. Note that the order of the records does not have to follow the preference value. In this example, sales.foo.com will be the least preferable server for delivery to foo.com. The following would have the same effect:

```
foo.com IN MX 0 mail1.foo.com
        IN MX 4 sales.foo.com
        IN MX 2 admin.foo.com
        IN MX 2 software.local.foo.com
```

Mail will be delivered to only one mail server. If the first is not accessible then the subsequent mail servers are tried until either the end of the list is reached or the mail is delivered.

Mail Delivery Using MX Records

Sendmail is one of the most common mail delivery programs used on the Internet. Microsoft Exchange Server is another SMTP-compatible mail delivery program. Both make use of MX records. The procedure for using MX records is detailed in RFC 974.

This section takes a closer look at how MX records are used. In particular, it examines how MX records can be used to prevent mail delivery loops where mail is continually passed between mail servers because it cannot be delivered to its final destination.

The mail delivery procedure includes the following steps:

1. Get the list of MX records from the DNS server.

2. Sort MX records by preference, lowest to highest.

3. Locate an MX record that matches the name of the current host.

4. Delete all MX records with a higher preference value than the current host if the current host is found in the list of MX records.

5. Try to deliver mail to one mail server starting from the beginning of the list.

NOTE: The matching that occurs in step 3 does not take into account any DNS aliases implemented using a CNAME resource record on most mail servers such as sendmail.

Proper operation using MX resource records depends on each mail server having access to a DNS server that has comparable MX resource record settings. If the MX resource records for the same mail destination are not the same on DNS servers used by different mail servers, mail can go undelivered or wind up in a never-ending loop. The two listings presented in this chapter are an example of comparable MX resource record definitions.

TIP: Use the same DNS zone for MX records for mail delivery servers in the same network. This means that all mail delivery servers will be using the same information for route determination that will eliminate the possibility of infinite routes.

In many cases, a DNS administrator will have to request that their ISP add an MX record to an external mail server host located at the organization's site so that mail can be delivered directly to the external mail server. This may not be the final destination, but it may forward the mail to another mail server on the local network, as shown in Figure 18-6.

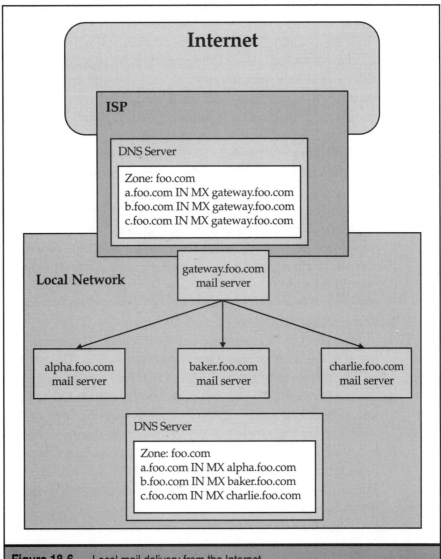

Figure 18-6.   Local mail delivery from the Internet

In this example, there are three mail servers, alpha.foo.com, baker.foo.com, and charlie.foo.com, that handle mail internally. They handle mail for the domains a.foo.com, b.foo.com, and c.foo.com, respectively. The ISP DNS server that manages the domain foo.com contains MX records to direct incoming mail to the gateway.foo.com server. Mail servers on the Internet that need to deliver mail to any of the three domains listed will locate the MX resource records from the ISP's DNS server. These mail servers then contact the gateway.foo.com mail server directly.

It is assumed that the servers on the local network will use the local DNS server shown in Figure 18-6. Notice that the MX records in this DNS server refer to the local mail servers, so when gateway.foo.com tries to forward mail it receives, it can locate the proper local mail server. Outgoing mail is normally handled by the ISP's mail server, which is not shown. The local mail servers will be configured to use the ISP's mail server to forward mail using the Internet and possibly MX records found in other DNS servers on the Internet.

Windows 2000 DNS server supports MX records, but they must be defined in the context of a domain or subdomain. Figure 18-7 shows the DNS MMC snap-in screen for adding a new resource record. To do so, select the domain or subdomain that the record should be added to. Select Action | Other New Records. Select the MX record from the Resource Record Type screen that is presented and click on the Create Record button.

The Host or Domain field can be left blank if the mail domain is the same as the domain that the record is defined in. The Mail Server field will be the name of the mail server that will receive or forward mail for the mail domain. The Mail Server Priority field is the MX preference value described earlier. Clicking the OK button stores the record.

To create the records in the DNS server shown in Figure 18-6, the foo.com domain must first be created. This is typically the domain associated with the zone. The Host or Domain field entry shown in Figure 18-7 would be "a," and the Mail Server field would be alpha.foo.com.

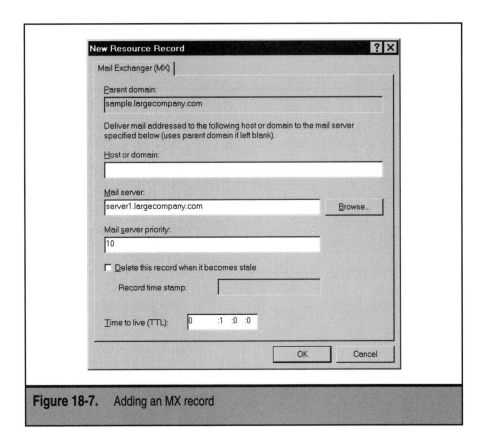

Figure 18-7. Adding an MX record

NOTE: Some DNS servers support wild card names with MX records. This would allow the ISP's DNS server to have a single MX resource record entry with a name of *.foo.com since the mail exchange name is the same for all three records. Windows 2000 DNS does not support wildcard entries, so individual entries, as shown in Figure 18-6, must be entered if the ISP DNS server is Windows 2000 DNS.

SUMMARY

If a network is connected to the Internet, DNS will be part of that connection. DNS is an integral part of the Internet and, with Active Directory's DNS requirements, DNS is an integral part of a Windows 2000 Active Directory network.

Much of this book deals with the details of DNS with respect to the network. This chapter deals with the interaction between DNS clients and servers on the network and their relationship with DNS clients and servers that are part of the Internet.

Unlike local networks where DNS is a public service that has very few restrictions, operation on the Internet typically requires more security. This chapter outlines various approaches to keep your network secure and still use DNS services. We also looked at network address translation and its effects on DNS use as well as the use of proxy DNS services.

Dial-up connections are commonly used with the Internet and bring up their own set of problems. Proper configuration of a local DNS server can be critical to dial-up connections, especially when connections are made automatically. Improper configuration can cause the connection to be made unnecessarily.

E-mail is another area where DNS services play a part. DNS comes into play for e-mail clients that normally use domain names to reference POP3, IMAP4, or SMTP mail servers. While it is possible to work with just IP addresses as with other IP-based services, this situation is almost unheard of. As such, every e-mail address will incorporate a domain name. The mail server that a mail client uses will process the domain name in an address, but a DNS server is normally involved if the mail is not local. MX resource records allow DNS administrators to control mail server operation.

Even if a network is currently isolated, it will probably not be long before it is connected to the Internet. DNS administrators that understand how DNS will interact with the Internet will be able to make such a connection in the future.

CHAPTER 19

Windows 2000 DNS Command Line Management and Utility Programs

T he Windows MMC DNS snap-in, which is generally used to manage the Windows 2000 DNS, DHCP, and WINS servers, is easy to use, partly because of its online help. It provides access to local services as well as services that are located on other Windows 2000 servers. However, as nice as the MMC DNS snap-in is, it is not the only way to manage Windows 2000 services. This chapter takes a look at the following command line management and utility programs:

▼ DNSCMD

■ IPCONFIG

■ NET

■ NETSH

▲ NSLOOKUP

The command line applications allow you to manage the Windows 2000 DNS, DHCP, and WINS services via batch files, and they provide a way to control the services by using a remote character-mode interface such as Telnet.

These command line applications are helpful in different ways. The DNSCMD program allows you to configure and determine the status of the Windows 2000 DNS server. IPCONFIG provides a way to experiment with a DHCP client and provides useful client information that can assist in debugging.

The NET application has a rather extensive comment set. Its primary use for DNS administrators is to start and stop services such as Windows DNS, DHCP, and WINS. The application can do much more; the NET section in this chapter examines the actions related to DNS services and presents only some of the less relevant actions.

The NETSH application is similar to the DNSCMD application in function but is designed to support the Windows 2000 DHCP and WINS services. It has a limited command set, but it can be a valuable tool when managing and debugging these services.

The NSLOOKUP application is a useful tool for querying a Windows 2000 DNS server. NSLOOKUP will work with any DNS server, and versions of the application can be found on almost every network platform.

These command line applications are handy even if most DNS, DHCP, and WINS management is performed using the respective MMC snap-ins. DNS administrators should have at least a passing familiarity with these applications. Some are useful debugging tools; others can streamline management chores, especially in large networks with many DNS, DHCP, and WINS servers. Each of these command line applications is covered in its respective section.

DNSCMD

The DNSCMD application provides command line control of local or remote Windows 2000 DNS servers. It can manage the cache, reset secondary DNS zones, and add and delete resource records from primary and Active Directory–integrated DNS zones.

NOTE: DNSCMD will not be installed when the Windows 2000 DNS service is installed. DNSCMD is part of the Windows 2000 Support Tools that are found on the Windows 2000 installation CD-ROM.

DNSCMD has a large number of available options. These are listed when the program is run without any arguments, as shown below:

```
C:\Program Files\Support Tools>dnscmd

USAGE:  DnsCmd <ServerName> <Command> [<Command Parameters>]

    <ServerName>:
            .                   -- local machine using LPC
        IP address              -- RPC over TCP/IP
        DNS name                -- RPC over TCP/IP
        other server name       -- RPC over named pipes
    <Command>:
        /Info                   -- Get server information
        /Config                 -- Reset server or zone configuration
        /EnumZones              -- Enumerate zones
        /Statistics             -- Query/clear server statistics data
        /ClearCache             -- Clear DNS server cache
        /WriteBackFiles         -- Write back all zone or root-hint datafile(s)
        /StartScavenging        -- Initiates server scavenging
        /ResetListenAddresses -- Select server IP address(es) to serve DNS requests
```

```
        /ResetForwarders         -- Set DNS servers to forward recursive queries to

        /ZoneInfo                -- View zone information
        /ZoneAdd                 -- Create a new zone on the DNS server
        /ZoneDelete              -- Delete a zone from DNS server or DS
        /ZonePause               -- Pause a zone
        /ZoneResume              -- Resume a zone
        /ZoneReload              -- Reload zone from its database (file or DS)
        /ZoneWriteBack           -- Write back zone to file
        /ZoneRefresh             -- Force refresh of secondary zone from master
        /ZoneUpdateFromDs        -- Update a DS integrated zone by data from DS
        /ZoneResetType           -- Change zone type Primary/Secondary/DSintegrated

        /ZoneResetSecondaries -- Reset secondary\notify information for a zone
        /ZoneResetScavengeServers-- Reset scavenging servers for a zone
        /ZoneResetMasters        -- Reset secondary zone's master servers
        /EnumRecords             -- Enumerate records at a name
        /RecordAdd               -- Create a record in zone or RootHints
        /RecordDelete            -- Delete a record from zone, RootHints or Cache data
        /NodeDelete              -- Delete all records at a name
        /AgeAllRecords           -- Force aging on node(s) in zone
<Command Parameters>:
    -- parameters specific to each Command
    dnscmd <CommandName> /? -- For help info on specific Command
```

DNSCMD performs one operation on one DNS server. The DNS server can be specified by name or address. If the local Windows 2000 computer is running a DNS service, it can be referenced using a period. An IP address, including a local IP address, can be used to designate a DNS server. A domain name can be used if it resolves to the IP address of the desired DNS server. This assumes that the DNS client on the computer that is running the DNSCMD command is referencing a DNS server that will resolve the name as desired.

Named pipes are an interprocess communication programming mechanism supported by Windows 2000. From an administrator's point of view, it is simply the NetBIOS name of the computer running the Windows 2000 DNS service. This allows reference to a computer using \\server1 instead of server1.largecompany.com, assuming these were the NetBIOS and DNS names for the same computer. For example, the following two command lines result in the same action:

```
DNSCMD \\server1 /zoneinfo largecompany.com
DNSCMD server1.largecompany.com /zoneinfo largecompany.com
```

NOTE: If a DNS server is set up to listen to specific IP addresses and an IP address is used to specify this DNS server, the specified IP address must match one that the DNS server is listening to. A DNS server can listen on all IP addresses assigned to a server or one or more specified IP addresses.

The server reference is always followed by a command option. The command may have zero or more arguments following it; these arguments are outlined in the following sections along with a description of the command.

If you are just starting to experiment with DNSCMD, check out the /Info, /Config, /EnumRecords, /EnumZones, /Statistics, and /ZoneInfo commands. These do not affect the operation of the DNS server or the contents of a zone or the cache; instead, they simply provide information about the current configuration.

The commands shown in Table 19-1 perform general nondestructive operations such as clearing the cache or reloading

Command	Operation Performed
/ClearCache	Clear DNS server cache
/StartScavenging	Initiate server scavenging
/WriteBackFiles	Write back all zone or root hint datafile(s)
/ZonePause	Pause a zone
/ZoneResume	Resume a zone
/ZoneReload	Reload zone from its database
/ZoneWriteBack	Write back zone to file
/ZoneRefresh	Force refresh of secondary zone from master
/ZoneUpdateFromDs	Update an Active Directory–integrated zone
/AgeAllRecords	Force aging on node(s) in zone

Table 19-1. Commands that Perform General Nondestructive Operations

zone information. The /ZonePause command will leave a zone in an inaccessible state, but no information will be lost.

The remaining commands perform operations that modify the configuration of the DNS server or one of the zones that it manages. These should be used only after the user understands a command's operation and implication. It is best to create a dummy zone to experiment with or to use a DNS server that is operating in a noncritical environment when experimenting with these commands. The commands include those shown in Table 19-2.

DNSCMD can be used from the command line, but it is typically used in batch files to perform a sequence of operations. The following

Command	Operation Performed
/ZoneResetType	Change zone type to Primary/Secondary/DSintegrated
/ResetListenAddresses	Select server IP address(es) to serve DNS requests
/ResetForwarders	Set DNS servers to forward recursive queries to
/ZoneResetSecondaries	Reset secondary\notify information for a zone
/ZoneResetScavengeServers	Reset scavenging servers for a zone
/ZoneResetMasters	Reset secondary zone's master servers
/ZoneAdd	Create a new zone on the DNS server
/ZoneDelete	Delete a zone from DNS server or DS
/RecordAdd	Create a record in zone or RootHints
/RecordDelete	Delete a record from zone, RootHints, or Cache data
/NodeDelete	Delete all records at a name

Table 19-2.   Commands that Modify the Configuration of the DNS Server or One of the Zones It Manages

sample batch file, DnsAddPrimaryZone.BAT, shows how DNSCMD can be used:

```
@ECHO OFF
; This batch file creates a new primary DNS zone
IF "%1" == '''' GOTO HELP
IF "%2" == '''' GOTO LOCAL
IF "%3" == '''' GOTO FULL
GOTO ERROR
:FULL
DNSCMD %1 /AddZone %2 /Primary /file %2.dns
DNSCMD %1 /ZoneInfo %2
GOTO DONE
:LOCAL
DNSCMD . /AddZone %1 /Primary /file %1.dns
DNSCMD . /ZoneInfo %1
GOTO DONE
:ERROR
ECHO *** Syntax error ***
:HELP
; Note: %0 is the name of the batch file.
ECHO SYNTAX:  %0 [DNS_Server] Zone_name
ECHO EXAMPLE: %0 10.10.10.1  foo.bar.com
ECHO EXAMPLE: %0 foo.bar.com
:DONE
```

This simple sample makes use of only two commands, but it does simplify and hide the use of DNSCMD. In this case, the zone file name is assumed to follow the Windows 2000 DNS convention of appending .dns to the zone name. The batch file also prints out the status of the zone after it is created.

Batch files can be as complex as necessary. They can even be generated by applications. For example, a Visual Basic application could process third-party DNS zone files or a hardware inventory report to create a batch file that would create a new zone file populated by information extracted from these sources.

DNSCMD can be very handy after you understand how to use the various commands.

DNSCMD /Info

The /Info command presents information about a Windows 2000 DNS server. When entered with no arguments, it presents information about the DNS server using the following layout:

```
C:\>dnscmd . /info
Query result:
Server info:
        ptr                    = 00075AD8
        server name            = server1.largecompany.com
        version                = C2000005
        DS container           = c
    Configuration:
        dwLogLevel                 = 00000000
        dwDebugLevel               = 00000000
        dwRpcProtocol              = FFFFFFFF
        dwNameCheckFlag            = 00000002
        cAddressAnswerLimit        = 0
        dwRecursionRetry           = 3
        dwRecursionTimeout         = 15
        dwDsPollingInterval        = 300
    Configuration Flags:
        fBootMethod                    = 3
        fAdminConfigured               = 1
        fAllowUpdate                   = 1
        fDsAvailable                   = 1
        fAutoReverseZones              = 1
        fAutoCacheUpdate               = 0
        fSlave                         = 0
        fNoRecursion                   = 0
```

```
        fRoundRobin              = 1
        fLocalNetPriority        = 1
        fStrictFileParsing       = 0
        fLooseWildcarding        = 0
        fBindSecondaries         = 1
        fWriteAuthorityNs        = 0
Aging Configuration:
        ScavengingInterval       = 0
        DefaultAgingState        = 0
        DefaultRefreshInterval   = 168
        DefaultNoRefreshInterval = 168
ServerAddresses:
        Addr Count = 3
                Addr[0] => 123.123.123.1
                Addr[1] => 192.168.0.1
                Addr[2] => 10.10.10.150
ListenAddresses:
        NULL IP Array.
Forwarders:
        NULL IP Array.
        forward timeout  = 5
        slave            = 0
Command completed successfully.
```

The complete listing is useful when an administrator wants an overview, but extracting details using programs like grep can be tedious and there is the potential for errors. The alternative is to display only the information that is desired and then use an extraction program to obtain the desired information.

NOTE: The grep program is a command file search and extraction program that processes a text file based upon command line arguments passed to grep. Grep is not included with Windows 2000, but free versions can be found on the Internet at www.shareware.com. It is also included with a number of other products.

The single argument for the /Info command may be one of the following:

BootMethod	RpcProtocol	LogLevel
EventlogLevel	NoRecursion	ForwardDelegations
ForwardingTimeout	IsSlave	SecureResponses
RecursionRetry	RecursionTimeout	MaxCacheTtl
MaxNegativeCacheTtl	RoundRobin	LocalNetPriority
AddressAnswerLimit	BindSecondaries	WriteAuthorityNs
NameCheckFlag	StrictFileParsing	UpdateOptions
DisableAutoReverseZones	SendPort	NoTcp
XfrConnectTimeout	DsPollingInterval	DsTombstoneInterval
ScavengingInterval	DefaultAgingState	DefaultNoRefreshInterval
DefaultRefreshInterval		

The /Info argument is case sensitive as shown in the following example.

```
C:\>dnscmd . /info scavenginginterval
Info query failed.
      Status = 9553 (0x00002551)


Command failed:  DNS_ERROR_INVALID_PROPERTY    9553 (00002551)

C:\>dnscmd . /info ScavengingInterval
Query result:
Dword:  0 (00000000)
Command completed successfully.
```

The argument names are self-explanatory. Although the same information is available from the DNS MMC snap-in, it is often faster to use the DNSCMD /Info, as with many command line utilities.

DNSCMD /Config

The /Config command is used to set attributes of a Windows 2000 DNS server or an existing zone. The command can have these two forms:

```
DnsCmd <ServerName> /Config <ServerProperty> <Value>
DnsCmd <ServerName> /Config <ZoneName> <ZoneProperty> <Value>
```

The <ZoneName> can be a normal DNS zone name or the string ..AllZones. In the latter case, the <ZoneProperty> for all the zones managed by the server is set to <Value>. The <Value> is assumed to be decimal unless it is prefixed with 0x, in which case it is a hexadecimal value.

Following are <ServerProperty> values:

/RpcProtocol	/LogLevel	/EventlogLevel
/NoRecursion	/ForwardDelegations	/ForwardingTimeout
/IsSlave	/SecureResponses	/RecursionRetry
/RecursionTimeout	/MaxCacheTtl	/MaxNegativeCacheTtl
/RoundRobin	/LocalNetPriority	/AddressAnswerLimit
/BindSecondaries	/WriteAuthorityNs	/NameCheckFlag
/StrictFileParsing	/UpdateOptions	/DisableAutoReverseZones
/SendPort	/NoTcp	/XfrConnectTimeout
/DsPollingInterval	/DsTombstoneInterval	/ScavengingInterval
/DefaultAgingState	/DefaultNoRefreshInterval	/DefaultRefreshInterval

The following is a list of <ZoneProperty> values:

▼ /SecureSecondaries

■ /AllowUpdate

■ /Aging

■ /RefreshInterval

▲ /NoRefreshInterval

DNSCMD /EnumZones

The /EnumZones command will list the specified DNS zones managed by the DNS server. It does not list the contents of the zones. Refer to the NSLOOKUP section for details on listing the contents of a zone.

The syntax for the /EnumZones command is

DnsCmd <ServerName> /EnumZones [<Filter1>] [<Filter2>]

With no arguments, the command will list all forward and reverse zones. It indicates whether a zone is an Active Directory–integrated

DNS zone using the designation DS. The filters allow a subset of zones to be presented. The <Filter1> values include the following:

- ▼ /Primary
- ■ /Secondary
- ■ /Cache
- ■ /Auto-Created
- ▲ /DS

The <Filter2> values include the following:

- ▼ /Forward
- ▲ /Reverse

If a filter is not included, all the options are assumed. It is not possible to include a list of filters such as /DS and /Cache.

DNSCMD /Statistics

The Windows DNS service maintains a number of statistics that can be useful in determining whether the service is running properly and the load being placed on the service. The statistical counters can be cleared to track statistics relative to that time. Only one set of statistics is maintained, so old information is lost if the counters are cleared.

The syntax for the /Statistics command is

```
DnsCmd <ServerName> /Statistics [<FilterValue> | <FilterName> | /Clear]
```

The /Clear argument will clear the statistical counters. The <FilterValue> and <FilterName> values are listed in Table 19-3.

A single <FilterName> can be used. The <FilterValue> can be any one listed in the table or it can be a logical combination. For example, 0x00000007 would display the statistics for Time, Query, and Query2.

DNSCMD /ClearCache

This is an easy one. The /ClearCache command clears the DNS service's cache. The command takes no arguments and simply

<FilterName>	<FilterValue> (hex value)
Time	0x00000001
Query	0x00000002
Query2	0x00000004
Recurse	0x00000008
Master	0x00000010
Secondary	0x00000020
Wins	0x00000040
Update	0x00000100
SkwanSec	0x00000200
Ds	0x00000400
Memory	0x00001000
PacketMem	0x00010000
SkwanSec	0x00020000
Dbase	0x00040000
Records	0x00080000
NbstatMem	0x00200000

Table 19-3.   DnsCmd /Statistics Arguments

indicates whether the operation succeeded or failed. Failure will occur if the user has insufficient access rights or if the server is inaccessible.

DNSCMD /WriteBackFiles

Changes made to a primary zone are not always written back to the zone file and are sometimes maintained by the DNS server in its local database. This makes dynamic DNS updates faster and allows changes to be made that may be undone by reloading the zone information.

The syntax for the /WriteBackFiles command is

DnsCmd <ServerName> /WriteBackFiles [<ZoneName>]

The /WriteBackFiles command updates all the primary zone files managed by the DNS server, including the root-hint file, if the command is used with no arguments. A specific zone file can be updated as well. The <ZoneName> must be the FQDN for the zone.

DNSCMD /StartScavenging

The Windows 2000 DNS server will periodically scavenge its internal database for resource records that have expired. Scavenging can reduce the size of the database and thereby improve performance.

Scavenging can be initiated using the /StartScavenging command. It can also be scheduled and initiated from the DNS MMC snap-in.

DNSCMD /ResetListenAddresses

The Windows 2000 DNS server can listen for DNS requests on all network adapters if the listen address list is empty. It will listen on specific adapters based upon the IP addresses they support if the list is not empty.

The syntax for the /ResetListenAddresses command is

DnsCmd <ServerName> /ResetListenAddresses [<IP Address> ...]

The /ResetListenAddresses command is used to set up this list. The list is emptied when the command starts. Zero or more IP addresses may be provided as arguments to the command. These IP addresses are then placed in the listen address list. The change affects server operation immediately.

DNSCMD /ResetForwarders

The Windows 2000 DNS server can forward DNS requests if it cannot resolve the request using local information in the server's DNS zone files or the DNS cache. Unresolved requests are sent to each DNS server in the forwarders list until the end of the list is encountered or the request is handled by a DNS server.

The syntax for the /ResetForwarders command is

DnsCmd <ServerName> /ResetForwarders [<IP Address> ...]
[/[No]Slave] [/Timeout <Time>]

The /ResetForwarders command is used to set up the forwarders
list. The list is emptied when the command starts. Zero or more IP
addresses may be provided as arguments to the command. These IP
addresses are then placed in the forwarder list. The change affects
server operation immediately.

The DNS server can be set up to act as a slave with the /Slave
argument. The default condition is /NoSlave. The /Timeout <Time>
value is the time the DNS server will wait for each DNS server in the
list to respond. The value is in seconds.

DNSCMD /ZoneInfo

The /ZoneInfo command is used to display a zone's properties. The
syntax for the /ZoneInfo command is

DnsCmd <ServerName> /ZoneInfo <ZoneName> [<ZoneProperty>]

The <ZoneName> must match a zone defined on the DNS server. All
zone property values will be displayed if there is no <ZoneProperty>.
A single zone property will be displayed if one of the <ZoneProperty>
values listed in Table 19-4 is used.

<ZoneProperty>	Description
AllowUpdate	Does zone allow dynamic DNS updates?
DSIntegrated	Is the zone an Active Directory–integrated DNS zone?
Aging	Is resource record aging enabled?
RefreshInterval	Refresh time in seconds
NoRefreshInterval	Is refresh enabled?

Table 19-4.   DnsCmd /ZoneInfo ZoneProperty Values

The DnsCmd /Config command can be used to set the values presented in this table.

DNSCMD /ZoneAdd

The /ZoneAdd command will add a new zone to a Windows 2000 DNS server. The syntax for the /ZoneAdd command is

DnsCmd <ServerName> /ZoneAdd <ZoneName> <ZoneType>

The <ZoneName> must be an FQDN that does not exist on the DNS server. The <ZoneType> includes the following information:

▼ /DsPrimary

■ /Primary /file <filename> [/load] [/a <AdminName>]

▲ /Secondary <MasterIPAddress> … [/file <filename>]

The /DsPrimary option is used to create an Active Directory–integrated DNS zone. This means that the Windows 2000 DNS server must be a domain controller with Active Directory installed. Primary and secondary DNS zones can be created on any Windows 2000 DNS server.

The /Primary option creates a primary DNS zone. The zone <filename> must be specified. Typically, it is the zone's FQDN plus .dns. The /load option indicates that the file already exists and that its contents are to be used for the zone. The /a option is used to set the administrator's e-mail address name in the zone's SOA record.

The /Secondary option creates a secondary DNS zone. There must be one <MasterIPAddress>, but there may be more. The IP address is the address of a DNS server that will provide the DNS zone information. The list of IP addresses is used to find a DNS server that will initially provide the zone information. The list is also used when the zone information needs to be refreshed. At least one of the DNS servers in the list must be available to update the secondary DNS zone, although the zone will be set up regardless of whether it can be initially updated.

DNSCMD /ZoneDelete

The /ZoneDelete command is used to delete a zone definition from a
Windows 2000 DNS server. The syntax for the /ZoneDelete
command is

DnsCmd <ServerName> /ZoneDelete <ZoneName> [/DsDel] [/f]

The <ZoneName> must be an FQDN, and it must exist on the
DNS server. Active Directory–integrated DNS zones, primary DNS
zones, and secondary zones can be deleted. DnsCmd will prompt
for verification if the /f option is not included. The /DsDel option
is only applicable for Active Directory–integrated DNS zones.
Normally, the zone will only be deleted from the DNS server and
the information will be left in the Active Directory database.
Adding the /DsDel option will remove the information from the
Active Directory database as well. This can only be done if the Active
Directory–integrated DNS zone is the last one defined in the Active
Directory domain.

DNSCMD /ZonePause and /ZoneResume

The NET program can be used to start and stop the Windows 2000
DNS service. /ZonePause and /ZoneResume are used to pause and
resume the zone. When paused, a zone will not be used to resolve
names, secondary DNS zones will not be updated, and the zone will
not be scavenged.

The /ZonePause command is followed by a single argument,
an FQDN. A paused zone can be restarted using the/ZoneResume
command.

DNSCMD /ZoneReload

Changes can be made to a primary DNS zone, but they will not be
updated until a /ZoneWriteBack command is performed. Primary
DNS zone information can come from a file or the Active Directory
database, depending upon how the primary DNS zone is configured.

The /ZoneReload command takes an FQDN as an argument. The file that a primary DNS zone uses is already defined when the zone is created.

See the sections on the DNSCMD /ZoneRefresh command for secondary DNS zones and /ZoneUpdateFromDs for Active Directory–integrated DNS zones.

DNSCMD /ZoneWriteBack

Changes made to a primary or Active Directory–integrated DNS zone will be saved when the /ZoneWriteBack command is executed. The argument is an FQDN. Changes can be discarded by using the /ZoneReload command.

DNSCMD /ZoneRefresh

A secondary DNS zone can be updated using the /ZoneRefresh command. A single argument is an FQDN of the secondary DNS zone. A secondary DNS zone will be updated when it is created and when the timeout interval for the zone has expired.

The /ZoneRefresh command is normally used on DNS servers with secondary zones after the related primary or Active Directory–integrated DNS zone has been changed. DNSCMD is often used to make these changes.

DNSCMD /ZoneUpdateFromDs

Active Directory–integrated DNS zones can be reloaded from the Active Directory database to clear changes made to the zone. This function is similar to the /ZoneReload and /ZoneRefresh commands for primary and secondary DNS zones.

The /ZoneUpdateFromDs command takes one argument, the FQDN of the Active Directory–integrated DNS zone.

DNSCMD /ZoneResetType

A zone's type can be changed just as it can from the DNS MMC snap-in. The syntax for the /ZoneResetType is

DnsCmd <ServerName> /ZoneResetType <ZoneName> <ZoneType> [<ZoneOption>]

The <ZoneName> is an FQDN of an existing DNS zone. The <ZoneType> may be one of the following:

▼ /DsPrimary

■ /Primary /file <filename>

▲ /Secondary <MasterIPAddress> … [/file <filename>]

The /DsPrimary option will change a primary or secondary DNS zone to an Active Directory–integrated DNS zone. The contents of the existing zone are moved to the Active Directory database.

The /Primary option sets up a primary DNS zone. The zone information is placed in the <filename> file.

The /Secondary options sets up a secondary DNS zone. Any existing zone information is lost since a secondary DNS zone obtains its information from one of the DNS servers in the MasterIPAddress list. The secondary zone's <filename> is optional. If it is not supplied, the <ZoneName> is used as part of the file name.

The <ZoneOption> may be /OverWrite_Mem or /OverWrite_Ds. The former uses information the Active Directory database. The latter uses information from the DNS server's local database to update the Active Directory database if an Active Directory–integrated DNS zone is created.

DNSCMD /ZoneResetSecondaries

Any DNS zone can be used to provide information to a secondary DNS zone on another DNS server. The /ZoneResetSecondaries command is used to configure how this process will work. The syntax for the /ZoneResetSecondaries command is

DnsCmd <ServerName> /ZoneResetSecondaries <ZoneName> [<Secure>] [<Notify>]

The <ZoneName> is an FQDN of an existing DNS zone. The <Secure> option may one of the following:

- ▼ /NoXfr
- ■ /NonSecure
- ■ /SecureNs
- ▲ /SecureList <SecondaryIPAddress> ...

The /NoXfr option disables secondary DNS zone updates. The /NonSecure option allows any DNS server to request a secondary DNS zone update for the zone. The /SecureNs option allows the DNS zone to be used only by DNS servers that have NS resource records listed in the zone. The /SecureList option specifies DNS servers by IP address that can request secondary DNS zone updates.

The <Notify> option may be one of the following:

- ▼ /NoNotify
- ■ /Notify
- ▲ /NotifyList <NotifyIPAddress> ...

The /NoNotify option indicates that the zone will not send out notification messages when changes are made to the zone. The /Notify option indicates that notification messages will be sent to all DNS servers that have NS resource records listed in the zone. The /NotifyList option indicates notification messages will be sent to DNS servers in the NotifyIPAddress list.

DNSCMD /ZoneResetScavengeServers

If scavenging is enabled for a zone, the /ZoneResetScavengeServers command can be used to specify what server can perform this operation. The syntax for the /ZoneResetScavengeServers command is

DnsCmd <ServerName> /ZoneResetScavengeServers
<ZoneName> [<ServerIPAddress> ...]

If the <ServerIPAddress> list is empty, any server can scavenge a zone; otherwise, only those DNS servers listed can do so.

DNSCMD /ZoneResetMasters

A secondary DNS zone receives its information from a master DNS server. The list of master DNS servers is set when the secondary DNS zone is created. The /ZoneResetMasters command is used to change this list. The syntax for this command is

DnsCmd <ServerName> /ZoneResetMasters <ZoneName>
<ServerIPAddress> ...

There must be at least one IP address in the <ServerIPAddress> list. As with any secondary DNS zone configuration, the master DNS server hierarchy should not include any circular references. For example, if DNS server B gets its secondary DNS zone information from DNS server A, then A should not be set up to get its secondary DNS zone information for the same zone as DNS server B.

DNSCMD /EnumRecords

The /EnumRecords command is used to display a set of resource records from a zone. It is not as powerful as the NSLOOKUP program, but it can come in handy when using DNSCMD to configure a DNS zone. The syntax for the /EnumRecords command is

DnsCmd <ServerName> /EnumRecords <ZoneName>
<NodeName> [<DataOptions>] [<ViewOptions>]

The /EnumRecords command lists all the resource records associated with a particular <NodeName> in the zone. If the <NodeName> is @, it means the zone root is used. The <NodeName> can be relative to the zone root or an FQDN. The latter always ends with a period.

The <DataOptions> include the following:

▼ /Type <RRType>

■ /Authority

■ /Glue

■ /Additional

■ /Node

■ /Child

▲ /StartChild <ChildName>

The /Type option is followed by a resource record type such as A, PTR, or NS. The default type is A. Only one type can be included at a time. The /Authority option indicates that authoritative data is also displayed. The /Glue option displays glue data, and /Additional displays any extra information associated with the node.

The /Node option specifies that only the named node will be displayed. Child nodes will not be displayed. This is the default. The /Child option displays all child nodes in addition to the specified node. The following will display all the child nodes in a zone:

```
DNSCMD . /EnumRecords @ /Child
```

NOTE: The /Child option is not recursive. Only the child nodes of the specified node are listed, not the children of subdomains. Subdomains are not listed.

The /StartChild option is similar to the /Child option except that the listing starts with the specified child node.

The <ViewOptions> include the following:

▼ /Continue

▲ /Detail

More than one of the <ViewOptions> can be included. The /Continue option will display all the requested information in the zone; if it is not used, only the first buffer of information will be displayed. The size of the buffer seems to be arbitrary, so use /Continue if all information must be displayed. The default condition is designed for very large zones that may require more than one buffer to deliver information.

The /Detail option changes the display from the default display format, which is similar to the zone file format, to a detailed list of attributes for each node.

DNSCMD /RecordAdd

The /RecordAdd command is used to add a new resource record to a zone. The syntax for this command is

> DnsCmd <ServerName> /RecordAdd <ZoneName>
> <NodeName> [/Aging] [<TTL>] <RRType> <RRData>

The layout is different than a zone file, but the details are the same with the exception of the /Aging option. The <TTL> option is the time-to-live in seconds. The <RRType> can be any valid type including SOA. The <RRDate> is specific to the <RRType>.

DNSCMD /RecordDelete

The /RecordDelete command is used to remove an existing resource record from a zone. The syntax for this command is

> DnsCmd <ServerName> /RecordDelete <ZoneName>
> <NodeName> <RRType> <RRData> [/f]

Only the matching resource record will be deleted. DnsCmd will prompt prior to the deletion if the /f option is not included.

DNSCMD /NodeDelete

The /NodeDelete command is used to remove all existing resource records for the matching node within a zone. The syntax for this command is

> DnsCmd <ServerName> /NodeDelete <ZoneName>
> <NodeName> [/Tree] [/f]

All resource records with the matching <NodeName> will be deleted. DnsCmd will prompt prior to the deletion if the /f option is not included. All nodes in the subdomain will be deleted if the /Tree option is included. The process is recursive.

DNSCMD /AgeAllRecords

The /AgeAllRecords command is used to age the specified resource records within a zone. The syntax for this command is

DnsCmd <ServerName> / AgeAllRecords <ZoneName> <NodeName> [/Tree] [/f]

All resource records with the matching <NodeName> will be aged. DnsCmd will prompt prior to aging if the /f option is not included. All nodes in the subdomain will be aged if the /Tree option is included. The process is recursive.

IPCONFIG

IPCONFIG is a client-oriented utility. It can display the current IP and adapter configuration details. It can flush the DNS client's resolver cache and release and renew the PC's IP address if DHCP is used.

IPCONFIG does not display routing information. The ROUTE command, not covered in this book, can provide this information. Run ROUTE with no parameters, and it will present a list of options that can be used with the ROUTE command.

Running IPCONFIG by itself will list an abbreviated status of the current IP configuration. Run IPCONFIG with an argument of /?, and the following listing will be presented:

```
C:\>ipconfig /?

Windows 2000 IP Configuration


USAGE:
```

```
ipconfig [/? | /all | /release [adapter] | /renew [adapter]
        | /flushdns | /registerdns
        | /showclassid adapter
        | /setclassid adapter [classidtoset] ]


adapter    Full name or pattern with '*' and '?' to 'match',
           * matches any character, ? matches one character.
Options
   /?            Display this help message.
   /all          Display full configuration information.
   /release      Release the IP address for the specified adapter.
   /renew        Renew the IP address for the specified adapter.
   /flushdns     Purges the DNS Resolver cache.
   /registerdns Refreshes all DHCP leases and re-registers DNS names
   /displaydns   Display the contents of the DNS Resolver Cache.
   /showclassid Displays all the dhcp class IDs allowed for adapter.
   /setclassid  Modifies the dhcp class id.
```

The /all option presents a complete listing of all IP-related configuration settings. This includes every adapter. If the adapter is configured with multiple IP addresses, each is listed, along with the netmask for the IP address. Additional details are also presented, such as whether DHCP, WINS, or IP routing is enabled. Even the NetBIOS node type is listed. The host (PC) name and primary DNS suffix are also presented. The PC's DNS name is the concatenation of these two. This will be the name that is sent to the PC's DNS server via dynamic DNS update.

The /release and /renew options are used to release IP addresses obtained from a DHCP server. The options are only applicable if one or more of the network adapters are configured to use DHCP. An error message will be displayed if these options are used and no network adapters use DHCP.

NOTE: IPCONFIG /renew will perform an implicit DHCP release if an adapter that uses DHCP has an IP address leased to it. The /release operation will release a leased IP address, but it will do nothing if the adapter or adapters do not have an IP address leased to them. An adapter without an IP address cannot be used until a /renew operation is performed to obtain an IP address.

The optional adapter name allows individual network adapters to be controlled on a multiadapter configuration. The full adapter name can be used as an argument for the /renew or /release option. A partial name can be used with the wildcard character "*". An adapter name of Foo* will match any network adapter starting with Foo, as in Foobar. An adapter name of *NE2000* will match any adapter that includes NE2000 in any part of the adapter's name.

NOTE: The wildcard operation for the /renew and /release arguments is different from the wildcard matching used for file names with applications such as Windows Explorer or the DIR command in a DOS window. In this case, only trailing wildcard characters are allowed. Embedded or leading wildcard characters cannot be used with these applications.

The /registerdns option is similar to /renew with no options, but it will also register the PC's DNS name with the DNS servers referenced by the DNS configuration for the network adapters.

The /flushdns option clears the contents of the DNS resolver cache. The /displaydns option lists the contents of the DNS resolver cache. The cache will fill as subsequent DNS requests are made and processed.

TIP: Be prepared for a long listing if the /displaydns option is used on a DNS server or a client that has been accessing different sites using TCP/IP. In the case of a DNS server, the DNS resolver cache will be used by the local DNS client if the PC references the DNS server on the PC. The cache will also contain any information obtained by the DNS server on behalf of other DNS clients that use the DNS server for name resolution. The number of entries can be very high if the DNS server is handling many DNS requests for noncached and nonlocal DNS information.

Some DHCP services, such as the Windows 2000 DHCP service, can download custom information to a DHCP client based on the client's class ID when an IP address is leased or the lease is renewed. This is handled in the same way that the default gateway and DNS server are given to the DHCP client.

The /showclassid option will display the current class ID setting for a specific adapter or a group of adapters if the PC has more than one. The /setclassid option can be used to change the class ID.

NET

The NET program performs a large number of actions, but in this book we will concentrate on only the few that are relevant to DNS, DHCP, and WINS service management. Basic NET command syntax is displayed when the program is run with no arguments. The HELP option provides more details.

The NET program is primarily used for three purposes: managing services, managing users and groups, and managing network resources. In this section, we will concentrate on service management. User and group management support can be used with DNS, DHCP, and WINS service security management, but these operations will not be covered in this book. Typically, these security management functions will be used to add or delete users from groups that manage these services. Network resource management allows network shares to be created, removed, and utilized. These operations are handy when managing files on a remote PC, but usually the shares will be created only once. The use of the NET program is handy when you need a large number of servers to be configured in the same way.

The syntax for the service management operations is

NET <Action> <Service>

The <Action> may be Start, Stop, or Pause. The <Service> option may be one of the following:

ALERTER	CLIENT SERVICE FOR NETWARE	CLIPBOARD SERVER
COMPUTER BROWSER	DHCP CLIENT	DHCP SERVER
DNS CLIENT	DNS SERVER	DIRECTORY REPLICATOR
EVENTLOG	LPDSVC	MESSENGER
NET LOGON	NETWORK DDE	NETWORK DDE DSDM

NETWORK MONITORING AGENT	NT LM SECURITY SUPPORT PROVIDER	PLUG AND PLAY
REMOTE ACCESS CONNECTION MANAGER	REMOTE ACCESS ISNSAP SERVICE	REMOTE ACCESS SERVER
REMOTE PROCEDURE CALL (RPC) LOCATOR	REMOTE PROCEDURE CALL (RPC) SERVICE	SERVER
SIMPLE TCP/IP SERVICES	SNMP	SPOOLER
TASK SCHEDULER	TCPIP NETBIOS HELPER	UPS
WORKSTATION	WINDOWS INTERNET NAMING SERVICE	

The <Service> option should be bounded by double quotes if the value listed above includes an embedded space. For example:

```
NET STOP "DNS SERVER"
```

Service names can also be found by starting the Services management application from Start | Program | Administrative Tools | Services. The names listed by this application are the complete list of services that can be started, paused, or stopped using the NET program.

In addition, the Start option can be used with no <Service> option. In this case, the list of currently running services is presented. This is handy when pausing or stopping a service.

Of course, the services that you are interested in include the DNS, DHCP, and WINS clients and servers. Service control is typically done in conjunction with changes to the configuration files associated with the services.

NETSH

The NETSH program is used to manage the Windows 2000 DHCP and WINS services. It is also used to configure network interfaces, RAS (Remote Access Service), and routing. Unlike the NET and DNSCMD programs, the NETSH program operates in one of three modes: per command, via a script file, or interactively.

In the per command mode, NETSH executes the command specified as arguments to the NETSH program. The program terminates when the command has been executed. The script file mode executes a sequence of commands found in a text script file. The file is specified as an argument to the NETSH program. The program terminates when all the commands have been executed. The interactive mode allows the user to enter commands. The *exit*, *quit*, and *bye* commands will terminate interactive mode and the NETSH program.

The syntax of the NETSH program is

NETSH [-a <AliasFile>] [-r <RemoteMachine>] [-c <Context>]
[<Command> | -f <ScriptFile>]

The <AliasFile> allows a set of aliases to be loaded before any NETSH command is processed. An alias allows one or more commands to be executed when the alias name is entered as a command. Aliases can be entered via the Alias command when in interactive mode or when using a script file.

The local computer is used by the NETSH program by default. Services on a remote machine can be managed by specifying the <RemoteMachine> name. This will be the NetBIOS name of the computer.

Interactive mode is entered if a <Command> or <ScriptFile> is not specified. Interactive mode operates in a specified context that can be changed. Commands are specific to the context. The default context is netsh.

The context names are also used to change from one context to another. The valid <Context> names include the following:

▼ aaaa

■ dhcp

■ interface

■ ras

■ routing

▲ wins

Some contexts have subcontexts. For example, the routing context has an ip and an ipx subcontext. As with a context, the subcontexts are entered by using the subcontext name as a command. However, these subcontext commands will only apply when NETSH is in the matching context. Some subcontexts have additional subcontexts.

A context and subcontext can be concatenated as a command in interactive mode to change to the specified subcontext. In interactive mode, the current context is part of the prompt as in the following:

```
routing ip nat>
```

This is the network address translation (NAT) subcontext for the IP protocol in the routing context. This context specification can also prefix a command for the context, in which case the command is executed with respect to the context. In interactive mode, the current context will be preserved when executing a context-specified command. The following example shows the prompts and commands but not the information presented by the command:

```
netsh> wins
wins> routing ip nat
routing ip nat> routing
routing > ip
routing ip> nat
routing ip nat> exit
```

In any context, the list of commands including subcontexts that can be entered can be displayed using the question mark (?) character. A more detailed description of the commands can be displayed by typing the command followed by the question mark. This is not true for subcontexts, but it is possible to switch to the subcontext and then to type ?.

There are global commands in addition to context-specific commands. These include the following:

bye	quit	exit
exec	list	help
?	show	set
alias	unalias	pushd
popd	dump	

We will not go into detail on NETSH commands because they are so numerous, but we will describe them briefly here.

The first three global commands have already been discussed. The exec command is used to execute commands from a script file. The list, help, and ? commands are used to display online help. Use the ? command with any command for details on the syntax and semantics of a command. The show and set commands are used to display and set global and context-sensitive attributes. The alias and unalias commands are used to set and clear an alias.

The pushd and popd commands are used to preserve and restore contexts. These are typically used in interactive mode or when using script files. The following interactive mode shows how these commands affect the context:

```
netsh> wins
wins> pushd
wins> routing ip nat
routing ip nat> routing
routing > ip
routing ip> popd
wins> exit
```

The dump command is used to generate a text file that can be used as a script file with NETSH to configure a compute using the computer's current settings. Comments, preceded by a pound sign (#), are included in the dump.

The next two sections take a look at the WINS and DHCP context-specific commands.

NETSH WINS Commands

The wins context of NETSH allows actions to be performed with the WINS server. As with most NETSH contexts, the wins server context has a large number of context-sensitive commands and attributes. Actually, the wins context has one context-sensitive command, *server*. The server command actually changes to a subcontext and it can accept an argument that is the server name. For example:

```
wins >server \\sampleserver1
wins server>
```

The Wins Server subcontext-sensitive commands are shown in Table 19-5.

Command	Description
add	Add an entry to table
check	Check table integrity
delete	Delete an entry from the table
init	Initiate an operation on the table
reset	Reset configuration entry in table
set	Set value of configuration entry in table
show	Show table entry

Table 19-5. NETSH WINS Server Subcontext Commands

The table lists only the command names. We will not go into detail on the syntax and semantics of these commands as this would make this chapter much larger than it already is. The following listing shows how to find out these details using a pair of commands:

```
wins server>add ?
Add Name          - Adds a name record to the server
Add Partner       - Adds a replication partner to the server
Add PNGServer     - Adds a list of Persona Non Grata Servers for
                    the current server
wins server>add name ?

To add a name record to the WINS server database.

Syntax:

        add name [Name=]ServerName [[Endchar=]16th char in Hex]
        [[Scope=]scopename] [[RecType=]RecordType] [[Group=]GroupType]
        [[Node=]NodeType] [IP=]{address1[,address2,address3]}

Parameters:

        Name              - The name to add and register in the WINS
                            server database.
```

Endchar   – If used, the 16th character of the name in
                 hexadecimal.

Scope   – If NetBIOS scope is used, the name of the
                 scope.

RecType   – The record type: 0–Static(default),
                 1–Dynamic.

Group   – The group type: 0–Unique, 1–Group, 2–Internet
                 3–Multihomed, 4–Domain Name.

Node   – The NetBIOS node type: 0–B Node, 1–P Node,
                 3–H Node.

IP   – The list of IP addresses separated by commas
                 and enclosed by {}.

Notes: Field tags (Name=, EndChar=) are optional. If
             EndChar and Group are both used, EndChar overrides the
             Group parameter. If used, tags must be applied to all
             field parameters in the command. If tags are omitted, a
             value must be provided for each of the supported fields
             in the specified command.

Examples: add name Name=HOSTA IP={10.0.0.1}
             add name HOSTB 20 SUBNETA 0 3 1 {10.0.0.2,10.0.0.3}

             The first example command adds a default NetBIOS record
             set of the 00h, 03h, and 20h records for a computer
             named HOSTA with a mapped IP address of 10.0.0.1. The
             second example command adds a 20h record for HOSTB, a
             multihomed computer with IP addresses 10.0.0.2 and
             10.0.0.3.

In this case, the online help command shows the add command's
three formats. The second online help command presents the lengthy
description for adding a WINS host entry. Typically a WINS entry
is added automatically but often a name must be added explicitly.
This can be done using this command syntax or using the WINS
MMC snap-in.

The table referred to in Table 19-5 is the WINS database. The delete command, as expected, is the converse of the add command. The init command has an extensive list of options that provide access to actions that the WINS server can perform such as replication, backup, and scavenging. The reset command is used to reset the statistics that the WINS server can display. The show command can display these statistics as well as table entries and attributes maintained by the WINS server. The set command can be used to set these attributes.

NETSH DHCP Commands

The NETSH DHCP commands are similar to the WINS commands except that the table being managed is the DHCP server's configuration table. This includes the scopes and multicast scopes that the Windows 2000 DHCP server supports.

As with the NETSH WINS commands, the first thing that is done is to select the server to manage. With the DHCP context, it is possible to simply deal with the current computer's Windows 2000 DHCP service, but the commands do not include multicast scope support. The following is a list of the commands that are applicable from the DHCP server subcontext:

```
dhcp server>?
list                          - Lists all the commands available.
dump                          - Dumps configuration to a text file.
help                          - Displays help.
?                             - Displays help.
add                           - Adds a configuration entry to a table.
delete                        - Deletes a configuration entry from a table.
initiate                      - Initiates an operation.
set                           - Sets configuration information.
show                          - Displays information.
scope <scope-ip-address>      - To switch to the scope identified by
                                the IP Address.
mscope <mscope-name>          - To switch to the mscope identified by
                                the MScope name.
```

The add command is used to add new scopes and definitions. Anything that can be done with the DHCP MMC snap-in can be done here, as long as you can find the command

NSLOOKUP

Versions of the NSLOOKUP program can be found on almost every operating system. Windows 2000 comes with its own NSLOOKUP program that will work with any DNS server. This is important because NSLOOKUP is used as a diagnostic tool, and diagnosing DNS problems often involves checking out details from a number of DNS servers.

NSLOOKUP can execute a single action using command line parameters, or it can operate in interactive mode. The syntax for the NSLOOKUP program is

NSLOOKUP [-<command> ...]
NSLOOKUP [-<command> ...] - <DnsServer>
NSLOOKUP [-<command> ...] <Query>
NSLOOKUP [-<command> ...] <Query> <DnsServer>

NSLOOKUP does most of its work by processing a <Query> that is either a domain name or an IP address. A domain name can be relative or an FQDN. By default, the computer's DNS server is used to process a query. This can be changed by designating a <DnsServer> by name or IP address.

NOTE: The hyphen before the <DnsServer> on the NSLOOKUP command line must be followed by a space, while the hyphen before a <command> must not use a space. If you type in the hyphen wrong, the two will get reversed. This typically results in NSLOOKUP trying to execute a <DnsServer> as a command or trying to look up a DNS server with the name of a <command>.

If no <Query> is provided, NSLOOKUP enters interactive mode; if a <Query> is provided, it performs the DNS query and terminates. Any <command> is executed before the query is made. The NSLOOKUP commands are listed in Table 19-6.

NSLOOKUP commands can be combined with output redirection such as >filename or >>filename that will create or append, respectively, all output to the designated file.

The *server* command is used to change the DNS server being used. The information being queried and other attributes are configured using the *set* command. If the <value> is not included with the <keyword> for this command, the attribute is displayed; if <value> is included, it is set to the new <value>. The <keyword>s are listed in Table 19-7.

Command	Description
help	List online help
exit	Exit from NSLOOKUP
finger [<username>]	Look up <username> via Finger server
ls [<lsOption>] <DomainName>	List information about or contents of <DomainName>
lserver <DomainName>	Set default domain
root	Alias for lserver ns.nic.ddn.mil
server <DnsServer>	Set DNS server to use for queries
set all	List all attribute values
set <keyword>[=<value>]	List or set an attribute
view <filename>	View redirected file contents

Table 19-6.   NSLOOKUP Commands

Syntax	Attribute Description	Default Value
set cl[ass][=<Class>]	Query class	IN
set [no]deb[ug]	Debug mode	nodebug
set [no]d2	Exhaustive debug mode	nod2
set [no]def[name]	Use default domain name for relative queries	defname
set do[main][=<DomainName>]	Set default domain name	.
set [no]ig[nore]	Ignore truncation errors	ignore
set po[rt][=<Port>]	DNS port number	53
set q[uerytype][=<RRType>]	Query type	A
set [no]rec[urse]	Recursive query	recurse
set ret[ry]	Retry timeout in seconds	4
set ro[ot]	DNS root	ns.nic.ddn.mil
set [no]sea[rch]	Search subdomains of default domain for relative queries	search
set srchl[ist] [<DomainName> [/<DomainName> ...]]	Default domain search list (up to 6 <DomainName>s)	
set ti[meout][=<Timeout>]	Query timeout in seconds	5
set ty[pe][=<RRType>]	Alias for querytype	A
set [no]v[c]	Virtual circuit operation	novc

Table 19-7.   NSLOOKUP SET Commands

The following is a list of simple command line requests using NSLOOKUP:

```
C:>nslookup wong1.dom  123.123.123.1
Server:  server1.largecompany.com
Address:  123.123.123.1


Name:   wong1.dom
Address:  123.123.123.8


C:>nslookup -type=MX foo.sample.largecompany.com 123.123.123.20
Server:  ns2.largecompany.com
Address:  123.123.123.20


foo.sample.largecompany.com    MX preference = 10, mail exchanger = mail.largecompany.com
foo.sample.largecompany.com    MX preference = 5, mail exchanger = 123.123.123.44
```

```
server1.largecompany.com          internet address = 123.123.123.1
mail.local.largecompany.com       internet address = 192.168.0.1
mail.test.largecompany.com        internet address = 10.10.10.150
```

The first command is a simple query that will check for address (A) resource records. The second command specifies mail exchange (MX) resource records. The results show that one mail server address is available where delivery is at a relative cost of 10, while four are available with a relative cost of 5.

The following is an interactive NSLOOKUP session.

```
C:\usr\local\bin>nslookup
Default Server:  server1.largecompany.com
Address:  123.123.123.1

> set type=ns
> largecompany.com
Server:  server1.largecompany.com
Address:  123.123.123.1

largecompany.com            nameserver = server1.largecompany.com
server1.largecompany.com          internet address = 123.123.123.1
server1.largecompany.com          internet address = 192.168.0.1
server1.largecompany.com          internet address = 10.10.10.150
> set type=a
> server1
Server:  server1.largecompany.com
Address:  123.123.123.1

Name:     server1.largecompany.com
Addresses:  123.123.123.1, 10.10.10.150, 192.168.0.1

>exit
```

This example shows some minor attribute changes and two searches. The first is for mail exchange (MX) records, while the second is for an address (A) resource record. The session is terminated by the last command. The ls command was not used, as this dumps a large amount of information for even a small domain. It can be handy when trying to determine what a domain or subdomain contains such as a subdomain used for dynamic DNS updates.

NSLOOKUP is one tool every DNS administrator should be aware of. It provides a quick way of verifying the operation of a DNS server as well as its links to other DNS servers.

SUMMARY

Network management has always involved command line utilities, and even with snazzy looking interfaces like MMC there is still a need for them. In many instances, command line operation will be more customizable and faster than using the graphical tools.

Custom applications can be written that perform these functions, but most network administrators will turn to programmers only as a last resort. Writing batch files using the command line programs presented in this chapter is usually sufficient.

The DNSCMD application is specific to the Windows 2000 DNS service. It allows configuration and diagnostics to be performed with relative ease. NSLOOKUP provides a service that is not available in the DNS MMC snap-in, the ability to resolve names. As noted, it is a handy debugging tool that can be used on any DNS client, including a PC running a Windows DNS service.

Like NSLOOKUP, IPCONFIG is a client-side diagnostic tool. IPCONFIG addresses both DNS and DHCP client support for a Windows 2000 workstation or server. It has more features than the Windows 9x version.

NET provides an extensive set of functions, but those appropriate for use with the Windows 2000 DNS, DHCP, and WINS services are limited. Still, without the NET command, many actions could not be performed via batch files because services wouldn't be able to be started or stopped using a batch file.

The NETSH command addresses Windows 2000 DHCP and WINS services in a fashion similar to DNSCMD and DNSSTAT, although NETSH provides an interactive as well as a command- and batch-oriented interface.

Keeping track of command line options and command line applications is no easy task, but these applications are typically incorporated into batch files. The batch file programmer, often the network administrator, simply needs to know what these applications are and what options they support when the batch file is being created and tested. Windows 2000's online help is a useful starting point, but trail-and-error is often an even better teacher.

CHAPTER 20

Remote DNS Management

M anaging a single DNS server is a snap if you can sit in front of the console and work with the management tools. Still, it would be convenient to be able to manage the DNS service, and other Windows 2000 services, from a Windows 2000 Professional workstation or from any Windows 2000 server. It would be better still if the management could be done from any workstation.

Windows 2000 is actually quite flexible when it comes to remote management. Most of the Microsoft Management Console (MMC) snap-ins that come with Windows 2000 can manage on any Windows 2000 computer on the network. Windows 2000 systems running the Windows 2000 Terminal Services provide a remote control environment where a client on the network can run a session on the Windows 2000 server and provide administrators access to management applications. Windows 2000 even comes with a limited Telnet server designed for remote management from almost any platform using a Telnet client. Also, some management applications like NETSH can connect to a remote Windows 2000 computer.

NOTE: NETSH and other command line–oriented applications can be found in Chapter 19. These utilize the Windows 2000 InterProcess Communication (IPC) protocol.

In the case of the MMC snap-ins, the usual graphical interface is used. With a Terminal Services client, an administrator can select from graphical or character mode management tools. Telnet is a character mode interface that restricts access to the latter.

"Remote Management via Active Directory" takes a look at how Active Directory–integrated DNS zones can handle some of the management chores automatically.

"Remote Management via MMC Snap-in" examines how the Windows 2000 MMC allows remote computers to be accessed. This feature is actually dependent upon the snap-ins, but the Windows 2000 bundle services, such as DNS and DHCP, provide this feature.

"Remote Management via Terminal Services" takes a look at the graphic environment available through a Terminal Services client.

"Remote Management via Telnet" takes a look at the Telnet server and how it is set up and managed. Windows 2000 comes with a limited Telnet server specifically for management tasks.

"Third-Party Tools" examines a few tools that can be used for remote management and for DNS testing and support. For example, DNS Expert can examine DNS zones supported by a Windows 2000 DNS server, but it works just as well with any DNS server since DNS Expert uses the standard DNS access protocol to communicate with the DNS server.

REMOTE MANAGEMENT VIA ACTIVE DIRECTORY

Active Directory's management feature is one reason that Windows 2000 DNS offers so much to DNS administrators when it operates in an Active Directory environment.

There are two aspects to Active Directory related management when it comes to Windows 2000 DNS. The first is the use of Active Directory–integrated DNS zones. As noted throughout this book, Active Directory–integrated DNS zones are automatically replicated in the Active Directory database of each domain controller in the Active Directory domain. Any changes made to these zones will automatically be replicated to other Windows 2000 DNS servers in the same domain. All that is required is that the Windows 2000 DNS servers be part of an Active Directory domain.

The other aspect of Active Directory related management is security. Windows 2000 DNS services and Active Directory–integrated DNS zones are secured by the Active Directory security system. Changes made to security groups for the DNS service will be effective regardless of where the change was made within the Windows 2000 Active Directory zone. In fact, many aspects can be controlled by network administrators who have the appropriate access rights from anywhere within an Active Directory forest.

While these two features of Active Directory may not seem important, they make the DNS services more secure and easier to manage than many DNS service alternatives. And although the security and management aspects are not unique to Windows 2000, the consistent integration of Active Directory with other Windows 2000–based services provides Windows 2000 with a significant number of advantages over the competition.

REMOTE MANAGEMENT VIA MMC SNAP-IN

Active Directory addresses many aspects of Windows 2000 DNS server management, but it is not a replacement for the DNS MMC snap-in. Likewise, the MMC snap-ins for other services such as DHCP and WINS are invaluable tools to network administrators.

The MMC snap-ins typically manage services located on the server from which the MMC application is run. Most also manage services located on other Windows 2000 servers. Active Directory is not a requirement for using most MMC snap-ins across the network.

The default operation for an MMC snap-in such as the Windows 2000 DNS MMC snap-in is to manage the DNS service on the local computer. To change the management to a service on a remote computer, it is simply a matter of selecting the root, noted as DNS, in the left pane and then selecting Action | Connect To Computer. This brings up the screen shown in Figure 20-1.

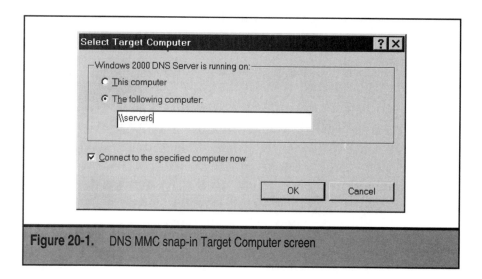

Figure 20-1. DNS MMC snap-in Target Computer screen

A remote computer must be identified using its NetBIOS name or its DNS domain name. In Figure 20-1, the NetBIOS name is used. The DNS domain name for this server is server1.largecompany.com. Both suffice. The first may have a leading "\\", but it is not required.

Finding a similar function in other MMC snap-ins is relatively easy but not identical. For example, for the DHCP MMC snap-in, the menu selection is Action | Add Server. The screen is similar to the one shown in Figure 20-1, but the DHCP MMC snap-in automatically lists authenticated DHCP servers, which makes it more friendly than the Windows 2000 DNS MMC snap-in.

The Windows 2000 DNS MMC snap-in supports any number of DNS servers, but it can only have a server listed once by the same name. Multiple copies of the MMC can be active at one time to provide different views of the same service. If the MMC is set up in author mode, it is possible to add new child windows. These child windows can be populated with MMC snap-ins. Multiple DNS snap-ins can be added, and each can manage the same DNS server. This is handy when it is useful to see different parts of a zone of a DNS server with a large number of resource records. The MMC is covered in Chapter 10. The DNS MMC snap-in is covered in Chapter 11.

NOTE: A Windows 2000 DNS server can be added to the same snap-in window more than once if different names are used. For example, server2 could be added as server2, \\server2, or server2.company.com, where the latter is the server's domain name.

Most DNS administrators will find the DNS MMC snap-in the best way to manage DNS resources. The MMC application will also be the most common way to manage other services, but there is one major restriction to using the MMC: it must be run on a computer running Windows 2000. This is not always possible in some networks, hence the other alternatives presented in this chapter, such as the use of the Windows 2000 Terminal Services.

REMOTE MANAGEMENT VIA TERMINAL SERVICES

The Windows 2000 Terminal Services provides a graphical multiuser interface to Windows 2000. It is essentially a client/server environment where a remote computer runs a Windows 2000 Terminal Services client and the Windows 2000 server runs the Windows 2000 Terminal Services service. The client connects to the server and opens a new session. The session is isolated from other Windows 2000 Terminal Services sessions, but it shares resources on the server such as memory and disk space. The Windows 2000 security system can be used to limit access to these sessions to specific and possibly unique resources.

The client is a graphical application that runs on the remote computer. Windows 95 and Windows 98 are just some of the clients that the Windows 2000 Terminal Services supports. When a session is started, an application is started on the server. The Windows 2000 Explorer application that manages a Windows 2000 desktop is the usual application. The applications run on the server but the input and output are handled by the client. Any additional application started will run on the server.

Obviously, applications such as the Windows 2000 MMC and its snap-ins can be run through a Windows 2000 Terminal Services client. The advantage to using them is that these applications can be run from many different platforms other than Windows 2000. The disadvantages tend to be rather minor to network administrators. The first is that, as with most remote control programs, there is a lag between input and output operations. The second is that each client must have a license. This is an additional cost but one that is often amortized among other uses. For example, if the Terminal Services server is used to run other applications on a regular basis, the occasional use as a network management console is only a minor addition.

It is not necessary to run the Windows 2000 Terminal Services server on all Windows 2000 servers that need to be managed. In fact, this tends to be a rather difficult way to manage multiple servers, since the graphical and command line management tools can do this job from a single computer. Using the Windows 2000 Terminal Services simply allows these Windows 2000–based services to be run on platforms that are unsuitable for the management tools.

Graphical management tools tend to be easier to use and have better online help than character mode tools, but character mode tools have several advantages. The DNS, DHCP, and WINS related character mode tools are covered in Chapter 19. These can be used from a Terminal Services client, but they can also be used from other character mode services such as Telnet.

REMOTE MANAGEMENT VIA TELNET

Telnet servers have been around for a very long time. A Telnet server can be accessed by a Telnet client. The relationship is similar to the Terminal Services described in the previous chapter except that the Telnet client is limited to a character mode display. The client is significantly simpler than the Windows 2000 Terminal Services graphical client. A Telnet client can also be found for every major operating system from a variety of sources.

Telnet servers for Windows are not a new item. The Georgia SoftWorks (**www.georgiasoftworks.com/**) Telnet Server for Windows NT/2000 is an industrial quality Telnet server. It has several advantages, such as a secure and encrypted client/server connection. Check out the Web site for more details.

Another Telnet client/server company is Pragma Systems, Inc. (**www.pragmasys.com/**). Its offerings are similar to Georgia SoftWorks in the Windows operating system environment. Pragma Systems supports Windows NT and Windows 2000.

The Telnet Server Services in Windows 2000 are a standard component that must be installed as part of the Windows 2000 Support Tools that come with Windows 2000. The services are not installed by default.

Nor is the Telnet server started by default. It is set to manual instead of automatic because the security associated with Telnet is more limited, and it can be considered a security concern. The Telnet client can be set up to use the NTLM recognition, but this feature is not available with many Telnet clients. The NTLM support allows the user name and password to be encrypted. Unfortunately, the NTLM support is not as secure as the Kerberos support used by Windows 2000.

The Windows 2000 Telnet server is managed by the character mode Telnet Server Administration program. This is started via

Start | Programs | Administrative Tools | Telnet Server Administration. The initial application response is shown in Figure 20-2.

The Telnet services can be started and stopped using this application, but this will not change the initial startup conditions. This must be done from the Services application that is started via Start | Programs | Administrative Tools | Services. This tool can also be used to start and stop the Telnet server service.

The Display/Change Registry Settings option allows you to change various settings including whether the NTLM support is used. That particular setting value is 0, 1, or 2. A 0 allows the server to work with any Telnet client, but the user name and password are sent unencrypted. Keep in mind that a user who has Telnet access must also have the ability to log on to the server. This is normally restricted to administrators.

WARNING: Sending a user name and password unencrypted is not recommended except where the security of the network can be guaranteed. Although this type of access will work over the Internet, it is not wise because it will involve an administrative user name and password.

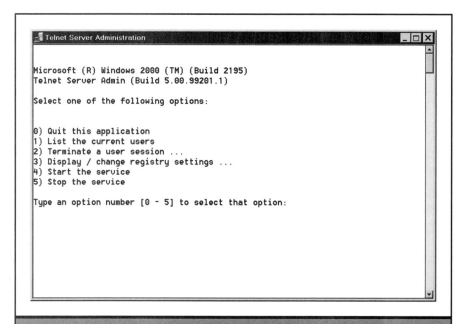

Figure 20-2. Telnet Server Administration screen

This incarnation of the Telnet server is limited to two simultaneous connections. This is a hard-coded limit. To support more than two sessions, network administrators need to install Microsoft's Services for UNIX (SFU) or one of the many third-party Telnet servers. SFU extends the session limit in addition to providing a variety of UNIX-related applications and services that are unrelated to the management of the DNS and DHCP services that we are concerned with.

A Telnet client can be used to access most of the features of Windows 2000 and Active Directory. Some of these applications are discussed in Chapter 19, but they are only the tip of the iceberg. It is possible to change directory security, add and delete groups, and perform a host of other actions using the appropriate application, most of which are bundled with Windows 2000. Figure 20-3 shows a sample Telnet client session.

Microsoft also publishes application programming interfaces (API) for most management interfaces for those network administrators with programming expertise or support available

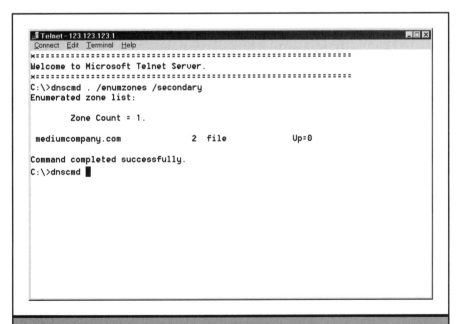

Figure 20-3.   Sample Telnet client session using DNSCMD

to them. This approach is not easy even with tools such as Microsoft Visual Basic, but it may be appropriate for repetitive tasks.

THIRD-PARTY TOOLS

The number of third-party DNS tools exceeds the scope of this book. The Internet tends to be the best source on old and new DNS tools as more are being developed all the time. Many run on Windows or Windows 2000 computers, while others may run only on platforms such as UNIX and Linux.

The advantage of many of these tools is that they use the standard DNS server interface and will operate with any DNS server, not just the Windows 2000 DNS server. This is especially important in a heterogeneous network with different types of DNS servers. A cross-platform DNS tool can help with problems related to server-to-server replication such as replication of a secondary DNS zone.

DNS Expert Professional

NSLOOKUP is really the only DNS diagnostic tool that is supplied with the Windows 2000 DNS service. It is a very handy tool, but it cannot hold a candle to tools like DNS Expert Professional from Men & Mice (**www.menandmice.com**).

DNS Expert Professional is designed for larger networks. The DNS Expert Standard edition is available for smaller networks; it is limited to a single zone. Both have the same level of functionality.

DNS Expert has four main tools: Ping, Trace Route, NsLookup, and Zone Analysis. Figure 20-4 shows the main DNS Expert screen as well as the NsLookup window.

DNS Expert would be rather pricey if it did not include the Zone Analysis tool, which is such a valuable tool that every DNS administrator should have it. Just take a look at the results screen in Figure 20-5 if you are not convinced.

The Zone Analysis tool is configured with a number of rules. You select a rule set and then select the DNS zone and DNS servers to be examined. Start up the Zone Analysis tool and wait for the results.

The Zone Analysis tool can apply as many or as few rules as necessary. For example, if you want to check MX records alone, just

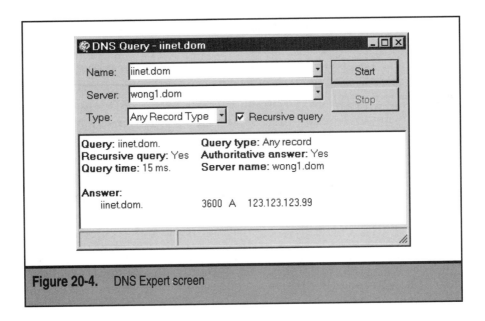

Figure 20-4. DNS Expert screen

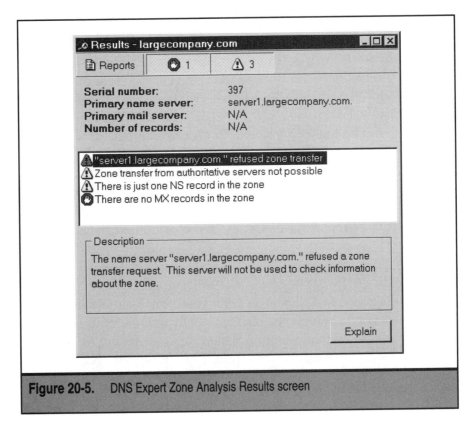

Figure 20-5. DNS Expert Zone Analysis Results screen

enable MX record related rules. It is just a matter of putting check marks in a box.

The Zone Analysis tool handles all major resource records. It can alert you to the lack of MX records or NS records. It can verify that DNS zones can be downloaded. This is only a sampling of what it can do—the complete set of rules is too extensive to list here.

A set of three rule sets is provided. These can be copied and modified. Modification is normally necessary when dealing with Windows 2000, as DNS Expert uses strict name checking. As of this writing, DNS Expert did not handle the more advanced naming options used by Microsoft's Windows 2000 DNS server, such as the leading underscore used with the Active Directory–related subdomains. Simply disabling the name checking gets rid of the numerous error messages normally encountered with the default rule sets and a Windows 2000 Active Directory DNS domain.

CyberKit

CyberKit (**www.cyberkit.net**) is more of a Swiss Army knife of network diagnostic tools. It has a graphical interface that provides a much needed polish to the usual character mode utilities such as PING and NSLOOKUP. CyberKit includes a number of additional utilities such as FINGER and TRACE ROUTE. Figure 20-6 shows the main screen for CyberKit. Its tabbed interface provides quick access to the various tools such as NSLOOKUP.

The price is right for CyberKit—it is postcardware. This means that you just download it from the Internet and send the author a postcard if you use CyberKit on a regular basis. Unless you have a similar tool already, CyberKit will wind up in your diagnostic toolkit.

FastLane DM/Manager

FastLane DM/Manager from FastLane Technologies, Inc. (**www.fastlanetech.com**) is actually a domain management and migration tool, but it does have some relevance to Windows 2000 DNS. As you have seen throughout this book, Windows 2000 DNS

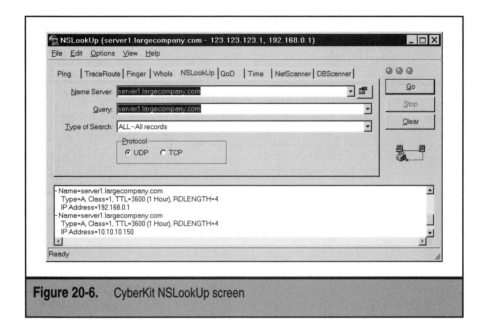

Figure 20-6.   CyberKit NSLookUp screen

will probably be tied to Windows 2000 Active Directory. Windows 2000 Active Directory is, in turn, tied to DNS support, typically Windows 2000 DNS. Therefore, proper configuration of the Active Directory domain environment is critical to the planning and configuration of the DNS system within a Windows 2000 network.

DM/Manager actually provides a number of features, but most of them will not be discussed in this section. The one feature that is of most interest is DM/Manager's ability to massage domain information without actually making changes until necessary. This allows network administrators to experiment with different domain hierarchies.

DM/Manager will not generate DNS domain hierarchy, but this is generally identical to the Windows 2000 hierarchy. DM/Manager can generate various reports that provide these kinds of details.

DM/Manager is normally used for migration of large networks from Windows NT to Windows 2000. Its advanced management capabilities are still useful under Windows 2000, but that is another story.

SUMMARY

With the Windows 2000 MMC snap-ins, many network administrators will not even realize that they can remotely manage a server. Once they do, however, they will save themselves a great deal of time. Of course, network administrators who manage large networks are probably already aware of the various remote management tools such as Telnet.

If a Windows 2000 computer is readily available, such as in a homogeneous Windows 2000 network, the Microsoft Management Console, with its extensive snap-in library, is a good choice for remote management. Most network administrators will have access to a Windows 2000 server or workstation.

The Windows 2000 Terminal Service client/server architecture is another approach to providing access to the graphical Windows 2000 management tools. Its configuration and support are more work for a network administrator unless the Terminal Services must be installed for other reasons.

Turning to a character mode interface like Telnet may seem like a step back, but it is an appropriate alternative since there is effectively no restriction on the client platform. Telnet clients abound in bundled, commercial, shareware, and freeware forms. It does take a bit more work to learn how to manage services using a character-based interface, but it is possible. It might also be the best choice in a heterogeneous environment that includes UNIX and Linux computers.

Third-party DNS tools can be invaluable. The tools bundled with Windows 2000 DNS services are fair, but they are definitely limited.

The bottom line is that the Windows 2000 DNS service and most other Windows 2000 services can be readily managed from a remote computer without major modifications to the Windows 2000 server.

CHAPTER 21

BIND and Windows 2000 DNS

Bind is a popular DNS service that predates Windows 2000 DNS and even Windows NT DNS. BIND version 8 and later can support Windows 2000 Active Directory domains. This chapter looks at the actual named program of BIND and the companion DHCP service, dhcpd.

Entire books have been written about BIND; it is an application as complex as Windows 2000 DNS. This chapter does not provide a detailed description of the operation, configuration, and maintenance of BIND. Instead, this chapter provides an overview of BIND that is sufficient to provide Windows 2000 DNS administrators with an idea of what services can be provided, how BIND can work with a Windows 2000 DNS server, and how BIND can provide Windows 2000 Active Directory support.

The "Comparison of BIND and Windows 2000 DNS" section takes a look at BIND and how the various features are configured. These are compared with Windows 2000 DNS support for the same kind of support.

"Using BIND with Windows 2000 DNS" examines how BIND can be used with Active Directory as well as how primary and secondary DNS zones are shared.

"BIND and Dynamic DNS Updates" takes a look at how BIND supports dynamic DNS updates from Windows 2000 computers.

"DHCPD" discusses the dhcpd application that is normally used in conjunction with BIND to provide IP leases. This feature is also provided by the Windows 2000 DHCP service.

COMPARISON OF BIND AND WINDOWS 2000 DNS

BIND is an extremely complex and very functional DNS server. It has many features not found in Windows 2000 DNS, and it can support Windows 2000 Active Directory, although there are areas where the two take a different approach. See the "BIND and Dynamic DNS Updates" section for one example.

The comparison presented here is not exhaustive; rather, this section is designed to present BIND basics. It should provide those who are unfamiliar with BIND a sufficient understanding of its configuration and operation so that they will be able to understand the information presented in the next section, "Using BIND with Windows 2000 DNS." The same is true for dynamic DNS update support, which is covered in the "BIND and Dynamic DNS Updates" section.

BIND comes in two flavors: BIND 4 and BIND 8. Each uses distinct configuration file definitions. BIND 8 will be the version presented in this chapter, as BIND 4 will not support Windows 2000 Active Directory servers.

NOTE: There are actually a number of different BIND versions. The primary version number is listed here. Versions prior to BIND 8 are compatible in file formats, but BIND 8 is required to support Windows 2000 Active Directory. This support is not required to support IP-based services that run on Windows 2000, so it is possible to have DNS servers that use versions prior to version 8 within a Windows 2000 network.

BIND 8, or simply BIND from here on, uses a two-level file hierarchy to define zones. Primary and secondary DNS zones are supported by BIND. These are stored in text files. Appendix A describes the DNS resource records used in these files, and Appendix B provides a detailed description of the configuration and zone file layout.

NOTE: The implementation and configuration details of BIND described in this chapter are based upon the Linux and UNIX versions. BIND is a publicly supported piece of software with source code that is freely available. Implementations for a variety of operating systems exist, and some commercial DNS server products are based upon BIND.

The top level of the two-level hierarchy is the named.conf file normally found in the /etc directory. The name of this file corresponds to the name of the DNS server application, *named*. This is also referred to as the name daemon. Typically, named will be run by the startup scripts when an operating system boots, and the program will continue to run until the server is stopped. This management aspect of named is beyond the scope of this book as it is operating system–specific. The "NAMED.CONF Configuration File" section addresses the named.conf file and its contents.

The second level of the two-level hierarchy consists of the primary and secondary DNS zone text files. The primary DNS zone text files are normally created and managed by the DNS administrator. The secondary DNS zone files are copies of information downloaded from a secondary DNS zone source such as the DNS server that has the primary DNS zone file. The section "BIND Zone File Basics" examines differences between BIND primary DNS zone files and Windows 2000 primary DNS zone files.

BIND is not restricted to Linux and UNIX. It can be found on a host of other operating systems including Windows. Len Conrad's Web site (**http://bind8nt.meiway.com/**) is a great source of information for BIND on Windows including an implementation by Larry Tremblay of the standard BIND 8 release.

NAMED.CONF Configuration File

The /etc/named.conf file is read by the named program when it starts. Command line arguments to named can change the file name and where the file is located, but this is typically done for migration or debugging purposes only.

The named.conf configuration file is used to set up named to handle primary or secondary DNS zones, provide caching services, act as a forwarding server, and so on. This file contains no information about the contents of a zone.

First, a couple general comments. The named.conf configuration file is line-oriented with respect to comments, but it's relatively free-form otherwise. There are three types of comments supported by BIND 8 in the named.conf file, as shown in the following list:

```
# Perl-style comment to the end of the line
// C++-style comment also to the end of the line
/* C-style comment that can span multiple lines
    until the matching character combination is found */
```

The Perl-style comments were the original comment style, and the C and C++ versions were added later. Comments can start midway into a line and apply only to information past that point.

All other named.conf statements end with a semicolon. This can be somewhat confusing as arguments within a statement also end with a semicolon. The following are named.conf statements:

▼ logging

■ options

■ zone

■ acl

■ key

■ trusted-keys

■ server

■ controls

▲ include

Some of these statements will be examined in more detail than other statements. A complete presentation is beyond the scope of this book; there are whole books written on the subject. Multiple statements of the same type can be found in a named.conf file. The general format for a statement is the statement name followed by a list of parameters or arguments, bracketed by a pair of curly brackets, followed by a semicolon. Parameters end with a semicolon and are statement specific. The following is a simple example of the options statement:

```
options {
  directory "/usr/local/named" ;
} ;
```

▼ The logging statement controls how and where log files are used. BIND has extensive logging capabilities.

■ The options statement specifies global parameters. These affect how the named application will operate as well as defaults for other statements such as the zone statement and the contents of the zone files.

■ A zone statement is required for each primary and secondary DNS zone. It is also used to define the named cache.

■ An acl (access control list) statement defines an IP address list used for access control. This list has a name associated with it so that the details can be referenced by this name in other named.conf statements.

■ The key statement defines security key information that is used in other statements to restrict access and services based upon digital keys.

■ The trusted-keys statement defines DNSSEC digital keys that are implicitly trusted by the named program.

■ The server statement contains configuration parameters for remote servers.

■ The controls statement addresses details associated with the ndc program, a debugging tool for BIND.

▲ The include statement is used to incorporate another text file into the configuration. The designated file is essentially inserted into the configuration file at this statement and processed accordingly by the named program.

The following sections take a closer look at each statement. A named.conf file will contain at least an options statement and one or more zone statements. The following is a simple named.conf file:

```
# Sample named.conf file
options {
  directory "/usr/local/named" ;
} ;
# Zone for the localhost name associated with 127.0.0.1
zone "0.0.127.in-addr.arpa" {
  type master ;
  file "db.127.0.0" ;
} ;
# Sample primary DNS zone
```

```
zone "smallcompany.com" {
  type master ;
  file "db.smallcompany.com" ;
} ;
# Sample secondary DNS zone
zone "largecompany.com" {
  type slave ;
  file "db.largecompany.com" ;
  masters { 123.45.67.1 ; 123.45.67.2 ; } ;
} ;
# Sample reverse lookup DNS zone
zone "67.45.123.in-addr.arpa" {
  type master ;
  file "db.123.45.67" ;
} ;
# Cache definition
zone "." {
  type hint ;
  file "db.cache" ;
} ;
```

This file defines a primary DNS zone for smallcompany.com and a secondary DNS zone from largecompany.com. The source of the information for the secondary zone comes from either the DNS server at 123.45.67.1 or at 123.45.67.2. Two reverse lookup primary DNS zones are defined. One defines the 123.45.67.0/24 IP address range, while the other handles 127.0.0.0/24. The latter is the default definition for a computer's internal IP address that is defined to be 127.0.0.1. The DNS cache is also defined.

This particular sample is relatively open. It does not allow dynamic DNS updates, but it will not refuse any DNS clients or secondary DNS replication requests. In many small- to medium-size networks using BIND, this type of named.conf file is all that is required. More complex configurations are required as more advanced features are used, such as secure access and multiple network adapter support on the server.

Logging Statement

The logging statement specifies how logging is to take place, where information is to be logged, and what information is to be logged. The syntax for the logging statement is

```
logging {
    [ channel <channel_name> {
      ( file <path_name>
        [ versions ( <number> | unlimited ) ]
        [ size <size_spec> ]
      | syslog ( kern | user | mail | daemon | auth | syslog |
          lpr | news | uucp | cron | authpriv | ftp |
          local0 | local1 | local2 | local3 |
          local4 | local5 | local6 | local7 )
      | null );
      [ severity ( critical | error | warning | notice |
          info | debug [ <level> ] | dynamic ); ]
      [ print-category <yes_or_no> ; ]
      [ print-severity <yes_or_no>; ]
      [ print-time <yes_or_no>; ]
    }; ]
    ...
    [ category <category_name> {
      <channel_name>; [ <channel_name>; ... ]
    }; ]
    ...
};
```

An explanation of this statement is beyond the scope of this chapter, but it should be obvious that BIND can provide almost any level of detail regarding the operation of the server for debugging purposes. There should be only one logging statement in the configuration file, although multiple channels and categories can be defined.

The logging statement can be used to debug the named.conf file, so it should always be the first statement in the file.

Options Statement

The options statement specifies one or more global parameters. Many statements have the same parameters available. If the parameter is given in another statement, it will be used; otherwise, the one in the options statement will be used. If neither is present, the initial defaults for named.conf are used.

The syntax for the options statement is

```
options {
    [ version <version_string>; ]
    [ directory <path_name>; ]
    [ named-xfer <path_name>; ]
    [ dump-file <path_name>; ]
    [ memstatistics-file <path_name>; ]
    [ pid-file <path_name>; ]
    [ statistics-file <path_name>; ]
    [ auth-nxdomain <yes_or_no>; ]
    [ deallocate-on-exit <yes_or_no>; ]
    [ dialup <yes_or_no>; ]
    [ fake-iquery <yes_or_no>; ]
    [ fetch-glue <yes_or_no>; ]
    [ has-old-clients <yes_or_no>; ]
    [ host-statistics <yes_or_no>; ]
    [ multiple-cnames <yes_or_no>; ]
    [ notify <yes_or_no>; ]
    [ recursion <yes_or_no>; ]
    [ rfc2308-type1 <yes_or_no>; ]
    [ use-id-pool <yes_or_no>; ]
    [ treat-cr-as-space <yes_or_no>; ]
    [ also-notify <yes_or_no>; ]
    [ forward ( only | first ); ]
    [ forwarders { [ <in_addr> ; [ <in_addr> ; ... ] ] }; ]
    [ check-names ( master | slave | response ) ( warn | fail | ignore); ]
    [ allow-query { <address_match_list> }; ]
    [ allow-recursion { <address_match_list> }; ]
    [ allow-transfer { <address_match_list> }; ]
    [ blackhole { <address_match_list> }; ]
```

```
        [ listen-on [ port <ip_port> ] { <address_match_list> }; ]
        [ query-source [ address ( <ip_addr> | * ) ]
                [ port ( <ip_port> | * ) ] ; ]
        [ lame-ttl <number>; ]
        [ max-transfer-time-in <number>; ]
        [ max-ncache-ttl <number>; ]
    };
```

It is possible to guess the purpose of many of the parameters based on their names. We will not examine all these options, but we will look at a couple that are found in the average named.conf file.

The directory parameter specifies the <path_name> to be used with any relative file names in the named.conf or zone files. Most file names are relative, and the typical path name is /var/local/named. The named.conf file itself is usually located in the /etc directory.

The default values for the option parameters keep BIND consistent with the DNS standards. It is possible to change these values so that the standards are not followed. This is possible so that DNS will be compatible with prior versions of BIND. For example, the multiple-cnames default is no. Multiple CNAME resource records with the same name were previously supported to allow a form of load balancing.

Another common parameter is forwarders. This can also be found in the zone statement. Using it here allows global forward references that are applicable to every request that cannot be resolved locally. The parameter is followed by a list of IP addresses of DNS servers.

NOTE: The check-names parameter is important to BIND DNS servers supporting Windows 2000 Active Directory. The typical value for this parameter in this instance is ignore since the Windows 2000 naming conventions conflict with the default checking done by BIND.

The allow-query, allow-recursion, allow-transfer, and blackhole parameters are found in more advanced BIND environments. The allow-query restricts what clients can access the server. The allow-recursion and allow-transfer parameters indicate whether the server will handle recursion and transfer requests respectively. The blackhole parameter specifies computers that should never be used to resolve queries or from which queries should be accepted.

Zone Statement

Other than the options statement, the zone statement is the one most commonly encountered in a named.conf file. One statement is required for each primary and secondary DNS zone and the cache. There are four layouts for the zone statement: one for a primary DNS zone, one for a secondary DNS zone, one for a forwarded DNS zone, and one for the cache. Only one of the latter may appear in the configuration file.

The syntax for the primary DNS zone statement is

```
zone <domain_name>  [ ( in I hs I hesiod I chaos ) ] {
    type master;
    file <path_name>;
    [ check-names ( warn I fail I ignore ); ]
    [ allow-update { <address_match_list> }; ]
    [ allow-query { <address_match_list> }; ]
    [ allow-transfer { <address_match_list> }; ]
    [ dialup <yes_or_no>; ]
    [ notify <yes_or_no>; ]
    [ also-notify { <ip_addr>; [ <ip_addr>; ... ] };
    [ pubkey <number> <number> <number> <string>; ]
};
```

The type master parameter identifies the primary DNS zone statement. The remaining arguments are specific to this statement type. Only the zone database file name must be included; all other arguments are optional. Secondary DNS zone support is controlled by allow-transfer, notify, and also-notify. Dynamic DNS updates are controlled by allow-update, and secured updates are used in conjunction with the pubkey argument.

The syntax for the secondary DNS zone statement is

```
zone <domain_name>  [ ( in I hs I hesiod I chaos ) ] {
    type ( slave I stub );
    [ file <path_name>; ]
    masters [ port <ip_port> ] { <ip_addr>; [ <ip_addr>; ... ] };
```

```
[ check-names ( warn | fail | ignore ); ]
[ allow-update { <address_match_list> }; ]
[ allow-query { <address_match_list> }; ]
[ allow-transfer { <address_match_list> }; ]
[ transfer-source <ip_addr>; ]
[ max-transfer-time-in <number>; ]
[ notify <yes_or_no>; ]
[ also-notify { <ip_addr>; [ <ip_addr>; ... ] };
[ pubkey <number> <number> <number> <string>; ]
};
```

The arguments for the secondary or slave DNS zone are similar to the primary DNS zone statement definition. Secondary DNS zone replication arguments such as allow-transfer indicate what DNS servers will be obtaining their secondary DNS zone information from this copy of the zone. The max-transfer-time-in specifies the number of seconds that a transfer is allowed to take.

The syntax for the forwarding zone statement is

```
zone <domain_name> [ ( in | hs | hesiod | chaos ) ] {
    type forward;
    [ forward ( only | first ); ]
    [ forwarders { [ <ip_addr> ; [ <ip_addr> ; ... ] ] }; ]
    [ check-names ( warn | fail | ignore ); ]
};
```

This syntax is relatively simple. The optional list of forwarders is part of the forwarders argument. If the list is not supplied, the options statement must include a list of forwarders. The list specified for this domain is specific to queries that include the <domain_name>.

The syntax for the cache statement is

```
zone "." [ ( in | hs | hesiod | chaos ) ] {
    type hint;
    file <path_name>;
    [ check-names ( warn | fail | ignore ); ]
};
```

▼ The cache statement is noted by a <domain_name> of "." and the type of hint. A file name is required. The naming checking feature is on by default, but it can be disabled.

▲ The zone statements can occur in any order. Zone statements should reference unique file names, and usually the file names include no path name. This is typically specified in the options statement.

Acl statement

The syntax for the acl statement is

    acl <name> { <address_match_list> } ;

This allows <name> to be used as a value for any argument in a statement that requires an <address_match_list>. The acl statement essentially defines what hosts, by IP address, can be used with respect to an argument. There are four predefined acl names: all, none, localhost, and localnets. The first allows all hosts, and the second allows no hosts. The localhost name matches all IP addresses associated with the computer that named is running on. The localnets name matches all IP addresses for all subnets support by each configured network adapter on the computer.

Key Statement

The key statement is used to define keys that will be used for authentication when authenticated communication is specified for the server or for a zone. The syntax for the key statement is

    key <key_id> {
        algorithm <algorithm_id>;
        secret <secret_string>;
    };

Multiple algorithms are supported, but they are based on support installed on the computer. The <secret_string> is the key. Access to the named.conf file should be restricted to administrators and the named application if keys are contained in the named.conf file.

Trusted-keys Statement

The trusted-keys statement is used to specify keys that are required to perform functions on a particular domain. The syntax for the trusted-keys statement is

```
trusted-keys {
    [ <domain_name> <flags> <protocol> <algorithm> <key> ; ]
    ...
};
```

Any number of keys can be defined.

Server Statement

The server statement contains details about a remote server. The syntax for the server statement is

```
server <ip_addr> {
    [ bogus <yes_or_no> ; ]
    [ transfers <number> ; ]
    [ transfer-format ( one-answer | many-answers ); ]
    [ keys { <key_id> [ <key_id> ... ] }; ]
};
```

The server is specified by an IP address. A bogus server is one that should not be used because it has been determined that its information is invalid or bogus. The transfer-format specifies whether a secondary DNS zone transfer should occur in one message or multiple messages. The latter is more efficient. Both methods are supported by Windows 2000. Earlier versions of BIND support the one message method.

Controls Statement

The controls statement is used in conjunction with the ndc program for debugging a BIND configuration. The syntax for the controls statement is

```
controls {
   [ inet <ip_addr>
     port <ip_port>
     allow { <address_match_list> ; }; ]
   [ unix <path_name>
     perm <number>
     owner <number>
     group <number> ; ]
};
```

The controls statement should be used only by those familiar with BIND and ndc.

Include Statement

The include statement is used to insert the contents of another file into the stream being processed by the named program. It cannot be using within a statement. The syntax for the include statement is

include "<file_name>" ;

The named.conf file is often a collection of include statements. In this case, each file typically contains different aspects of the configuration such as defaults set up by the options statement, security information, and zone definitions.

BIND Zone File Basics

BIND zone files are a superset of those used by Windows 2000. The details of the zone files are outlined in Appendixes A and B. As with Windows 2000, a BIND zone file must have one SOA resource record and it can contain one or more NS resource records to indicate which DNS servers are authoritative for the zone.

Two meta-statements are supported by BIND:

$ORIGIN <DomainName>
$INCLUDE <FileName>

These statements are normally used together to make zone management easier, especially when subdomains are used within a zone. In this case, the contents of each subdomain can be placed in a separate file.

The $ORIGIN statement is used in conjunction with the relative domain name shortcut used in a zone file. Normally the default domain is added to a relative domain to generate a FQDN for use with a resource record. The $ORIGIN statement changes the default domain so any subsequent resource records will use the new value. This includes any resource records in a file that is added to the zone via the $INCLUDE statement.

The following lines define address resource records using FQDN:

```
able.my.bar.com.       A 123.45.67.1
baker.my.bar.com.      A 123.45.67.2
server1.your.bar.com.  A 123.45.67.44
server2.your.bar.com.  A 123.45.67.45
```

This is equivalent to this definition

```
$ORIGIN my.bar.com.
$INCLUDE "my.bar.com.db"
$ORIGIN bar.com.
$INCLUDE "your.bar.com.db"
```

plus the file contents of my.bar.com.db

```
# File: my.bar.com.db
able      A 123.45.67.1
baker     A 123.45.67.2
```

and the file your.bar.com.db

```
# File: your.bar.com.db
server1 A 123.45.67.44
server2 A 123.45.67.45
```

USING BIND WITH WINDOWS 2000 DNS

BIND can work with Windows 2000 in five ways:

1. A BIND secondary DNS zone references a Windows 2000 DNS server.

2. A Windows 2000 secondary DNS zone references a BIND DNS server.

3. BIND provides support for a Windows 2000 Active Directory zone.

4. BIND forwards requests to a Windows 2000 DNS server.

5. Windows 2000 forwards requests to a BIND DNS server.

The first three items in this list are covered in more detail in the sections "BIND Secondary DNS Zone Referencing a Windows 2000 DNS Server," "Windows 2000 Secondary DNS Zone Referencing a BIND DNS Server," and "Using BIND to support Windows 2000 Active Directory."

The forwarding requests are a bit simpler and are covered right here. Setting up named.conf so that unresolved requests are forwarded is a matter of putting the IP address list of DNS servers including any Windows 2000 DNS servers in either the options forwarders list or the zone's forwarders list.

```
# Sample named.conf file
options {
  directory "/usr/local/named" ;
  forwarders { 129.22.67.1 ; 129.22.14.121 ; } ;
} ;
# Sample forwarding DNS zone
zone "smallcompany.com" {
  type forward ;
  forwarders { 123.45.67.54 ; } ;
} ;
```

In this case, a pair of DNS servers handles all unresolved requests except for the zone smallcompany.com. The DNS server with an IP address of 123.45.67.54 is used in this instance. A typical environment would be to have this forwarding DNS server use a local DNS server for the specific zone of smallcompany.com and use two ISP-based DNS servers for all other requests.

Having the Windows 2000 DNS server forward requests to a BIND server is simply a matter of making sure the check box Enabled Forwarders is checked and adding the BIND server's IP address in the list on the Forwards tab of the Windows 2000 DNS server's Property screen. Windows 2000 does not have a zone level forwarding mechanism.

BIND Secondary DNS Zone Referencing a Windows 2000 DNS Server

The zone statement definition in the "Zone Statement" section provides sufficient details on how to reference the source of a secondary DNS zone including those from the Windows 2000 DNS server. The following is a sample named.conf file that references a Windows 2000 DNS server with an IP address of 129.33.11.155. The zone name is largecompany.com. It may be an Active Directory–integrated, primary, or secondary DNS zone.

```
# Sample named.conf file
options {
  directory "/usr/local/named" ;
} ;
# Zone for the localhost name associated with 127.0.0.1
zone "0.0.127.in-addr.arpa" {
  type master ;
  file "db.127.0.0" ;
} ;
# Sample secondary DNS zone
zone "largecompany.com" {
  type slave ;
  file "db.largecompany.com" ;
```

```
    allow-updates { 123.45.67.0/24 ; } ;
    masters { 129.33.11.155 ; } ;
} ;
# Cache definition
zone "." {
  type hint ;
  file "db.cache" ;
} ;
```

This secondary DNS zone is also set up to forward dynamic DNS updates to the Windows 2000 DNS server. Of course, the Windows 2000 DNS server must be set up for dynamic DNS updates as well.

Some changes may be necessary on the Windows 2000 DNS server side. Using the Windows 2000 DNS MMC snap-in, select the zone largecompany.com. Then select Action | Properties. From the zone's Properties screen, select the Zone Transfers tab. The Allow Zone Transfers check box must be checked. If To Any Server is selected, everything should be ready. If Only To Servers Listed On The Name Servers Tab is selected, the IP address of the BIND server must be on the list that is located on the Name Servers tab screen. If Only To The Following Servers is selected, the IP address of the BIND server must be on the list that is on the Zone Transfers screen. Use the Notify button if the Windows 2000 DNS server should send a notification message to the BIND server when updates occur.

Windows 2000 Secondary DNS Zone Referencing a BIND DNS Server

Setting up Windows 2000 with a secondary DNS zone that is sourced from a BIND server is a relatively simple chore. The idea is the same as in the previous section, but the point-of-view changes.

To start with, the named.conf file must be set up with a primary or secondary DNS zone. The following has a primary DNS zone called myprimary.com:

```
# Sample named.conf file
options {
  directory "/usr/local/named" ;
```

```
} ;
# Zone for the localhost name associated with 127.0.0.1
zone "0.0.127.in-addr.arpa" {
  type master ;
  file "db.127.0.0" ;
} ;
# Sample primary DNS zone
zone "myprimary.com" {
  type master ;
  file "db.myprimary.com" ;
  allow-transfer { 123.45.67.0/24 ; } ;
  notify yes ;
} ;
# Cache definition
zone "." {
  type hint ;
  file "db.cache" ;
} ;
```

The zone myprimary.com is set up to allow transfers from any
DNS server with an IP address in the range of 123.45.67.0 to
123.45.67.254. As long as the Windows 2000 DNS server has an IP
address in that range, the BIND server will deliver the goods. The
BIND server will also notify the Windows 2000 DNS server of changes
once the Windows 2000 DNS server makes the initial contact.

A secondary DNS zone must be created on the Windows 2000
DNS server using the New Zone Wizard. The IP address of the BIND
server must be entered on the Master DNS Servers screen in the IP
address list.

Using BIND to Support Windows 2000 Active Directory

BIND can provide support for Windows 2000 Active Directory
domain controllers. In this case, the BIND server will host the
primary DNS zone for an Active Directory zone of the same name. In
the following example, the zone name is ad.sample.com:

```
# Sample named.conf file for Windows 2000 Active Directory support
options {
```

```
      directory "/usr/local/named" ;
} ;
# Zone for the localhost name associated with 127.0.0.1
zone "0.0.127.in-addr.arpa" {
   type master ;
   file "db.127.0.0" ;
} ;
# Sample primary DNS zone
zone "ad.sample.com" {
   type master ;
   file "db.ad.sample.com" ;
   allow-transfer { 123.45.67.0/24 ; } ;
   notify yes ;
   allow-update { 123.45.67.0/24 ; };
} ;
# Sample primary DNS zone
zone "_msdcs.ad.sample.com" {
   type master ;
   file "db._msdcs.ad.sample.com" ;
   allow-transfer { 123.45.67.0/24 ; } ;
   notify yes ;
   check-names ignore;
   allow-update { 123.45.67.0/24 ; };
} ;
# Cache definition
zone "." {
   type hint ;
   file "db.cache" ;
} ;
```

It is possible to have a single primary DNS zone, but Microsoft recommends that the _msdcs subdomain be split from the parent domain, as shown above. This allows two things to take place. First, Active Directory details are handled in their own zone definition. Second, the rest of the parent zone, ad.sample.com in this case, can be set up for full error checking and independent dynamic DNS update support compared to the subdomain, which will need name checking turned off and dynamic DNS update support enabled.

The reason for this configuration is that the Windows 2000 Active Directory support places address resource records for global catalog servers in the gc._msdcs subdomain. Unfortunately, BIND will generate an error in response to the dynamic DNS update used to add these records to the subdomain.

Additional subdomain zones will have to be created if controls need to be applied to the other Active Directory subdomains, including domains, _sites, _tcp, and _udp. SRV resource records are added using dynamic DNS updates, so the allow-update must be included unless the DNS administrator manually edits the zone file to add or remove the SRV resource records as needed. The check-names does not have to be set to ignore since the conflict mentioned above with address resource records will not occur.

BIND AND DYNAMIC DNS UPDATES

The latest version of BIND supports dynamic DNS updates from a variety of sources including Windows 2000 computers. Chapter 13 examines client configuration, and Chapter 15 discusses dynamic DNS updates in more detail. This section presents BIND's configuration to support dynamic DNS updates.

Dynamic DNS updates are enabled on a per zone basis. A single line is added to the zone definition contained in the named.conf file. The following is a sample zone definition that includes the allow-update line:

```
zone "largecompany.com" {
        type master;
        file "largecompany.com.db";
        check-names ignore;
        allow-update { 123.45.67.1 ; 123.45.68.0/24 };
} ;
```

This definition allows dynamic DNS updates to the largecompany.com zone from two groups of computers based on the arguments to the allow-update statement. The allow-update statement indicates that dynamic DNS updates are allowed. Dynamic DNS updates are ignored if this statement is not included.

NOTE: The check-names statement was included to disable the name checking that will cause a problem if a Windows 2000 Active Directory domain controller needs to update the zone using SRV records that are in a subdomain with an underscore in the name.

The allow-update argument list can contain individual IP addresses and netmask defined ranges as shown in the example. Items in the list can also be prefixed by an exclamation point (!), in which case the address or range is excluded.

The list can also contain references to named acl definitions, described earlier in this chapter, and key ID names. This makes use of BIND's secure dynamic update support, which is not compatible with Windows 2000 dynamic DNS update support. This type of support can be included, but if Windows 2000 computers will have to use dynamic DNS updates, the IP addresses for the Windows 2000 computers must be included in the allow-update argument list. Windows 2000 computers will first attempt a Windows 2000 secure update that will fail. A normal, nonsecure update will be sent next and should succeed if the named.conf file is set up as just noted.

TIP: Split subzone definitions into their own zone definitions when using dynamic DNS updates so that finer security control can be maintained. For example, Windows 2000 domain controllers need to update the _msdcs, _tcp, _udp, and _sites zones. These can be restricted to fixed IP addresses associated with the Windows 2000 domain controller computers. Likewise, the DNS address resource records, A, associated with these computers can be entered in a nondynamic DNS update zone.

BIND's dynamic DNS update support does not provide the secured dynamic DNS update support found in the Windows 2000 DNS service that utilizes Kerberos, so it is important to restrict use of dynamic DNS updates. On the other hand, BIND supports key-based security originally specified in RFC 2065. Windows 2000 does not support this mechanism. Actually, the two mechanisms are very similar but incompatible.

Dynamic DNS updates are often used in conjunction with computers that obtain their IP address from a DHCP server. It is possible to use the Windows 2000 DHCP server and its dynamic DNS update proxy support so that updates are restricted to the DHCP server.

Dynamic DNS updates are useful DNS server features that are not restricted to Windows 2000 DNS. They are not a requirement for Windows 2000 Active Directory support, but they can significantly ease the burden of support for DNS.

DHCPD

Windows 2000 DHCP and WINS servers are discussed in this book because of their relationship with Windows 2000 DNS. WINS support tends to be unique to Windows operating systems with server implementations for Windows NT and Windows 2000 whereas DHCP support is more universal.

A popular implementation of a DHCP server under UNIX and Linux is dhcpd. Environments that use BIND often incorporate DHCP support using dhcpd. As with BIND, we will provide a brief overview of dhcpd for network administrators who may have to consider migration to Windows 2000 DHCP.

The dhcpd program is normally run from a startup script. The script may use a number of command line arguments; these are described in the online documentation for dhcpd. The /etc/dhcpd.conf text file holds the configuration information for dhcpd. This section provides a simplified view of the dhcpd.conf file.

NOTE: The dhcpd program, also known as a daemon, provides BOOTP support as well as DHCP support. BOOTP support is not presented in this book.

The dhcpd.conf file consists of a set of subnet definitions. These definitions describe the range of IP addresses that may be leased as well as information that may be dispersed when an IP address is leased. The following is a sample subnet definition:

```
subnet 123.45.67.0 netmask 255.255.255.0 {
  range 123.45.67.50 123.45.67.75 ;
  range 123.45.67.100 123.45.67.200 ;
  default-lease-time 600 ;
  max-lease-time 6000 ;
  option subnet-mask 255.255.255.0 ;
  option routers 123.45.67.254 ;
  option domain-name-servers 123.45.67.250, 239.10.34.10 ;
  option domain-name "sample.com" ;
} ;
```

The first line specifies the subnet range and netmask for the
network adapter for which the program will provide IP leases. In this
case, the IP address for the network adapter might be 123.45.67.10.
This subnet has two ranges of IP addresses that will be used for
leases. These include 123.45.67.50 through 123.45.67.75 and
123.45.67.100 through 123.45.67.200. The default-lease-time and
max-lease-time values control lease length.

The option lines specify information that will be delivered with a
leased IP address. The Windows 2000 DHCP service can be
configured to deliver this same information. The option names are
self-explanatory. Multiple value options such as the 123.45.67.250,
239.10.34.10 for domain-name-servers are supported by both dhcpd
and Windows 2000 DHCP.

Multiple subnet definitions may be included in the
/etc/dhcpd.conf file. This will occur when the server has more than
one IP address. If a subnet definition does not exist for an IP, dhcpd
will not provide IP leases for that subnet.

This information should be sufficient to migrate dhcpd support to
the Windows 2000 DHCP service. For example, it is possible to
convert the previous example into a Windows 2000 DHCP scope by
doing the following:

1. Start up the DHCP MMC snap-in (see Chapter 14).

2. Run the New Scope Wizard using Action | New Scope.

3. In the IP Address Range screen, set the subnet mask to
    255.255.255.0, as shown in the example.

4. Enter a starting IP address of 123.45.67.50 and an ending IP address of 123.45.67.200.

5. Unlike dhcpd, which uses multiple ranges, the Windows 2000 DHCP services uses a single range but multiple exclusionary ranges. In this case, add an exclusion range of 123.45.67.76 to 123.45.67.99 in the Add Exclusions screen.

6. The options can be added in the New Scope Wizard or later by selecting Scope Options under the new scope.

7. Select Action | Configure Options. The router 123.45.67.254 matches the Windows 2000 DHCP 003 Router option. The domain-name-server matches 006 DNS Servers. The domain-name matches the 015 DNS Domain Name option. Every dhcpd scope option should have a Windows 2000 DHCP scope option.

In general, migration from dhcpd to Windows 2000 DHCP is significantly easier than migrating from BIND to Windows 2000 DNS. Windows 2000 DHCP's dynamic DNS update proxy can be enabled as well. This feature is not in the current dhcpd implementation.

SUMMARY

The Windows 2000 Active Directory system is dependent upon DNS server support. While the Windows 2000 DNS service is an ideal platform to support Active Directory, there are many alternative DNS services, including BIND. Given BIND's prevalence on the Internet and in large networks, it is likely that DNS administrators will need a background in BIND.

BIND has sufficient features to support Windows 2000 and Active Directory, but upgrading to the latest version of BIND may be necessary. In particular, BIND must support SRV records and, preferably, dynamic DNS updates as well.

Windows 2000 DNS server is unique in that it is the only DNS server to support Active Directory–secured dynamic DNS updates. This may be a security issue in some environments.

APPENDIX A

DNS
Resource Records

NS resource records are contained within a DNS zone. The DNS zone file format covered in Appendix B contains the resource records defined in this appendix. The description in this appendix includes the text format for each resource record used with DNS zone files. Active Directory–integrated DNS zones keep the same information that is stored in a zone file, but this information is kept in binary format within the Active Directory database maintained on each Windows 2000 domain controller.

NOTE: An Active Directory database does not cross Active Directory domains. This means that Active Directory–integrated DNS zone information in the database will be bound by the domain. The zone information can be replicated using secondary DNS zones.

There are a large number of different DNS resource record types, but only a few are regularly used. These include SOA, A, PTR, MX, NS, CNAME, and SRV. These are used throughout this book. Some are covered in specific sections such as the mail exchange (MX) resource record that is described in Chapter 18.

RFCs define the syntax and semantics of the DNS system including the syntax and semantics of DNS resource records. Chapter 2 lists all RFCs supported by Windows 2000 DNS. Table A-1 covers the RFCs that relate to this appendix.

The DNS resource record text format has the following syntax:

[<name>] [<class>] [<ttl>] <type> <data>

This syntax and the overall DNS zone file format are covered in more detail in Appendix B. The <name> field can be a relative domain name or FQDN. It may also be @, which indicates that the zone's domain name will be used. The examples in this appendix have arbitrary <name> values.

The <class> value used with DNS servers for TCP/IP support is IN for Internet. This is the only type of class supported by the Windows 2000 DNS server. The <ttl> field is the time-to-live in seconds. The <ttl> field is normally not included and is not included in the examples in this appendix. The <type> field matches one of the Type: lines found in the "DNS Resource Record Types" section. This field

RFC	Title
1034	Domain Names—Concepts and Facilities
1035	Domain Names—Implementation and Specification
1101	DNS Encoding of Network Names and Other Types
1464	Using the Domain Name System to Store Arbitrary String Attributes
1664	Using the Internet DNS to Distribute Mail Address Mapping Tables
1706	DNS NSAP Resource Records
1712	DNS Encoding of Geographical Location
1886	DNS Extensions to Support IP Version 6
1912	Common DNS Operational and Configuration Errors
2052	A DNS RR for Specifying the Location of Services (DNS SRV)
2181	Clarifications to the DNS Specification

Table A-1. RFCs Supported by Windows 2000

determines the resource record type. The <data> field is specific to the resource record type.

DNS RESOURCE RECORD TYPES

Type   A

Name   Host address

RFC   1035

Description   Maps a domain <name> to an <IPv4Address> (32-bit Internet Protocol version 4 address).

Syntax   [<name>] [<class>] [<ttl>] A <IPv4Address>

Data   <IPv4Address> – 32-bit IP address

Example   server1.largecompany.com. IN A 123.45.67.1

Type   AAAA

Name   IPv6 host address

RFC   1886

Description   Maps a domain <name> to an <IPv6Address> (128-bit Internet Protocol version 6 address).

Syntax   [<name>] [<class>] [<ttl>] AAAA <IPv6Address>

Data   <IPv6Address> – 128-bit IPv6 address

Example   ipv6_server1.mediumcompany.com. IN AAAA 4321:0:12:34:56: 78:90:0ab

Type   AFSDB

Name   Andrew File System Database

RFC   1183

Description   Maps a domain <name> to an AFS <ServerHostName>. The <subtype> indicates the type of server. This resource record will only be found in networks using or referencing an Andrew File System.

Syntax   [<name>] [<class>] [<ttl>] AFSDB <subtype > <ServerHostName>

Data   <subtype> – A value of 1 indicates an AFS version 3.0 volume location server. A value of 2 indicates an authenticated name server holding the cell-root directory node for the server that uses either Open Software Foundation's (OSF) DCE authenticated cell-naming system or HP's Network Computing Architecture (NCA).

<ServerHostName> - name of AFS location server

Example   afs.foo.com.   AFSDB   1   server1.afs.foo.com.

Type   ATMA

Name   Asynchronous Transfer Mode address

RFC   ATM Name System Specification Version 1.0

Description   Maps a <name> to an ATM address referenced in the <AtmAddress> field. Check out the ATM Forum (www.atmforum.com) on the Internet for more details.

Syntax   [<name>] [<class>] [<ttl>] ATMA <AtmAddress>

Data   <AtmAddress> – ATM address

Example   atm-host ATMA
41.0123.00330123000000000000.00914f000012.00

Type   CNAME

Name   Canonical name

RFC   1035

Description   Maps a domain <name> to a <CanonicalName>. The <CanonicalName> must resolve to a valid DNS domain name.

Syntax   [<name>] [<class>] [<ttl>] CNAME <CanonicalName>

Data   <CanonicalName> – Relative domain name or FQDN

Example   www.foo.com. CNAME server1.foo.com.

Type   HINFO

Name   Host information

RFC   1035, 1700

Description   Indicates the type of CPU and operating system associated with the domain <name>. This is normally paired with an address resource record, A, or an IPv6 address resource record, AAAA. Some applications can use special procedures to communicate with the host based on the operating system and CPU type.

Syntax   [<name>] [<class>] [<ttl>] HINFO <CpuType> <OsType>

Data   <CpuType> – See RFC 1700, examples: INTEL-486, VAX-11/780
<OsType> – See RFC 1700, examples: WIN32, UNIX

Example   server1.mediumcompany.com.   HINFO   INTEL-486 UNIX

Type   ISDN

Name   Integrated Services Digital Network (ISDN)

RFC   1183

Description   Maps a domain <name> to an ISDN telephone number. The telephone number should follow ITU-T E.163/E.164 international telephone numbering standards.

Syntax   [<name>] [<class>] [<ttl>] ISDN <IsdnAddress> <SubAddress>

Data   <IsdnAddress> – ISDN telephone number
<SubAddress> – ISDN device number

Example   server1-isdn.mediumcompany.com. ISDN 1215551234 001

Type   MB

Name   Mailbox (MB) resource record

RFC   1035, experimental

Description   Specifies that a domain <name> mailbox will be serviced by a <MailServer>. The <name> translates to a more conventional e-mail address using the same encoding as the SOA resource record. For example, mailbox.foo.com translates to mailbox@foo.com.

Syntax   [<name>] [<class>] [<ttl>] MB <MailServer>

Data   <MailServer> – Relative or FQDN of the mail server host

Example   mailbox.mediumcompany.com.   MB
              mailserver.mediumcompany.com

Type   MD

Name   Mail destination

RFC   1035

Description   Superseded by MX resource record.

Type   MF

Name   Mail forwarder

RFC   1035

Description   Superseded by MX resource record.

Type MG

Name Mail group

RFC 1035, experimental

Description Specifies that the domain <name> mail group contains <MailboxName> as part of the group. The <MailboxName> should have a matching mailbox (MB) resource record in the current zone. Multiple MG records with the same <name> are used to populate a mail group.

Syntax: [<name>] [<class>] [<ttl>] MG <MailboxName>

Data <MailboxName> – Relative or FQDN of a mailbox

Example administrators.mediumcompany.com. MG
admin1.mediumcompany.com
administrators.mediumcompany.com. MG
admin2.mediumcompany.com

Type MINFO

Name Mailbox mail list information

RFC 1035, experimental

Description Specifies a domain mailbox for a responsible person for a <name>d resource. An error mailbox is also specified. These can be the same mailbox.

Syntax [<name>] [<class>] [<ttl>] MINFO <ResponsibleMailbox>
<ErrorMailbox>

Data <ResponsibleMailbox> – Relative or FQDN of an MB-defined mailbox
<ErrorMailbox> – Relative or FQDN of an MB-defined mailbox

Example info.foo.com. MINFO responsible-mbox.foo.com error-mbox. foo.com

Type   MR

Name   Mailbox renamed

RFC   1035, experimental

Description   Indicates that the domain mailbox <name> has been changed to <NewMailbox>. The MR resource record is normally used to forward mail for a user who has a new mailbox name.

Syntax   [<name>] [<class>] [<ttl>] MR <NewMailbox>

Data   <NewMailbox> – Relative or FQDN of an MB-defined mailbox

Example   old-mbox.mediumcompany.com.   MR new-renamed-mbox.
              mediumcompany.com

Type   MX

Name   Mail exchanger

RFC   1035

Description   Mail for a domain <name> is to be delivered to the specified <MailServer>. Check out Chapter 18 for more details on how the MX record is used.

Syntax   [<name>] [<class>] [<ttl>] MX <Preference> <MailServer>

Data   <Preference> – Two-digit preference associated with the <MailServer>
              <MailServer> – Relative or FQDN of the host mail server

Example   mediumcompany.com.   MX 20 mailserver1.mediumcompany.com

Type   NS

Name   Name Server

RFC   1035

Description   Indicates that the <DnsServer> is an authoritative DNS server for the domain <name>. Multiple authoritative servers can be defined using multiple NS resource records.

Syntax   [<name>] [<class>] [<ttl>] NS <DnsServer>

Data   <DnsServer> – Relative or FQDN of a DNS server

Example   mediumcompany.com.   NS ns1.mediumcompany.com

Type   PTR

Name   Pointer

RFC   1035

Description   Maps an address in the form of a <name> to a <ResourceName>. The <name> normally follows the reverse lookup format associated with the in-addr.arpa domain tree used to provide reverse lookups. See Chapter 2 for more details on reverse lookups and in-addr.arpa.

Syntax   [<name>] [<class>] [<ttl>] PTR <ResourceName>

Data   <ResourceName> – FQDN

Example   123.0.0.10.in-addr.arpa.   PTR host.mediumcompany.com.
              123   PTR host.mediumcompany.com.

Type   RP

Name   Responsible Person

RFC   1183

Description Specifies the <MailboxName> for a responsible person and a <TextRecordName> description for the domain <name> or for the responsible person, usually the latter.

Syntax [<name>] [<class>] [<ttl>] <MailboxName> <TextRecordName>

Data <MailboxName> – Name of associated MB record
<TextRecordName> – Name of associated TXT record

Example foo.com.   RP   admin.foo.com. admin-info.foo.com.
admin-info.foo.com.   TXT "Bill Wong, (555) 555-1212"
admin.foo.com.   MB mailserver1.foo.com.

Type RT

Name Route through

RFC 1183, experimental

Description Provides a way of determining the proper route to a domain, <name>. Multiple RT records for the same domain can exist. The <Preference> provides a way to prioritize route selection.

Syntax [<name>] [<class>] [<ttl>] RT <Preference> <IntermediateHost>

Data <Preference> – Two-digit preference value used in a fashion similar to the same field in the MX resource record to determine the best router when multiple routes are available
<IntermediateHost> – Relative or FQDN of router

Example mediumcompany.com. RT 20 router.foo.com

Type SOA

Name Start of Authority

RFC   1035

Description   Defines the domain's attributes. This includes the primary <NameServer> and the <MailBox> for the domain. The SOA record is discussed in more detail in Chapters 2 and 3.

Syntax   [<name>] [<class>] [<ttl>] SOA <NameServer> <MailBox> (<SerialNo> <Refresh> <Retry> <Expiration> <MinTtl>)

Data   <NameServer> – Relative or FQDN (preferred) for the primary DNS server
   <MailBox> – Mailbox for the domain
   <SerialNo> – Sequence number
   <Refresh> – Refresh time in seconds
   <Retry> – Retry time in seconds
   <Expiration> – Expiration time in seconds
   <MinTtl> – Minimum time-to-live in seconds

Example   mydomain.com. IN SOA ns1.mydomain.com admin.mydomain.com (
            1 ; Serial number
            10800 ; Refresh (seconds)
            3600 ; Retry (seconds)
            604800 ; Expiration (seconds)
            86400) ; Minimum TTL (seconds)

Type   SRV

Name   Service locator

RFC   2052, 1700

Description   Specifies a well-known service is available from a <Host> at a specific <Port>. Multiple hosts for the service can be defined for the service using multiple SRV resource records. The type of service is normally noted as part of the domain <name>. Windows 2000 uses the SRV record to locate services such as Active Directory domain controllers and Lightweight Directory Access Protocol (LDAP) services. LDAP normally operates on TCP port 389. RFC 1700 defines a symbolic name for well-known services such as _telnet and _smtp. The <Preference> and <Weight> fields can be used in a load-balancing mechanism when multiple servers are available. Zero values can be used if load balancing is not needed.

Syntax   [<name>] [<class>] [<ttl>] SRV <Preference > <Weight> <Port> <Host>

Data   <Preference > – 0 to 65535
         <Weight> – 0 to 65535
         <Port> – 0 to 65535
         <Host> – Relative or FQDN for a host

Example   _ldap._tcp.ms-dcs.foo.com   SRV 0 0   389 dc1.foo.com

Type   TXT

Name   Text

RFC   1035

Description   Provides a descriptive text for the domain <name>. A TXT resource record can be defined in conjunction with any resource record.

Syntax   [<name>] [<class>] [<ttl>] TXT "<String>"

Data   <String> – Text string

Example   mediumcompany.com.   TXT "This is a sample text record for this domain name."

Type   WKS

Name   Well-known service

RFC 1035

Description Describes well-known TCP/IP services supported by a particular protocol by a host at a specific IP address. Multiple WKS resource records can define multiple services and protocols for the same <name>
and <Address>.

Syntax [<name>] [<class>] [<ttl>] WKS <Address> <Protocol> (<Service> ...)

Data <Address> – IP address
<Protocol> – TCP, UDP
<Service> – telnet, smtp, ftp, shell, domain

Example mediumcompany.com. WKS 10.0.0.1 TCP (telnet smtp ftp)

Type X25

Name X.25

RFC 1183, experimental

Description Maps a domain <name> to a Public Switched Data Network (PSDN) address number specified by <PsdnNumber>. The <PsdnNumber> should follow the X.121 international numbering plan.

Syntax [<name>] [<class>] [<ttl>] X25 <PsdnNumber>

Data <PsdnNumber> – X.25 PSDN number

Example mediumcompany.com. X25 5550133377

APPENDIX B

DNS Zone Files

DNS administrators who deal with Windows 2000 using only the DNS MMC snap-in may never encounter DNS zone files, but it is still a good idea to know the format for these files. This is especially true in a heterogeneous DNS environment that includes BIND (see Chapter 21).

The layout for DNS zone files is covered in RFC 1035. Definitions for most DNS resource records are covered in Appendix A. A zone file is used for primary and secondary zones for Windows 2000 DNS and BIND. A binary form of a zone file is stored in a Windows 2000 Active Directory database for Active Directory–integrated DNS zones.

This appendix is divided into two parts, "DNS Control Files" and "DNS Zone File Layout."

Control files are used by BIND but not by Windows 2000. Still, Windows 2000 has similar data structures to manage DNS zones. The first section compares the two.

This zone file layout section addresses the layout supported by Windows 2000 as well as extensions that are supported by BIND.

DNS CONTROL FILES

DNS servers utilize a two-level layout hierarchy, as shown in Figure B-1. The top level contains information about domains, and zone information is contained in the second level. BIND utilizes files at both levels. Windows 2000 uses a combination of the Windows 2000 registry, files, and, if Active Directory–integrated DNS zones are used, the Active Directory database.

Chapter 21 discussed BIND and the contents of the top level control file and zone database files. The contents of the control file will not be replicated here. The zone database file contents are covered in the "DNS Zone File Layout" section.

On UNIX and Linux, the top level control file is /etc/named.conf. It is a text file like the zone files. The top level control file contains the names of the zone files.

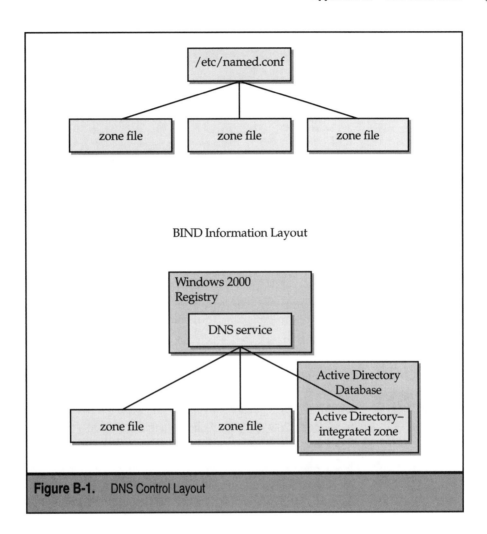

Figure B-1. DNS Control Layout

Windows 2000 DNS control information is kept in the Windows 2000 registry. The information can be found in the following registry key:

MyComputer\HKEY_LOCAL_MACHINE\SYSTEM\ CurrentControlSet\Services\DNS

The contents of this key can be viewed using the Windows 2000 Registry Editor, REGEDIT.EXE, as shown in Figure B-2.

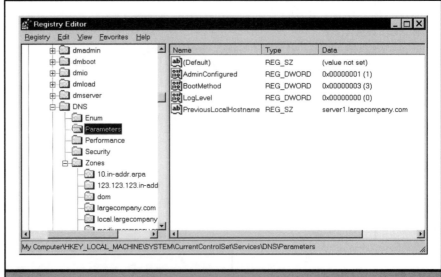

Figure B-2. Windows 2000 DNS registry entries

WARNING: It is possible to make changes to the DNS configuration using the Windows 2000 Registry Editor, but this is definitely not recommended. Most changes can be made using DNSCMD, discussed in Chapter 19, and the DNS MMC snap-in, discussed in Chapter 11. There are some values that can only be changed using the Registry Editor but these should only be done as noted in application notes for the Windows 2000 DNS service.

The zones managed by the Windows 2000 DNS service are enumerated under the Zone key. The key names under the Zone key are the names of the zones. Most zone-related attributes are self-explanatory. For example, primary DNS zones have a registry key named DatabaseFile that contains the name of the zone file.

Whereas the BIND control file configuration is well defined, the Windows 2000 DNS registry information is not. In general, stick to the DNS MMC snap-in for DNS service and zone configuration. Experts can use DNSCMD as well.

DNS ZONE FILE LAYOUT

The DNS zone file layout is relatively simple. It is a text file that contains blank lines, comment lines, and resource records. Comments start with a semicolon (;). There must be one SOA resource record that should be the first resource record in the file. The description of the DNS resource records is covered in Appendix A.

This description of the zone file layout is accurate for Windows 2000 DNS zone files used with primary and secondary DNS zones. These files are compatible with BIND. BIND also supports meta-statements that Windows 2000 does not. The "DNS Zone File Meta-statements" section addresses this feature.

General DNS Zone File Layout

A DNS zone file is a line-oriented text file. A semicolon indicates the remaining part of a line is a comment to be ignored when parsing the DNS zone file.

The contents of the DNS zone file are the DNS resource records presented in Appendix A. The order in which these records are presented is not important except when shortcuts are used. A shortcut eliminates the <name> associated with a DNS resource record. When there is no <name>, the <name> of the prior resource record is assumed. Take the following DNS zone file snippet, for example. This code

```
server1.foo.com.      A 123.45.67.89
server1.foo.com.      NS foo.com.
server1.foo.com.      HINFO "x86" "Windows NT"
```

is the same as this:

```
server1.foo.com.      A 123.45.67.89
                      NS foo.com.
                      HINFO "x86" "Windows NT"
```

This can be shortened further if the DNS zone file defines the foo.com. zone. In this case, the snippet can be shortened to

```
server1               A 123.45.67.89
                      NS foo.com.
                      HINFO "x86" "Windows NT"
```

In addition, the at character (@) can be used in place of the zone name. This is normally used with the SOA or NS resource records, as in

```
@ IN SOA wong1.dom. administrator.dom. (
    23        ; serial number
    3600      ; refresh
    600       ; retry
    86400     ; expire
    3600  )   ; minimum TTL


@ NS ns1.wong1.dom.
@ NS ns2.wong1.dom.
```

Of course, the two shortcuts can be combined to give you this:

```
@ IN SOA wong1.dom. administrator.dom. (
    23        ; serial number
    3600      ; refresh
    600       ; retry
    86400     ; expire
    3600  )   ; minimum TTL


  NS ns1.wong1.dom.
  NS ns2.wong1.dom.
```

Care must be taken with any positional shortcuts. Inserting another DNS resource record between the SOA and NS resource records in the previous example will change the semantics of the NS resource records. This is often the way that DNS zone files are corrupted by inexperienced DNS administrators.

DNS Zone File Meta-statements

BIND supports meta-statements that are not supported by the Windows 2000 DNS service. If files with these statements are to be migrated to Windows 2000, the files must be merged using a text editor. Chapter 17 addresses migration issues including an alternative that moves a zone from one DNS server to another using a secondary DNS zone.

The meta-statements that are supported by BIND but not Windows 2000 include $ORIGIN and $INCLUDE. These are designed to make management of DNS zone files easier.

> **NOTE:**   See Chapter 17 for details on ways to convert DNS zone files with meta-statements to DNS zones files that Windows 2000 can use.

The following is the syntax for the $ORIGIN statement:

$ORIGIN <DomainName>

The $ORIGIN statement changes the default domain name to <DomainName>. Initially, this value is the domain name associated with the DNS zone file. This is found in the DNS control file for BIND and some other DNS servers. This information is found in the Windows 2000 registry for the Windows 2000 DNS server.

The purpose of the $ORIGIN statement is to allow subsequent DNS resource records to use relative domain names that then incorporate the default domain when they are converted to a FQDN. The following is an example without the $ORIGIN statement:

```
able.foo.com.    A 123.45.67.1
baker.foo.com.   A 123.45.67.2
server1.bar.com. A 23.45.67.44
server2.bar.com. A 23.45.67.45
```

The example matches the following example with the $ORIGIN statement:

```
$ORIGIN foo.com.
able  A 123.45.67.1
baker A 123.45.67.2
$ORIGIN bar.com.
server1 A 23.45.67.44
server2 A 23.45.67.45
```

The $ORIGIN statement is most often used with the $INCLUDE statement. This allows the included file to be defined using relative domain names. The same file can be used as a zone file simply by the addition of an SOA resource record. The syntax for the $INCLUDE file is

$INCLUDE <FileName>

The following is a typical example of the $ORIGIN and $INCLUDE statements used together:

```
; Define subdomain1.foo.com.
$ORIGIN subdomain1.foo.com.
$INCLUDE db.subdomain1.foo.com
; Define subdomain2.foo.com.
$ORIGIN subdomain2.foo.com.
$INCLUDE db.subdomain2.foo.com
```

SAMPLE DNS ZONE FILES

The next few sections discuss a number of sample DNS zone files. An Active Directory DNS zone file illustrates how a domain controller advertises its services. This type of configuration will be found on any DNS zone supporting an Active Directory domain. Sample files are also presented to show how DNS files can be defined with and without shortcuts. The use of shortcuts makes management at the file level easier.

Windows 2000 Active Directory DNS Zone File

The following is a sample DNS zone file. It was created by converting an Active Directory–integrated DNS zone to a primary DNS zone after an Active Directory domain controller was set up.

```
;
;   Database file largecompany.com.dns for largecompany.com zone.
;      Zone version:  397
;


@ IN SOA server1.largecompany.com.  admin.largecompany.com. (
        397             ; serial number
        900             ; refresh
```

```
        600             ; retry
        86400           ; expire
        3600            ) ; minimum TTL


;
;  Zone NS records
;
@       NS    server1.largecompany.com.
@       NS    server2.largecompany.com.
;
;  Zone records
;
@       600   A    10.10.10.150
@       600   A    123.123.123.1
@       600   A    192.168.0.1
a788b3c3-1c8f-416f-ae72-6e38dc86e7ec._msdcs 600 CNAME
        server1.largecompany.com.
_kerberos._tcp.Default-First-Site-Name._sites.dc._msdcs 600 SRV 0 100 88
        server1.largecompany.com.
_ldap._tcp.Default-First-Site-Name._sites.dc._msdcs 600 SRV 0 100 389
        server1.largecompany.com.
_kerberos._tcp.dc._msdcs 600 SRV 0 100 88
        server1.largecompany.com.
_ldap._tcp.dc._msdcs    600 SRV 0 100 389
        server1.largecompany.com.
_ldap._tcp.7606e4ba-6a7d-4971-a25e-ba8754e8ee0d.domains._msdcs
        600 SRV 0 100 389 server1.largecompany.com.
gc._msdcs     600 A 10.10.10.150
              600 A 123.123.123.1
              600 A 192.168.0.1
_ldap._tcp.Default-First-Site-Name._sites.gc._msdcs 600 SRV
        0 100 3268 server1.largecompany.com.
_ldap._tcp.gc._msdcs    600 SRV 0 100 3268
        server1.largecompany.com.
_ldap._tcp.pdc._msdcs   600 SRV 0 100 389
        server1.largecompany.com.
_gc._tcp.Default-First-Site-Name._sites 600 SRV 0 100 3268
        server1.largecompany.com.
_kerberos._tcp.Default-First-Site-Name._sites 600 SRV
        0 100 88 server1.largecompany.com.
_ldap._tcp.Default-First-Site-Name._sites 600 SRV
        0 100 389 server1.largecompany.com.
```

```
_gc._tcp   600 SRV 0 100 3268 server1.largecompany.com.
_kerberos._tcp   600 SRV 0 100 88 server1.largecompany.com.
_kpasswd._tcp   600 SRV 0 100 464 server1.largecompany.com.
_ldap._tcp   600 SRV 0 100 389 server1.largecompany.com.
_kerberos._udp   600 SRV 0 100 88 server1.largecompany.com.
_kpasswd._udp   600 SRV 0 100 464 server1.largecompany.com.
ann       A  123.123.123.119
bob       A  123.123.123.114
ftp       CNAME  server2.largecompany.com.
jenn      A  123.123.123.111
john      A  123.123.123.110
lab1      A  123.123.123.100
lab2      A  123.123.123.101
lab3      A  123.123.123.103
lab5      A  123.123.123.104
laura     A  123.123.123.112
linux     A  123.123.123.21


;
;  Delegated sub-zone:  local.largecompany.com.
;
local NS server2.largecompany.com.
;  End delegation

sales       A       123.123.123.120
@           MX 5    sales.largecompany.com.
            MX 10   server1.largecompany.com.
server1     A       10.10.10.150
            A       192.168.0.1
            A       123.123.123.1
server2     A       123.123.123.2
techsupport A       123.123.123.141
www         CNAME   server1.largecompany.com.
```

The Windows 2000 DNS service places the SOA record first using
the @ shortcut. This is followed by the two NS resource records that
define the authoritative name servers for the DNS zone. These use
FQDN. The relative address resource records, A, for server1 and
server2 are found later in the file.

Server1 is the first domain controller in this Active Directory
DNS zone. The server has three IP addresses because server1 has two
Ethernet adapters and a modem link that has a fixed IP address. It

was a busy system that also doubled as a router and a remote access gateway. Most servers will have a single network adapter. The server was also known as server1 so it responds to largecompany.com. and server1.largecompany.com.

Things start to get a bit complicated with the subdomain definitions used by Active Directory. For example, the CNAME resource record named a788b3c3-1c8f-416f-ae72-6e38dc86e7ec._msdcs references the domain controller server1.largecompany.com. The resource record is part of the _msdcs subdomain. The number is a unique identifier generated by the Active Directory installation program.

There are a number of SRV resource records used to define the various services for Windows 2000, such as ldap and kerberos. All these resource records are added to the zone automatically when the domain controller starts up. This is done using dynamic DNS updates.

The Active Directory subdomain definitions are followed by more command address and CNAME definitions. This includes a number of named workstations, the FTP and Web servers that have relative names of ftp and www. There is even a delegated subzone and some mail exchange resource records. This was added to make things interesting. It indicates that the subdomain local.largecompany.com. will be handled by server2.largecompany.com.'s DNS server. The mail exchange resource records, MX, use the @ sign shortcut. The two mail servers, sales.largecompany.com and server1.largecompany.com, are set up to handle mail for largecompany.com.

The Active Directory subdomain _msdcs can get quite large as the number of domain controllers for the domain increases. Likewise, the _sites subdomain will be filled as more sites are defined typically in a distributed network.

The next two sections present a simpler DNS zone file to show how resource record naming makes life simpler for DNS administrators who deal with DNS zone files directly.

Simple DNS Zone File with No Shortcuts

The following is a sample DNS zone file. It defines a zone named wong1.dom. It was a Windows NT network that was eventually upgraded to Windows 2000. The zone file in the "Simple DNS Zone

File with Shortcuts" section was actually the zone file created using the Windows NT DNS service. The following is a version that uses none of the shortcuts mentioned earlier:

```
;   Database file wong1.dom.dns for wong1.dom zone.
;       Zone version:  23
wong1.dom. IN  SOA server1.wong1.dom.  administrator.wong1.dom. (
        23              ; serial number
        3600            ; refresh
        600             ; retry
        86400           ; expire
        3600        )  ; minimum TTL
;  Zone NS records
wong1.dom.                  NS server1.wong1.dom.
wong1.dom.                  NS linux.wong1.dom.
;  Zone records
router.wong1.dom.   A       123.123.123.99
linux.wong1.dom.    A       123.123.123.21
server2.wong1.dom.  A       123.123.123.19
server1.wong1.dom.  A       123.123.123.8
server1.wong1.dom.  HINFO        "x86" "Windows NT"
ftp.wong1.dom.      CNAME server1.wong1.dom.
www.wong1.dom.      CNAME server1.wong1.dom.
```

There is no ambiguity defining a DNS zone file in this fashion, as the semantics will not change even if the zone name is changed. This is usually a disadvantage, and the extra text needed to accomplish this is another reason that a fully qualified DNS zone file is rarely used. Generally, the file discussed in the next section is what will be used.

Simple DNS Zone File with Shortcuts

The following is a sample DNS zone file that matches the one in the previous section, assuming that the DNS zone name is wong1.dom. All the resource record names are relative, but the SOA and the CNAME resource records use FQDN. If the domain name is changed, the FQDNs must be changed. These can be relative as well, in which case the zone's domain name can be changed simply by changing the name in the zone definition in the DNS control file or the Windows registry. The latter is normally handled by the DNS MMC snap-in under Windows 2000.

```
;  Database file wong1.dom.dns for wong1.dom zone.
;      Zone version:  23
@ IN SOA server1.wong1.dom.  administrator.wong1.dom. (
        23              ; serial number
        3600            ; refresh
        600             ; retry
        86400           ; expire
        3600        ) ; minimum TTL
;  Zone NS records
@                       NS          server1.wong1.dom.
@                       NS          linux.wong1.dom.
;  Zone records
router                  A       123.123.123.99
linux                   A       123.123.123.21
server2                 A       123.123.123.19
server1                 A       123.123.123.8
                        HINFO       "x86" "Windows NT"
ftp                     CNAME server1.wong1.dom.
www                     CNAME server1.wong1.dom.
```

Reverse Lookup DNS Zone File

The following is a sample of a reverse lookup DNS zone file. It has the same layout as the primary DNS zone files already presented. The only difference is that the resource records after the name server definitions are all PTR resource records. This DNS zone file handles resolution for IP addresses of the form 123.123.123.xxx. The file name is 123.123.123.in-addr.arpa.dns. The file uses shortcuts.

```
;  Database file 123.123.123.in-addr.arpa.dns
;      for 123.123.123.in-addr.arpa zone.
;      Zone version:  20
@ IN  SOA server1.largecompany.com.
      administrator.largecompany.com. (
      20              ; serial number
      900             ; refresh
      600             ; retry
      86400           ; expire
      3600        ) ; minimum TTL
```

```
;   Zone NS records
@ NS           server1.largecompany.com.
  NS           server2.largecompany.com.
;   WINSR (NBSTAT) lookup record
@ WINSR        L2 C900 (largecompany.com. )
;   Zone records
1     1200 PTR server1.largecompany.com.
120        PTR sales.largecompany.com.
141        PTR techsupport.largecompany.com.
2          PTR server2.largecompany.com.
99         PTR router.largecompany.com.
21         PTR linux.wong1.dom.
8          PTR server1.wong1.dom.
```

Note that subnet 123.123.123.0/24 was used by two zones: largecompany.com. and wong1.dom. Also notice that the PTR resource record that links 123.123.123.1 to server1.largecompanyt.com. includes a TTL of 1200 seconds.

APPENDIX C

DHCP Options

T his appendix lists the various DHCP options that can be used for messages between a DHCP client and server to lease an IP address. The information can be ignored selectively by the DHCP client, although most clients will use all the information that they can.

Chapter 14 covers the Windows 2000 DHCP service including configuration and references to this appendix.

DHCP OPTION DEFINITIONS

The Pad option is used to align DHCP packers to a word boundary, and the End option indicates the end of a list of DHCP information. DHCP options supported by the Windows 2000 DHCP server are listed in Table C-1. Table C-2 lists the DHCP message types. These types are used in the DHCP protocol and are not directly accessible by the user.

NOTE: Option codes 0, 1, and 255 are handled automatically by the DHCP clients and servers when messages are generated. They will not appear in any configuration options presented by the DHCP MMC snap-in.

Code	Name	Description
0	Pad	Filler to word-align other options.
255	End	Indicates the end of a list of options or a list of suboptions when a vendor-specific option list is included (see option Code 43 for more details).
1	Subnet Mask	Subnet mask for client's IP address. Example: 255.255.255.0.

Table C-1. DHCP Options

Code	Name	Description
2	Time Offset	Time offset in seconds from Universal Coordinated Time (UCT) for the subnet from the zero meridian (Greenwich mean time).
3	Router	List of IP addresses of routers that a client can use.
4	Time Server	List of IP addresses of RFC 868–compliant timer servers.
5	IEN Name Server	List of IP addresses for Internet Engineering Note–compatible name servers. See code 6 for DNS name server list.
6	DNS Server	List of IP addresses for DNS servers.
7	Log Server	List of IP addresses for MIT-LCS UDP–compatible log servers.
8	Cookie Server	List of IP addresses for RFC 865–compliant cookie servers.
9	LPR Server	List of IP addresses for RFC 1179–compliant line printer (LPR) servers.
10	Impress Server	List of IP addresses for Imagen Impress servers.
11	Resource Location Server	List of IP addresses for RFC 887–compliant Resource Location servers.

Table C-1.   DHCP Options *(continued)*

Code	Name	Description
12	Host Name	Fully qualified domain name (FQDN) normally constructed from the computer name provided in the DHCPREQUEST and a domain suffix set at the DHCP server.
13	Boot File Size	Unsigned 16-bit integer value that specifies the number of 512-byte blocks that make up the boot record for the client.
14	Merit Dump File	Specifies the name of a file on the client that is to be dumped in the event of a client failure.
15	DNS Domain Name	Domain name suffix that the client should use for resolving simple domain names.
16	Swap Server	IP address of the swap server for the client.
17	Root Path	Root path for client.
18	Extension Path	Specifies the file name of a boot file that can be downloaded using the Trivial File Transfer Protocol (TFTP). Similar to the BOOTP response from a BOOTP server.
19	Enable IP Forwarding	Enables IP forwarding by the DHCP client.

Table C-1. DHCP Options *(continued)*

Code	Name	Description
20	Enable Nonlocal Source Routing	Enables DHCP client to use source routing for nonlocal IP address destinations.
21	Policy Filter	List of IP addresses and address mask pairs that make up a filter for nonlocal source.
22	Maximum Datagram Reassembly Size	Specifies the maximum number of bytes for datagram reassembly. The minimum size is 576 bytes.
23	Default IP Time to Live	An 8-bit integer that specifies the default time to live in seconds for outgoing datagrams.
24	Path MTU Aging Timeout	A 32-bit unsigned integer that specifies the Path Maximum Transmission Unit (MTU) value in seconds.
25	Path MTU Plateau Table	Specifies a table of 16-bit unsigned integers for the plateau table. The minimum value is 68. The table is ordered smallest to largest.
26	Interface MTU	Specifies the MTU size that can be used with a host adapter.
27	All Subnets Are Local	Specifies whether the DHCP client assumes that subnets on the intranet use the same MTU.

Table C-1.   DHCP Options *(continued)*

Code	Name	Description
28	Broadcast Address	Specifies the IP address to be used for broadcast datagrams. The default is 255.255.255.255.
29	Perform Mask Discovery	Specifies whether the DHCP client can use the Internet Control Message Protocol (ICMP) for subnet mask discovery.
30	Mask Supplier	Specifies whether the DHCP client will respond to subnet mask requests using ICMP.
31	Perform Router Discovery	Specifies whether the DHCP client will use the router discovery method specified by RFC 1256.
32	Router Solicitation Address	Specifies the IP address of the server that handles router solicitation requests.
33	Static Router	Specifies static routes. The destination IP address and router IP address pairs indicate the router to be used for messages to a specific destination.
34	Traffic Encapsulation	Specifies whether the DHCP client negotiates the use of trailers when using address resolution protocol (ARP) as described in RFC 983.

Table C-1.   DHCP Options *(continued)*

Code	Name	Description
35	ARP Cache Timeout	Specifies ARP cache timeout value in seconds.
36	Ethernet Encapsulation	A value of 0 specifies that the DHCP client uses Ethernet v.2 (RFC 894) encapsulation versus a value of 1 that specifies IEEE 802.3 (RFC 1042) encapsulation.
37	TCP Default TTL	Specifies the default 8-bit time-to-live value in seconds for the DHCP client when sending TCP segments.
38	TCP Keepalive Interval	Specifies the interval the DHCP client waits before sending a keepalive message to a TCP connection. A value of 0 disables keepalive messages.
40	NIS Domain Name	Specifies the Network Information Service (NIS) domain name.
41	NIS Servers	Specifies a list of IP addresses for NIS servers.
42	NTP Servers	Specifies an IP address list in order of preference for Network Time Protocol (NTP) servers.
43	Vendor Specific Information	Specifies information for vendor-specific DHCP clients.

Table C-1. DHCP Options *(continued)*

Code	Name	Description
44	WINS Server	Specifies list of IP addresses of WINS servers or NetBIOS name servers (NBNS) to be used by a WINS client.
45	NetBIOS Datagram Distribution Server	List of IP addresses of NetBIOS datagram distribution servers.
46	NetBIOS Node Type	Node Type, Values: 0—b-node, 1—p-node, 4—m-node, 8—h-node.
47	NetBIOS Scope ID	Specifies the NetBIOS over TCP/IP scope ID for the DHCP client.
48	X Window System Font Servers	Specifies an IP address list of X Window System font servers.
49	X Window System Display Manager Servers	Specifies a list of IP addresses of X Window System display manager servers.
50	Requested IP Address	Included in a DHCP message from a DCHP client to a DHCP server to request a lease on the specified IP address.
51	IP Address Lease Time	A DHCP client can request a specific lease time in seconds. A DHCP server will indicate the lease time when an IP address is leased.

Table C-1.   DHCP Options *(continued)*

Code	Name	Description
52	Option Overload	Specifies whether the standard sname and file fields are overloaded. This option extends the options area. Values: 1—file field, 2—sname field, 3—file and sname fields
53	DHCP Message Type	See Table D-2.
54	Server Identifier	Specifies the IP address of the DHCP server involved in a DHCP lease request.
55	Parameter Request List	Sent by a DHCP client to the DHCP server to request the specified set of options. Options are listed in order of preference.
56	Optional Message	Text message normally sent by DHCP server with a negative acknowledgement or by the DHCP client when it declines a lease.
57	Maximum Message Size	A 16-bit integer that specifies the maximum message size in bytes. The default is 576.
58	Renewal Time Value	Specifies the time in seconds before which a DHCP client should request a lease renewal. It is typically 50 percent of the lease time.

Table C-1.   DHCP Options *(continued)*

Code	Name	Description
59	Rebinding Time Value	Specifies the time in seconds before which a DHCP client should enter the rebinding state. It is typically 87.5 percent of the lease time.
60	Vendor Class Identifier	Specifies vendor-specific class identification information.
61	Unique Client Identifier	An identifier that a DHCP client can give to the DHCP server to uniquely identify the client. This is often a media access control (MAC) number.
64	NIS+ Domain Name	Specifies the NIS+ domain name for the DHCP client.
66	TFTP Server Name	Name of TFTP server used to download a boot file.
67	Boot File Name	Boot file name to be downloaded from the TFTP server.
68	Mobile IP Home Agents	Specifies a list of IP addresses of mobile IP home agents available to the DHCP client.
69	Simple Mail Transport Protocol (SMTP) Server	Specifies a list of IP addresses of SMTP servers that the DHCP client can use for sending e-mail.

Table C-1.   DHCP Options *(continued)*

Code	Name	Description
70	Post Office Protocol (POP3) Servers	Specifies a list of IP addresses of POP3 servers that the DHCP client can use for picking up e-mail.
71	Network News Transport Protocol (NNTP) Servers	Specifies a list of IP addresses of NNTP servers that the DHCP client can use.
72	World Wide Web Servers	Specifies a list of IP addresses of Web servers that the DHCP client can use.
73	Finger Servers	Specifies a list of IP addresses of Finger servers that the DHCP client can use.
74	Internet Relay Chat (IRC) Servers	Specifies a list of IP addresses of IRC servers that the DHCP client can use.
75	StreetTalk Servers	Specifies a list of IP addresses of StreetTalk servers that the DHCP client can use.
76	StreetTalk Directory Assistance Servers	Specifies a list of IP addresses of StreetTalk Directory Assistance servers that the DHCP client can use.
77	User Class Information	Specifies user-class information that can be used by class-specific clients.

Table C-1. DHCP Options *(continued)*

Type	Name	Message Type
1	DHCPDISCOVER	Discovery
2	DHCPOFFER	Offer
3	DHCPREQUEST	Request
4	DHCPDECLINE	Decline
5	DHCPACK	Positive acknowledgement
6	DHCPNAK	Negative acknowledgement
7	DHCPRELEASE	Release
8	DHCPINFORM	Information

Table C-2.   DHCP Message Type

Index

Note: Page numbers for illustrations and tables are in italics.

A

E

F

G

H

Z